JUDGMENT:

THE LAST TRUMP AND THE FALL OF AMERICA

JUDGMENT:

THE LAST TRUMP AND THE FALL OF AMERICA

ALFRED FUKA TOFIBAM

ARPress
ILLUMINATING IDEAS.
EMPOWERING VOICES

ARPress
45 Dan Road Suite 5
Canton MA 02021
Hotline: 1(888) 821-0229
Fax: 1(508) 545-7580

Ordering Information:
Quantity sales. Special discounts are available on quantity purchases by corporations, associations, and others. For details, contact the publisher at the address above.

Printed in the United States of America.

ISBN-13:   Paperback   979-8-89389-540-7
           eBook   979-8-89389-541-4

Library of Congress Control Number:

Contents

PART ONE: THE FALL OF THE NATIONS

Introduction i

Chapter 1 : Introduction to Bible Prophecy 1

Chapter 2 : Understanding Satan 28

Chapter 3 : Israel's Blunder 34

Chapter 4 : Satan and His Counterfeit Plan 40

Chapter 5 : Satan in the Gospels and Epistles 59

Chapter 6 : Satan's Attack on the Early Church 71

Chapter 7 : Satan Transforms Into An Angel of Light. 80

Chapter 8 : The Roman Empire Goes Abroad (Colonialism). 111

Chapter 9 : Birth of New Rome (Babylon), USA.. 132

Chapter 10 : Apostasy: Then And Now. 159

Chapter 11 : The Strife For World Domination
in the Modern Era 192

Chapter 12 : The Modern World: A World Divided 250

Chapter 13 : The Fall of the Free World 291

Chapter 14 : Ah, Sovereign LORD! 374

PART TWO : THE BRIDE OF CHRIST

Chapter 15 : The Diverse Nature of the Bride 390

Chapter 16 : An Interview Into the Kingdom of God 400

Chapter 17 : The Gospel of Salvation 415

Chapter 18 : The Cost of Discipleship:

Following Jesus Christ. 430

Chapter 19 : Behold! Jesus is Coming! 445

Chapters 20 : The Millennium 473

APPENDIX

Bibliography 492

Notes 495

INTRODUCTION

" *T*he word of the LORD came to me: 'Son of man, set your face
against Jerusalem and preach against the sanctuary [church].
*Prophesy against the land of Israel [the world] and say to her: 'This
is what the LORD says: I am against you. ...Because I am going to cut
off the righteous and the wicked, my sword will be unleashed against
everyone from south to north.* ... 'Therefore groan, son of man! Groan
before them with broken heart and bitter grief. And when they ask
you, 'Why are you groaning?' you shall say, 'Because of the news
that is coming. Every heart will melt and every hand go limp; every
spirit will become faint and every knee become as weak as water.' It
is coming! It will surely take place, declares the Sovereign LORD"
(Ezek. 21:1-7).

Many have undertaken to investigate into and write about prophesies
concerning the end of the last days and the second coming of Jesus
Christ. Countless books abound, but to the extent that I have read
them, there seems to be something missing. It is my hope that this
book will fill the missing link or at least shed some light on the
subject.

God's plan is perfect and can never be thwarted. What he has
promised he will fulfill to the dot. Jesus said that heaven and earth
shall pass away but his word shall not pass away. This echoed the
prediction of Isaiah in chapter 40:6-8; *"All men are like grass and
all their glory like the flowers of the field. The grass withers and the
flowers fall ...* **but the word of our God stands forever.***"* Thus, the
word of God will stand forever, while all the nations in all their glory
will pass away; *"Surely the nations are like a drop in a bucket; they
are regarded as dust on the scales; he weighs the islands as though
they were fine dust. ... Before him all nations are as nothing; they are*

regarded by him as worthless and less than nothing" (vv.15-17). **God has bound himself with an oath to do what he has promised to do;** *"I will not violate my covenant or alter what my lips have uttered"* (Ps. 89:34). Therefore, we can count on his word and faithfulness.

I am confident about what I am going to say but would like to say the following. Prophecy cannot be fully understood until it is fulfilled completely. This makes it hard to predict into prophecy. Even the prophets did not understand what they were writing about (1 Pet. 1:10-12). Even the angels do not understand. Even when Jesus was with the disciples, they did not understand fully until after his death, resurrection, ascension, and the coming of the Holy Spirit. Even then, Peter did not completely get it (Acts 10; Gal. 2). Paul finally captions this lack of complete knowledge of prophecy in 1 Corinthians 13:9-12, when he says; *"For we know in part and we prophesy in part, but when perfection comes, the imperfect disappears. ... Now we see but a poor reflection as in a mirror; then we shall see face to face. Now I know in part; then I shall know fully, even as I am fully known."*

However, this does not imply that we should neglect prophecy either (that's the devil's wish). If we neglect prophecy, we will be ignorant when Jesus is revealed, just like the people of his days on earth (Matt 22:29). We must search out for the things upon which our hope lies just like Daniel of old and the Berean believers (Dan. 9:1-2; Acts 17:11; John 5:39). The Holy Spirit inspired the Scriptures, and he equally interprets the Scriptures. Besides, we overcome by the blood of Jesus (no fear of death; Rev. 12:11), and by the testimony of Jesus, which is the spirit of prophecy (Rev. 19:10). God equally asks us to ask him of things to come (Is. 45:11). Again, Amos declares that; **"Surely the Sovereign LORD does nothing without revealing his plans to his servants the prophets"** (Amos 3:7; cf. Gen. 18:17). It is to our detriment if we fail to study prophecy, especially prophecies about the second coming of Jesus Christ.

It is evident from Scriptures that the prophetic office was not an easy one. It had to be authenticated in that what the prophet said must come true (Deut. 18:15-22). Thus, there is always the possibility of someone speaking presumptuously in the name of the LORD, hence false prophets. Again, if a prophet failed to speak or disobeyed what

God had commanded him, the prophet equally faced the risk of death (1 Kings 13:21-24). The most difficult thing about the prophetic office was that the true prophet often had to go alone. He had to stand against the sins of the people, against their own nations, and against other nations (even the whole world!). This meant rejection from the people. The true prophet was often resented, maltreated, and even killed (Heb. 11:32-38). It is precisely in this light that Jeremiah cried out;

> *"O LORD, you persuaded me, and I was persuaded; you overpowered me and prevailed.* **I am ridiculed all day long; everyone mocks me. Whenever I speak, I cry out proclaiming violence and destruction. So the word of the LORD has brought me insult and reproach all day long. But if I say 'I will not mention him or speak any more in his name,' his word is in my heart like a fire, a fire shut up in my bones. I am weary of holding it in; indeed, I cannot.** *I hear many whispering, 'Terror on every side! Report him! Let's report him!' All my friends are waiting for me to slip, saying, 'Perhaps he will be deceived; then we will prevail over him and take our revenge on him'"* (Jer. 20:7-10).

Truth and reality may be bitter, but they must be spoken. And the one who stands for truth and reality will be persecuted! Prophecy, therefore, is dangerous territory. If you venture in this terrain, expect opposition, resentment, and the possibility of even losing your life. Prophecy, in many ways exposes Satan, and once you unveil him, he relentlessly pursues you. The only way to defeat him is to stand fearlessly in the face of persecution and death; *"They overcame him by the blood of the lamb and by the word of their testimony;* **they did not love their lives so much as to shrink from death"** (Rev. 12:11).

On the contrary, false prophets, who were always in great numbers, enjoyed a good time with the people, in as much as their message was intended to please rather than rebuke the people. They sat in kings' palaces and were well-fed in order to deceive the people with pleasantries and false visions and dreams. The more they were fed, the more they fabricated their false prophecies, fantasies, and imaginations.

Again, it is to our disadvantage if we do not pay attention to the prophecies about the second coming of Christ, which are like a light shining in a dark place (world); *"And we have the word of the prophets made more certain, **and you will do well to pay attention to it,** as a light shining in a dark place, until the day dawns and the morning star* [Jesus Christ] *rises in in your hearts"* (2 Pet. 1:19). The timetable for the current world events (judgments in the day of wrath) is clearly charted out in the prophets (Rev. 10:7). To keep current, you must eat and breathe Scripture, especially the prophets. The second coming of Jesus Christ is the most significant event that will happen in these last days of the present age (in the midst of the judgments on moral depravity and wickedness; Rev. 16). It is an event that the whole world (believers and unbelievers alike) is looking forward to and wondering about with anxiety and impatience. While unbelievers maybe waiting for that day in fear, doubt, and the threat of judgment and hell; believers do so with great anticipation, because it is the ultimate hope of the believer. However, some believers are anxious about the event just to excite themselves and show-off rather than live a holy life. It is important to note that the purpose of prophecy is not to satisfy our curiosity, but to humble us and call us to live holy lives.

Jesus' teaching focused a lot on the age to come. He took a great deal of time talking about his second coming to his disciples, who were anxious to know the exact time. The answers he gave to their questions about the time of his coming implied the following. He wanted believers to be watchful and prepared, rather than to know the exact day or hour. Thus, it is unnecessary to make predictions. Many have tried and failed. However, he gave them (and us) characteristics of the world situation by which believers can judge for themselves what is happening. The book of Revelation promises us a blessing if we read and pay attention to the prophetic word; ***"Blessed is the one who reads the words of this prophecy, and blessed are those who hear it and take to heart what is written in it, because the time is near"*** (Rev. 1:3).

Blowing a trumpet sounds a very archaic practice. Who blows a trumpet or a ram's horn these days? I remember when I was growing up, how an appointed person in my village will go around blowing a ram's horn to rally people for community labor, and one person would keep blowing the horn while the villagers worked. Even today, a special ram's horn is sounded when the chieftain of my tribe is passing wherever there are people in public or when he is arriving at an occasion. The sounding horn alerts the people that the chief is coming so that they should pay the due respect. Apart from the book of Revelation, there is not much about trumpet blowing these days. What kind of trumpets are the people or angels in the book blowing? Do human beings hear these trumpets or is it just symbolic? Or are the trumpets just sounding in ways that people do not really understand that they are sounding? Are people going to recognize the last trumpet blast?

Why did God introduce the blowing of trumpets or ram's horns in Israel? How often was the trumpet blown in Israel? Here are some occasions during which the trumpet was blown or will be blown.

1. The trumpet was blown to call people to the presence of God and for worship (Ex. 19:13c, 16-19).

2. The trumpet was blown to call people to assemble and for battle (Num. 10:1-10; Jos. 6:4-9, 13).

3. The trumpet was blown to declare the peoples' sins (Is. 58:1ff; this time, raising a voice).

4. The trumpet was blown to call people to repentance (Joel 2:12-17).

5. The trumpets are being blown to bring judgment (Rev. 8; 9).

6. **The Last Trumpet [this book]** is being blown for the battle of the day of the LORD (Is. 18:3; Joel 2:1- 2; Zech. 9:14-15); for the gathering of believers (Matt. 24:31; 1 Cor. 15:52, 1 Thess. 4; Rev. 11:15); and for the Re-gathering of Israel at the appearing (Is. 27:13).

When the trumpet of the Lord shall sound, and time shall be no more, will you be there?

CHAPTER 1

INTRODUCTION TO BIBLE PROPHECY

" And we have the word of the prophets made more certain, and you will do well to pay careful attention to it, as to a light shining in a dark place, until the day dawns and the morning star rises in your hearts. Above all, you must understand that no prophecy of Scripture came about by the prophet's own interpretation. For prophecy never had its origin in the will of man, but men spoke from God as they were carried along by the Holy Spirit" (2 Pet. 1:19-21).

After the angel of Jesus revealed the book of Revelation to John, John wanted to worship the angel.

*"At this I fell at his feet to worship him. But he said to me, 'Do not do it! I am a fellow servant with you and with your brothers who hold to the testimony of Jesus. Worship God! **For the testimony of Jesus is the spirit of prophecy.**'"* (Rev. 19:10)

What the Jews Regarded as Prophecy

According to the Jews, prophecy is divided into two sections: The **Former Prophets and The Latter Prophets.** The latter prophets are divided into two according to length of book: **Major and Minor Prophets, as we have them in our English Bibles. But I regard the whole Bible as prophecy!** While the divisions above are obviously discernible and are correct, a thorough reading of the Bible shows that from Genesis to Revelation, each book of the Bible has recordings that have prophetic significance. Consider what Jesus did with the two disciples on the road to Emmaus; *"And beginning with Moses and all the Prophets, he explained to them what was said in all the Scriptures concerning himself"* (Luke 24:25-27). Thus, all

1

of Scripture is prophecy! This assertion will become clearer as we continue in this study.

The Bible is the Living Word of the Living God, and therefore, is a book for all times (Heb. 4:12, 13, Acts. 7:38). The whole Bible, from Genesis to Revelation, is looking forward to the consummation of redemption and human history, which will be climaxed in the second coming of Jesus Christ (King of kings or President of presidents, and Lord of lords). Even exhortations to holy living focus our eyes on the coming Savior and King.

Prophecy

Prophecy can be defined as; **confronting the evil** of the time with the aim of calling people to repentance or otherwise face God's judgment (this is the greater content of prophecy); that is, prophecy is God's message to the contemporary generation. **The prophet confronted the king** and his idolatrous practices, national idolatry, and **false prophets** (who were fond of promising peace, security, prosperity, but no judgment). **The prophet confronted the priests,** who failed in their duties of teaching the law to the people; **merchants,** who used false balances and unjust scales (unfairness in trade); **judges,** who favored the rich and gave no justice to the poor or the under-privileged (alien, widow, fatherless, poor); **greedy women,** who lived in luxury and chased after empty beauty; **evil and sinful nations** (world) that did not know or acknowledge God. Prophets were preachers of their day!

Notice the usage of the word "confront" or "confronting" as the attitude or demeanor of the prophet as required by God. Yah commanded Ezekiel; *"Son of man, **confront Jerusalem with her detestable practices …"*** Again, we read; *"Son of man, will you judge her? Will you judge this city of bloodshed? Then **confront her with all her detestable practices …"*** (Ezek. 16:1, 2; 22:2ff). While prophets were specially chosen, anyone who loved God and his word and hated sin and evil, could equally distinguish and frown upon the evil and sin of the society (the remnant).

Prophecy as Forth-telling: This is to declare beforehand what will happen in the immediate future, and sometimes with conditionality: if this, then that; if not that, then this. This also includes prophecies of the restoration of Judah after the Babylonian captivity. God relents and withholds judgment if those warned or threatened repent (Jonah 3:4-10), which explains conditionality.

Prophecy as Foretelling: This is predicting the future sometimes with or without precise details. Both forth-telling and foretelling were almost always attached to the present situation that the prophet was addressing. In the process of both, the prophet was revealed the glory of the Christ in his first and second advents almost as if they were one single event (Is. 61:1-3; Luke 4:18-19; Matt. 3:11, 12; Notice the **break or gaps** in both prophecies. As we study Bible prophecy, we should watch out for such gaps). The promises of deliverance, redemption, restoration, and threats of judgment in most prophecies, ultimately pointed forward to Christ in both advents (first and second comings). It was the Spirit of the Christ that moved the prophets (2 Pet. 1:20-21)!

Prophet

A prophet is defined popularly as **someone who can foretell or predict the future.** To the **Greeks**, a prophet was "one who speaks for a god and interpret his will to man." To the **Hebrews**, a prophet is "one called," that is, called by God, to speak for him. The Hebrew prophet, therefore, is God's mouthpiece. A prophet is also known by other names such as: seer, man of God, watchman, messenger of the LORD (Yah), and man of the Spirit.

Function: The Hebrew prophet provided significant spiritual, military, and judicial leadership; advised kings or confronted them when they disobeyed God's word; reminded the people of the Law (the curses and blessings); called the people to repent or face judgment; declared God's judgment on sinful nations; in short, they were preachers of justice and righteousness!

Apocalypse

Apocalypse means to reveal or unveil. It is that part of prophecy that reveals an overview or panorama of human history (with saints usually persecuted and even killed) using diverse symbols, images, and numbers, and culminating in final judgment and redemption at the end of the age and ushering in God's everlasting kingdom for the saints. This revelation comes mostly through dreams and visions.

The Prophets: What Kind of People Were They?

Prophets were ordinary people like you and I that God called to use them to reveal his plan to the rest of mankind (James 5:17). Once called, the prophet responded and acted in obedience and faith (Heb. 11). There were both writing and non-writing prophets: **non-writing:** Abraham; Gen. 20:7; Israelite elders prophesying; Num. 11:23-29; Saul and a procession of prophets prophesying; 1 Sam. 10:9-13; Joshua and the Judges; Samuel and a school of prophets at Ramah; 1 Sam. 19:18-24; Elijah and Elisha and a company of prophets at Bethel, Jericho and Gilgal; 2 Kings 2:3-5; 4:38; etc.; **writing prophets:** David and the Psalms, see Acts 2:29-31; the four major and twelve minor prophets.

Paul declared that prophecy in the early church was going to cease (1 Cor. 13). I do not know when this was to happen. Some believe prophecy ceased after Revelation was penned because only the Apostles were inspired to write Scripture (John 16:12-15; 17:20; Heb. 1:1-2), or when the canon of Scripture was put together. Some spiritual gifts ceased or became less operational even in the apostolic era (Phil. 2:26-27; 2 Cor. 12:7-9). Some believe that perfection in 1 Corinthians 13:8-9 refers to the second coming, when prophecy and tongues will cease. Given that believers in Revelation 19:10 are said to overcome by the testimony of Jesus, which is the spirit of prophecy, prophecy is present in the church today. But this does not necessarily mean the ability to predict the future, rather, the ability to understand or interpret prophecy and to edify the body of believers. The Bible is complete in relation to our salvation and the second coming of Jesus Christ, and we are waiting for fulfillment. There may be some vision or dream or prophecy, for a particular group of believers, but not necessarily for the whole body of Christ. We must always exercise caution and not accept anything that does not conform to or contradict the Scripture (1 Cor. 14:29). We are also commanded; *"Do not put out the Spirit's fire; do not treat prophecies with contempt. Test everything. Hold on to the good"* (1 Thess. 5:19-21).

The Prophet Must Obey or Face Consequences

Once God called a prophet, the prophet in turn had to obey and act in faith or face drastic consequences. Prophetic ministry was/is never easy!

Abraham: He obeyed God all his life but wavered and succumbed to his wife's temptation as they waited for God's timing for the promised son. The result was the birth of **Ishmael**, who has lived in hostility toward **Isaac**, the child of promise, until today (Gen. 15:1-4; 17:15-17; 18:9-5)! In Genesis 16, Ishmael's fate was pronounced, and this has continued until today! Are you surprised about the Arab-Jewish conflict and terrorism? Here is the origin—it's a **prophetic destiny of Ishmael and his descendants;** *"He will be a wild donkey of a man; his hand will be against everyone and everyone's hand against him, and he will live in hostility toward his brothers"* (Gen. 16:12). Ishmael was given a tremendous blessing (17:18-21; perhaps Arab oil!). The only difference between Ishmael and Isaac is that the covenant to bless the world was to be through Isaac. Even from ancient times, there was hostility between Ishmael and Isaac (Gen. 21:8-13; 25:9-18). The Arabs and Jews up to today have lived in hostility toward each other! Politicians, European and American, especially from Nixon, have tried to solve the problem, but only God himself can and will solve it! President Bush (and the Quartet, USA, UNO, EU, RUSSIA) in his Roadmap to Peace, insisted that the Holy Land must be divided between the Jews and the Palestinian (his speech in Jordan on June 4, 2003), but this is a fatal mistake that provokes God himself (Joel 3:1-3; Zech. 12:2-5). All of this is because of Abraham's faltering in respect to God's promise.

Moses: When he was called, he refused to go alone, and Aaron became his mouthpiece. Moses obeyed God all his life except for one instance, because of the rebellion of the Israelites, which cost him heavily (Num. 20:2-12; 34:1-6). He only saw the Promised Land but did not enter it. Do not add or subtract from God's command (Prov. 30:5-6)! No one is indispensable to God.

Samson: He succumbed to his wife, Delilah, by revealing his God-given secret to her, and perished with the ungodly as a result (Jud. 16:15-30). In this light, remember Jesus' warning; *"If anyone comes to me and does not hate his father and mother, his wife and children, his brothers and sisters—yes, even his own life—he cannot be my disciple"* (Luke 14:26).

The Man of God from Judah (1 Kings 13:1-24): This man of God was strictly warned by God not to eat anything where he went to carry out his mission, but he disobeyed and ate. As a result, he was killed. Contrast with Paul, who always obeyed (Acts 21:10-14; 20:22-24)! DO NOT peddle the word of God for money; freely you have received freely you must give (Matt. 10:7-8; 2 Cor. 2:17; 1 Tim. 6:3-5, 9- 10).

The Prophet Often Went OR Goes Alone

Moses: In some cases, Moses bore the burden of the Israelites with his assistants, but at other times he stood alone. In Exodus 32, Aaron, Moses' assistant, led the people into idolatry by making the golden calf. Moses had to stand alone on God's side and **confronted the people.** In Numbers 12:1-2, Aaron and Miriam, Moses' siblings, turned against him because he had married a racially different woman (a Cushite). This was the first case of visible racism in the Bible and its judgment was harsh. The LORD struck Miriam with leprosy. Because she had discriminated against this black woman because of her skin or race, God cursed her skin by turning it leprous (as white as snow) as a result (vv.9-15). Thus, from the onset, God has always frowned at racism because he made all men in his own image.

Elijah (1 Kings 18:22; 19:10, 14): Israel had abandoned the LORD their God and went a whoring after Baal. Elijah was alone on God's side as **he confronted the people** and the prophets of Baal; *"So Ahab sent word throughout all Israel and assembled the prophets at Mount*

Carmel. Elijah went before the people and said, 'How long will you waver between two opinions? If the LORD is God, follow him; but if Baal is God, follow him.' But the people said nothing. Then Elijah said to them, 'I am the only one of the LORD'S prophets left, but Baal has four hundred and fifty prophets." The encounter was fierce as Elijah challenged the prophets of Baal to call on him to answer by fire. Only the LORD God of Elijah answered by fire and all of Baal's prophets were killed.

Jeremiah: Jeremiah had a difficult ministry. He ministered alone (except sometimes for his secretary, Baruch) and was often mistreated—he was thrown in jail; thrown into a cistern; and other harsh treatments. Nobody listened to him, but he stood alone for the LORD at all times for about forty-seven years!

The Prophet Was/Is Often Hated, Rejected or Regarded as a Traitor

Prophets were/are often hated or rejected for their message. This hatred and rejection were/are mostly done by God's own people (so they believe to be), especially the deeply and devoutly religious! [They often thought; "We are God's chosen people, we can't be judged or taken into exile. God cannot destroy his people or his Temple." This reminds us of the Pharisees, who continued to rely on the fact that they were Abraham's descendants, but John the Baptist and Jesus reminded them that they were a brood of vipers and children of the devil, respectively (Matt. 3:7-10; John 8:31-47). They relied on their religious heritage just like some are doing today! They insist that theirs is a Judeo-Christian worldview: the pride of the West, which has sunk into utter depravity. Do not live in the past (Ezek. 18:24); therefore, hear the warning (Ezek. 33:11, 14-15)].

This rejection was especially because the prophetic ministry was/is intentionally confrontational (for God commanded and intends it to be so). **But the people hated confrontation just as is the case in our day;** *"These are rebellious people, deceitful children, children unwilling to listen to the LORD'S instruction. They say to the seers, 'See no more visions!' and to the prophets, 'Give us no more visions of what is right! Tell us pleasant things, prophesy* *illusions. Leave this way, get off the path, and **stop confronting us with the Holy One of Israel!**'"* (Is. 30:9-11). **No one wants to be confronted nor are people willing to confront others in the name of the LORD.** We have become men pleasers, preferring to polish the sins of the people rather than confront them, and hence, we are in danger of judgment. We want what is pleasant and comfortable to us; we want illusions but not what is right, not what pleases the LORD.

Elijah: He was persecuted by **Jezebel** because he had killed the prophets of Baal at Mount Carmel (1 Kings 19:1-5). The wicked king, Ahab, Jezebel's husband, had said to Elijah; ***"Is that you, you troubler of Israel?"*** (I Kings 18:17). Elisha, Elijah's successor, was equally rejected (2 Kings 2:23-24). Thus, prophets are sometimes regarded as troublemakers, as disturbers of the peace and of the status quo.

Jeremiah: He was threatened with death; **considered a traitor and accused of preaching desertion to Israeli soldiers.** As a result, he was thrown in jail and into a cistern (11:18-19; 26:2-15; 32:1-15; 36:1- 32; 37:11-38). At the end, he was helped out of the cistern by a foreigner, an Ethiopian (38:7-13).

In any case, the prophet had to be willing to do his duty (Jer. 20:7-9; 1 Cor. 9:16,17).

The prophets were sometimes considered as **maniacs, insane, demon-possessed** (Hos. 9:7-9; Acts 26:24; Luke 7:33; John 8:48-53); **or conspirators** (Amos 7:10-13; Jer. 29:26-27). During Jesus' time on earth, the high priest, Caiaphas, had predicted that it was better for one person to die for the nation than for the Romans to come and take over the nation (John 11:45-53). **Jesus' accusers not only considered him demon-possessed but saw him as unpatriotic and a disturber of the peace, who deserved to be eliminated.** In a similar way today, most prefer absolute patriotism, political stability, and peace at all costs, with compromise of spiritual demands, rather than spiritual renewal that may upset the political status quo or seem unpatriotic. Jesus declared that Jerusalem killed the prophets, the same place he was going to die (Matt. 23:29-39). Eventually, Jesus was persecuted, rejected, and killed by the religious community, who preferred Caesar as their king rather than their true King, Jesus (John 19:1- 16).

It is rather surprising that the prophets were often heeded and helped by foreigners (Jer. 40:1-6; Judah was removed as divine discipline for her sin; but in Jonah 3; the people of Nineveh repented after the preaching of Jonah. In Daniel 4, Nebuchadnezzar did not attack Daniel after he interpreted his dream; he was to spend seven years in the bush!).

Prophets Often Endured Difficult or Even Bizarre Circumstances

The Prophets faced Death Daily (Heb. 11:32-40). The writer of Hebrews summarizes that; *"... the world was not worthy of them."* Only persistent and vibrant faith can endure and overcome the devil's world (1 John 5:19, 3-4). We must equally travel this road of faith to overcome like they did. Some of the bizarre circumstances they went through were designed by God to illustrate his plan, an event, or a point of doctrine.

Abraham (Gen. 22:1-12): God commanded Abraham to take the only child of promise and sacrifice him to God. Abraham obeyed God. In the process of sacrificing Isaac, God provided a lamb for the sacrifice. We see here that God tests his children. Job is another example of such tests.

Samson (Jud. 14:1-4, 10, 20; 15:1-8): God caused him to marry a Philistine woman (through ordinary circumstances—Samson fell in love with the woman), because he was seeking an occasion to confront the Philistines.

Isaiah (Is. 20:1-4): He went around stripped (with bare feet and bare buttocks) for three years, to illustrate what will be done to the Egyptians by the Assyrians.

Ezekiel (Ezek. 4:1-5:6; 24:15-21): Ezekiel had to lie (sleep) on each side of his body for a specific number of days and eat certain foods cooked in specific ways. God also took away his wife (she died) but commanded him not to weep. This was to illustrate to the Israelites that God would take away the temple, the delight of their eyes, in which they took pride but were unfaithful to God.

Jonah (Jonah 1:15-2:10): He was in the belly of a fish for three days, which depicted Jesus' burial and resurrection.

We do not know exactly how the prophets received their revelation. But most people believe that it was ecstatic yet rational (given the poetic constructions). As one person has said; "God 'speaks to His prophets, not in magical processes or through the visions of poor phrenetics, but by a clear intelligible word addressed to the intellect and the heart. The characteristic of a true prophet is that he retains his consciousness and self-control under revelation.'"[i] Nevertheless, we cannot fully comprehend what the prophets went through when they were receiving revelation or visions. Daniel said that sometimes, he laid ill for days after receiving some visions.

True Versus False Prophets

The issue of false prophets is the most critical thing about Bible prophecy. It was a problem then, and it is a problem now. How could one distinguish between a true and a false prophet? God himself gave the most distinguishing characteristic. **A True Prophet** was one whose predictions came true (Deut. 18:14-22; 1 Kings 17:1; 18:1); and whose message was from God (Num. 12:6). A true prophet's message was based on the blessings and curses in the law. He was/is God's direct mouthpiece. On the other hand, **False Prophets** (there were always many at a time), were those who dreamed their own dreams and saw their own visions, illusions, and delusions. They gave false hopes and promises of peace and blessings to the people even when they had abandoned God's covenant (law) and went after strange gods and idols (Jer. 6:13-15; 14:11-16). They were serving their own self-interests (financial, position or status, fame, men pleasers, etc.), and thus deceived the people (1 Kings 22:1-38; Mic. 2:6; 3:5-11). They equally turned the people to idolatry (1 Kings 18:25-40) and prophesied lies and their imaginations (Jer. 5:30-31; 23:9-40). They were/are greatly condemned (Ezek. 13; 2 Pet. 2).

In the New Testament we do not have writing prophets (except for Revelation), although the apostles' writings have some prophetic overtones. Prophecy was/is a spiritual gift that is given to be used at particular times for particular purposes and in the local church for edification (Acts 13:1-3; 20:22-24; 21:9-11; Eph. 4:11; 1 Cor. 12:7-11, 29; 14:3-5). In a sense, preaching is prophesying. However, Paul declared that prophecies and other spiritual gifts like speaking in tongues were going to cease (1 Cor. 13:8-10). I believe that most of the sign gifts were foundational and temporary (that is, to confirm the Word of the Apostles; Eph. 2:19, 20; Heb. 1:1; 2:4), although God cannot be limited. Jesus continues to work in his church today by his Spirit through his word, the sword of the Spirit (Eph. 6:17). What we need today is to pay careful attention to the written prophetic word (2 Pet. 1:19), by interpreting, but not by prophesying. We need the spiritual gifts of wisdom, knowledge, discernment, faith, love, and distinguishing between spirits and false prophets (1 Cor. 12:7-10; 13; 1 John 4:1-6).

The business of new prophecies today is done by false prophets, and you should avoid them (Matt. 24:4-14, 22-27; 2 Thess. 2:8-12; 1 Tim. 4:1-4; 2 Tim. 4:1-5; 2 Pet. 2; Jude). False prophets can perform miracles, signs and wonders, and counterfeiting everything that Jesus does. This is the work of Satan through his false apostles, who have transformed into angels of light and penetrated the ranks of believers. They are counterfeiters, pseudo-Christs, antichrists, who pose "in place" of Christ. **Take note of the word counterfeit: that is, that which is not genuine; pretended; a forgery or an imitation; that which resembles closely. Counterfeit Christianity is so close to genuine Christianity so much so that if you do not cling to the truth of the Bible, you will be deceived.** Notice how the word truth comes up again and again wherever the subject of false Christianity or antichrist comes up. **If you do not know the truth, you cannot identify the counterfeit.** How many of us can identify counterfeit money? In most cases, only those specifically trained can do so. So, if you do not know the truth well, you will not be able to identify counterfeit Christianity and its antichrist.

The Prophet's Message

The prophet's message was not his own; it was God's message through him to others (primarily God's people and then the surrounding nations). The Father, the Son, and the Holy Spirit, is the source and origin of the prophet's message. The prophets were God's mouthpieces.

The Origin of the Prophet's Message

God the Father: The formula, "Thus says the LORD," or "Says the LORD Almighty," indicates the source of the Prophet's message (Num. 2:6-8; Is. 1:20; 3:15; 4:9; 7:7; 8:1; 28:22; Jer. 49:1, 7; Ezek.6:11). The message was from God and the prophet was just a mouthpiece.

The Holy Spirit: It is written; *"Above all, you must understand that no prophecy of Scripture came about by the prophet's own interpretation. For prophecy never had its origin in the will of man, but men spoke from God as they were carried along by the Holy Spirit"* (2 Pet. 1:19-21; cf. Num. 11:25; John 16:5-14; Acts 20:22-24; 21:10-11; Rev. 2:7, 11, 17; 3:6, 13, 22; 4:2; 22:17). Also, 2 Timothy 3:16 says that; *"All Scripture is God-breathed ..."*

Jesus Christ: The pre-incarnate Christ [LORD] was the source of prophecy. After he ascended into heaven, he became the direct source of prophecy; *"The revelation of Jesus Christ which God gave him to show his servants what must soon take place. ..."* Again, it is written; *"I, Jesus, have sent my angel to give you this testimony for the churches. ..."* (Rev. 1:1; 22:16)

The Prophets as Covenant (Law) Enforcers

The prophet's message was not necessarily new; he only tried to turn the people from their idolatry and sin to the covenant that God had made with their forefathers. Therefore, to understand the prophets properly, it is important to understand the covenant that God made with Israel at Mount Sinai (Exodus 20 to Deuteronomy 31). The covenant specified their moral or ethical, cultic (sacrificial system), and civil obligations. The LORD their God promised them blessings or curses depending on their obedience or disobedience to the covenant, respectively. Some of the moral obligations, blessings and curses are recorded in the following passages: Exodus 20:1-17; 23:1-13; Leviticus 18, 19, 20, 22:17- 33; 26. The covenant was conditional as Israel was required to obey all that the LORD had commanded (Deut. 27:9-26; 28; then Deut. 30:1-10). The covenant demanded exclusive worship of the one true God, Yah; sound economics, and good treatment of the poor, widow, fatherless, and alien (Deut. 15:1-11). God warned them never to stray or disobey (Deut. 30:11-20; 1 Kings 9:1-9). Disobedience would lead to drastic consequences. Even after making the covenant with Israel, God predicted their disposition to forsake him and follow other gods (Deut. 31:14-29)! There are repeated echoes in the prophets concerning the forsaking of the covenant (Jer. 11:1-17; Ezek. 5:5-7; etc.). There were three parts to the covenant: the moral, the cultic, and the civil (though the Israelites regarded the law as a whole unit). God's moral law was to remain binding through all generations, even until today. The cultic law was fulfilled in Jesus Christ, while the civil law was abrogated, since God was no longer going to deal with his new people (the church) as a civil nation (though we can derive some implications from that civil law for today—for example, on private property; Ex. 21-22ff).

The Purpose of the Prophet's Message

The prophet's message was never intended for excitement or for the prophet's self-importance, nor was it for economic or private gain as is often the case with prophets today!

Firstly, the message was designed to reprimand or rebuke the people$r sins and religious hypocrisies; and to call them to repentance (Isa. 1, 28, 29; 10:5-19; Jer. 2-4:4; 9:12-14; 11).

Secondly, the message was intended to declare impending judgment on Israel and/or Judah if they failed to repent of their idolatry, sin, and pride (Jer. 4:5-5:31). God is merciful, compassionate, slow to anger and quick to forgive; he relents if people repent (Jer. 15:19-21; Jonah 3). The message also declared the impending judgment of idolatrous, proud, and sinful nations (Isa. 13-24).

Thirdly, the prophet also declared the distant future; that is, restoration and redemption in Christ, and the final judgment and eternal reign of King Jesus (Isa. 7, 9, 11, 12, 25, 26, 32, 42, 49, 53, 61ff, Jer. 23:1-8; 31:31-34; 33:14-18; Zech. 14).

Fourthly, the prophet's message was also intended to prove God's existence, and thus, distinguished him from all other gods, because he was and can declare the future or the end from the beginning (Isa. 43:8-13; 44:7-8; 45:20-21; Jer. 1:12; Ezek. 21:6-7; and of course, Daniel and Revelation). This not only demonstrates God's omniscience and foreknowledge, but also his providential guidance of all human history; the God of all mankind (Jer. 32:27)! God's self-vindication at the end of days will largely be based on the fact that he declared beforehand what has been happening in the world until the day Christ is revealed.

Fifthly, the prophet's message also has implications for us, the church; *"And we have the word of the prophets made more certain,* **and you will do well to pay attention to it,** *as a light shining in a dark place, until the day dawns and the morning star rises in your hearts"* (2 Pet. 2:19). The mystery of end- time events (our days) are all written in the prophets, and the more you read the prophets, the more you understand the events as they are being fulfilled (Rev. 10:5-7). Thus, the prophetic message is still valid for our days, and much more so. Therefore, we can correct our ways by learning from the sins of the Israelites; their complacency, religious hypocrisy, and backsliding (Amos 5:18-27; 6:1-7; Isa. 1:10-17).

However, we must distinguish what was specifically promised only to Israel (for instance, promise of land and covenant blessings) from what was promised to the church. In fact, there are not many direct promises to the church, though we still live by the moral law and derive implications from the prophets (and the rest of the Old Testament) for ourselves. The experience of the Israelites and the experience of the surrounding nations serve as examples for us (1 Cor. 10:1-11). Apocalyptic passages and other passages (especially messianic and millennial) that apply to the end time deserve our careful study. The New Testament is the direct prophetic word for the church. The blessing for the Christian is to carry the cross daily, to be hated, persecuted, and rejected by the world, and to suffer for Christ's sake (Matt. 5:11-12; Mark 10:29-31; Luke 14:25-27; Acts 14:22b; 2 Tim. 3:10-13).

Interpreting the Prophets

One important feature in interpreting Bible prophecy is to understand the literary structure of the material. Most of prophecy is neither narrative nor prose—it is mostly poetry. The prophets used contemporary idioms to rephrase the law; using the known to express the unknown and physical reality to convey spiritual reality and truth. Usually, they would use graphic physical depictions to get the people's attention to the spiritual lesson they wanted them to get. A prominent example is the constant usage of adultery to point out idolatry.

Some Aspects of Prophecy

Typology:
Definition: a. An event or events, object or objects, individual or individuals, and idea or ideas, that point forward to future ones or anticipate God's activity later in history. The former is a prototype of the latter. Only when the latter has occurred or is occurring can we be able to understand its prototype that pointed to it.

Jesus was the first to interpret Scripture in this manner and so did the apostles after him. The Church Fathers followed in their footsteps, but modern interpreters have questioned whether believers after the apostles have such a prerogative or not. Because typology can be abused as some Church Fathers did, they argue, it is advisable to stick with what Jesus and the apostles interpreted as typological (they were inspired, as those who deny this prerogative say). However, I do not believe that Jesus and the apostles exhausted all the typologies prefigured in the Old Testament. In some cases, even their words are types that point forward to the end of the age (2 Pet. 2:1).

It should be noted that typology does not suggest or signify two levels of meaning (*sensus plenior*—**deeper or fuller meaning**), as some suggest, or that the author intended or understood two levels of meanings. True typologies were known only by God, who inspired them and thus, set the pattern. Typologies are introduced by words like "just as," or "like," and others. Some examples include John 3:14-15 and Numbers 21:4-9; where Jesus said; *"**Just as** Moses lifted up the snake in the desert, so the Son of Man must be lifted up, that everyone who believes in him may have eternal life."* Then Matthew 2:13-15 and Hosea 11:1, where it is written; *"When Israel was a child, I loved him, and out of Egypt I called my son."* This statement referred to the nation of Israel when they came out of Egypt, but also typologically pointed forward to Joseph's flight to and from Egypt when Jesus was born. (cf. also1 Cor. 10:1-4 and Exod. 14:19-22; Ex. 17:6 and Num. 20:9-12; the water from the rock, which rock represented Christ. Heb. 3:2, 3; 7:1-3, 11, 15, 16 and Gen. 14:18-20).

b. Typology refers to events or predictions that had immediate and distant fulfillment. The LORD revealed an event in the prophets' immediate future that anticipated an event of a similar kind and even greater in the distant future. Think of a cone with increasing circles.

> "It should be noted, of course, that some of the prophecies of the near future were set against the background of the great, eschatological future, and sometimes they seem to blend. ... The reason for this is that the Bible regularly sees God's acts in temporal history in light of His overall plan for all of human history. Thus the temporal is to be seen in light of the eternal plan."[ii]

Some examples include:

Son of David (2 Sam. 7:11-16 and Matt. 22:41-45). Solomon was the immediate son of David, but this pointed forward to Jesus Christ, although the Christ is David's Lord.

The Day of the LORD (day of vengeance or day of reckoning; Amos 5:18-20; Isa. 2:6-4:1; 13:6-13; 24; 61:2bff; 63:1-6; etc.), and the **Day of our Lord Jesus Christ** (1 Cor. 1:8; 5:5; 2 Pet. 3:10-13; Parts of Revelation). The day of the LORD was historically fulfilled for Israel, Judah, and the nations, but it equally typologically pointed forward to the Day of the LORD/Lord/Christ at the end of the age (now). The Day of the LORD was/is usually accompanied by deliverance for the godly and those who repent (Isa. 13:6-24:23 and 19:19-25; 25, 26, 27). This confirms the cry of Habakkuk that in wrath God should remember mercy (Hab. 3:2). The Apostle Peter says that even in the Day of the Lord, believers are looking forward to the new age (new heaven and earth; 2 Pet. 3:13). A look through the book of Revelation reveals that during wrath, the saints overcome (the promise to all 7 churches; and also 12:10- 11, 17; 13:10; 14:12, 13); and join with the King of kings to conquer the enemies of God, the armies of the Antichrist (Rev. 17:14; 19). The saints will receive the kingdoms of the earth (Rev. 11:15-18; 20:4; cf. Dan. 2:34-35, 44-45; 7:13-14, 26-27; note how the saints are oppressed in Daniel 7:21-22, 25, just before they are delivered, same as in Revelation).

The Day of the LORD refers to the day or period when God punishes Israel or the nations (and ultimately the whole world) for their sins and rebellion against God (and his Christ) through an invasion or natural disasters (hail, drought, hurricanes, snow, wind, rain and flood, terror, crime, war, etc.). It is a devastation of world powers in descending order of world influence and importance from the top (superpowers) to the bottom: Babylon (Isa. 13:1-14:23), Assyria (Isa. 14:24-27), Philistine (Isa. 14:28-32), Moab (Isa. 15; 16), Damascus (17), Cush (18), Egypt (19), Egypt and Cush (20), Babylon (21:1-10; again for emphasis because Babylon was the greatest or number one! Babylon comes up again in Isaiah chapters 46 and 47), Edom (Isa. 21:11-12), Arabia (Isa. 21:13- 17), Jerusalem (Isa. 22), Tyre (Isa. 23), the whole earth (Isa. 24)!

NOTE:

1. The Day of the LORD was historically fulfilled for these nations and so also was deliverance and restoration for Jerusalem, but all pointed forward to the day of Christ—judgment for the wicked at the end of the age, deliverance and redemption for the Church, and restoration for Israel and Jerusalem (Messianic Age—Age of Gentiles or The West over!).

2. Except for God's supernatural judgment (ten plagues) in Egypt (while Israel was kept from the judgments), God used one nation to judge another; that is, using evil to judge evil. But the pride

of the instrument of judgment would eventually lead to the judgment of that nation. **The Day of the LORD for Israel and for the nations was called the Day of God's wrath (war, invasion, terror, famine, drought, devastation, calamity, snowstorm, hail, etc.;** Job 38:2-23; Isa. 10:5; 13:3, 6, 9; 26:20, 21; with the righteous preserved; Isa. 42:25; Ezek. 9:8).

3. **How the historical Day of the LORD was fulfilled:** In Exodus 7-11, God punished Egypt with ten plagues, but preserved Israel. In Isaiah 8:1-8, God used Assyria as his instrument of judgment to judge Damascus and Judah. Isaiah had prophesied earlier about this day of the LORD to be executed by Assyria on Judah in Isaiah 2:6-4:1. After Assyria was used as God's instrument of judgment (*"the rod of my anger, in whose hand is the club of my wrath,"* Isa. 10:5) against Judah, God in turn would judge Assyria for her destructive spirit and pride; *"When the LORD has finished all his work against Mount Zion and Jerusalem, he will say, 'I will punish the king of Assyria for the willful pride of his heart and the haughty look in his eyes"* (Isa. 10:6-19, 24-25; 14:24-32). God eventually judged Assyria by using his next instrument of judgment, Babylon and her king, Nebuchadnezzar (Jer. 25:8-14, 27:1-11). Babylon rose to superpower status by crushing the reigning superpower, Assyria, in 610 BC, and by crushing Egypt, the long-time superpower, at the battle of Carchemish in 605 BC. **Babylon fulfilled God's Day of wrath for these two nations as prophesied by Isaiah. Babylon equally fulfilled the LORD'S Day of wrath for the surrounding nations that Isaiah had prophesied against:** Edom, Moab, Ammon, Tyre and Sidon, Philistia, Gaza, and all the surrounding nations that Babylon crushed in her ascendancy to supremacy (Jer. 25:15-33). Judah was attacked by Egypt in 609 BC, beginning the day of the LORD for her. In 605 BC, Babylon subdued Judah, taking some Israelites, including Daniel the prophet, as captives to Babylon. In 597 more captives were taken to Babylon including Ezekiel the prophet. And finally in 586 BC, Jerusalem, the temple, the palaces, and every fine house, were burned down by the Babylonians and all the strong were taken to exile in Babylon (Jer. 39 and 52). Then, in Jeremiah 50-51, Jeremiah prophesied about the coming destruction of Babylon herself; that had been God's destructive instrument of judgment on other nations. In Daniel 4:24-

37, Nebuchadnezzar, God's servant, was punished and humbled for his pride (he walked with animals in the bush for seven years), and he repented. We are reminded that before this time, he had previously acknowledged God (Dan. 2:46-47) but remained proud and arrogant (Dan. 3:1-23). Finally, he acknowledged God after having been in the bush for seven years (Dan. 3:24-4:3). In Daniel 5, Babylon under Nebuchadnezzar's son, Belshazzar, finally fell to Darius, the Mede, and then to Cyrus, the Persian (God's anointed and captain of the LORD'S armies; Isa. 45; fulfilled in Ezra 1). Thus, we see that the day of the LORD or day of wrath is primarily fulfilled by war and terror, and secondarily by natural disaster.

After the Medo-Persians came the Greeks, the Romans, the Barbarians, and the Medieval Papacy (Babylonian Church). From the Barbarians came seven prominent colonial empires (Rev. 13:1-10): the Portuguese, Spaniards, French, Dutch, Anglo-Saxons, Italians, Germans; then from all these (and the rest of the world), the Americans, the eight, which is of the seven (Rev. 17:9-11); as depicted in the dreams of Nebuchadnezzar and Daniel (Dan. 2 and 7; that is, the history and fall of Western civilization—The Age of Gentiles, at Christ's second coming! Very soon!). For Russia, see Ezekiel 38 and 39 (now being fulfilled in the Russia-Ukraine war).

The question we may pause to ask is "Why does God call evil pagans his servants (Jer. **25:9; 27:6; Dan. 2:37-38; 5:18-19; Isa. 45:1, 4); and even uses them to carry out and/or reveal his plan?"** Notice that it is God who brings nations and empires to greatness: whether Israel, Assyria, Babylon, Media, Persia, and great nations of today (Dan. 2:37-38; 5:18-19). So why does God judge, destroy, and bring them down or bring them to an end? Do you think that God does not want people to have a happy time? Do you really think that God controls history and that both prosperity and disaster come from him (prophecy and apocalypse; Isa. 45:7; Amos 3:6; Mic. 2:3)? In fact, the Bible asserts that God moves the hearts of ALL the kings of the world, yet he will punish them for their arrogance, pride, and wickedness (Prov. 16:4)!

Evidence shows that at the height of every great civilization and human achievement, man always turns his back on God, becomes proud, and enthrones power or strength (military; Hab. 1:11; Mic. 2:1), wealth, money, pleasure, man (statues, idols—national idolatry; Dan. 3; an image of gold— modern equivalents like the Statue of Liberty and The Washington Monument), as god (Matt. 16:26). From God's warning to the Israelites (Ezek. 16); then Tyre (Ezek. 26-28); Babylon (Isa. 13-14); Nebuchadnezzar and Belshazzar (Dan. 4:24-31; 5); the rich fool (Luke 12:13-21); the wealthy of the world (James 5:1-6); and Jesus' saying that it is hard for the rich to enter heaven (Mark 10:17-25); we must be on the alert and examine ourselves, lest the deceitfulness of power and riches choke us, and the same fate befall us. The Bible warns;

"Those who cling to worthless idols forfeit the grace that could be theirs" **(Jonah 2:8).**
"Though grace is shown to the wicked, they do not learn righteousness; even in the land of uprightness, they go on doing evil and regard not the majesty of the LORD" **(Isa. 26:10).**
"I hate those who cling to worthless idols; I trust in the LORD" **(Psa. 31:6).**
"Pride goes before destruction, a haughty spirit before a fall" **(Prov. 16:18).**
"The fear of the LORD is to hate evil; I hate pride and arrogance, evil behavior and perverse speech" **(Prov. 8:13).**

However, this disposition and attitude to displace God and worship man and idols, does not surprise God, it just happens that God knows that man will behave this way (Deut. 8:10-20), but he will judge man severely!

4. Babylon, the greatest superpower of antiquity, comes up again and again in the prophets, and comes up again in Revelation 17 and 18. With the threat of judgment, God's people are always commanded to flee or come out of Babylon (Isa. 48:20; Jer. 50:8; Rev. 18:4). John the Apostle exhorts us; *"Dear children, keep yourselves from idols"* (1 John 5:21). He also says; *"Do not love the world or anything in the world. If anyone loves the world, the love of the Father is not in him. For everything in the world--the cravings of sinful man, the lust of the eyes and the boastings of what he has and does-- comes not*

from the Father but from the world. The world and its desires pass away, but the man who does the will of God lives forever" (1 John 2:15-17).

Figurative (Allegory and Analogy):

Allegory: An allegory is **an imaginary story** told to represent an actual physical event or circumstance. The *Oxford Illustrated American Dictionary,* defines allegory as; "a story, picture, etc., in which the meaning is represented symbolically." It is a kind of parable, but it is distinguished from a parable in that a parable is a fictional or imaginary story designed to teach or illustrate a moral or spiritual truth/lesson. There is a correlation of events and features in an allegory but not necessarily in a parable. The Church Fathers overextended the use of typology to allegory and allegorized the Old Testament in many illegitimate ways. Some examples of allegory are found in Ezekiel 16, 17, and 23.

Some have allegorized (typology?) the seven days of creation (a day with Lord is like a thousand years and a thousand years like a day; 2 Pet. 3:8), to represent the 7,000 years of modern human history until the new heaven and the new earth. Thus, by the year 2,000, we entered the seventh day of rest, the Millennium. So, Messiah will descend on ZION!

Analogy: An analogy is an **event that occurs similar in nature or parallel** to another event of a different kind. It is to speak figuratively. This also relates in some way to allegory. An example of an analogy is found in Galatians 4:21-31.

Shadow of Things to Come:

These include Laws or Events in Israel's history that pointed forward to a future reality. Most of these laws/events were/are fulfilled in Jesus Christ (Heb. 10:1).

Sabbath: The seventh day of rest (Gen. 2:2-3; Exod. 20:8-11; then Col. 2:13-17). The Sabbaths, feasts and their cycle of celebration were fulfilled in Jesus Christ (Matt. 5:17, 18). Is the Sabbath binding on believers today? How can you enforce it? Especially in an age of businesses operating 24 hours a day, seven days a week? Can it become a national issue as others are agitating? Or was the Sabbath only intended for the Israelites (Exod. 31:12-17)? The penalty for violating the Sabbath was death! Who among us actually keeps the Sabbath (see Isa. 58:13-14; Jer. 17:19-27)?

The Pharisees and the Sabbath: They strictly regulated the Sabbath with additional and complicated rules (about 39 in all!). They condemned Jesus for doing miracles on the Sabbath (Luke 13:10-17).

Jesus and the Sabbath: It was his custom to minister on the Sabbath (Luke 4:14-16). He violated the Pharisees' rules concerning the Sabbath (Luke 6:1-11). He is Lord of the Sabbath, which was made for man and not man for the Sabbath! He cited the commandments a few times without including the Sabbath (Luke 18:20). Perhaps, it was a given, given that he always taught on the Sabbath and everybody understood it to be the day of rest and worship. He rested in the grave on the Sabbath (Luke 23:53-56). Thus, Jesus did not teach his followers to break the Sabbath, since the women rested on the Sabbath and could only go to see Jesus in the tomb after the Sabbath. Therefore, until his death, Jesus and his disciples kept the Sabbath and he did not command them in any way to change the Sabbath.

The Apostles and Early Disciples and the Sabbath: It was their custom to minister on the Sabbath and sometimes everyday (Acts 13:14, 44; 16:13; 17:2;16-17; 18:4). The early church met on the Sabbath and on the first day (resurrection day) of the week for breaking of bread. The apostles did not command the keeping of the Sabbath, even when citing the commandments (Rom. 13:9, 10); but they did not abrogate the Sabbath either. Perhaps, Sabbath keeping was also a given to them! Nevertheless, no one should judge you concerning a Sabbath (Col. 2:13-17).

The First Day of the Week: The first day of the week was the resurrection day and the day for post resurrection meetings (Matt. 28:1-10; Luke 24:1-8; John 20:1-3, 19). It was the day for meeting and breaking of bread and study of the Apostles' word (Acts 2:46,

47; 20:7-12). It was the weekly meeting day during which offering and/or gifts were collected (1 Cor. 16:1-2). Thus, the early church, predominantly Israelites, met on both the Sabbath and on the first day of the week (Sunday).

How then did we come to meet only on Sunday? Long story! By the second, third and fourth centuries AD, the church was becoming predominantly Gentile. There was a growing tendency to distinguish Christianity from Judaism and some began to prefer Sunday over the Sabbath. There was an anti-Semitic twist to this preference. **Eventually, Constantine, the first supposed Christian Roman Emperor, decreed the observance of only one day for the Christians, Sunday (which also happened to coincide with the venerable day of his pagan Unconquered Sun-god worship).** This, of course, was confusion—when people gathered on Sunday: were they worshiping the venerable Sun or the exalted Son? The devil loves confusion (Babel)! The Roman Catholic Church maintains the exclusive claims of having changed the Sabbath from Saturday to Sunday! This explains the prominence of Sunday over Saturday or Sabbath as the day of Christian worship. **Is Sunday, therefore the Sabbath? No!** Can keeping the commandments then bring salvation? No! (Gal. 3:19-25; Rom. 3:20, 27- 28). Should we therefore toss the commandments out of the window? Absolutely not! (Rom. 3:31; 7:12- 14; 8:1-4; Rev. 12:17). The problem is not God's law (moral), it is us, who are sinful and no longer want to rest (to our own detriment; Hag. 1:5-6).

However, there still remains a Sabbath-rest (Millennium—when Christ will restore all things) for those who will defeat the devil and persevere to the end (Heb. 4:1-11). During this time all the Sabbaths of the LORD will be restored and celebrated (Isa. 66:24). But for now, here is my conclusion: in addition to Colossians 2:16-17; *"Therefore, do not let anyone judge you by what you eat or drink, or with regard to a **religious festival, a New Moon celebration or a Sabbath day. These are a shadow of the things that were to come; the reality, however, is found in Christ.**"* See also Romans 14:5, 6; *"One man consider one day more sacred than another; another man considers everyday alike. Each one should be fully convinced* *in his own mind. He who regards one day as special, does so to the Lord."* In this light, **no empire or nation can legislate or enforce the Sabbath, Saturday or Sunday!**

Patterns:

These are historical events or circumstances that repeat themselves as a pattern of judgment or redemption (see Eccl. 1:9-10 for cycles of moral history). Examples include: the recurrent events of Judges (2:6-11, 16; 3:7, 9; and the rest of the book); the sin of Sodom and Gomorrah (Gen. **18:20; 19:29); Israel sometime in her life was likened to Sodom and Gomorrah (Ezek. 16 esp. 46-52; Isa. 1:2-17). Jesus intimated that the days of his coming will be like the days of Sodom and Gomorrah. Our days indeed, are like the days of Sodom and Gomorrah (Luke 17:28-33; see also spiritual Sodom;** Rev. 11:7, 8). Thus, destruction will fall on our generation as it fell on Sodom and Gomorrah, and only believers will be delivered as Lot and his family was delivered then! But remember Lot's wife! She looked back at the world and became a pillar of salt (Gen. 19:26; Luke 17:32, 33)! She loved this world; its beautiful cities, wealth, and its glory or splendor—Satan's cosmic system both religious and political. This is why John warns against love of the world in 1 John 2:15-17; *"Do not love the world or anything in the world. If anyone loves the world, the love of the Father is not in him."* Heaven and earth (all civilization, irrespective of how beautiful it is—including America the beautiful) will pass away, but only the Word of God will stand forever and those who obey it! Choose today whom you will serve! Are you going to serve the world and money? Idols made with human hands? Or will you serve Christ? **Sodom, therefore, is a symbol of depravity or grievous sin, and where this pattern is repeated, judgment and destruction are inevitable.**

Another parallel event (a pattern of evil) pointing out these days close to the coming of the Lord is the days of Noah prior to the Flood (Gen. 6:1-9; Matt. 24:37-39). There is a group of people here called the **sons of God or sons of the gods** [These were fallen angels or demonized humans or deified humans, since they could lust. They were like the kings, rulers, and judges of old, who claimed they were gods (Psalm 82:1, 6-7; Ezek. 28:2, 6, 9; Acts 11:21-23). Roman emperors, for example, were deified]. **Notice the watchword: *lust,* which is a universal disease in our days! Sexual perversion in our day seems to be demonically influenced—rampant sexual immorality, homosexuality, lesbianism, divorce, cohabitation, violent sex (rape), child rape (molestation), pornography (visual and slide), sodomy or oral sex (touching each other's genitals with the mouth); lasciviousness, lewdness, concupiscence, indecency and impropriety—almost everything, especially in Western society today, that is not sexy is considered out of fashion.**

We pause here to consider the sexual revolution in the USA in the 1960s (Satan deceived Eve); the commercialization of sex (whether dress, lotion, etc., is it sexy?); adult and child prostitution; sex slavery (pimps—with the arc stretching from Asia through Russia, and Europe to North America). Jesus warns that; *"But I tell you that anyone who looks at a woman lustfully has already committed adultery with her in his heart"* (Matt. 5:28). Yet, our civilized culture thrives on the promotion of lust and illicit sex. **Hollywood and pornography have become the wide gates that lead to destruction, and many are walking that path without blushing. Nothing can be more antichristian and satanic or demonic!**

Another class of people in Noah's day that parallel our days is **Giants.** Men of renown: stars, actors, celebrities, sports stars, heroes and heroines, warriors, etc.; these have become icons and idols of worship in our days!

Another watchword concerning Noah's days is **Wickedness.** There is increase crime, organized crime—national and international (The Mafia, drug trafficking), gangs; drug addiction and epidemics, with drugs like cocaine, heroin, marijuana, ecstasy, Methamphetamine, etc.; gun violence and murder (with the USA toping the chart among industrialized nations), suicide, abortion, kidnapping, terrorism, and the like. Wickedness, indeed, is the watchword for our society! Thus, **every inclination and the thoughts of the heart of man were evil all the time, so it is today!** Doing that which is contrary to God and hurtful to others, both individual and organized evil (political and religious crusade arrogance), have become the norm rather than the exception.

During this wicked and moral decadence, **Noah was blameless and a preacher of righteousness.** He acted faithfully and built the ark of safety. Are you blameless and righteous? Will you be spared like Noah? **The most shocking thing is that only eight people were saved out of that whole generation!** Are only a few people going to be saved (Luke 13:23-27; Matt. 7:21-23)? Will the Son of Man come and find faith on the earth (Luke 18:8)? **Many people want to enter heaven on their OWN CONDITIONS and by DOING THEIR OWN WILL, but not by God's condition, nor are they willing to do God's Will!** Are you in the ark of safety, Jesus Christ? Are you standing on the rock? Will the door be closed on you even as you warm the church bench paying lip services but worshipping the devil (Matt. 7:21-23)?

These two events (destruction during Noah's time and destruction of Sodom and Gomorrah) were a pattern of things that pointed forward to the destruction that will come upon the wicked, unrepentant, and hypocrites, when the Lord Jesus Christ returns—there will be weeping and gnashing of teeth (2 Pet. 2:1-9). Are our days worse than the days of Noah and the days of Lot? YES! We have the Word of God unlike them, yet we go on sinning! Their major sins were sexual perversion, overeating, unconcerned (apathy/complacency), arrogance, haughtiness, which illustrates the cycle of human civilization (Ezek. 16:49, 50a). The Lord hates these things (Prov. 8:13). Save yourselves from the wrath that is being poured out on the earth, oh brood of vipers!

Stop and ponder the following questions: Where do you fall? Are you with Noah in the ark? Are you a Lot? Are you Lot's sons-in-law to-be (Gen. 19:12-14), who were warned but failed to escape? Or are you Lot's wife? Where your treasure is there your heart will be also! Do not work for food that spoils, but for food that endures to eternal life, which the Son of Man will give you (John 6:27). Do not cling to worthless idols that will be destroyed soon (Jonah 2:8; 1 John 5:25).

Other passages that enumerate the sins of the last days include: Rom. 1:18-32; 1 Tim. 4:1-5; 2 Tim. 3:1-13; 4:1-5; 1 Thess. 4:15-5:9; 2 Thess. 2:1-12; James 5:1-6; Dan. 12; Matt. 24; Luke

21:5-36; Rev. 9:20-21; 16:21. Could we be actually experiencing a time of distress now, a time of judgment, especially as recorded in Luke 21:25-26? Emphatically Yes! He who has eyes, let him open and see; and let him who has ears, let him listen! If anyone is to be led into captivity, into captivity he will go!

Apocalypse (Greek: to reveal or unveil):

In apocalypse, redemptive and historical events are revealed in symbols, images, and numbers through visions or dreams. In interpretation, clues should be searched within the apocalypse itself, related apocalypse, and in history. Apocalypse, like the rest of prophecy, is mostly understood during or after fulfillment. Some **examples include: Ezekiel 1; God or Son of Man on his throne; Ezekiel 37:1-14;** restoration from Babylon and final restoration at the end of the age, that is, the resurrection of Israel; **15- 28; Daniel 2:** five superpowers from Babylon to the present modern western civilization, with the USA at the top, equivalent in power to Rome; in fact, the greatest superpower in all of human history (deeply divided—the political situation in the US today, just before Christ descends; especially verses 41-45). Rise up, oh Zion, for your redemption is near! **Daniel 7:** similar to dream of statue in Daniel 2, but with some details; with the horn waging war against the saints, especially verses 20-27. Relate to Revelation 12:1-3; 13; 17. Most of Revelation chapters 4-16 is apocalypse; so also, is Zechariah 5:5-11, which relates to Revelation 17; two kinds of women are presented, where one represents the true church and another the false church. **Babylon stands for** the epitome of civilization, the standard of wickedness and degeneration; that is, what is considered the civilized world today is turning from God toward degeneration, while the Third World or Developing World is receiving the gospel; the first shall be last and the last first!

Wake up! The end is upon us! Stand in the gap; blow the trumpet; warn the wicked, the hypocrites and the complacent; FLEE FROM BABYLON!

CHAPTER 2

UNDERSTANDING SATAN

Satan in the Old Testament

Satan is one of the major characters in the Scripture. His name suggests his character; he is the arch enemy or adversary of God and his plan. He is the epitome and perpetrator of evil. He is the blueprint of the spirit of disobedience to God (Eph. 2:2). As to his origin, the Bible shows that he was created, but when he was created, only God knows. However, since he began his activity with our first parents, Adam and Eve, we can rightly assume that he was created before Adam and Eve. As we shall see, since the time that he lost his position before God, Satan still lives in God's presence.

Satan in Eden; Genesis 3

Satan is first mentioned in the Bible in Genesis chapter three, right at the beginning of human life. His last mention would be at the beginning and end of the Millennium. He is introduced in Genesis chapter three as the serpent, an animal among creatures of God. From this passage, we learn the following things about Satan.

1. He is crafty; always having an evil intent.

2. He attacks from the weak side, that is, Adam was in charge, but he came to the woman. He tempts man on his area of weakness, and uses natural desires to lead men astray.

3. He creates doubts about the word and command of God; *"Did God really say, 'You must not eat from any tree in the garden'?"* (v.1). He twists God's word to suit his diabolic purposes. By his cunning attitude and pressure, he deceived Eve, making her even to add to God's words. God had commanded them not to *"eat from the tree of the knowledge of good and evil ...,"* but Eve added *"... and you must not touch it ..."* (v.3). When you fail to follow all the commands of God, you have inadvertently fallen into Satan's trap. He feeds on mental laziness and ignorance of the word of God. Where biblical illiteracy is prevalent, Satan succeeds the most.

4. He is a liar. He twists and contradicts the word of God. He said to the woman; *"You will not surely die"* (v.4). To be sure, Satan will quote the word, but to suit his schemes and agenda.

5. He claims to have the secrets to make humans be like God or gods; *"For God knows that when you eat of it your eyes will be opened, and you will be like God, knowing good and evil"* (v.5).

6. He causes chaos. The man and the woman began to blame each other for their disobedience to God's command; *"The man said, 'The woman you put here with me--she gave me some fruit from the tree, and I ate"* (v.12).

7. Satan's fate was decreed from the beginning; *"So the LORD said to the serpent, 'Because you have done this, cursed are you above all the livestock and all the animals! You will crawl on your belly and you will eat dust all the days of your life. And I will put enmity between you and the woman, and between your offspring and hers; he will crust your head, and you will strike his heel'"* (vv.14-15).

The woman's offspring ultimately referred to Jesus Christ. He crushed Satan's head on the cross at the same time that Satan stroke his heel. Since the cross, Satan has always been determined to destroy those who trust in Jesus Christ and obey God (Rev. 12:17).

While humans have the volition (freewill) and potential to reject evil and sin, Satan is behind every evil and sinful action. In the course of time, as Adam and Eve's children, Cain and Abel, brought offerings to the LORD, Abel's was accepted but Cain's was rejected. Filled with anger, Cain murdered Abel. Commenting on this passage, John writes; *"Do not be like Cain, who belonged to the evil one and murdered his brother. And why did he murder him? Because his own actions were evil and his brother's were righteous"* (1 John 3:12). When Cain became angry that his offering was not accepted, God said to him; *"If you do what is right, will you not be accepted."* Thus, we see that Satan instigated the first murder, and since then, all murders until now. That is why Jesus says of Satan; *"... He was a murderer from the beginning, not holding to the truth, for there is no truth in him ..."* (John 8:44).

Genesis 6:1-7

Satan, as we will see later, has a host of fallen angels or demons (devils) with him who carry out his plans. The appellation "sons of God" seems to refer to these fallen angels (cf. Job 1:6). However, Psalm 82 gives us a clue as to their identity. God is said to preside in judgment among the gods; *"God presides in the great assembly; he gives judgment among the "gods"* (v.1). These "gods" are referred to as sons of the Most High, men and rulers (judges); *" 'I said, 'You are "gods"; you are all sons of the Most High.' But you will die like mere men; you will fall like every other ruler"* (vv.6-7). Therefore, though called "gods," "sons of the Most High," or "sons of God," these creatures were mere men. The activities thus described, imply that those referred to in Genesis 6, were human beings, who were perhaps deified as gods. They were probably corrupt and perverted leaders, kings, judges, princes, and heroes. Our concern is mostly about the activity of these satanic beings. Activities that suggest they were humans include:

1. They were human in appearance since they could marry.

2. They lusted after the daughters of men (sexual perversion).

3. They were heroes, therefore, brave and famous men (renown).

4. Resulting from this was the fact that the human heart became exceedingly wicked; *"The LORD saw how great man's*

wickedness on the earth had become, and that every inclination of the thoughts of his heart was only evil all the time" (v.5).

No matter the identity of these individuals, it is clear that Satan's activities were visibly manifested to the highest degree. Men were in alliance with Satan and his humanized demons against God. Satan is described as the spirit that works in the children of disobedience; *"As for you, you were dead in your transgressions and sins, in which you used to live when you followed the ways of this world and of **the ruler of the kingdom of the air, the spirit who is now at work in those who are disobedient"*** (Eph. 2:1-2). Satan is the spirit behind all disobedience as it began in the Garden of Eden with Adam and Eve.

Job 1:6ff and 2:1ff

Job is another instance where Satan's character is revealed; he is the accuser of those who love and obey God. In fact, the word "Satan" means accuser or adversary. As already said, Satan still lives in the presence of God. In verse 6, he was among the "sons of God" or divine beings (angels) as they came to present themselves before the LORD. His brief conversation with the LORD reveals his jurisdiction; *"The LORD said to Satan, 'Where have you come from'? Satan answered the LORD, 'From roaming through the earth and going back and forth in it'"* (v.7; cf. 1 Pet. 5:8). When God challenged him concerning the blamelessness and uprightness of Job, Satan immediately accused Job before God; *"Does Job fear God for nothing?' Satan replied. 'Have you not put a hedge around him and his household and everything he has? .... "* (1:9-11). Satan challenged God that if Job's wealth was taken away, Job would curse God to his face. When this test against Job failed, Satan challenged God to afflict Job's body with disease. Again, Job passed the test although his wife failed, by asking Job to curse God and die (v. 9-10).

Isaiah 14:3-20 And Ezekiel 28:1-19.

These two passages depict Satan personified or incarnated in the rulers of Babylon and Tyre. The passages point backward to the original fall of Satan, and also forward to his final fall before the beginning of the millennial reign of Christ. Because we will deal with these passages in detail later, I will just mention a few things here. It is apparent that God gave man authority to rule over the earth and subdue it (Gen. 1:28). Man gave over this mandate to Satan and man's attempt to dominate the world is tainted and satanically motivated. Isaiah 14:3-20 shows that:

1. Satan originally lived or lives in heaven.

2. He was the first among God's creation--the morning star, son of the dawn. These descriptions come close to those of Jesus--the bright morning star (Rev. 22:16).

3. Satan laid/is laying low the nations.

4. Satan's ambition was/is to raise his throne above the stars of God (nations) and enthrone himself in the mount of assembly or the church (cf. 2 Thess. 2:2-12).

5. Satan wanted/wants to be like the Most High, thus usurping God's place, authority and power. Ezekiel 28:1-19 further shows that:

6. Satan's major problem is pride (because of his beauty).

7. He wanted/wants to be a god with an exalted throne. Remember this is what he promised to Eve,

8. "You will be like God."

9. Satan was/is the model of perfection, full of wisdom, and perfect in beauty.

10. He was the anointed guardian cherub. He is an expert in trade (dishonest trade), which has caused him to sin.

Other Mentions of Satanic Activity in the Old Testament

Satan may not be mentioned specifically in some parts of the Old Testament, but there is evidence that his activities are manifested through the activities of certain individuals. It is important to note that any activity that God prohibits has an evil or satanic origin. Satan and his demons are behind every form of idolatry, some of which include: divination, sorcery, consulting mediums and spirits, child sacrifice (abortion as modern equivalent), worship of Molech, interpreting of omens, witchcraft, casting spells, necromancy, astrology (worship of starry host), and the like. In Zechariah 3:1-2, Satan is introduced as the accuser, who was standing before Joshua (high priest symbolizing Christ yet to come). The LORD sternly rebuked him (cf. Jude 9).

CHAPTER 3

ISRAEL'S BLUNDER

After Adam and Eve's rebellion, man was left on his own to seek God. In Genesis 6, we see Noah as a man who was blameless and found grace before God. God revealed himself to Noah, but there was no written revelation yet. Even in God's dealings with Abraham and his immediate progeny, there was no written revelation. Beginning with Moses, God was to be the direct ruler of his people, Israel, through those he would choose and put his Spirit in them. Joshua followed Moses, then God raised up rulers (Judges), to lead Israel. The priests (Levites) were to handle matters related to worship.

Israel Asked for a King

The Israelites were not satisfied with God's leadership through the judges and the priests. They looked at the leadership style of their pagan neighbors and wanted to imitate them. They started to ask for a king by requesting one Judge, Gideon, to be their king, but he refused; *"The Israelites said to Gideon, 'Rule over us--you, your son and your grandson--because you have saved us out of the hand of Midian.' But Gideon told them, 'I will not rule over you, nor will my son rule over you. **The LORD will rule over you**'"* (Jud. 8:22-23). Again, in the days of Samuel, the judge and prophet, **the Israelites rejected the LORD'S leadership and requested for a king to rule over them as was the case with other pagan nations** surrounding them; *"So all the elders of Israel gathered together and came to Samuel at Ramah. They said to him, 'You are old, and your sons do not walk in your ways; **now appoint a king to lead us, such as all the other nations have**'"* (1 Sam. 8:4-5; How the people of God always want to go the way of the world, even today! Jesus warned the disciples against Gentile systems). This made Samuel very angry, and he prayed to the LORD; *"And the LORD told him: 'Listen to all that the people are saying to you; it is not you they have rejected, but they have rejected me as their king'"* (v.7). The LORD, through Samuel, warned the Israelites of the disadvantages of asking for a king, but they insisted to have a king anyway; *"But the people refused to listen to Samuel. 'No!' they said. 'We want a king over us. Then we will be like all the other nations, with a king to lead us and to go out before us and fight our battles.'"* Thus, the people rejected God's kingship and preferred human kingship, though the LORD had up to then, fought their battles for them. The Jews would again cry out before Jesus' crucifixion; *"We have no king but Caesar!"* God's people living in disobedience are always prone to go with human viewpoint rather than divine viewpoint. They prefer the way of the world (Satan's way) and paganism to God's way.

Saul is Made King

Although the people rejected God's kingship, God did not abandon them, he condescended and went ahead and gave them a king. The LORD selected a young man, Saul, tall and handsome, whom Samuel anointed as king over Israel. The LORD'S Spirit came upon Saul in power and he prophesied. However, Saul later failed to carry out the LORD'S specific instruction to annihilate the sinful Amalekites and everything that belonged to them; *"But Saul and the army spared Agag and the best of the sheep and cattle, the fat calves and lambs--everything that was good ..."* (1 Sam. 15:9). God was displeased with Saul and to further aggravate the situation, Saul said that he spared the best sheep and cattle in order to sacrifice to the LORD. This made Samuel angry; *"But Samuel replied: 'Does the LORD delight in burnt offerings and sacrifices as much as in obeying the voice of the LORD? **To obey is better than sacrifice,** and to heed is better than the fat of rams. **For rebellion is like the sin of divination, and arrogance like the evil of idolatry.** Because you have rejected the word of the LORD, he has rejected you as king'"* (1 Sam. 15:22-23). The verdict against Saul was clear and the gravity of the sin illustrated. If only we can learn from Saul's failure! Saul began to give excuses as to why he did what he did (like, I was afraid of the people and so I gave in to them), but the verdict was already reached and could not be changed. So, the LORD was grieved that he had made Saul as king over Israel.

The Spirit of the LORD departed from Saul, and an evil spirit from the LORD tormented him. Saul's life and leadership spiraled downward, and he was filled with evil and murderous thoughts toward David, who was to replace him as king. He killed the priests, and resorted to witchcraft and divination for help because the LORD would not speak to him again. He consulted a witch at Endor (1 Sam. 28). Eventually, Saul went to war against the Philistines and in the face of defeat took his own life (1 Sam. 31). What a tragic end to an excellent beginning! When God gives over anyone, nothing can reverse the course. Disobedience is a terrible sin that we must avoid at all cost. As it was with Adam, so it was with Saul. What about you? It was not only this occasion that Saul had acted presumptuously. As the king and hence the civil leader, he had once taken upon himself to execute spiritual duties, which only the priest, Samuel, had the prerogative to execute (1 Sam. 13:7b-14). He was equally rejected as king because of this. This is a solemn reminder that only God can hold both civil or political power and spiritual power at the same time or only the specific leader that he has commissioned these offices to. Any other person who tries to sway both civil and spiritual power like Saul is a usurper; like the Antichrist is doing/would do in these last days.

David is Made King

Once Saul was rejected as king, the LORD chose David to replace him. David is said to have been ruddy, with a fine appearance and handsome features. He was brave, a warrior, and eloquent, and the LORD was with him. He proved his bravery by defeating the Philistine giant, Goliath. He entered Saul's service, but Saul became jealous of him, and tried to kill him. As David fled from Saul, he went through many difficulties. He had opportunities to kill Saul but dared not lay a hand upon the LORD'S anointed.

David's life before he finally settled on the throne in Israel is an example of patience. Sometimes we see the end at the beginning, but we must be patient and go through the thistles and thorns until God brings us to our victory and destination. No foolishness, presumption, and short-cuts are allowed. David first became king over Judah and then later, over all of Israel. He conquered Jerusalem, defeated the Philistines, and brought the Ark of the Covenant to Jerusalem. David was a warrior, and his conquests were phenomenal. He expanded the borders of Israel to include almost all the promised territory. David was a great king and a great prophet (the Psalms) and earned the title of *"a man after God's own heart."* Nevertheless, he blundered in a few things. He committed adultery with one of his general's wife, and then conspired for the murder of the general in order to take the general's wife, Bathsheba, as his own wife. God was not happy with David because of what he had done; *"... But the thing David had done displeased the LORD"* (2 Sam. 11:27). God sent Nathan, the Prophet, to rebuke David. David repented but evil did not depart from his house. One of his sons, Amnon, raped his half-sister, Tamar; and his son, Absalom, conspired against him to take over the kingdom and David fled from him.

Solomon is Made King

When David had had rest from his enemies, he settled in his palace. He wanted to build a house for the LORD, but the LORD revealed to David through Nathan, the prophet, that he will establish his house forever, and give him a son to sit on his throne forever, too (2 Sam. 7:11-16).

This prophecy was fulfilled in in Solomon, who had a long, restful, and prosperous reign. However, Solomon was just a type, and pointed forward to the Christ, who will, at his second coming, sit on the throne of David that will last forever. Christ's throne and kingdom will last forever. The magnificence and splendor of Solomon's kingdom was a foreshadow of what Christ's kingdom will be, and many times better.

Solomon became king in place of his father David, though one of David's sons, Adonijah, attempted to usurp the throne. It is written;

"So Solomon sat on the throne of the LORD as king in place of his father David" (1 Chron. 29:23). Once established on the throne, Solomon made the right choice toward God. When God appeared to him in a dream and asked him to ask whatever he wanted, Solomon asked for a discerning heart. God gave him wisdom and added riches and honor as well! (1 Kings 3:9- 13).

So great was Solomon's wisdom that he wrote many proverbs, songs, and other achievements. Many came from all over the world to listen to his wisdom. He built a magnificent temple and palace and accumulated much gold and chariots. Despite his wisdom and splendor, Solomon blundered. He married many foreign wives (700 wives and 300 concubines), who turned his heart away to foreign gods. God became angry with Solomon. He raised up enemies against Solomon, and his very own son, Jeroboam, rebelled against him. Eventually, God split the kingdom into two, Judah and Israel, because of Solomon's sins. We see here again that, just as in the case of Adam and Saul, obedience brings blessing, but disobedience brings a curse. We must always allow God in control as king of our lives.

The Hebrew Prophets and God's Plan Till the Coming Millennium Revealed

With the promise of an eternal throne to David and typified in Solomon, God began to reveal his plan for the coming millennium following the second coming of Christ. Throughout the Psalms, prophecies are given of the coming of the Messiah (first and second advents) to sit on David's throne (Ps. 2; 72) Down the tunnel, the LORD revealed to the prophets events that will occur to the Israelites (captivity and restoration) until the Messiah comes. A large gap (Church Age) would exist between the first and second advent (for instance, Isaiah 61:1-2a speaks of the first advent, while 2b-11 speaks of the second advent).

No prophet had a better view of this time of peace and glory of Christ than Isaiah. Christ himself will rule as King of kings and Lord of lords. He will be the ideal king and will rule the world with justice, righteousness, equity, and with an iron scepter (his powerful Word).

The Millennium will be a time of righteousness: righteous judgment, of peace among wildlife, and of peace among the nations(Is. 11; 12). Nations will flock to Jesus Christ for righteousness and will praise God (Is. 30:19-26; 32:1-8). It will be a time of restoration of what went wrong in Eden and beyond (Is. 35; 54; 62); a time of everlasting salvation (Is. 51:1-16); a time of glory in Zion (Is. 60); a time of universal knowledge of God (Is. 11:9; Hab. 2:14; Jer. 31:33-34); a time of prosperity for the nations (Ps. 72:7,16); a time of new creation and longevity of life (Is. 65:17-25).

In his earthly ministry, Jesus referred again and again to the age to come (the Millennium). He focused his teaching on this present age and how it will end. He gave many promises that will be fulfilled in the age to come. One of these promises is recorded in John 14:1-3; *"Do not let your hearts be troubled. Trust in God; trust also in me. In my Father's house are many rooms; if it were not so I would have told you. I am going there to prepare a place for you. And if I go and prepare a place for you, I will come back and take you to be with me that you also may be where I am,"*

God began to reveal this timetable by 1000 BC through Samuel the prophet. In fact, he even began earlier when he gave the promise to Abraham to bless all nations through him (about 2000 BC). Later, we will examine what was happening in the world outside of Israel at the very time. Satan, the master counterfeiter, began to reveal his own millennium to those who serve him around the world. We will equally see how this counterfeit has spanned the centuries in religions, philosophies, political ideologies, and the new age movements.

CHAPTER 4

SATAN AND HIS COUNTERFEIT PLAN

Since the time that Satan rebelled against God and led astray several of the angels to be with him, he has been working hard to make himself god and to make mankind to serve and worship him. When Adam and Eve disobeyed in the garden, Satan took over dominion of this world and became its god. As an invisible personality (spirit of disobedience; Eph. 2:2), he works relentlessly through the cultures and hearts of men in order to be recognized as god. Since he was God's first creature and servant, he knows part of God's plan for mankind, and in attempt to set himself up as god, he imitates God's plan. As we shall see, Satan is the master planner behind all religions, philosophies, and political ideologies. He take's advantage of man's religiosity to enslave man and bid him to do his will. He is the inventor of every religion that does not honor God as revealed in the Holy Scriptures and incarnated in Jesus Christ.

Primitive Religions

God created man in his own image and likeness, and thus, man was meant for a relationship and fellowship with God. Therefore, there is something inherent in man that longs for God. Simply put, man is a religious being. His religiosity, if not fulfilled, creates a void in him. When this void is not filled by God, Satan fills it with all kinds of false religions and philosophies. The Bible shows that mankind has one ancestor, no matter where he came to be found on the surface of the earth. It is written; *"From one man he* [God] *made every nation of men, that they should inhabit the whole earth; and he determined the times set for them and the exact places where they should live. God did this so that men would seek him and perhaps reach out for him and find him, though he is not far from each one of us"* (Acts 17:26- 27). God deliberately scattered mankind over the whole earth so that they may find him and worship him (Gen. 11:8). However, since man relinquished his position to Satan, Satan is using all kinds of superstitions and religions to enslave man and prevent him from seeking the one and only true God. Because of man's ignorance, Satan has blinded man and men have resorted to the worship of the heavenly hosts (sun, moon, stars, planets, etc.); every imaginable created thing like trees, birds, animals, rivers, springs, stones, spirits (demons), ancestral spirits, gods (created by their imaginations), idols (of wood, gold, silver, stone), cast images of revered leaders, and many others. These false religions and superstitions were/are manifested through witchcraft, sorcery, ritual, divination, prayer, necromancy, casting spells, consulting mediums, and the like; and were/are regulated by chiefs, priests, shamans, and a host of others. These primitive religious practices and superstitions have continued till today in both uncivilized and civilized cultures. Sometimes the old stuff is repackaged in new baggage—occultism.

We will note here that all these practices are forbidden by God; *"Let no one be found among you who sacrifices his son or daughter in the fire, who practices divination or sorcery, interprets omens, engages in witchcraft, or casts spells, or who is a medium or spiritist or who consults the dead"* (Deut. 18:10-11). God had equally warned against the worship of heavenly starry hosts like the sun, moon, stars, or planets; *"And when you look up to the sky and see the sun, the moon and the stars--all the heavenly array—do not be enticed into bowing down to them and worshiping things the LORD your God has apportioned to all the nations under heaven"* (Deut. 4:19).

Eastern Religions

By about 2000 BC, most primitive religions were developing into organized religions. This happened to be the same time that God called Abraham out of the idolatry of the Chaldeans and promised to bless the whole world through him. One of the earliest of these religions was Hinduism, from which other religions would later develop. The rest of these religions that continue to today include: Jainism, Buddhism, Sikhism, Chinese religions, Daoism, Confucianism, Shinto, and Zoroastrianism. These religions center around their founders and moralistic and behavioral teachings, regarding men and women, children, and the society. Some, like Hinduism are polytheistic (worship of many gods) and observe high and rigorous spiritual lives, with self-control as a major goal. Asceticism is highly cherished in some of these religions, especially Buddhism. Buddhism has a strict moral code (The Ten Precepts[iii]) for its monks, the first five of which apply also to the laity. In Buddhism, the eightfold path highlights its optimum spirituality.[iv] In a sense, these religions represent a culture, a worldview, a way of life. Some may have a concept of a Supreme Being, but as to how he can be known, or how he relates to mankind, is only speculative. It can be concluded that despite the moral correctness within these religions, their epistemology about God and how he can be reached, are only doctrines of Satan and his demons. Thus, Satan is the force behind their distorted epistemology about God, if they have any concept of God at all.

Ancient Egyptians and Babylonians

Here we can trace how primitive beliefs and religions and village deities evolved into city, government, and national deities. There was a multiplicity of gods (polytheism) in almost every primitive society; or in short, superstitions and the doctrines of demons. The Egyptians had strong religious beliefs that to an extent shaped their national life, though they were highly polytheistic. As one person has said; "Certainly few peoples honored more gods and goddesses; the deities worshiped by the Egyptians numbered in thousands. These spirits were conceived in a confusing variety of forms—as animals, humans, birds, plants, inanimate forms, abstractions, and mixtures of any three of these forms."[v] With the passage of time, these deities narrowed down, and some became national deities. For instance, Horus, Amon, Ra - the sun god, and Osiris (and his wife Isis) - grantor of a happy life after death. The Egyptians had a strong belief in the afterlife and a final judgment, where the heart of the individual will be weighed on a balance against the goddess of truth. Thus, Egyptian religion was concerned about a good and moral life for its adherents.

Babylonian religion evolved from village to city to national gods, and at the center of their worship was the temple—a center for social life, where sacrifices were made to the gods. Like the earlier inhabitants of the river valleys, the Mesopotamians, Babylonians were polytheistic, with countless numbers of deities. Some of the deities that came to prominence include: An (Anu) - the sky- god; Enlil (Bel) - the air-god; Enki (Ea, god of earth and water); Nanna (Sin) - the moon god; Utu (Shamash) - the sun god; Isthar became the universal goddess of love and fertility, and was later worshipped as the planet Venus - the queen of heaven.[vi] When Babylon rose to prominence, Marduk became her most prominent national god. These deities served various functions and under them were lesser spirits that could bring blessings or misfortunes to the people.

Greek Mythology and Philosophy

Among the Greeks, the primitive gods gave way to more prominent gods of much importance and prominence. These gods evolved as people began to conglomerate in cities and nations. The Greek city-state began to form after a series of invasions and influx into Asia Minor of Aryan or Indo-Europeans (from the north) such as the Achaeans, Dorians, Ionians, and Aeolians. In this influx deities emerged, chief among whom were: Zeus (Pater), the chief god - sky-father and rainmaker (known as Dyaus Pitar to Indo-Aryans; and Jupiter to the Romans); Demeter, the earth-mother; Hestia (sister of Zeus), virgin goddess of the hearth; Rhea; Athena; Hermes; Hera; Apollo; Aphrodite; Dionysus; Artemis, Poseidon, and Ares (some of these gods are mentioned in the book of Acts). These deities were immanent and mundane and were readily invoked during daily activities, but others like Hades (god of the underworld) and Ouranos (the god of heaven), were transcendent and believed in but not worshipped in Greek homes.[vii] The gods were believed to have great power over humans, sometimes blessing or cursing them. Around these deities arose myths (Greek mythology) concerning origins— including the origin of the gods themselves (Homer). Later, early Greek philosophers further refined the idea of the gods, and tried as hard as they could to come up with the idea of a Super Being (monotheism) rather than many gods (polytheism). From the start,

"Greek philosophy began as monism: everything in the universe is some form or other of one thing." This one thing, "Whatever it was, it was creative or divine, …. Xenophanes was sure that the creative power was 'one god greatest among gods and men, not like mortals in form, nor yet in mind. He sees all over, thinks all over, and hears all over.'"[viii] Plato came to conceive of this being as;

> "There was above them, and behind all other beings and things, a Creator, or Artisan, who had identified himself with the highest of all values, the Good. He it was who in the beginning beheld the realm of ideal forms, which not even he created, and was inspired by them to make a world that participated in their structure and that, in mountains, plains, and seas, gods, humans, and animals, bodied forth the good, the beautiful, and true in various degrees. As for man or woman, each is a soul in a body, and the soul needs to grow toward the highest good, that it may no longer have to suffer continued rebirth [reincarnation?] but go into that state in which it may, like God, behold and enjoy forever the hierarchy of the ideal forms, in all their truth, beauty, and goodness."[ix]

Plato disliked the superstition of worship and attempts to please or manipulate the gods. He was no friend of atheism or superstition; "Firm in his beliefs, Plato in his old age contended that atheism or any assertion that God is indifferent to humankind or can be bought off by gifts or offerings should be treated as dangerous to society."[x] Aristotle too, broke with traditional polytheism and "in considering the highest kind of being, he had to posit God the Prime Mover, that is, a being causing all the movements of celestial and terrestrial bodies by attraction toward himself, while being himself actually without motion."[xi] Thus, in their thinking, we see how man attempts to reach God purely from reason without inherited religion. Did they find God or merely found new religions different from the traditional superstitions and mythology?

Rome, Etruscans Influence, and the Rest of Europe

The Italian peninsular was first inhabited by non-Indo-European peoples. The shaping of the religion of the Romans (Latins) was much influenced by or borrowed from the Etruscans, Greeks, Egyptians, and the Middle East. The Roman religion was therefore eclectic. Chief among their deities included: Diana; Jupiter - the great sky-father, who was the most exalted of the gods known as Optimus Maximus, and who brought rain and sunshine; Janus - god of the door and defender of the threshold; Vesta - god of the hearth (fire); Mars and Quirinus - gods of war (the Romans regarded themselves as children of Mars); Neptunus; and Saturnus; just to name a few. Most of these gods (whose statues were erected in temples) were honored in ceremonies during state holidays, for Roman religion was nationalized into a state cult--the empire itself deified (Dea Roma), and later on, the emperors (the Imperial Cult—with statues of emperors erected). Magic, charms, taboos, and reading of omens, were part and parcel of Roman religion. When the Romans came in contact with the Etruscans, they adopted some of their deities, some of which include: Juno (associated with Jupiter as married partners), and Minerva - goddess of wisdom and patroness of arts and trades. From the Greeks, the Romans borrowed the following: Hermes as Mercury - god of commerce; Aphrodite as Venus - goddess of love, who united with Mars in love; Fortuna - goddess of luck and good fortune.

The rest of the European peoples had developed their own superstitious concepts of the gods and religion. **The Celts,** who spread throughout Europe (to the British Isles, France/Gaul, Spain, Italy, Greece, and Asia Minor), were described by an outsider as worshipping Mercury, Apollo, Mars, Jupiter, Minerva, and Dispater - god of the underworld. They also worshipped animals and trees; "The Celts found divinity in nature all around them, for they revered it in the sky, mountains, stones, trees, lakes, rivers, springs, the sea, and every kind of animal--the boar, the bear, the bull, the horse, the hare, the ram, the stag, even the crow, and many female as well as male creatures--the cow, for example. ... Some Celtic gods and goddesses were part animal and part human in shape."[xii] Fertility (fruitfulness) was much celebrated and there were many fertility-powers and mother-goddesses. **The Maypole dance in Europe and America is a survival of the Celtic May Day festival:** "There was a May king and a May queen who symbolized, or were thought of as incarnations of, the vegetation spirits in and below ground. ...

Roman sources report incidences of human sacrifice and their own steps taken to suppress the practice."[xiii]

The Teutons (Anglo-Saxons, Jutes, Saxons, Alamanni, Lombards, Frisians, Franks, Goths, Scandinavians, and Vandals) had their own line of gods and goddesses. Chief among them were Tiw or Tiwa - the sky-god; Donar (Thumor or Thor) - god of thunder and rain; Wodan or Odin - god of earth, magic, the dead, war, and wisdom (knowing all and seeing all); Freyr and Feyja (the divine May king and queen) - symbolized fruitfulness and wealth; Balder, whose mother was Frigg, consort of Odin and queen of the gods, was the kindest, most noble and gentle of the gods. Death intrigued the Teutons; "Until the corpse of a man decayed, it could harm as a specter or vampire ..., and the corpse itself was in danger of being torn to pieces by wolves out of hell, by horse-shaped demons, or by swooping eagles, such as the giant wind-demon Hraesvelg. On the other hand, the spirits of the dead, if they had been good in life and were faithfully reverenced after death, could bring good fortune to their descendants."[xiv]

Strangely enough, is the Celts and Teutons belief in a day of doom and the end of the world or recreation of the world. The Celts believed that a doomsday would eventually come and overwhelm both men and the gods, "... when fire and water would swallow up the earth, the sky would fall, and all humankind would perish, to make way for a new heaven and earth and a new race of men."[xv] The Teutons on the other hand, in Snorri's Epic, also believed in a doomsday;

> "Then the final battle of the world would take place on the plains of earth, with the gods and the heroes of Valhalla going down in defeat; humankind would suffer apparent extinction, and the earth would be burned up by the victorious forces of fire and chaos.
>
> After a while a new earth would emerge from the sea, and the sons of Wodan and Thor, together with Balder and Hodr released from Hel, would establish a new and more promising world order. Human life would begin again from two survivors of the Gotterndammerung and its accompanying world conflagration.

This remarkable conception of time and history links the Teutonic peoples with those of India, who also believe, and still do, in world cycles."[xvi]

As we shall see later, these Roman and European gods are still honored or worshipped today in one form or another, especially in the nomenclature of our solar system, names of the Gregorian calendar and days of the week. Their names are still extant as words or titles; for instance: Valhalla, Titan, Juno, Jupiter, just to name a few. The Roman Catholic religion is replete with this pagan terminology and much of these pagan practices are a veneer of Christianity.

The Americas

The New World, as it came to be called, was indeed not new! It was inhabited by people, who, to some extent, were civilized, and were deeply religious--with many religious ceremonies and rituals, including prayers. Like many other tribal peoples elsewhere in the world, they were varied in their interpretation of the world, religious views, and worship. Some tribes had/have creation myths, but others do not, just as each tribe had/has its own religion (and we will not examine each here). However, few things were common among the peoples: a fascination with the supernatural, nature, and polytheism or many gods;

"There were many gods in the Indians' pantheon, and many different beliefs about the origin of man and this earth, about spiritual realms, and about afterlife. Some of the spirits were benign, some were evil, but all had to be placated. One tribe would have elaborate ceremonies to enlist the aid or avoid the wrath of supernatural beings; another would have few, if any, rites but would live by a set of rules calculated to appease the unseen powers."[xvii]

Animism was common among all the peoples, that is, the belief that "all living things—plants as well as animals—had souls and were to be shown proper respect and consideration."[xviii]

The Cherokees, for instance, had a creation myth in which the plants and animals came first before man; they believed that the earth was suspended by four cords that gives it its horizontal spatial order; they divided living things into orders—some of which (the anomalous ones, like bats, flying squirrel, Venus fly-trap, pitcher plant, beetle, etc.) were attributed special powers and significance. They believed that each creature not only had a soul, "but a double, separable from the flesh-and-blood body."[xix] They believed in spirits, supreme among whom was the Sun (generally considered female) and her consort, the Moon. Everyday life was enmeshed in religious ritual, with priests, medicine men, sorcerers, diviners, etc., playing important roles. Rituals were performed from birth to puberty, marriage, warfare, and death. The spirit of the dead was believed to live on and needed respectful attention, otherwise they could harm the living (as we have seen with the Teutons above).

The Mayans too, for instance, had an elaborate cosmology. In their cosmology, they believed that; "The sky was supported by four gods, the Bacabs. ... they were children of Hunab Ku, 'single existing god,' a remote creator deity. ... Apparently the world rested upon a huge crocodile-like dragon, or perhaps on four of them—many deities appearing in four aspects, ..."[xx] Creation to them, took three attempts: first the creator gods spoke and the earth (land) appeared— then vegetation and speechless animals, and mud creatures who could speak; second, wood creatures who could speak yet unintelligent; then, "In the third attempt the ancestors of the Quiche Maya were made from the quintessential provender, a gruel of yellow and white maize. This time the original four were *too* gifted; so the gods, not wishing humans to be so nearly their equal, dulled their vision with a bit of mist. Wives were created for them. Then the morning star appeared, the sun arose, and the humans worshipped their makers."[xxi] With their elaborate calendric system, the Mayans believed "that history repeats itself, so that one can prepare for repetitions of good or evil eras if the calculations are accurate enough."[xxii] The Mayans had an elaborate religious system, with magnificent temples or ceremonial centers, and a hierarchical priesthood. They had many deities as well, which have been classified into four categories: [xxiii] (1) celestial and remote; the most prominent of which is Itzama - often identified as son to Hunab Ku, the "single existing god." "Itzama in his special manifestation as Kinich Ahau, the sun god, is spouse to the moon goddess Ixchel. (2) fertility and domestic; the most prominent is *Chac,* the rain god. Ah Mun is the god of all crops especially corn, and Ixchel is the patroness of pregnancy, childbirth, medicine, and weaving. (She is often confused with Our Mother or Virgin Mary, where the Catholic religion meets Mayan religion). (3) death and war; the chief deities here are *Ah Puch,* the god of death ("As chief demon, Hunhau, he presided over the lowest of the nine Maya underworlds"[xxiv] and *Ixtab,* the goddess of suicide. (4) calendric and ceremonial; "The calendric and ceremonial deities sponsored the thirteen segments of the upper world and the nine levels of the lower world. There was a single god for each world level, but each segment could also be conceived as having a separate sponsoring deity."[xxv] As would be expected, "Each stage of a person's life was dominated by calendric horoscopes interpreted by priests."[xxvi] There were rituals performed from birth and naming of children to puberty and marriage, and then death.

African Traditional Religions

The African customs, traditions, and practices that can be termed religious, have, of late been referred to as African Traditional Religions. That, of course, is the best description as of now, but that is a misnomer. There really is nothing as African Traditional Religions, if by religion we mean an organized system of worship with a priesthood and centers of worship. Each African tribe has its distinct customs, traditions, and practices, which they simply consider their way of life handed down to them by their ancestors. However, much of what goes on can readily be described as religious. There is probably thousands of extant tribes and many ethno-linguistic groups, though some have a common heritage or can be grouped together. In talking about religion, especially in Sub-Saharan Africa, Scott notes; "First, traditional Africa was composed of at least eight hundred distinct ethno-linguistic groups …, each having its own language and identity, and each with its own conceptions regarding the spirits and the spirit realm. No two are *exactly* alike, though we will find some themes which appear to have been almost universal."[xxvii] He notes again that, "Further, we must note that there was no such thing as one single 'traditional' understanding commonly found across the sub-Saharan part of the continent."xxviii The two most common and almost universal beliefs among the sub-Saharan peoples of Africa were belief in the one high Creator God, and the spirit realm (though their perceptions were never identical). For instance, the Western Sudanic and Tropical West African peoples (in respect to God or the spirits), believe in a pantheon of minor divinities who serve the high god and control elements of nature, locations, and aspects of human endeavor; while the Bantu peoples have no deities between God and man—the role of deities (spirits or gods) is served more by the ancestors; and the Nilotic see God more as "spirit" and less anthropomorphic—and God takes a direct role in human affairs. xxix Generally speaking, the High Creator God is remote and is not readily available to assist mankind; the idea of God as a personal, loving and saving God was never present. Therefore, he was not frequently consulted, and even to reach him, intermediaries were required, hence the existence of the spirit realm—with the spirits sent to approach and placate him. Sometimes, this God is not available for help and the diviners, witchdoctors, and herbalist play the role.

For a comprehensive coverage of the spirit realm (whose existence is a given among all the peoples), researchers have classified them into five major categories: divinities, nature spirits, evil spirits, guardian spirits, and human spirits.xxx

(1) Divinities:

"The number of such deities varied from tribe to tribe, and even within each tribe. ... The divinities were variously thought to originate from one of three sources. First, some were thought to have been created with the rest of the world .... Second, some were thought to have at one time been ancestral kings, heroes, or champions, who had passed from personal memory of the tribe and were deified, ... Third, and finally, some were thought to be the personification of natural forces or objects (thunder, lightning, sun, moon, etc.; ...). The impact of these deities on daily life varied from divinity to divinity as well as from tribe to tribe. Some were widely worshipped, others ignored. These were the beings who actually controlled the world, serving as the hands of God. ... Man was entirely dependent on them, and they could please or disappoint him. Though of a different order from mankind, they had very human limitations, being subject to hunger, anger, and jealousy. Because of their power, it was advisable to always 'seek to be on the best of terms with them.' ... Sacrifice to and worship of the minor divinities was sometimes a means to worship the high God (the lower ones serving as intermediaries)."[xxxi]

(2) Nature Spirits: Not clearly distinguished from the divinities, these were spirits (or gods) directly tied to: natural objects, such as the sun, the sky, the earth, the sea, rivers, or mountains; natural phenomena, such as storms, thunder, wind, and diseases; natural resources, such as iron or blacksmithing and farming.

(3) Malicious or Evil Spirits: these could cause evil though they could also be employed for protection; some were sadistic, and others believed to be the spirits of bad men who died. Significantly absent in their spirit world is any malevolent spirit equivalent to the biblical devil.

(4)"Doubles" or Guardian Spirits:

"A guardian spirit was thought to be intimately linked to one person, serving him or her in a special capacity. Belief in this type of spirit was spread particularly throughout West Africa .... The Yoruba believed that every person was looked after by a "double" (called *enikeji*), who derived his existence from the person's soul. Being a spirit, the double was thought to have a better understanding of the work of the spirit realm than his human counterpart, and served as guide, protector, and bringer of good fortune."[xxxii]

(5) Human Spirits: these are the "ancestors" or "living dead." Death is not seen as the end of life but as a passage into a different type of existence. Scot summarizes;

"Shortly after death, the ancestor was thought to be still interested in the living, doing things (good or bad) to ensure that his descendants remembered him. Not everyone who died achieved ancestral status; generally this was limited to adults (usually male) who had children before dying .... The ancestors were generally seen as vital members of the family. In some tribes, almost no major decision would be made without consulting them (through diviners, dreams, omens, etc.; ...). They were included in the major events of life, seen in the offerings, sacrifices, and libations given to them. If neglected for too long, they could trouble the family as a reminder of their needs. ... Finally, they were not thought of or prayed to as if they were gods—they were usually treated as superior elders, but not as objects of worship ...."[xxxiii]

The spirits performed myriad activities, most of which were negative. They could bring medical problems like insanity, causing infertility, birth deformities, etc.; causing social problems like loss of employment, social status, failure, etc.; empowering objects; appearing to the living; possessing animals or people and making them witches or sorcerers; etc. (In a sense, could these evil spirits be classified as demons?) Because of their malevolent activities, people had to protect themselves from the spirits and especially those who harness them, like sorcerers and witches. This remedial role was played by the witchdoctors, who helped to identify witches; diviners who could foretell the future and wade off evil spirits and witches; and herbalists, who are generally regarded as healers. All these three helpers supplied people with charms or fetishes that were/are thought to protect the holder from evil spirits, sorcerers, and witches.

In the community life of the people, the important men who performed traditional roles were the kings or chiefs and their representatives; the cultic societies mostly for men and some for women; the tribal or clan head; the village head; etc. They performed the land, family, and tribal rituals.

Supreme Deity (Philosophy), Morality, Truth, Conscience, and Religion

Given the above analysis, what can we conclude about human experience with God/god or the gods? Can we legitimately conclude that the experience of those in primitive religions, other religions, and philosophy, was a true experience of/with the one true God? Did the philosophers find God or just a Supreme Being? The biblical answer to all these questions is an emphatic no. If these religions or philosophies were sufficient means to reach God, it would have been needless for God to have called Abraham out of his pagan polytheistic nation and family to serve the Most High God. In short, there would have been no need for revealed religion if polytheistic religions and philosophy could have been pathways to God. Natural religion (though it may have a right appraisal of nature), is not a sufficient pathway to God; at best, it only results in idolatry and nature-worship (Rom. 1:20-23).

Or what can we say about the philosophers and poets? Did they find God? These too, in all their reason, only ended up in idolatry or vanity. Philosophy is deceptive in as much as it depends on traditions (reason and wisdom), but the world through wisdom cannot know God. Paul told the Colossians; *"See to it that no one takes you captive through hollow and deceptive philosophy, which depends on human tradition and the basic principles of this world rather than on Christ"* (Col. 2:8). Again, he says; *"For since in the wisdom of God the world through its wisdom did not know him ..."* (1 Co. 1:21). We only need to review the history of philosophy and see how many came to know Christ through their philosophical search!

One may ask, "Is there truth in other religions other than Christianity?" Of course, yes! All truth is truth and as someone has said, all truth is God's truth. Paul did accept the fact that the Athenian poetic expression, "We are his offspring" (Acts 17:28), was true. However, despite some truths in other religions, only the Bible contains absolute truth about God and how he can be reached, and thus, is the standard for judging all truth. Although the Athenians knew that all were God's offspring, they did not know this God personally. They called him "The Unknown God" (Acts 17:23).

Again, another question to ask is; "Is there true morality in other religions and/or cultures? Yes! Almost all religions and cultures have moralistic elements, though morality might find different expressions in different religions and cultures. However, just like with truth, the Bible is the source of absolute morality. The Bible judges all religions and cultures; it is supra-cultural. Conscience (expression of the Imago Dei) explains why there is truth and morality in all religions and cultures, and perhaps, why man is generally religious. Since man came from the hand of God and was made in the image and likeness of God, **there is a consciousness of God in ALL mankind,** though in his fallen state of sin, man cannot reach God by his own efforts. Paul explains that God will judge those who have not heard the revealed gospel of Jesus Christ based on natural law imprinted on their consciences (Rom. 2:14-15). Thus, conscience serves as a moral code or judge of human morality across all cultures. Nevertheless, conscience cannot be the final arbiter of human morality, the Bible is. There are several reasons why conscience cannot play the role of final arbiter of morality, some of which include the following. Conscience can be under-informed or misinformed. Conscience can also be corrupted. Conscience can be seared or hardened by evil and sin, to the extent that right is regarded as wrong and wrong regarded as right, bad as good and good as bad, or conscience can become insensitive to wrong or bad (2 Tim. 4:2; Is. 4:20). Only an informed and redeemed conscience can bear testimony to that which is right, good, true, and godly (Rom. 9:1; 1 Tim. 1:5, 19).

Civilization

Civilization is man's ability and ingenuity to accomplish things or develop himself and his environment to better his conditions of life—socially, religiously, economically, and politically. This is a good incentive and achievement. But as we shall see in this chapter and later, man's very achievements become his source of condemnation. Why? Because at the height of his achievement; man becomes proud and boastful of his strength, genius, and success in wealth, economics, and military. Apostle John characterizes this as love of the world—the cravings of sinful man, the lust of his eyes and the boasting of what he has and does—these come not from the Father but from the world (1 John 2:15- 16). The prophet Jeremiah also cries out against such an arrogant spirit; *"Let not the wise man boast of his wisdom or the strong man boast of his strength or the rich man boast of his riches, but let him who boasts boast in this: that he understands and knows me, that I am the LORD ... "* (Jer. 9:23-24). The epitome of this folly, arrogance, and pride of the civilized, began at Babel, when men wanted to reach heaven by their own efforts and achievement; ***"They said to each other, 'Let's make bricks and bake them thoroughly.' ... 'Come, let us build ourselves a city, with a tower that reaches to*** *the heavens, so that we may make a name for ourselves ..."* (Gen. 11:3-4). [In this connection, we are reminded of the king of Babylon (Satan-incarnate), who says he will ascend to heaven and raise his throne above the stars of God. Babylon's king is described as a tree that grew and touched the sky/heaven; that is, a depiction of his strength, greatness, glory, and dominion (Is. 14:13; Dan. 4:11, 22). Again, when Jerusalem fell in 586 BC, Jeremiah described the fall as; *"He* [God] *has hurled down the splendor of Israel from heaven to earth,"* that is, from honor and glory to dishonor (Lam. 2:2-3)]. So, what does it mean for humans to reach heaven or build a city with a tower that reaches to the heavens? It means to be great, to be strong, to be prosperous, and to be glorious; that is, to reach great splendor and a superpower status. It means to be the greatest civilization at a time. That is what the people at Babel aspired to do! To build a city, a nation, an empire, with a tower that reaches the heavens, so that they may make a name for themselves. And what they were unable to do, or God stopped them short of doing, modern man has done. The city of man that was foiled at Babel has reached that stage again and even beyond, and the supreme court of heaven is pondering the matter now; *"But the LORD came* [is coming down] *to see the city and the tower that the men were* [are] *building. The LORD said* [is saying], *'If as one people speaking the same language* [a united nations speaking a universal English] *they have begun to do this, then nothing they plan to do will be impossible for them. Come, let us* [the LORD and the holy ones] *go down and confuse their language so they will not understand each other* [let us go down and judge them]*"* (Gen. 11:5-7; cf. Dan. 4:13-14, 17; 7:9-11, 26).

We have seen that as men built cities and nations, they created deities and worshipped them. We see this right from the first pages of the Bible, where Cain built a city and named it after his son, Enoch (Gen. 4:17). After the flood, we are told that Nimrod, who became a mighty warrior (a conquering empire builder--a tyrant) on the earth and in the presence of the LORD, built the first center of his kingdom in Babylon, and later built Nineveh (of the Assyrians). As was the case then, "Many cities and nations had for their chief god their founder; such was the case with Nimrod. To make this God more real and honorable, images were made to represent him; later the images themselves came to be worshipped. ...Thus, the chief god of Babylon, and Nineveh, Nimrod, had images referring to him. These images glorified his attributes as protector, leader, god of war, knowledge, etc."xxxiv From the deified Nimrod came gods (variant forms of his name) like Chemosh (the god of the Moabites), Moloch (the Ammonite deity), Merodach (the deity Marduk, worshipped as the supreme deity of the Babylonians), Remphan (a god identified or connected with the planet Saturn), Tamuz (the Sumerian son-god), and Baal (the Canaanite deity), as mentioned in the Bible. Nimrod is still revered today by Free Masons as one of their founders. [Talk about images of founders in the likeness of Nimrod—look on the surface of the earth today, they are everywhere—Buddha, Stalin, Washington, Moa Tse Tung, just to name a few. Romans 1:22 states; *"Although they claimed to be wise, they became fools and **exchanged the glory of the immortal God for images made to look like mortal man and birds and animals and reptiles."*** This is humanism—the worship of man: Me first; us first!]. Daniel 10:13 speaks of the prince of Persia, the invisible demonic principality that controlled the lives of the Persians. Thus, there are national gods—spirits (or the spirit of a nation) that oppose God. Every civilized nation has this demonic spirit (prince of) that controls that nation and its citizens, and this spirit opposes God. It is the spirit of civilization united against God—come let us burn bricks and build a city, with a tower reaching to the heavens, and make a name for ourselves. It is the arrogant spirit of national pride and greatness--"We the people." You may pause to ponder, "What is the spirit of my nation or national spirit?" Is that spirit in defiance or submission to God?

The rebellion at Babel was a demonstration of how man resists and disobeys God by virtue of his achievement. The pages of the Bible are filled with the rise and fall of civilizations or great empires (Egypt, Assyria, Babylon, Median and Persia, Greece, Rome, and other smaller civilizations like Elam, Ammon, Edom, Philistine, Moab, Tyre, etc.). At the height or zenith of each of these civilizations, their pride and arrogance equaled that of Satan as illustrated in the case of Babylon and Tyre in Isaiah 13-14 and Ezekiel 26-28, respectively. [Satan always wants to sit on top impersonating through the proud, the rich, the powerful and the dominant. He controls the empires that rule the world at any given era or time. He has undisputed claims to the nations and their splendor; "*Again, the devil took him* [Jesus] *to a very high mountain* [the greatest nation on earth] *and showed him all the kingdoms of the world and their splendor. 'All this I will give you,' he said, 'If you will bow down and worship me*" (Matt. 4:8-9). The nations and their splendor are Satan's].

The irony is that God allows or enables man to develop his environment and accumulate wealth (civilization), for he is sovereign over all our talents and ingenuity. In the case of Babylon we read; "*You, O king* [Nebuchadnezzar], *are the king of kings. The God of heaven has given you dominion and power and might and glory; ....*" "*O king* [Belshazzar], *the Most High God gave your father Nebuchadnezzar sovereignty and greatness and glory and splendor*" (Dan. 2:37; 5:18). In fact, every talent and skill we have is from God. He expects us to give him all the credit and glory for all our achievement and to acknowledge his sovereignty over all mankind and all that man has and does. However, at the height of all human achievement (civilization), man always wants to receive the glory and give credit to himself, hence impersonating Satan—the god of this world (human civilizations and systems operating outside of God's moral norms and dictates). Of Belshazzar, king of Babylon, it is said; "*As they drank the wine, they praised the gods of gold and silver, of bronze, iron, wood and stone*" (Dan. 5:4). At the zenith of his power, Nebuchadnezzar, despite repeated evidences that there was the Most High God (Dan. 2:46-47; 3:28-4:3), built an image of gold and commanded his people to worship it (Dan. 3:1-7; the symbol of the Babylonian kingdom and glory), and credited the glory of the kingdom to himself; **"... He said, 'Is not this the great Babylon I have built as the royal residence, by my mighty power and for the glory of my majesty?'"** (Dan. 4:30; this resonates with our modern phrase, "We the People!"). God has strictly warned against such an attitude (Deut. 8:10-20; esp. 14, 17, 18). **As a result, he had to eat grass with the animals for seven years, at the end of which he declared; *"Now, I, Nebuchadnezzar, praise and exalt the king of heaven, because everything he does is right and all his ways are just. And those who walk in pride he is able to humble"*** (Dan. 4:37; cf. Pr. 8:13; 16:18).

It happened that through this same Nebuchadnezzar, God opened the annals of the future and revealed the fate of all human civilizations to him, including our end-time Babylon, over which Satan is reigning. After this satanic Babylon is destroyed, the kingdom of God will be officially and physically inaugurated on earth. I will discuss this in detail in later chapters. The example of the king of Babylon still does not seem to ring a bell in the minds of the proud, the rich, and the powerful of today. What has been will be again; *"What has been will be again, what has been done will be done again; there is nothing new under the sun"* (Eccl. 1:9).

CHAPTER 5

SATAN IN THE GOSPELS AND EPISTLES

Is Satan ever quiet? No! He roams the earth to and fro seeking whom he may devour. He works day and night to make sure that his kingdom stands. What the Bible does not do for us is to give a chronological account of Satan from his prehistoric fall (?) through history to his final expulsion from heaven. Nevertheless, as we have seen, and will continue to see, the Scriptures only make clear his activities and human activities that imply satanic influence or involvement.

It is in the New Testament that we see Satan in full gear of operation. This is because the one to crush his head was on the scene. A decisive invisible battle that had been going on for ages was about to end. It is not as though he was not active during the inter-testament period. However, the New Testament brings out in some detail, Satan's identity and how he operates. A clear understanding of his modus operandi will help us to understand how he is working in our societies today. Satan commands a large army of fallen angels (demons), who do his will. Satan works indirectly by influencing people to do his will (demon influence), and directly by taking up residence in individuals (demon possession).

Herod (Matthew 2)

One of the ways Satan influences people is through quest or lust for power and dominance. Satan likes to dominate and since he cannot physically control people, he impersonates through pagan or unbelieving leaders, who want to dominate and rule over people.

We see the first example of this in the life of King Herod (Matt. 2). Satan knew that his head would be crushed by Jesus when he would die for the sins of mankind. Once Jesus came into the world, Satan was determined to eliminate him. When Herod heard from the Magi that Jesus was born, who would be the King of the Jews (and ultimately the King of the world), he was disturbed; "A king that will displace me or even be above me?" he must have wondered. Herod was theologically correct (he knew the Christ was to be born), and so were the chief priests and the teachers of the law (who knew exactly where the Christ was to be born). But did King Herod go to worship this king and pay homage to him? No! At least he pretended to the Magi that this was his intention. However, he actually wanted to kill this newborn king (vv.13-14). Behind all of Herod's actions, was the god of this world, Satan. Satan lost his battle here as God supernaturally protected the infant King by sending his family to Egypt. But did Satan surrender or give up or learn his lesson? No!

The Temptation of Jesus (Matthew 4:1-11)

About thirty years later, after Herod's assault against the infant King, Jesus, Satan came out in the open and confronted Jesus as he was about to begin his public ministry. As it is written; *"Then Jesus was led by the Spirit into the desert to be tempted by the devil"* (v.1). We are not told what form the devil was from the brief intercourse here, but we can note the following about Satan and his character, and the method Jesus used to defeat him.

First, Satan tempts us through our legitimate desires, especially when we are vulnerable. Jesus had fasted for forty days and was hungry, and the devil said to him; *"If you are the Son of God, tell these stones to become bread"* (v.3). Notice that it was through the desire to eat that Satan deceived Eve!

Secondly, Satan creates doubt about our identity—He said to Jesus; *"If you are the Son of God, ... "* Just like he did to Eve, *"you will be like God ...."*

Thirdly, Satan's challenges are sometimes foolish; *"... tell these stones to become bread."* We will note here that God can do the impossible, but he will not do the foolish to entertain the devil's demands or human curiosity. The Pharisees would later demand a sign from Jesus as proof that he is the Christ just as the devil did here.

Jesus launched his first defense, and guess what? It was not from the fact that he was deity (Son of God as Satan had rightly said) but from the word of God! *"Jesus answered, 'It is written: Man does not live by bread alone, but on every word that comes from the mouth of God'"* (v.4). Well, I do not need to belabor the point--we must live by EVERY WORD that comes from the mouth of God, even to the last jot or iota. If only believers would eat up the word of God, the sword of the Spirit (Ezek. 2:7-8; Eph. 6:17)! The word is the sum of the believer's armor. Remember what happened in Eden with Eve when Satan came to her? She failed to rely on God's word! How people are led astray today because of ignorance, disobedience, and failure to rely on every word of God! They no longer say; "It is written!" How many people serve Satan today because of bread (their stomachs; Phil. 3:18,19)!

Fourthly, Satan knows the Bible very well, but always misquotes it (out of context) or misapplies it (vv.5,6); *"Then the devil took him to the holy city and had him stand on the highest point of the temple. 'If you are the Son of God,' he said, 'throw yourself down. For it is written: 'He will command his angels concerning you, and they will lift you up in their hands, so that you will not strike your foot against a stone.'"* Satan was directly challenging Jesus' deity--would he jump off from the highest point of the temple to satisfy Satan's whims?

Jesus again fired a second ballistic missile FROM THE WORD; *"Jesus answered him, 'It is written: Do not put the Lord your God to the test'"* (v.7). By this statement, Jesus had actually implied, "I am the Lord God."

Fifthly, Satan possesses all the kingdoms of the earth/world and gives them to whomever he pleases, if only they bow down before him. That is what he wanted Jesus to do; *"Again, the devil took him to a very high mountain and showed him all the kingdoms of the world and their splendor. 'All this I will give to you,' 'if you will bow down and worship me'"* (vv.8, 9). Satan probably looked down the future (and he knew all the promises of the millennial reign of Jesus the Christ), that is, our times today, and was challenging Jesus to take a short cut to his own throne! Here, we see the trap set for those who aspire for power and dominion over the peoples of the world. They will do whatever it takes, even with Satan's assistance to rule the world. Beware! Did you know that many great world leaders dabble with the occult and secret societies like Freemasonry and Rosicrucian, and others? And hence, they worship of Satan? They seek his power to dominate people and the world.

Jesus already knew that the kingdoms of the world belonged to him (Ps. 2:8; Rev. 11:15) though they were/are temporarily under Satan's control (cf. Heb. 2:8; Rev. 12:9). Jesus knew the way to his throne and would not deter from it--the cross (suffering and death, Luke. 24:26; Phil. 2:8; Heb. 12:1-2). Therefore; *"Jesus said to him, 'Away from me, Satan! For it is written: Worship the Lord your God, and serve him only. Then the devil left him ... '"* (vv.10, 11). Again, the power of the word prevailed. If you neglect the word of God or do not study it diligently and apply it, Satan will get you! James admonishes us; *"Submit yourselves, then, to God. Resist the devil, and he will flee away from you."* For we know that our *"... enemy the devil prowls around like a roaring lion looking for someone to devour. Resist him ...."* (James. 4:7; 1 Pet. 5:8, 9) This is the resistance that Jesus demonstrated here, and it is through the word of God. Therefore, knowledge and practice of the word of God should be the priority of every believer, who hopes to resist and overcome Satan.

We shall see later how these particular characteristics of Satan delineated here have played out as he deceived people down the centuries and continues to do same today.

Satanic or Demonic Influence

Satan also works indirectly to influence men to do his will. While this is mostly on unbelievers, believers living in sin (out of fellowship with God) might equally fall under the influence of Satan and his demons.

The Scribes, Pharisees, and the Jewish Religious Leaders: These religionists of Jesus' day were those who opposed Jesus the most. Scriptures show that they were the devil's mouthpieces! While these were not demon-possessed (that is, with demons living in them), they were demon-influenced; they were advancing the kingdom of Satan. The irony of the matter is that they were deceived themselves because they thought that they were doing God's service as they opposed Jesus. In fact, they accused Jesus of driving out demons by the prince of the demons (Beelzebub or Satan; Matt. 12:22-28). When Jesus discussed about the freedom that he gives to those who believe in him by repenting from their sins, these blind religionists insisted that they were Abraham's children and had never been enslaved, and therefore were free (John 8:31-47; The freedom Jesus was talking of here was freedom from slavery to sin). Jesus assured them that they were doing what they see their father (Satan) do (that is, they were seeking to kill him, which was Satan's intension). They became adamant; *"'We are not illegitimate children,' they protested. 'The only Father we have is God himself.'"* (v.41b) But Jesus said to them; *"You belong to your father, the devil, and you want to carry out your father's desire. He was a murderer from the beginning, not holding to the truth, for there is no truth in him. When he lies, he speaks his native language, for he is a liar and the father of lies"* (v.44). What an irony! This people's intentions were satanic, yet they believed wholeheartedly that they were serving God. They were carrying out Satan's desires in the name of God! This is the most subtle form of satanic influence because the people serving Satan are self-deceived in as much as they think that they are serving God. This deception is flourishing today, where many are serving Satan thinking that they are serving God! It has been the case throughout church history, where religionists persecuted and killed followers of Christ in the name of God.

Peter (Matthew 16:13-28): This blessed apostle, one of the first to be called by Jesus, was a man of vibrant faith. He was always the first to act (he walked on the water, acknowledged the deity of Jesus, cut off the high priest's servant's ear). However, just as Satan tempts the strong most, he did it to Peter. When Jesus asked his disciples who they thought he was; *"Simon Peter answered, 'You* *are the Christ, the Son of the living God.'"* Jesus then assured them (Peter) that he will build his church upon that confession (thought by others that the church was to be built on Peter, the rock), and that the gates of hell shall not prevail against that church. How was this church to be built? By the death of Jesus on the cross and the resurrection (he had said, if I be lifted up from the earth, I will draw all men to myself). Death on the cross was going to be God's decisive victory over Satan (Gen. 3:15; he [Christ] will crush your head, and you [Satan] will strike his heel). In fact, it was the very reason for which Jesus Christ came into the world, and in his earthly ministry he looked forward to it (Is. 53). When Jesus began to tell his disciples of his suffering, death, and resurrection; Satan used Peter to oppose the prime of his ministry—death on a cross. It is recorded; *"Peter took him aside and began to rebuke him. 'Never, Lord!' he said. 'This shall never happen to you!'"* Rebuke Jesus! Jesus immediately recognized Satan's influence behind Peter's rebuke. Then *"Jesus turned and said to Peter, 'Get behind me, Satan! You are a stumbling block to me; you do not have in mind the things of God, but the things of men.'"* In Jesus' counter rebuke, we see **a succinct definition of Satanism or satanic influence: not having in mind the things of God, but preoccupied with the things of men.** Satanism is love of the world. Lift up your eyes and see how many are under Satan's influence around you!

Satan thought that he could persuade Jesus to avoid the cross by disobeying God the Father. But Jesus obeyed the Father and carried out his mission; *"... he humbled himself and became obedient to death—even death on a cross!"* (Phil. 2:8). As we shall see later, the cross is a stumbling block to Satan, and he fights relentlessly to remove it from the cause of Christ. He promises freedom with a compromise for people to avoid the cross (suffering and persecution; Matt. 16:24-25), just as he did through Peter to persuade Jesus to avoid the cross. And indeed, many who claim to follow Christ today try to avoid the cross at all costs. They would rather vie for and defend religious freedom than accept persecution and suffering as a promise and blessing to believers (Matt. 5:11-12; Acts 14:22; 2 Tim. 3:12-13). Few today actually carry the cross. They are claimants for religious freedom but fail to realize the subtlety of Satan behind such manipulations. As it is written; *"They promise them freedom, while they themselves are slaves of depravity ... "* (2 Pet. 2, esp. v.19). They prefer a Christ without a cross! There is no Christianity without a cross! If there is no cross, that Christianity is a compromise with Satan! Are you in Satan's trap here? Break free!

Judas: As we saw in the case of Job, Satan is always moving to and fro among God's children. He was able to infiltrate the ranks of Jesus' disciples (There is no group of believers today—church or denomination, in which Satan is not present). Satan infiltrated Jesus' disciples, so he will equally infiltrate our fellowships today. Satan had his agent among the disciples and has many agents among believers today. Judas observed every move and plan, yet he had his secret satanic agenda. We know that Judas was a thief and used to help himself with the money in the bag (John 12:4- 6). Thus, he had a love for money (which is a root of all kinds of evil) and this would become an avenue for Satan to use him to betray Jesus; *"Then one of the twelve--the one called Judas Iscariot--went to the chief priests and asked, 'What are you willing to give me if I hand him over to you?' So they counted out for him thirty pieces of silver. From then on Judas watched for an opportunity to hand him over"* (Matt. 26:14-16; cf. Zech. 11:12-13). In John's account of the last supper, we read of Satan's influence on Judas; *"The evening meal was being served, and **the devil had already prompted Judas Iscariot**, son of Simon, to betray Jesus"* (John 13:2). When Jesus dipped the bread in the dish, he gave it to Judas, and *"As soon as Judas took the bread, **Satan entered him**"* (John 13:27). That was Satan at work through the love of money. Perhaps, someone would say "I could never have behaved liked Judas." Guess what? Millions today, including professing Christians, are betraying Jesus because of their love for money. Jesus, at one point had directly referred to Judas as a devil; *"Then Jesus replied, 'Have I not chosen you, the Twelve? Yet one of you is a devil!'"* (John 6:70).

From these three accounts (the religious leaders, Peter, and Judas); we may conclude that Satan does not know every detail or specifics of God's plan. Through Peter, he wanted Jesus to avoid the cross, but through the religious leaders and Judas, Jesus was betrayed, falsely accused and crucified. Perhaps, they thought they were putting an end to Jesus' ministry, but Peter later declared; *"This man was handed over to you by God's set purpose and foreknowledge; and you, with the help of wicked men, put him to death by nailing him to the cross"* (Acts 2:23). Satan can only act within the bounds set for him by God just as was the case with Job. He can use anyone who opens himself to him by sin or disobedience to God (for instance, Eve).

Demon Possession

Demon possession is a situation where a demon or demons take over the personality of an individual, resulting in an abnormal behavior or some kind of sickness. In this case, the individual is said to be bound by Satan (Luke 13:16). There are several instances of demon-possession recorded in the gospels, some of which include the following.

Matthew 8:28-34: Demon possession was manifested in living in the tombs and violence. The demons recognized Jesus as the Son of God!

Matthew 17:14: Demon possession was manifested in seizures.

Mark 9:14-27: Here, demon possession was manifested in foaming, gnashing of teeth, deafness, dumbness, and muteness.

Jesus' ministry was a constant confrontation with Satan and his demons. In all the confrontations, Jesus overpowered and cast out the demon or demons. In all instances where the demons spoke, they recognized the deity of Jesus as the Son of God, who had authority over them (Matt. 8:29- 31; Mark. 1:23-26).

We should note that not all sicknesses that Jesus healed were a result of demon possession (Matt. 9:1-8). Jesus equally gave his disciples and us authority over the demons and all kinds of sicknesses (Matt. 10:8ff).

Not All Cases of Sin Imply Demon Influence or Demon Possession

While all sinners are under the dominion of Satan—the ruler of the kingdom of the air or darkness (Eph. 2:1-3; Col. 1:13), not all cases of individual sin are satanically induced. Jeremiah 17:7 states that; *"The heart is deceitful above all things and beyond cure."* Thus, from the heart of man comes sin as Jesus puts it; *"What comes out of a man is what makes him unclean: For from within, out of men's hearts, come evil thoughts, sexual immorality, theft, murder, adultery, greed, malice, deceit, lewdness, envy, slander, arrogance and folly. All these evils come from inside and make a man unclean"* (Mark. 7:20- 23). James describes the process of human sinning as follows; *"... but each one is tempted when, by his own evil desire, he is dragged away and enticed. Then, after desire has conceived, it gives birth to sin; ..."* (James. 1:14, 15). This is a demonstration that man is incurably sinful and can commit any sinful act on his own, even when Satan is not in charge. There is no transfer of guilt by saying that the devil made me do it.

Satan's Head Crushed; His Fate Sealed

Jesus' death on the cross was a decisive victory over Satan and his demons. No doubt, Satan worked so hard to persuade Jesus to avoid the cross. On the cross, the human predicament of sin was settled forever: Jesus became the perfect atonement (sacrifice for sin) and propitiation (appeasement or satisfaction and aversion of God's wrath) for mankind's sin. Sins were paid for once and for all. When Jesus was approaching his death, he declared; *"Now is the time for judgment on this world; now the prince of this world will be driven out. But I, when I am lifted up from the earth, will draw all men to myself"* (John 12:31-32). While Satan looked at the cross as a place of defeat, it was actually on the cross that he was defeated, and his fate sealed forever.

However, we know that Satan has not given up yet, he is still fighting for the souls of men to bring them with him to hell. Jesus declared about Satan and those who follow him; *"Then he will say to the ones on the left, 'Depart from me you who are cursed, into the eternal fire prepared for the devil and his angels"* (Matt. 25:41).

Satan is doomed and all those who follow him. Despite the triumphal march of the Church, Satan is still active and launching his assault against faithful followers of Jesus Christ and deceiving unbelievers. In the end, all things will be placed under Jesus' feet, as it is written; *"The LORD says to my Lord: 'Sit at my right hand until I make your enemies a footstool for your feet'"* (Ps. 110:1). There is no hope for Satan and those who follow him. He is a defeated roaring lion.

Satan in the Epistles

The apostolic writings also help to show us the character of Satan and his agents, human and demonic.

Satan is described as the god of this age, who blinds the minds of unbelievers so that they cannot see the light of the gospel of the glory of Christ (2 Co. 4:4). Jesus describes him as snatching away the word from those who hear it and do not understand (Matt. 13:19). He controls the minds of unbelievers and the societal systems at every level—socio-cultural, economic, justice, organized evil, and even religion.

Satan masquerades as an angel of light. He hides himself and his inner motives and puts on a façade as a do-gooder, but he is a wolf in sheep clothing. Paul used this expression about some people who were posing as apostles and secretly penetrating the ranks of believers in the church at Corinth (2 Co. 11:1-15; 12:11; Rom. 16:17-20). Their cunning and deceptive strategies are likened to that of the serpent with Eve (2 Co. 11:3). Of this category are all classes of false apostles, false prophets, false teachers, and those who preach another gospel, who are led by deceiving spirits and who teach doctrines of demons (Gal. 1:8,9; 1 Tim. 4:1-3; 2 Pet. 2; Jude 3-16).

Satan uses the love of money and wealth to trap people in his net (Phil. 3:18, 19; 1 Tim 6:3-10; Matt. 13:7,22). Jesus declares; *"You cannot serve both God and money"* (Matt. 6:24; 21:12).

Satan holds people in slavery by their fear of death (Heb. 2:14-15).

Satan controls the whole world and is leading it astray (1 John 5:19; Rev. 12:9).

Satan is introduced in the gospels as Beelzebub (Lord of the flies), the prince of the demons. Some people use him to drive out demons. The Pharisees falsely accused Jesus of driving out demons by Beelzebub (Matt. 12:22-28).

Demons are fallen angels, who are reserved in chains and darkness until the Day of Judgment (2 Pet. 2:4; Jude 6). Their activities are identified with the activities of sinful men, who lived in Noah's day and in Sodom and Gomorrah.

Satan, as the enemy of believers, is like a roaring lion that prowls around looking for someone to devour (1 Pet. 5:8). He uses many schemes and devises to attack believers (2 Co. 2:10-11; Eph. 6:16).

Demons are behind all kinds of idolatry and occultism, even in our day (1 Co. 10:20-21).

Victory Over Satan and Demons

Jesus had complete victory over Satan when he tempted him and throughout his ministry. He cast out demons by the word of his command every time he came face to face with them (Matt. 8:28-34). He gave the disciples authority to drive out demons (Matt. 10:8; Luke. 10:17; Mark. 16:15-18; Matt. 28:18; Acts 16:16-18). Jesus' decisive and final victory over Satan and his demons was on the cross (John 12: 31-33; 16:33; 19:30; Col. 2:15). The ability to drive out demons became less frequent after the apostolic era. We do not see it commanded in the epistles. However, when confronted with demons and the Spirit prompts, the spiritual leader can drive out demons in the name of Jesus. Again, this is of rare occurrence today. Exorcism is not a mandate for believers. Believers are commanded in the Epistles to resist Satan and his demons. To do this, we must understand and do the following.

First, Satan is a master schemer, and we must be aware of his schemes. We are specifically warned about anger and an unforgiving spirit, which are channels of satanic influence (2 Co. 2:10-11; Eph. 4:26-27). Every form of external enticement to sin: sex, murder, violence, lies, falsehood, false teaching, etc., are schemes of the devil and demons.

Secondly, believers must put on the full armor of God in order to fight Satan, principalities, rulers, powers and authorities in the dark world; the spiritual forces of evil in the heavenly realms; and all satanic schemes. The full armor of God includes: truth, the gospel light, righteousness, faith, the hope of salvation, the sword of the spirit, which is the word of God (as used by Jesus in Matthew 4:1-11), and prayer (Eph. 6:10-18; 2 Co. 10:3-6; 1 John 5:4). The one who is fully armed with this armory will have complete victory over Satan and his demonic agents.

Thirdly, do not love the world—the system of sin and evil; all kinds of cravings and inordinate desires—lust, sexual immorality (sexually explicit screen material, pornography; half naked or nude people in public or screen are satanic agents—demonic, aimed at seducing and bringing many to hell; Pr. 5:3-6; 7:6-27. In fact, only the demon-possessed can appear naked, half-naked or nude in public or screen), power lust, arrogance, boasting and pride, love of material possessions, love of money, etc. (1 John 2:15-17; James 4:1-10). Resist the devil by avoiding these things and put on humility as Jesus did (Phil. 2:1-5; Rom. 12:3).

Fourthly, as a believer, he that is in you (the Father, Jesus Christ, and the Holy Spirit) is stronger than he that is in the world (Satan, his demons, and agents), as stated in 1 John 4:1-4. In the NAME OF JESUS, we are more than conquerors and have victory over Satan, his demons and agents. However, we are not given the mandate to go hunting for Satan and his demons to drive them out or bind him or send them to the abyss (Jude 8, 9; 2 Pet. 2:10, 11; Zech. 3:1-3). Jesus himself shall arrest Satan at his arrival (Rom. 16:20; Rev. 20:2, 3). As of now, Satan continues to be in the presence of God. It is sheer ignorance and arrogance for a believer to think that he can bind Satan or cast him into the abyss.

CHAPTER 6

SATAN'S ATTACK ON THE EARLY CHURCH

Will Satan ever learn his lesson to accept defeat? No! He still thinks that he can justify his case before God and make himself as high as God. Even though he knows his fate, he continues to attack God by attacking the ones God has chosen to reveal his glory through--believers in Jesus. As his name rightly means, he accuses believers moment by moment before God (Zech. 3:1-3; Rev. 12:10). As the people of God progress from one age to another, Satan adjusts his plan of attack accordingly, in attempt to foil God's plan. When Jesus died on the cross, Satan thought he had won the battle, but three days later, he was dumbfounded as death gave birth to life—Jesus rose from the dead to live forever (Rev. 1:18)!

Satan's Attack on the Resurrection

When the Holy Spirit descended upon the disciples at Pentecost, Peter addressed the crowd and said of the resurrection; *"This man was handed over to you by God's set purpose and foreknowledge; and you, with the help of wicked men, put him to death by nailing him to the cross. **But God raised him from the dead, freeing him from the agony of death, because it was impossible for death to keep its hold on him"*** (Acts 2:23-24). But, before this day, a lot had transpired concerning the resurrection of Jesus. When Jesus hung on the cross, the soldiers and the people insulted him, because to them, this was the end of his ministry (Matt. 27:37-44). Unfortunately, they were ignorant of the word of God--Jesus would rise from the dead in three days (Matt. 28:1-10). Because Satan could not keep Jesus in the grave, he devised a plan to explain away the resurrection; "...

*some of the guards went into the city and reported to the chief priests
everything that had happened.* **When the chief priests had met with
the elders and devised a plan, they gave the soldiers a large sum
of money, telling them, 'You are to say, His disciples came during
the night and stole him away while we were asleep;** *if this report
gets to the governor, we will satisfy him and keep you out of trouble.'
So the soldiers took the money and did as they were instructed. And
this story had been widely circulated among the Jews to this very
day"* (Matt. 28:11-15). The resurrection, since then, has remained a
stumbling block to Satan until our modern days. Satan knew that the
hope of Jesus' followers depended upon his coming back to life and
that if he made it to appear as a hoax, then he had succeeded. Later
in modern history, many theories would be put forward in attempt to
deny the resurrection.

The Way (Church) is Born

When Jesus was arrested, the disciples were scattered (Zech.
13:7; Matt. 26:56). Even Peter, who followed him to his trial, finally
denied him as Jesus had predicted. After the crucifixion, the disciples
returned to their normal lives, for they did not believe that Jesus would
resurrect in three days. Though unbelieving, they finally accepted the
resurrection after many proofs (Jesus appeared to them again and
again). According to the predetermined plan of God, the Father sent
the Holy Spirit (fifty days after the resurrection and ten days after
the ascension into heaven) on the day of Pentecost (Acts 2). The
timid and fearful disciples were transformed into fiery preachers and
witnesses to the resurrection. Thus, the Church was born, and the
gates of hell could not and cannot prevail against her.

Satan's Determination to Crush the Church

After the Church was born, Satan launched an attack against her,
and this continued in various forms until this very day. The rest of
the second part of this book would be an attempt to trace this satanic
attack on the Church and how it will end. We will begin by tracing
Satan's attack on the early church as recorded in the book of Acts.
For about three centuries after the church was born, Satan's main
tool against her was persecution. The disciples and early Christians

suffered greatly and most of them paid it with their lives. Persecution was both religious and secular.

Acts 4:1-21: Peter and John had just healed a crippled beggar, and the religious leaders became furious. Dumbfounded by the reality of the miracle and by the fact that on account of the miracle many were believing in Jesus as the Christ, they tried to stop Peter and John from speaking to anyone in the name of Jesus; *"But Peter and John replied, 'Judge for yourselves whether it is right in God's sight to obey you rather than God. For we cannot help speaking about what we have seen and heard.'"* (vv.19, 20)

Acts 5:17-41: The high priest, his associates, and the Sadducees; filled with jealousy, arrested the apostles and put them in jail. But the jail gates could not keep them in as an angel of the Lord opened the gates and let them out. These religious leaders threatened to kill the disciples, but one of them, Gamaliel, a Pharisee, warned them that they should be careful lest they find themselves fighting against God. They flogged the disciples and commanded them again not to speak in the name of Jesus and sent them away.

Acts 6:8-8:8: Stephen, a man full of God's grace and power, was falsely accused of blasphemy against Moses and against God and was brought to the Sanhedrin (the Jewish ruling council). Stephen rehearsed the story of the Israelites, starting from Abraham and ending up to the current time by charging the religious leaders of resisting the Holy Spirit. They stoned Stephen to death with Saul (who would later become Paul, the great apostle) giving approval to his death. A great persecution arose after Stephen's death and the believers were scattered from Jerusalem to diverse places. However, this persecution only helped to expand the Church as; *"Those who had been scattered preached the word wherever they went"* (Acts 8:4). Saul continued to destroy the Church with orders from the high priest and the Jewish ruling council (the Sanhedrin), going from house to house and city to city, and dragging off men and women and putting them in prison and some to death.

Acts 12: King Herod had arrested some of the believers and had killed James with the sword. Because this pleased the Jews, he proceeded to arrest Peter also, and put him in prison. The Lord intervened and sent his angel and delivered Peter. Herod, in his arrogance, was stricken dead by God, but the gospel continued to spread.

Saul and the Rest of Acts: Saul, the persecutor, was eventually confronted by the risen Jesus Christ, and he was converted to become one of the greatest apostles. He carried the gospel to the Gentiles (non-Jews) and suffered a lot of persecution in the hands of both religious leaders and secular authorities (Acts 16:16-26; 17:5-9; 18:12-17; 21:27-28:31). Paul was finally brought to Rome, the capital of the Roman Empire, where he continued to testify about the Christ until his execution. For a summary of the persecution of Paul, see 2 Corinthians 11:16-33. Details about the deaths of the apostles are not recorded in the Bible, but legend holds that all of them were killed through persecutions except John, who lived into a good old age.

The Church Breaks Away from Judaism

As the Church continued to grow and many Jews and some priests became followers of Christ, persecution also increased. The Jews led a rebellion in AD 66 against the Roman occupiers, and by AD 70, Jerusalem was destroyed by the Roman army. To be noted is that, in its early stages, Christianity was not regarded as a new religion, but a sect of Judaism, which believed the messianic age had begun. But with the Jewish rebellion, Christians (now largely Gentiles) began to distance themselves from the Jews. The Roman Empire began to recognize Christianity as a separate religion from Judaism. Persecution, that had been largely from the Jews, now turned into the hands of the Romans.

Persecution From Nero to Constantine

We must not forget our old foe, Satan, the great accuser of the believers and God's archenemy. Although he is not a physical being, he uses humans through their personal ambitions, to fight against Jesus Christ and his Church. Nero was the first Roman emperor to launch an organized persecution against the Church. When part of the city of Rome burned down, he accused the Christians for having masterminded the arson. Many Christians were arrested and killed in the arenas by animals (believers were eaten alive), some by crucifixion, some burnt at the stake, and others in other cruel ways.

Another persecution from Roman authorities that affected both Jews and Christians was launched by Emperor Domitian. Persecution continued into the second century and the test for Christians was this: "Pray to the gods, burn incense before the image of emperors, or curse Christ."[xxxv] Those who failed to perform these rites or recant their faith were executed. Emperor Trajan formulated a policy toward the punishment of Christians that lasted until the third century. Prominent among those executed were: Ignatius of Antioch, Polycarp (who was asked to worship the emperor, swear by the emperor or curse Christ). Persecution became fierce again under Marcus Aurelius. During this time, persecution was not only in the realm of suffering, but also in the realm of the intellect, which some Christian apologist undertook to defend as Gonzalez writes; "Much more difficult to refute was the criticism of a number of cultured pagans who had taken the trouble to learn about Christianity and claimed that it was intellectually wanting."[xxxvi] They insisted that; "Christians were an ignorant lot whose doctrines, although preached under a cloak of wisdom, were foolish and even self-contradictory."[xxxvii] These enemies of Christianity (servants of Satan) regarded Christians as culturally uncivilized and concluded that; "… Christianity was a religion of barbarians who derived their teaching, not from Greeks or Romans, but from Jews, a primitive people whose best teachers never rose to the level of Greek philosophers."[xxxviii] Such a classification of Christians has continued until the present, where Christians are regarded as half-wits, ignoramus, unscientific, and bigots, but time will prove whether Christians indeed are barbarians and ignoramus or not.

However, Christians were not under constant persecution. There were times that they enjoyed some relative peace though Trajan's policy was still in effect (that is, he had decreed that in the punishment of Christians, the state should not seek them out, but if accused and they refused to recant, they should be punished). In the third century, Emperor Septimius Severus wanted religious harmony within the empire under the **Unconquered Sun**, and thus, promoted religious syncretism. Jews and Christians objected, and he outlawed their spread—conversion was punishable by death. In 202 AD, the edict of Septimius was issued, after which persecution increased. New converts and their teachers became prime targets. After a while, persecution subsided, but resurfaced again when Decius, who wanted to restore Rome's glory by restoring her ancient pagan religions, became emperor. Those who refused to worship the gods were accused of causing the downfall of the empire and were therefore, guilty of high treason. Since killing the Christians resulted instead in more people turning to Christianity, Decius's goal was to force Christians to recant or become apostates. Christians responded to this differently: "Some ran to obey the imperial command. Others stood firm for a while, but when brought before the imperial authorities offered the required sacrifices to the gods. Still others obtained fraudulent certificates without actually worshiping the gods. And there was a significant number who resolved to stand firm and refuse to obey the edict."[xxxix]

In the third century, this vicious and diabolical persecution broke out again under Diocletian, because of the Christians' attitude toward the army. Some Christians were against military service, and to ensure order in the army, some Christians were expelled and some even executed. This persecution of Christians later extended to the burning of churches and Christian sacred writings, and removal or execution of Christians from the government. As was always the case, the way out was either to recant, burn incense to the image of the emperor, or sacrifice to the gods. This was the cruelest persecution of all. It finally ended by April 30, AD 311, with the edict of Galerius that granted pardon, peace, and some freedom to the Christians. Imperial persecution officially ended when Constantine became sole emperor of the Roman Empire and issued the Edict of Milan in AD 313.

Thus, the price of being a Christian in these first centuries was very high—you had to pay it with your life. As we saw right from the case of Herod at Jesus' birth, to say that Jesus Christ is king within the Roman Empire, was to say inadvertently that you rejected the kingship of the emperor or that you submitted to a king higher than him. This claim to Jesus' kingship earned Jesus his death as it is written; *"From then on, Pilate tried to set Jesus free, but the Jews kept shouting, 'If you let this man go, you are no friend of Caesar.* **Anyone who claims to be king opposes Caesar.'** *... 'Here is your king,' Pilate said to the Jews. But they shouted, 'Take him away! Take him away! Crucify him!' 'Shall I crucify your king?' Pilate asked. 'We have no king but Caesar,' the chief priests answered"* (John 19:12-15). The same claim would lead to the persecution of all who followed Jesus as we have seen under these emperors. If these emperors did not stand for Jesus, the King of kings, they stood with or for Satan, Jesus' adversary. By rejecting Christ, they were indeed, antichrists, the perpetrators of the mystery of wickedness (2 Thess. 2:7).

Early Christian Heresies

Apostle Paul had warned the elders at Ephesus; *"I know that after I leave, savage wolves will come in among you and will not spare the flock. Even from your own number men will arise and distort the truth in order to draw away disciples after them"* (Acts 20:29-30). Of such people, he had also said that just as Satan masquerades as an angel of light, so do his servants—false apostles, deceitful workmen, who masquerade as servants of righteousness to enter the Church- -wolves in sheep clothing. John had also said this about them; *"Dear children, this is the last hour; and as you have heard that the antichrist is coming, even now many antichrists have come .... Who is a liar? It is the man who denies that Jesus is the Christ. Such a man is the antichrist--he denies the Father and the Son"* (1 John 2:18-22). Again John says; *"Many deceivers who do not acknowledge Jesus Christ as coming in the flesh, have gone out into the world. Any such person is the deceiver and antichrist"* (2 John 7).

Satan did not only launch his attack against the Church through persecution and intellectual assault, but also secretly sent his apostles into the Church to introduce destructive heresies. Paul declared that savage wolves would come in clandestinely and subvert believers, and that even some within the Church will lead people astray. John was very specific about those he labelled antichrists: they are those who deny that Jesus has come in the flesh or is the Christ. At the time

John and Paul wrote, these super-apostles, wolves, and antichrists, were already harassing the Church. Some of the full-blown heresies that plagued the Church include the following.

Gnosticism: Derived from the Greek word *gnosis*, meaning "knowledge," Gnostics claimed to possess a special mystical knowledge reserved only for those with true understanding. This knowledge, according to them, was the secret key to salvation.[xl] To Gnostics, all matter is evil or unreal and the human is an eternal spirit trapped in prison--the body. Christ, to Christian Gnostics, was the heavenly messenger sent to give mankind this knowledge. "Since Christ is a heavenly messenger, and since body and matter are evil, most Christian Gnostics rejected the notion that Christ had a body like ours."[xli] Thus, Christ only appeared or seemed to be human (docetism) but was not. This led to a denial of creation as good, and a denial of the incarnation and the resurrection. Gnostics were, therefore, full-blown antichrists (Satan's apostles) according to John's definition of antichrist.

Marcion: Marcion was another antichrist, who believed that the world was evil, and therefore, its creator must be either evil or ignorant. He concluded that the God and Father of Jesus Christ (loving, gracious, and just), was not the same Jehovah, the God of the Old Testament, who was vindictive and punitive. Thus, to Marcion, "Jesus was not really born of Mary, since such a thing would have made him subject to Jehovah. Rather he simply appeared as a grown man .... Naturally, at the end there will be no judgment, since the supreme God is absolutely loving, and will simply forgive us."[xlii] This in many respects sounds like some stuff out there today.

Arianism: The major issue at stake with Arianism was whether the Word of God (Jesus Christ) was co-eternal with God or not. Arianism (that bears the name of its chief proponent, Arius) argued that; "There was when he was not."[xliii] According to Arius, the Word was not God, but the first of all creatures. Thus, God had not lived in the flesh. Again, just as John has stated, such arguments are the spirit of antichrist. The response to this heresy was clear and simple: the Word was/is co-eternal and co-equal with God (John 1:1, 14; Col. 2:9). This heresy was so serious that a church council was held at Nicea in AD

325, in which it was confirmed that the Word, Jesus Christ, was/is God. He was Immanuel--God with us in human flesh dwelling. This heresy has been revived in modern days by the Jehovah's Witnesses, who deny that Jesus is God just like the Father.

Other Christological Heresies: In the fourth and fifth centuries, other heresies developed concerning the humanity of Jesus Christ, and how the divine was united with the human. First, Apollinaris argued that in Jesus the Word of God took the place of the rational soul. This implied that Jesus was human in every way but did not have a human intellect. The flaw in this argument is that a human being without a human intellect cannot be fully human. Secondly, Nestorius argued that; "In Jesus there were two natures and two persons; one divine and one human. The human nature and person were born of Mary; the divine were not."[xliv] Thirdly, there was Eutyches, who argued that "While the Savior was 'of one substance with the Father,' he was 'not of one substance with us.'"[xlv]

To resolve these antichrist teachings, the Church met at Chalcedon and came out with the following declaration; "… we all with one voice teach that it is to be confessed that our Lord Jesus Christ is one and the same God, perfect in divinity, and perfect in humanity, true God and true human, with a rational soul and body, of one substance with the Father in every way like us, with the only exception of sin, begotten of the Father before all time in his divinity, …."[xlvi] We will equally note here that in the hypostasis (union of two natures—divine and human in one person), it was the divine that took on humanity and not humanity taking on the divine (John 1:14; Phil. 2:5-8; Heb. 2:14). Anyone who rejects either the deity or humanity of Jesus Christ is an antichrist.

CHAPTER 7

SATAN TRANSFORMS INTO AN ANGEL OF LIGHT

"*For such men are false apostles, deceitful workmen, masquerading as apostles of Christ. And no wonder, for Satan himself masquerades as an angel of light. It is not surprising, then, if his servants masquerade as servants of righteousness. Their end will be what their actions deserve*" (2 Co. 11:13- 15).

Satan had tried without success to stop Jesus from going to the cross, and for three centuries, he equally tried without success to stop Jesus' followers through persecution and death. The cross in one sense means suffering, persecution, and sometimes even death. Jesus went through all three. He bore the cross, which Satan, through Peter wanted him to avoid. Satan, of course, is always working hard. He uses as many tactics and schemes as possible. Obviously, his external hostile and heinous assault through persecution and killing was not succeeding, so he decided to launch an offensive from within. If you cannot beat them from without, join them and beat them from within! Therefore, Satan transformed himself into an angel of light so that it would be difficult to recognize him from within. He had to appeal to human nature to obscure the cross of Christ. In fact, he literally removed it—"Christians, you do not need to suffer anymore; I will grant you religious freedom within my kingdom or empire!"

Jesus' commands concerning the cross, that is, suffering and persecution were plain and clear. When Peter rebuked Jesus for saying that he was going to suffer in the hands of the religious leaders and be killed; *"Jesus turned and said to Peter, 'Get behind me, Satan! You are a stumbling block to me; you do not have in mind the things of God, but the things of men.'"* The passage goes ahead to say that; *"Then Jesus said to his disciples, 'If anyone would come after me, he must deny himself and take up the cross and follow me'"* (Matt. 16:23-23). Following Jesus means taking up the cross; *"... anyone who does not take his cross and follow me is not worthy of me"* (Matt. 10:38). Jesus also says; *"Blessed are you when people insult you, persecute you and falsely say all kinds of evil against you because of me"* (Matt. 5:11). Apostle Paul reiterates the same thing; *"... We must go through many hardships to enter the kingdom of God"* (Acts 14:22b). Again, Paul says; *"In fact, everyone who wants to live a godly life in Christ Jesus will be persecuted, ..."* (2 Tim. 3:12). Peter equally admonishes the Christians; *"Therefore, since Christ suffered in his body, arm yourselves also with the same attitude, ... Dear friends, do not be surprised at the painful trial you are suffering, as though something strange were happening to you. But rejoice that you participate in the sufferings of Christ, so that you may be overjoyed when his glory is revealed. If you are insulted because of the name of Christ, you are blessed, for the Spirit of glory and of God rests on you"* (1 Pet. 4:1, 12-14).

With all these stern commands and admonitions, the early Christians knew too well what it meant to follow Jesus Christ. In fact, they rejoiced when they went through beatings and suffering, as it is written; *"... They called the apostles in and had them flogged. Then they ordered them not to speak in the name of Jesus, and let them go. The apostles left the Sanhedrin, rejoicing because they had been counted worthy of suffering disgrace for the Name"* (Acts 5:40-41). The martyrdom of Ignatius of Antioch by AD 107 also indicates how Christians rejoiced in suffering for Christ. He had been condemned to death by the Roman authorities and on his way to Rome for execution; "Somehow, Ignatius heard that Christians in Rome were considering the possibility of freeing him from death. He did not look at this with favor. He was ready to seal his witness with his blood ...."[xlvii] Ignatius faced death with courage because he knew that by his death, he will become a witness for Christ. With such courage from the martyrs, and with the fact that by such deaths more were turning to Christ, Satan saw that through hardships, persecution, and death, the Church continued to grow (the blood of the martyrs is the seed of the gospel); so why not remove this cross from them? Thus, persecution was going to end officially within the Roman Empire, and whether this was good or bad for the Church, has been subject to debate for centuries.

Constantine and the Gangrene of Union of Church and State

Much has been written about Constantine, the supposed first Christian Emperor of the Roman Empire. Was his vision of the cross at Milvian Bridge from Christ? Was he truly converted or born again? Was his effort to unite the empire and the Church of negative or positive consequence to Christianity? These questions and many others about Constantine are difficult to answer given that only God truly knows the heart of men. At best, we can only be subjective, and at worst, wrong. However, with the help of the Scriptures and events that transpired in Constantine's life and the Church during his lifetime, we have some help in answering some of these questions.

We know that not every revelation or vision is from God/ Christ. Therefore, the veracity of Constantine's vision is known only between him and God. Again, as to whether he was truly born again, only he and God know. Nevertheless, Constantine's activities from his conversion to his death can help us to conclude certain things about his conversion.

What things in Constantine's life proved that he was a Christian or not? Jesus had warned his followers; *"Watch out for false prophets. They come to you in sheep's clothing, but inwardly they are ferocious wolves. **By their fruit you will recognize them ...**"* (Matt. 7:15-18). So, what kind of fruit did Constantine bear? Even though he took many positive steps toward the Church such as: ending official persecution; supervising theological councils; making the Roman nobility receptive to Christianity; offering financial favor to the bishops; etc. (and it was politically expedient to do so since Christianity had become a force to reckon with), the following activities make his conversion questionable.

1. He continued to worship the *Unconquered Sun.*

2. Both Christians and pagan priests partook in the great ceremonies during the founding of Constantinople.[xlviii]

3. He determined his own religious practices, and even intervened in the life of the Church, considering himself as "bishop of bishops."[xlix] (Of course, the "bishop of bishops" is Christ alone--thus, Constantine was a usurper, posing in the place of Christ--an antichrist).

4. He repeatedly took part in pagan rites in which no Christian would partake.

5. He was not baptized until on his death bed. Eusebius, an Arian bishop, baptized him (a bishop like Paul, after a vision from Christ took baptism right away; Acts 9, why not this "bishop of bishops"?).

6. He served other gods (syncretism) and acknowledged their reality and power—thus serving two masters, which is impossible according to Jesus Christ (Matt. 6:24).

7. He continued to accept the title of High Priest, Supreme Pontiff of paganism, a prerogative of emperors, and partook in all sorts of pagan ceremonies. After his death, the Roman senate declared him a god.

8. Coins minted in his reign bore names and symbols of ancient gods, as well as the monogram for the name of Christ, the chi rho.[l]

9. He decreed in AD 324 that all soldiers should worship the supreme God on the first day of the week, Sunday--the resurrection day for Christians. However, it was also the day of the *Unconquered Sun.* Thus, pagans and Christians could worship together, as pagans did not see any need to oppose such syncretism.

By their fruit you shall know them! So, did Constantine see the power of God in his vision? If so, does seeing the power of God necessarily imply submission and obeisance to that power? We can note the example of Nebuchadnezzar of Babylon, who, after acknowledging God, still went ahead with his idolatry, pride, and arrogance against God. Whatever conclusions we may make about Constantine, it is clear that Satan had become an internal disguised enemy, posing as a bishop or apostle of Christ--the tares were successfully and officially sown among the wheat (Matt. 13:24-30), and the cross removed from imperial Christianity by a veneer of religious freedom. The enemy, Satan, had cunningly sown his virus in Christ's body. Constantine, by his policies and influence, would affect Western Christianity in largely negative ways, which have continued until this very day. **In fact, Christianity became "Constantianity," a Christianity without a cross, in which the world and paganism invaded and inhabited the Church.** A Christianity where Caesar and God are united. Roman paganism then put on a new face, disguised as Christianity. A keen observer of this "Constantianity" with the cross removed has noted in what he calls 'The End of Christendom":

> "We are being compelled to return to a much more biblical and radical position—that of being a minority in the world but not of it. Few Christians are aware that the 1,700 years of a politicized Christianity as the ideology of the ruling elite are rapidly drawing to a close. Whether we like it or not, the concept of the **imperial Church** dominated the thinking of Roman Emperors from Constantine onwards through the papacy, the Reformation and the nineteenth century mission movement. Its marks are also visible in the largely Protestant Moral Majority or Religious Right in the USA and the efforts of Russian Orthodox to eliminate every alternative religious opinion today. The era of Constantine Christendom is ending. A Church deprived of political power is freed from the burden of trying to use human power to dominate and influence the world."[li]

This succinct and almost prophetic declaration is an honest and objective recognition of the fact that with Constantine, a new form of Christianity ("Constantianity") was born, and that has affected the Church negatively until this very second. We must note here that God is not some desperate deity out there seeking for some important personalities (VIPs) to acknowledge him. He is the supreme God, who commands men everywhere (irrespective of their social status) to repent and escape the wrath to come. He does not need political thrones to change the world. He chooses the weak and despised things of this world (even the unschooled and ignoble) to confound the wise, the strong and powerful, and the rich (1 Co. 1:26-29; James 2:1-7).

Imperial Christianity

"To the angel of the church in Pergamum write: These are the words of him who has the sharp, double-edged sword. I know where you live--where Satan has his throne" (Rev. 2:12-13a).

When Jesus Christ walked this earth, he made it clear that his kingdom is not of this world like were the kingdoms of the Caesars, the kings, and the governors; *"Jesus said, 'My kingdom is not of this world. If it were, my servants would fight to prevent my arrest from the Jews. But now my kingdom is from another place"* (John 18:36). Christ and Caesar were forever to remain separate until Christ returns to set up his everlasting kingdom—then and only then, will Caesar and Christ be united in one person. However, with the supposed conversion of Constantine and the endorsement of Christianity by the Roman Empire, an unfortunate and unholy marriage between Christ's bride and Caesar occurred. Or should I say that Satan began to deceive Christ's bride just as he did to Eve? Apostle Paul had cautioned; *"I am jealous for you with a godly jealousy. I promised you to one husband, to Christ, so that I might present you as a pure virgin to him. But I am afraid that just as Eve was deceived by the serpent's cunning, your minds may somehow be led astray from your sincere and pure devotion to Christ"* (2 Co. 11:2-3; Remember that this is the same passage where Paul says that Satan masquerades as an angel of light; vv.13-14). Christ had told the people to give to Caesar what is Caesar's (tribute, tax, submission, honor), and to God what is God's (worship, trust, complete devotion and allegiance), but with God and Caesar united, this could mean utter chaos and confusion. As far as I am concerned, this illegal marriage between the state and the Church represented the official planting of the tares and weeds in Christ's wheat farm. Jesus had earlier alerted his followers;

*"Jesus told them another parable: 'The kingdom of God is like a man who sowed seed in his field. **But while everyone was sleeping, his enemy came and sowed weeds among the wheat and went away.** When the wheat sprouted and formed heads, then the weeds also appeared. The owner's servants came to him and said, 'Sir, didn't you sow good seed in your field? Where then did the weeds come from?' 'An enemy did this,' he replied. The servants asked him, 'Do you want us to go and pull them up?' 'No, he answered, 'because while you are pulling the weeds, you may root up the wheat with them. Let both grow together until the harvest. At that time I will tell the harvesters: First collect the weeds and tie them in bundles to be burned; then gather the wheat and bring it into my barn'"* (Matt. 13:24-30).

Satan had successfully sown his seed in the Church, and it quickly sprouted up. His throne was transferred into the Church of Jesus Christ. Satan had again embarked on his age-old insinuating plan of usurping God's throne and impersonating God, as it is written; *"You* [Satan] *said in your heart, 'I will ascend to heaven; I will raise my throne above the stars of God; I will sit enthroned on the mount of assembly, on the utmost heights of the sacred mountain* [think of the Church here], *I will ascend above the tops of the clouds; I will make myself like the Most High"* (Is. 14:13-14). Very soon, his seed began to choke the wheat, and now he is smiling that his rebellion is coming to fruition.

Implications of Church/State Union

The union of Church and state had many implications for the Church from AD 312 until at least the Protestant Reformation. Even the Protestants did not reform this evil, as some of them still went ahead to organize national or state churches. Some of these implications include the following.

1. Syncretism entered the Church as Christians and pagans celebrated imperial ceremonies side by side. Incense, which was used as a sign of respect for the emperor, began appearing in Christian churches. Officiating ministers began dressing in more luxurious garments.[lii] Christian feast days were strategically placed to

co-inside with pagan feast days. The birth of Christ originally celebrated on January 6, Epiphany, was placed by the Latin West on December 25th, a date for a pagan festival (Saturnalia, celebrated with revelry and gift exchanges). Sunday too, which was the pagan feast day of the venerable *Unconquered Sun,* was officially decreed as the Christian day of worship.

2. The cross (persecution) was officially removed from Christianity.

3. The direction the Church would take in most instances was directed by the whims and authority of the emperor. For instance, Arianism enjoyed some favorable moments because the emperor at times would be pro-Arianism (Constantius in AD 353 threatened bishops and they accepted Arianism). Even Constantine died at the hands of an Arian bishop.

4. Augustine, Bishop of Hippo in North Africa, articulated for the Church and empire, the theory of just war, which has been unfortunately used by the Western Church till this day.

5. Christian ministers came to be called 'priests.'

6. The Church often compromised her role as ecclesiastical leaders blindly supported and obeyed civil leaders, who sometimes determined who would occupy which bishopric.

7. Bishops who followed independent policies were often persecuted by the emperor or empress.

8. "Theological discussion came to be tainted with the ever-present possibility of appealing to the emperor to take one's side, and thus crushing an enemy one could not overcome by mere argument,"[liii] whether one was right or wrong.

9. Sometimes pagans were forcibly converted and baptized.

10. In the ninth century, Emperor Charlemagne (founder of the famous Holy Roman Empire, that was neither Roman nor holy), felt called to rule his people both in civil and ecclesiastical matters, thus, appointing bishops and handling other things.

11. The clergy were offered imperial riches that would eventually corrupt them.

12. Roman paganism crept into and became part and parcel of the Church (syncretism).

Changes in the Church Until Development of the Papacy (Roman Catholic Church—RCC)

In the first three centuries of the Church's existence, it was possible to ask; "What has Caesar to do with Christ?" Or "What has Rome to do with Jerusalem?" But by the fourth century after Constantine joined the Church, Caesar had everything to do with Christ and Rome was becoming a holy city, with the same stature as Jerusalem or even replacing her. The following changes were noticeable in the Church.

1. Christian ministers and writers began to show biases and preferences to certain emperors over others.

2. The development of the cult of relics surfaced as bodies of martyrs were unearthed and parts of them placed in churches.

3. Relics eventually led to superstition.

4. Big church buildings (basilicas) were built that contrasted the simple house churches that Christians met in.

5. The simple poor Church of Christ was adorned with riches (seen as divine favor), which eventually led the Church astray.

6. A clerical aristocracy developed like the social structure of the empire. This clerical hierarchy, with the bishops at the top, who were separated from the people (called laity), was/is antithetical to Christ's injunction; *"Let the greatest among you be the one who serves."*

7. The eschatological hope of the early Church was abandoned in favor of the present circumstances. Those who would return to such a hope would be branded later as heretics.

8. A ruthless hatred for the Jews began (anti-Semitism; they were accused for killing Christ) in which Jews were hunted, persecuted, ostracized, and even killed. The most reminiscent example is the Spanish Inquisition, during which many Jews perished.

9. Augustine speculated on a place of purification (purgatory) for those who died in sin, where they would spend some time before going to heaven. This speculation was made Church dogma by Pope Gregory. Later, it was believed that masses offered on behalf of these people in purgatory could improve or even reverse their situation (What a dangerous and misleading heresy!).

Development of the Papacy (Birth of the Antichrist System)

Someone has remarked that it takes only one step to stray. Jesus Christ had made it unmistakably clear that whoever wants to be greatest in the kingdom of God must humble himself like a little child or must be the one who serves. He deliberately contrasted leadership within the Church to Gentile hierarchical leadership when the disciples were anxious about greatness and high positions in the Church. While they were arguing about this; *"Jesus called them together and said, 'You know that the rulers of the Gentiles lord it over them, and their high officials exercise authority over them. Not so with you. Instead, whoever wants to become great among you must be your servant, and whoever wants to be first must be your slave--'"* (Matt. 20:25-27). One would think that this admonition is crystal clear and plain to the least literate person, but despite this, the Papacy developed and has continued hitherto. The Papacy, then and now, is in direct violation of this teaching of the Lord Jesus Christ, head of the Church. How did this come about? With imperial religion came clerical aristocracy that began to imitate the imperial hierarchy. The fight against heresy also helped in the development of the Papacy as the Church needed some authoritative structure to condemn what they deemed heresies. It also developed as the bishops of major cities like Alexandria, Antioch, Constantinople, and Rome, fought among themselves as to whose bishopric had authority over the others. In the struggle, the bishop of Rome succeeded to establish his primacy over the others. **The bishop of Rome came to be called "Pope" or "father," in direct violation of Christ's command in Matthew**

23:9; *"And do not call anyone on earth 'father,' for you have one Father, and he is in heaven."* The pope became of prominence when the empire was crumbling in the face of the barbarian invasions. Pope Leo, the first pope in the modern sense, was the one who negotiated with the Vandals to avert the burning of Rome in AD 455. It was Leo, who argued strongly "...that Jesus had made Peter and his successors the rock on which the church was to be built, and that therefore, the bishop of Rome, Peter's direct successor, is the head of the church."[liv] Thus, the **heretical argument for universal papal authority** was firmly established or enshrined as dogma.

The Papacy became a significant authoritative seat both spiritually and politically from the fifth to the sixteenth century when the Protestant Reformation began. [This significant union occurred in 538 AD, when emperor Justinian signed a decree "constituting the Bishop of Rome as the head of all Churches in [Western Europe]"[lv] This began the arrogance and blasphemy of the Papacy]. Some who occupied the post used it to reform the Church and promote sound and biblical doctrine, but others used it to promote all sorts of corruption and doctrinal heresies. It is not my intension here to cover the medieval Papacy and its achievements and failures, but just to highlight how Satan used the post (for the dragon, Satan, had given his authority and seat/throne to the beast; Rev. 13:2) to derail biblical Christianity. **Heresies postulated, confirmed and promulgated by the Papacy include the following:**

1. Pope Gregory confirmed the heresy of purgatory as dogma. He believed that the living could help the dead out of purgatory by offering masses on their behalf or favor. He also believed that in the mass or communion, Christ was sacrificed anew. That is, the mass is a sacrifice. (This is totally against the assertion of Scripture that Christ was sacrificed once for all; Heb. 10:10). Gregory also encouraged superstition.

2. The popes at times became puppets of emperors.

3. The papacy became a throne to be coveted and fought for, leading to deadly rivalries during the medieval period. Some even obtained the post by bribery, deceit, and violence. Popes

were strangled, imprisoned, etc., and sometimes, there were two or even three popes. Aristocratic families laid hold of the Papacy. Bishoprics were bought and sold; a practice known as simony. All sorts of corruption, including nepotism, were practiced.[lvi]

4. The heresy regarding communion was also developed: the Roman Catholic Church, as the Western Church came to be called, believed, and taught that after consecration, the bread and wine become the actual body and blood of Jesus Christ; a heresy that is theologically known as transubstantiation. This heresy has not abated.

5. Universal clerical celibacy (doctrines of demons) became accepted dogma and in the process of implementation, married priests had to set aside their wives. While celibacy can be a gift or a voluntary choice (Matt. 19:11-12; 1 Co. 7:7), Paul warned about false teachers, who will appear in later times and forbid men from marrying; *"The Spirit clearly says that in later times some will abandon the faith and follow deceiving spirits and things taught by demons.* **Such teachings come through hypocritical liars, whose consciences have been seared as with a hot iron. They forbid people to marry and order them to abstain from certain foods,** *which God created to be received with thanksgiving by those who believe and who know the truth"* (1 Tim. 4:1-3).

6. The wrong theory (taught as doctrine) of just war led to one of the greatest mistakes in Western civilization—the crusades, an offensive against Islam.

7. The Church practiced anti-Semitism--convert Jews or kill them or exterminate them. Jews were compelled to wear distinctive garments in Christian lands, etc.

8. Those who challenged these heretical teachings of the Roman Church were presented and burnt at the stake as heretics.

9. Priests became the sole interpreters of the Scriptures, and their teachings were binding and unquestionable. This was one of Satan's successful strategies—to keep the people ignorant of the word of God, lest he be exposed. Church tradition (Canon Law)

became par in authority with the Scripture, and sometimes, even surpassing Scripture.

10. The people came to regard the pope as more than human and that for salvation all human creatures must be under the Roman Pontiff. Thus, the pope had replaced Christ as mediator between God and man. Any sane person need not look any further for the antichrist (one who poses as Christ or in place of Christ). The pope claimed to be God's very representative on earth—the Vicar of Christ, God's vice regent, God himself, the Holy Father! This was/is the most arrogant form of blasphemy (Rev. 13:5; 2 Thess. 2:3-4)!

11. Some popes used the papacy as a political weapon and waged wars on their rivals and on emperors.

12. All in all, by the time of the Protestant Reformation and European nationalism, the Papacy was the greatest universal spiritual and political seat on earth—the seat of the antichrist, Satan's earthly representative. Nevertheless, the wheat was still thriving among the weeds, and some ran and took root in the wilderness.

The Church in the Wilderness

Christ had vehemently declared that the gates of hell will not prevail against his Church. Although the tares were planted in the Church, God preserved the wheat in an extraordinary way. Despite its extreme asceticism (punishment of the body to achieve the life of the Spirit, legalism, exclusivism of the monks, and development of self-righteousness and eventual corruption), monasticism was a step in the right direction, that preserved biblical Christianity at a time when the imperial Church was at its lowest ebb. It is important to note that monasticism began even before Constantine, though much of it was sparked by the corruption of imperial Christianity. Their reaction was provoked by the following.

First, the monastics saw imperial Christianity and pagans flocking to the Church as a great apostasy (which of course, was true; 2 Thess. 2:2).

Secondly, those who accepted the riches of the state, the lack of persecution, and a false sense of security proved weak to stand trial. Therefore; **"This in turn convinced others that security and comfortable living were the greatest enemies of the Church, and that these enemies proved stronger during periods of relative peace. Now, when the peace of the church seemed assured, many of these people saw that very assurance as a snare of Satan."**[lvii] *(emphasis mine).* Indeed, it was a snare of Satan, which has remained in the Western Church until today—a false security, a false assurance, and comfortable living; a false peace and a façade of religious freedom (Rev. 3:17; 2 Tim. 3:12-13).

Thirdly, Monasticism per se, was not founded by the Church; it began even in opposition to the church hierarchy. Later, most priests who made an impact in the hierarchy of the Roman Church were either monks or priests influenced by the monastic life. Prominent among these were Augustine, Athanasius, Basil, John Chrysostom, and Gregory the Great.

It was not only the monastics that tried to maintain biblical Christianity. There were many others too, and anyone who attempted to do so faced either the wrath of the official imperial church or the imperial wrath or both. John Chrysostom was one of the voices in the wilderness, who sought to reform the life of the clergy (who had become rich and lived in luxury). Some clergy claiming to be celibate had in their homes "spiritual sisters."[lviii] The powerful and the rich, including the impress at Constantinople rose against John. The empress attempted to bribe him with money (what a satanic plot), but that did not close his mouth. He was falsely accused by other bishops and was exiled by an imperial edict. Thus, the Church (bishops) and crown (emperor), both satanic agents, persecuted John to death. (Jesus had said that a time would come when one who kills you, that is, believers, would think he is doing God's service. This was exactly fulfilled by the action of the imperial and papal persecution). The enemy had succeeded to establish himself and operate from within. He was now an internal enemy posing as an apostle of Jesus Christ!

Another great contribution of monks to the Church and Western civilization was the laborious work on copying the Bible and other books, which were preserved for future generations. Monasteries also became centers of learning and hospitality. The monasteries were the reforming agents in the Roman Church when the Papacy was decaying. The monasteries provided the Church with priests and popes, who were zealous in reforming the Church. The two mendicant orders, Franciscans and Dominicans (though with their distorted view of poverty) advanced the mission of the Church by preaching to and serving the poor. They later played a big part in preaching to and defending the Native Americans against colonial slavery and exploitation. Though these Orders operated with papal approval, I do not hesitate to call them sects of the Roman Catholic Church.

One story that is unfortunately left untold in general church history is the continuity of Christianity in Africa after Satan infiltrated and took over the European church (that deserves a separate volume). Church history largely ignores this history of the church, which is rather unfortunate. When the barbarians (the northern European Teutonic and Germanic tribes) seized the Roman Empire, and later, when Muslims wiped out Christianity in Roman North Africa, a remnant church remained—the Egyptian Coptic Church and the Ethiopian Church. These churches continued down the centuries and are still thriving today. The Ethiopian Church in particular, maintains a close tradition with Judaism and has been less influenced by Western Christianity; "It has grown directly from Christianity's Jewish roots, without the admixture of Hellenism."[lix] They have kept the seventh day Sabbath holy until today (Sunday was also kept), and kept many other Jewish dietary laws. Their practices have been adopted by some modern African churches; "Many modern African prophetic churches keep the Sabbath holy, and adopt dietary and other prohibitions similar to those laid down in Leviticus, as the Ethiopians do."[lx] Indeed, the woman was hidden in the desert and kept out of the reach of the dragon (operating through the Roman Church) and was determined to keep the commandments of God and the testimony of Jesus (as quoted at the beginning of this section).

Ringing the Alarm Bell

Other groups sought reformation outside the Church, unlike the monks. Circumstances led them to eventually break from the Roman Church. They were not satisfied to see the weeds and the wheat growing together. They might not have intended to break away from the Church, but persecution forced them to. Christ had instructed his followers that if they were persecuted in one town, they should flee to another (Matt. 10:23). Two cannot walk together except they agree to do so (Amos 3:3). It was evident to these early reformers that Satan had not only invaded the Church but was on the throne. The papal system was no longer Christ's representative on earth (vicar of Christ as the popes claim) but rather the devil's representative (vicar of Satan), the antichrist.

The Waldensians: They were so named because of their founder, Peter Waldo. The Waldensians devoted themselves to a life of poverty and preaching. They were strict in following the Bible, parts of which they translated to the vernacular, and sought earnestly to return to apostolic teachings. They were rejected, condemned, anathematized, excommunicated, persecuted, and some killed in the flames by the Roman Church. They continued preaching until they finally joined the Protestant Reformation. They are still extant in some European countries, especially Italy.

Albigensians: These originated in Southern France. They claimed that the orthodox Christians were too worldly. These, too, faced the same fate, and even worse, as the Waldensians. The Papacy persecuted them with all their full vent of barbarity. They were displaced from their livelihoods and territories, yet they kept the testimony of Jesus Christ.

John Wycliffe: He was one of the early reformers, who sought to reform both the life and doctrines of the Church. What was wrong with the Roman Church and its Papacy according to Wycliffe?

1. Wycliffe asserted and insisted that; "All legitimate dominion come from God. But such dominion is characterized by the example of Christ, who came to serve, not to be served. Any

Lordship used for the profit of the ruler rather than for that of the governed is not true dominion, but usurpation."[lxi]

2. Again, he declared that; "Any ecclesiastical authority that collects taxes for its own benefit, or seek to extend its power beyond the sphere of spiritual matters is illegitimate."[lxii] In respect to civil power, he affirmed the the limits of its dominion. To him, civil authority must not exert dominion over spiritual matters. (Unfortunately, this is strikingly true even with modern Protestantism in today's America, where spiritual and political powers are operating hand-in-glove).

3. He argued that the Church is the body of all who are predestined, and that the Bible ought to be put back in their hands and in their language. The prerogative to read and interpret the Bible was not exclusively to the supposed experts (bishops or priests). (Again, we note that even Protestantism today, has voluntarily relapsed into this error, in which theologians are the interpreters and most Christians no longer read their Bibles as they should. Thus, we see experts again in control, hence apostasy).

4. Wycliffe rejected the doctrine of transubstantiation. He argued that the body of Christ is indeed present in the bread but without destroying it just as the divine did not destroy the human in the incarnation.

5. He was declared a heretic and was imprisoned for some time. When he died his body was later exhumed and burned. (In his lifetime, he made a mistake of coveting money).

6. Wycliffe's followers came to be called "Lollards" (Mumblers). They believed that: The Bible should be returned to the people; Pastors should not hold civil office; images, clerical celibacy, and pilgrimages were abominations. (Of course, we have a resurgence of pilgrimages today, the Holy Land Tours). They also rejected prayers for the dead.

John Huss: He was another great forerunner of the reformation, but "He had no intention of altering the traditional doctrines of the Church, but only of restoring Christian life, and particularly the life of the clergy, to its highest ideals."[lxiii] He held to transubstantiation though he followed Wycliffe's philosophical views. He concluded that an unworthy pope is not to be obeyed. He also concluded "that the Bible is the final authority by which the pope as well as any Christian is to be judged. A pope who does not obey the Bible is not to be obeyed."[lxiv] On indulgences, he concluded "that only God can grant forgiveness, and that to sell what comes only from God is a usurpation."[lxv] Huss was condemned by the council of Constance (AD 1415), imprisoned, and finally executed by burning at the stake, and his colleague, Jerome, was also burned a few days later.

The Taborites: They were an apocalyptic movement among the peasants that existed even before the time of Huss. They agreed with Huss in many aspects but rejected everything that was not found in Scripture. With the **Hussites** (who retained everything except what was explicitly rejected by the Bible), and the **Horebites,** these groups agreed on Four Articles[lxvi]:

1. The word was to be preached freely throughout the kingdom of Bohemia.

2. Communion would be given in both kinds—cup also to the laity.

3. The clergy should be deprived of its wealth and live in "apostolic poverty."

4. Gross and public sin, especially simony (selling of bishoprics), would be properly punished.

The Catholics and the Germans repeatedly launched crusades against the Bohemian Christians, who defeated them on most occasions. Finally, negotiations were made, and the Bohemians rejoined the Church, but many left the established Church and formed the *Unitas Fratum or Union of Brethren*, who later became the **Moravians** during the reformation.

Girolamo Savonarola: He began expounding Scripture in a garden and then in the Church. He condemned the evils of the time contrasting the true Christian life to the life of luxury, thereby offending many among the powerful. He sold a great deal of the property of the convent and gave the proceeds to the poor. He reformed the inner life of the community of monks. He recommended that the gold and silver of the churches should be sold to feed the poor. He emphasized study and many people studied Latin, Greek, Hebrew, Arabic and Chaldean. He was "convinced that the luxuries of the time, and all the things that the rich value so much, were vanity, and that lust for them was at the root of all the evils that he deplored."[lxvii] Because of war and intrigue, the pope took harsh measures against him. He was seized by a mob, tortured, tried by papal legates, and condemned as a heretic, then turned over to secular authorities (together with his closest collaborators), and was hanged and burned.

Do you want to preach truth and stand for it? Do you want to expose Satan and his agents? He will come after you for he neither loves the truth nor those who stand for it. Indeed, everyone who wants to live a godly life in Christ Jesus WILL BE PERSECUTED, while evil men and impostors (Satan's agents—at that time, the Papacy and its priests and followers) will go from bad to worse, deceiving and themselves being deceived (2 Tim. 3:12-13). In all the cases we have seen above, all who stood for biblical Christianity were persecuted by both arms of Satan (the papacy and secular authorities). Jesus had told his disciples that a time would come when those who kill believers will think that they are doing God some good service. Was this the Church of Christ? No! It was the church of Satan, the antichrist.

Attempts at Restoration

If the Church that was supposed to represent and preach Christ on earth had become an agent of Satan—the antichrist; what were those who desired to stay true to the gospel of Christ to do? Were they to allow the weeds to continue to choke the wheat, especially when they were not allowed in the Church? It is apparent that when Martin Luther set out to correct the wrong doctrines of the Roman Church, his intention was not to break from the Church. He rather wanted a reformation of the Church and a return to the simple apostolic faith. The Papacy and the priesthood were fast decaying and descending rapidly into the abyss, rather than ascending up to heaven. Humanists, like Erasmus and others, were calling for a reformation of both the doctrine and practice of the Church.

Martin Luther: Luther, who was a monk and later a priest, had gone through a torturous path before finding the truth of the gospel: justification by faith. Knowing God is that simple, but religionists are always prone to complicate things and make God to be so remote and reaching him such a laborious and intricate task. This is what the Pharisees did, and Jesus had to rebuke them very sharply; *"They tie up heavy loads and put them on men's shoulders, but they themselves are not willing to lift a finger to move them. ... Woe to you teachers of the law and Pharisees, you hypocrites! You shut the kingdom of heaven in men's faces. You yourselves do not enter nor will you let those enter who are trying to"* (Matt. 23:4, 14). Luther was blinded by this Pharisaism until the Lord opened his eyes and he found the following wrong in the Roman Church.

1. The indulgences (buying forgiveness with money) that sparked his opposition against which he wrote the Ninety-five Theses. He questioned their efficacy and pointed out how the German people were exploited by the Papacy.

2. Luther supported Huss as he declared that the council of "Constance had erred in condemning Huss, and that a Christian with the support of Scripture has more authority than all popes and councils against that support."[lxviii]

3. Luther burned the papal bull that condemned him and his books. This marked the final break with Rome.

4. Luther's success depended on political circumstances. Luther saw a distinction between church and state--kingdom of gospel and kingdom of law. He believed that; "In the kingdom of the gospel, civil authorities have no power. In that which refers to this second kingdom, Christians are not subject to the state, and owe it no allegiance."[lxix] However, Christians were under the authority of the state. (Here, we note that not being subject and owing allegiance to the state, but under the state is distinguished). Luther was not a pacifist. He justified going to war for self-

defense to Lutheran princes. He supported and was convinced that civil authorities were under obligation to crush the peasant and Anabaptist movements, which he called subversive. (One wonders: What if the empire was to crush him too as subversive?).

5. Luther's ruling prince, Frederick the Wise protected him from the assault of the Papacy and empire. German nationalists supported him because they saw him as a mouthpiece of German outrage in the face of the abuses and exploitation of Rome. Luther equally challenged the empire when he refused to recant when he was asked to do so at the diet of Worms.

6. Luther concluded that the Bible has authority over the Church, pope, and tradition.

7. He rejected the five other sacraments, which were invented and instituted by the Roman Church, and accepted only Baptism and Communion. He, however, did accept infant baptism, since to him, salvation was only God's initiative.

8. He rejected transubstantiation but was not ready to reduce communion to a mere sign or symbol of spiritual realities.

9. He retained all traditional uses that did not contradict the Bible. Those who followed him came to be known as Lutherans. Lutherianism later spread beyond Germany to other nations and became the state church of some European nations.

Ulrich Zwingli: He was a mercenary soldier and priest, who began to preach against "pilgrimages as a means of salvation." He also rejected the indulgences. He preached against laws of fasting and abstinence and declared that priestly celibacy was unbiblical. His main goal was to restore biblical faith and practice. Many priests, monks, nuns, were married because of his influence. He taught that Communion was to be given in both kinds (bread and the cup) to the laity. He differed with Luther in that, to him, communion was symbolic. "For him, the material elements, and the physical actions that accompany them, can be no more than signs or symbols of spiritual reality."[lxx] He also emphasized general public education with no distinctions.

He recommended war and himself died in battle. He was strongly supported by the council of government at Zurich.

Anabaptists: This group of reformers carried the Reformation to its logical conclusion, beyond Luther and Zwingli. First, they acknowledged that there is always a marked difference or contrast between the Church and the society, hence persecution, which is what the primitive Christians went through (2 Tim. 3:12; 1 Pet. 4:3-4, 12-16). Secondly, they recognized that; "The compromise between Church and state that took place as a result of Constantine's conversion was itself a betrayal of primitive Christianity."[lxxi] To belong to the true Church is a matter of personal decision, and not by birth right (John 1:12-13). Thus, they taught that infant baptism must be rejected. They believed that pacifism was an essential element in Christianity—Christians ought not to take up arms to defend themselves (correct), nor their country (wrong). They called themselves the "Brethren"; under the leadership of George Blaurock and Conrad Grebel (who baptized each other by sprinkling). They began adult baptism and later adopted baptism by immersion. This earned them the name "Anabaptists" or "Rebaptizers." They were greatly persecuted by both the Roman Catholic Church and Protestants alike, such as Luther and Zwingli. Many of them were killed: "The martyrs were many—probably more than those who died during the three centuries of persecution before the time of Constantine."[lxxii] It is sad to hear that even Luther and Zwingli, who sought reformation and both supported by the state, became instruments of Satan in persecuting those who sought a return to the Bible. It doesn't take much for a believer to be influenced by Satan to do his will. The evil union between church and state had continued even in the Reformation Church.

Later, Anabaptists became radical. Rejecting earlier pacifism, they resorted to violent revolution. They attempted to establish New Jerusalem in Munster, announcing that the Day of the Lord was near. This, however, was a wrong move. We are never commanded in the New Testament to take up arms as Christians or to establish New Jerusalem.

Menno Simons, a Dutch Catholic priest, later reorganized the Anabaptists. His followers became and are still known as Mennonites. Insisting on pacifism, they had nothing to do with the revolutionary Anabaptists. Menno Simons felt that Christians ought not to offer any oaths nor occupy positions requiring oaths. Christians should obey civil authorities, as long as what is required of them is not contrary to Scripture. They adopted adult baptism by pouring. They believed that neither baptism nor communion conferred grace. These were outward signs of what takes place inwardly between God and the believer. They also practiced foot washing. They were greatly persecuted but they still survive up to the present.

John Calvin: He systematized Protestant doctrines and rejected the "false sacraments" of Rome and defended Christian freedom. On communion, he affirmed that the presence of Christ is real although spiritual, thus, not only symbolic. Those who followed him became known as "Calvinists" or "Reformed."

More Reformation in Europe Until the 1800s

The cry of the reformers *"Sola Scriptura"* was plain and effective. The Bible was returned to the common man (laity) and men sought ways to live out the faith. Nevertheless, much of the reform (except for early Anabaptists, Mennonites, and others), had political overtones. Therefore, much of what happened in Europe was not necessarily a return to the Bible (though this was true in some circles) but attempts to achieve political independence from the Papacy and her so-called Holy Roman Empire.

England: In England, it was the issue of marriage that caused Henry VIII to break with Rome (his divorces, remarriages, and taking of more wives—he ended up with the sixth). The marital problems produced different heirs to the throne of England that would follow different policies toward the English (Anglican) Church (some pro-Catholic like Mary Tudor and pro-Protestant like Elizabeth). Henry VIII was not seeking for reformation, but "As Henry saw matters, what was needed was not a reformation … but rather a restoration of the rights of the crown against undue papal intervention."[lxxiii] With the final break in 1534, the king was made supreme head of the Church of England. The mistake in this is that no one, not to talk of a secular sovereign, can be head of the Church. Jesus Christ alone is the head of the Church. Thus, this was and is a usurpation copied from the Roman Church. During this darkness, Sir Thomas More objected and refused to swear loyalty to the king as head of the Church. This earned him imprisonment. He was condemned to death; "But after he had been condemned to death he openly declared that, in order to clear his conscience, he wished to be clear that he did not believe that a layman such as the king could be the head of the church, nor that any human being had the authority to change the laws of the church."[lxxiv] Thus, even those who sought reformation soon became instruments of Satan—killing in the name of God.

There were few steps taken toward reformation during the reign of Edward VI, even in the midst of this political reformation. Thomas Cranmer ordered the Bible to be translated into English and placed in every church. The cup in communion was restored to the laity and clergy were allowed to marry. Images were withdrawn from churches and new liturgy for the Church of England and the Book of Common Prayer were developed.

Under Mary Tudor (1553-1558), whose goal was to restore Roman Catholicism in England, there was open persecution of Protestant leaders. "Almost three hundred of them were burnt while countless others were imprisoned or went on exile."[lxxv] Thus, this queen, who later became known as "Bloody Mary," had her satanic mark on the Church of Jesus Christ and has gone down in the annals of persecutors. Thomas Cranmer, one of the prominent English reformers, before dying, rejected the pope and his false doctrine, calling him Christ's enemy and antichrist.

Next on the throne of England was Elizabeth (1558-1603), who accepted only a moderate form of Protestantism. Under her, the "Thirty Nine Articles" that formed the basis for the Church of England, were promulgated. Under her also, many Catholics were equally executed. Toward the end of her reign the "Puritans" (those who insisted on the need to restore the pure practices and doctrines of the New Testament) became prominent. **The Puritans objected to the following:** the use of the cross; certain priestly garments; and the celebration of communion on an altar. **They stressed the following:** the need for a sober life, guarded by commandments of Scripture and lacking in luxury and ostentation; the need to keep the Lord's Day, devoting it to exclusively religious exercises and the practice of charity; they were opposed to bishops or episcopacy as a later invention not found in the Bible; the need to avoid drunkenness, particularly among the ministers; the need to avoid licentiousness— theater, not only because immorality was often depicted, but also because of the "duplicity" implicit in acting. **There were different groups of Puritans: (1) Independents:** These stressed that each congregation ought to be independent of all others. They became a big movement and denomination. **(2) Baptists:** These stressed that baptism ought to be administered to believing adults only. They also came to adhere to some distinctive beliefs. They have become one of the largest Christian denominations. **(3) Those of Anabaptist persuasion** were systematically persecuted. (Here again, we note the fact that, if you call yourself a Christian, and in one form or another persecute another Christian, the truth is that you are serving Satan, the accuser of the brethren, irrespective of your belief system— Protestant or not).

As noted earlier, much of the reformation in Europe was politically motivated. Spiritual reform and political reform were often mixed. Thus, in many cases, national religion was adopted. The unholy marriage between church and state continued and continues to plague the Church, even among Protestants. Even with the Puritan reformation in England, religion and politics were constantly mixed. The Constantinian gangrene of uniting church and state was not removed. James I of England sought to strengthen the episcopacy (which Puritans opposed) to increase his own power. Some conservative bishops joined the king in affirming that bishops as well as kings rule by divine right (This was a satanic lie—both are placed there by God but not in the sense implied here). The Puritans who controlled parliament were opposed to these views. Charles I (James's Son), who continued his father's policies (recognizing the divine right of kings), continuously clashed with the Puritan parliament, thus resulting in a civil war between Puritans and the king. The Puritans, who originally sought spiritual reformation, formed a militia and under **Oliver Cromwell (who was convinced that they were waging a holy war)** eventually executed the English Sovereign, Charles I. The Puritan Cromwellian Protectorate took measures toward legislation of religion and to reform both church and state. (This, of course, was a grave mistake). We must note here that the union of church and state was wrong and that no one can bring religious change by legislation. Throughout the Puritan reformation, there was open hatred for Catholics, an unfortunate situation. Christ had commanded his followers not to return evil with evil, but to pray for those who despitefully use you and persecute you and bless rather than curse.

Scotland: At the heat of the Protestant Reformation on the continent, the doctrines of the Lollards and the Hussites had found followers in Scotland. Some Scots who had studied in Germany brought the reformation to the country but from 1528, such preachers were persecuted and killed by the Scottish parliament. John Knox became the most prominent Scottish reformer and together with his followers, organized the Reformed Church of Scotland and Presbyterianism as their polity.

The Spread of Lutheranism: As Lutheranism continued to take root in Germany, and as German princes took up the cause of Protestantism, the imperial and papal dominance over Germany continued to wane. Some bishops, because of personal ambitions, declared for Protestantism as they saw the emperor's power diminish in Germany. In the Scandinavian countries monarchs took up the reformation as their cause and sometimes, Protestant beliefs were joined with royalist convictions. The Danish Church subscribed to the Confession of Augsburg and by 1560, Sweden was a Protestant country, with a Lutheran ecclesiastical hierarchy.

Thus, we see that much of the Protestant Reformation became more a political movement than a spiritual restoration. As Gonzalez concludes; "Eventually, even some who were involved in the wars of religion gave signs that political and personal considerations were paramount. Typical was the case of Henry IV of France, who repeatedly changed his religion in order to save his life or achieve his political goals."[lxxvi] Protestant German princes and their ministers made use of religion in order to further their political agendas. One of the bloodiest of the religious wars, the Thirty Years War, was provoked by Bohemian Protestants. Thus, not only Catholics were aggressors, but Protestants were equally guilty. Using religion (in this case Christianity) as a pretext for war is unbiblical (at least according to the New Testament), and a misrepresentation of Christianity.

Again, no sooner was the Protestant Reformation begun did they fall into cold formalism and tradition, as had the Roman Church:

> "Theologians in the seventeenth and eighteenth centuries zealously defended the teachings of the great figures of the sixteenth, but without the creativity of that earlier generation. Their style became increasingly rigid, cold, and academic. Their goal was no longer to be entirely opened to the Word of God, but rather to uphold and clarify what others said before them. Dogma was often substituted for faith, and orthodoxy for love. Reformed, Lutheran, and Catholic alike developed orthodoxies to which one had to adhere strictly or be counted out of the faith."[lxxvii]

It is rather unfortunate that this crisp description captures the mindset of these various traditions until today. Such rigidity has hijacked the Christian faith into academia--the university and the seminary classroom. There is a great stress on the letter (line upon line, which in itself is not bad) yet void of the Spirit (2 Co. 3:6). Theologians are full of knowledge, which puffs up, and can discuss every theological detail, but without love (1 Co. 8:1-3; 13). They use their tradition to interpret Scripture rather than be open to the word of God. Thus, Protestants jumped out of the Roman boat (tradition) and built their own boat (tradition). This was and continues to be a grave mistake. (By saying this, I am not suggesting anti-intellectualism for Christians).

The Spiritualist Movements: Those who sought more intense personal faith and piety distinguished themselves from the cold orthodoxy. As Gonzalez writes;

> "The seemingly endless debates on dogma, and the intolerance of Christians among themselves, led many to seek refuge in a

purely spiritual religion. Some in attempt to do this started seeing visions and rejecting the leadership of the church. Such was the case with Jacob Boehme who concluded 'that the leadership of the church had built a veritable tower of Babel with its interminable quibbling debates.'"[lxxviii]

However, in his over-reaction, "He exalted the freedom of the Spirit, the inner life, and direct individual revelation. He declared, for instance, that since the 'letter kills; believers ought not to be guided by Scripture, but by the Holy Spirit, who inspired the biblical writers and even now inspires believers."[lxxix] This, of course, was a wrong conclusion. The word of God is the sword of the Spirit (Eph. 6:17) and even if there is any new revelation, it must be consistent with Scripture (1 Thess. 5:19- 21).

The most prominent of the spiritualist movements were the Quakers, whose founder was George Fox. A devoted student of Scripture, he came to the "conviction that all the sects that abounded in England were wrong, and their worship was abomination before God."[lxxx] He disapproved of buildings called "churches" and of pastors working for a salary. To him, hymns, orders of worship, sermons, sacraments, creeds, and ministers were all human hindrances to the freedom of the Spirit. He also stressed the "inner light," a seed that exist in all human beings (both saved and unsaved). By this he rejected the Calvinist doctrine of total depravity as a denial of the love of God. "Thanks to this light, pagans can be saved as well as Christians.... It is rather the capability we all have to recognize and accept the blessing of God."[lxxxi] It is not intellect, conscience or natural reason. George Fox became an interruptive speaker at others' meetings, beginning with Baptists. Quakers rejected baptism and communion. Decision making was not by majority vote but by the Spirit. Fox argued that ultimate truth was in the Spirit, who inspired Scripture, and not in Scripture itself (wrong). He was pacifist. Quakers rejected the swearing of oaths and refused to pay tithes. They were greatly persecuted.

Another spiritualist movement of great significance was pietism that began in Germany. It was equally a response to the dogmatism of the theologians. It was begun by Philip Jakob Spener. The

Pietism stressed Bible study and devotion. Spener, depending on the priesthood of the believer, suggested that there be less emphasis on the differences between laity and clergy. He called on preachers to set aside the polemical and academic tone (display of knowledge). He insisted on the need to turn constantly to Scriptures, and to read them with a spirit of devotion and piety. He also emphasized sanctification. In his apocalyptic zeal, he became convinced that the prophecies of the book of Revelation were being fulfilled and predicted that the end was near. (Some of these reforms or demands for spirituality were not welcome by the Church, which felt secure and comfortable; Rev. 3:14ff). **Pietism eventually gave birth to Protestant missions that caught fire with the Moravians, who from 1732, sent missionaries to Africa, India, South and North America.**

Low Countries (today Netherlands, Belgium, Luxemburg): There was some reformation in this region before the coming of Protestantism. They were greatly persecuted by the emperor, Charles V, and "Tens of thousands died for their faith. The leaders were burnt, their followers beheaded, and their women were buried alive."[lxxxii] In the midst of such persecution, some Protestants resorted to armed rebellion resulting in more persecution. At the end, the Netherlands emerged Protestant, and Belgium and Luxemburg Catholic.

France: Protestantism had a hard time taking root in France, a Catholic country. Depending on the political situation, they were tolerated or persecuted resulting in exile for some. The French Protestants, the **Huguenots**, as they were called, were sometimes persecuted, and many lost their lives. At times, there was armed confrontation between Protestants and Catholics. The most memorable tragedy against the Huguenots was the **St. Bartholomew's Day Massacre,** in which tens of thousands lost their lives. The pope deplored the bloodshed, but ordered a celebration and that "the same be done every year in memory of such glorious deeds."[lxxxiii] Protestants and Catholics continued in a series of wars that sort of ended on April 13, 1598, when Henry IV, who had changed his religion at least five times, issued the Edict of Nantes. The edict granted the Huguenots freedom of worship in all places where they had their churches except in Paris.

And where was our old foe, Satan, in all these wars of religion? He probably thought he could quench the fire of the Reformation, and where impossible, he caused Protestants to take up arms and fight. Satan enjoys it when wars of religion are fought, because this brings him glory rather than God! Thus, in the face of reform, the dragon could not stand by to see his kingdom invaded and his authority challenged. He had to launch a defensive offensive. He had to spew water like a river to overtake the woman (Rev. 12:15).

The Catholic Response: The Roman Church responded to the Protestant Reformation with a counter reform. As Gonzalez writes;

> "Luther and Calvin, for instance, always insisted that the power of the Word was such that, as long as the Roman Church continued reading it, and even though the pope and his advisors might refuse to listen to it, there was always in the Roman communion a 'vestige of the church,' and they therefore awaited the day when the ancient church would once again hearken to the Word, and reforms such as they advocated would take place."[lxxxiv]

This 'vestige of the church' has remained in the Roman Church until today, but the needed reformation (that is, at least of doctrine) has never taken place. Only more heresies have been added to the old ones.

In the face of the Protestant Reformation, measures were taken to reform the Catholic Church, although the reform was mostly clerical rather than doctrinal. Francisco Jimenez de Cisneros under Isabella of Spain took measures to reform the clergy, convents, and monasteries. Unfortunately, it was under them that the infamous *Inquisition* (the barbaric, systematic, search, capture, and execution of perceived enemies of the Roman Church) prevailed. Even with scholarly reformation, doctrinal reformation was not allowed, and opponents (so-called heretics) were mercilessly persecuted. Anti-Semitism reached its climax during this time and there were many forced conversions of Jews and Moslems. During this period, the Society of Jesus (Jesuits), founded by Ignatius Loyola, became one of the main instruments (satanic tool) of the Catholic offensive against Protestantism. The Council of Trent brought a lot of reformation to the Roman Church, especially the clergy. However, they failed to reform the following heretical doctrines. They decreed that: tradition has an authority parallel to that of Scripture; the sacraments are seven; the mass is a true sacrifice that can be offered for the benefit of the diseased; communion in both kinds is not necessary (bread only); justification is based on good works done through collaboration between grace and the believer.

CHAPTER 8.

THE ROMAN EMPIRE GOES ABROAD (COLONIALISM)

About 2,500 years ago, God used a pagan king, Nebuchadnezzar, and the prophet Daniel, to reveal the timetable of Western civilization from that time until the second coming of Christ. **In his dream, Nebuchadnezzar saw a beautiful and magnificent statue,** which together with its interpretation, were as follows;

"You looked, O king, and there before you stood a statue—an enormous, dazzling statue, awesome in appearance. The head of the statue was made of pure gold, its chest and arms of silver, its belly and thighs of bronze, its feet partly of iron and partly of baked clay.... You O king, ... You are that head of gold. After you, another kingdom will arise, inferior to yours. Next, a third kingdom, one of bronze, will rule over the whole earth. **Finally, there will be a fourth kingdom, strong as iron—for as iron breaks and smashes everything—and as iron breaks things into pieces, so it will break all the others.** *Just as you saw that the feet and toes were partly of baked clay and partly of iron, so this will be a divided kingdom; yet it will have some of the strength of iron in it, even as you saw iron mixed with clay. As the toes were partly iron and partly clay, so this kingdom will be partly strong and partly brittle. And just as you saw the iron mixed with baked clay, so the people will be a mixture and will not remain united, any more than iron mixes with clay"* (Dan. 2:31-43).

The elements and the empires represented on the statue are as follows:

1. Head of pure gold = Babylonian Empire.

2. Chest and Arms of silver = Medo-Persian Empire.

3. Belly and thighs of bronze = Greek Empire.

4. Legs of iron = Roman Empire.

5. Feet partly iron and partly baked clay = Later Roman empire [the ten barbarian kingdoms that supplanted the Roman Empire] or modern Europe and its daughter-nations overseas, or what we call today the "Western World." This includes continental European nations and nations descended from Europe such as Canada, USA, Australia, New Zealand, and parts of South America. **The Roman Empire is described as strong as iron and breaking to pieces and crushing everything in its path. This depicts political and imperial strength that extended to the ends of the earth (European colonial imperialism).**

The Bible asserts that at the testimony of two or three witnesses, let a matter be established. So, God presented the same situation as concerns Western civilization to Daniel in a vision. **In his vision, Daniel saw** *"Four great beasts, each different from the others, came out of the sea* [peoples, nations and tongues]*"* (Dan. 7:3-28). These four beasts or kingdoms represented the following:

1. The First like a lion with eagle's wings = Babylon.

2. The Second like a bear = Medo-Persia.

3. Third like a leopard = Greece.

4. The Fourth **terrifying and frightening and very powerful** = Roman Empire; *"It had large iron teeth; it crushed and devoured its victims and trampled underfoot whatever was left. It was different from all the former beasts* [kingdoms]*, and it **had ten horns*** [ten barbarian kingdoms]*."*

Daniel was puzzled by this description of the Roman Empire; *"Then I wanted to know the true meaning of the fourth beast, which was different from all the others and was terrifying, with its iron teeth and bronze claws—the beast that crushed and devoured its victims and trampled underfoot whatever was left"* (v.19). He was given the following explanation; *"He gave me this explanation: 'The fourth beast is a fourth kingdom that will appear on the earth. It will be different from other kingdoms and **will devour the whole earth, trampling it down and crushing it**'"* (v.23).

A little horn comes up among the ten horns; *"While I was thinking about the horns, there before me was another horn, a little one, which came up among them* [the Papacy rose to power amidst the 10 barbarian kingdoms]*; and three of the first horns were uprooted before it* [the barbarian kingdoms: Heruli, Vandals, and Ostrogoths, were uprooted by Papal Rome]. *This horn had eyes like the eyes of a man* [Pope as spokesperson for the Papacy] *and a mouth that spoke boastfully* [papal claims to universal authority, Vicar of Christ, God on earth, Holy Father, etc.]*"* (Dan. 7:8). Daniel saw more about this little horn; *"As I watched, this little horn was waging war against the saints and defeating them* [papal persecution as we have seen through the medieval period and up through the Protestant Reformation], *until the Ancient of Days came and pronounced judgment in favor of the saints of the Most High, and the time came when they possessed the kingdom* [which time is still to come though the Papacy was weakened in 1798, when the Pope was taken captive by French troops and papal political power was broken, ensuring some freedom for believers (this was seven years after the bill of rights in the USA that guaranteed religious freedom)]*"* (vv.21-23). However, the time will fully come when Jesus Christ physically arrives and will completely and finally deliver the believers. This little horn (religious-political kingdom with pope at the head) took his stand against God himself; *"He will speak against the Most High* [all papal claims as vicar of Christ, Holy Father, absolution, etc.] *and oppress his saints* [persecution] *and try to change the set times* [see the Gregorian calendar now in use and what existed before then] *and the laws* [Catholics do not have the second commandment in the Decalogue, number four has been changed from Saturday to Sunday, and number ten is divided into two]. *The saints will be handed over to him for a time, times and half a time* [3 ½ years or 1260 days or years, from 538 AD to 1798]. The time here also typologically points to the three and a half years of the Great Tribulation at the end of time. Summarizing the above about the ten toes and the ten horns, we have the following:

Barbarian Tribe   **Modern country**

1.	Suevi	Portugal
2.	Visigoths	Spain
3.	Franks	France
4.	Alemani	Germany
5.	Burgundians	Dutch
6.	Lombards	Italy
7.	Anglo-Saxons	Britain ➔USA, Canada, Australia, New Zealand
8.	Heruli	Uprooted by Papacy
9.	Vandals	Uprooted by Papacy
10.	Ostrogoths	Uprooted by Papacy

The rest of this chapter discusses the ramifications of this fourth kingdom (Roman Empire) and its ten horns or toes (the ten Barbarian kingdoms or rather, the seven that remained), and how they have affected the whole earth. **The history of these seven nations in foreign affairs describes the history of European colonialism and imperialism, with its destructive methodology: devouring, crushing, and trampling the whole earth, unlike any other peoples of the earth.**

Legend holds it that Rome was founded by Romulus and Remus in 753 BC and was built on a cluster of seven hills.[lxxxv] Rome later became a republic and gradually began to conquer much of the Italian peninsular. Soon, Rome began to expand overseas and by 44 BC, the Roman Empire consisted of much of the land surrounding the Mediterranean Sea. By the time Jesus Christ was born, Rome controlled the holy land and Roman domination continued around the Mediterranean Sea extending as far east to Mesopotamia and far west to Britain. Rome continued its supremacy in the region until it was overrun by the barbarian kingdoms during the fourth and fifth centuries AD. Even with the barbarian invasions, Roman civilization was preserved especially by the Church, as some of the barbarians adopted or were converted to Christianity. The Roman Empire, now called the Holy Roman Empire (with church and state united), was revived in the eight century AD by the Carolingian kings (the most prominent of whom was Charlemagne) and consisted of much of what is today Western Europe. By this time, England and France were somewhat or relatively independent. By the time the Holy Roman Empire finally died, Western Europe had disintegrated into nation-states, but the mark of Rome (Roman law and the sum of Western civilization until then—thought, architecture, art, etc.) remained in them until today. The Western world is essentially a Roman world!

The Rise of Humanism

By the twelfth and thirteenth centuries, medieval civilization had begun to wane, giving way to the Renaissance as people sought to revive the glories of classical antiquity. A noticeable aspect of the Renaissance was humanism. **In one sense, humanism was a return to the humanities like literature, poetry, and art. In another sense, humanism was the tendency to place humans at the center of the universe, making man the measure of all things.** [lxxxvi] Man and his achievement became center stage and in a subtle way, turning attention from the Creator to the creature. Humans became centers of attention, hence, the birth of modern humanism. This paradigm shift from societal to individual achievement was manifested in the arts, as important figures of the past and present (then) were sculptured and honored. Men were becoming gods! *"I said, 'You are "gods"; you are sons of the Most High.' But you will die like mere men; you will fall like every other ruler"* (Ps. 82:6, 7). Of this attitude of making and honoring human figures in images and statues, Paul writes; *"Although they claimed to be wise, they became fools, **and exchanged the glory of the immortal God for images made to look like mortal man** and birds and animals and reptiles"* (Rom. 1:22-23). Even in the church, sculptures of important figures, Bible characters, and so-called saints, were erected. This humanism has continued up to this day, with statues of important people and celebrities, especially political figures, erected all over the face of the earth (like the Egyptian Pharaohs on the hills and pyramids).

The Rise of European Nationalism

By the fourteenth and fifteenth centuries the Papacy as a center of authority and political power was declining, partly due to clerical corruption and partly because of the rise of nationalism among various European peoples. As already mentioned, Britain and France were to an extent independent from the Holy Roman Empire. By this time, the concept or idea of identity as a nation began to take hold in the minds of most Europeans, who had previously just considered themselves as natives of a county or city. These nationalist sentiments undermined and weakened the papal claims to universal authority. Before this final decline, the Papacy was the greatest and strongest seat of both spiritual and political power on earth behind which Satan hid to exert his power over the hearts of men—the antichrist!

Nationalism changed the face of Europe and ultimately the rest of the modern world. The nation states that developed in order of power and influence (even global influence) included: Spain, Portugal, France, Dutch, Britain, and later, Germany and Italy. **These nations and other European nations would begin to aspire and compete to build overseas empires (that is, Rome going abroad—ruthlessly devouring, crushing, and trampling everything in its path).**

Modern European Colonialism

The history of mankind is a story of conquest and domination since the time men were scattered at Babel. Any ethnic groups that merged, if at all this happened, must have fought each other and the weaker submitted to and was absorbed by the stronger. The history of western civilization; the Mesopotamians, Egyptians, Assyrians, Babylonians, Persians, Greeks, Romans, and Europeans; is a story of conquest and domination. Sacred history revolves around these great western civilizations and will end there (not excluding the rest of the world). God himself set this clock in motion, and that is why he foretells it before it happens and will bring it to a close and begin the New Age. **We will concern ourselves here with modern European colonialism as it developed after the crumbling of the Roman Empire.** In fact, the Roman Empire in a sense actually became

Europe, and thus, has never crumbled. It will only crumble at the coming of Christ.

Before we delve into this subject, let us examine Acts 17:26-27, which states; *"From one man* [Adam] *he* [God] *made every nation of men, that they should inhabit the whole earth; and **he determined the times set for them and the exact places where they should live.** God did this so that men would seek him and perhaps reach out for him and find him, though he is not far from each one of us."* God scattered all the peoples over the whole earth and even **determined the exact places** where they should live. **At the beginning of modern European colonialism, every continent was occupied with indigenous peoples**—Aboriginals in Australia, Chinese in China, Indians and other Asians in Asia, Europeans in Europe, Africans in Africa, Native Americans or Indians in North and South America, and you can name the rest. **Therefore, the displacement of peoples by the colonizing and marauding Europeans (the Roman Empire going abroad) is described in Sacred History as a <u>devouring, crushing,</u> and <u>trampling underfoot</u> of its victims** (Dan. 7:19). We shall see why and how.

In the book of Daniel, the Roman Empire is described as having ten horns. (Horns can stand for kings or kingdoms; Dan. 7:24). The book of Revelation gives the same vision with some details and a stunning linkage is made with Satan directly. Rome/Europe is described as being in alliance with the dragon or Satan; *"Then another sign appeared in heaven: an enormous red dragon with seven heads and ten horns and seven crowns on his head"* (Rev. 12:3). This is a depiction of Satan, the ancient serpent called the devil (see Rev. 12:9), which happens to be identical to the Roman Empire as described in Daniel, except for the addition of seven heads and seven crowns. Satan comes down to the shore of the sea (peoples of the earth--Europe then) and a beast or an empire or kingdom is born; *"And the dragon* [Satan] *stood on the shore of the sea. And I saw a beast coming out of the sea. He had ten horns and seven heads, with ten crowns on his horns, and on each head a blasphemous name"* (Rev. 13:1). Satan and the beast (Roman Empire/Europe) are united, as Satan gives over his power and mandate to the empire (whose identity is Satan's); *"... **The dragon** [Satan] **gave the beast** [Roman Empire/Europe] **his power and his throne and great authority"** (Rev. 13:2b). It is unmistakably clear here that Satan's throne is on earth, and he has someone on it, who has been given authority to carry out Satan's plan! For a further understanding of the issue, Jesus gives his servants more clues; *"Then the angel carried me away in the spirit into a desert. There I saw a woman* [which means it is a Church--Papacy] *sitting on a scarlet beast* [Roman Empire/Europe] *that was covered with blasphemous names and had seven heads and ten horns* [this is the identical wording for Satan's description in Rev. 12:3] *... This woman was drunk with the blood of the saints, the blood of those who bore testimony to Jesus* [martyrs]" (Rev. 17:3,6).

How do we know this woman is a church? Because the Church of Jesus Christ is described in the same context as a woman! *"A great and wondrous sign appeared in heaven: **a woman clothed with the sun**, with the moon under her feet and a crown of twelve stars* [twelve apostles]*"* (Rev. 12:1-2). Of the persecution of Christ's Church by the dragon or Satan or Papacy, it is written; *"When the dragon saw that he had been hurled to the earth, he pursued the woman who gave birth to the male child. The woman was given the two wings of a great eagle, so that she might fly to the place prepared for her in the desert, where she would be taken care of for a time, times and half a time, out of the serpent's reach"* (Rev. 12:13-17). A further identification of the woman drunk with the blood of the saints and the beast she rides is given as follows; *"This calls for a mind with wisdom. **The seven heads are seven hills** [Rome was/is built on seven hills as earlier said] on which the woman sits. **They are also seven kings** [seven barbarian tribes that survived the Papacy and their modern nations or kingdoms; Portugal, Spain, Dutch, France, Italy, Germany, Britain]. Five have fallen, one is, the other has not yet come; but when he does come, he must remain for a little while. **The beast who once was** [Babylon] **and is not, is an eighth king** [USA]. **He belongs to the seven** [USA out of Britain and the other six nations] and is going to his destruction"* (Rev. 17:9-11; cf. 18). We see only seven kings here or seven horns out of ten because the Papacy uprooted the other three horns.

How have these seven kings (colonial kingdoms or empires) and the eighth colonial power (all offspring of Rome) influenced and shaped the modern world? Before we examine that question, let us examine the motive of the colonial impulse. **Given that Europe is identified with or as Satan, let us consider the following passage that best describes the European colonial impulse. Jesus said;** *"The thief comes only to steal, and kill, and destroy"* (John 10:10a). These three words perfectly describe the whole colonial enterprise of the modern era: **destroying, killing,** and **stealing;** or as described in Daniel before: **devouring, crushing, smashing, breaking to pieces,** and **trampling underfoot** (Dan. 2:40; 7:7, 19).

Some of the motives for colonialism included:

1. European curiosity in the rest of the world provoked by better navigation and new military capability.

2. Europeans wanted a new route to tap the riches of the East. (The first in this venture were the Portuguese).

3. Europeans wanted to capture the gold trade in Western Africa. They developed a lucrative trade in gold, ivory, sugar, and slaves.

4. Greed and Profit: When Vasco da Gama returned from India, his return cargo sold for sixty times the cost of his expedition.[lxxxvii] This provoked the curiosity of many adventurers, who hurried to the East Indies and carved out a large commercial and political empire.

5. As would later be followed by the Spaniards, English, French and Dutch, Europeans went out in search of gold, silver, any precious gem, and riches. They were bent on exploitation. **If it meant killing and destroying before stealing, they did not hesitate to do so.** Bent on building overseas empires and a lucrative trade, some Europeans left their home without any hope of ever returning and **wherever they settled, they mistreated the indigenous peoples and displaced some permanently.** The side effects of this savage and barbarous behavior is still lingering and affecting many people today--you just need to keep current

with indigenous peoples where Europeans settled, especially in the Americas.

The Practice of Colonialism

While colonialism was practiced by most European nations, the degree of their activities differed from country to country. Seven of these nations that built strong overseas empires include the following. (The eighth, USA, which is of the seven, is excluded in this section).

Portugal: The Portuguese began first by discovering a sea route to the East. In 1510, a Portuguese expedition took over Arab, Indian, and Malayan trading centers in India. Also, "Portuguese ships carried slaves and ivory from Africa to India where they were exchanged for spices, cloth, and glassware."[lxxxviii] "On his second voyage in 1502, Vasco da Gama threatened to burn the town of Kilwa (in present day Tanzania) unless the ruling sultan acknowledged the supremacy of the king of Portugal and paid an annual tribute in gold. Lacking the power to resist, the sultan capitulated."[lxxxix] Later, when the port of Sofala in Mozambique fell to the Portuguese, Portugal controlled the gold shipped from the interior. Mombasa in present-day Kenya, resisted the Portuguese, but the Portuguese, after looting the ancient and wealthy city, burned it down and sailed away. In summary; "By their actions, Europeans destroyed the older systems of Indian Ocean trade which had brought wealth and cultural enrichment to many parts of Asia and Africa."[xc] The Portuguese were disparaged in their racial discrimination, with the Bantu peoples, their main target of scorn: "The Bantu-speaking coastal peoples were regarded by the Portuguese as a lower caste and were relegated to menial jobs."[xci] Some of them they captured as slaves, especially those along the coastal areas. The Portuguese saw Angola as a source of slaves and using force, established a Portuguese colony there. They also established another colony on the East Coast of Africa in Mozambique. On the Portuguese overall impact on Africa, Fred Burke concludes that Portugal's influence on Africa was largely negative because her interest was narrowly commercial.[xcii] Their rule was harsh and did not foster appreciation of European civilization among Africans.

On the Orient, Portugal saw that she could not conquer the Indians, Chinese, and Japanese, and thus, settled for a policy of trade. This helped them to establish many trading posts. Westward, Portugal had laid claim on Brazil, whose wood served as a source of wealth; and later, sugar cane, the growing and processing of which required cheap labor, resulting in enslaving of Indians. Without sufficient slaves, the Portuguese began importing slaves from Africa. **Thus, in a nutshell, we see that the colonizers were ruthless, cruel, brutal, and licentious. They devoured, crushed, destroyed, and trampled everything on their path, and stole all that they could get away with.**

Spain: It is sometimes difficult to separate colonialism from religious imperialism. Since I intend to treat religious imperialism in a separate section, I will attempt to draw a line between the two. Christopher Columbus discovered the Americas in 1492. But before the Europeans arrived in the Americas, the natives had built great civilizations. The Aztecs of Mexico, the Incas of Peru, and the Mayans in the Yucatan peninsula.[xciii] Despite their civilization and self-reliance; "The beautiful native American civilizations were no match for the marauding Europeans. Spanish military men, particularly those of the lesser nobility, were part of a centuries-old tradition of crusading for Church, crown, and profit."[xciv] The Spaniards overcame the Aztecs by a combination of treachery, tactics, weapons, and determination. "They slaughtered and looted the poorly armed Aztecs without mercy."[xcv] They equally slew the primitively armed Incan troops by their thousands. A record is given about an Incan chief captured by the Spanish general, Pizarro: "Pizarro promised to free the Incan chieftain in return for a ransom of gold objects sufficient to fill a room seventeen by twenty-two feet to a height of nine feet, plus a larger amount of silver. This ransom was collected and paid, but Pizarro ... had him put to death anyway."[xcvi] The gold and silver that arrived in Spain was worth $10 million. Talk about savagery and exploitation! Thus, the Indians were exploited and decimated by the Spaniards and by their imported diseases.

The *encomiendas* (trusts), were developed, where the Indians were entrusted to a settler (*encomenderos),* who was to civilize the

Indians and teach them Christian doctrine, and the Indians would work for him in exchange. As Gonzalez comments: "The result was even worse than out-right slavery, for those who held trusts—the *encomenderos*—had no investment in the Indians, and therefore no reason to be concerned for their well-being."[xcvii] At times rape was added to mistreatment and exploitation. Indians in the Carribean were ordered to pay a quarterly tax to the Spaniards in gold or cotton; and defaulters were hunted with dogs. **Again, in summary, the colonizers had come to steal, kill, and destroy by whatever means possible.** One of the major incentives that motivated European expansionism was the advent of new commodities like spices, coffee, tea, sugar, dyes, tropical fruits, fine textiles, tapestries, precious stones, potatoes, corn, tobacco, chocolate, etc. The most precious of these commodities was black slaves, whom the Europeans bought from Africa for their mines and plantations.

Dutch: The Dutch became the intra-continental merchants of the exploits of the colonialists. By 1602, the Dutch founded the Dutch East India Company that made exorbitant profits. The Dutch expanded in the East by driving out the Portuguese. They had limited success in penetrating China and Japan, and force could not work. By 1652, the Dutch established a way station at the Cape of Good Hope at the Southern tip of Africa. More Dutch and other Europeans settled inland and by the time of British colonization in the seventeenth century, the Dutch descendants (Boers) were sort of an independent country. They would be remembered in modern history for their egregious and discriminatory Apartheid policy towards blacks. In later imperialism, the Dutch East Indies included much of what is today Indonesia.

Britain: The British came in later in the discovery adventure. By 1600 they had established the East India Company after having displaced the Portuguese. First, the British were interested only in trade, but were later involved politically in India. Between 1763 and 1871, Europe was involved in internal struggles and; "Imperial powers such as Spain, Portugal, and France, lost many of their overseas holdings during this period, leaving Great Britain as the only Western nation with an extensive empire."[xcviii] By 1839, the

British forced themselves on the Chinese. Even with other European rivals, the British got the lion's share. Between 1871 and 1914, British fingers and tentacles were all over Asia. African colonization was slow in coming, especially the interior, but in 1884, Europeans captured and divided this elephant into pieces among themselves. Britain had a significant chunk—Sierra Leone, Gold Coast (Ghana), Nigeria, Egypt, Sudan, Uganda, Kenya, much of Southern Africa, and Somaliland. The British were the most successful in building an overseas empire; "By 1914 the British Empire included one-fourth of all the land and people of the earth."[xcix] The British Empire also included self-governing dominions such as Canada, Australia, New Zealand, and the Union of South Africa. She also had other dominions in Central America and numerous islands. Her empire still survives today, consisting of 60 nations in the British Commonwealth. Britain's richest imperial prize was India, from whom Britain took more out than she brought in.

France: The French, like the British, came into the discovery venture later than the Portuguese and the Spanish. Nevertheless, they did and continue to do their own exploits. France has always been a rival of Great Britain. France entered the Eastern scene later than Britain and by 1740 had made some progress, but her success was limited because of wars with Britain. "The French took large areas in Sourtheast China and Hainan Island as their sphere."[c] They detached Indochina from Chinese sovereignty and soon had posts in east India. The French had (and continue to have) their greatest exploits in Africa. Since then, until today, she has remained a parasite in Africa that does not care whether the host plant survives or not. Her empire stretched from the Mediterranean to West Africa, and to central Africa. As always, the French clashed with the British in attempt to establish an all-French axis across Africa from West to East.

Germany: When other Europeans were having their exploits (feasts) overseas, Germany was still divided or under the shadow of the Holy Roman Empire. But during the new era of imperialism (late 1800s), Germany had colonies (posts) in the East—Kiao-chow (China), Mariana I, Carolinal, and Papua New Guinea. The Germans also got a share of Africa, with colonies in Togoland, Kamerun (Cameroon), Southwest Africa (now Namibia), and East Africa (mostly Tanzania).

Italy: Like Germany, Italy did not unify until later, and equally came in late in the overseas empire building. Italy did not have a post in the East. In the scramble for Africa, Italy had only a few tiny strips of land in today's Libya, Eritrea, and Somaliland. Her attempts to subdue Ethiopia were met with fierce resistance. For a time (1889-1896), Ethiopia was an Italian protectorate.

Other European countries with less significant colonial impulse were Denmark, Belgium, and Sweden. Thus, through colonialism, Europe (Rome's offspring) came to dominate the whole globe. Between 1871 and 1914 (and even until today), the whole world was practically under European domination. Why? Because of economic advancement and military capability: "The rapid expansion of industry in Europe and the United States created demand for greater markets, new sources for raw materials, and investment outlets for surplus capital."[ci] This economic impetus for colonialism became one of the precursors of modern global economy and marked the birth of Mystery Babylon (the global capitalist commercial empire) that is materializing more and more in our very eyes. Europe came to dominate the world and the global economy by displacing their competitors, as one historian has concluded;

> "The brilliant Aztec and Incan civilizations of Mexico and Peru were destroyed. The tribes of American Indians were exterminated, absorbed, or confined to reservations. The Moslems, Hindu, Buddhist, and Confucian civilizations of Asia and Africa were virtually enslaved by the aggressive European imperialists. ... The rise of capitalism not only changed the nature of European society; it also provided much of the explosive force that enabled tiny Europe to dominate most of the rest of the world."[cii]

Nationalism and national pride were other catalysts for European domination of the globe: "The competitive struggle for national prestige among Western nations; and imperial conquest became a measure of status, proof that a nation had become first-rate."[ciii] In their national egotism, Europeans reasoned that the privileged were bringing the blessings of civilization to the backward peoples--"the lesser breeds" of the earth. Another factor that brought the world under European domination was Christian missions.

Missions and Religious Imperialism

When discussing the end-times, Jesus said; *"And this gospel of the kingdom will be preached in the whole world as a testimony to all nations, and then the end will come. ... And he will send his angels with a loud trumpet call, and they will gather his elect from the four winds, from one end of the heavens to the other"* (Matt. 24:14,31).

It is difficult to say anything on religious imperialism, especially due to the difficulty of separating true missions from religious imperialism (that went hand-in-glove with colonialism); and especially as one who has benefited from both. Nevertheless, something can still be said according to evidence of history. There are countless missionaries who went out under the conviction of and call of God to bring the good news to a lost world (the heathen), but it cannot be denied that some went out for the expansion of the western empires and whose actions fulfilled Matthew 23:13-14;

> *"Woe to you, teachers of the law and Pharisees, you hypocrites! You shut the kingdom of heaven in men's faces. You yourselves do not enter, nor will you let those enter who are trying to enter. Woe to you, teachers of the law and Pharisees, you hypocrites!* ***You travel over land and sea to win a single convert, and when he becomes one, you make him twice as much a son of hell as you are."***

In most cases, first went the discoverers and second came the colonizers, and thirdly came the missionaries. Religious imperialism sounds as a negative term. While it is true to some extent, it is equally true that during the discoverers and colonizers, **there were some who went out in sincere faith with the genuine hope of converting the heathen to Jesus Christ.** Most of the first missionaries were Catholic, at which time Protestantism was still shaping itself and gaining ground in Europe. **Colonialism was the advancement of**

the satanic kingdom (killing, stealing, destroying), but missions was the advancement of the kingdom of God (the gathering of the elect). Religious imperialism was Satan's strategy to discredit or plant tares within the kingdom of God (true missions).

Catholic Missions (in the New World): In the New World, the Spaniards followed the crusade spirit or principles in conquering Indians, just as they had used against the Moors in Spain. But there were those who loved and fought for the indigenous peoples. The friars (Franciscans and Dominicans), and sometimes Jesuits, with their vows of poverty and simplicity of lifestyle, "Made it possible to live among the Indians, and to see the disastrous results of colonial policies."[civ] Most Dominicans took up the defense of the Indians. They objected to Indian slavery; rejected the *encomiendas* and *encomenderos*; they objected to the exploitation of Indians, with some, such as Las Casas, who "Openly declared that Christain faith was incompatible with the exploitation of the Indians by the Spanish."[cv] (The Spanish crown again and again, enacted laws for the protection of the Indians, though the colonial settlers refused to follow the laws). Another Domincan, Francisco de Vitoria questioned the right of the Spanish to take the territories of the Indians. "Throughout the colonial period, however, there were in Spanish America, Christians who protested against the exploitation of the Indians, and who devoted their lives to the betterment of their lot."[cvi] In Mexico, Indians rushed for baptism--since the Christian God had defeated their gods, they thought it wise to submit to the powerful Christian God. Most of the work was done by the friars, who, in time, gained the respect of and even loved the Indians.

However, there are some few mistakes to be noted here: (1) Some Indians were baptized without having been instructed in the faith. (2) Indian education was opposed by some, not that Indians were incapable of learning, but; "On the contrary, what was said was that if they learned how to read and write, they would be able to communicate among themselves from one ocean to the other, and that this would make them dangerous. This fear lay behind the low level of low education given to the Indians for several generations."[cvii] This is an attitude that has prevailed in almost all mission fields, both Catholic and Protestant; and clearly violates Jesus' command to teach converts everything he had commanded the disciples (Matt. 28:19-20). Paul had reiterated the same injunction when he said to Timothy; *"And the things you have heard me say in the presence of many witnesses entrust to reliable men who will also be qualified to teach others"* (2 Tim 2:2). Any missionary who fails to continue this pattern, because he thinks he is superior to the people to whom he has brought the gospel, is not a servant of Christ. In the space of three years, Jesus replicated himself in the disciples to the point that he called them friends and not servants, because they knew his complete mission (John 15:14-15). Jesus also said that it is sufficient for the servant to be like the Master, and that his servants would do even greater works than he did (John 14:12). Any minister or missionary who fails to reproduce himself in the lives of those he leads does not qualify as a servant of Christ. This was and still continues to be a terrible failure in the mission field (both Catholic and Protestant). As was the case, "The Dominicans declared that Indians should not be ordained or educated at all," implying they had a low regard for them. The Franciscans had a slightly different view. Gonzalez records the following about Juan da Estrada Ravago, a Franciscan in Central America: "He learned the language of the Indians and, with a single exception, refrained from violence against them. He traveled throughout the area teaching the Christian faith, baptizing people, and building churches. With his own resources he bought clothes, food and seeds for both Indians and settlers."[cviii] Again, we see that it is difficult to draw a line between who was sincere and who was not sincere in the mission field. The weeds and tares were/are growing together.

In Columbia and Venezuela: Luis Bettran among others "sought to bring Christianity to the Indians, and to undo the evil done by the *conquistadores* and settlers."[cix] He equally sought justice for them. The Jesuit Pedro Claver; "Had ample opportunity to see the suffering of black slaves, and therefore when he was finally allowed to make his final vows in 1622 he added a further vow to his signature; *Petrus Claver, aethiopum semper servus*--Pedro Claver, forever a servant to blacks."[cx] He argued that slaves were brothers in Christ and were to be treated as equals. He undertook to care for the blacks in their deplorable conditions from the time they arrived in the cramped packed ships, to barracks until they were sold. He took care of the sick and abandoned and "Took upon himself the task of cleaning the sores of infected blacks, who had been cast out to die."[cxi] Other Europeans did not associate with him because he spent most of his time among slaves. "Those who had anything to do with him mostly tried to dissuade him from his labors, for they feared that giving the slaves a sense of dignity was a dangerous thing to do."[cxii]

With the demise and conquest of the Inca Empire; "… the most remarkable figure of that early period was the Dominican Gil Gonzalez de San Nicolas, who spent many years as a missionary among the Indians of Chile and came to the conclusion that the war that was being waged against them was unjust. To attack others with the sole purpose of taking their lands and property, he declared, was a mortal sin, and therefore those who were involved in such activities should be denied the consolation of penance."[cxiii] Where the Spanish settlers were close, they became a hindrance to missionary work and even destroyed it. Thus, the white colonialists, both Spanish and Portuguese, were the worst enemies of missions. Their hatred against the Jesuits was that they did not allow them to enslave the Indians. After all is said, it is also clear that to some extent, Christianity was used to exploit the Indians.

In Africa and the East, the Portuguese first established churches on the West coast of Africa, Congo/Angola, mostly for the Portuguese and a few Africans. Portuguese Priests arrived in Mozambique in 1506, not seeking to convert Africans, but as chaplains to the Portuguese garrisons. A Jesuit Priest, Gonzalo de Silveira, converted the king of Zimbabwe, who later killed him. Many pioneer missionaries after him for the next fifty years were equally martyred. This is the unfortunate news about missions--many pioneer missionaries all over the world, like this one, were martyred by the same people to whom they brought the good news. As easy as it may sound, pioneer mission work has never been easy, and continues to be as dangerous today as in those days. It is often easy to rationalize the treatment of natives by the Europeans but forget the savage treatment that some got from the natives.

Francis Xavier, a Jesuit, was sent to the East by the king of Portugal. He had success with the indigenous people of India, mostly those of the lower castes--sort of a social conversion. These lower caste members felt privileged to associate with the Europeans, resulting in opposition to Christianity from the upper castes. Xavier later went to Japan and died in transit to enter China. One discernable mistake here is that; "Xavier and his fellow missionaries did not make a clear distinction between European culture and the Christian faith. When their converts were baptized, they were given "Christian," that is, Portuguese names, and encouraged to dress in Western clothes."[cxiv] (This mistake of presenting western culture as "Christian" continues to this day, and many who arrive in western culture from the very mission fields are stunned when they go searching for a "Christian" culture and find none! And sometimes, not even in the church!). Catholics would later enter China, which was closed to any foreign influence.

Back in Brazil in the New World, the missionaries worked in collaboration with the colonizers: "The missionaries were grateful for the support of the Portuguese, and in exchange offered the labor of the Indians in what practically amounted to slavery."[cxv] Such activities perplexed the native Indians provoking diverse reactions. The Indian reaction took the form of messianic cults—such movements allowed oppressed blacks and Indians a sense of dignity that official Christianity denied them. Gonzalez concludes that; "All told, the story of Christianity in Brazil, as in so many other lands in that period of colonial expansion, is not an inspiring one. It would be many years before the negative consequences of such inauspicious beginnings could be overcome."[cxvi]

Catholic missions in the West and East coast of Africa were sporadic. Mission effort was mostly by chaplains, who came to serve in the slave trading posts. Effort in the interior was very limited. The slave trade will leave a lasting wound between the African and the European that is very difficult to heal.

Protestant Missions: Protestants came in late after the Catholics in overseas missions. As mentioned earlier, Protestant missions began by the early 1700s after the Pietist revival in Europe. As early as 1707, the king of Denmark sent missionaries to his colonies in India. The zeal for overseas missions was caught by the Moravians, whose missionaries traveled to the Caribbean, Africa, India, South America, and North America.[cxvii] Missions picked up impetus by 1792, when the first missionary society (Baptist Missionary Society) pioneered by William Carey was founded in Great Britain. Shortly thereafter, many other missionary societies were formed that sent missionaries to nearly every inhabited continent. It was an all-out effort to gather the elect into the kingdom of the Great King. It was not an easy endeavor. Civilization barriers, language barriers, rough terrain, racial barriers, disease, just to name a few, stood in the way of evangelization. The cruelest of these barriers was disease. Many missionaries lost their lives to disease, and some died just a few days or years in the field. The hardships were untold; the rough terrain and civilization gap, made things difficult to almost unbearable for many missionaries. Nevertheless, many endured the hardships, and the fruit of their labors is clearly seen in the expanding third world church today. Some of the other barriers were overcome with great difficulty and in others (especially race) seeds of mistrust were sown that have never been successfully uprooted. The attitude of better-than-thou and superior-than-thee, that prevailed also contributed to this mistrust and has continued hitherto.

Sometimes the mission effort was tied closely to the colonial impulse, especially trade, leading to false conversions (let's accept the gospel and open up for trade). The close collaboration of missionaries with the colonialists made Christianity to be seen as a threat, an outside influence that undermined local authority. Thus, the indigenous people sometimes saw missionaries with the same lenses that they saw the colonialists. Therefore, in a sense, colonialism tainted the missionary enterprise, because for many indigenous people, both enterprises were inseparable. Nevertheless, even if there was collaboration in some instances, there were others in which colonialism clashed with the mission enterprise.

In a concluding note, we as humans, must always exercise caution when offering a critique of a Christian endeavor, because we do not know men's hearts. That exclusive right belongs to God and the Lord of the Church, Jesus Christ. The best thing we can say is to echo Paul's words in Philippians 1:12-18 on men's motives in preaching the gospel;

> *"It is true that some preach Christ out of envy and rivalry, but others out of goodwill. The Latter do so in love, knowing that I am put here for the defense of the gospel. The former preach Christ out of selfish ambition, not sincerely, supposing that they can stir up trouble for me while I am in chains. But what does it matter? The important thing is that in every way, whether from false motives or true, Christ is preached. And because of this I rejoice."*

CHAPTER 9

BIRTH OF NEW ROME (BABYLON), USA

" *As men moved eastward, they found a plain in Shinar* [Babylonia] *and settled there.*" (Gen. 11:2)

"I looked, and there before me was a white horse! Its rider held a bow, and he was given a crown, and he rode out as a conqueror bent on conquest." (Rev. 6:2)

America is not only an extension of the Roman Empire (Europe), but the epitome of European/Western civilization, in fact, the epitome of all human civilization of all time. She is the summation of all human genius, and all that humanity can achieve and can be, while still being human. In the previous chapter, we saw that the ten toes of Nebuchadnezzar's image and the ten horns of the fourth beast in Daniel's dream, pointed forward to the barbarian tribes that finally formed the prominent nations of Europe. Three of these tribes were uprooted by the Papacy and the other seven gave birth to Portugal, Spain, Dutch, France, Italy, Germany, and Britain. Out of these seven, especially from Britain, came an eighth, USA; *"The beast who once was* [Babylon]*, and now is not, is an eighth king. He belongs to the seven and is going to his destruction"* (Rev. 17:11). Only the USA of the nations of the West has come to surpass Babylon in glory, and to equal or surpass Rome in power. From this last world power or superpower (the sole superpower right now), will come or has come the final world dictator, who is the political arm of the antichrist (Dan. 8:23-25; 11:36-45). Surprised and in disbelief! The most important thing to note is that it will be during the supremacy of this last superpower that the rock that was cut out without human hands,

Jesus Christ, will crush all civilization and install the everlasting kingdom of God; *"While you were watching, a rock was cut out, but without human hands* [no human or military assistance]. *It struck the statue on its feet* [the apex of western civilization] *of iron and clay and smashed them. Then the iron, clay, bronze, the silver and gold were broken to pieces at the same time and became like chaff on the threshing in the summer. The wind swept them away without leaving a trace* [But the beast was captured, and with him the false prophet … The two of them were thrown alive into the fiery lake of burning sulfur; Rev. 19:20]. *But the rock that struck the statue became a huge mountain and filled the whole earth* [The kingdom of the world has become the kingdom of our Lord and of his Christ, and they will reign for ever and ever; Rev. 11:15b]*"* (Dan. 2:34-35).

Rome/Europe, in the dream (Dan. 2) and in the vision (Dan. 7), is represented by iron. Thus, the iron of the feet represents the European-Americans. The clay of the feet represents the minorities or so-called colored peoples—Blacks, Hispanics, Jews, Asians, etc. (a mixture of peoples—the ultimate melting pot of the world). What America lacks that Rome had is unity through the sole authority of the emperor. Because of by-partisanship; Republicans and Democrats, the president does not have absolute power as did the emperors and kings.

America was not only founded as the New World, but as New Europe. Names such as New England, New York, New France, New Sweden, New Netherlands, New Amsterdam, etc., were evidence that the Old World was wearing a new garb: from Old Babylon to New Babylon; Old Rome to New Rome. America has been perceived as the last empire: *NOVUS ORDO SECLORUM*—The New Order of the Ages (see the reverse side of the dollar bill).

An important question to ponder on is; "Was it economics or religion that necessitated the settling of the New World?" It is hard to distinguish between the religious dream and the economic or secular dream of those who crossed the Atlantic Ocean to found the New World. Which of these dreams was overriding and which of them has eclipsed the other in modern times? Or are both still as real as they were 400 years ago? In other words; "What was the American dream then?" and "What is the American dream now?" The dream then, was primarily economic and secondarily religious; but now, it is largely economic—wealth and freedom, being the hallmarks. The overall dream had been expressed as follows:

> "The dream of America as a place of unique opportunity—for liberty, abundance, security, and peace - appeared in England soon after Columbus' discovery. This dream found a classic expression in *Utopia,* a book written by Sir Thomas More ..., which described society on an imaginary island supposedly discovered by a companion of Americus Vespucius in the waters of the New World. Life in Utopia was as nearly perfect as human beings guided by reason and good will could make it. Though the Utopians lived comfortably enough, they scorned the mere accumulation of only material things, and while all were expected to keep busy, none was oppressed or overworked. They enjoyed complete freedom of thought but were careful not to offend one another in the expression of their beliefs."[cxviii]

Apart from liberty, life on this western island (USA) today is far from being what Thomas More envisioned. While there may be apparent comfort (and the rising psychological traumas does not necessarily suggest so); human beings on this island are far from being perfect, especially those who claim to be guided by reason; none seem to scorn the accumulation of material things (in fact, it is the very ethos of existence for most people on this island); and while there is a great and superb work ethic, oppression still prevails and many are overworked—even the elderly! Far from being "careful not to offend one another in the expression of their beliefs," people on this island now seem to be at each other's throat in respect to expressing their views (the culture wars). Crime and murder are common place—in fact, the most outrageous in the industrialized world. In short, Utopia has not been realized.

Primarily and objectively speaking, it was the economic impetus that set the pace for the first settlers: "The initial ventures were undertaken by joint stock companies specifically chartered by the royal government to plant settlers in the New World. The first English colony was established in Jamestown, Virginia, in 1607."[cxix]

America was first settled mostly by the British during the colonial era. The driving forces for settlement included the founding of overseas empires, economic expansion, and religious dissent in England. Of Britain, it has been recorded that; "Her colonization was essentially a business enterprise, a product of the new age. But it was motivated by ideals of a better life as well as by the search for power and profit."cxx Thus, the first venture was economic, and to say that it was religious is a misrepresentation. Only in about thirteen years later, after the first settlers, did the first English religious pilgrims arrive at the scene; "Only a little later, in 1620, a group of puritans despairing of finding religious freedom in Stuart England, founded a colony at Plymouth, Massachusetts."cxxi Putting the facts clear would help much in our modern day in which many claim that the founding of the colonies was purely religious in origin--though it is true that Massachusetts was. It cannot, however, be denied that the pilgrims too, had economic dreams in mind--if not for anything else, but survival. Thus, before the *Mayflower* expedition of the Pilgrim Fathers, there had been *Godspeed, Discovery,* and *Sarah Constant.*cxxii Much, of course, can be said, and has been said about early Puritanism in America; its influence on American life until the present; and its great impact on world Christianity. That would be the subject of a different enquiry, and many books already abound.

Another motive for the colonization of the New World by the British was the founding of an overseas empire like other rival continental Europeans. The modern English empire in the New World has gone through many struggles, especially in eliminating and assimilating other rival Europeans that settled in North America, like the Spanish, Dutch, French, Germans, Russians, etc. It was also a hard struggle to push down the Mexicans; not to talk of the decimation and displacement of the natives.

Europeans and Native Americans

"From one man he [God] *made every nation of men, that they should inhabit the whole earth; and **he determined the times set for them and the exact places where they should live"** (Acts 17:26).

"Woe to him who builds a city with bloodshed and establishes a town by crime! Has not the LORD *Almighty determined that the people's labor is only fuel for the fire, that nations exhaust themselves for nothing?"* (Hab. 2:12-13; cf. Jer. 51:58).

"Woe to the city of blood, full of lies, full of plunder, never without victims!" (Nah. 3:1).

The founding of America and her later history in respect to the natives of the land has never been the best of relations. In many ways, there have been positive and negatives effects, accusations and counter accusations, with each side justifying their actions. The First impressions by the native peoples seemed to have been positive; "In most cases the American natives were very hospitable to the European upon his first approach."[cxxiii] A story is told of a native who courageously rescued a drowned European. On another positive note, the natives had a prepared space for settlers, which otherwise would have been difficult for them: "The Indian 'Old fields,' especially in New England attracted incoming settlers as convenient places to begin settlement, and the newcomers eagerly adopted the cultivation of native crops especially corn. Without the clearings and the crops that the Indians provided, the Englishmen would have had greater difficulty than they did in getting a start in the New World."[cxxiv] The settlers themselves seemed to have begun in a good footing with the natives also, establishing trade and building relationships: "To the Englishmen the Indians were of interest as customers for English goods and as suppliers of woodland commodities, especially hides and skins."[cxxv] **A great missionary effort was made by Europeans to convert the natives to Christianity, but there was more resistance than success. The natives saw the settlers as occupiers and in a sense resented their conqueror and occupier God.** In the course of time, relations turned sour, and the natives tried through military campaigns to resist the occupiers. The settlers had to respond. Thus, the missionary effort soon turned to massacre and elimination; "… by 1619 about fifty missionaries had already entered the wilds to convert native souls. But most of the colonists soon changed their image of the Indian. After a few massacres they began to consider him as a wild beast fit only to be slaughtered."[cxxvi] Also, "… the

Puritans viewed the red men as 'pernicious creatures' who deserved extermination unless they would adopt the white man's ways. ... About 400 Indians were burned to death or killed when trying to escape, and most of the survivors were hunted down, captured, and sold as slaves. The Pequot tribe was almost wiped out."[cxxvii] (This happened when the Pequots took to the warpath as a means of resistance). Wars with the natives (the Indian wars) continued for a time. The natives in the New World, and particularly in North America, would suffer severely; "The Indians of North America suffered a less dramatic but perhaps ultimately more ignominious fate at the hands of Europeans."[cxxviii] That is in comparison to those of South America. "The English settlers pursued a more ruthless policy toward the native Americans...."[cxxix] It is reported that before the settlers set foot on North America (in the 1500s), there were about 9 million or more natives in the land, but by the turn of the twentieth century (1900s), there were only about 250,000 natives! Many were permanently striped of their land and permanently displaced and forced into concentration camps or reservations, where there is no hope of ever being proprietors of their own land.

Europeans and Negroes

"Woe to him who builds his realm by unjust gain to set his nest on high, to escape the clutches of ruin. You have plotted the ruin of many peoples, shaming your own house and forfeiting your life. The stones of the wall will cry out, and the beams of the woodwork will echo it" (Hab. 2:9-11).

Slavery

Slavery is, of course, an ancient institution that at times seems to be given biblical sanction. But the slavery of the black man in the Americas has been such a gruesome, inhuman, and savage practice that will always reverberate in the annals of eternal sacred history, like the slavery of the Israelites in ancient Egypt. Thus, it deserves some attention here (just highlights and nothing exhaustive).

The enslavement of Africans did not begin with the Europeans. It is recorded that; "At the dawn of the Christian era, slaves from

Africa were common in India and, somewhat later, in Arabia, Persia, Indonesia, and China."**cxxx** When Arabs established trade links with East Africa, they also began to trade in slaves from the interior. As it was; "The Arabs were not interested in most of Africa's raw materials. Their chief reason for establishing contacts with the interior was to acquire ivory, slaves, and gold...."cxxxi Thus, "Long before Africans were carried in chains to the New World, they were being sold in the slave markets of the East. Large numbers of African slaves were living in medieval India, Indonesia, Egypt, Turkey, and Persia."cxxxii However, they seem to have been treated fairly by their Muslim masters as some African slaves were appointed to important positions within the Bengal kingdom: "These slaves apparently were not regarded by the Arabs as inferior. Indeed, some were held in high esteem because of their superior intelligence or skills. Slaves in Muslim households frequently were granted their freedom and raised to positions of responsibility."cxxxiii These, of course, are stunning revelations, given that ever since the European met the African, he has regarded him as inferior and even sub-human, resulting in the worst treatment ever received by a human from another human, based primarily on mere skin color. (Perhaps, this historical connection may explain why some Blacks in America embrace Islam).

By the early 1500s the Portuguese had overtaken the Arabs as trade masters in the East African Coast and Indian Ocean. The Portuguese carried slaves and ivory from Africa to India, where they were exchanged for spices, cloth, and glassware. Spain soon followed Portugal in the slave business as the demand for this precious commodity proved valuable, especially in the New World. Africans themselves became involved in this profitable business as the coastal Africans raided those in the interior to capture slaves to sell to the Europeans. It is recorded that "The number of Africans victimized by slave-raiders increased tremendously when the New World demands for slaves were added to those of the Arabs in the East."cxxxiv It was not only the New World needed slaves. Some slaves were taken to Europe though not in large numbers: "But the number of African slaves purchased for labor in Europe remained small, partly because there was a plentiful supply of cheap labor in Europe."cxxxv **The slave business brought great profits to the Europeans;**

"The wealth that slavery brought first to Portugal and Spain, and later and increasingly to Holland, England, and France, helped to finance technical and industrial advances in Europe.… The profits were enormous. It was not only the industrialization of Western Europe but the rapid settlement and agricultural development of the Americas were facilitated by the profits from the slave trade and the labor of the African slave."[cxxxvi]

(And just as a side comment, now that the West is far advanced industrially, they throw scorn at Africa!). For three centuries (sixteenth to nineteenth), Europe's primary interest in Africa was procuring slaves;

"Relations between European governments and the rulers of African kingdoms were limited to agreements for the procurement of slaves. There was no significant exchange of culture and knowledge. One of the reasons why few missionaries or explorers visited Africa during this period was that the slave trade was so inhuman that those involved in it wanted no observers who might report its horrors."[cxxxvii]

The slave trade crippled Africa's progress and the effects are still felt today. Fred Burke comments as follows; "Africa's development was impeded by the coming of the most dreadful era in that continent's history: the long centuries of forcible transport which took millions of Africans from the land of their birth to another continent and life in bondage. In the Americas black people were to provide the sweat and muscle to build a new civilization while their own civilization in Africa declined."[cxxxviii] The African became the machinery to build a new civilization in which he was neither wanted nor accepted, and with the advent of the industrial revolution, he was discarded and tossed into the wilderness to languish and vanish. Africa was deprived of her talented, healthy, and finest men. In all, about 50 million were displaced within three centuries. The transportation across the Atlantic was callous and brutal. Many lost their lives and were thrown into the sea (no doubt Revelation 20:13 says that at the judgment, the seas will give up their dead). Once in the Americas, they were screened for sale as a trader would presort his goods; then seasoned and sold, and those too weak and sick to be sold were abandoned to die. Talk about savagery! In all, 35 million died during African slave raids and on the way to the coast; 3 million died on shipboard; and 5 million died during "seasoning" in the New World. [Compared to those who died in WW I and WW II, and given the population then, the ratio is higher, making the slave trade the real first world war and universal carnage of humans, largely fought by one people against an innocent, defenseless and non-attacking peoples (Ps. 10:1-11; James 5:6). Surely, God is dead because he cannot see!]. About 10 million survived to build the economy of the New World, and their descendants were eventually dished out and continue to suffer after the arrival of the machine.

Slavery in the New World

The plantation system in the New World demanded labor and someone had to provide that labor:

> "It was the establishment of the plantation system in the New World that sparked a new interest of Europeans in Africa. The plantations needed labor; African slaves could provide the commodity. Portuguese, Dutch, English, French, and North American traders and adventurers, acting with the support of their governments, established a series of trading posts along West African coast stretching from modern Senegal to Angola chiefly for the purpose of purchasing slaves to be transported to the New World."**cxxxix**

It was a cruel and savage process: "The cruelties and humiliation inflicted on them were designed to strip Africans of their pride and self-respect. Slave owners tried to instill in young Africans a feeling of inferiority. The suffering endured by Africans brought about a deep-seated bitterness which lingers among their Afro-American descendants down to the present."[cxl] Many tried to justify their treatment of Blacks with the excuse that Blacks were inferior and less than human. From this inhuman behavior came one of the most evils of all times, racism, which some have gone as far as to describe as coming from Satan himself:

"Racial prejudice was an outgrowth of African slavery and not its cause. Arguments purporting to establish the inherent inferiority of Negroes began to appear when guilt-ridden Europeans and Americans who had profited or acquiesced in the slave trade felt compelled to find reasons to justify their inhuman actions. Captains and owners of slave ships, middle-class investors in the slave traffic, and perhaps even kings and queens slept better after persuading themselves that slavery was justified on the grounds that Africans were 'not quite human.'"[cxli]

Even with the abolition of slavery, racism, or discrimination against Blacks, especially in America, continued in subtle forms like segregation, which in some cases was legislated by the constitution and promoted in some churches; "In 1892, the Supreme Court approved segregation, as long as blacks were treated as 'separate, but equal.' **Then the long series of 'Jim Crow laws' ensued, effectively excluding blacks from public places, from the right to vote, from good public education, and so forth. Meanwhile, southern white churches continued their racist teachings and practices.**"[cxlii] The civil rights movement of the 1960s only began the healing process, which still has a long way to go, given that there is still racism, racial prejudice, and racial profiling.

There is, however, a subtle twist to racism. One would have thought that without peoples of color, as they are so-called, racism would be non-existent, but unfortunately, this is not the case. Not only did the whites consider themselves superior to other races, but the Anglo-Saxons also considered themselves even more superior to continental Europeans!

"Thus, late in the century [nineteenth] the general secretary of the Evangelical Alliance, Josiah Strong, declared that God was preparing the Anglo-Saxon race for a greater moment, 'the final competition of races.' Then that race, representing 'the largest liberty, the purest Christianity, the highest civilization,' would fulfil its God-given destiny of dispossessing the weaker ones, assimilating others, and moulding the rest, so as to 'Anglo-Saxonize' humankind."[cxliii]

The liberal wing of Protestantism in America held to a similar view. They "… held that Protestantism and freedom of opinion were the great contribution of the Nordic races against the tyranny and Catholicism of the Southern European races, and that therefore people of Nordic origin had the responsibility of civilizing the 'backward' races of the rest of the world."**cxliv**

These quotations demonstrate the folly, arrogance, pride, and ignorance of man, who has never known God, and who lives in Satan's chambers. So, where were the Bible and Christianity during the enterprises of slavery, racism, and segregation? How could people practice such Satanism with the Bible in hand? **Racism and the idea of racial superiority betray the following biblical teachings:**

1. Racism betrays the fact that man was created in the image and likeness of God, and therefore, all men are equal before him, and all reflect him (Gen. 1:27-28).

2. Racism also betrays the fact that all races (or different peoples) originated from one man--Adam, as stated in Acts 17:26, and therefore, no peoples, race, or nation, are superior or inferior to the others.

3. **Racism is a denial of the incarnation** (God in the flesh as Jesus Christ). Implied in racial superiority is the fact that if Christ was Anglo-Saxon, he would not have taken on the inferior flesh of continental Europeans; or that if he was white, he would not have become black (or colored), because that would mean becoming inferior and less than human. But Jesus left all the glory above to become human!

4. We must never debase others, lest we risk going to hell; "*But I tell you that anyone who is angry with his brother will be subject to judgment. Again, anyone who says to his brother 'Raca'* [a term of contempt] *is answerable to the Sanhedrin. But anyone who says, 'You fool!' will be in danger of the fire of hell*" (Matt. 5:22). To say that someone is less than human, is to imply that he is not even fit to be called a fool—he is less than a fool!

5. Being racist risk the danger of retribution at the last judgment according to the golden rule; *"So in everything, do to others what you would have them do to you"* (Matt. 7:12).

6. Racism places us in danger of breaking the two great commandments: Love the Lord with all your heart, soul, and strength; and love your neighbor as yourself (Mark. 12:29-31). Apostle John further illustrates this in 1 John 3:14-15, which states; *"We know that we have passed from death to life, because we love our brothers. **Anyone who does not love remains in death. Anyone who hates his brother is a murderer, and you know that no murderer has eternal life in him.**"* You cannot love someone whom you racially discriminate against. Racism is hatred and hence, murderous.

7. Racism demonstrates sublime ignorance, in as much as our human anatomy, biological make-up, and intelligence, are basically the same. Color is only skin-deep or is it not!

8. As believers in Jesus Christ, we have this treasure (spiritual life) in jars of clay; *"But we have this treasure in jars of clay to show that this all-surpassing power is from God and not from us"* (2 Co. 4:7). We are all clay and all our flesh (white, pink, red, tan, brown or black) rot after death and go back to dust from whence we all came! *"... the LORD God formed the man from the dust of the ground ... until you return to the ground, since from it you were taken; for dust you are and to dust you will return"* (Gen. 2:7; 3:19). Skin complexion is deceptive. What matters is whether we have Jesus Christ in us, the treasure in jars of clay otherwise we are nothing, no matter our skin complexion, whether we glow like sapphires or like bronze.

9. It was (and it is) on account of beauty that Satan fell or would fall! *"You were the model of perfection, full of wisdom and perfect in beauty ... Through your widespread trade you were filled with violence, and you sinned. ... Your heart became proud on account of your beauty, and you corrupted your wisdom because of your splendor. So I threw you to the earth; ... "* (Ezek. 28:11-19).

10. To glory in outward appearance is humanistic and worldly; it is earthy; but God looks on the inside. Your worth is determined by who you are in your heart and not on how you look on the outside. This is illustrated in the choice of David as king rather than his elegant brothers; *"When they arrived, Samuel saw Eliab and thought, 'Surely the LORD'S anointed stands here before the LORD.' But the LORD said to Samuel, 'Do not consider his appearance or his height, for I have rejected him. **The LORD does not look at the things man looks at. Man looks at the outward appearance, but the LORD looks at the heart'"*** (1 Sam. 16:6-7).

11. The first punishment for racism in Scripture was a curse of leprosy! It is written; *"Miriam and Aaron began to talk against Moses because of his Cushite* [Ethiopian/black] *wife, for he had married a Cushite. ... And the LORD heard this. ... And the anger of the LORD burned against them, and he left them. When the cloud lifted from above the Tent, there stood Miriam--leprous, like snow."* (Num. 12:1-15)

12. The black cannot change his skin; God gave it to him! *"Can the Ethiopian* [Cushite/black] *change his skin or the leopard its spots?* (Jer. 13:23). God makes it categorically clear that even the Israelites, who were chosen, are not different to him than the Cushites or Ethiopians; *"'Are not you Israelites the same to me as the Cushites?' declares the LORD"* (Amos 9:7).

Voices in the Wilderness

"In him [Jesus Christ] *was life, and that life was the light of men. The light shines in the darkness, but the darkness has not understood it."* (John 1:4-5)

God always ensures that he shines light where there is darkness and evil. It does not always take a crowd for him to shine that light. One individual (as my brother is fond of saying; "One with the Lord is the majority") or just a few are sufficient for him to witness to the wickedness of men who suppress the truth by their evil behavior (Rom. 1:18-19). Just like in South America, there were in North America, those who objected to the European's treatment of the Indian

and the encroachment on his land, and the treatment of black slaves. Through these individuals, God continued to bear witness during the darkness that prevailed so that the perpetrators were without excuse.

Roger Williams: Even though the Puritans sought religious freedom for themselves, they were intolerant to any person who disagreed with them. Roger Williams not only wanted religious freedom (liberty of conscience in matters pertaining to God—Worship), but a very pure and strict church. He strongly believed that the land belonged to the Indians, and therefore, that the colonial enterprise was unjust and illegal. As a result of such views (perceived as dangerous by the colonialists), he was rejected in the first Puritan colony of Massachusetts; "Making friends with the neighboring Indians, he concluded that the land belonged to them and not to the king or to the Massachusetts Bay company. The colonial government, considering Williams a dangerous man, decided to deport him, but he escaped."[cxlv] His flight was in the winter (and his persecutors did not care whether he would freeze to death) and he spent about fourteen weeks in the cold. He eventually bought land from the Indians and founded Providence that led to the founding of Rhode Island. William also advocated complete freedom of worship in contrast to the Puritans (who had strict religious laws abiding on all citizens of the colony), and absolute separation of church and state. Thus, he was able to discern this Constantinian unholy alliance that plunged Europe into such religious wars, chaos, and apostasy. Concerning the Puritans who merged civil authority with ecclesiastical authority; "… he declared that Puritans in the colony erred in granting the civil authorities power to enforce those commandments that had to do with an individual's relation with God."[cxlvi] Other dissenters like the Baptist, who followed in William's footsteps and belief system, were equally persecuted by the Puritans.

William Penn: After whom Pennsylvania is named, was an outstanding and prominent Quaker, another dissenting group in England. He was a strong defendant of religious freedom and tolerance. As he sailed out to the New World; "His purpose was to found a new colony in which there would be complete religious freedom."[cxlvii] His goal was unlike the other colonies that were founded as religious states and marked by religious intolerance. Pennsylvania, following the example of Rhode Island, practiced religious freedom. The religious intolerance of the colonies often led to persecution. In Massachusetts for example; "Quakers were persecuted, condemned to exile, and even mutilated and executed."[cxlviii] The two Williams advocated for freedom of worship, and hence separation of church and state.

Transplanted Englishmen

The settlement of North America was largely an English venture as earlier mentioned. Most of the first settlers were of English descent, and the venture has come to be described as Transplanted English Men.[cxlix] Not until later in the 1800s, did the settlers begin to develop a distinctly new identity--American. From the start, the settlers saw themselves as an extension of the English empire. More and more English people would settle in North America, though people of other European nationalities--Spanish, Dutch, Swedish, French, German, Russian, etc., would also settle in the land, claiming it for their European nations of origin. At the end of the day, the English became prominent, and to avoid another Europe with diverse languages, they assimilated the other peoples. Thus, English became the dominant and national language. Of course, this was not done without difficulty, and in some cases, matters were decided on the battlefield. At the end, only New England, New York, etc., remained, while New France, New Netherlands, New Amsterdam, New Sweden, etc., disappeared. The English conquered the Spanish, Dutch, Swedish, French (the Louisiana Purchase), Mexican, and bought Alaska from Russia. The English gradually absorbed the other Europeans and their languages, and hence, the rest of the world that immigrated to their shores. In effect, the Anglo-American Empire was born and has triumphantly thrived hitherto. The white horse conqueror of the Apocalypse was and has been on the move; *"I looked, and there before me was a white horse! Its rider held a bow, and he was given a crown, and he rode out as a conqueror bent on conquest."* (Rev. 6:2)

Founding of the USA

"Then I saw another beast, coming out of the earth. He had two horns like a lamb, but he spoke like a dragon. He exercised all the

146

authority of the first beast on his behalf, and made the earth and its inhabitants worship the first beast, whose fatal wound had been healed. And he performed great and miraculous signs, even causing fire to come down from heaven to earth in full view of men." (Rev. 13:11-13)

The colonies that settled America finally rejected the British royal crown and constituted themselves as the United States of America. Thus, the thirteen colonies that settled the East Coast of North America decided and founded a tiny nation that would become big and great and would surpass every nation and empire that ever existed on planet earth. Her influence would be felt to every corner of the globe. That nation was to become a beacon of freedom unlike any other that ever existed in the world and would ultimately lead the world into an advanced stage of civilization. It would become a magnet for immigrants from the rest of Europe and the rest of the world. The rest is history that cannot be told here! I am concerned here with the prophetic destiny of this great nation.

Prophesy is not history, although it gives a panorama of man's entire history. Daniel was given a picture of the distant future that revealed the end of the Roman Empire and eventually Europe, her daughter-nations, and the rest of the world (human civilization as we know it now). John, the Revelator, also saw the panorama of Western civilization in its final glory and fall. John describes two beasts, that is, empires or kingdoms in Revelation 13. The first beast as we have seen is Rome/Europe and is identical to or is identified as the dragon or Satan. This beast is described as having come out of the sea (peoples). That is, Rome/Europe rose as an empire from the ruins of previous empires. But the second beast is described as coming out of the earth. Thus, this refers to a significant world empire that would come into existence on a new land not previously occupied by any empire. This second beast is directly connected to the first beast as it exercises the authority of the first beast. The only significant world power that has existed after the Roman Empire that fits these descriptions is the United States. She eventually became a colonial power like other European nations (the eighth of the seven; Rev. 17:11), and much more as an imperialistic one.

Another significant characteristic of this beast is that it has two horns like a lamb. The New Testament uses the imagery of lamb to refer to the meek and innocent Jesus Christ (John 1:29; Rev. 5:6; 17:14). The lamb-likeness refers to the meek, gospel loving, and innocence of this beast (USA) at her founding. In a nutshell, it is not an overstatement to say that the Puritans were pioneers or founders of America (though they came thirteen years after the settlement of the Virginia Company). It is an historical mistake to talk or refer to the founders of the USA implying only those who fought the war of independence and united the thirteen colonies. The early settlers of the colonies basically founded religious communities or states, both Protestant and Catholic, though not exclusively. Whether these communities or colonies were ideal in their religious practice or not, it is clear that they were "Christian" communities in a sense. Thus, these humble beginnings gave America the semblance of a lamb. Horns also represent powers and could very well stand for the two power structures: Protestantism and Republicanism. One would wish that the description only ended here with the lamb, but it doesn't.

Unfortunately, this beast, although having two horns like a lamb, unlike a lamb, spoke like a dragon. How is this possible? The religious phase of America somewhere along the line gradually gave way to the dragon phase. [It is my contention that by the declaration of independence, America began to develop the characteristics of a dragon (becoming in status just like any other empire clearly discernible from the fact that the state was separate from the religious institutions), and ever since, the Republic, as a secular and political entity, has increasingly drawn closer to the dragon until it now speaks like it.]

First, I would like to ask, "Was the empire or nation founded on July 4, 1776, a child of the Protestant Reformation, the Puritan Reformation, or the Enlightenment?" It cannot be denied that the genius of America's founding fathers gave birth to the best political entity since the dawn of civilization, and the prominence of the USA today attests to that fact. However, while these men are revered, venerated, and even worshipped, we must not overlook the precursors to their genius. The political philosophy of the new Republic was not an American genius; it was a product of European political philosophers, derived purely from reason. **John Locke, one of the British Enlightenment thinkers**, had argued strongly for the natural rights of human beings, which are life, liberty, and property. He also argued that "The powers of the government, however, whether monarchical or popular, are strictly limited. No government may violate the individual's right to life, liberty, and property. If it does, the people who set it up can and should overthrow it."[cl] **Another Enlightenment political philosopher, Baron de Montesquieu**, reflecting on the current monarchies of Europe then, suggested that "Since power corrupts ... government should be exercised by three powers that would balance and limit each other: the legislative, the executive, and the judicial."[cli] **This enlightenment political philosophy was the inspiration of the American Patriots, especially Thomas Jefferson**, "... who wrote many of Locke's ideas into the Declaration of Independence, frequently using his exact words. They likewise appear in the United States Constitution ..."[clii] Again, "On July 4, 1776, congress issued the Declaration of Independence, the work of Thomas Jefferson, one of the radical leaders. Its magnificent preamble, leaning heavily on the political philosophy of John Locke and the European disciples of the Enlightenment, stated in strong words the doctrines of natural rights and government by contract."[cliii] Given this evidence, would anyone with a functioning brain say that the nation founded was "Christian?" There is neither explicit quotes from the Bible nor anything to suggest the inclusion of Christianity. **Enlightenment and natural law (deism) were the brainchild and blueprint of the Republic.** To suggest that the documents of the Republic are "Christian" because of the mention of "nature's God" or "Creator," is to say that Africa, south of the Sahara, was "Christian" before the arrival of the missionaries, because they believed in a "Creator God!" To make such a conclusion is to commit spiritual, academic, and historical suicide!

Much has been said about the religion of America's founding fathers, and those who argue that the Republic was founded as a "Christian" nation popularize it a lot. Like in the case of Constantine, no one stands as judge of another's faith, but by their fruits, we can understand them. **Source after source indicates that some of the** prominent founding fathers were Freemasons—including the first president of the Republic, and others were deists. We know Freemasons have a high disregard for the deity of Christ. Anyone who dabbles with the deity of Christ is called antichrist (1 John 2:22-23; 4:2-3). Thomas Jefferson's disdain for the supernatural (Jesus' divinity and miracles) has been clearly noted, but he was the most radical leader of the revolution and a major contributor to the early documents. Another thing to note is that, to acknowledge religion does not necessarily mean to be "born again" just like Nebuchadnezzar acknowledged God, but still went ahead to erect an idolatrous statue for his kingdom. Any experienced politician in a religious community would consider it expedient to consider the religion of the people. A proper understanding of the cult of Freemasonry is mandatory for anyone who wants to understand the Christian origins of the American Republic. **To say, of course, that the Republic was a brainchild of the Enlightenment is not to disregard the fact that Christianity also played a strong influence.** The rule of law, that basically keeps the nation on a successful path, was a contribution of Calvinistic theology as practiced by the Puritans. To be sure, there were many Christian men involved in the founding of the nation and in the writing of the early documents. However, for thc Republic per se, state religion was disestablished when the union was founded--the Republic had no legislated national religion! This was good for both the Republic and Christianity, and the first Amendment on the Bill of Rights ensured that this would be the case. Any deviation from this at any point would harm the cause of both the Republic and Christianity—in fact it could even invoke divine displeasure.

Republicanism is of course as old as the Greek city state and philosophers, and as old as Rome. **The distinctive feature of American Republicanism is that it was/is attached to the wealthy—to whom franchise was limited from the start. Far from being a government of the nobility, it is a government of the elite—the rich and strong (property owners from the start), a government for the elite by the elite. The word Democracy is just a veneer for this elitist governance (Republicanism).** This political philosophy was encapsulated in Alexander Hamilton's doctrine. He was aristocratic in his political philosophy and was convinced that what the new nation needed most was order and that only a powerful central government based on the support of people of wealth could provide that order. He fashioned a national economic policy intended to favor the wealthy and to tie their interests to a strong central government. That philosophy is still well and alive in the Republic today—the poor and commoner cannot mount the throne.

USA: "Christian" or Not?

This is a complex subject that has been treated in many books and continues to be debated among American Christians and non-Christians alike. Whether the USA is a "Christian" nation or not, depends on whom you asked the question. Many Americans and almost the rest of the world believe in a "Christian" America. But is that true? Does the evidence support the conclusion or otherwise? What does it mean for a nation to be "Christian?" Did the founding fathers found a "Christian" Republic or a secular one? What would they say if they were alive today? It is very difficult to say what makes a nation "Christian": is it its constitution; its laws; its governance; or just its people? Can a nation per se, be "Christian?" We will note, first, that only individuals can become Christians. The Great Commission commanded the apostles to make disciples of every nation but not to make nations "Christian" or disciples. Since the coming of Jesus Christ, God ceased working with nations as his instrument of bringing about his kingdom; he has been using the church. It is very dangerous for a nation or people within it, to class a nation as "Christian" in as much as this would mean that that nation must live up to the biblical expectation--and no single nation on earth comes close to that. In fact, it is explicit from Scripture that Satan directly rules the nations since the time he took over in the garden from Adam and Eve (Job 1:6-7; Matt. 4:8-9; 1 John 5:19; Rev. 12:9).

To state it in simple terms, the USA is a Republic, governed by its three branches of government according to its constitution (inspired by the Enlightenment). If the USA was a "Christian" nation, it would be a theocracy, governed by the Priest, Prophet, and King, Jesus Christ, in whose physical absence, his constitution (the Bible) stands. To mess up these two entities (The USA and Christianity) or merge them into one is spiritual and intellectual suicide. In fact, it is chaos and a satanic deception. Here is one person's definition of what a "Christian" nation should entail (if we accept the misnomer):

> "For a nation, its primary purpose must be to minister the name of Jesus Christ alone, without regard to any other gods or philosophies. Its primary charter must be initial agreement with the Bible, and all positions of authority must be held by individuals who meet the biblical criteria necessary for disciples of Christ. [The US Constitution clearly states that "… no religious Test shall ever be required as a qualification to any Office or public Trust under the United States." Article VI]. A true Christian nation would be a theocracy administered through God's prophets. His law would reign supreme in the hearts and minds of that nation's founders, all of whom would have to be men who are truly born again by the Spirit of God. The nation would also have to have been created in response to a covenant initiated by God with its founders."[cliv]

Such a nation does not exist on earth, after the dissolution of the Israeli nation 2000 years ago.

However, many have continued to argue for a "Christian" America. They use among many other arguments, the following to justify their position: the vision of the Pilgrims in the *Mayflower* and their covenant contract; the nation founded as a city on a hill; Bible-based constitutions of the colonies; the perceived divine mission of the first colonies and the nation ever since in conjunction with the chosen nation or people theme; the New Israel theme with divine mandate (which will imply the displacement of natural Israel); faith of the founding fathers; most first institutions of the nation were Christian; just to cite a few. From a naïve legal standpoint, some equally argue that the usage of the words "Nature's God" and "Creator," in the preamble of the United States Constitution, confirms the fact that the USA is a "Christian" nation or was founded as such. But, if it were, the first amendment on the Bill of rights would have been unnecessary. That itself, spells out the fact that the Republic was not a "Christian" state. There is also the historical argument that points to the Christian heritage or tradition. There are equally arguments based on public statements about God: "In God We Trust" on currency added later in the early 1900s; and "One Nation Under God" on the Pledge of Allegiance to the Flag and the Republic.

Granted that the above arguments are true, let us assess America according to Old Testament standards and the belief of the first Puritan settlers, who saw themselves as a New Israel. If we can accept the tenability of the New Israel argument, we should also note that it is possible for God's people to turn their backs on him just like the Israelites of old. Israel was called and planted by God in the Promised Land, but the same God uprooted and scattered them (exile) because of sin and disobedience. We see the same desperate attempt by the Israelites in the days of Jeremiah and Ezekiel to justify that they were God's people, and that the temple was God's, and therefore, could not be destroyed in the face of prophetic pronouncements that they will face God's wrath and go on exile. Religious heritage does not matter when a people turn their backs on God and turn to idolatry, detestable or abominable practices and blatant sin. God turns his back on his people if they no longer follow his ways and obey him. Even if it was true that the nation was founded as a "Christian" nation; that is no longer the case. The nation does not live up to that claim. Worse still, we must realize that we do not live in the past! What might have been true of seventeenth century America (if that is tenable) might not or is not necessarily true of twenty first century America. The Scripture argues vehemently that the same people who were delivered from Egypt were the same people whom God swore that they will never enter his rest because they disobeyed (Num. 32:10-12; Heb. 3:12-19). The issue, therefore, is not whether the USA is a "Christian" nation or not, but whether the nation or its people obey God?

There are, of course, arguments that refute the above arguments for a "Christian" America. The founding documents and their framers (and some were Christians) and their context— the Declaration of Independence and the Constitution, and then, the first Amendment, do not suggest that America was founded as a 'Christian" nation. The language and earlier interpretations, for instance, words like denomination, religion (Jews and Muslims were in mind also), God, Creator, probably did not have the same meaning to the framers, some of whom were deists and other occultists. The disestablishment of the religion of the states at the founding of the Union shows clearly that no one denomination or religion was endorsed as a federal religion (this does not suggest irreligion). Therefore, even public statements about God; if by "God" it is meant the "God" of the Bible, are illegal or unconstitutional and at worst, blasphemous (for not every American is "Christian") because they violate the third commandment (Ex. 20:7; *"You shall not misuse the name of the LORD your God, for the LORD will not hold anyone guiltless who misuses his name."*). But, if it is just the pluralistic "God" or generic "god" common to all mankind, then Christians are badly deceived. They are caught in Satan's trap. To prove the point further, if the word "God" is replaced by "Jesus Christ" (for instance, "In Jesus Christ We Trust" or "One Nation Under Jesus Christ"), and still means the same thing, then, he is the God of the Bible. Even in that case, it remains blasphemy—taking the name of God in vain.

Again, historically speaking, can anyone answer confidently and affirmatively to the questions; "Is the history of the USA a history of a "Christian" nation, a holy empire?" "Does the president and senate or House of Representatives (government) make policies with the Bible in hand?" Far from being so! Sources show that it may not be an exaggeration to say that the nation's leadership history is a triumph of the cult of Freemasonry. Consider the following: "Some very famous Americans have been Masons—including 14 United States presidents (George Washington, for one), 18 vice presidents, 5 chief justices of the Supreme Court, Paul Revere, Benjamin Franklin, James Monroe, Alexander Hamilton, ..."[clv] To this list is added some Unitarian Universalists (deny the Trinity by denying the deity of Christ—hence antichrist!): "Certainly Unitarian Universalism has influenced many prestigious individuals. Past Unitarian Universalists include five U.S. presidents (John Adams, Thomas Jefferson, John Quincy Adams, Milliard Fillmore, and William Taft); ... eight U.S. Supreme Court justices; ...."[clvi] At the end of the day, more people have ruled the U.S., who deserved to be called antichrist than those who might have been for Christ or pro-Christ or other. The history of the empire is equally that of aggression, militarism, expansionism, and suppression of peoples of non-European origin (decimation of natives, slavery, racism, segregation, etc.). I guess if that is the history of a "Christian" nation, not even the chimps in the jungle would have anything to do with Christianity!

Furthermore, there is no biblical argument for "Christian" nations. There is nothing as such! It is a misnomer to think like that—it is deception and confusion, just like the Europeans believed in a "Holy Roman Empire," when in fact, the empire was neither Roman nor holy. Are we any different than they or it is just because they were Catholics? The underlying conception inspires both if you do believe in a "Christian" America. That being the case, the best thing we have learned about the Holy Roman Empire is that we are replicating it, while still holding it in contempt. The Constantinian gangrene (union of church and state) had eaten deep into the church and basically destroyed Christianity in Europe, for Caesar and Christ were to remain separated forever. That is why Christ did not send the apostles to go and make "Christian" nations but to make disciples of every nation (peoples). Christ's kingdom is not of this world, and thus, no human kingdom can be identified with the kingdom of Christ. When one argues for a "Christian" nation, that one is going against Christ. This is a fatal mistake and a great deception that is sweeping many into the wrong direction. Instead of fighting for the kingdom of Christ, such individuals are fighting for the kingdom of man, which they mistakenly identify as the kingdom of Christ. Nationalistic religion is different from biblical Christianity! The USA just happens to be a secular nation that right from its founding up to today, has always had many professing Christians within its borders (so it is believed). We must look beyond the earthly kingdoms of men that are under the dominion and direction of Satan and are all destined for destruction. The only extant "Christian" nation today is the Church—the expectant Bride of Christ! As it is written; *"**But our citizenship is in heaven.** And we eagerly await a Savior from there, the Lord Jesus Christ, who, by the power that enables him to bring everything under his control, will transform our lowly bodies so that they will be like his glorious body"* (Phil. 3:19-21). This contrasts with those whose minds are on earthly things, the splendor of the kingdoms of men—they are religious nationalists (Phil. 3:18; cf. Matt. 16:23).

The Pros And Cons of Colonialism

Is colonialism always wrong or bad? Of course not! God himself was the first colonialist, though the earth and all that is in it belong to him and he does as he pleases, and no one can ask him why or what have you done (Dan. 4:34-35)? God called Abraham out of Ur of the Chaldeans and promised him land that was occupied by other peoples. When he brought Israel out of Egypt, he commanded them to destroy completely the inhabitants of Canaan because of their sin and then occupy the land.

In many ways, God is the one who allows superpowers to conquer and dominate other peoples. He is the one who brought Assyria against Israel to discipline them by removing them from the land. God equally brought Babylon against Judah and gave the surrounding nations into the hands of Nebuchadnezzar, whom he called his servant (Jer. 24, 25). When the time of the Babylonians was up as they were lifted with pride and arrogance, God brought the Medes and the Persians against them. In a similar manner, against the Persians, he brought the Greeks, and against the Greeks he brought the Romans. It was the Romans who occupied Palestine at the time of Jesus Christ. As a colonial power, Rome built the roads and brought other privileges to Palestine and kept the peace—*Pax Romana*; a perfect time for God to bring forth his Son into the world.

Thus, we see that colonialism is not always bad or out of God's providential guidance and control. The following may be regarded as the pros of modern colonialism. Colonialism gave birth to world trade, hence, improving standards of living worldwide. Colonialism opened routes for missionaries for the spread of the gospel. Also, education and learning were brought to the colonized lands. The colonized peoples benefited from modern European civilization: rail roads, cities, agriculture, health, and medical advancement, resulting in high life expectancy, and a host of others.

On the other hand, the following can be delineated as the cons of colonialism. There was the destruction of indigenous civilizations: for instance, the Aztec, Mayan, Incan of Mexico and Peru, Asia, and Africa. There has also been the extermination, absorption, displacement, and confinement to reservations of some indigenous peoples. Many indigenous people are landless in their ancestral land while foreigners to their land own vast estates. This is especially true in lands where Europeans settled permanently, particularly in the Americas and Australia. Most of these indigenous peoples are landless or have less land to survive on, which can be very difficult in agrarian societies. For a time there was virtual enslavement and domination of the globe by the Europeans. Another sad side of colonialism has been the dehumanizing of other races especially the Blacks (who were variously described as inferior and sub-human from their first contact with the European), who for a time were reduced to slavery and servitude, a condition they have not emerged from completely, and even those who have emerged live with grudges, stigma, trauma, and are still considered stereotypes. The plantation system, where the colonized were and remain the suppliers of raw materials for the Western industrialists, remains a deplorable form of exploitation. **Such exploitation and looting of natural resources, which has continued until now, is storing up wrath of God for the exploiters;** *"For I, the LORD, love justice; I hate robbery and iniquity."* (Is. 61:8)

There was and remains, an imbalance in trade. Even with improved agriculture and the industrial revolution, colonies were not allowed to compete with the colonial masters, hence economic stagnation, and poverty until today. As a result (and the colonized are partly to be blamed) economic dependencies were created, which condition is still affecting most of sub-Saharan Africa today. Some colonial methods like the French policy of assimilation (French citizens abroad), deceived many to think that they belonged to France (and now immigration into France has been tightened, thus, many are realizing that they were never French citizens abroad anyway).

Summarizing the effect of colonialism on Africa, one historian has observed: "On a whole, the development of sub-Saharan Africa was seriously impeded by the encounter of its peoples with the Western Europeans during the seventeen and the eighteenth centuries. Africa's human resources were depleted, her natural resources plundered, and her political and social structures disoriented."[clvii]

Compared to the Moslems before them; "The Europeans gave little in return, especially when compared to what the Moslems of North Africa had contributed to the enrichment of sub-Saharan Africa prior to 1500."[clviii] **Permanent damage was inflicted upon Africa. First, there was universal savagery— within three centuries, and about more than 35 million people were killed and millions displaced, at a time when Europe and her New World daughters, were building their economies. The African was made the beast of burden before the machine came to replace him.** Africa was depleted of her strong and industrious, to lay the foundation of America. This explains in part why sub-Saharan Africa still lags today. Every policy was turned against the African and determined to cripple him forever. The worst form of racism, Apartheid, was practiced in South Africa. A few years ago, a prominent world leader put his stamp of approval on this when he arrogantly declared that South Africa is the only thriving economy of the African continent. However, though we look backward (and God will call the past to account; Ps. 10:12-15), since we cannot erase history, we are on the way forward. The dead shall rise, and the weak shall be strong, because God has become their refuge. Lastly, since the colonizers sometimes worked hand in hand with the missionaries, Christianity came to be resented and still is resented in parts of Africa, Japan, China, and other places, as an imperialistic tool of Western domination. What a bad seed to plant in the kingdom of Christ (Matt. 13:24-30)! **So that is how far the Roman Empire has devoured, crushed, and trampled the whole earth. That is how far the thief (Satan) has killed, destroyed, and stolen from the world.**

CHAPTER 10

APOSTASY: THEN AND NOW

Satan Attacks the Word of God (From Eden to Early 1800s)

If there is anything Satan attacks most, it is the word of God. This is precisely because God's word reveals God, his character, his plan, the only hope of man, and the demise of Satan. Whatever God has spoken is true and must be fulfilled; *"The LORD said to me [Jeremiah], 'You have seen correctly, for I am watching to see that my word is fulfilled'"* (Jer. 1:12). Jesus says; *"I tell you the truth, until heaven and earth disappear, not the smallest letter, not the stroke of a pen, will by any means disappear from the Law until everything is accomplished"* (Matt. 5:18). **God is not a man that he should change his mind or his word, WHAT HE HAS SAID HE MUST DO;** *"... but I will not take my love from him, nor will I ever betray my faithfulness. I will not violate my covenant or **alter what my lips have uttered**. Once for all, I have sworn by my holiness--and I will not lie to David—"* (Ps. 89:33-35). The word of God is established in heaven forever—it is eternal; *"Your word, O LORD, is eternal; it stands firm in the heavens"* (Ps. 119:89,152). God has exalted his word above everything else; *"... for you have exalted above all things your name and your word"* (Ps. 138:2). God made it categorically clear to the Israelites; *"**... that man does not live on bread alone but on every word that comes from the mouth of the LORD"*** (Deut. 8:3; cf. Matt. 4:4). Jesus reiterated the same fact when Satan tempted him in the desert. By using the written word of God only to defeat Satan, Jesus proved the importance and reliability of the word of God. In his life and ministry, Jesus relied on the word of God; he taught it, fulfilled it, and did not break or violate it (John 5:37-40; 7:16). He confirmed the fact that Scripture cannot be broken since what God has spoken or promised, he must do or fulfill (John 10:35; 17:12). He is the God of prophecy, who makes known the future and the end to his prophets and makes sure that their predictions are fulfilled. As it is written; *"Surely the Sovereign LORD does nothing without revealing his plan to his servants the prophets." "I am the LORD, ... who carries out the words of his servants and fulfills the predictions of his messengers"* (Amos 3:7; Is. 44:24-26). This, of course, ought to remind us of something. If the Bible says it, believe it, trust in it, and wait for it, no matter how dark things may seem, for God will fulfill it at the proper time; *"For the revelation awaits an appointed time; it speaks of the end and will not prove false. Though it linger, wait for it; it will certainly come and will not delay."* (Hab. 2:3) Again, not a single word of God is useless or should be taken lightly. Pay attention to all of Scripture, not only parts. Avoid picking and choosing what to believe and what to ignore; what to claim and what not to claim. Avoid selective hermeneutics (interpretation).

The word of God is true and must be fulfilled, and because it describes in detail Satan's doom, Satan fights relentlessly against it in as many ways as he possibly can. From the Garden of Eden until today, Satan is bent on attacking and countering the word of God. But we are glad of one thing: he cannot destroy it completely! He can only go as far as God allows him. When Satan came to Eve in the Garden of Eden, he started by questioning God's word; "Did God really say?" Since then that has been his tactic: to question the veracity and integrity of God's word, and to create doubts about it—"Has God really said?"

When God gave the law to Israel, he commanded them over and over in Deuteronomy that they should observe and obey all his commands, statutes, decrees, and laws, without turning to the right or to the left. Whenever they obeyed God by paying attention to his word, they triumphed and prospered, but whenever they disobeyed by turning to other gods, they were vanquished. What else can we say but that Satan from time-to-time seduced Israel to depart from God's law and turn to other gods!

Note again that when Satan realizes that you will not turn away from the word of God, he decides to quote it to you out of context. When Jesus retorted to him that man does not live on bread alone but on every word that proceeds from the mouth of the LORD, Satan went ahead to misquote Psalm 91:11-12 concerning angelic protection (Matt. 4:6). The word of God must always be quoted or read in context. Satan specializes in quoting Scripture out of context in order to create doubt and deception. The apostles in their earlier days had to face Satan through the pseudo-apostles, who penetrated the ranks of the Church and contradicted and countered the word of God by their teachings.

We have already seen how the Gnostics in the second century tried to manipulate Scripture (and their apostles are extant today running around with the Gnostic gospels!). In the third and fourth centuries, the Church recognized the canon of Scripture as consisting of 66 books as we have them today (that is, for Protestants). In the medieval period, the satanic and elitist priesthood in attempt to hide the truth of the Scripture from the people withheld the Scripture from them. They lied to the people by creating the impression that only the priests had the prerogative to interpret the Bible. Thus, they shut the truth of God's word from the people and introduced destructive heresies. People were unable to recognize the paganism that was cloaked in the name of Christianity that pervaded the Church. Not only so, Canon Law (church law) and tradition came to command the same authority as Scripture, and sometimes, taking precedence over Scripture. This evil persisted for a while until God began to shine the light through John Wycliffe (and others before and after him). He challenged the priestly prerogative to interpret Scripture and insisted that the Bible ought to be put back in the hands of the believers and in their language (for the Bible was only available in the scholarly language, Latin). The tide was turning, and the light was beginning to shine in the dark, and Satan could not hide the word of God any longer. With the Protestant Reformation came the dictum: *Sola Scriptura*; Scripture alone!

However, shortly after the Reformers, their followers build traditions around the Reformers' interpretations: Lutherans, Calvinists

(Reformed), etc., that became stronger than Scripture itself. This seems to be evident in most Christian movements or denominations of later Protestantism until today: whether Presbyterian, Baptist, Methodist, Adventist, Pentecostal, Charismatic, and many others. Each movement begins with the Bible and the Bible alone (no creed but the Bible), but the doctrines of the founders develop into traditions that become more important and normative than Scripture or seem to carry or command the same authority as Scripture. Thus, tradition becomes preferable than openness to the Bible, although all may still claim to be Bible-believing denominations. In many cases, this is a natural or unconscious development, a true characteristic of human nature. But those who are wise would never exalt tradition above Scripture or regard tradition in par with Scripture. They would always be on the alert for any such developments. They live above denomination! Of course, this does not suggest that everyone is wrong or that tradition is wrong. Even the Bible and the Bible alone is a tradition! Therefore, tradition with openness to Scripture is what should be practiced.

The Enlightenment

> *"The wrath of God is being revealed from heaven against the godlessness and wickedness of* **men who suppress the truth by wickedness**, *since what may be known about God is plain to them, because God has made it plain to them.... For although they knew God, they neither glorified him as God nor gave thanks to him, but* **their thinking became futile and their foolish hearts were darkened. Although they claimed to be wise they became fools,** *and exchanged the glory of the immortal God for images made to look like mortal man and birds and animals and reptiles."* (Rom. 1:18-23)

The Enlightenment, otherwise known as the age of reason, represented a radical break with the past and tradition (what men held to be true until then) and biblical revelation as sources of truth. It focused on what man could or can do based on reason or human intellect. The Enlightenment was unlike the renaissance that called for a return to the ancient classics. It was unlike the Protestant Reformation that stressed a return to supernatural revelation. The Enlightenment thinkers questioned everything that existed before their time and subjected it to critical reasoning as they saw it. As historians assert, they argued that; "All we know and all we can know is what we perceive through our senses and interpret with our reason. There are no such things as innate ideas or revealed truth."[clix] This was an open and complete denial of God and revelation (Bible). The Enlightenment thinkers asserted the following on nature: that; "Nature is governed by a few simple and unchangeable laws."[clx] In a sense, by acknowledging the fixed state of nature but denying revealed truth, they perfectly fit the description of the people in the verses above; *"... since what may be known about God is plain to them, ... For since the creation of the world God's invisible qualities--his eternal power and divine nature--have been clearly seen, being understood from what has been made* [nature], *so that men are without excuse"* (vv.19-20). They failed to realize that just as the laws of nature are unchangeable, so also are the moral laws of the world, that is, God's revelation. Both the natural universe and the moral universe are perfectly ordered by the one who created them and as much as we cannot tamper with the laws of nature, so we should not tamper with the laws of God (revealed truth--Bible). Rejecting the law of God or Christ, for that matter, would be like one jumping out of an airplane at a high altitude but refusing a parachute. In this case, that individual will plunge to the ground and break into pieces according to the laws of physics. In like manner, rejecting God and his word would mean to crash into eternal oblivion and perish in torments.

On Change and progress (I will limit to the moral and the philosophical), the philosophers asserted that; "Change and progress work hand in hand as human beings work to perfect themselves and their society."[clxi] REALLY! No one can deny the reality of change and progress, but far from perfecting themselves and their society, men are becoming worse and worse as society progresses. They are more prone to do evil and to invent more ways of doing evil as Paul explains;

"Furthermore, since they did not think it worthwhile to retain the knowledge of God, he gave them over to a depraved mind, to do what ought not to be done. They have become filled with

every kind of wickedness, evil, greed and depravity. They are full of envy, murder, strife, deceit and malice. They are gossips, slanderers, God-haters, insolent, arrogant and boastful; they invent ways of doing evil [various new ways of sin and crime], *they disobey their parents; they are senseless, faithless, heartless, ruthless.*" (Rom. 1:28-31)

The only person, among the Enlightenment thinkers, who seemed to have had a realistic view of society and progress was Jean Jacques Rousseau; "According to him, what we call 'progress' is not really such, for what in truth has happened is that humankind have progressively departed from its natural state and fallen into artificiality."clxii And so it has continued in that trend until almost all of us seem to be wearing masks—hypocrisy or political correctness! On human beings and their potential, the philosophers were also very hopeful. They asserted that; "Human beings are naturally rational and good, but the proponents of mystic religions have distorted human thinking and prevented proper progress by preaching false doctrines of original sin and divine moral laws. Rid people of these religious hindrances and they can and will build for themselves a more perfect society."clxiii Surely, when the people forsake the law the wicked prosper; right is called wrong and wrong right. Such optimism about man is in direct contrast to God's view of man. In fact, it is a direct affront on God himself. When you spurn the word of God you are rejecting God himself. Men are born in sin and are by nature objects of wrath (Eph. 2:1-3). And what can we say? Has this secular enlightened optimism about man brought a perfect society? Far from the truth! Crime, greed, and the vices listed above continue to increase even in the best civilized societies, especially as divine law/revelation is rejected. We see more and more laws enacted every day to check human maladjusted behavior. (For instance, in progressed and civilized societies like Europe, where secularism took root first and then the USA, just to cite these two). Those who have rid themselves of religion are far from being virtuous or perfect.

These were some of the general concepts of the Enlightenment and how they related to divine revelation. This does not suggest that the Enlightenment was only negative or that reason is always wrong.

The Enlightenment was only wrong in its rejection of revelation and biblical doctrines and in its optimistic predictions on how reason would lead people to develop a perfect society, which time has proven wrong. We can use our reason as much as we want, but when it comes to truth about God (metaphysical epistemology) and morality, the Bible is the absolute source and authority, and is dependable. (It is complete though not exhaustive, especially when it relates to new ways of doing evil. We must derive implications to apply to present circumstances.)

Some of the Enlightenment philosophers were deists (though not atheist per se, these discounted the significance of certain historical events and revelation, especially the significance of Jesus Christ), and some articulated political philosophies that became the hallmark of modern governments, especially Republicanism. (It is not my intention to critique various forms of government here, but good as Republicanism and democracy are, I admire monarchy, which is what Christ's kingdom will be--a theocratic monarchy). The Deists believed that "Some infinite Divine Being must have created it [universe] and set it in motion. However, the finite mind of human beings cannot comprehend the infinite. Therefore, God is unknowable. Furthermore, God, having set his perfect mechanical laws in motion, will never tamper with them nor interfere in human affairs. God is impersonal."[clxiv]

Notice that believe in a Divine Being or that God exists is not sufficient for salvation nor does it mean true worship. This is the case of those described in Romans 1:21; *"For although they knew God, they neither glorified him as God nor gave thanks to him, but their minds became futile and their foolish hearts were darkened. Although they claimed to be wise, they became fools …."* It is also written: *"Where is the wise man? Where is the scholar? Where is the philosopher of this age? Has not God made foolish the wisdom of the world?"* (1 Co. 1:20) Again God says; *"I am the LORD, who overthrows the learning of the wise and turns it into nonsense, …."* (Is. 44:24-25) Even the devil and his demons believe that there is one God and shudder, but they do not accept him as God or subject themselves in worship of him (James 2:19). In short, the God of deism is not the God revealed in Jesus Christ, who is the only way to the one God and Father (John 14:6). Indeed, God is infinite, and the finite human mind cannot completely comprehend him (Rom 11:33); but we can know him to the extent that he has made himself known, and this is through the very revelation that the Deists rejected (Jer. 9:24; Matt. 11:27; 1 Co. 2:10-16). Contrary to their claim that God is impersonal and does not interfere in human affairs, the opposite is true. God is personal and providentially guides and directs human history to his desired end: the global kingdom of God. Deism was/ is subtle. Deists or freethinkers, as they were also known (free from orthodoxy and Protestants squabbles), were not necessarily atheists; they were simply tired of sectarian orthodoxy. However, to avoid this sectarianism, they made the grave mistake of rejecting revealed religion or particular revelation in preference to natural religion. This, of course, pits them against God himself, for to reject God's revelation is to reject God himself, and his ultimate revelation, Jesus Christ.

The greatest contribution of the Enlightenment philosophers was in government. This was begun by men like John Locke of England and followed later by French thinkers like Voltaire (one of the forerunners of the French Revolution), Baron de Montesquieu, and Jean Jacques Rousseau. They rejected despotism and monarchy in favor of a republic. "Since power corrupts, Montesquieu suggested that government should be exercised by three powers that would balance and limit each other: the legislative, the executive, and the judicial."[clxv] Locke also argued for the natural rights of human beings, which are life, liberty and property. This theory of government and the rights of humans became the gospel for the American revolutionaries and "Jefferson wrote many of Locke's ideas into the Declaration of Independence, frequently using his exact words. They likewise appear in the United States Constitution and numerous French declarations of liberty." (As noted earlier) This illustrates vividly why I argued earlier that the American Republic was more a child of the Enlightenment than of the Protestant or Puritan Reformations. Like the Enlightenment thinkers, some of the American founding fathers were optimistic that natural means could ensure both personal virtue and social perfection; "… many of America's founding fathers had very minimal views concerning the fall of humans, and almost all were highly optimistic about the capacities of human reason to discover natural law unaided by revelation. Thomas Jefferson, the author of the Declaration, especially repudiated the idea of subordinating his thought to biblical principles."clxvi **This is another proof that America's founding documents came from the Enlightenment and were not even remotely Christian, as some erroneously argue.** Well, all these Enlightenment thinkers and their disciples in North America were wrong in their optimism and positivism about man—look at Western society today! Reason has not brought us anywhere. We are far from personal virtue and social perfection resulting from natural law and human reason. We are not even close. In fact, most people who are driven by Enlightenment and human positivism thinking are given over to vice and avarice.

Let us pause here for a reality check on the optimism of the Enlightenment. One only needs to look at the world today in general and the democratically stable Western nations in particular and ask whether such optimism on humanity has come to fruition. We are increasingly becoming depraved, greedy, and corrupt. To back up a little bit, the ancient philosopher, **Plato, had predicted that the political society would progress to the point when a Philosopher-King, the ideal ruler, and the epitome of an intellectual and philosophical aristocracy, would rule the world ushering in the reign of peace.** Well, the world has progressed politically, and we have a political tier, but those who rule on top do not come close to being philosopher-kings. Not even an enlightened despot as Voltaire suggested.clxvii As we will see in later chapters, the only philosophers that gave the right predictions concerning progress and change in human behavior and society (it will increasingly become evil and wicked, given to all forms of vice) were Jesus Christ and his apostles.

Some of these philosophers had gone past Satan, though they were still in his camp (not good servants). Satan will never go so far as to reject revelation because he knows that God exists and that is why he is trying to usurp him. Denying revelation would mean that Satan can no longer deceive people using religion or from within religion. Besides, Satan is not more powerful than God, and therefore, cannot destroy God's revelation (He can only go as far as God allows him). Satan cannot try to be God if he believed that there is no God. It is abysmal ignorance to deny the existence of God (it is foolishness); *"A fool* [morally deficient person] *says in his heart, 'There is no God.' They are corrupt, their deeds are vile; there is no one who does good."* (Ps. 14:1; cf. Rom. 1:22) **These Enlightenment philosophers were, indeed, antichrists, though they did not cooperate with Satan directly.**

New Philosophies

The Enlightenment marked the beginning of a new era in human intellectual history. Men discarded tradition and revelation and began to formulate new philosophies of life that have persisted till today or are the underlying principles or modus operandi of modern life.

Sociology: This discipline was founded and named by Auguste Comte, who divided history into three epochs. The first epoch was religious, the second metaphysical, and the third was "specific or positive, when truth would be discovered by the scientific gathering of factual data. Comte had utter scorn for the first [religious] …. Comte's religion was the worship of humanity [… *and they worshiped and served created things rather than the Creator* …; Rom. 1:25], and he had great faith in its future."[clxviii] **Sociologists "were the most persistently and pointedly hostile to religion. Supernatural religion** [especially Christianity] **had no place whatever in Comte's positivism,** humanity itself being the object of worship."[clxix] *(emphasis mine).*

Psychology: What is it? Psychology was popularized by Sigmund Freud, who "… concluded that much of human behavior is irrational, unconscious, and instinctual. He argued that conflict is a basic condition of life, particularly conflict between our innate biological drives (such as sex or aggression) and our social selves. These conflicts are worked out in a mostly unconscious level and in stages during childhood. These conflicts invariably cause frustration. …"[clxx] This became the basis for modern psychology and psychoanalysis. Psychologists were equally hostile to religion. **"Psychologists**

typically viewed religion as a fantasy or illusion created by human beings."[clxxi] *(emphasis mine)*.

Darwinism/Evolution: The major theses of this discipline was/is that; plant and animal species/life as we have it today, came by a slow process of evolution from simpler forms through a process of natural selection--survival of the fittest. Evolutionists concluded that humans evolved from more primitive species by the same process as plants and animals—macro evolution (evolution across species, e.g. man from apes). The missing link, of course, which they continue to search for, has not yet been found. The only reason the missing link has not been found is that there is none! However, we note that there is micro evolution (changes within the same species over a period due to environment and diet). Evolution from the start has always been the enemy of creationism (the Biblical teaching that all of nature has its origin from God, its Creator. see Genesis 1 and 2 and Job 38-40). The Bible does not answer every detail about origins (the processes of creation). God reserves the right not to reveal everything to humans. Therefore, it is not a matter of the Bible not containing everything that is scientifically discovered, but whether God intended to reveal it to us. Secret things belong to the LORD; *"The secret things belong to the LORD our God, but the things revealed belong to us and to our children forever, that we may follow all the words of this law"* (Deut. 29:29). Faith provides the missing ingredient to understand completely God's creative work; *"By faith we understand that the universe was formed at God's command, so that what is seen was not made out of what was visible."* (Heb. 11:3)

Evolutionists equally had their optimistic assumptions on human progress. If evolution could provide a whole way of life; "Humanity in this view, was advancing from simpler to more complex tasks, from a primitive to a sophisticated state of existence. **Christianity, in this reading, may have been helpful in aiding primitives cope, but it was a primitive religion, and as such needed to be carefully reconsidered."**[clxxii] *(emphasis mine)*. Intellectuals followed the same line of reasoning: "In the same academic circles, great optimism prevailed regarding the human creature and its capabilities. Thanks to evolution and progress, the day was at hand when humans would be able to solve problems until then insoluble, thus bringing in a new age of joy, freedom, justice, peace, and abundance."[clxxiii] Thus, the evolution theory (which has remained a theory since) made its way into schools as scientific fact, seriously attacking and undermining creationism. The famous encounter of evolution and creationism was the Monkey Scopes Trial (in the US in 1925), which apparently crowned Darwin as creator over against God, the Creator.

Naturalism: Naturalism is the philosophical belief that "nothing exists outside the material, mechanistic ..., natural order. ... A naturalist believes that the physical universe is the sum of all that is."[clxxiv] For the naturalist, the universe is a closed system, outside of which there is nothing, and everything that happens must be explained as having its cause from within the system. "Naturalists believe that everything that happens within nature has its cause on something else that exists within the natural order."[clxxv] Such a philosophy has no room for God or the supernatural. Nature is all that exists; a materialistic, self-explanatory, totally uniform, and deterministic system.

Anthropology: "Anthropologists dug into the human race's distant past to unearth the primitive origins of its culture, of which religion is always an important part. **Nearly all of them concluded that religion is based on primitive superstition.**"[clxxvi] *(emphasis mine)*. Sir James Frazer published his book that showed "a vast and fascinating history of early myths, superstition, and cults from which he believed that present-day religions, including Christianity, are derived."[clxxvii]

Republicanism: This became the most favorite and preferable form of government stemming from the Enlightenment, as opposed to monarchy, aristocracy, and despotism. In Republicanism, a large group of elected officials rule on behalf of the people and only the most qualified citizens, most often, the rich or property owners, have the right of franchise. The populace is deceived to think that their vote counts! The best example is the American Republic at its birth. Republicanism easily degenerates into a democracy when every citizen is given the right of franchise. To some extent, America is presently a democracy within a Republic.

Democracy: This is the system of government in which everyone has the right to vote (at least of specified voting age) and whoever has the most votes goes to office. Democracy has its positive and negative aspects that space will not allow me to include here. But suffice it to say that it has come to be accepted as the universal gospel of governance that offers opportunity for all (so it is believed). Where democracy exists, it tolerates Christianity, but neutralizes its effect to nearly zero. It offers false security to Christians to think that everything is alright but when a lot is amiss. Democracy at the end of the day is a hidden, if not an explicit form of the antichrist system.

Marxism: Marxism is a form of socialism that was advocated by Karl Marx, a brilliant German Jew, who, with Friedrich Engels, wrote the *Communist Manifesto* in 1848. Marx argued that;

> "Economic interests and motivations underlie the most critical actions of human beings…. Societies are formed around the means of production, around the principal ways that human beings make a living. The political system, the religious system, and the cultural system that develop must conform to the necessities of the economic system and the social system which form around the economic realities of life…. Societies are broadly divided into the haves and the have-nots. The haves are the owners of the means of economic production; the have-nots are the exploited laborers for these haves. The haves and have-nots are opposing classes with opposing interests…."[clxxviii]

Marx had a great disdain for capitalism (competitive and providing illegitimate profits from surplus value to the capitalist at the expense of the laborers; a modern example would be the first world and third world technological divide, with cash crops and manufactured goods exchange]. Marx envisioned a time when the capitalist system would be destroyed or overthrown by the working class leading to a classless socialist society. Socialism was and is openly atheistic—that is, anti-God. The history of the former USSR from the Bolsheviks revolution of 1917 until its collapse in 1979 summarizes the communist experiment and debacle.

Capitalism: Capitalism is the most revered trade system of the so-called free world and ultimately the rest of the world. The world trading system changed hands from Feudalism (where few wealthy lords controlled the means of exchange) to Mercantilism (semi government-controlled system) and finally to capitalism (free trade, that is sometimes not free as purported). Capitalism gives rise to maximum production of goods and services and maximum profits. America's economic history is the success story of modern capitalism. Capitalism fosters great amassing of wealth (materialism), avarice, and the most hideous hedonism. It is the system whose collapse spans many pages of Scripture. While not necessarily bad, it is the system behind which Satan is openly hiding (Is. 14, Ezek. 28)!

On an ending note, most of these new philosophies were in one way or the other, implicitly, or explicitly hostile to Christianity. Where explicit, Christianity was openly persecuted, but where implicit, they neutralized and diffused Christianity, which is the most deceptive.

Science and God

While the Bible makes statements that may have geographic or scientific implications, it is not a textbook of any of these disciplines. However, whenever the Bible makes such statements, they are true. For instance, Job declared that; *"He* [God] *spreads out the northern skies over empty space; he suspends the earth over nothing"* (Job 26:7ff). Some have argued about the statement that the sun stood still for Joshua (10:12-13). This statement was not designed to teach about the rotation of the earth; it was based on observation.

God is not against factual science. Factual science is an investigation into what God created out of nothing and placed there. We tap into his created universe and turn one substance into another, but we cannot create anything out of nothing. Factual natural science (physical and chemical) are not a problem (I believe in it and use it every day--all the positive achievements in science, especially Physics, Chemistry, Mathematics, Biology and Medicine, Technology, etc.). The early fights between scientists from Copernicus and following, with the Church (both Catholic and Protestant), was due to ignorance and misinformation. **God never fights science, only scientists fight**

God. Notice I said, scientists, not science. Science never fights God, only scientists do!

However, there is always cause for concern about the ethical implications of science--using life humans for experiments, messing up with life (genetics to some extent), stem cells, or any other ethical implications generated by scientific advancement. Theories like evolution not yet proven but mere hypothesis, that are presented as facts are always cause for concern. Social implications of science such as invention of things that cause evil (Rom. 1:30): firearms (crime, war), guns, machine guns, bombs like the atomic bomb, nuclear weapons, biological weapons, continuous military technology, etc., are equally cause for concern. Man risks extinction by man and man continues to live in fear of man and the earth is increasingly becoming an unsafe place to live on; for instance, homicides and terrorism. Good science has become man's best friend (medical science, mechanized agriculture leading to more production, technology, etc.), but at the same time, science has also invented man's worst enemy. The line of evil of these dangerous weapons goes from the heart of the inventor to the user (Is. 54:16).

Here again, we note that man's positivism and optimism in science, has not solved the problem of man's heart. Such optimism as; "The marvelous achievements of the scientists caused many to place great faith in people and in their ability to do for themselves whatever needed to be done.... **In fact, there appeared to many, at the end of the nineteenth century to be less and less place and need for God,**"[clxxix] *(emphasis mine)* has not materialized at all. Darwin's supporters had; "... proclaimed that scientists would very soon be solving all the remaining mysteries of life and even creating life."[clxxx] But I would like to ask, "Where are they now?" Have these optimistic assertions come true? The Bible asserts that the heart of man is wicked above all things (Jer. 17:9, 10), and filled with madness (Eccl. 9:3), and can only be cured by God, who created it. But if we reject him, we will get nowhere. At best, we are only deluding ourselves and racing at a very high speed toward the bottomless pit—the abyss.

Critical Scholarship (Satan's Apostles in the Church)

"For such men are false apostles, deceitful workmen, masquerading as apostles of Christ. And no wonder, for Satan himself masquerades as an angel of light. It is not surprising, then, if his servants masquerade as servants of righteousness. Their end will be what their action deserves" (2 Co. 11:13-15).

Critical scholarship was the search for error and fraud in the Bible, and a questioning of its historicity and authenticity. Higher Critics like David Strauss; *"... stripped Christ of his divinity and undertook to explain in natural terms the miracles and prophesies recorded in the New Testament. Strauss asserted that the New Testament was a very unreliable document...."*[clxxxi] Ernest Renan declared that Christ was man, not God. He embarked on the humanization of Christ. Historical Critics raised doubts about the historical authenticity of several, if not most books of the Bible. All that seemed extraordinary or miraculous was to be rejected. Thus, *"Although they claimed to be wise, they became fools ..."* (Rom. 1:22). Now where are they? *"Where is the wise man? Where is the scholar? Where is the philosopher of this age? Has not God made foolish the wisdom of this world?"* (1 Co. 1:20). Again, Paul writes about these self-proclaimed scholars; *"Do not deceive yourselves. If any one of you thinks he is wise by the standards of this age, he should become a 'fool' so that he may become wise. For the wisdom of this world is foolishness in God's sight. As it is written: 'He catches the wise in their craftiness'"* (1 Co. 3:18-19).

The Rise of Modernism

To the modernists (radical liberals), *"... Christianity and the Bible were little more than another religion and a great book among many."*[clxxxii] They especially disliked fundamentalism with its five cardinal beliefs on Christianity (verbal inspiration and inerrancy of Scripture, the divinity of Jesus Christ and the Virgin birth, the atonement as a substitute for sinners, his physical resurrection, and the impending return). Fundamentalism came to be disliked by many. Modernism was a reaction to the challenges and assaults on Christianity by science, by surrendering to these challenges.

Modernists attempted to change the doctrines of the church to conform to Critical and Higher criticism of the Bible. "They would reject the supernatural and deny the divinity of Christ. They would make the Bible a book of good literature and high ethical ideals; Christ, a great social reformer; and the church, an instrument for the promotion of good will, wholesome fellowship, racial tolerance, temperance, charity, patriotism, and so on."[clxxxiii] This was blatant apostasy! "Modernists were Protestants, who felt that it was necessary for the Christian faith to adjust self-consciously to the norms defining modern culture."[clxxxiv] They attempted to give new meanings to Christian truths while retaining terminology; for instance, reconciliation, atonement, etc. This attempt is most dangerous as it deceives though looking like the real thing. Their new theology gave modern reason a more central role in religion. Modernism triumphed in centers of higher learning rather than the churches. Some taught that Jesus came to realize God as his Father and that Paul was at variance with what Jesus taught. Modernism did set the tone for the study of religion in academic circles, college and university alike. The tares had been sown and they would choke the seed terribly throughout the twentieth century, particularly in North America and wherever it spread.

Liberal Scholarship

Liberal scholarship was a reaction to modern science and an acceptance of modernity. What they sought to do was to reconcile science (especially evolutionary theory) with revelation by reinterpreting Genesis chapter one. They "... endeavored to show that on the theory of evolution is God's method of creation, religion and science can indeed be reconciled. The biblical story of creation has to be taken as devout, prescientific theorizing, poetically if not literally true, its essence not disproved, though its form requires reinterpretation."[clxxxv]

The father of modern Protestant liberalism was Friedrich Schleiermacher. He "... was the first professional Protestant theologian to call for sweeping changes in Protestant orthodoxy to encounter and come to terms with the *Zeitgeist* of modernity. The result was the birth of liberal Protestant theology."[clxxxvi] Two tenets of the New Protestant

Liberal Theology that developed at the turn of the twentieth century were: "(1) the necessity of reconstructing traditional Christian thought in the light of modern culture, philosophy and science; and (2) the necessity of discovering Christianity's true essence apart from the layers of traditional dogma that were no longer relevant or even possible to believe in light of modern thought."[clxxxvii] These aimed at sweeping away orthodoxy and authoritarian traditionalism. They held an inflated over-optimism about success in the future; "... All of them saw modern thought as a necessary tool of interpretation and most of them gave it a guiding and even controlling authority in determining the essence of Christian truth."[clxxxviii] Some discarded entirely any literal belief in the supernatural or miraculous. Some simply downplayed or neglected the supernatural (see 2 Peter 2 concerning these scoffers). Some downplayed and others rejected completely doctrines such as the Trinity and deity of Christ, while others reinterpreted them. They attempted to construct a Christian theology compatible with the best of modern philosophy, science, and biblical scholarship. Protestant liberalism appealed to and gained acceptance among the intellectual elite in the United States; "But most liberals were committed Christians whose very commitment drove them to respond to the intellectual challenges of their time in the hope of making the faith credible for modern people,"[clxxxix] that is, as they saw it. Liberalism gave birth to the "social gospel," though not all liberals subscribed or believed in it. The social gospel, propounded by the Baptist leader, Walter Rauschenbush, was devoted "... to exploring and showing the relationship between the demands of the gospel and the misery in which the urban masses live."[cxc] Rauschenbush "... insisted that the social and economic life of the nation [USA] should conform to the requirements of the gospel, ..."[cxci] Thus, he and those who followed him, were dedicated to the plight of the poor. They were concerned about the great inequity and social injustice resulting from the practice of capitalism.

Rise of False Prophets and Occultism

The last three centuries have seen the rise of many false religions and cults, especially within what is called "Christendom." What has happened is what we can say, that the powers, authorities, rulers, and principalities that be (Eph. 6:12), settled in our midst to visibly promote the work of the devil. Some of them had always existed but had a significant influence especially in the past 300 years. Many politicians, as we have seen, who held sway over the lives of many, became involved in this occultism. Examples: Rose Croix or Rosicrucian, Freemasonry, Illuminati, Theosophy, Christian Science, Mormonism, and other Christian and Hindu-based cults and occult groups.

Voices in the Wilderness

There were those who launched a concerted effort to combat the threats posed by modernism, liberalism, and evolutionary science. These began to appear by mid nineteenth century (within many denominations) and by the turn of the twentieth century, the overt movement became known as Fundamentalism. They sought to defend what they considered as the fundamental orthodox doctrines of the Christian faith. These included: (1) the verbal inspiration and inerrancy of the Scripture, (2) the deity of Jesus Christ, (3) the incarnation or virgin birth of Jesus Christ, (4) the substitution death or atonement of Jesus Christ on the cross, and (5) the physical resurrection and impending physical return of Jesus Christ. Fundamentalism came to be defined as "anti-liberal" because it saw liberalism as a denial of the faith (antichrist). Fundamentalism became a defender of orthodox doctrine. With this movement came a new hermeneutic, dispensationalism, as a major thought and method of interpretation. There were many other denominations that held tenaciously to the biblical faith and teaching (the advent and holiness movements), who were not necessarily labeled fundamentalists.

Attempts at Church Unity

Ecumenism: The search for unity among Christians began mostly in the twentieth century. A driving force behind it was the missionary movement, where missionaries had to cooperate in Bible translation, who had to go to which area and who to the other area. "The great forerunner of the ecumenical movement was none other than William Carey, who suggested that an international missionary conference be convened at Cape Town in 1810."[cxcii] However, his call was not heeded until 1910, when the first missionary conference was gathered in Edinburgh, Scotland. The main subject of discussion was pioneer missions. There was no discussion of Protestant missions in Catholic and Orthodox lands. The cooperation born at this conference would eventually give birth to the World Council of Churches in 1948. Doctrine, and denominational doctrinal distinctive, however, were not discussed in the 1910 conference. The "Life and Work Movement," another ecumenical body of the conference, took resolution toward practical Christianity. Some of their positive outcomes were: (1) "From the beginning, this movement took a firm stance against every form of exploitation or imperialism." (2) "It also noted a 'general resentment against white imperialism' that threatened to break into open conflict." (3) Also, "... its final documents included a strong word against every form of totalitarianism, and the condemnation of war as a method to solve international conflict."[cxciii] This progress ended as follows: "Finally, on August 22, 1948, the First Assembly of the World Council of Churches was called into order in Amsterdam. One hundred and seven churches from forty-four nations were part of it."[cxciv] "With the Cold War beginning, the council called on all churches to reject both communism and liberal capitalism."[cxcv]

However, despite its positive goals, this ecumenism began to pave the way back to Rome and the Papacy (MYSTERY BABYLON THE GREAT; Rev. 17:5). Thus, the calls of the Protestant Reformers were being neutralized or repudiated. Not only so, but ecumenism has also come to embrace most if not all world religions, and thus, is out rightly antichrist because it undermines the Christian exclusive dictum; *"Salvation is found in no one else, for there is no other name under heaven given to men by which we must be saved,"* except the name of Jesus (Acts 4:12). Jesus says; *"I am the way and the truth and the life. No one comes to the Father except through me"* (John 14:6). Jesus is not a way among other ways! Ecumenism is an enemy of Jesus Christ—it is antichrist.

Western Syncretism (Imprints of Ancient European Paganism/ Religions on Christianity)

Nationalism: We had noted earlier how the ancient peoples developed the concept of gods--from village gods to city gods and to national gods. [For instance, Egypt, Mesopotamia/Babylon (Bel and Marduk), Assyria, Greeks (Zeus as the chief god, also known as Pater and Sky father, known to the Romans as Jupiter), Demeter - the earth mother, virgin goddess of the hearth, sister of Zeus]. Like it was in the case of Nimrod, these gods all related to the founders or the spirit of the founders of the village, city, nation or empire, who came to be revered. These spirits hold strong sway over the lives of the people who revere them. A biblical example is the Prince of Persia in Daniel 10:13, who prevented the angel from getting to Daniel on time. Sometimes this nationalism even resulted in state or emperor worship like in Daniel 3 and the Roman Empire (Caesar is Lord; Caesar is God's son, and hence, is worshipped). The rise of nationalism in the West gave rise to such nationalistic deities or spirit (s)--the spirit other than God that unites and controls the people. "Nationalism may be defined as feelings of common cultural identity and loyalty to one's country."[cxcvi] The most common factor is language; second by a historical tradition of unity; sometimes religion and also natural boundaries.

The revolutions of the late 1700s gave rise to a new kind of nationalism. Americans united under the spirit of Freedom (from Britain), Unity, and the Rights of man (Bill of Rights). The democratic spirit since then has become a universal god, sought and worshipped by almost all peoples. On the other hand, the French Revolution was the dawning of a new era and gave birth to a new and more radical kind of nationalism. The people were in control of their own affairs and government. In France, "Nationalism acquired attributes of religion. Such mass dynamism made revolutionary and Napoleonic armies irresistible."[cxcvii] At the turn of the twentieth century, Christianity in the USA became identified with patriotism by some. The Evangelist, Billy Sunday had "claimed that 'Christianity and Patriotism are synonymous terms'..."[cxcviii] That deception has continued to the present day, where reciting the Pledge of Allegiance has become a religious fervor. This close identification of Christianity with patriotism is very dangerous--Caesar (under Satan) and the Christianity (under Christ) are different. Once the devil convinces or deceives the people to identify his cause with the cause of Christ, he has succeeded greatly. And such cases of nationalism are nothing short of idolatry. Glimpses of such nationalism are revealed in the book of Revelation as the worship of the beast (empire or kingdom or nation).

Venus: She was the Summerian queen of the heavens and goddess of love and fertility. She is still honored today as the planet Venus! She was also known as Ishtar, a universal goddess, "the queen of heaven and the stars" (Jer. 44:18-25).

Astrology: This is the attempt to read the will of the gods in the dispositions of the heavenly bodies like planets, sun, moon, stars; and predicting the course of individual lives and world events.[cxcix] Astrology was the precursor to Astronomy, horoscope, etc., and the Zodiac by Hindu, Muslim, and western people. We know that horoscope columns are a regular feature in many newspapers, at least in the US.

Rome: The Romans borrowed much from the Etruscans and others like the Egyptians, the Babylonians, and other Eastern peoples. **"The religion of Numa"** of earlier Romans was associated with charms, taboos, and the reading of omens. **Jupiter** was chief of the gods and his most exalted title was **Optimus Maximus** (closely related to Pontifex Maximus, the Roman high priest, that is, the emperor; and this came to refer to the pope). The Roman capital was built on the Capitoline hill, hence called Jupiter Capitolinus. **"Janus** was the **Numen** in the door, defending the threshold ..."[cc] Some Patron deities of the home were **Ceres, Juno, and Jupiter; while Mars and Quirinus** were war gods. **"Hermes** came to Rome also, but under the name of **Mercury**, for he was to be the god of commerce (mercantura)"[cci] **The Religion of the Roman State:** This was the domestic cult nationalized, with king as chief priest during the monarchy. A lot of ceremonies and sacrifices were performed. Some deities to whom these ceremonies were dedicated are familiar words in usage today: **Faunus, Flora, Janus, Jupiter, Mars, Neptunus, Saturnus, Vesta, etc.**

"For one thing, Rome itself was like a deity (**Dea Roma**) and no longer needed the help of the old gods in the old way. The educated classes, enlightened or disillusioned by Greek philosophy, pursued the atheistic way of the Epicureans, or the pantheistic way of the Stoics, or else lapsed into indifference. … Religion was something to discuss pleasantly over the dinner table or with friends in a moment of leisure, but apart from its value as a political binding element, it was of no vital concern to thinking persons."[ccii]

(Does that ring a bell in your head of our modern era? That is why malignant nationalism is considered idolatry—the worship or deification of the nation or the worship of the beast.) This attitude later gave way to the divinization of the emperors, where their statues were build and erected within the empire and revered, a practice still alive and well today in many nations.

The Celts: The Celts worshipped a god called **Mercury**. They also worshipped **Apollo, Mars, Jupiter,** and **Minerva.** The Celts celebrated many ceremonies dedicated to gods; "Among the recurrent ceremonies of Celts was the **May Day** festival. It has survived in a token form as the **Maypole Dance** in Europe and America."[cciii]

The Teutons (Anglo-Saxons, Jutes, Saxons, Alamanni, Lombards, Frisians, Franks, Goths, Scandinavians, Vandals) had the following in common: The sky-god, who was also god of law, fertility, and war, and was called **Tiw or Tiwaz**--who is now remembered in the Anglo-Saxon word **Tuesday. Donar (Thurmor or Thor)** was the red-bearded god of thunder and rain; "He became the chief god in Norway and Iceland. (We now have his name in **Thursday.**)"[cciv] **Wodan or Odin** was the god of the earth, magic, and the dead; he was all-knowing and all-seeing, and the source of wisdom of seers and poets: "(We still honor him today in our **Wednesday.**)"[ccv] "**Freyr and Freyja** were the divine **May King** and **May Queen** whose magical embrace brought the revival of life in spring."[ccvi] **Balder** was the most notable god of the gods and goddesses of seasons (spring, summer, and autumn): "His mother Frigg, consort of Odin and queen of the gods (for whom **Friday** is named), took oaths from all things not to hurt him, but she neglected to pledge **the mistletoe.**"[ccvii] In respect to the dead the Teutons believed that; "Until the corpse of a man decayed, it could do harm as a **specter or vampire** (a belief the Norse shared with the Chinese…), and the corpse itself was in danger of being torn to pieces by wolves out of hell, by horse-shaped demons, or by swooping eagles, such as the giant wind-demon Hraesvelg. On the other hand, the spirits of the dead, if they had been good in life and were faithfully reverenced after death, could bring good fortune to their descendants."[ccviii] (The idea of Vampires is still prominent in the West today). **Valhalla**, a great hall in the sky was used for keeping fallen warriors.

More on Week Days: Greg Dues writes that in pre-Christian times days were named after the sun, moon, and visible planets, which were considered by the pagans to have divine power and were honored as deities (forbidden in the Bible in Deut. 4:19). He states that;

"When the Germanic peoples gained influence in the Roman Empire, they renamed four week days after their own gods. These names remain today among people whose language derives from ancient Germanic tribes, including English-speaking people:

Sunday - day of the sun
Monday - day of the moon
Tuesday - Tiw's day, god of war
Wednesday - god Woden's day
Thursday - god Thor's day
Friday - Frigg's day, goddess of love
Saturday - day of Saturn."[ccix]

In part one, I briefly discussed something on **the Sabbath day in relation to Sunday**. Here, I want to note that Catholicism claims exclusive authority in making Sunday the Christian day of rest, which poses concern for any serious Bible student and follower of Jesus Christ. Greg Dues, writing from a Catholic perspective, explains how the venerable day of the sun became the Christian Sabbath (so it is believed). He writes in *Catholic Customs & Traditions*;

"The first followers of Jesus were Jews. For a while they continued to observe Sabbath (Hebrew *shabbath*, to 'leave off' or 'to rest') traditions. They dedicated this seventh, or last, day of the week to the one God, Yahweh, in accord with the Genesis creation story (Genesis 2:1-3) and the Third [sic] Commandment: 'Remember to keep holy the Sabbath day' (Exodus 20:8). The Jewish Sabbath provided a regular rhythm to life with traditions that emphasized rest or absence of work and physical activities. It was also a day of assembly and a feast day."ccx

He continues to write on the first day of the week; "From the very beginning those who believed Jesus was the Christ gathered together weekly on the first day of the Jewish week, the anniversary of his being raised from the dead. ... This special day was reckoned by early Christians from sunset to sunset, as were all days according to Jewish custom. The first Christian assemblies were, therefore, most probably in the evening of the Sabbath."ccxi At this time, the first day of the week (Sunday) was still a workday. The switch from Saturday (Sabbath) to Sunday Evening, as Greg writes, came as follows; "Soon, however, Christians had their own special day—the first day of the week (Acts 20:7). On Sunday evening of the first day of the week and the end of a regular workday, those who believed Jesus was the Christ would gather in one of their homes, a primitive house-church, for a meal (1 Corinthians 11:17- 22)."ccxii This, of course, was largely for the breaking of bread (Eucharist or Lord Supper), not a regular Sabbath worship, for it was Paul's custom to go and preach in the synagogue on the Sabbath, during which the law was read and exhortations given (Acts 16:13; 17:2; 18:4). These meetings were later moved to Sunday Morning, as Greg explains; "In the early 2nd century, this Eucharistic ritual was moved to before dawn on Sunday, the first day of the week. This change may have been caused by persecution. A decree of Emperor Trajan forbade suspicious gatherings in the evening. A time before dawn was necessary because Sunday was still an ordinary workday."ccxiii This morning service included other worship activities and "Afterwards people went about their daily work and chores. **During the first centuries of Christianity the notion of resting on this special day was unheard of."ccxiv** *(emphasis mine).* On the title, "Sunday," Greg writes;

> **"The popular title, 'Sunday' is a contribution from the Germanic peoples and is an example of how culture and pagan traditions influenced Christian religious traditions.**

This title comes from pre-Christian worship of the sun. ...
This association of the Christians' greatest day with the sun is
also fitting because the sun is life-giving and never defeated,
an annual lesson experienced on the occasion of the winter
solstice."[ccxv] *(emphasis mine)*

I will live it up to you to chew that analogy and whether Sunday
worship tantamount to sun worship or not! Greg continues to say
that; "Sunday had no particular themes in early Christianity until the
seasons of the church year evolved."[ccxvi] This, of course, came when
the church was paganized (Romanized or Babylonized) from the
fourth century AD. At least, we see that early Christians met on both
days. They worshipped on the Sabbath (Saturday) and broke bread
on Sunday (First day of the week).

How did Sunday come to be regarded as the day of rest almost
an equivalent of the Hebrew Sabbath? Greg writes;

"During the first three centuries of Christianity there was no
particular tradition or discipline of avoiding work and other
activities on Sunday. ... It became popular to observe Sunday
as a day of rest only as the economic situation of Christians
improved. ... A weekly day of rest was also linked to a human
need, recognized by Roman civil authority, for a regular 'break'
from the monotony of work. **On March 3, 321, Emperor
Constantine ordered a weekly holiday on the 'venerable day
of the sun.' His motive, however, was probably based, more
on his devotion to the cult of the sun, as his father before him,
than on Christian conviction.** His decree did give this special
Christian day the same privileges enjoyed by pagan feast days
scattered through the year."[ccxvii] *(emphasis mine).*

This is the official link of paganism (especially sun worship)
with the worship of the Son on the sun's day of worship. So Christians
could worship the Son and pagans or Christo-pagans could also
worship the sun at the same time. That, friends, is Babylon, Babel-
-confusion; tares that look so closely like the wheat that the simple
cannot differentiate! Not to confuse Sunday with the Jewish Sabbath,

the Roman religion helped to make the distinction between the two. Greg continues to write;

"The motive for assembling for worship on Sunday, as we have seen, was not linked at first to the Jewish Sabbath and the Third Commandment [sic]. Nor was the motive refraining from physical work on Sunday. When early Christian writers interpreted the Third Commandment for the baptized, they counseled abstinence from sinful activity on Sunday and all days. **St. Jerome and later the Council of Orleans (538) condemned any connection between Jewish Sabbath laws of rest and the Christian Sunday.** It became increasingly common, however, to understand the Ten Commandments with a Christian content. **A church discipline enforcing Sunday rest became common as a result. In 589, the Council of Narbonne called for severe punishment including whipping, for anyone who worked on Sunday.** In 789, Emperor Charlemagne forbade all work on Sunday as a violation of the Third Commandment. This prohibition crossed over into universal church law."[ccxviii] (*emphasis mine*).

Thus, according to church tradition (Roman Catholic), Sunday is not the equivalent of the Jewish Sabbath, commanded in the Fourth Commandment, which the Catholics call the Third Commandment. [Catholics have erased the Second Commandment that forbids idol worship, since idols are the center of their worship. Just as Catholics have changed God's laws and the set times— the solar calendar (Dan. 7:25), and now have only eight of the Ten Commandments, Protestants who worship on Sunday equally have only nine of the Ten Commandments, since Sunday is not the Sabbath!]

Advent Wreath: Greg writes; "This custom originated with Lutherans in Germany in the 16th century and quickly became popular in other areas. **Along with the Christmas tree, it is probably an example of Christianizing practices popular from pre-Christian times.** There had always been a festival of burning special lights and fire at the end of November and beginning of December in Germanic lands as the darkness of winter becomes more severe."[ccxix] (*emphasis mine).* **The**

right term for these practices is syncretism--mixing pagan beliefs and traditions with Christianity.

Christmas: Greg also writes; "... **Christmas incorporates numerous pre-Christian traditions concerning the winter solstice** along with the legends of St. Nicolas that gave rise to the modern creation of Santa Claus."[ccxx] (*emphasis mine*). We note that concerning the birth day of Jesus Christ, no one knows the exact date, and there is remote possibility (if not near impossibility) that he was born in December! Greg explains that the choice of December 25 might have been due to the symbolism that the time portrayed. He explains;

> "Earthy symbolism is very powerful at this time of the year in the northern hemisphere. Each year Christians, along with the general population, noticed that beginning with the fall equinox, the darkness of night began creeping up on daylight as days became shorter and nights longer. At the winter solstice this situation changed and the light of day began again to defeat the darkness of night. The winter solstice occurred on December 25 on the Julian calendar and became the popular date for Christmas. ... a five-day pagan harvest festival of Saturnalia devoted to Saturn, the god of agriculture, occurred shortly before the winter solstice. It was celebrated with gift exchanges, feasting, and excesses."[ccxxi]

Another strong pagan influence that contributed to a December Christmas came from a Persian religion, Mithraism. Greg puts it this way;

> "Mithraism, a pagan sun cult popular in the Roman Empire during primitive Christianity, promoted this natural symbolism. Devotees of Mithra, a Persian deity, celebrated the birthday of their sun god with a festival called *dies natalis Solis Invicti* (Latin, 'birthday of the unconquered sun') at winter solstice. In 274, Emperor Aurelian proclaimed this Sun god the principal divine patron of the Roman Empire. He promulgated the feast throughout the empire in an effort to promote unity by way of a uniform monotheism."[ccxxii]

Thus, Christmas, though very popular as a Christian festival, is a veneer of paganism. This is a very hard nut for many to swallow, but we must always consider whether to obey God or men (our traditions, in this case, clearly from paganism). Greg concludes that; "Some popular Christmas traditions are considered religious but are only indirectly so. They reflect a Christianization of pre-Christian customs, especially traditions related to the winter solstice and the symbolism of light and dark in the northern hemisphere. This is the case with Christmas trees traditions and Christmas lights of all shapes, sizes, and colors."[ccxxiii] On the Christmas tree, Greg explains;

"Most Christmas traditions associated with evergreens and trees are related somehow to pre-Christian practices. The use of evergreens and wreaths as a symbol of life was popular already among the ancient Egyptians, Chinese, and Hebrews. **Teutonic and Scandinavian peoples worshiped trees and decorated houses and barns with evergreens at the New Year to scare away demons.**

The Christmas tree, as did so many other Christmas traditions, originated in Germany. ... Children were so delighted with this tree that parents were persuaded to have one in the home, especially when these plays were forbidden in churches because of abuses."[ccxxiv] (*emphasis mine*).

This is how the tradition of the Christmas tree came to be! Close to these are other traditions like the Mistletoe, the Holly, Poinsettia, Santa Claus, and a host of others. Other traditions also surround Easter (name of doubtful origin) like the fertility theme derived from pre-Christian pagan fertility cults with the symbolism of eggs and bunnies. Greg continues to write;

"In ancient Egypt and Persia friends exchanged decorated eggs at the spring equinox, the beginning of their new year. These eggs were a symbol of fertility for them because the coming forth of a live creature from an egg was so surprising to people of ancient times. Christians of the Near East adopted this tradition, and the Easter egg became a religious symbol. ...The custom of decorating trees outdoors with decorated, hollow Easter eggs originated in Germany.

Easter egg hunts, and even the egg-rolling on the White House lawn, are contemporary versions of egg games played on Easter for centuries in European countries. **Easter Bunnies:** Little children are usually told that the Easter eggs are brought by the Easter Bunny. Rabbits are part of pre-Christian fertility symbolism because of their reputation to reproduce rapidly. Their association with Easter eggs goes back several hundred years to vague legends in Germany. ...The Easter Bunny has never had a religious meaning."ccxxv

Other related traditions include: Prayers to saints, purgatory, memorialization of fallen heroes (memorial days), ancestral cults, which are all forms of ancestor worship in various forms among different peoples of the world, including much of Christendom.

Some Months of the Year: "January honors the Roman god Janus; March honors the Roman god of war; May was named for Maia, the Roman goddess of spring; June—Juno, the patron god of marriage; December honors Saturn, the god of harvest."ccxxvi

All this is tradition. And it is overt syncretism—paganism posing as Christianity. Christ strictly warned the Pharisees against nullifying the commands of God by their traditions. The same trap is well and alive 2000 years later! Beware! God had strictly warned the Israelites not to practice any of the abominations (especially pagan religious practices) of the Canaanites as they were going in to possess the land of Canaan. They were to wipe them out completely, together with such practices, including the worship of heavenly bodies; *"And when you look up to the sky and see the sun, the moon and the stars--all the heavenly array—do not be enticed to bowing down to them and worshiping things the LORD your God has apportioned to all the nations under heaven"* (Deut. 4:19; cf. 18:9-13). But the Israelites did not drive out completely the people from the land, and their religious practices became a snare to them, and they indulged in Canaanite pagan worship and idolatry. This was obviously the mistake of Christianity as it penetrated Europe. Instead of stamping out paganism and idolatry, paganism penetrated the Church (as we saw from the days of Constantine), and in many instances, these pagan practices were carried on, even until today, as Christian tradition. Patrick Johnstone sums it up as follows; "We need to stop mourning the decline of Christianity in Europe and many parts of the West and **realize that the coming of Christianity did not convert Europe, but 'baptized' the paganism that still has to be adequately confronted with the claims of Christ.**"ccxxvii (*emphasis mine*). We also need to understand that the use of the wreath was a pagan practice--in the worship of Zeus (Acts 14:13). **Paul had vehemently warned;** *"No, but the sacrifices of pagans [Gentiles] ar offered to demons, not to God, and I do not want you to be participants with demons"* (1 Co. 10:20). Behind all these pagan gods are demons, which we seem to acknowledge in subtle forms today in our traditions, words, and names. This paganism is even continuing today in the Church as Christian tradition, both in Catholicism and Protestantism. Should Christ visit the Church today, most Christians will reject him if he challenges these human and pagan traditions just as the Pharisees did 2,000 years ago. It is always important to ask, "If this is not found in the Bible, why am I doing it? Is it possible to disobey God by doing these things?" You must never treat such matters as trivial. You will be obeying men and demons (Satan) rather than God. In short, Roman Catholicism remained a Babylonian religion and Protestantism has largely remained a Teutonic religion. The current Western calendar and most of "Christian" tradition are still very pagan, a tribute to the European gods and demons. Christianity in some respect has remained a solar religion (sun worship). This is full-blown syncretism.

The East Invades the West.

We saw earlier how through the missionary efforts, Christianity attempted to make a headway in the East (Asia). We also saw how Christianity was regarded as a foreign influence or more still, as a colonizing tool. Christianity was not readily accepted by most Asians, Japanese, Chinese, Indians, and others. They already had established religions such as Hinduism, Buddhism, Taoism, Jainism, Shinto, etc. These religions that resisted Christianity, in many subtle ways, have rather made in-roads in the West in the last half of the twentieth Century more than Christianity did in the East. Rather than Christians evangelizing the East, the East is succeeding in de-evangelizing the West, as many in the West are abandoning the faith of their forefathers. Theosophy, the New Age Movement, Hare Krishna, occultism, and other cults, are all off-shoots of Hinduism or have borrowed largely from Hinduism and Buddhism, whose mysticism has been made appealing through practices such as Transcendental Meditation and Yoga. A survey of these religions, the cults, and the occult, shows one central theme: they teach that man is divine, and just needs to discover his divinity or God-realization, Self-realization, Self-actualization, Enlightenment, or discover the spark of the divine from within. Enlightenment, they believe, would show that the soul (*atman*) is identical with the universal soul (*Brahman*). This, of course, is Satan's old lie to Eve; "you will be like God" or "you will be gods." Mysticism is part and parcel of these Eastern religions and claims to be a pathway to true spirituality or a pathway to God whoever he is perceived to be.

The New "God" of All: MONEY

A survey across religions reveals that one thing happens to all religions with the passing of time, especially regarding the priesthood in general and worshippers in particular. There always seem to be a shift from the original founders' commands. They all seem to drift toward a new god: money; and from reality to hypocrisy. This is true of all world religions: Hindu, Buddhist, Shinto, Judaism, Islam, and even Christianity. This god, money, is the strongest; most influential; and the most worshipped god today across the religious spectrum. All religions have compromised in one way or the other to worship money. That is why Revelation records that toward the end of days (now), the whole world will worship the beast, probably because of her monetary grip over people, since almost everyone desires to have money and to live a wealthy, happy, and prosperous life. It is written: *"Men worshiped the dragon* [Satan] *because he had given authority to the beast, and they also worshiped the beast and asked, 'Who is like the beast? Who can make war against him?'"* *"... they did not stop worshiping demons, and idols of gold, silver,* [money] *bronze, stone and wood ..."* (Rev. 13:4; 9:20; cf. 18). We will recall that this is precisely what Satan demanded of Jesus; *"Again, the devil took him to a very high mountain and showed him all the **kingdoms of** *the world and their splendor. 'All this I will give to you,' he said, 'if you bow down and worship me.' Jesus said to him, 'Away from me Satan! For it is written: 'Worship the Lord your God, and serve him only'"* (Matt. 4:8-10). Jesus could not bow to Satan to obtain the splendor (money and wealth) of the nations. He refused to serve Satan. But where Jesus succeeded, mankind has failed terribly; they have bowed and served Satan by eating his bait, money. Jesus had categorically stated; *"No one can serve two masters. Either he will hate the one and love the other, or he will be devoted to the one and despise the other. You cannot serve* [worship] *both God and Money"* (Matt. 6:24). It is the attempt of the modern church to disprove Jesus' statement as she grasps for and worships wealth just as the world is doing; *"You say, 'I am rich; I have acquired wealth and do not need a thing.' But you do not realize that you are wretched, pitiful, poor, blind and naked"* (Rev. 3:17). As such, the riches and wealth are choking the fruitfulness of the church (of course, not all of the church—there is a remnant); *"Other* [seed] *fell among thorns, which grew up and choked the plants. ... The one who received the seed that fell among thorns is the man who hears the word, but the worries of this life and the deceitfulness of wealth choke it, making it unfruitful"* (Matt. 13:7, 22; cf. 6:25-34).

CHAPTER 11

THE STRIFE FOR WORLD DOMINATION IN THE MODERN ERA

"I looked, and there before me was a white horse! Its rider held a bow, and he was given a crown, and he rode out as a conqueror bent on conquest. … Then another horse came out, a fiery red one. Its rider was given power to take peace from the earth and to make men slay each other. To him was given a *large sword*" (Rev. 6:2, 4).

The strife for earth domination is as old as the Egyptian and Mesopotamian empires in the Near East. This, however, excluded places like the Americas, Sub-Saharan Africa, and the Far East (not as though there were no strives in these places). The age of discovery, beginning from the thirteenth Century, marked the modern era of strife for complete global domination. The impact of this was seen in colonialism as we discussed. However, that era did not see a single Western nation dominating the whole globe. This, of course, does not mean that they did not try to. To dominate the globe, any single European nation had to dominate Europe first, and the attempts to do so brought untold bloodshed and damage to Europe and the rest of the world. It is this era of strife, beginning with the French Revolution that I want to discuss here.

Let us imagine for a moment the animal world. Which is the strongest animal or king of the beast? Obviously, it is the lion, but I believe the other animals tried it out before they finally surrendered to the lion. Think of the world as a jungle full of many types of beasts and of various strengths. The animals in the jungle must have fought against each other so that each class knows its strength and which other class of animals it can or cannot defeat. By so doing, they now know who should bow to whom, and who roars in the jungle and every other beast hides, or who is the king of the jungle. These contests certainly arrived at the lion being the king of the beasts. But we may note that even as the king of the beasts, the lion, despite his strength, may not successfully handle bees and other similar insects! The nations of the earth in the modern era have been engaged in this fierce jungle fight and rivalry, and one by one, some have succumbed to the others, until there is at least, a king of the jungle, or is it? Being the king of the jungle is such a coveted position that no nation bows to the other, though they appear to do so. They may do it in public but secretly, they continue to find ways to beat the leading nation and climb to the top of the world. Because it is a coveted position, no one who holds it will ever live in peace and security. The position will continue to be contested for until the Lord Jesus Christ returns and puts an end to such strife, folly, and arrogance of men although after a thousand years, Satan will instigate the rebellion and strife again (Rev. 20:7-10).

The history of intrigue, war, and strife for domination, is as old as the history of mankind. Thousands of wars have been fought and the number has increased throughout the twentieth century, especially the last 100 or so years. In the beginning of modern man's history, God gave Adam the authority to rule over his creation (Gen. 1:28; Ps. 8:5, 6). But at that very beginning, Adam gave over that privilege of dominion to Satan, whose methodology to rule over the world is built on evil and murder (John 8:44). This evil began with Cain (who was of the evil one), who murdered his brother, Abel (Gen. 4:8; 1 John 3:12).

The first account of war in the Bible in Genesis 14 shows us that the desire to conquer and dominate; the formation of alliances; and the greed to grab plunder or booty was practiced from the beginning of human civilization. This spirit of empire building, making a great name for ourselves— heroes and men of renown (Gen. 6:1-4), and building towers reaching up to the heavens (self- magnification while despising God) in defiance to God's supremacy, has never abated since the beginning of mankind hitherto. The study of history is the study of war, conquest, and domination. Every group of people strives to be super-group or race by exerting their supremacy and arrogance over other groups or races of people. Space will not permit me to trace the history of wars for the past 6000 years. One of the themes of this book has been to trace western history as revealed to Nebuchadnezzar and Daniel, from Babylon, Medo-Persia, Greece, Rome, Barbarians, Papacy, and to Modern Babylon. For the modern era, Europeans not only strove for dominance among themselves, but they also equally strove to extend their dominance over the rest of the world by building overseas empires through colonialism. In their struggle, the European nations unintentionally passed on the baton to America.

The Bible frequently describes this strife for dominance as the churning of the seas or waters, or the raging of nations:

*"**Why do the nations conspire** [rage] **and the peoples plot in vain?** The kings of the earth take their stand and the **rulers gather together against the LORD and against his Anointed One.** 'Let us break their chains,' they say, 'and throw off their fetters"* (Ps. 2:1-3) *"**But the wicked are like the tossing sea, which cannot rest,** whose waves cast up mire and mud. 'There is no peace,' says my God, 'for the wicked'"* (Is. 57:20-21).

David cried out; *"Rebuke the beast among the reeds, the herd of bulls among the calves of the nations.... Scatter the nations who delight in war"* (Ps. 68:30).

*"Daniel said: 'In my vision at night I looked, and there before me were the **four winds of heaven churning up the great sea.** Four beasts, each different from the others, came up out of the sea'"* (Dan. 7:2-3).

*"And the **dragon stood on the shore of the sea. And I saw a beast coming out of the sea.** He had ten horns and seven heads, with ten crowns on his horns."* (Rev. 13:1)

*"Then the angel said to me, '**The waters you saw, where the prostitute sits, are peoples, multitudes, nations and languages"*** (Rev. 17:15).

We saw earlier that Daniel 7:7 depicted Rome and subsequent western civilization until the second coming of Christ. Roman dominance and supremacy were overcome by the Barbarians, but in its place the Papacy emerged, and persecuted the remnant church sending her to the wilderness. There was apparent peace with the Church on top and the kings of Europe in a kind of submission. The Holy Roman Empire survived for some time until European nationalism, during which the different ethnic peoples of Europe fought for their independence. Once they acquired their independence, they began to aspire for overseas empires. This resulted in the horrible and destructive history of colonialism, whose wounds and scars are still fresh in places like North and South America, and Africa (see chapter 12). The dragon and the gods had gone crazy! They were mad at the nations and bent on dispossessing and occupying them. The mystery of iniquity, which is the spirit of antichrist, was at work (2 Thess. 2:7, 8). The colonial impulse was first trade, but it later extended to the competitive spirit of building overseas empires under the pretext of bringing the white man's civilization to the backwards peoples (the white man's burden).

European history shows that this striving for dominance was on nationalistic lines. The main players as we have seen were the Portuguese, Spanish, Dutch, English, and French. Because the Germans and Italians were still scattered under the guise of the Holy Roman Empire, they came in late in the venture and would be the last to cause more havoc in the twentieth century.

Before modern democracy, championed by America, the nations of Europe were governed by kings—they were monarchies (monarchy is the form of government where the king or queen is head of a kingdom). As I said earlier, the wars of religion in Europe in the sixteenth and seventeenth centuries were more on nationalistic lines though under the guise of religion (Protestantism). The big picture of this modern strife is depicted in Revelation 6:2-4. The white horse depicts the American Revolution in as much as the nation founded in 1776 has been a militaristic empire, bent on conquest and continues to conquer. There is no biblical description that the empire of the rider on the white horse is conquered by any earthly power. The USA is the only earthly power that remains unconquered. She will eventually take on the Prince of Peace, who will defeat her but not with human power or arsenal;

> *"In the later part of their reign* [Age of the Gentiles], *when rebels have become completely wicked* [the current moral rebellion of this generation], *a stern-faced king* [popularly known as the Antichrist], *a master of intrigue, will arise. He will become very strong, but not by his own power. He will cause astounding devastation and will succeed in whatever he does* [bent on conquest; Rev. 6:2]. *He will destroy the mighty men and holy people* [capture or deceive the church and the Jews]. *He will cause deceit to prosper, and will consider himself superior* [Ezek. 28:1-19]. *When they feel secure, he will destroy many and take his stand against the Prince of princes* [Jesus Christ at the second coming]. *Yet he will be destroyed, but not with human power"* (Dan. 8:23-25).

Christ's victory over this western evil trinity (dragon, beast, and false prophet) and the rest of the world is recorded as follows; *"Then I saw the beast and the kings of the earth and their armies gathered together to make war against the rider on the white horse* [Jesus Christ] *and his army. But the beast was captured, and with him the false prophet who had performed the miraculous signs on his behalf"* (Rev.19:19-20; cf. 13).

There has been constant warring without rest between the kingdoms of the earth since the history of man. In the last stages of human history, the dragon has taken the stage and is ready to face the Lion of Judah as he did in the wilderness (Matt. 4:1-11). This is going to be the most interesting battle (Armageddon) of all time, in that the outcome of the battle was documented before there was man on earth, and the results were made known to believers in the Lamb. Another interesting thing is that the dragon-lion-bear-leopard quartet (Rev. 13) has every imaginable weapon of destruction ever devised by man, but the Lamb and his army have only one weapon: the truth, which is the Word of God (Rev.19:11-15; cf. Ps. 45:4)! He will soon assert his right to kingship and rulership of his Father's world.

The French Revolution

"When you hear of wars and uprisings, do not be frightened. These things must happen first, but the end will not come right away." (Luke 21:9)

One may argue for the legitimacy of the American Revolution, but the spirit of revolution that it set in place resonated in Europe and continues to resonate around the world today. The blueprint for internal political revolutions in rejecting monarchies began with the French Revolution. The spirit of this revolution can be likened to the description of the second horseman of the apocalypse; *"Then another horse came out, a fiery red one. Its rider was given power to take peace from the earth and to make men slay each other. To him was given a large sword"* (Rev. 6:4). The French revolution opened a new door of warfare, a door for men to slay each other within the same nation. It was a bloody revolution. The history of revolutions that followed is a history of men slaying each other; it is a history of bloodshed; it is a history of men slaying their own kin to assert their supremacy. It is a history of nations raging; a history of seas churning up. In fact, it is a history of the spirit of antichrist trying to assert dominion over the earth without Christ. The triumph of the French Revolution was the triumph of atheism, irreligion, and humanism over Christianity. It was this revolution that struck the dead blow on the Papacy setting it in decline. As is the case, each revolution is usually characterized by a political ideology. And since the eighteenth century, one ideology after another has risen in Europe: Napoleon, socialism, communism, fascism, Nazism, liberalism, and democracy (which triumphed over the others). The French Revolution came out of years of political dissatisfaction and struggle against feeble and despotic monarchies. The forerunners were the Enlightenment and the political philosophies articulated by the philosophers. The revolution had great impact around the world, especially in South America, and has served as a blueprint for several revolutions around the world since then.

Things Bringing The World Closer Together

Since the time of Prince Henry, the Navigator and the coming of Europeans to the Americas, the world has continued to shrink and to get closer. The underlying factor is commerce, which happens to be the cause of the eventual downfall of Satan and Babylon the Great (Rev. 18). This cross-continental commerce laid the groundwork for end-time Babylon the Great. The Industrial Revolution that began in Great Britain became the accelerator for bringing the world closer together as manufactured goods in Europe were carried abroad in search for markets and raw materials. As technology increased, new means of transportation were developed, even bringing the world closer, especially by the beginning of the nineteenth century. The steam engine, locomotive engine, rails, and steamships, made transportation easier; and the telegraph, telephone and fax, made communication also easier. The invention of the automobile and the airplane virtually made transportation very cheap. Indeed, they virtually made the world one—the precursor of the present global village.

Events Bringing the World Closer Together

The twentieth century was the century of world unity—the formation of a global community. Some of the events that have enhanced or sparked these efforts at unity were never intended for that purpose. Because the rider on the red fiery horse had taken peace from the earth and made men to slay each other (war and revolutions), there was need for global peace. Thus, the global empire arose because of petit empires trying to rise to the top of the world. It is apparent that at the turn of the twentieth century, no individual or nation was hoping of uniting the world under its thumb since the time of Napoleon. Nevertheless, the seas were churning. From the French Revolution, European nations struggled among themselves for supremacy in Europe. (The English had always struggled with the French for European domination, and Germany's attempts brought about the two devastating world wars). Great Britain had built a large and strong overseas empire much to the envy of her continental rivals, especially France. The English had succeeded to ward off the French in the New World by seizing their American empire in 1763.

The English had done same to the Dutch in the New World by 1664, thus remaining the major colonizing power in North America.[ccxxviii]

When Napoleon seized power in France, he hoped to become master of a united Europe as he began to build his military machine. At that time a new but old form of warfare began--the forming of alliances. [There seems to be one unmistakable trend in the history of these wars: once a country builds a strong military and is wealthy enough, war on perceived enemies is inevitable for any and every reason. Sometimes war is just fueled by the desire to build an empire.] Britain, in alliance with Austria and Russia, declared war on Napoleon's France. To the East, Napoleon defeated Austria and Russia and for a time become master of continental Europe after the treaty of Tilsit in 1807. Thus, France had her day as master of Europe. At this time; "The Holy Roman Empire was at long last abolished, and its hundreds of little principalities greatly consolidated."[ccxxix] French influence was felt all over Europe and "By 1808, all Europe except the British Isles and the Balkan peninsular ... was under French control or French influence. No conqueror has so dominated Europe."[ccxxx] So, under Napoleon, the French had their taste of European domination, though excluding Great Britain. Napoleon became a virtual dictator. This, however, lasted for a very short time. By 1815 at Waterloo in Belgium, Napoleon's dream came to a halt.

The spirit of domination (mystery of iniquity), at least in Europe, did not die with Napoleon. The Congress of Vienna (1814-1815) did its best to restrain France. The Austrian Prince, Klemes Metternich became the most dominant diplomat in post-Napoleonic continental Europe. In the alliances that emerged after Vienna, he determined to make "An international military police force that would suppress any liberal or national movements."[ccxxxi] The alliance (concert of Europe) succeeded to police Europe for a while until Great Britain disagreed with the Metternich system. However, Metternich's system continued to be successful over the Germanies--including Prussia and Austria. His rule was semi-dictatorial toward German nationalism--probably beginning a formal secret police (spies) that has become the hallmark of global influence today with countries that have global influence like Russia and America. Thus, Metternich, for a time dominated a large part of Europe.

Great Britain remained separated from continental Europe, thanks to her natural barrier of water, and would be the only European power to build a large and successful global empire. Thus, while not having dominated Europe, her dominance was felt to all the four corners of the earth. Her empire would at one time comprise ¼ of the earth's land and peoples.

World War I

All the tumultuous political revolutions in Europe built up to the first devastating clash in the strife for world dominance. This clash was of such a large scale that it was given a befitting name: World War I. It was the first time that most nations of the world, particularly European nations, engaged each other in battle. James had warned the believers; *"What causes fights and quarrels among you? Don't they come from your desires that battle within you? You want something but don't get it. You kill and covet, but you cannot have what you want. You quarrel and fight"* (James 4:1-2).

The Germans had suffered repression under the Metternich system. When the system crumbled in 1848, German nationalism began to burgeon. At the helm of German nationalism and military built-up (a military machine up to then unknown to the world) and campaigns, was the iron chancellor, Otto E. L. Von Bismarck. His efforts eventually unified the Germans into a single nation. Crushing France in a decisive war in 1871, "The German Empire had now [then] replaced France as the dominant power on the European continent and became a new rival of Great Britain for world hegemony."[ccxxxii] Thus, Great Britain felt threatened and,

> "In the face of Germany's swift rise to power and prestige, the British took renewed pride in their dominant navy and in their empire. ... many well-to-do Britishers thought themselves to be so superior to the other peoples of Europe that they became the most unpopular of all travelers on the continent. To some observers,

it appeared that Great Britain was as big a bully on the seas and overseas as Germany was on the continent of Europe."[ccxxxiii]

(This seems to be the same fate with America today). Despite this inflated pride and pump, Britain would finally be humiliated after WW II as America replaced her as the most dominant world power.

Meanwhile, the German Empire continued to grow; "The German Empire possessed the world's most powerful army, a large energetic, and disciplined population, a rapidly growing industrial machine, a fervent and restless national spirit."[ccxxxiv] With the rise of Germany, military alliances seemed the only secure thing to do. Germany entered alliance with Austria-Hungary and Italy, called the Triple Alliance, while Britain, France, and Russia formed the Triple Entente. The world was uneasy about Germany's strength; "As the industry and wealth of the German Empire came to match and complement the strength of her army, the rest of the world became increasingly uneasy."[ccxxxv] When Wilhelm II became the Kaiser of Germany, his policies, contrary to Bismarck's, became the precursor for WW I. Germany's supremacy was not only in military build-up, she had become a strong economic power such that;

"By 1914 Germany was a close second to Great Britain in industry and commerce; in many areas such as the production of steel and machinery, Germany far outstripped Britain. In the up-and- coming chemical and electrical industries and in scientific agriculture and forestry, Germany was far in advance of all other nations. Germany was also first in the application of science to industry and industrial scientific research."[ccxxxvi]

Thus, we see that, once an empire or nation has a strong army and a thriving economy, its next goal is to rise to the top of the world and assert its supremacy, and any other empire or nation that stands on their way must face its wrath. It was true then, and it is true now! This competitive spirit is the real cause of wars. Such precursors always lie hidden until an opportunity arises. The immediate cause of WW I, the assassination of Archduke Ferdinand and his wife, only served as the last straw on the camel's back, to unleash the military showdown that was inevitable, given the military build-ups of the last three decades among the great powers. By August 1914, Europe, and ultimately the rest of the world, was on full-scale war, and by 1918, when the war was over, Europe was in a pool of blood and the dreams of western civilization almost shattered. It was a demonstration that the civilized can also act like barbarians when they aspire to rise to the top of the world. The war ended with the Treaty of Versailles, which treated Germany very harshly, only planting a seed that would germinate into the Second World War two decades later.

The Road Back to Babel

"Then they said, 'Come, let us build ourselves a city, with a tower that reaches to the heavens, so that we may make a name for ourselves and not be scattered over the face of the whole earth'" (Gen. 11:4).

"For you know very well that the day of the Lord will come like a thief in the night. While people are saying, 'Peace and safety,' destruction will come on them suddenly, as labor pains on a pregnant woman, and they will not escape" (1 Thess. 5:2-3).

The peace settlement at Versailles was the first human attempt in modern history to bring about peace among the nations in a global scale. It was the first attempt in which different nations came together or united for control of the globe. No longer were nations to work in isolation, but in unity to foster world peace. The result of the peace talks was the formation of the first universal/international organization, the League of Nations. Although the peace conference included many statesmen from allied nations, the British, French, and American representatives, were the most recognizable. Of the "Big Four," Woodrow Wilson of the USA was the most prominent, especially with the enunciation of his fourteen points, the last of which was the brainchild behind the formation of **the League of Nations.** He called for a general association of nations "that would settle peaceably the tensions and conflicts that were certain to arise in the future."[ccxxxvii] **So a kind of a world government was set up to arbitrate global conflicts.** However, this world government was weak and bound to fail in as much as the USA as well as other bigger powers such as Britain and France, were unwilling to surrender their absolute sovereignty to a world government. In fact, the United

States did not even join the League, and Great Britain and France soon lost faith in the League. Nevertheless, the foundation stone was laid, and nations had come together and united saying; "Let us unite and live in peace and safety." They were conspiring together against the LORD and his Anointed One (Ps. 2:1-3). The road to Babel was being paved.

Communism/Socialism (Anti-God; Atheistic)

As early as the second half of the eighteenth century, following the industrial revolution, some thinkers had begun to advocate for economic planning that based "society on cooperation and community rather than competitive individualism."[ccxxxviii] They advocated for the abolition of private property, and the doing away of economic competition, which they saw as the source of much evil. Some advocated communal living, which some tried though it was short-lived.

The nineteenth century saw a different form of socialism that was organized and revolutionary—that advocated by Karl Marx. He deplored the spirit of competitive capitalism, which would continue into the twentieth century with the rise of corporate business. The industrialists paid the workers as little as possible but got from them as much work as possible (a practice that has continued until today even with the existence of labor unions). Even among the companies; "The giant corporations were ruthless in dealing with each other. In this era of unrestrained competition, the big and strong frequently destroyed the small and weak."[ccxxxix] (This practice has only gotten worse in our days!). Socialism continued to mushroom as Marx continued to write; "According to Marx, historically, capitalism was doomed to be overthrown by a revolution of the working class and replaced by a socialist system."[ccxl] Socialism gained ground in some western countries like Germany and France.

Marx's propositions finally took root in Russia in the Bolsheviks revolution of 1917. By this time, Russia was lagging in the industrial and political advancements in Western Europe and the United States. World War I in a way precipitated the communist revolution in Russia. Increasingly under the dictatorial hand of Czar Nicholas

II, and in the face of Russian losses against Germany, Russia deteriorated into social unrest. During this chaos, the Bolsheviks seized the opportunity and rose to power. Their strategy of success was the genius of Lenin: the party was neither open nor democratic, but rather consisted of elites, a highly trained and constantly purged group dedicated to Marxist revolutionaries. The socialist revolution included both the industrial working class and the peasants. Once they gained power, the Bolsheviks abolished capitalism and nationalized both industry and agriculture. Church land was expropriated by the state. Before this time, the Church in Russia had become too close to the Czarist government despite its dictatorship over the centuries. [This is always a grave mistake for the church to become too close or identified with a particular government. The mistakes and failures of the government are always considered as those of the church that supported it. Such a government always falls with the church. It was the case with the French Revolution and would be the case for any church today that closely identifies with a particular government. It seems most people never learn the lessons of history!]

The communist experiment went on through the 1920s and 1930s, during which Stalin eliminated as many opponents as possible. Nevertheless, the Communists had their own successes—the rapid industrialization and mechanization of agriculture (Stalin's five-year plans), so much so that by 1941, "The Soviet Union was the fourth largest industrial power in the world. In a number of categories, it had surpassed both Great Britain and Germany and was second only to the United States."[ccxli] The Communists introduced an aggressive and successful educational system; eliminated class distinction and discrimination against women.

However, the effects of communism on the entire globe have been devastating, especially wherever it came face to face with western capitalist democracy. From the start, the Communists were determined to spread their ideology to the whole world. This immediately provoked the antagonism and isolation from the capitalist West, though at some points, they had to cooperate in order to contain Nazi Germany. Things took a different turn after World War II, with the beginning of the infamous Cold War. The manifestation of the Cold War around the globe resulted in carnage after carnage, during which millions lost their lives (in Asia, South America, and Africa).

The most devastating effect of Communism was the persecution of Christians wherever it took root. Communism was/is out rightly anti-God, that is, atheistic and humanistic. Many Christians have been killed by the Communists in proportions similar to those killed by the medieval Papacy;

"The Church in Russia has suffered the most severe and sustained persecution of any nation in recent history. All deaths in the *gulags* (prison camps) between 1920 and 1990 are reckoned at 20 million; a further 16 million perished *en route* to them— many were Christians. It is reckoned 200,000 Christian leaders were martyred and a further 500,000 imprisoned. There were 100,000 church-owned buildings in 1920 (mainly Orthodox); by 1940 only 1,000 were in use by Christians, the rest being seized or destroyed. Structures and ministries were emasculated or manipulated, leadership cowed into compliance and compromise, Christians discriminated against, their children harassed and denied educational opportunities, and millions consigned to years of imprisonment, exile or psychiatric 'treatment.'"[ccxlii]

Democracy/Capitalism (Anti-Christ)

I must start this section with a disclaimer. It is not my intention to evaluate forms of government. I just want to treat democracy as a form of governing ideology that has influenced the world for the past 200 years or so. Democracy is an old ideology developed by the Greeks in their city-state of Athens. It did not remain a popular form of governance as time passed on. In subsequent empires, emperors and monarchs governed by personal whims and the whims of their nobilities. Some kings from the medieval period even claimed to rule by divine right. Democracy is closely associated with freedom and the rights of the people. Its precursor in modern times was the Magna Charta, in which the king of England granted some powers (concessions or rights) to the parliament (people). Democracy was in effect, a rebellion against monarchism. It emphasizes the rights of the people to life, freedom, and property; the right of the people to choose their own leaders; and the rule of law. No government may violate these fundamental rights and principles. According to the proponents of democracy, any government that violates these principles should be overthrown by the people. Thus, in a democracy, the power comes from the governed. The story of the United States is a story of democracy in progress to some extent, though with its own ups and downs and limitations. That statement needs some qualification because the USA is not a democracy per se—it is a Republic. A democracy stands if most people are civil and law abiding. When most people lack integrity, decency, and civility, anarchy will prevail in the name of democracy. It may be rather surprising that democracy promoted abroad (majority wins the vote) by the USA is not the same democracy practiced at home (democracy within a republic)!

Because democracy is closely tied with capitalism (free enterprise), it has brought in an era of immense wealth, and has become the undisputed political ideology of this age. As is the case today, no one can fight democracy in as much as no one can fight success. Democracy is the accepted form of government for most of the world except for some pockets of communist resistance here and there, Islamic theocracies, and a few dictatorships. In some cases, the spread of democracy secretly undermines foreign governments, topples some, even eliminates some foreign leaders, and where possible, it is forced on a people. It is the new form of colonial imperialism.

Capitalistic democracy offers a compromise to Christianity, unlike communism that persecutes it, but in many instances, democracy neutralizes the effectiveness of Christianity. Many Christians may seem to hail democracy as a God-given governmental system--the only alternative, but in a subtle way, democracy has virtually destroyed Christianity. Democracy may seem to offer some sense of freedom, justice, fairness, and security, but it has destroyed the cross and the carrying of the cross. Just look at Christianity in democratic Western Europe and lately North America. While capitalistic democracy has brought about untold wealth, it has at the same time swept professing Christians off their feet with materialism. Capitalistic democracy has come to define life in terms of economic success (more is better) in clear contrast to the biblical definition of life. Jesus said; *"Watch out! Be on your guard against all kinds of greed; a man's life does not consist in the abundance of his possessions"* (Luke 12:15). Economic success seems to be the measure of the true value of man and the ethos of life. It may be too late for Christians to realize how, by embracing democracy and capitalism they have embraced the world and love for the world. Should Christians therefore oppose democracy? Absolutely not! Christians are not called to oppose any governments. But we must be wise in any system devised by man, where Jesus Christ is not the center. Democracy, as the god of the new age, in short, is anti-Christ, unlike communism that is anti-God.

Hitler and the Third Reich (a Prototype of End-time Antichrist)

We saw earlier that by the beginning of the twentieth century, the seas were churning as the waters (and its waves) surged back and forth. The beasts out of the sea continued to juggle among themselves to see who will rise to the top of the world. The settlements at Versailles after WWI were not satisfactory to the belligerents, and the world government (League of Nations) was too weak to assert power over the nations. The big powers did not cede their sovereignty (at the time the USA was practicing its policy of Isolationism) over to the League. Aspiration for world dominance continued to mushroom in continental Europe. Between 1918 and 1938, Germany and Italy, and to a lesser extent, Spain, continued to stir up emotions that resulted in another blood pool—World War II. New political ideologies would arise during this period. The most notable were Fascism and Nazism.

Fascism was a political ideology that was basically authoritarian and dictatorial and was backed by the military. Benito Mussolini of Italy was the first to build a fascist state. Italy, though with the allies, did not get what she wished for during the Peace Settlements at Versailles. Italy had desired "acquisitions east of the Adriatic and the Turkish and German provinces in Asia and Africa ...,"[ccxliii] but these were denied her. They were hoping to build their own overseas empire, and thus, "These frustrations were severe blows to Italian national pride."[ccxliv] Things took a downturn in Italy, and during this, Mussolini rose to power with his fascist party. The ideological ethos of fascism was nationalism-- "malignant nationalism run wild."[ccxlv] At the heart of this nationalism, Mussolini asserted: "'**The goal,' he cried, 'is always Empire! To build a city, to found a colony, to establish an empire, these are the prodigies of the human spirit**.... Discipline at home that we may present the granite block of a single national will.... War alone brings up the the [sic] highest tension all human energy and puts the stamp of nobility upon the people who have the courage to meet it.'"[ccxlvi] *(emphasis mine)*.

The cry is evident, "Empire!" Why? Why found a colony? Why establish an empire? Why make war? To assert their dominance and hegemony over the other peoples. **This cry of empire or colony is at the heart of all nationalistic and imperialistic expansionism or dominance, that is well and alive today, though it may be veiled.** Each nation, especially the superpowers, fosters this spirit of nationalism and imperialism as they consider themselves better than others, and hence, qualify to assert their dominance over the peoples of the earth. To build this empire, Mussolini built a powerful army and navy (as is the case with imperial superpowers today), thus, recovering Italy's national pride.

Nazism: After Versailles, a weak and liberal democracy was imposed on Germany. Reparation demands on her were considered unbearable. The US helped them pay most of the reparations by providing loans. However, "The spirit of revenge toward the former Allies filled the hearts of many Germans."[ccxlvii] In the midst of these frustrations, Adolf Hitler became a figure of national hope for Germany. Hitler was a nationalist socialist, who borrowed more in ideology from fascism. His ideology (Nazism) was built around the basic philosophy of the German master-race and hatred for the Jews. This master race according to him was "superior to and destined to conquer and rule other peoples."[ccxlviii] (This echoed the Anglo-Saxon sentiment in the USA, both nationally and in the church, that the Anglo-Saxons represented the most civilized people, and therefore, were obliged to bring their superior civilization to the rest of the inferior races of the world; in fact, to Anglo-Saxonize the world as others did put it). Here, the echo again is evident: conquest and domination of all other peoples! This was the spirit of world dominion—the spirit of antichrist! Hitler's foreign policy was stronger than his domestic policy (as is the case with any nation aspiring to dominate the globe. It has been the spirit of empires since the beginning of time). To achieve this world dominance; "Militarism, indomitable will, pride, aggressiveness, and brute strength were held to be virtues; [while] gentleness, peacefulness, tolerance, pity, and modesty, vices."[ccxlix] Has such a spirit stopped since then? We see it today with the superpowers! The Nazi political maneuver was dubious and they "exaggerated and exploited the Communist threat."[ccl] [Some politicians always take advantage of an external threat (whether communism or terrorism) to guise their domestic ineptness].

Hitler was the epitome of dictatorship. Free speech, press, rival political parties, were all abolished. He had a sophisticated secret police and an elaborate propaganda machine. Youths were indoctrinated—the Hitler-youth. He empowered German nationalism and promoted an anti-Christian (antichrist) ideology, though he manipulated and controlled religion (you must always be watchful of any politician, who manipulates religion to his own ends). Clergy who resisted were eliminated. Hitler, however, achieved much internally—superhighways, airfields, hospitals, apartment buildings, and many other things, were built. Thus, the people came to trust such a patriotic nationalist, who vowed to elevate the German people to the top of the world—surely a nice feeling! Hitler was in league with Italy and Japan, who both aspired for world hegemony, too. In their attempt to rise to world dominion, they plunged the world again into another world war, WW II.

World War II (1938-1945): A Time of Terror

Often, causes of wars can be complex to discuss since most causes advanced may not really be the reason for a war. Germany emerged from WWI defeated and was reduced to nothing by the Versailles Peace settlements. The burden on her was enormous and her sense of national pride was terribly marred. This would prepare the way for war again. The Germans were just waiting for an opportunity to assert their supremacy again.

The USA had emerged as the strongest power both militarily and economically after WWI. Although the Americans pioneered the formation of the League of Nations, they did not become an active member. In the 1920s, she was practicing the policy of Isolationism. America's refusal to join the League eventually led to the failure of the League, especially when the USA did not support Britain and France against Japanese aggression on China. This action or inaction helped convince Mussolini and Hitler that they could safely launch aggressions of their own. [In this respect, is there reason to believe that America's isolationism was one of the indirect causes of WWII? In a sense, the USA helped to kill the League she helped to found, that is, by her refusal to help Britain and France against Japanese aggression.]

Mussolini began by invading Ethiopia and in his thinking; "This was to be the first step in the restoration of the ancient Roman Empire."[ccli] *(emphasis mine)* Thus, we see that it is not a stretch to say that European nations seeking to build overseas empires represented the Roman Empire going abroad, which confirms Daniel's description that the fourth world empire (Rome) will devour the whole earth, trampling underfoot, and crushing anything in its path. Mussolini's action provoked economic sanctions (Article XVI of the League), which could have only succeeded with the cooperation of the USA. However, isolationism prevailed in America and American oil companies continued to sell oil to Italy. [Economic sanctions would become a tool in the hands of the Global Empire, especially the USA, to punish nations that do not comply to global Babylon. The Bible records this about the beast out of the earth (USA); *"He also forced everyone, small and great, rich and poor, free and slave, to receive a mark on his hand or on his forehead, **so that no one could buy or sell unless he had the mark**, which is the name of the beast or the number of his name"* (Rev. 13:16-17). Throughout the rest of the twentieth century up to this very moment, every nation that does not comply to international demands or cooperate with Global Babylon, must be ostracized, and levied economic sanctions—not being able to buy or sell. It is useless to continue to push this prophecy into the future when it is being fulfilled before our very eyes!]

Germany, on her part, began by occupying the demilitarized Rhineland against the terms of Versailles. Britain refused to help France. Civil war broke out in Spain and became a testing ground for Mussolini and Hitler's new weapons as they supported General Franco of Spain. By 1938 Hitler began his military march toward Eastern Europe: Austria, Czechoslovakia (which was in alliance with Russia and France). Hitler was appeased at the Munich Conference, especially by British and French Premiers, who granted Hitler the Sudeten areas of Czechoslovakia without Czech or Russian notice. Despite the appeasement, Hitler overran the rest of Czechoslovakia. He signed a peace pact with Russia (Stalin) to guarantee Russian neutrality as he attacked Poland. When Hitler attacked Poland, Britain and France declared war on Germany, thus sparking WWII.

Germany continued its assault with victory over victory: Poland, Denmark, Norway, Luxembourg, Netherlands, Belgium (though with heavy resistance—Britain and France came in in support of Belgium). France attacked and this led to partial surrender from Germany. Britain, although partially defeated stood its ground. Hitler began to overrun Russia, but winter halted him though he announced partial victory. As if German havoc was not enough, Japan, in her military aggression in December 1941, attacked the USA (that was still tied down by Isolationism) at Pearl Harbor. At this time, the die was cast, and the world powers (in the jungle strife for world supremacy) were all out to settle who was going to be king of the jungle through military conquest. It was as though the gods had gone crazy, the seas were churning, and world dominance was up for grasp.

Hitler's dream almost came true for a while. Like Napoleon, he almost dominated all of Europe.

"By 1942 Hitler ruled most of continental Europe from the English Channel to Moscow. He had initiated his 'New Order'--basically a program of racial imperialism--in the lands he controlled. The conquered people were used according to their ranking in Hitler's racial hierarchy. Those more directly related to the Nazi conception of the 'Aryan race,' such as the Scandinavians, the Anglo-Saxons, and the Dutch, were treated well and would supposedly be absorbed into the Nazi Empire as partners with the

Germans. The 'Latin races,' such as the French, were considered clearly inferior but tolerable as supportive cogs in the New Order. Slavs were toward the bottom of Hitler's ranking; they were to be isolated, shoved aside, and treated as slaves. Large numbers of Russians, Poles, and others were removed from their lands and turned into slave laborers, more often than not perishing under the harsh conditions of their new existence.

Lowest on Hitler's scale were the Jews and such other groups as socialists, gypsies, intellectuals, Jehovah's Witnesses, and the mentally ill. These people were systematically hunted, rounded up, transported to concentration camps, and exterminated."[cclii]

[We will note that racism has always been at the heart of Satanism— when a particular people think of themselves as better and superior to others, and therefore should degrade them, especially through subjugation—slavery. Satan, in his beauty aspired to raise his throne above the stars of God, that is, to raise himself and his people above the rest of the peoples of the world; Is. 14:13]

The attack on Pearl Harbor brought the USA fully into the war-- and things began to change in favor of the allied forces. The Atlantic Charter guaranteed that the Allied forces were not fighting for territorial gain. A union of nations and the Big three--Britain, USA, and Russia, fought fiercely against the Axis headed by Germany and Japan. Russia forced Germany to retreat until Russia entered Berlin. However, Russia had lost at least 20 million people. The Anglo-American forces defeated the Axis in North Africa, and assaulted Germany from the English Channel. The Normandy bombardment on June 6, 1944 (D Day), finally led to German surrender on May 8, 1945.

In the Pacific, Japan was still holding out, but was steadily driven back by the better American forces. On Japan's main Island, "The United States decided to use the bomb to shock Japan to surrender. On August 6, 1945, the first atomic bomb to be used in warfare destroyed the Japanese city of Hiroshima…. August 9, [1945] the second and last atomic bomb then in existence demolished the industrial city of Nagasaki."[ccliii] This forced Japan to surrender on August 14, 1945.

By the usage of the atomic bomb, the statement was clear: men had produced the most dangerous weapon of mass destruction and would use it. It was literally fire raining down from heaven! *"And he performed great miraculous signs, even causing fire to come down from heaven to earth in full view of men"* (Rev. 13:13). This ushered in the destructive and evil era of nuclear weapons that has plagued the world since then. Although there is noise and camouflage about nuclear disarmament, no nuclear power will ever disarm until the King of kings arrives. They will only do so when the elements burn up in the day of the Lord; *"But the day of the Lord will come like a thief. The heavens will disappear with a roar;* **the elements will be destroyed by fire,** *and the earth and everything in it will be laid bare.... That day will bring about the destruction of the heavens by fire, and* **the elements will melt in the heat"** (2 Pet.3:10-12). Although there is also noise that nuclear weapons must not be found in the wrong hands, it is certain that there are no right hands to possess nuclear weapons in as much as the atomic bomb was used. How right are the right hands?

Christians who pretentiously hide behind nuclear arsenal are self-deceived. They are in the wrong army, **for to the LORD it is *"Not by might nor by power, but by my Spirit, says the LORD Almighty"*** (Zech. 4:6). Such Christians have substituted the power of the Holy Spirit with nuclear power, while at the same time deceiving themselves that the possession of such weapons serves as a deterrence. The reality is that the possession of such weapons continues to provoke and fuel other nations to aspire and develop nuclear weapons. You cannot defend yourself with a gun and deny another person from defending himself with a gun, too. **There will never be any nuclear disarmament as long as the present nuclear powers maintain their stockpiles and as long as they write the rules of the game.** How long are we going to keep deceiving ourselves and others?

The aftermath of WWII was devastating. About 30-50 million lives were lost and untold mass destruction. Neither Germany, Italy, nor Japan, rose to the top of the world. Their empire building aspirations had all shattered. Britain, Russia, and America were raised to the top, with America above them, ushering in a new era of domination. America had indeed, like Charles Martel, saved the civilized world from tyranny. Nevertheless, the struggle between American capitalism and Russian communism, would usher in another era of war and carnage (see Cold War ahead). The end of the war brought about the disintegration of the British and French overseas empires as colonialism ended (or did colonialism end? It only gave birth to indirect control and manipulation—neocolonialism). With the difficulties facing Britain, the British Empire began to dismantle (it formerly consisted of ¼ of the world's land and peoples!). Many of her colonies gained independence. Her old glory (the sun had begun to set over the empire over which the sun never set) began to fade; "Furthermore, it was difficult for Britishers to adjust to their greatly diminished place in the world. Many could still remember the glamorous days when Britain ruled the seas and an empire over which the sun never set."[ccliv] She would lose first place as the foremost industrial nation and go through many political and economic setbacks as the decades passed by, with escalation of violence and lawlessness even right down to the 1980s. What goes up must come down. Nevertheless, the British Empire remained in an undercover form—the British Commonwealth.

France was also badly affected and humiliated. To add to this was the effect of the US-Russian cold war on her. Her overseas empire began to crumble as well with humiliating wars with Indochina and Algeria. However, almost all independent former French colonies voted to remain with the French Union. Such were the losses of WWI and many more!

Again, we want to ask; "Where do wars come from?"; *"What causes fights and quarrels among you? Don't they come from your desires that battle within you* [the greatest of these battles is the desire to dominate!]*? You want something but don't get it. You kill and covet, but you cannot have what you want. You quarrel and fight"* (James 4:1-3a). We are reminded of Hitler's thirst for living space for his super-race. And in our modern day, we see how the **covetousness for oil** is at the center of wars in the Middle East!

The Ticking Clock of the Time of the End

The end of WWII led to the formation of many organizations aimed at world unity or world government, both political and religious. All these organizations are directly and indirectly against God's plan for the "Age to Come."

Birth of The United Nations Organization (UNO):

"Now, brothers, about times and dates we do not need to write to you, for you know very well that the *day of the Lord will come like a thief in the night. While people are saying, 'Peace and safety,' destruction will come on them suddenly, as labor pains on a pregnant woman, and they will not escape"* (1 Thess. 5:1-3).

"*Peace and safety*" were the cry and yearning of the world after seeing the devastation caused by war. It was and still is their hope that wars will come to an end. That is why the UNO was founded. But that dream has never come true and will never come true until the Prince of peace arrives. It was decreed from heaven that; "*The people of the ruler who will come will destroy the city and the sanctuary.* **The end will come like a flood: War will continue until the end, and desolations have been decreed"** (Dan. 9:26). Not many people, that is, sane people, want war, not me; but things that cause wars will continue to happen as we have seen in James 4:1-6. [The desire to dominate, greed, covetousness, pride, folly and arrogance, and madness or insanity, etc., will continue to rage in the minds of the naïve and simpletons] It was for world peace that the UNO was founded. The world needed peace, co-existence, and interdependence. At the Yalta Conference after the war, the United Nations Charter was signed by the Big Three: Churchill of Britain, Roosevelt of America, and Stalin of Russia. Not everything was agreed upon smoothly by the Big three—especially Russian influence in Eastern Europe. Disagreements will spill over to tension and the nuclear standoffs of the Cold War.

The United Nations has had its successes and failures. Its agencies like WHO, UNESCO, etc., have benefited and continue to benefit the world greatly. Nevertheless, the UNO represents nations untied together (world government) against God and his Anointed (Ps. 2). They honestly believe that they can achieve peace without Christ or his constitution (Bible).

Birth of the Cult of the American Republic:

The Roman Republic had the cult of the state (Dea Roma), at the top of which was the Emperor, Lord of the Empire. He was worshipped and some emperors were deified after their death. The emperor was the Pontifex Maximus of the religion of the empire. This idea was borrowed by the Papacy, where the pope became the supreme Pontiff (Pontifex Maximus), holding both spiritual and political power such that denying one was denying both. As we noted earlier, from the French revolution, nationalism took on religious characteristics, which followed in the footsteps of the Roman spirit. The careful stipulation of separation of church and state in the USA ensured that spiritual and political authority would always be separated. However, the merging of nationalism or patriotism with Christianity as one, has blurred that distinction in the USA. The fact that patriotism and Christianity have come to be viewed as one and the same thing has made nationalism of religious proportions or significance. Steps toward Union of Church and state in the US are delicate to trace, but it is evident that a civil religion is in vogue. When citizens come to pledge allegiance to a flag and the Republic, it is evident that the Cult of the Republic has been born. [Recall that this is precisely what God will demand of his people from the nations, as Isaiah puts it; *"In that day five cities in Egypt will speak the language of Canaan and **swear** [pledge] **allegiance to the LORD Almighty"*** (Is. 19:18)]. This is, therefore, an imitation of God or usurpation. To make things deceptive, "Under God" was inserted to blind those who are uncritically patriotic. Christ asks us not to swear (pledge) at all, and anything beyond "yes" and "no" is from the evil one or Satan (Matt. 5:33-37). The irony here that illustrates that "God" on the pledge has nothing to do with the God of the Bible is that the same God that children acknowledge in school in the pledge cannot be prayed to at the same spot! Who is that God? He is the God of pluralism, the generic god, not the God of the Bible! Thus, like Rome, the American Republic has the cult of the state, except that instead of deifying the president, the Republic itself is deified (Think again before you fire your missile at me, it may boomerang!).

Scripture clearly teaches on the place of Government (Rom. 13:1-7; 1 Peter 2:13-17). But which government? To be sure, Christ lived under the Roman empire, where Caesar was worshipped as lord or son of god. Jesus respected its laws and accepted its authority (John 19:10-11), and calls on his followers to do likewise, for government is instituted by God. However, he made a clear distinction between God and Caesar. The apostles who commanded the believers to respect and honor government, were under Rome and Roman governors. These same governors persecuted them, and even Christ had stated that believers will be persecuted by governors (Matt. 10:17-20; Rev. 10:9-11; 1 Tim 2:1ff; 2 Co. 11:16ff). Christ does not say that we should obey only democratic governments; he requires us to obey and honor all governments or any governing authority, if doing so does not tantamount to giving Caesar what is God's. Thus, even the communist or Islamic theocracies, must equally be respected and obeyed. After all, the Roman government that the believers were commanded to obey was anything but democratic. We must not make the mistake to think that it is only about 200 years ago that governments that deserve our respect were founded. In respecting and obeying governments, however, what is due God, that is, worship, reverence, and unwavering allegiance, must never be given to government or governor or nation; this would be idolatry. Should you want to argue that nobody worships or reveres his country, be reminded that the whole world is worshipping the dragon and the beast (Rev. 13:4). This does not necessarily mean building temples and having orders of worship. You worship whatever takes first place in your heart! If it is the empire or nation, that's worship.

There are some Old Testament examples of individuals like the three Hebrew men and Daniel, who respected and obeyed a pagan government—they were, in fact, even part of it. However, when nationalism and patriotism took on idolatrous characteristics, they defied such nationalism (Dan. 3; 6)! The three men refused to bow to the national statue (symbol of the Babylonian pride) and were thrown into a furnace. Daniel refused to pay homage to the king (in our case the empire) and was thrown into the lions' den. It requires extraordinary and exclusive devotion to Christ and spiritual discernment (which is available to all who want it and search for it) to be able to detect such nationalistic idolatry. To be sure, ALL nations are under the leadership of the devil (Matt. 4:8,9; Rev. 12:9; 1 John 5:19). Therefore, never follow a state blindly. Again, do not be cajoled by the appellation "Christian" nation or the usage of the word "God."

Birth of World Council of Churches (mostly a North American effort):

We saw in the previous chapter that there were attempts at Church unity prompted by missionary zeal and cooperation, which led to the formation of the World Council of Churches in 1948. Positive as this might have appeared to be, it was the beginning steps of Protestant return to Rome (the Papacy, whose wound had begun to heal). John records the following about the Papacy.

> *"One of the seven angels who had the seven bowls came and said to me, 'Come, I will show you the punishment of the great prostitute* [Papacy], *who sits on many waters. With her the kings of the earth committed adultery* [many nations have their ambassadors and embassies in the Vatican State] *and the inhabitants of the earth were intoxicated with the wine of her adulteries* [false doctrines and idolatry].' ... *There I saw a woman* [Papal Church] *sitting on a scarlet beast* [Europe—EU] *that was covered with blasphemous names and had seven heads and ten horns* [this beast is identical with the dragon or Satan; Rev. 12:3; 13:1-2]. *The woman was dressed in purple and scarlet, and was glittering with gold, precious stones, and pearls* [she is very rich, and purple her official color]. *She held a golden cup in her hand, filled with abominable things and the filth of her adulteries. This title was written on her forehead: MYSTERY BABYLON THE GREAT THE MOTHER OF PROSTITUTES* [false doctrines] *AND OF THE ABOMINATIONS OF THE EARTH. I saw the woman was drunk with the blood of the saints* [papal persecution], *the blood of those who bore testimony to Jesus"* (Rev. 17:1-6).

John equally records the following about **Protestant return to the Papacy;** *"Then I saw another beast* [Protestant USA; and there is a significant Catholic population in the US], *coming out of the earth. He had two horns like a lamb* [Predominantly Christian], *but he spoke like a dragon* [Satan]. *He exercised all the authority of the first beast on his behalf* [swaying political and religious power in one, like the Papacy, with many Catholic traditions unchanged], *and made the earth and its inhabitants worship* [serve or acknowledge Catholic traditions; see section on Western Syncretism] *the first beast, whose wound* [Papal capture and political power broken in 1798] *had been healed* [Papal political resurgence since the 1930s after the Lateran treaties with Mussolini]" (Rev. 13:11-12).

Christian political activism and especially, the battle over moral issues, have brought Catholics and Evangelicals together in the United States.[cclv] Their united effort has virtually united the two beasts of Revelation 13, Mystery Babylon the Great, and Babylon of Revelation 17 and 18. This union has been precipitated by the culture wars in the US. We will note that genuine Christianity is concerned about absolute morality and ethical behavior, but genuine morality and ethical behavior in themselves do not constitute genuine Christianity. The Pharisees were highly and genuinely moralistic and ethical to the letter, but they missed the Son of Man! It is possible that the overt culture wars have nothing to do with biblical Christianity; it has everything to do with religion, which is what Babylon is all about.

Birth of European Economic Community (EEC ➜ European Union):

The USA virtually reshaped the West Germans, organizing them into a free state different from the East under Soviet communist control. They reconstructed the German economy and that of the rest of Europe. The Marshal plan provided economic assistance or aid for the reconstruction of European economies and resuscitated the ravished and devastated Europe. This laid the groundwork for European economic integration. There was increase cooperation among Western European countries leading to the formation of the Organization of European Economic Cooperation (OEEC), and the European Coal and Steel Community. There was also political integration: "In 1949 several nations in Western Europe took an initial step toward political integration by setting up the Council of Europe. Many hoped that this organization would develop into a parliament of Europe with real political power."cclvi [As we now know, this dream and hope has come true with the European Union and a parliament] From the Coal and Steel industry formed by France and Germany, and later joined by Italy, Belgium, Luxembourg, and the Netherlands, came the European Economic Community (Common Market). "Its purpose was to eliminate tariff barriers, cut restrictions on the flow of labor and capital, and generally integrate the economies of the member nations."cclvii The success of this organization has continued to increase until today. Nation after nation continued to join the original six—Great Britain, Ireland, Denmark, Greece, Portugal, Spain, and now, some Eastern European nations have joined. The European Union now consists of about 27 member-states, and more are on the waiting list.

The Cold War (1945-1989)

*"Jesus answered" 'Watch out that no one deceives you. For many will come in my name, claiming, 'I am the Christ,' **and will deceive many**. You will hear of wars and rumors of wars but see to it that you are not alarmed. Such things must happen, but the end is still to come. Nation will rise against nation, and kingdom against kingdom. There will be famines and earthquakes in various places. All these things are the beginning of birth pains'"* (Matt. 24:4-8).

A new kind of struggle emerged after the defeat of Germany and her belligerents. The great powers that emerged from the war began to compete against each other for superpower status. This struggle was mostly between the United States and Russia, though it had global ramifications. This struggle came to be called the "Cold War." It was characterized by the stockpile of the most dangerous and sophisticated weapons of mass destruction (WMD) the world has ever known and will ever know— the nuclear arms race. It was a war between liberal democratic capitalism and totalitarian communism. Russia, and her satellite states, that came to be known as USSR (Union of Soviet Socialist Republics), strove to spread communism in Western Europe and the rest of the world, while the USA strove to contain such influence and to spread liberal democracy (or call it freedom) to the rest of the world. "It was a war fought in almost all ways except open military conflict, and the threat of military force was always present. At times, the Cold War became violent, but the two superpowers never came together in direct armed combat."cclviii Europe became split between West and East by what Churchill of England had described as the iron curtain "dividing a free and democratic West from an East under totalitarian rule."

The US and her Allies favored free elections in Eastern Europe, but the Soviet Union wanted control, in which she succeeded as most of Eastern Europe turned to communist hands and control by 1950, including East Germany. America's effort was captioned in the Truman Doctrine—supporting free peoples everywhere, who are resisting attempted subjugation from outsiders. "The United States would draw a military ring around the Soviet Union and its satellites from Manchuria to Norway. It was a policy of military containment."cclix In the course of events, diplomacy between the United States and the Soviet Union came to a halt. Both did not agree on the control of atomic weapons, and thus, embarked on the production of such nuclear weapons, whose spread has plagued the world hitherto. The possession of a nuclear weapon has come to mean the boosting of national ego, and every warrior-nation aspires for one.

The Marshal Plan launched by the US to reconstruct Europe was greeted with skepticism by Russia: "The Soviet Union regarded the Marshall Plan as an American scheme to shore up Europe's and its own tottering capitalism, to lure away the Soviet satellites, and to make the European countries economic dependencies of the United States."cclx The USA took further steps to consolidate her military strength against the communist Soviet Union by organizing the military alliance known as North Atlantic Treaty Organization (NATO) with other Western European countries. NATO has continued since then until today. The Soviet Union countered the Marshall Plan and NATO by establishing the Council for Economic Mutual Assistance and the Warsaw Pact Organization. Thus, Europe was split into two: the West under US leadership and the East under Russian leadership.

> "Both sides were pitted against each other in a world-wide war of propaganda. Political struggles almost everywhere, whether purely internal matters or not, became potential fields for a victory or defeat in a Cold War competition. This competition expanded during the following decades to the non-Western world and to a variety of fields not usually thought of as political, from exploration of space to the Olympic games."[cclxi]

France became caught in the middle of the Cold War. She felt as though her world prestigious position was eclipsed by the superpowers and thus struggled for her identity and prestige independent from American domination. The French leader, who emerged after WWII, De Gaulle, sought to restore French hegemony:

> "In foreign affairs, de Gaulle set out to restore France's 'greatness'—its prestige in world affairs and its hegemony in Western Europe, He also sought to make Western Europe a 'third force' independent of both American and Soviet domination. To achieve these ends, he created at great cost an independent nuclear striking force, cultivated cordial relations with Germany, withdrew France's military from NATO because of its domination by the United States, and vetoed Great Britain's entry into the European Common Market because of its close ties to its Commonwealth associates and to the United States."[cclxii]

How does this relate to our subject matter? The nuclear arms race was the strife for greatness, prestige, world hegemony, and domination. A nuclear striking force boosts national ego, supremacy, and a sense of competition as a recognizable world power. The possession of nuclear weapons was and has always been a matter of national ego and international prominence! Every nuclear power commands some respect from other nations. During the Cold War, China exploded its first nuclear device in 1964, and India in 1974, boosting their national egos, respectively.

This West-East Cold War manifested itself in many wars around the world (wars and rumors of wars): the Korean War (1950-53); Cuban Missile Crisis, in which Russia placed its missiles in Cuba that almost resulted in all-out war; Vietnam, where the Northern Vietnamese were supported by communist Russia and communist China, and Southern Vietnam by the USA. It is reported that:

> "The Vietnam war was one of the most destructive wars in history. Millions of Indochinese had been killed, maimed, or left homeless--their lands and forests ruined for the foreseeable future. The intervention of the United States in the civil war in Vietnam for the purpose of containing communism (Russian and Chinese, it was believed) resulted in greater bombing [by the USA] and destruction than in World War II."[cclxiii]

(During the same period, the US supported a dictatorship in Pakistan). Tensions soon gave way to peaceful co-existence—cooperation rather than confrontation. The Berlin Wall, that finally collapsed in 1989, and the Soviet invasion of Afghanistan in 1979, were all marks of the Cold War. Other continents like South America and Africa, experimented and flirted with communism, much of which still lingers on today. In all the instances, tensions existed with the West, particularly the USA, and in some cases, the USA supported dictatorships in these continents just to counter communism.

It was the Reagan administration that took a tougher stand toward the Soviet Union and communism, reviving Cold War rhetoric and increasing arms build-up, and the deployment of American missiles in Europe. Reagan and Pope John Paul II, eventually contributed to the downfall of communism in 1989.

The Cold War had a strong psychological effect on Americans even though they were experiencing hitherto unknown prosperity: "During these prosperous decades after World War II the American people were often harassed by anxiety, unrest, fear, and violence. … they were seized by a morbid fear of the Soviet Union and communism. Many journalists, military leaders, politicians, and business and professional people exploited this fear."[cclxiv] [It is always the case that such people take advantage of external threats to hold the people hostage or launch their careers. It was communism then, and terrorism now] The collapse of communism, far from anything, has not brought about the end of wars and rumors of wars. Since the 1990s, the world has seen many civil wars and international conflicts than ever before, and within the same period, a new threat to international peace, terrorism, has heightened.

Independence From European and American Imperialism

Much of South America had gained her independence in the early 1800s, even before Africa was colonized. In Africa, the ancient kingdom of Ethiopia had remained independent until the Italian invasion. Liberia, founded by Freed Slaves in 1847, had remained independent during the colonial period. Generally, from 1957-1962, most African nations became independent from the European imperialists, except a few. These later gained independence through fierce fighting and resistance by the Europeans and White minorities within their borders. After her emancipation, Africa's economy steadily declined since the 1960s (time of her independence) until now, perhaps due to ineffective leadership and poor economic planning. Corruption and embezzlement have helped to aggravate the situation. After independence, a new form of colonialism— neocolonialism (a new form of exploitation and slavery), developed, in which most African nations have largely remained economic dependencies of European nations. This dependency is a direct product of colonial policies and continues to help Europeans to deplete African resources and raw materials, and to benefit from her cheap agricultural products.

Many Asian nations became independent too within this period. In 1971, East Pakistan gained independence as Bangladesh, then Ceylon, Burma, and Malaya, from Britain. The Dutch East Indies gained independence from the Dutch as Indonesia, after some resistance. Then, India from Britain; Indochina as Vietnam from the French after years of war, with America aiding France. France also freed Laos and Cambodia, which America undertook to establish its power within them. With independence, came dictatorships, that have plagued and continue to plague these developing nations.

The last half of the twentieth century has equally seen the development of more things that continue to bring the world together. There has been accelerated technology; for instance, TV, Space satellites, Computer, and internet; easy flight across oceans, international corporations (MTC), just to mention a few. Within this time too, there are more signs that point to the second coming of Jesus Christ. Some of these include increase in erratic weather, earthquakes, pestilences and new diseases, famines, persecution, and others.

Islam: Then and Now

Islam Then:

One would have to begin by asking, "Is Allah identical with the God of the Bible? That is, Yahweh or Jehovah, who has been manifested in the flesh as Jesus Christ?" From my knowledge of Islam, I can say that the answer to that question is an emphatic, no! If Allah was Yahweh (Jesus Christ), his followers would not be antagonistic to both Jews and Christians (although in Islam's original tenets, the peoples of the BOOK are to be respected). In short, Christianity is built upon the truth that God was manifested in the flesh and dwelled among men in the person of Jesus Christ. **Thus, Jesus is 100 percent deity, and therefore equal with God. Islam denies that truth and reduces Jesus Christ to a mere prophet of God and a human being, who is even less in status than Muhammad.** The Islamic motto affirms the unity of Allah and Muhammad's preeminence over all prophets; "There is no god but God (Allah) and Muhammad is Allah's prophet (messenger)." Islam acknowledges people like Abraham, Moses, and Jesus Christ as prophets; "But Muhammad is the last and greatest of them all, the 'seal' of those who appeared before him. None is his equal, either in knowledge or in authority; none has received or handed down so perfect a revelation."[cclxv] In every respect, therefore, Allah is different from Yahweh, who is manifested in Jesus Christ. Of the prophets and revelation, it is written; *"In the past God spoke to our forefathers through the prophets at many times and in various ways, **but in these last days he has spoken to us by his Son,** whom he has appointed heir of all things, and through whom he made the universe"* (Heb. 1:1-

2). **There is, therefore, no revelation or prophet that supersedes Jesus Christ. Either the Bible is right about Jesus Christ and Islam wrong, or Islam is right and the Bible wrong.** Time will prove who is wrong.

"Allah (meaning God or 'the deity,' like the Hebrew *El* and the Babylonian *Bel*; ...) was vaguely conceived as the creator, a far-off high-god, venerated by Muhammad's tribe, the Ouraysh."[cclxvi] Central to Islam is the Ka'ba, or "cube," a holy shrine in which is found a black stone that was venerated in Arabia, which was believed to have fallen from heaven from the days of Adam. This holy shrine was an ancient shrine (in Arabian pagan polytheism) that was adopted by Muhammad into Islam. However, Mohammad was vehemently against all forms of polytheism, propounding the unity of Allah (the core of Islam). Islam is a devout and moralistic religion, epitomized in the Five Pillars of Islam (The Creed, Prayer, Almsgiving, Fasting during Ramadan, Pilgrimage).

Islam began as a religion of conquest and domination, both spiritually (by the prophet) and militarily (political theocracy). Muhammad began by subduing Medina, Mecca, surrounding Arab tribes, and then, the entire Arabia, through warfare. Thus, the sword took care of those who hesitated to swear allegiance to the prophet and his message and mission. Islam expanded beyond Arabia by the sword. Their first campaign against Damascus (Syria) brought them head-on with Christians (in the Byzantine Empire). Next in the conquest line was Jerusalem, then the whole of Palestine, Egypt, and North Africa, and then Spain. They would have overrun the whole of Europe, but they were stopped by Charles Martel in 732 AD at the battle of Tours. Thus, from about 622 AD to 732 AD, Islam almost overran the Mediterranean world. To the Far East, they penetrated Iraq and Persia, and went as far as India, and to the Northwest, Asia Minor. **In short, Islam was an empire on the move, aimed at world conquest and domination.** It was and still is, a religion of dominion, that seeks to dominate or subdue the world in submission to Allah. There is, therefore, no doubt why Islam clashes with those who dominate the earth, a position they have always coveted or strove for.

After the death of Muhammad, there were internal power squabbles as to who was the legitimate successor to the prophet. The Islamic empire did not remain a unitary political structure. The empire eventually fell apart into separate autonomous political states. Four significant Islamic empires later arose: the Uzbek, the Safawi, the Mughal, and the Ottoman. The Ottoman empire became very strong and large, covering the whole of Asia Minor, part of Eastern Europe, Palestine, and Egypt. It survived until WWI, after which it was broken up.

Islam: A Sect of Judaism and/or Christianity?

This may be an interesting connection to make! Is there a sense in which Islam can be regarded as a sect of Judaism and/or Christianity, assuming for the moment that Allah is just the Arabic name for God? Given that Islam, in many respects, seems to be a reaction to or an attempt to improve or correct, or even pollute and twist Judaism and Christianity (especially Jesus' birth, deity, death, and resurrection), it will not be far-fetched to assert that it could be considered a sect of both. I understand that adherents of all these three religions might be furious at me for making such a connection, but evidence seems to support the claim. It is not clear (and perhaps only clear to Muhammad) how Muhammad became receptive to ideas of God paralleling those of Jews and Christians. For instance, believe in angels, last judgment, and eschatology--last day (one of the Hadiths claims the 12th Mahdi to come is Jesus. This is the case with especially the Sunnis, but not the Shi'ites).[cclxvii] The belief is that Jesus will come back to earth at the end of days, kill the Antichrist and establish the religion of Islam. He will then rule for 40 years and be buried beside Muhammad. These events will happen in the "Final Hour" at the close of history. This hour is hidden but there are some characteristics that can hint the time is near: unnatural disasters, moral decadence, disappearance of godly wisdom, drunkenness, sexual sin, injustice, rampant moral corruption, less truth and honesty and piety; then Messiah will come and destroy the false messiah and establish peace and righteousness on earth (sounds very much like Christian eschatology, right?).

How does Islam view Judaism and Christianity? Evidence show that Islam began with an attitude of friendliness toward Jews and Christians (Peoples of the Book). But this attitude changed with time, especially as they charged Jews and Christians for breaching their covenants with God. They claim these two religions have corrupted their original Scriptures by concealing God's word; verbally distorting the message of their books; not believing all parts of it; and not knowing what their own Scriptures really teach. They also charge Christians of wrong doctrinal beliefs like the incarnation, deity of Christ and the Trinity (hence polytheism), original sin, sacraments, images, and other church laws. As such, Muslims claim that the Qu'ran fulfills and even supersedes the incomplete revelations of Jews and Christians. At the end of the day, to some Muslims, Jews and Christians are only unbelievers—infidels.

Muhammad's high regard for the "Book" and "Peoples of the Book" (Jews and Christians) may imply that he was well acquainted with the Book (Bible) itself. Evidence shows that he was at least influenced by Nestorian Christians. (As we saw earlier, the Nestorians believed that there were two natures and persons in Jesus; the human born of Mary, and the divine was not). **Since Muslims acknowledge that before Muhammad's revelations, he had received truths and moral laws made known through the prophets such as Abraham, Moses, and Jesus, it implies that he was acquainted with or accepted Judaism and Christianity.** Even if one denies that Islam is not a sect of these religions, I perceive that it could very well be, or at least, is an eclectic of Arabian pagan beliefs fused together with Judeo-Christian beliefs, and Muhammad's visions.

The following evidence further authenticate the fact that Islam in a sense, is a sect or an outgrowth of Judaism and Christianity, though deviant in many respects.

First, in respect to monotheism and parallel practices and claims to the prophets, one can conclude that these two religions served as an inspiration to Islam. There is a striking similarity between the Hebrew *shema*; *"Hear, O Israel: The LORD our God, the LORD is one"* (Deut. 6:4), and the Islamic motto; *"la ilaha illa Allah—There is no god but God."* Thus, all three religions are committed to the unity of God, and are vehemently opposed to any form of polytheism or idolatry (making an image to represent God).

Secondly, by every indication, Muhammad was influenced by Judaism and Christianity before he received his revelations and/or formulated his belief system; "He had apparently been struck by the belief common to both Jews and Christians that there would be a last judgment and a punishment of idolaters by everlasting fire. The one true God, they said, could not be represented by an image but only by prophetic spokespersons."[cclxviii] Khadija, Muhammad's first wife, and her cousin, Waraqa, and Muhammad's slave-boy, Zaid, who had some influence on Muhammad, were all Christians or well acquainted with Christianity.[cclxix]

Thirdly, Gabriel and Michael are both angels in Judaism and Christianity. Muhammad believed it was Gabriel who spoke to him, though he doubted himself and the revelations for a while. But Muhammad, "… finally came to look upon himself as being miraculously enough, a true prophet (*nabi*) and apostle *(rasul)* of Allah, that is to say, a messenger of the one and only true God already known to the Jews and Christians."[cclxx] The question is "Did Gabriel really speak to Muhammad?" Only Muhammad and God know the answer to that question. But if Gabriel spoke to him, then, Islam is a sect of both Judaism and Christianity.

Fourthly, Muhammad's message echoes Judaism and Christianity's message, especially teachings on morality and the last day and final judgment. Islamic teaching is rigorously devoted to religious duty and right conduct (though in a legalistic sense), whether Muslims live up to it. Central to Islamic belief is believe in one God, the Last Day, angels, the Book (Christian Bible), and the Prophets. There is extensive teaching on giving of alms to the needy and poor; respect to parents; no murder, especially infanticide and abortion; respect of others' property, especially orphans; good conduct in marriage; non-aggression (though Islam spread by the sword!); no wine or gambling; and the like.

So, why did God give birth to Islam? Or why did God allow Muhammad to found Islam? Did God just decide to reveal himself to Ishmael's descendants in a different manner to keep them separate until Christ (Mahdi) returns and bring them in? God had promised Ishmael; *"And Abraham said to God, 'If only Ishmael might live under your blessing!' ... And as for Ishmael, I have heard you; I will surely bless him; I will make him fruitful and will greatly increase his numbers. He will be the father of twelve rulers* [could this explain the teaching about the twelve Mahdis in Islam?] *and I will make him into a great nation"* (Gen. 17:18, 20). Again, in Genesis 21:13,17-18, we read; *"I will make the son of the maidservant into a nation also, because he is your* [Abraham's] *offspring. ... God heard the boy crying, and the angel of God called to Hagar from heaven and said to her, 'What is the matter, Hagar? Do not be afraid; God has heard the boy crying as he lies there. Lift the boy up and take him by the hand, for I will make him into a great nation.'"* **God always keeps his promises, and we cannot underestimate this promise of making Ishmael into a great nation.** We can only marvel at the great history of Arabs and the fact that they sit on the black gold (oil) of today, which is greatly coveted and fought for by the West. Could it be true that by the sixth century AD, Christianity had become so corrupted as we saw in our earlier narrative (the papacy and its idolatry) and men therefore needed new revelation? As it is recorded in Acts 10:34-35; *"Then Peter began to speak: 'I now realize how true it is that God does not show favoritism but accepts men from every nation who fear him and do what is right."* Did Islam really supersede Judaism and Christianity as Muhammad and his followers claim? Are the Christian Scriptures corrupted, misunderstood, and falsified to suite the pagan concepts brought into the church by pagan Rome? Has western syncretism corrupted and polluted Christianity?

Islam Now

Islam is no doubt, a universal monotheistic religion with a large following (about 1.3 billion) and is still growing (by proselytism at a rate of 2.17 percent in contrast to Christianity's 1.43 percent). The Islamic empire consists of about 57 countries united in the Islamic Conference, and all other Muslims around the world. One can only ask, "Is the old dream of Muhammad to subdue and dominate the whole world under the will of Allah still the aspiration of Islam today or not?" Though united in a sense, Islam has its own internal and sectarian squabbles (especially the Sunni and Shi'ite sects) and seems to be struggling for identity and a universal expression because nationalistic expressions differ from country to country. For instance, Egypt, Saudi Arabia, Iraq, Iran, Pakistan, Indonesia, Morocco, and others, have their own different nationalistic expressions of Islam. The Islamic Empire (Islamic Conference) or Islamic nations lack a united political will (which they have sought to establish—Pan-Islamic Unity, Arab League, etc.) to perhaps, achieve Allah's universal theocracy?

Terrorism

One aspect of Islam that has drawn international attention and is embroiling the whole world today, is terrorism. How can a religion of universal brotherhood and peace bring such unrest and havoc to planet earth? There is no simple answer to that question. Much of the answer though, has to do with some historical events that had planted the seeds of hatred that have never been reconciled. A few that deserve mentioning include the following.[cclxxi] First, it was the Muslim initial advance into Western Europe that was stopped at the battle of Tours in 732 by Charles Martel. Second came the Christian assault on Muslims during the infamous crusades of the medieval period. Third, was the Turkish Ottoman invasion and occupation of Eastern Europe for a long time (about 1,200 years). Fourth, was the European colonial domination of many Muslim lands, under whose shelter emerged the state of Israel, whose existence continues to fuel Muslim hatred. Fifth, Muslim hatred resulting from their failure to wipe out Israel during the Yom Kippur war of 1973. Muslims continue to see the West, particularly America, as protectors and supporters of Israel. Lastly, Muslims abhor and detest what the perceive as the invasion of immoral Western culture into the Muslim World and society, especially through the Media and movie industry. To many Muslims, there is no difference between Hollywood and the "Christian" West. There could very well be a disdain for what appears to be Western democratic imperialism that threatens to destabilize Islamic theocracies.

These, and many other events, have inspired some Muslims (or Muslims) to use religion to carry out their wickedness and evil (and unfortunately, some Christians have done and still do the same mistake today. We must note that the Christian/Western assault on Islam, for instance, the Crusades, and other western actions, are not representative of biblical Christianity. They have more to do with Satan than with Jesus Christ, who never mandated his followers to take up arms to advance his cause--not then, not now!). **While we have seen that God promised great blessings to Ishmael and his descendants, there is a striking prophetic pronouncement about his fate;** *"He will be a wild donkey of a man; his hand will be against everyone and everyone's hand against him, and he will live in hostility toward his brothers"* (Gen. 16:12). Talk about terrorism and hatred for the Jews by the descendants of Ishmael, there is no blueprint than this! The Bible further says; *"Altogether, Ishmael lived a hundred and thirty-seven years. ... His descendants settled in the area from Havilah to shur, near the border of Egypt, as you go toward Asshur.* ***And they lived in hostility toward all their brothers"*** (Gen. 25:17-18; TO THIS VERY DAY!). The Ishmaelites and Jews are from one blood, Abraham. They share the same DNA and genes. Solomon says *"An offended brother is more unyielding than a fortified city, ..."* (Pr. 18:19). It is easier to reconcile a city than an offended brother! Ishmael's descendants obviously believe it was unfair for God to give the promise of blessing to Isaac, thirteen years, Ishmael's junior, as sons of Abraham. The solution to the Jewish-Palestinian or Arab problem lies in the hands of one person, God himself. As an outsider, beware when you meddle in their affairs, for the brothers may reconcile and turn against you.

Sometimes or even most often, it is not religion that is bad, but individuals that use religion to do evil under the guise of religion or use religion to justify their evil and wickedness (recall that some White Christians in the United States used the Bible to defend their enslavement of Negroes, segregation, and racism). Modern terrorism might very well have arisen from the frustration of the inability to realize the Islamic old dream—subduing the whole world in submission to Allah and establishing Islamic hegemony and supremacy over the world. At the heart of this is the belief in "Jihad" or holy war, and the justification to carry it out against perceived enemies (infidels), and sometimes, there is ambition for territorial gain. Even without desire for territorial expansion, there is the desire to raise the crescent above the world, and whoever stands in the way or stands on top of the world, is ruthlessly attacked. Terrorism is an extreme form of this Jihad, especially directed against the West in general, and the USA in particular, because of what they deem western immorality and promiscuous libertinism, and support for Israel. So, what do the terrorists believe? Kill in the name of Allah? Kill the infidels and go to paradise?

Islam/Terrorists Versus the West/USA; A Clash of Worldviews?

Is the West and/or America identical with Christianity? Is the appellation "Christian Nation" or "Christian West" deceptive and confusing? Are both Western "Christians" and Muslims wrong in the usage of these appellations? To equate America with Christianity is a grave mistake and a misnomer. It is great confusion that has caused untold damage to both Christians and Muslims. These two entities (Christianity and America) have nothing in common (except for apostate Christianity that identifies national goals and patriotism with Christianity). Christianity and America are 180 degrees out of phase and set their agendas following opposing masters. Christianity is under Jesus Christ and receives its orders from him, and America, like any other nation on planet earth, is under Satan. To miss this fact would lead to great deception that will end up in the wrong destination with drastic consequences. Again, one may pause and asked; "Is the Muslim accusation of America as having been given over to immorality, promiscuity, lasciviousness, concupiscence, wantonness, immodesty, indecency, and supremacist imperialism, true? Is biblical Christianity for or against these vices?

A clash of civilizations?

Is terrorism simply a product of being uncivilized or hater of civilization? Are Muslims that uncivilized? To answer those questions affirmatively will imply lack of understanding of what is going on, and even an historical mistake. In the medieval period (the

dark ages in Europe), Islamic knowledge and advancement exceeded
that of the West. The Muslims had made great strides in the study of
antiquities, the classical writings, and in science, than the Christian
West. As Noss writes;

> "The Christian West came to be grateful for these Arabic writings.
> When the Muslim conquests had ended and the Mediterranean
> basin ceased to be in turmoil ..., the Christian West found itself far
> less informed than were the Muslim lands about Plato, Aristotle,
> medicine, mathematics, astronomy, and science generally. ... But
> beyond this the considerable contributions of Muslim science
> and philosophy were also discovered. By rendering this service,
> the Muslim world greatly stimulated the development of Western
> thought."[cclxxii]

Thus, the issue of Islamic terrorism is not that of being uncivilized.
To simply label terrorists as uncivilized will never get to the root of
the problem. After all, what does it mean to be civilized? There are
home-grown terrorists even in the best supposedly civilized societies,
who commit homicides in great numbers.

A clash of opposite moral systems?

There is no denial (except for those who have nothing to do
with reality) that the West has been swept over by wantonness and
evil concupiscence, and what Hollywood portrays on morality seems
to be the norm rather than the exception (at least, it is passionately
consumed by many). It is an extreme form of moral depravity. On
the other hand, Islam is an expression of rigid morality, steeped in
legalistic suppression. Sadly, some western Christians (or are they
really Christians?) have come to accept Hollywood (which is a direct
opposite of biblical morality) as the norm and consume it more than
they do the Bible. As such, Muslims have come to identify so-called
"Christian America" with Hollywood. It seems that to the Muslim,
America is Hollywood, and Hollywood is America. And therefore,
the moral depravity portrayed by Hollywood has become the window
through which the Muslim sees America (militaristic imperialism not
excluded). This misnomer is very destructive, both to the American
and to the Muslim. Some American Christians regard America as

a "Christian" nation, and most Muslims have come to the same erroneous conclusion, and therefore, regard everything American as "Christian." Who is right and who is wrong? Without a doubt, both are terribly wrong, and unless both have a correct and true view, and make a distinction between America and Christianity, there will never be an end to the Muslim-American fight. [A note on personal observation: if entering heaven was a matter of devoutness and external morality, more Muslims might probably enter heaven than would "Christians." Christian libertinism has abandoned biblical morality and decency]. Lastly, can Islamic theocracy ever co-exist with western democracy and its version of freedom?

God and Terror?

This is a delicate, sensitive, and difficult issue at this time in human history to discuss. For a beginning note, we must understand that God uses evil to judge evil. As we saw earlier, he used the proud and warring Assyrians to judge the Israelites (Northern kingdom), and in turn used the ruthless, impetuous, and proud Babylonians (the hammer of the earth), to judge Assyria and surrounding nations (Hab. 1:6-11; Jer. 27:1-7). Concerning the fall of the economic giant and tyrant, Tyre, God says; *"I am going to bring foreigners against you, the most ruthless of nations* [like terrorists]; *they will draw swords against your beauty and wisdom and pierce your shining splendor"* (Ezek. 18:7). Surprising still, it is stated that; *"Surely the wrath of men brings you* [God] *praise, ... "* (Ps. 76:10).

The word terror obviously did not come into existence from Islamic terrorism. Terrorism is an old atrocious behavior from time immemorial. Besides the verse in Ezekiel quoted above, what does the Bible say about terror? Or does terrorism preclude the fact that God is not sovereign and is incapable of averting it? Or, if God is still sovereign, why does he allow terrorism and how does it play into his overall plan? [We must be reminded that there are many people capable of and do perform terrorists acts and murders, who may be considered as civilized and who have nothing to do with Islam. It is a sad note that Americans kill each other with guns more than in any other western industrialized nation, with homicides in their thousands annually. This civil unrest and crime wave happened in ancient Egypt because Egypt was lifted against God, and God himself caused this to happen to them; *"I* [God] *will stir up Egyptian against Egyptian— brother will fight against brother, neighbor against neighbor, ... The Egyptians will lose heart, and I will bring their plans to nothing; they will consult the idols and the spirits of the dead, the mediums and the spiritists."* Again, God states that, *"On that day* [day of the LORD] *men will be stricken by the LORD with great panic. Each man will seize the hand of another, and they will attack each other."* (Is. 19:2-3; Zech. 14:13)]

Connect the Following:

1. God exclusively and emphatically states that if there is terror in the city, the people should come and consult him for he himself has caused it! *"When disaster comes to a city, has not the LORD caused it?"* (Amos 3:6).

2. God says that he creates evil and disaster in respect to raising up Cyrus to attack and capture Babylon; *"I form the light and create darkness, I bring prosperity and create disaster; I, the LORD, do all these things"* (Is. 45:7).

3. **When the people disobey God and reject his word, he brings terror on them.** To the Israelites he said; ***"'But if you will not listen to me and carry out all these commands, and if you reject my decrees and abhor my laws and fail to carry out all my commands and so violate my covenant, then I will do this to you: I will bring upon you sudden terror, wasting diseases and fever that will destroy your sight and drain away your life ...'"*** (Lev. 26:14-16). As was the case, Israel rejected God, his laws, decrees, and commands, and God brought terror upon her. God has not changed nor is he a respecter of persons-- reject his laws, terror will be your lot!

4. *"For this is what the LORD says:* **'I will make you a terror to yourself and to all your friends** ..." (Jer. 20:4).

5. *"Although **I had him spread terror in the land of the living**, Pharaoh and all his hordes will be laid among the uncircumcised,*

with those who killed by the sword, declares the Sovereign LORD" (Ezek. 32:32).

6. About the Persians, who were to destroy Babylon (in the day of God's wrath), the LORD said; *"I have commanded my holy ones; I have summoned my warriors to carry out my wrath*--those who rejoice in my triumph. ... The LORD Almighty is mustering an army for war. They come from faraway lands, from the ends of the heavens--the LORD and the weapons of his wrath--to destroy the whole country. Wail, for the day of the LORD is near; it will come like destruction from the Almighty. Because of this, all hands will go limp, everyman's heart will melt. **Terror will seize them, pain and anguish will grip them; they will writhe like a woman in labor. They will look aghast at each other, their faces aflame"* (Is. 13:3-8).

7. **Terror or terrorism is a form of judgment;** *"The LORD, **the LORD Almighty, has a day of tumult and trampling and terror in the valley of decision, a day of battering down walls** and crying out to the mountains"* (Is. 22:5).

8. **Terrorism is a sign of the day of the Lord, a day of judgment, a day of wrath;** *"Terror and pit and snare await you, O people of the earth. Whoever flees at the sound of terror will fall into a pit;* whoever climbs out of the pit will be caught in a snare. The floodgates of the heavens are opened, the foundations of the earth shake. ... "* (Is. 24:17-22).

9. **God is determined to bring down Babylon;** *" 'Even if Babylon reaches the sky and fortifies her lofty stronghold, **I will send destroyers against her,'** declares the LORD"* (Jer. 51:53).

10. In respect to **the end-times in which we are living,** that is, the time preceding the appearing of *Yeshua Meshiach* (Jesus Christ), it is written; *"There will be signs in the sun, moon, and stars. On earth, nations will be in anguish and perplexity at the roaring and tossing of the sea* [hurricanes]. ***Men will faint from terror,*** *apprehensive of what is coming on the world, for the heavenly bodies will be shaken"* (Luke 21:25-26).

So, **the right and best thing to do about terrorism is to go to God** and ask him; "Lord, what are you saying to us by these things?" If we just embark on waging war, there will never be an end! As it is the case, **God has everything under control, including terrorism.** The other question we may ask is, "Have we done anything to deserve terrorism or to have provoked it?" Have we rejected and disobeyed God's laws and commands? Let him who is blind open his eyes and see, and let him who loves ignorance, stick his head in the sand; that will not stop the wind from exposing their nakedness or stop the reality clock from ticking.

When the terrorists shall have finished their evil and work of wrath, they too shall be ruthlessly judged, even as they are being judged today.

"This is what the Sovereign LORD says: I am against you, Mount Seir, and will stretch out my hand against you and make you a desolate waste. I will turn your towns into ruins and you will be desolate. Then you will know that I am the LORD. **'Because you harbored an ancient hostility** *and delivered the Israelites over to the sword at the time of their calamity, the time their punishment reached its climax, therefore as surely as I live, declares the Sovereign LORD,* **I will give you over to bloodshed and it will pursue you. Since you did not hate bloodshed, bloodshed will pursue you"** (Ezek. 35:1-15).

However, the one who faithfully follows the LORD will NEVER be AFRAID of TERROR, even if it strikes next door.

"He who dwells in the shelter of the Most High will rest in the shadow of the Almighty. I will say of the LORD, 'He is my refuge and my fortress, my God in whom I trust.' Surely he will save you from the fowler's snare and from the deadly pestilence. He will cover you with his feathers, and under his wings you will find refuge; his faithfulness will be your shield and rampart. **You will not fear the terror of night nor the arrow that flies by day, nor the pestilence that stalks in darkness, nor the plague that destroys at midday.** *A thousand may fall at your side, ten thousand at your right hand, but* **it will not come near you. You will only observe**

with your eyes and see the punishment of the wicked. ..." (Ps. 91:1-16).

Again,

"So do not fear, for I am with you; do not be dismayed, for I am your God, I will strengthen you and help you; I will uphold you with my righteous right hand" (Is. 41:10).

" 'See, it is I who created the blacksmith [the bomb, gun, rocket, explosives, and missile maker] *who fans the coals into flame and forges a weapon fit for its work. And **it is I who have created the destroyer to work havoc**; **no weapon forged against you will prevail, and you will refute every tongue that accuses you.** This is the heritage of the servants of the LORD, and this is their vindication from me,' declares the LORD"* (Is. 54:16-17).

The Lord will protect you and his wrath (or terror) will pass over you and he will rescue you; *"Go, my people, enter your rooms and shut the doors behind you; hide yourselves for a little while until his wrath has passed by." "Like birds hovering overhead, the LORD Almighty will shield Jerusalem* [his people]; *he will shield it and deliver it, he will 'pass over' it and will rescue it"* (Is. 26:20; 31:5).

God and the History and End of Gentile Civilization

It may surprise a Bible reader if I say that the Bible is the history of the other side of modern civilization (from God's viewpoint or perspective) from about BC 4,000 to AD 3,000; a period of about 7,000 years (6 days or 6,000 years of creation and 1 day or 1000 years of rest or Sabbath). Within this period, God's plan for the creation of mankind is revealed—eternal salvation!

The Bible sits as a visible, yet hidden record of human civilization, that is, especially civilizations that have had global impact. God affected or touched each one of them at its center, even though he might have been dealing with only a few people at a time—Adam, Noah, Abraham, the Hebrews, Daniel, et cetera. Modern civilization, as it began 6000 years ago, is man's effort to make his environment an Eden (a beautiful place) and to make conditions of life better.

Civilization began along the Nile rivers (the Pishon, in Havilah and the Gihon, in Cush or Ethiopia), and extended (or perhaps started simultaneously) to Mesopotamia (Babylon) between the two rivers—the Tigris and the Euphrates. It is equally here that life begins in the Bible—in the Garden of Eden!

> *"Now the LORD God had planted a garden in the east, in Eden; and there he put the man he had formed. ... A river watering the garden flowed from Eden; from there it was separated into four headwaters. The name of the first is the Pishon; it winds through the entire land of Havilah, ... The name of the second river is the Gihon; it winds through the entire land of Cush. The name of the third river is the Tigris; it runs along the east side of Asshur. And the fourth river is the Euphrates"* (Gen. 2:8, 10, 14).

These rivers are known as the cradles of human civilization. Thus, Eden stretched from the rivers of Egypt to the rivers of Mesopotamia. These first civilizations became corrupted, and God judged them with the waters of the flood (Gen. 6-9). Before this time, we are told that Cain was the first to begin building a city—the center of human civilization and sin; *"So Cain went out from the LORD'S presence and lived in the land of Nod, east of Eden. Cain lay with his wife, and she became pregnant and gave birth to Enoch. Cain was then building a city, and he named it after his son Enoch"* (Gen. 4:16-17).

Thus, the first civilization was begun by someone described as "of the evil one" (Satan); *"Do not be like Cain, who belonged to the evil one and murdered his brother"* (1 John 3:12). After the flood, men began to regroup again and united in rebellion against God at Babel (Babylon), and God scattered mankind throughout the surface of the whole earth (Gen. 10-11). It was from the Mesopotamian (Babylonian) civilization (Ur), that God called out Abram (about 2,000 BC). In a sense, just as life began in Eden, salvation history (call of Abram) also began in Eden; *"The LORD had said to Abram, 'Leave your country, your people and your father's household and go to the land I will show you. 'I will make you into a great nation and I will bless you; I will make your name great, and you will be a blessing. I will bless those who bless you, and whosoever curses you I will curse;*

*and **all peoples on earth will be blessed through you**'"* (Gen. 12:1-3). Universal salvation (all peoples on earth shall be blessed through you) in Jesus Christ, son of Abraham, is the fulfillment of this 4,000 years old promise, that will soon be consummated. Thus, out of ruins came a promise—redemption.

When God left the Mesopotamian civilization, he headed back to the other cradle of civilization (the Nile in Egypt) to make his presence felt there just as he had begun with Adam and Eve at the start. God did this by bringing Abraham to Egypt through natural circumstances (to ensure that he went to Egypt); *"Now there was famine in the land, and Abram went down to Egypt to live for a while because the famine was severe"* (Gen. 12:10). Why would God use famine to bring Abram to Egypt? God made his presence felt in Egypt through a surprising way: the beauty of Abram's wife and Abram's lie about her (Gen. 12:11-20)! God even made Abram rich in the process! Pharaoh had taken Abram's wife, Sarah, thus, the LORD judged Pharaoh; *"But the LORD inflicted serious diseases on Pharaoh and his household because of Abram's wife Sarai."*

Because the Canaanites occupied the land God had promised to Abraham, and because Abraham's descendants were still few, God brought them to Egypt (Gen. 15:13-14) again to build them into a nation (in Goshen). When they were big as a nation, God judged Egyptian civilization (ten plagues; Ex. 7-11, the most prominent civilization at the time in the Near East, whose supremacy lasted for a long time) and brought his people out (with plunder from Egypt; Ex. 12:36). God then used the Israelites to judge the pagan Canaanite civilizations by uprooting them.

The next major civilization was Assyria, and it felt the presence or influence of God as they met Israel, the northern Kingdom. God, at some point judged the Assyrians because of their harassment of his people (by slaying 185,000 Assyrian troops in one night! Is. 37:32-36). Eventually, God judged Israel because of their sins by allowing Assyria to take them into captivity in BC 721. However, the Israelites who went to Assyria carried the worship of God with them there. God finally judged Assyria through Babylonian conquest.

Thus, next in line came Babylon, the greatest superpower of antiquity. Babylon felt the influence of God when God made his presence felt through the Jews that were carried into exile by Babylon. Through the three Hebrew men and Daniel (see the book of Daniel), God showed to Nebuchadnezzar and the Babylonians that he is the Most High God, and besides him there is no other. After making his presence felt, he judged the Babylonians and brought back the Jews to their land. Through the Babylonian king, God revealed the timeline of western civilization (Median and Persia, Greece, Rome, Papacy, and Modern Europe and her daughter-nations) and how they will be judged before the inauguration of the everlasting kingdom of God. Of the Roman era, apostle Paul said that at just the right time God brought forth his Son into the world. The Roman world was a magnificent one and provided the right time for the beginning of the visible kingdom of God. There were good roads and hence, transportation, good communication, ordered society (law), relative peace (Pax Romana); and the center of what would become modern western civilization. Rome, herself, was judged in 476 AD as she was overrun by the Barbarians, ushering in the dark ages. Medieval civilization (or de-civilization?) was judged by the Protestant Reformation, as God made himself known in a unique way again.

Civilization then shifted to the New World carrying God with it then, but as the epitome of modern (or all) civilization, the New World is now overcome by wealth, money, and sin; and is lifted in pride and arrogance, also mingled with folly. You do not need a high IQ to figure out the outcome if you have been following the pattern of God and civilization as I have tried to delineate here. The New World (that has hatched New Israel, the Church, like Egypt hatched Old Israel) will be judged but the Church will be delivered with plunder from her! [By using the appellation New Israel here, I do not imply that the Church has replaced Israel, natural Israel is still in God's plan and will be delivered].

Thus, God has made his presence and influence felt in all important world civilizations and has consecutively judged them while at the same time delivering his faithful ones. Civilization began in Egypt-Babylon and has ended in Spiritual Egypt-New

Babylon! Old Egypt was judged through Moses and Babylon of old was judged through God's anointed one, Cyrus the Persian (Is. 45-47). New Egypt-Babylon will be judged by God's anointed one now (Rev. 18-19). It is not a matter of if, but a matter of when. This abrupt and tragic end of the present civilization was revealed to Nebuchadnezzar as follows:

"While you were watching, a rock was cut out, but not by human hands. It struck the statue [representing all western civilization] *on its feet of iron and clay* [the last and most prominent of western civilization] *and smashed them. Then the iron, the clay, the bronze, the silver and the gold* [named in reversed order: from the most recent--New Babylon to the old—Ancient Babylon] *were broken to pieces at the same time and became like chaff on a threshing floor in the summer. The wind swept them away without leaving a trace* [western civilization in its present form will be wiped out and forgotten completely!]. *But the rock that struck the statue became a huge mountain and filled the whole earth* (That is, the soon to be inaugurated Universal Kingdom of Christ). ... *'In the time of those kings,* **the God of heaven will set up a kingdom that will never be destroyed,** *nor will it be left to another people.* **It will crush all those kingdoms and bring them to an end,** *but it will itself endure forever"* (Dan. 2:34-35,44). That is the end of the matter!

Thus, Christ will engage these decadent and depraved civilizations (called beasts) in the last fight of the ages—Armageddon. He will defeat them with great triumph; *"Then I saw the beast and the kings of the earth and their armies gathered together to make war against the rider on the white horse and his army. But the beast was captured, and with him the false prophet* [the second lamb-like beast in Rev. 13:11] *who had performed the miraculous signs on his behalf. ... The two of them were thrown alive into the fiery lake of burning sulfur"* (Rev. 19:19-21). This marks the end of the Age of the Gentiles. Goodbye! Adios kingdoms of men!

Through civilization, mankind has made great strides. He has conquered hard weather conditions like extreme cold and heat; conquered the seas (ships), the skies (airplanes, shuttles, space station, airwaves); conquered the planets, the moon (landing man on the moon), and has even attempted to conquer the sun.

However, there is one thing that man in all his genius, has not been able to conquer, because it needs external help (Jesus Christ) to be conquered—the human heart! The human heart is the wildest and most uncivilized thing--the Unconquered Heart. We can tame the wildest beasts—lions, tigers, and others, but we are unable to tame the human heart! This is because man has a freewill (volition) and is prone to do and consistently chooses evil! It is human choice to be wicked or to be good; to practice virtue or vice; to do right or wrong; to acknowledge and obey God or reject him. The power of good and evil lies in human volition. Solomon declared; ***"This only have I found: God made man upright, but men have gone in search of many schemes"*** (Eccl. 7:29). The human heart is the source of all human evil, and is becoming more and more evil or depraved and uncivilized (de-civilization) with the progress of civilization:

> *"Furthermore,* ***since they did not think it worthwhile to retain the knowledge of God,*** *he gave them over to a depraved mind, to do what ought not to be done. They have become filled with every kind of wickedness, evil, greed and depravity. They are full of envy, murder, strife, deceit and malice. They are gossips, slanderers, God-haters, insolent, arrogant and boastful;* ***they invent ways of doing evil,*** *they disobey their parents;* ***they are senseless, faithless, heartless, ruthless. Although they know God's righteous decree that those who do such things deserve death, they not only continue to do these very things but also approve of those who practice them"*** (Rom. 1:28-32).

This is the perpetual state of many so-called civilized people today (not excluding the uncivilized). The heart of the so-called civilized man has sunk into utter depravity. This is how the LORD describes the human heart; *"The heart is deceitful above all things and beyond cure. Who can understand it?* (Jer. 17:9). Of the human heart, the Spirit cries out; *"The hearts of men, moreover, are full of evil and there is madness in their hearts while they live, ... "* (Eccl. 9:3). Jesus echoed the wickedness and madness of the human heart when

he declared that; *"What comes out of a man makes him 'unclean.'
For out from within, out of men's hearts, come evil thoughts, sexual
immorality, theft, murder, adultery, greed, malice, deceit, lewdness,
envy, slander, arrogance and folly. All these evils come from inside
and make a man 'unclean'* (Mark 7:20-23).

God will judge the wicked heart and cast the unrepentant heart
into the fires of hell; *"I the LORD search the heart and examine the
mind, to reward a man according to his conduct, according to what
his deeds deserve"* (Jer. 17:10). God will do this by his powerful
word from which he has made know to men what is evil or good;
*"For the word of God is living and active. Sharper than any double-
edged sword, it penetrates even to dividing soul and spirit, joints and
marrow; it judges the thoughts and attitudes of the heart. Nothing
in all creation is hidden from God's sight. Everything is uncovered
and laid bare before the eyes of him to whom we must give account"*
(Heb. 4:12-13). Jesus said, *"As for the person who hears my words
but does not keep them, I do not judge him. ... There is a judge for
the one who rejects me and does not accept my words; that very word
which I spoke will condemn him at the last day"* (John 12:47-48).

Conclusion On Chapter 11

The spirit of civilization, of the city of man, is the spirit of
rebellion. It is the spirit of the Age of the Gentiles as demonstrated at
Babel. It is the spirit of intrigue and warfare. It is the spirit of Satan
trying to dominate the earth after deceiving Adam and Eve and taking
away their rightful domination of the earth under God. Nevertheless,
this spirit of restless and raging dominion is under the auspices of
God's providence. This explains why God is not allowing complete
domination by one nation or groups of people. As one empire goes
down, another one comes up; and as one struggle goes down, then
another one comes up. The world had thought if they could contain
Hitler, then, there will be world peace, but came communism and
the Cold War. So, the world thought again, if only we can bring
down communism and hence end the Cold War, then peace will
come. However, before the Cold War officially ended, terrorism was
lurking at the corner. Now the delusion is, if only we will get rid
of terrorism, then there will be peace and safety, or the world will

be safer! Only a naïve and spiritually blind person will think that way. The truth is, there will be no peace until the Prince of Peace takes over. Sometimes, it is important to understand why nations rage at each other—in summation, it is supremacy and domination—overweening pride, arrogance, and folly!

When God placed man on the earth, he gave him the right to subdue the earth and rule over it in peace and tranquility. But man gave over the privilege to Satan, and Satan's attempt to dominate and subdue the earth is pursued in wickedness and murder. And we may ask, "Why all these murders, warfare, and churning of the seas?" Summarized in one word: the answer is dominance—the aspiration by one people (particularly the strong and rich) to exert their supremacy over others (especially the weak, poor, and helpless). Because most people desire to dominate the rest of the other peoples, warfare and murder are bound to occur, and would continue until Satan is captured. Warfare may be given fancy and captivating names, but one thing underlies them all—we want to dominate, we want to lead, and you follow. We are up or want to be up there and you must be down there—that's our lot, and that's your lot. When there are two or more groups of peoples aspiring for the same position (dominance of the world) at the same time, war is inevitable. In modern history, this explains the reason for the French aggression under Napoleon, Italian under Mussolini, German under Hitler, the Cold War, and now, terrorism.

The West, particularly the USA, is sitting on top of the world, a position coveted by all who aspire for world dominance since the history of ancient empires. Islam from the start had always aspired to subdue the world in submission to Allah's will by willing conversion or sword. Terrorism might very well be a result of frustration because of failure to achieve that age-old goal. People in the West seem to be frustrated about terrorism—why are they doing this to us? Why would people glory in killing the innocent, including themselves? One thing they overlook is that for a long time they (the West) have been sitting on the rest of the world, a position that others would want to occupy. The flip side to this is to ask, why all this western dominance? Why do we want to dominate and sit upon others? Why all this suppression? Why all this arrogance? The psyche of the westerner and particularly the American, seems to revolve on "We are richer and better than they and we have to tell them what to do." To be oblivious to the outcome of such thinking and action is to bury your head in the sand and remain blind to objective reality. Have you ever been in a neighborhood where one man seems to have it all and tries to tell the rest what they should be and do? How do you feel about that man? Just bow down at his feet? Have you ever been in a class with a bully? What were/are your reactions toward him? Just kneel before him? Have you ever been in a group with an obvious beautiful girl or woman, who thinks she is all in all and must tell the rest of the girls or women what to do and how to look? What was/ is your reaction? Just kneel before her? From these little things, you can understand the big picture of why the world will always continue in tumult, warfare, terror, and carnage. If you have always submitted to the arrogant neighbor; if you have always knelt before the bully; if you have always bowed to the beautiful and kissed their feet; know for certain that not everybody has and would. Thus, there will never be peace! Men will continue to fight and kill.

The issue is not that of being civilized or not (that is an ignorant approach to the problem), but the quest for dominance. The Cold War did not exist because the Soviet Union was uncivilized, it existed because each superpower was vying for complete and sole supremacy over the other and the rest of the world. America's third millennium apparently imperialistic dominance has bred and will only continue to breed more quarrels. The Spirit says, *"Pride only breeds quarrels, but wisdom is found in those who take advice." "All this I saw, as I applied my mind to everything done under the sun.* **There is a time when a man lords it over others to his own hurt.***" "Wisdom is better than weapons of war, but one sinner destroys much good"* (Pr. 13:10; Eccl. 8:9; 9:18).

The most interesting part of the current world chaos is the role of religion. The terrorist, obviously inspired by hatred or perhaps, even jealousy, believes he is doing the **will of Allah**. The war commander on the other hand believes that he is doing the **will of God,** as the Commander-in-Chief expresses; "Freedom is not only America's gift to the world, it is God's gift to the world!" Inherent in this statement is the belief that democracy is God's gift to the world. Nothing can be far from the truth and antithetical (antichrist) to God's freedom given by Jesus Christ; *"Then you will know the truth, and **the truth will set you free.**" "So if the Son sets you free, you will be free indeed"* (John 8:32, 36). Note that truth is the opposite of lie, then go and do your homework. Of liars it is said (within the same context as above); *"You belong to your father, the devil, and you want to carry out your father's desire. He was a murderer from the beginning, not holding to the truth, for there is no truth in him. When he lies, he speaks his native language, for he is a liar and the father of lies"* (John 8:44). So, who sets people free? The Son, that is, Jesus Christ! The Son and America are not identical. One is a pseudo form of the other or its antithesis. If you need brain surgery to understand, please contact a surgeon. Evil and wickedness, when they hide behind religion (the opium of the people as one man once said), constitute one of the worst forms of evil. Such evil is intolerant, and it persecutes, destroys, and kills, all in the name of God. As it is written; *"They will put you out of the synagogue; in fact, **a time is coming when anyone who kills you will think he is offering a service to God.** They will do such things because they have not known the Father or me* [Jesus Christ]*"* (John 16:2-3). Both on each side believe they are serving God and dying in the struggle means entering heaven. So, whose heaven is it going to be? Jesus Christ warns; *"'Not everyone who says to me, 'Lord, Lord,' will enter the kingdom of heaven, but only he who does the will of my Father who is in heaven. Many will say to me on that day, 'Lord, Lord, did we not prophesy in your name, and in your name drive out demons and perform many miracles?' Then I will tell them plainly, 'I never knew you. Away from me, you evildoers!'"* (Matt. 7:21-23). Yes, there are evil doers, who think that they are doing God's service. If I know God at all, he has nothing to do with murderers and killers, whomever they purport to be serving. God has nothing to do with hatred or pride or dominance. In fact, he says; *"To fear God is to hate evil; I hate pride and arrogance, evil behavior and perverse speech"* (Pr. 8:13).

So, we see here that the issue of world chaos today is dominance—control, supremacy; just as it has been since the beginning of empires.

It is all about covetousness (do not forget about the oil too); *"What causes fights and quarrels among you? Don't they come from your desires that battle within you? You want something but don't get it. You kill and covet, but you cannot have because you do not ask God"* (Js. 4:1-2). When religious tyranny clasps hands with political tyranny, they unleash havoc and unfathomable devastation to the society (and now ultimately to the world). It is even worse than degeneracy (moral decay). Here is a succinct summary:

> "Degeneration is *disorganized evil* in contrast to political or religious tyranny, which is *organized evil.* A dictator monopolizes evil as he restricts freedom and controls the populace [mostly through fear]; degenerate himself, the despot suppresses degeneracy by forcing strict morality upon the people. To secure power, organized evil attacks disorganized evil [culture wars] *and* persecutes Christianity [Biblical Christianity]; disorganized evil does not persecute but co-exist with Christianity."[cclxxiii]

When degeneration (moral and ethical decline—rampant crime, violence, sexual perversion, drug addiction, etc.), religious tyranny (apostasy), and political tyranny grip one society at the same time (which is pathetic), then the dark ages are ushered in. True Christians may soon, even in the age of freedom, face the worst form of persecution like that in the dark ages from apostate Christianity.

CHAPTER 12

THE MODERN WORLD: A WORLD DIVIDED

" *Y**ou who turn justice into bitterness and cast righteousness to the ground* (he who made the Pleiades and Orion [Constellations of stars], *who turns blackness into dawn and darkens day into night, who calls for the waters of the sea and pours them out over the face of the land—the LORD is his name— he flashes destruction on the stronghold and brings the fortified city to ruin),* **you hate the one who reproves in court and despise him who tells the truth. You trample on the poor and force him to give you grain. Therefore, though you have built stone mansions, you will not live in them; though you have planted lush vineyards, you will not drink their wine.** *For I know how many are your offenses and how great your sins. You oppress the righteous and take bribes and you deprive the poor of justice in the courts. Therefore the prudent man keeps quiet in such times* [surely not me], *for the times are evil"* (Amos 5:7-13).

For a while as I observed the world, I was surprised that even the popular Christian worldview in respect to the division of the world into first world and third world is no different from the secular worldview. In fact, it even appeared that secularists seem to have a heart for poor than some Christians do. Popular Christian theology lacks a biblical coverage of the subject of poverty. How could this be, given that the Bible from cover to cover has an obvious theology of the poor, the oppressed, the weak, the powerless, the helpless, like orphans and widows, and the alien? Little is written on the subject. Then I began to tell myself that something was wrong with my thinking (or perhaps with the Bible) because most have a different view. However, I still wanted to put down my view (which I believe is biblical) in a book. In December of 2003 I sat down at my table and wrote down the outline of this book, including this chapter. In 2005 while still in the process of writing, I went to a bookstore and started browsing around. I saw a book for one dollar with an interesting title; *Rich Christians In an Age of Hunger,* by Ronald J. Sider. So, I bought the book, went home, and devoured the pages with amazement. Ronald Sider had elaborately covered this subject in the most biblical way and with conclusions I was hesitant to make, given that they would indict most of the "Christian" West. Folks, something is seriously wrong with our theology of the poor in the West. Most Western Christians have a wrong view and act wrongly when it comes to the poor, oppressed, helpless, and aliens. When you are the oppressor, you became blind to your actions or tend to justify them!

There was a time I was conversing with my mother-in-law on the state of poverty, especially in the third world. She made a comment as follows: "Why is it that the rest of the world is not just like North America and Europe with abundance for most if not all." I was quick to tell her that in a large sense the world is the way it is because of the European's creation. Wherever the Europeans went (thanks to their genius and ingenuity as pioneers of modern civilization and war technology), they built a nice civilization if they wanted. However, where they built a civilization, they reduced the indigenous people to nothing and shoved them to the corner (that is, depriving them of most of their land). Where they did not build a civilization, they ensured that they exploited and depleted the resources and carry them back to Europe, a practice that continues today. These may appear as overstatements, but there is more evidence that validates them, than disprove them. This, of course, is a delicate subject and needs careful handling.

The twentieth century was the century of economic expansion and great accumulation of wealth through capital investment, innovation, invention, and technology. Materialism and greed also greatly enhanced this acquisition of wealth. Capitalism, unlike Communism, enabled people to advance and accumulate wealth at a fast pace. While others, particularly the West and Japan, took advantage of new technology, others lagged or were even made to lag through the international trade policies of the big capitalist industrialized nations. Right from the industrial revolution, those who had the capital took the advantage to enrich themselves, and sometimes at the expense of the poor workers. These differences in capital have resulted in a world divided on economic and technological lines (Technological Divide— TD)—the first or developed world and the third or developing world. While the developed world is relaxing (or is it?) in affluence, most in the third world are wallowing in poverty, grinding their teeth, and struggling for survival. The gap seems to widen geometrically each year, with the rich getting richer and the poor getting poorer.

The Third World

The appellation "Third World" used to refer to nations that did not belong to the group of nations considered developed or industrialized. The categorization has changed in the past few decades to include *Low-income countries (3.1 billion people), Lower-middle-income countries (1.1 billion people), Upper-middle-income countries (501 million), and High-income countries (812 million people).* [cclxxiv] Within the Low-come countries (3.1 billion people) are the desperately poorest people of the earth (1.3 billion people). The rest of the two billion are very poor and live on less than two dollars a day. There are significant deaths per year resulting from preventable diseases, malnutrition and malnutrition-related diseases, and there are millions who go hungry every day, not to mention the various famines in some areas of the world. So how poor are the poor? Why are they poor? Their Lot in Life? No!

The causes of poverty are complex to delineate. They range from: the fact that some of the poor are people who have been displaced from their lands either by colonizers or by war or disaster; uneven distribution of land and natural resources; their resources exploited by the rich and powerful; reliance on subsistence agriculture in an age of mechanized agriculture; illiteracy; ignorance; laziness and lack of initiative; lack of capital; lack of technology; individual wrong choices; great inequalities of power; wrong governments, that are corrupt and inept or lack economic strategies; and a product of colonialism and colonial trade policies. Colonies were never allowed to compete with mother countries and were/are largely seen as sources of raw materials and markets for finished goods, which was/ is for the advantage of the powerful industrialized nations. These colonial evils have left a negative lasting impact on the colonized. In relation to European influence in sub-Saharan Africa, someone has written:

> "What they wanted were the valuable raw materials of Africa and then before long the Africans themselves—as slaves to perform the arduous labor of creating a rich agricultural establishment in the New World. ... On the whole, the development of sub-Saharan Africa was seriously impeded by the encounter of its peoples with the western Europeans ... Africa's human resources were depleted, her natural resources plundered, and her political and social structures disoriented. The Europeans gave little in return, especially when compared to what the Moslems of North Africa had contributed to the enrichment of sub-Saharan Africa prior to 1500."[cclxxv]

Ronald Sider puts it this way:

> "Economic historians still argue about the economic impact on colonized nations. But there is little doubt that colonialism is one reason for some poverty, even today. ... It is now generally recognized by historians that many of the civilizations Europe 'discovered' were highly developed in many ways; their most obvious 'deficiency' was their lack of modern military technology. True, the civilizations of Asia, Africa, and the Americas were different in that they were not 'Christian,' but how Christian were the European colonizers? ... Most 'Mother' countries used their colonies to enhance their own national status in the world community. ...The creation of colonies was extremely useful. Preoccupied with the status of the mother country, colonizers seldom exhibited much regard for economic, social, and cultural conditions of the indigenous peoples."[cclxxvi]

Sub-Saharan Africa was badly affected the most because the cream of her manpower was sapped to build the New World agricultural economy. Even with the independence of African nations, colonialism is still depriving that continent of its resources (neocolonialism, by which Africa seems not to be in control of her destiny). Most African nations are still economic dependencies (the source for cheap raw materials and market for finished goods) to the advantage of her master nations.

Another major factor that causes poverty in the Third World is the lack of good government and structures that foster economic development. In most poor countries the governments are corrupt and government officials deplete the national treasures, reap the benefits from natural resources, and make matters worse by banking the embezzled money in Western accounts (capital flight), which help western economies to the detriment of their own national economies. Within such nations are wealthy elites who work hand-in-glove with the corrupt governments, further worsening the plight of the poor of these nations. As a result, in most cases the economy is matching backwards, and poverty continues to deepen. Thus, the Third World in a way accelerates its own poverty. To further make things worse, these Third World nations spend very extravagantly on the military at the expense of the education and health of its citizens and economic development. Lack of education and technology is another contributing factor. And even in education, the few who are educated prefer working in the West (brain drain), where there are more opportunities and advantages. They want a ready-made economy and do not want to bear the pains of building an economy from scratch. They play the blame game with the corrupt governments, each accusing the other of corruption on the one hand and unpatriotic on the other hand.

Poverty's complex causes extend to the global trade imbalances—both in currencies and trade policies. The wealthy industrialized nations (G7) virtually write the rules of world trade and design the rules to favor themselves. Not only so, but these rich nations also control most of the world's natural resources. The issue here, however, is not to play the blame game, but to assess the reality of the situation with objectivity and a sense of justice.

The Developed World: A great and Positive Achievement

Western economic advancement can be traced back as far as civilization began. But there are a few discernable economic systems that have developed in the past 2000 years. In the medieval period was feudalism, in which the feudal lords virtually controlled the economic lives of their dependents and the people. After feudalism came mercantilism, which, unlike feudalism (individual based), was a national economic policy "… based on the conviction that the economic well-being of a nation depended on directing the total national economy in a way that would produce a favorable balance of money coming into the economy."[cclxxvii] This method of wealth collection gave birth to the colonial era, in which the Europeans went out to reap the nations of their riches; "Among other things, this policy saw colonies as a source of cheap food and raw materials and an outlet for manufactured goods that would return a profit to the mother country."[cclxxviii] This, of course, is a reality that I need not comment on any further than to state that the West began to accumulate wealth by robbing the world. This is not to say that the West was not wealthy.

The Industrial Revolution changed the phase of economic expansion forever from the nineteenth century until the present. It began in Great Britain and quickly spread to continental Europe and the USA. Again, with vast overseas empires, the western nations quickly increased their wealth to unheard of proportions until then. Through economic liberalism and capital investment, the industrial capitalists took the advantage and amassed great wealth. Although workers were/are sometimes exploited, disciplined hard work and the dream of a better life contributed immensely to the wealth built-up of western industrialized nations. Hard Work itself became the most revered virtue. If the West is rich, it is because they have worked hard! There is no short-cut to riches--you must work hard!

Innovation and technological research, invention, and advancement, have continued to push the West ahead in wealth accumulation. This technological divide (TD) determines who is rich and who is poor today. Also, the existence of good and stable political systems—the rule of Law, good economic policies (for instance, government subsidies), and planning, are some of the hallmarks of western economic success. While colonialism seems to stand in the face of everything, it cannot be denied that belief in God and seeing the world as a place to take care of for him, has also been one of the driving forces behind western economic achievement.

Again, good banking and investment, and good financial institutions (control of World Bank and International Monetary Fund) have also led to the great wealth of the West. Because of the control of these institutions and control of world trade, and because of their shrewdness and wisdom in exploiting the wealth and resources of others (colonialism then, and multinational corporations now), the West has also accumulated much wealth. However, this is a very dangerous situation because God calls this attitude of amassing wealth, Satanism! It is what will lead to the downfall of Satan and his allies:

"By your great wisdom and understanding [economic ingenuity] *you have gained wealth for yourself and amassed gold and silver in your treasuries. By your great skill in trading you have increased your wealth, and because of your wealth your heart has grown proud. ... Through your widespread trade you were filled with violence, and you sinned. I drove you in disgrace from the mount of God, ... By your many sins and dishonest trade you have desecrated your sanctuaries. So I made a fire come out from you, and it consumed you, and I reduced you to ashes on the ground in the sight of all who were watching"* (Ezek. 28:4-5,16,18).

In this satanic web, the developing world remains a source for raw materials (for instance, minerals, coffee, cocoa, cotton; etc.) and a market for industrial finished products. High money values and rate of exchange too affect the Developed World/Third World wealth divide (from the Pound to the Dollar, and now to the Euro). Ronald Sider comments on this Developed/Third World divide as follows: "With a few exceptions, the rich countries are in the northern hemisphere.

The poor countries are more to the south. The north-south division is one of the most dangerous fault lines in the world today."[cclxxix]

Ronald Sider dedicates chapter eight of his book to delineating painstakingly, the economic *Structural Injustice Today*. This economic injustice is virtually practiced by the West. **These unjust structures directly or indirectly create poverty in many parts of the world (I call it Economic Terrorism).** Ron suggests "that some starvation results from the economic structures that wealthy nations like the U.S. erect for their own advantage."[cclxxx] As another person has said, the developed West is strangling the underdeveloped world and has kept a "stranglehold ... on the throats of the Third World." Ron continues to say that; "I do believe, ..., that affluent nations have played a part in establishing economic structures that contribute to some of today's hunger and starvation."[cclxxxi] Ron outlines seven areas (six of which are discussed here) in which the West is part of the unjust structures that contribute to world poverty and hunger.

Market Economies

The market economy is not bad. It is the unjust rules and unfairness that underlie its practice that are bad and fall short of biblical standards. The first problem Ron cites is that "at least a quarter of the world's people lack capital to participate in any major way in the global market economy." Thus, the market economy mostly serves the rich since what it offers, only the rich can pay for. It is staggering to hear that; "Today, 20 percent of the world's people receive 83 % of the world's income." It is sad to note that, the success of the market economy wherever it happens, ushers in pervasive cultural perversion. Ron continues to assert that; "The most obvious perhaps is the seeping materialism and consumerism that floods the world as country after country joins the global market. Material possessions and the money that buys them become all important to more and more people. ... In fact, more and more people value money more than marriage, parenting, or even honesty."[cclxxxii] The most chilling thing about materialism and consumerism is that Jesus calls it paganism! Materialism is equal to paganism! Jesus warns; *"Therefore, I tell you, do not worry about your life, what you will eat or drink; or about your body, what you will wear. ... And why do you*

*worry about clothes? ... So do not worry, saying 'What shall we eat?'
or 'What shall we drink?' or 'What shall we wear?'* **For the pagans**
[Gentiles or Westerners] **run after all these things, ...** " (Matt. 6:26-
32).

Consumerism promotes vices such as wastefulness, self-
indulgence, and the like, as virtues. The evil of this commercialization
is promoted through relentless advertising. Ron comments;
"Television ads showing sensuous, light-skinned women suggest that
older women can shed the aging skin, tanned and wrinkled by years of
hard labor in the sun."[cclxxxiii] Materialism has become the god of many
in the West as Ron comments; "The ever more affluent standard of
living is the god of twentieth-century North America, and the adman
is its prophet."[cclxxxiv] Advertising creates a global lust for ever-more
consumption. "Perhaps the most demonic part of advertising is that
it attempts to persuade us that material possessions will bring joy and
fulfillment."[cclxxxv] However, nothing can be far from the truth!

In market economies, profits are sought no matter what evil
it takes to get there. The markets corrupt the culture by rewarding
immoral actions—whether it is pornography, child molestation or
child pornography, if it brings profits, it is readily accepted. People
have become hedonistic, pleasure seekers, self-absorbed, rash, proud,
boastful—just because of what they have—it is a sign of the times of
the end (2 Tim. 3:1-5). The market economy is destroying anything
in its path on its way to profits!

International Trade

Again, we are reminded that trade and dishonest trade will
lead to Satan's downfall as quoted above. It is very easy even to the
dumbest person to be able to figure out the end of the nations that rob
poor countries according to the Bible. Ron writes:

"The industrialized nations have shaped the patterns of
international trade for their own economic purposes. In colonial
days, ..., mother countries regularly made sure that economic
affairs were organized to their own advantage. Such advantage
was largely achieved through manipulation of commodity

trade. Western colonial nations adopted policies that increased the quantity of goods they wanted from their colonies and at the same time discouraged efforts in the colonies to develop or improve manufacturing capacities. As a result, many colonies became unnecessarily dependent on shipping primary products to and purchasing expensive manufactured products from their 'mother' countries."[cclxxxvi]

This cycle of manipulation and dependency has not been broken, not for many Third World nations. Ron continues:

"Although colonialism ended decades ago, industrialized nations have continued, over the past several decades, to manipulate international trade by imposing restrictive tariffs and import quotas to keep out many of the goods (especially processed and manufactured goods) produced in the developed countries. **Tariff structures and import quotas affecting the poor nations are in fact one fundamental aspect of systemic injustice today.**
Major European countries (members of the EEC) charge four times as high tariff on cloth imported from poor nations as from developed countries. During the 1980s, 20 of the 24 industrialized counties increased their protection against manufactured or processed products from the developed countries. … The World Bank estimates that trade barriers imposed by the rich nations on goods from poor nations cost poor nations $50 to $100 billion a year.

Typically, developed countries have allowed many agricultural and other primary products (minerals, cocoa, rubber, sisal, and so on) to enter relatively duty free. But they have been less generous with manufactured goods. The more manufacturing and processing done by the poor country, the higher the tariff rich nations charged."[cclxxxvii] *(emphasis mine)*

In the colonial days such restrictions were designed to limit competition. However, "Today restrictions are maintained largely because their removal would threaten the interest of certain well-organized and politically entrenched groups. Both labor and management in the developed countries want to be able to buy cheap raw materials to profit from processing and manufacturing them here. They also want to hinder other countries' efforts at processing and manufacturing because those products, when imported, would directly compete with the domestic industry."cclxxxviii

And the story can continue. The rich nations do everything within their means and power, to protect their selfish interests and impoverish the poorest of the poor, who rely mostly on primary products. These people work hard under the harshest conditions (and I speak from experience--I know what it means to work in a coffee farm and earn practically nothing, while the coffee dealer in the West throws away food from his table and piles up money in stock markets). No one who has ever heard about God and justice would condone such robbery and injustice, yet the irony here is that those who promote it have the Bible in hand and answer present as "Christendom!"

The Debt of Very Poor Nations

It is assumed that money borrowed from poor nations goes to help the poor people. But a careful analysis would show that most of this money is largely wasted on projects that benefit the people very little. In most cases the money winds up in the hands of corrupt leaders, who siphon the money back to western bank accounts, while the nations creep deeper into debt and poverty. Bad management lavished military spending, and poor economic planning, all contribute to this indebtedness. As a result, debt repayment is done at the expense of national education and health care. Ron concludes; "Overall, African governments spend more on debt repayment than on basic education and health care." Of the truth as Solomon said: *"The rich rule over the poor, and the borrower is servant to the lender"* (Pr. 22:7).

Natural Resources and Environment

Rapid industrialization has hazardous effects on the environment and pose many risks to human life. Environmental pollution and degradation is endangering future generations—chemicals, pesticides, oil spills, industrial emissions, greenhouse gases (like carbon dioxide, methane, nitrous oxide--all contribute to global warming), carbon emissions from burning fossil fuel, etc., are all destroying the environment, fresh water supply, and polluting the air. This negative effect is proportionate to industrialization with the USA and China leading at the top.

Consider also energy consumption;

"A comparison of energy usage underscores our affluence. Because of a lengthening list of luxuries—numerous electrical gadgets and toys, large, air-conditioned cars, skyscrapers, and so on—North Americans consume more than twice as much energy per person as their counterparts in industrialized countries like Japan and Switzerland. And we use 25 times as much as the average Brazilian, 60 times the average Indian, 191 times the average Nigerian, and 351 times the average Ethiopian."[cclxxxix]

Apparently, God provided the world with resources to be consumed by just a few people out of the many people in the world! That is self-centeredness and selfishness. **The West is putting itself on the wrong side of divine favor because God will destroy those who destroy the earth** (Rev. 11:18). Ron makes the following comparison in respect to over-consumption;

"The U.S. will add about 50 million people to its population over the next forty years, and those 50 million will have approximately the same global impact in terms of resource consumption as 2 billion more people in India. Due to over-consumption, small numbers of affluent people strain the earth's limited resources far more than much larger numbers of poor people. ... Those of us in developed countries make up only one-fifth of the world's population. But we 'control 85 percent of its income and consume 70 percent of its energy, 75 percent of its metals, and 85 percent of its wood. [We also] produce two-thirds of all greenhouse gases.'"[ccxc]

Ron concludes; "The facts are clear. North Americans, Europeans, and Japanese devour an incredibly unequal share of the world's available resources."[ccxci]

No doubt the Scripture says that *"We know that the whole creation has been groaning as in pains of childbirth right up to the present time,"* and that creation itself waits for its liberation together with the sons of God (Rom. 8:19ff). We too, wait in hope for the trumpet of the seventh angel so that God will destroy those who destroy the earth (Rev. 11:15-18). It is rather paradoxical that those who destroy the earth claim they are Christians! Would they not have been good stewards of what God has given them and share it with the poor (and not steal from them instead), rather than devour most of the earth's resources? The Lord has promised that the meek shall inherit the earth (Matt. 5:5)! Shall the very meek (Western Christians) destroy their inheritance for selfish temporal pleasure? Or are they the meek at all? Or do they want to deplete the earth's resources and destroy the earth before they depart to their dry and weary land (hell)? Like in the days of Amos, many are longing for the day of the Lord or the rapture but;

> *"Woe to you who long for the day of the LORD! Why do you long for the day of the LORD? That day will be darkness, not light. It will be as though a man fled from a lion only to meet a bear, as though he entered the house and rested his hand on the wall only to have a snake bite him. Will not the day of the LORD be darkness, not light--pitch-dark, without a ray of brightness? 'I hate, I despise your religious feasts; I cannot stand your assemblies. Even though you bring me burnt offerings and grain offerings, I will not accept them. Though you bring choice fellowship offerings, I will have no regard for them. Away with the noise of your songs! I will not listen to the music of your harps.* **But let justice roll on like a river, righteousness like a never-failing stream**" (Amos 5:18-24).

Yes! Justice! Even in trade and in the treatment of the poor and the environment and its resources! As we will see later, Amos was wailing against complacent people, who claimed to worship God (or did they?), but who had grown rich by oppressing and exploiting the poor. In our day, the same evil is alarming, yet we are in church every day! Away with the noise of your songs and offerings, for the Lord desires mercy not sacrifice! Next time when you sip a cup of coffee, or eat a banana, think about the Ugandan poor coffee grower, who works the coffee but eats grass, or the Ecuadorian banana farmer, who sweats each day but goes home with an empty stomach. Or when you crave chocolate, think of the Cameroonian or Ivorian cocoa farmer, who works hard in the mosquito-infested forest to produce the cocoa bean, but neither has enough to eat nor enough to pay for the medication for malaria. The spoil of the poor is in your hands! The Bible warns;

"Food gained by fraud tastes sweet to a man, but he ends up with a mouth full of gravel."

"Do not exploit the poor because they are poor and do not crush the needy in court, for **the LORD will take up their case and will plunder those who plunder them.**"

"The LORD takes his place in court; he rises to judge the people. The LORD enters into judgment against the elders and leaders of his people: **'It is you who have ruined my vineyard; the plunder from the poor is in your houses. What do you mean by crushing my people and grinding the faces of the poor?'** *declares the LORD, the LORD Almighty"* (Pr. 20:17; 22:22-23; Is. 3:13-15; cf. Is. 1:4-17).

Food Consumption and Food Imports

Even when people in poor nations are languishing in poverty, their countries still export food to developed nations. How can this be? Colonial powers encouraged the colonized to produce cash crops at the expense of agricultural crops for local consumption. So even in famine, these plantation owners continue to export their food because the developed countries can pay much for it unlike the starving national population. So, the elites of the poor nations are in full complicity with their wealthy western friends, while their brothers are suffering. As Ron puts it; "They send us cotton, beef, coffee, bananas, or other agricultural products, and we send them the goods they desire in return. The system favors the wealthy, and the poor suffer."[ccxcii] The greatest paradox on the food issue is that while lack of food and famines are devastating millions or even billions in the poor countries, gluttony or overeating is devastating millions in the wealthy nations! Obesity, especially in America, has reached epidemic proportions, with billions of dollars spent annually on obesity and obesity-related diseases. Indeed, Sodom has resurrected as explained by Ezekiel 16:49-50: *"Now this was the sin of your sister Sodom: She and her daughters were **arrogant, overfed** and **unconcerned;** they did not help the poor and needy. They were **haughty** and **did detestable things** [abominations like homosexuality] before me. Therefore I did away with them as you have seen,"*

Sooner or later, the fate of Sodom will overcome America, if there is no repentance.

Multinational Corporations in the Third World

The availability of cheap raw materials and cheap labor in the Third World has led to a new frontier in slavery [Made in ...]. These Multinational Corporations take advantage of these advantages and invest in these poor nations to maximize profits. Goods are produced at a very cheap cost but are sold at exorbitant prices when the goods are taken abroad. Laborers are paid cents a day. One may argue that these corporations provide employment in the poor nations (and they do) to people who otherwise would have been unemployed, but that is not an excuse for the exploitation that goes on. Well, it is business as usual! No doubt, the multinational corporations have their own positive effects, but the adverse effects are just as devastating.

Those who knowing or unknowing participate and benefit from this system are as guilty as the perpetrators. They are largely silent because they are the benefactors and beneficiaries. It sure feels good to fill up your closet with cheap goods or fill your refrigerator with farm produce produced by virtually slave labor from developing nations. It is equally sinful to participate in evil social systems and societal structures that unfairly benefit some and harm others, especially the poor. Ron notes; "If we are members of a privileged group that profits from structural evil, and if we have at least some understanding of the evil yet fail to do what God wants us to do to change things, we stand guilty before God. Social evil is just as displeasing to God as personal evil. And it is more subtle."[ccxciii]

Behind these economic and social evils, stands the god of this world, Satan himself, who leads the whole world astray (Rev. 12:9; 18:23; 1 John 5:19). To fully participate in such social evil is to embrace Satan's cosmic system (love of the world; 1 John 2:15-17) and his modus operandi. No doubt, behind such an economic façade and thievery, God identifies Satan.

Most in the West associate poor and begging to anyone they see coming from the Third world. And to that, I want to draw your attention to an illustration from the King of the world, who not only owns all the riches of the world but owns your very life (Luke 16:19-31). The King tells the story of a poor beggar, Lazarus, who sat at the gate of a wealthy man desiring to eat from the rich man's table. The rich man did not give Lazarus anything to eat. Rather, only the dogs licked his wounds. Both men died and the beggar was carried to Abraham's bosom, but the rich man was carried to hell. From hell he looked up and saw Lazarus at Abraham's side, and begged Abraham to allow Lazarus to dip his finger in cool water and cool his tongue in the torments of the fires of hell. But Abraham reminded him of his earthly life of wealth and pump, and how he despised Lazarus when he lived in his abundance. He equally reminded him that there exists a chasm between them, and neither can cross to the other. This story illustrates to us that we should be mindful the way we treat the poor (not to mention in the cases we exploit them), for it just may happen that at the end, the poor end up in heaven and the rich end up in the torments of hell. Again, Jesus warns; *"But woe to you who are rich, for you have already received your comfort. Woe to you who are well fed now, for you will go hungry. Woe to you who laugh now, for you will mourn and weep"* (Luke 6:24-25).

Western society now stands at the same pitiful condition as the Rich fool in Luke 12:15-21.

*"Then he said to them, '**Watch out! Be on your guard against all kinds of greed; a man's life does not consist in the abundance of his possessions.**' And he told them this parable: 'The ground of a certain rich man produced a good crop. He thought to himself, 'What shall I do? I have no place to store my crops.' Then he said, 'This is what I'll do. I will tear down my barns and build bigger*

ones, and there I will store all my grain and my goods. And I'll say to myself, 'You have plenty of good things laid up for many years. Take life easy; eat, drink and be merry." But God said to him, 'You fool! This very night your life will be demanded from you. Then who will get what you have prepared for yourself?' This is how it will be with anyone who stores up things for himself but is not rich toward God."

The ground of the Rich West, indeed, has produced an abundant crop, and new barns are being built (Wall Street, Blackrock, and other Investment firms) and a lot of wealth hoarded up in these last days (James 5:1-6). But the writing is on the wall, the life of the West is being demanded by God! Western society has come to define man in terms of how much he has and does (in terms of economic value). On the contrary, **Jesus warns; "... *a man's life does not consist in the abundance of his possessions."*** But the devil cunningly says; "A man's life consists in the abundance of his possessions. Live your dream now! More and bigger and more expensive are better and bring happiness." Again, Jesus says; *"Sell your possessions and give to the poor. Provide purses for yourselves that will not wear out, a treasure in heaven that will not be exhausted, where no thief comes near and no moth destroys. For where your treasure is, there your heart will be also"* (Luke 12:33-34). But Satan says; "Hoard up for yourselves wealth here on earth and amass from the poor as much as you are shrewd enough to do so, save enough, and you will enjoy your old life. Take life easy, eat, drink, and be merry, this is all there is to life." No doubt Jesus says; *"I tell you the truth, it is hard for a rich man to enter the kingdom of heaven. ... it is easier for a camel to go through the eye of a needle than for a rich man to enter the kingdom of God"* (Matt. 19:23-24).

The apostle John strictly warns against materialism (amassing earthly possessions), which is paganism or worldliness;

*"**Do not love the world or anything in the world. If anyone loves the world, the love of the Father is not in him. For everything in the world—the cravings of sinful man** [moral degeneracy], **the lust of his eyes** [covetousness, envy, greed] **and the boasting** [pride] **of what he has and does— comes not from the Father***

but from the world [Satan's cosmic operating evil system]. *The world and its desires pass away, but the man who does the will of God lives forever"* (1 John 2:15-17).

James echoes the same warning; *"You adulterous people, don't you know that friendship with the world is hatred toward God? Anyone who chooses to be a friend of the world* [Satan's diabolic system] *becomes an enemy of God"* (James 4:4). Are you a friend of the world? Are you an enemy of God because you choose materialism over giving to the poor (heavenly banking or saving)? The only way to have a retirement bank account in heaven is to cast your possessions, including money, upon the waters (Eccl. 11:1)— give to God by giving to the poor. As it is written; *"He who is kind to the poor lends to the LORD, and he will reward him for what he has done"* (Pr. 19:17). Will you enter heaven with an empty bank account? You be your judge!

The G7 (Free World) and the Global Caste

Many of us dislike and loathe the caste system in India/Hinduism. However, the "Christian" West has built a solid economic caste and work night and day to maintain it, making sure that the lower caste members (the poor, especially the third world) stay where they are economically, so that the West can continue to profit. This is how the G7, and other industrialized nations control world trade under the leadership of America. If Hinduism is doing it, it is bad and evil, but if the "Christian" West is doing it, it is good and acceptable. **Right from the colonial period as we have seen, the West has been building this economic caste and continues to strive hard to maintain it today.** But this caste will be turned upside down! To be forewarned is to be forearmed: there are many who are first who will be last and there are many who are last who will be first. If only you know what that means! A man's life does not consist in the abundance of his possessions! Whoever mistreats the poor mocks their Maker!

Materialism and love for possessions is what the Book of Revelation calls the worship of the beast. The upward mobility to profit from this system (that has become a magnet for the peoples of the earth) is the worship of the beasts and equals Satanism—the worship of the dragon. This is precisely what Satan demanded from Jesus to give him the kingdoms of the world;

"Again, the devil took him to a very high mountain and showed him all the kingdoms of the world and their splendor [riches and wealth]. *'All this I will give to you,' he said, 'if you **bow down and <u>worship</u> me.'** Jesus said to him. 'Away from me Satan! For it is written; '**<u>Worship</u> the Lord your God, and <u>serve</u> him only"*** (Matt. 4:8-10).

Later, Jesus would use the same language about money, thereby identifying money with Satan; *"**No one can <u>serve</u> two masters**. Either he will hate the one and love the other or he will be devoted to the one and despise the other. **You cannot <u>serve</u> God and Money!"*** The world is worshipping the dragon, Satan (worshipping the beasts), by serving or worshipping money (Rev. 13:4). Satan had the audacity to try to divert Jesus to worship wealth and money. Jesus passed the test and gives power to his followers to do the same. However, millions upon millions who profess the name of Christ (Christians) have fallen into this trap of worshipping Satan by serving money and material possessions (which equal paganism). Of such people it is written;

*"People who want to get rich fall into temptation and a trap and into many foolish and harmful desires that plunge men into ruin and destruction. **For the love of money is a root of all kinds of evil**. Some people, eager for money, have wandered from the faith and pierced themselves with many griefs."*

They are hedonists; *"... **lovers of themselves, lovers of money, ... lovers of pleasure** [fun] **rather than lovers of God**--having a form of godliness but denying its power."* Again, *"They claim to know God, but by their actions they deny him. They are detestable, disobedient and unfit for doing anything good"* (1 Tim. 6:9-10; 2 Tim. 3:2-5; Tit. 2:16).

Of their unfruitfulness, Jesus says; *"Other seed fell among thorns, which grew up and choked the plants. ... The one who received the seed that fell among the thorns is the man who hears the word, but the worries of this life and the deceitfulness of wealth choke it, making it unfruitful."*

Again, he says about such hypocrites; *"Not all who say to me, 'Lord, Lord,' will enter the kingdom of heaven, but only he who does the will of my Father who is in heaven. **Many will say to me on that day, 'Lord, Lord, did we not prophesy in your name, ... Then I will tell them plainly, 'I never knew you. Away from me, you evil doers!"*** (Matt. 13:7, 22; 7:21-23).

Money should be our servant and not vice versa. Money is meant to serve us. We are not meant to serve money. **When you serve/worship money, you despise God,** no matter how much of that money is given to the church or charity. For God desires mercy and obedience, but not sacrifice. For the sacrifice of the wicked is an abomination to God, how much more when brought with evil intent (Pr. 15:8; 21:27)! You cannot buy God or eternal life with money;

"Hear this, all you peoples; listen, all who live in the this world. ... Why should I fear when evil days come, when wicked deceivers surround me--those who trust in their wealth and boast of their great riches? No man can redeem the life of another or give to God a ransom for him--the ransom for a life is costly, no payment is ever enough [except the ransom paid by Jesus Christ] --that he should live on forever and not see decay. ...But man, despite his riches, does not endure; he is like the beasts that perish. This is the fate of those who trust in themselves, and of their followers, who approve their sayings" (Ps. 49:1-13).

Again, the Psalmist cries out,

*"But as for me, **my feet had almost slipped; I had nearly lost my foothold. For I envied the arrogant when I saw the prosperity of the wicked.** They have no struggles; their bodies are healthy and strong. They are free from the burdens common to man; they are not plagued by human ills. **Therefore pride is their necklace; they clothe themselves with violence.** ... That is what the wicked are like, always carefree, they increase in wealth. ... **When I tried to understand all this, it was oppressive to me till I entered the***

sanctuary of God; then I understood their final destiny. Surely you place them on slippery ground; you cast them down to ruin. How suddenly are they destroyed, <u>completely swept away by terrors</u>! As a dream when one awakes, so when you arise, O Lord, you will despise them as fantasies (Ps. 73:2-6, 12, 16-20).

God's Plight for the Poor (Widow, Fatherless, Alien, and The Oppressed)

I do not need to belabor the point: the doctrine of poverty is a central doctrine of Scripture. That modern theology has largely neglected this, and it is not one of the central doctrines of Christian theology, simply means that modern theologians do not follow God's heartbeat or understand his word completely. From the Law of Moses through the prophets to Jesus Christ and the apostles, God is concerned about the poor, especially the oppressed, the widows, the fatherless, and the alien. Mistreating these classes of people is a direct affront at God, their maker.

Again, I will borrow Ron's definition of the poor here. He explains;

"The Hebrew words for poor are *ani, anaw, ebyon, dal,* and *ras. Ani* (and *anaw*, which originally had approximately the same meaning) denotes one who is 'wrongfully impoverished or dispossessed.' *Ebyon* refers to a beggar imploring charity. *Dal* connotes a thin, weakly person such as an impoverished, deprived peasant. Unlike the others, *ras* is an essentially neutral term. In their persistent polemic against the oppression of the poor, the prophets used the terms *ebyon, ani,* and *dal.* In the New Testament, the primary word for the poor is *ptochos*, which refers to someone, like a beggar, who is completely destitute and must seek help from others. It is the Greek equivalent of *ani* and *dal.* Thus, the primary connotation of 'the poor' in the Scripture has to do with low economic status usually due to calamity or some form of oppression.

The Scriptures also teach that some folks are poor because they are lazy and slothful (e.g. Proverbs 6:6-11; 19:15; 20:13; 21:25; 24:30-34). ... The most common biblical connotation of 'the poor,' however, relates to those who are economically impoverished due to calamity or exploitation."^{ccxciv}

A Brief Biblical Survey of God's Plight for the Poor

In giving the Law to the Israelites, Yahweh repeatedly commanded them to take care of the poor, the widows, and the alien; that is, the helpless of their society.

In Exodus 22:21-24, we read; *"Do not mistreat an alien or oppress him, for you were aliens in Egypt. **Do not take advantage of a widow or an orphan. If you do and they cry out to me, I will certainly hear their cry. My anger will be aroused, and I will kill you** with the sword; your wives will become widows and your children fatherless."*

Again, in Leviticus 19:9-10, 33-34, we read; *"When you reap the harvest of your land, do not reap to the very edges of your field or gather the gleanings of your harvest. Do not go over your vineyard a second time or pick up the grapes that have fallen. Leave them for the poor and the alien. I am the LORD your God."*

More about the plight of the helpless of society is recorded in Deuteronomy;

> *"When you have finished setting aside a tenth of all your produce in the third year, the year of the tithe, you shall give it to the Levite, the alien, the fatherless and the widow, so that they may eat in your towns and be satisfied. Then say to the LORD your God: 'I have removed from my house the sacred portion and have given it to the Levite, the alien, the fatherless and the widow, according to all you commanded"* (26:12-13; cf. 14:28-29).

Again, Yahweh declares;

> *"If there is a poor man among your brothers in any of the towns of the land that the LORD your God is giving you, **do not be hardhearted or tightfisted toward your poor brother.** Rather be openhanded and freely lend him whatever he needs. Be careful not to harbor this wicked thought: 'The seventh year, the year of*

*canceling debts, is near,' so that you **do not show ill will toward your needy brother and give him nothing. He may then appeal to the LORD against you, and you will be found guilty of sin.** Give generously to him and do so without a grudging heart; then because of this the LORD your God will bless you in all your work and in everything you put your hand to do. **There will always be poor people in the land. Therefore I command you to be openhanded toward your brothers and toward the poor and needy in your land"** (15:7-11; cf. Matt. 26:11).

A word to the wise is enough, right? The verses above speak for themselves. Hear and obey the message! We emphasize tithing in the church today, but how much of it is used to take care of the poor, widows, fatherless, and the aliens? Are we not guilty of disobedience? Do we not only want from Yahweh what will benefit us? Crowning the care for the helpless was the year of Jubilee, in which special privileges were granted to the poor and the alien (Lev. 25:8-54).

The prophets bemoaned over and over the mistreatment of the helpless—poor, widows, fatherless, and aliens. They called for justice and mercy for all in general and these underprivileged classes in particular. When Jesus walked the earth, he had special sympathy and compassion for the poor and outcasts of society. He gave them a comforting word and great promises (Luke 6:20-21). In Psalm 9:9, 18, it is written; *"The LORD is a refuge for the oppressed, a stronghold in times of trouble." "But the needy will not always be forgotten, nor the hope of the afflicted ever perish."*

Jesus commands the rich to sell their wealth (stocks) and give the money to the poor before they can follow him or have eternal life! Failure to heed this command means that the rich cannot enter the kingdom of God (Matt. 19:16-24). Jesus also intimates the fact that there will always be poor people among us as cited above (Matt. 26:9-11). This will always be the case, at least, because the rich oppressors will always be selfish and hoard rather than share their wealth. **However, Jesus was rich, yet became poor for our sake (2 Co. 8:9), so we ought to become poor for the sake of others.**

Care for the poor was a major spiritual goal for Paul. He could not think of faith in Jesus Christ without thinking about the poor. He was eager to care for the poor! *"All they asked was that we should* **continue to remember the poor, the very thing I was <u>eager to do</u>"** (Gal. 2:10). Just as Jesus commands the rich to sell their possessions and store up their treasure in heaven by giving to the poor, Paul commands the rich to do likewise;

> *"Command those who are rich in the present world not to be arrogant nor to put their hope in wealth, which is so uncertain, but to put their hope in God, who richly provides us with everything for our enjoyment. Command them to do good, to be rich in good deeds, and to be generous and willing to share. In this way they will lay up treasure for themselves as a firm foundation for the coming age, so that they may take hold of the life that is truly life"* (1 Tim. 6:17-19).

James and John also define **true love as sharing with those who do not have** (James 2:14-16; 1 John 3:16-20).

There is, therefore, a direct correlation between treatment of the poor and eternal life and storing up treasure for the age to come or heaven. To give to the poor is to invest, to save in an eternal retirement bank account (in heaven)! In fact, **giving to the poor is described as lending to God;** *"He who is kind to the poor lends to the LORD, and he will reward him for what he has done"* (Pr. 19:17). However, the opposite is true, **to mistreat, oppress, scorn, or deny justice to the poor, is to affront God himself.**

"He who oppresses the poor shows contempt for their maker but whoever is kind to the needy honors God."

"He who mocks the poor shows contempt for their maker; whoever gloats over disaster will not go unpunished."

"He who oppresses the poor to increase his wealth and he who gives gifts to the rich—both come to poverty." "If a man shuts his ears to the cry of the poor, he too will cry out and not be answered." (Pr. 14:31; 17:5; 22:16; 21:13)

God is Against the Oppressive, Exploitative, and Dominant Rich

"Why, O LORD, do you stand far off? Why do you hide yourself in times of trouble? **In his arrogance the wicked man hunts down the weak, who are caught in the schemes he devices.** *He boasts of the cravings of his heart; he blesses the greedy and reviles the LORD. In his pride the wicked does not seek him; in all his thoughts there is no room for God. His ways are always prosperous; he is haughty ... He lies in wait near the villages; from ambush he murders the innocent, watching in secret for his victims. He lies in wait like a lion in cover; he lies in wait to catch the helpless; he catches the helpless and drags them off in his nest. His victims are crushed, they collapse; they fall under his strength. He says to himself, 'God has forgotten; he covers his face and never sees.'* **Arise, LORD! Lift up your hand, O God. Do not forget the helpless. ... But you O God, do see trouble and grief; you consider it to take it in hand. The victim commits himself to you; you are the helper of the fatherless.** *Break the arm of the wicked and evil man;* **call him to account for the wickedness that would not be found out. ... You hear, O LORD, the desire of the afflicted; you encourage them, and you listen to their cry, defending the fatherless and the oppressed, in order that man, who is of the earth, may terrify no more"** (Ps. 10).

"The LORD takes his place in court; he rises to judge the people. The LORD enters into judgment against the elders and the leaders of the people: 'It is you who have ruined my vineyard; **the plunder from the poor is in your houses. What do you mean by crushing my people and grinding the faces of the poor?'** *declares the LORD Almighty"* (Is. 3:14-15).

"Woe to those who make unjust laws, to those who issue oppressive decrees [especially regarding trade, e.g. G7 and WTO], **to deprive the poor of their rights and withhold justice from the oppressed of my people, making widows their prey and robbing the fatherless. What will you do on the day of reckoning, when disaster comes from afar?** [cf. Pr. 11:4; **"Wealth is worthless in the day of wrath ..."**] *To whom will you run for help? Where will you leave your riches? Nothing will remain but to cringe among the captives* *or fall among the slain. Yet for all this, his anger is not turned away, his hand is still upraised"* (Is. 10:1-4).

"Go up and down the streets of Jerusalem [any city today], *look around and consider, search through her squares. If you can find but one person who deals honestly and seeks the truth, I will forgive this city.* **Although they say, 'As surely as the LORD lives,' still they are swearing falsely** [that is, even the rich oppressors claim to worship God—"God bless you," they say!]**.'** ... *'Why should I forgive you? Your children have forsaken me and sworn by gods that are not gods. I supplied all their needs, yet they committed adultery and thronged to the houses of prostitutes.* **They are well-fed, lusty stallions, each neighing for another man's wife. Should I not punish them for this?'** *declares the LORD.* **'Should I not avenge myself on such a nation as this?** ... *They have lied about the LORD; they said, 'He will do nothing! No harm will come to us; we will never see sword or famine. The prophets are but wind and the word is not in them; so let what they say be done to them'* ... **Hear this, you foolish and senseless people, who have eyes but do not see, who have ears but do not hear; Should you not fear me?'** *declares the LORD.* **Should you not tremble in my presence?** ... *But these people have stubborn and rebellious hearts, they have turned aside and gone away. They do not say to themselves, 'Let us fear the LORD our God, ... Your wrongdoings have kept these away; your sins have deprived you of good.* '**Among my people are wicked men who lie in wait like men who snare birds and like those who set traps to catch men. Like cages full of birds, their houses are full of deceit; they become rich and powerful and have grown fat and sleek. Their evil deeds have no limit; they do not plead the case of the fatherless to win it, they do not defend the rights of the poor. Should I not punish them for this?' Should I not avenge myself on such a nation as this?"* (Jer. 5:1-2, 7-9, 12-13, 21-29).

"The LORD roars from Zion and thunders from Jerusalem; The pastures of the shepherds dry up, and the top of Carmel withers. ... This is what the LORD says: **'For three sins of Israel, even four, I will not turn back my wrath. They sell the righteous for silver, and the needy for a pair of sandals. They trample on the**

heads of the poor as upon the dust of the ground and deny justice to the oppressed. Father and son use the same girl [or like fathers today using their own girls!]. *Hear this word, you cows of Bashan on Mount Samaria,* **you women who oppress the poor and crush the needy and say to your husbands, 'Bring us some drinks!' The Sovereign LORD has sworn by his holiness: 'The time will surely come when you will be taken away with hooks, the last of you with fishhooks.** *You will each go straight out through breaks in the wall, and you will be cast out toward Harmon,' declares the LORD.* **You who turn justice into bitterness and cast righteousness to the ground ... you hate the one who reproves in court and despise him who tells the truth** [It is apparent that no rich oppressor will heed the message of this book. They will probably want to eat me up]. **You trample on the poor and force him to give you grain** [Like getting at low-cost agricultural products from the Third World but sell to them manufactured products at exorbitant prices]. *Therefore, though you have built stone mansions, you will not live in them; though you have planted lush vineyards, you will not drink their wine. For I know how many are your offenses and how great your sins.* **You oppress the righteous and take bribes and you deprive the poor of justice in the courts.** *... Seek good, not evil, that you may live. ... Hate evil, love good; maintain justice in the courts. ... There will be wailing in all the streets and cries of anguish in every public square. The farmers will be summoned to weep and the mourners to wail.* **There will be wailing in all the vineyards, for I will pass through your midst,' declares the LORD.** *... Woe to you who are complacent in Zion, and to you who feel secure on Mount Samaria,* **you notable men of the foremost nation** [Like the superpower nation leading the world now], **to whom the people of Israel come** [Israel's modern current ally]*!* *...* **You put off the evil day and bring near the reign of terror.** *You lie on beds inlaid with ivory and lounge on your couches. You dine on choice lambs and fattened calves. ... You drink wine by the bowlful and use the finest lotions, but you do not grieve over the ruin of Joseph.* **Therefore you will be among the first to go into exile; your feasting and lounging will end.** *... The time is ripe for my people Israel* [then and now, and the world]; *I will spare them no longer. 'In that day* [The Day of the LORD—judgment],*'* declares the Sovereign LORD, 'the songs in the temple will turn to wailing. Many, many bodies--flung everywhere! Silence!' **Hear this, you who trample the needy and do away with the poor of the land, saying, 'When will the New Moon be over that we may sell grain, and the Sabbath be ended that we may market wheat?' --skimping the measure, boosting the price and cheating with dishonest scales** [This is precisely what the industrialized nations do, they boost the price of their goods but buy Third World goods at cheap prices!], **buying the poor with silver and the needy for a pair of sandals, selling even the sweepings of wheat.** The LORD has sworn by the Pride of Jacob: **'I will never forget anything they have done. ... Surely the eyes of the Sovereign LORD are on the sinful kingdom. I will destroy it from the face of the earth**—[Watch out, you, rich oppressive nations!]" (Amos 1:2; 2:6-7; 4:1-3; 5:7-17; 6:1-7; 8:2-7; 9:8).

"Woe to those who plan iniquity, to those who plot evil on their beds! At morning's light they carry it out because it is in their power to do it [Like the most powerful nation or nations of the world, doing as they please and dictate]. They covet fields and seize them, and houses, and take them. They defraud a man of his home, a fellowman of his inheritance [modern equivalent of displacing people from their ancestral lands]. **Therefore, the LORD says: 'I am planning disaster against this people, from which you cannot save yourselves. You will no longer walk proudly, for it will be a time of calamity. ... Am I still to forget, O wicked house, your ill-gotten treasures and the short ephah** [By dishonest scales, strong currencies, and trade, they amass wealth from other under-privileged nations], **which is accursed? Shall I acquit a man with dishonest scales, with a bag of false weights? Her rich men are violent; her people are liars and their tongues speak deceitfully. Therefore, I have begun to destroy you** [Sad to say it, but the downfall of the West has just begun, and will not be reversed], **to ruin you because of your sins.** You will eat but not be satisfied; your stomach will still be empty. You will store up but save nothing [The increase deficit, individual bankruptcies and debts of the people, are just symptoms of this irreversible downturn], because what you save I will give to the sword. ... " (Mic. 2:1- 3; 6:10-15).

"See, he is puffed up; his desires are not upright--... indeed, wine betrays him; he is arrogant and never at rest. Because he is as greedy as the grave and like death is never satisfied, he gathers to himself all the nations and takes captive all peoples [That is, the foremost nation takes captives from all the world]. *'Will not all of them taunt him with ridicule and scorn, saying, '**Woe to him who piles up stolen goods and makes himself wealthy by extortion! How long must this go on?' Will not your debtors suddenly arise? Will they not wake up and make you tremble? Then you will become their victim. Because you have plundered many nations, the peoples who are left will plunder you*** [Aha!]. *For you have shed men's blood; you have destroyed lands and cities and everyone in them.' '**Woe to him who builds his realm by unjust gain, to set his nest on high, to escape the clutches of ruin! You have plotted the ruin of many peoples, shaming your own house and forfeiting your life.*** The stones of the wall will cry out, and the beams of the woodwork will echo it. **Woe to him who builds a city with bloodshed and establishes a town by crime! Has not the LORD Almighty determined that the people's labor is only fuel for the fire, that the nations exhaust themselves for nothing?*** ... You will be filled with shame instead of glory. Now it is your turn! Drink and be exposed! **The cup from the LORD'S right hand is coming around you, and disgrace will cover your glory"*** (Hab. 2:4-13,16).

"Woe to you who are rich, for you have already received your comfort. Woe to you who are well fed now, for you will go hungry. Woe to you who laugh now, for you will mourn and weep" (Luke 6:24- 25).

*"Now listen, you who say, 'Today or tomorrow we will go to this or that city, spend a year there, carry on business and make money.' Why, you do not even know what will happen tomorrow. What is your life? You are a mist that appears for a little while and then vanishes. Instead you ought to say, 'If it is the Lord's will, we will live and do this or that.' As it is, you boast and brag. **All such boasting is evil. Anyone, then, who knows the good he ought to do and doesn't do it, sins. Now listen, you rich people, weep and wail because of the misery that is coming upon you.*** Your wealth has rotted, and moths*

have eaten your clothes. Your gold and silver, are corroded. Their corrosion will testify against you and eat your flesh like fire. You have hoarded wealth in the last days [For instance, the Stock Markets and Investments]. *Look! The wages you failed to pay the workmen who mowed your fields are crying out against you* [like the exploitation by colonial plantation systems of long ago and the multinational corporations now and stealing from those who produce cash crops for the developed world]. *The cries of the harvesters* [Don't the rich farmers pay the poor aliens meager sums?] *have reached the ears of the Lord Almighty. You have lived on earth in luxury and self-indulgence. You have fattened yourselves in the day of slaughter. You have condemned and murdered innocent men, who were not opposing you"* (James 4:13-5:6).

Yahweh **will rise and defend the poor, the oppressed and the exploited; the widows, fatherless, and the aliens; the exploited workers and the helpless.** There will be weeping and gnashing of teeth for the rich oppressors and exploiters. As it is written; ***"Do not defraud your neighbor or rob him. Do not hold back the wages of the hired man overnight."*** (Lev. 19:13) Again, Yahweh says, ***"'So I will come near you for judgment. I will be quick to testify against sorcerers, adulterers and perjurers, against those who defraud laborers of their wages, who oppress the widows and the fatherless, and deprive aliens of justice, but do not fear me,' says the LORD Almighty"*** (Mal. 3:5).

If we do not defend the poor and the alien, and only show them injustice and contempt, they will cry out to Yah, and he will rise on behalf of justice and defend them by crushing their oppressors. They will laugh and eat, while the oppressors wail and weep and go hungry. Consider the following:

*"For the LORD your God is the God of gods and Lord of lords, **the great God, mighty and awesome**, who shows no partiality and accepts no bribes. **He defends the cause of the fatherless and the widow, and loves the alien, giving him food and clothing"*** (Deut. 10:17-18).

"'Do not keep talking so proudly or let your mouth speak such arrogance, for the LORD is a God who knows, and by him deeds are weighed. The bows of the warriors are broken, but those who stumbled are armed with strength. Those who were full hire themselves out for food, but those who were hungry hunger no more. ... The Lord sends poverty and wealth; he humbles and he exalts. **He raises the poor from the dust and lifts the needy from the ash heap; he seats them with princes and has them inherit a throne in honor"** (1 Sam. 2:3-8).

"'Because of the oppression of the weak and the groaning of the needy, I will now arise,' says the LORD. 'I will protect them from those who malign them.'"

"You evildoers frustrate the plans of the poor, but the LORD is their refuge."

"Contend, O LORD, with those who contend with me; fight against those who fight against me. Take up shield and buckler; arise and come to my aid. ... Then my soul will rejoice in the LORD and delight in his salvation. **My whole being will exclaim, 'Who is like you, O LORD? You rescue the poor from those too strong for them, the poor and needy from those who rob them.'"**

"A little while, and the wicked will be no more; though you look for them, they will not be found. **But the meek will inherit the land and enjoy great peace.** The wicked plot against the righteous and gnash their teeth at them; **but the LORD laughs at the wicked, for he knows their day is coming. The wicked draw the sword and bend the bow to bring down the poor and needy, to slay those whose ways are upright. But their swords will pierce their own hearts, and their bows will be broken. Better the little that the righteous have than the wealth of many wicked; for the power of the wicked will be broken,** but the LORD upholds the righteous."

"I am in pain and distress; may your salvation, O God, protect me. I will praise God's name in song and glorify him with thanksgiving. This will please the LORD more than an ox, ...**The poor will see** *and be glad—you who seek God, may your hearts live! The LORD hears the needy and does not despise his captive people."*

"How long will you defend the unjust and show partiality to the wicked? **Defend the cause of the weak and fatherless; maintain the rights of the poor and oppressed. Rescue the weak and needy; deliver them from the hand of the wicked"** (Ps. 12:5; 14:6; 35:1-2, 9-10; 37:10-17; 69:29-33; 82:2-4).

"Speak up for those who cannot speak for themselves, for the rights of all who are destitute. Speak up and judge fairly; defend the rights of the poor and needy" (Pr. 31:8-9).

"Do not exploit the poor because they are poor and do not crush the needy in court, for the LORD will take up their case and will plunder those who plunder them" (Pr. 22:22-23).

Ronald Sider launches a strong diatribe in his book against the rich West that virtually oppresses the whole world, depriving the poor of their rights. He writes, "Regardless of what we do or say at 11:00 A.M. on Sunday morning, rich Christians who neglect the poor are not the people of God."[ccxcv] The fundamental problem for the complacency and indifferentism of rich "Christians" toward the poor, is that of theology. They simply have not been taught or have refused to perceive oppression and poverty through biblical lenses. Ron asserts:

"It is that our theology itself has been unbiblical. By largely ignoring the central biblical teaching of God's special concern for the poor, our theology has been profoundly unorthodox. ... We have allowed the economic values of our affluent, materialistic society to shape our thinking and acting toward the poor. ... Unless we drastically reshape both our theology and our church life so that God's concern for the poor and oppressed is as central in our theology and programs as it is in Scripture, we will demonstrate to the world that our verbal commitment to *sola scriptura* is a dishonest ideological support for an unjust, materialistic status quo. According to the Bible, it is central to the very nature of God to demand justice for the poor and oppressed."[ccxcvi]

When we knowingly or unknowingly [and we live in the information age that nobody can afford not to know!] participate in such evil social systems, we are equally guilty before God. Jesus intimates this when he says, *"The kings of the Gentiles lord it over them; and those who exercise authority over them call themselves Benefactors"* (Luke 22:25). When we become benefactors and even beneficiaries to an evil system and do not cry out against its injustices because we benefit from it, we sin, and are guilty before God. The spoil or plunder of the poor is in your houses, and you will give an account to God on the day of judgment. As Ron asserts:

"Neglect of the biblical teaching on structural injustice or institutionalized evil is one of the most deadly omissions in many parts of the church today. Christians frequently restrict ethics to a narrow class of 'personal' sins. In a study of over fifteen hundred ministers, researchers discovered that theologically conservative pastors spoke out on sins such as drug abuse and sexual misconduct, but failed to preach about the sins of institutionalized racism and unjust economic structures that destroy just as many people."ccxcvii

When we are evil doers, we keep our mouths shut! The apostle Paul thunders against this attitude when he says,

"...you, then, who teach others, do you not teach yourself? You who preach against stealing, do you not steal? You who say that people should not commit adultery, do you not commit adultery? You who abhor idols, do you not rob temples? You who brag about the law [now the Bible] *do you dishonor God by breaking the law? As it is written: 'God's name is blasphemed among the Gentiles* [unbelievers today] *because of you* [hypocritical Christians]'" (Rom. 2:21-24).

We clearly see the speck in others' eyes, but do not see the plank in our own eyes. We endorse and participate in such evil systems, yet continue to claim we are Christians, making the rest of the world wonder what kind of Christ we believe in--the Christ of justice and mercy or the Christ of injustice, fraud, and robbery! We choose to condemn the sins we hate but endorse and commit the ones we affirm (selective interpretation). We claim to know God but deny him by our actions (Tit. 2:16). Ron comments: "In the twentieth century, evangelicals have become imbalanced in their stand against sin, expressing concern and moral outrage about individual sinful acts while ignoring, perhaps even participating in, evil social structures. But the Bible condemns both. ... Sexual sins and economic injustice are equally displeasing to God. ... Economic injustice is just as abominable to our God as drunkenness."[ccxcviii] Ron continues; "God hates evil economic structures and unjust legal systems because they destroy people by the hundreds and thousands and millions [Economic Terrorism]. We can be sure that the just Lord of the universe will destroy wicked rulers and unjust social institutions."[ccxcix] Have I not said that the day of the Lord will be mourning, wailing, and gnashing of teeth to many who sing "Hallelujahs and Amen" every Sunday morning, yet exploit the poor and endorse evil social and unjust economic structures that defraud the helpless?

God Calls for Justice in Economics: Right Scales, Measures, Weights, and Laws

"Do not use dishonest standards when measuring length, weight or quantity. Use honest scales and honest weights, an honest ephah [used for dry measure] *and an honest hin* [used for liquid measure]. *I am the LORD your God, ..."* (Lev. 19:35-36).

"Differing weights and differing measures—the LORD detests them both." "Food gained by fraud tastes sweet to a man, but he ends up with a mouth full of gravel." "The LORD detests differing weights, and dishonest scales do not please him." "To do what is right and just is more acceptable to the LORD than sacrifice [church giving and service of any kind, and charity]. *" "A fortune made by a lying tongue is a fleeting vapor and a deadly snare"* (Pr. 20:10,17,23; 21:3,6).

Of Satan's kingdom, it is written: *"By your wisdom and understanding you have gained wealth for yourself and amassed gold and silver in your treasuries. By your great skill you have increased your wealth, and because of your wealth your heart has gone proud. ... Through your widespread trade you were filled with violence, and you sinned. ... By your many sins and dishonest trade you have desecrated your sanctuaries* [Many churches are accomplices to these evil systems of thievery or at least fail to preach against them]. *So I made a fire come out from you, and it consumed you, and I reduced you to ashes on the ground in the sight of all who were watching"* (Ezek. 28:4, 16, 18).

Dishonest trade (scales, measures, skimping, boosting prices, unjust standards, injustice, etc.) is hereby portrayed as the major cause of the fall of this end-time satanic economic monster. God equally accused Babylon of swallowing up the delicacies of other nations, probably through dishonest trade; *"Nebuchadnezzar king of Babylon has devoured us, he has thrown us into confusion, he has made us an empty jar. **Like a serpent** [Dragon] **he has swallowed us and filled his stomach with our delicacies,** and then spewed us out* (Jer. 51:34; Notice that Satan, who is leading the whole world astray is called the serpent; Rev. 12:3-9; You will be wise if you pay attention to these hints at Satan's identity).

Are Riches Always Wrong? By no means!

You could be a billionaire or even have more and be the greatest saint at the same time! This is true, if you follow God's law and economic principles and commands to acquire the wealth and give it away proportionately or appropriately. The Bible itself states that; *"You will be made rich in every way so that you can be made rich in every occasion, and through us your generosity will result in thanksgiving to God"* (2 Co. 9:11). It is God himself who gives riches to all people and the ability to make riches, both righteous and wicked. Without God no one will be able to make riches. He gives men life and breath, and wisdom and strength to make wealth.

Some of the greatest saints in the Bible were wealthy individuals. Consider Abraham; *"Abram had become very wealthy in livestock and in silver and gold"* (Gen. 13:2). However, when it came to tithe, he gave a tenth of all he had (Gen. 14:18-20). When occasion arose for him to acquire booty and add to his wealth, he gave up the opportunity, demonstrating that he was not covetous or greedy; *"But Abraham said to the king of Sodom, 'I have raised my hand to the LORD, God Most High, Creator of heaven and earth, and have taken an oath that I will accept nothing belonging to you, not even a thread or the throng of a sandal, so that you will never be able to say, 'I made Abram rich'"* (Gen. 14:22-23).

Thus, we see that wealth acquired through honest effort and fair or just trade, and used according to God's command, is never a problem (though it could be a snare and a source of much temptation). **It is our attitude toward wealth but not wealth itself that is the problem. Oppression and exploitation of the poor and helpless, defrauding, dishonest scales, and unjust/unfair trade, robbing or stealing, cheating, greed, covetousness, and the like, are what lead to the condemnation of the rich.**

Also consider Job;

"In the land of Uz there lived a man whose name was Job. This man was blameless and upright; he feared God and shunned evil. He had seven sons and three daughters, and he owned seven thousand sheep, three thousand camels, five hundred yoke of oxen and five hundred donkeys, and had a large number of servants. He was the greatest man among all the people of the East" (Job 1:1-3).

Yes, the greatest and richest man can be blameless and upright, because he fears God and shuns evil—all evil. I presume that he paid all his many servants fairly and used honest scales to acquire or sell his merchandise; and gave to the poor accordingly [which explains his greatness among the people of the East]. Such a rich man will never be at odds with God, even if he is a billionaire! Job's attitude was what mattered. He did not put his trust in wealth as he said; ***"If I have put my trust in gold or said to pure gold, 'You are my security*** [and how many today give their all for financial security!]***,' if I have rejoiced over my great wealth, the fortune my hands had gained, ... then these also would be sins to be judged, for I would have been unfaithful to God on high"*** (Job 31:24-28). Yes, trust in wealth, especially as one's security, and rejoicing in wealth, are sins that will be judged severely. Even when God permitted Satan to take away Job's wealth, he was still able to worship God!

"At all this [loss of all his wealth], *Job got up and tore his robe and shaved his head. Then **he fell to the ground in worship** and said: 'Naked I came from my mother's womb, and naked I will depart. The LORD gave and the LORD has taken away; may the name of the LORD be praised.' In all this, Job did not sin by charging God with wrongdoing"* (Job 1:20-22).

And how many would crash today or turn against God after a financial collapse? How many people committed suicide because of the financial depression of the late 1920s? Wealth has become the trust, security, and anchor of the wealthy; a worthless idol that will lead many to hell; *"Those who cling to worthless idols* [wealth] *forfeit the grace that could be theirs"* (Jonah 2:8). At the end of his ordeal, God prospered Job beyond his previous estate and wealth, proving that God himself gives us riches (Job 42:12-13).

However, riches always drive out godliness by bringing in complacency, pride, arrogance, selfishness, self-dependence, self-indulgence, apathy, and an attitude of "I am better than you," "we are the richest or we are richer than you," an inflated sense of self, and similar evils. Wealth and success are the hardest things to handle, which always bring down unwatchful Christians. God gave warning against such an attitude to Israel, should they become rich, which warning the "Christian" West has neglected or fallen into;

*"When you have eaten and are satisfied, praise the LORD your God for the good land he has given you. **Be careful that you do not forget the LORD your God, failing to observe his commands, his laws and his decrees** that I am giving you this day. Otherwise, when you eat and are satisfied, when you build fine houses and settle down, and when your herds and flocks grow large and your silver and gold increase and all you have is multiplied, **then your heart will become proud and you forget the LORD your God, ... You may say to yourself, 'My power and the strength of my hands have produced this wealth for me.'** But remember the LORD your God, for it is he who gives you the ability to produce wealth, ... **If you ever forget the LORD your God and follow other gods and worship and bow down to them, I testify against you today that you will surely be destroyed"** (Deut. 8:10-19).

This is precisely what happened to the Israelites, and God destroyed them. God's people can handle all kinds of trials, even persecution and death, but when it comes to wealth, they always seem to be ensnared.

If you are rich and want to be perfect (to be right with God), obey the commandments in 1 Timothy 6:17-19 and Matthew 19:21. There will always be poor people among us until Christ comes back because we do not obey God's commands to share since we are incurably (and there is sufficient grace to cure us; Tit. 2:11) selfish. The poor are a source of blessing to the rich. The existence of the poor is a great opportunity for the rich to swell up their bank accounts in heaven, but many are preparing an iron cell for themselves in hell because of the poor. Some even use the poor to earn their living by using devious charity and ministry schemes. Will the poor be your joy in heaven or your agony in hell? There is no neutral ground—you must have an attitude toward the poor, the oppressed, and the aliens, and that attitude has much to do with your eternal destiny!

The LORD'S Claim to the Earth and all its Riches

Not only does God give ability to men to make wealth, but he owns all the people and their wealth! Whether it is the diamonds, the gold, the silver, the precious gems, or any other mineral, the oil, and the like, all belong to him. He is the Creator and Landlord of all that we tap from his earth, and as such, we must use the wealth according to his dictates. If we do not, as we do today, he will come and lay his rightful claim to the wealth and drive the wicked custodians to everlasting dungeons.

Here are Yahweh's claims; *"The earth is the LORD'S, and everything in it, the world, and all who live in it; for he founded it upon the seas and established it upon the waters"* (Ps. 24:1-2). Again, he says; *"I have no need of a bull from your stall or of goats from your pens, for every animal of the forest is mine, and the cattle on a thousand hills. I know every bird in the mountains, and the creatures of the field are mine. If I were hungry I would not tell you, for the world is mine, and all that is in it"* (Ps. 50:9- 11). The Sovereign LORD declares; *"The silver is mind and the gold is mine"* (Hag.

2:8). Yahweh is the God of all mankind and their possessions; *"Rise up, O God, judge the earth, for all the nations are your inheritance"* (Ps. 82:8). *"I am the LORD, the God of all mankind. Is anything too hard for me?"* (Jer. 32:27).

It is God who gives life and breath and the ability and conditions necessary to all to make riches. He has set the seasons in place and waters the earth abundantly with snow, rain, and the rivers, and gives it light and life from the sun (Matt. 5:45; Acts 14:17). If he shuts up the sky so that it should not rain, even the most technologically advanced will not produce food! At the height of her glory, God reminded Belshazzar that it was he who raised Babylon to that status and could equally bring them down to nothing (Dan. 5:18-23). God holds in his hand the life and ways of all mankind and does with them as he pleases, and directs them for his purposes; *"The LORD works out everything for his own ends--even the wicked for a day of disaster"* (Pr. 16:4)

Perhaps one would argue "I am rich because I worked hard, so why do I have to give up my wealth to the poor?" Thou ignorant man, consider this, it is God who gives all men the ability to produce wealth. He not only owns the earth and all the wealth that comes from it, but he also owns your very life! *"... he himself gives all men life and breath and everything else. ... For in him we live and move and have our being. ... We are his offspring"* (1 Tim. 6:13a; Acts 17:25, 28). We must not make the mistake of many in the West that the blessing of wealth is evidence of being Christians. Yes, it may be the case, but God equally gives ability to all men, not only Christians, to produce wealth, whether Muslim, Hindu, Buddhist, Atheist, Japanese Shinto, and others. It is a grave mistake to rely on the fact that wealth is a sign that God is in our midst. In fact, the wicked prosper many times over than Christians! Jeremiah cries out and complains about the prosperity of the wicked as follows; *"You are always righteous, O LORD, when I bring a case before you. Yet I would speak with you about your justice: Why does the way of the wicked prosper? Why do all the faithless live at ease? You have planted them, and they have taken root; they grow and bear fruit. **You are always on their lips but far from their hearts**"* (Jer. 12:1-2).

God not only owns all the wealth of the wicked, but he would at the end strip and plunder them of their wealth and give it as an inheritance to the righteous. He will plunder those who plunder the poor now and give their wealth to the poor who serve him; *"A man can do nothing better than to eat and drink and find satisfaction in his work. This too, I see, is from the hand of God, for without him, who can eat or find enjoyment?* **To the man who pleases him, God gives wisdom, knowledge and happiness, but to the sinner he gives the task of gathering and storing up wealth to hand it over to the one who pleases God"** (Eccl. 2:24-26; cf. Is. 18:7; 23:18; 45:14). So, either the rich give willingly to the poor and receive a reward or at the end lose all to the poor and eat gravel and languish in burning sulfur! We must give back to God all that is his. We must be good custodians and stewards of what he has placed in our care.

A Petition to God

Given therefore, that even Christians have remained racially conscious and divided, and that they equally strive to maintain the status quo on the First World/Third World divide, I have launched a petition to God to partition heaven according to colors, and into First World heaven (rich and wealthy and with all comfort) and Third World heaven (poor and destitute and without any comfort). This, I hope will satisfy those who think that color is what makes them better than others before God, and those who think that living in affluence makes them better before God than the poor. If God is going to reject my petition, (and I am afraid he will), then many will be shocked and disappointed when the trumpet shall sound. For it is God who says; *"'Do not consider his appearance or his height* [color, beauty, handsomeness], *for I have rejected him. The LORD does not look at the things man looks at. Man looks at the outward appearance* [which is primarily what racism is all about], *but the LORD looks at the heart.'"* Proverbs echoes this in chapter 31:30; *"Charm is deceptive, and beauty is fleeting; ...."* If we live in this life and our primary identity is our skin color or how much possessions we have, as appears to be the case in most instances, it is clear evidence that we are not heading to heaven. If there will be no racial or economic caste in heaven, and we live and promote a caste system in on earth, even in Christendom (especially in economics and wealth build up), we are in danger of hell fire. There are many who are first who shall be last and there are many who are last who shall be first. The truth of this saying is staggering as we are already seeing it being fulfilled— Christianity is fast declining in the First World but gaining ground in the Third World (1 Co. 1:26-29; James 2:5-7). Let us consider Jesus' warning again; *"But woe to you who are rich, for you have already received your comfort. Woe to you who are well fed now, for you will go hungry. Woe to you who laugh now, for you will mourn and weep"* (Luke 6:24-25).

CHAPTER 13

THE FALL OF THE FREE WORLD

A s we have seen, God gave a panorama of Gentile history and how it will end through Nebuchanezzar and Daniel the prophet. Isaiah and Ezekiel, and most of the prophets, also saw a glimpse of the final fall of the Gentile world, which is depicted as the fall of Satan and his angels. It is at this time that Satan and his angels (who rebelled long ago but remained in heaven; Job 1:6) will be expelled finally from heaven (Rev. 12:3-4,7-9). **This time of world civilization is referred to biblically as the "Times of the Gentiles."** It is the time of trampling underfoot of Jerusalem, which also represents mankind's trampling of God's laws and commands (Ps. 2:1-3). Jesus spoke about the Age of the Gentiles as follows; *"Jerusalem will be trampled on by the Gentiles until the times of the Gentiles are fulfilled"* (Luke 21:24b). This is echoed in Revelation 11:2; *"But exclude the outer court; do not measure it, because it has been given to the Gentiles. They will trample on the holy city for 42 months."*

Typology Revisited

In chapter one, I defined typology as event or events, object, or objects, individual or individuals, and idea or ideas, that point forward to future ones or anticipate God's activity later in history. The former is a prototype of the latter. Only when the latter has occurred or is occurring can we be able to understand its prototype (former). Typologies are events or predictions that have immediate and distant fulfillment or patterns of recurrence. The LORD revealed an event in the prophet's immediate future that anticipated an event or events of a similar kind and even greater, in the distant future.

Typology Illustrated: Typology may not necessarily mean literal fulfillment. It simply means that what is occurring is similar or a type of what occurred before. The most striking example is the usage of the word "sodomy" in our modern times, to refer to excessive sexual immorality and sexual perversion, especially homosexual activity, and oral sex. [The *Oxford Illustrated American Dictionary,* defines *Sodom* as "a wicked or depraved place," and *sodomy* as "sexual intercourse involving anal or oral [mouth] copulation [sex]."] Therefore, when a place is referred to as Sodom, this does not imply that the city or nation in question has literally become Sodom or that the individual so described lived in Sodom of old (a Sodomite). It simply means that the city or nation or individual is **acting like the people of Sodom did. They are a type of Sodom. They are repeating a pattern like that of Sodom. In this chapter, I will connect the fact that the fall of the free world will typologically represent the fall of Satan.** Consensus on biblical interpretation holds that the fall of Satan depicted in Isaiah 14 (fall of Babylon and her king) and Ezekiel 28 (fall of Tyre and her the king), both typologically point to the fall of Satan at the end of time (that is, by the fall of the Antichrist, king of Babylon, as in Revelation 18). Solomon's statement on moral history that; *"What has been will be again, what has been done will be done again; there is nothing new under the sun. Is there anything of which one can say, 'Look! This is something new'? It was here already, long ago; it was here before our time"* (Eccl. 1:9-10), helps to explain typology. What has been will be again! If not identical, it would be similar and even of a greater magnitude.

Sodom and Gomorrah

Of these cities, it is written; *"Then the LORD said, 'The outcry against Sodom and Gomorrah is so great and their sin so grievous that I will go down and see if what they have done is as bad as the outcry that has reached me. If not, I will know"* (Gen. 18:20-21). Again, we read in Genesis 19:4-5; *"Before they had gone to bed, all the men from every part of the city of Sodom—both young and old-- surrounded the house. They called out to Lot, 'Where are those men who came to you tonight? Bring them out to us so that we can have sex with them.'* Yes, the outcry about the wickedness and sin of Sodom and Gomorrah was great, and their homosexual activity was alarming. It was same for both the old and the young. They had all become depraved perverts and had corrupted their ways. We learn more about their evil from other parts of Scripture—they became a bad legend and a by-word. Israel at some points in her history was likened to Sodom, which means they were depraved to the same degree as the Sodomites. **Two passages of Scripture help to highlight what else was going on wrong in Sodom, which expands the definition of sodomy, not only limiting it to sexual perversion, but also including gross sin, especially rebellion and hypocritical worship** (Is. 1:2-17); **overfeeding or gluttony, arrogance, haughtiness or pride, and apathy or being unconcerned** (Ezek. 16:46-50). Thus, any modern city or nation that displays these characteristics, can be legitimately called Sodom. As you read the Bible, look at the world, what do you see? What are the practical implications or significances for our day and society? Also, when prophets prophesy lies, they are likened to Sodomites (Jer. 23:9-14).

Egypt

What was wrong with her? What legend or prototype did she become? Is it like any powerful nations today (Is.19-20)? Egypt was full of national idols (statues or heads of Pharaohs on hills and/or pyramids) and the Egyptians were swollen up with pride and arrogance. **God crushed Egypt by causing civil strife, crime, and murder amongst themselves.** Finally, Egypt was destroyed and exiled by Assyria. Egypt trusted in and consulted her idols, spirits of the dead, mediums, spiritists, wise counselors (who were indeed, fools), senseless advisers, foolish officials, deceptive leaders who led Egypt astray. The LORD himself had poured upon these wise men, a spirit of dizziness and they staggered like drunkards. Egypt became a prototype of strong and proud superpowers.

Tyre

What was wrong with her? What kind of prototype did she become? **Tyre was an economic giant that exalted herself above the rest of the nations and against Jerusalem.** She boasted that she was perfect in beauty and had her domain on the high seas (strong naval power), and excellent architects that built here to perfection. The LORD said of her prosperity; *"Your wealth, merchandise and wares, your mariners, seamen and shipwrights, your merchants and all your soldiers, and everyone else on board will sink into the heart of the sea on the day of your shipwreck"* (Ezek. 27:27; cf. Rev. 18). Is Tyre like any prosperous or economic giant or nation today that receives as many sea containers as possible and merchandise annually and is also a strong naval power with domain on the seas (from sea to sea)?

Babylon

What was wrong with Babylon, the greatest superpower of antiquity (whose leader, Nebuchadnezzar, was once called God's servant; Jer. 25:9; 27:6; 51:7)? Is Babylon like any nation or nations today? Babylon was the greatest superpower of antiquity (Is. 13-14:23). The day of the LORD or day of Wrath for them equaled invasion, war, and disaster. This day of wrath was historically fulfilled but is yet future according to Revelation 18! Thus, Babylon of old was just a prototype. Babylon would be attacked and vanquished by the LORD'S army then (Medes/Persians; Dan. 5:30), and now, by the Prince of Peace.

Is the Free World Actually Free?

Definition

What is freedom or liberty? Is there any universal consensus as to the definition of this mysterious word or concept? Who defines freedom? The *Oxford Illustrated American Dictionary* defines *free* as

"1 not in bondage to or under the control of another, having personal rights and social and political liberty. 2 (of a nation or its citizens) not subject to foreign domination nor to despotic government; having national and civil liberty … 3 **a** unrestricted; not restrained or fixed. **b** not confined or imprisoned, **c** released from ties or duties, **d** unrestrained as to action; independent," etc.

That is freedom as we define it and see it today. But freedom or liberty is defined largely by the person using the expression and, in most cases, the usage must be understood in the context. The word "freedom" or "liberty" does not always mean the same thing in all situations and to all people. Their meaning is always tied to the person using the word or to the context in which it is used.

One of the most important things about freedom is that it goes with responsibility. Freedom is not irresponsibility. We are responsible for every free decision and action that we make or take. For every free action there are consequences. Life in general is a product of free choices. Every human action result from a choice, and each choice has consequences. In freedom (volition) lies the power of life and death (Deut. 30:15-20) and the power of evil and virtue; *"And the LORD God commanded the man, 'You are free to eat from any tree in the garden; but you must not eat from the tree of the knowledge of good and evil, for when you eat of it you will surely die"* (Gen. 2:16-17). Thus, the difference between good and evil lies in freedom. Freedom is what led to Satan's fall. Freedom is what led to man's fall. Freedom will make the difference between who goes to heaven and who goes to hell! Your freedom will determine your destiny. In a sense, freedom is the origin of evil.

Types of Freedoms

The context of a word determines its meaning and/or depends on who uses it. Just as an illustration, the word "liberty" was commonly used during the American revolutionary war both in the churches and on the political platform. In most cases it was used as meaning the same thing. But in the true context, the word as used by politicians had nothing in common with the word as used by Paul, the apostle, from whom the pastors of the era derived their meaning. Freedom from Britain was not identical with freedom to which Christ Jesus has called believers (Gal. 5:1). In this context, believers are freed from the yoke of slavery, which is the law, particularly circumcision. To equate this freedom with that strove for against Britain, is reading into the text. When this distinction is not made, a lot of misunderstanding sets in, which can be very misleading.

God is Free: God is a free being and can do anything and everything as he pleases and no one can ask him, "What are you doing?" (Dan. 4:34-35). He is not under any restrain but acts freely according to his plan and will. He is not responsible to anyone but himself, that is, his integrity. God can only be restrained in respect to his spoken word. What he has said or promised, he is bound by it and will do it (Ps. 89:34). This is in conformity to his integrity, for he is not a man that he should change his mind or lie. No one can give God counsel as to what to do (Rom. 11:33-35).

Angelic Freedom: Angels are God's creatures or spirits (sometimes appearing in human form; Gen. 18-19:29; Heb. 13:1-2) that are in the presence of God. The Angels delight in God's creative work (Job 38:4-7). They worship and serve God (and serve the redeemed) and do his bidding as messengers (Ps. 103:20-21; 148:2-5; Heb. 1:14; see angels in the book of Revelation). They are higher, stronger, and more powerful than humans (Ps. 8:5; Col. 1:16). Although stronger than humans, angels are limited in knowledge in respect to human salvation (1 Pet. 1:12). While they are powerful now and above humans, redeemed mankind will be above them in the age to come, as believers are elevated to a superior status with Jesus Christ, which is above that of the angels (Heb. 1:4-14; 2:5-9,16). The world to come or the age to come (Millennium/eternity) is subjected to redeemed mankind but not to angels, which is why believers shall judge the angels (1 Co. 6:3).

Angels are free beings—they have volition. Angels know God very well though not completely, yet they have the freedom to obey or disobey him. This is precisely what happened or has happened to some angels under the leading angel, Satan, who has become God's number one enemy, aspiring to be as God. In their freedom, angels chose or have chosen to rebel against God by disobeying his word. These angels, now known as demons, actively oppose God and his plan, but will be judged at the end (Eph. 6:12; 2 Pet. 2:4; Jude 6). Satan and his demons will be condemned because they willingly and freely disobey God and his word. The difference between obedience and disobedience, therefore, is freedom. There is no freedom without responsibility or consequences. What you plant that you will reap. [In this chapter, I have likened the free world's freedom to angelic freedom—they know 100 percent that it is against God and his word, but they choose to do it anyway!].

Adam and Eve's Freedom: Freedom of choice (volition) is God's greatest gift to man. It is what makes us human. A free God who made man in his image, could only make humans that are free as he is. Freedom is essential to any relationship. Life will be meaningless if there were no options. It is because God loves his creatures that he has given them volition. From the onset, God made man in his own image, and that image included freedom, for God is a free being. With freedom, was the option to obey or disobey God. Freedom is the gift that God lovingly endowed our first parents (Adam and Eve). Would they appreciate, respect, and obey the one who had freely given them life and everything? **God does not and will never coerce anyone to obey him** nor will he ever take away human freedom. He is not interested in creating robots! Not then, not now, not in the age to come! It is written; *"And the LORD God commanded the man, 'You are free to eat from any tree in the garden; but you must not eat from the tree of the knowledge of good and evil, for when you eat of it you will surely die"* (Gen. 2:16- 17). **God's freedom has boundaries--his word.** But Adam and his wife freely chose to disobey the voice (word) of God because they were not satisfied only to be in the image of God, they wanted to be like God himself. So, the tempter (Satan) said to the woman;

> *"For God knows that when you eat of it your eyes will be opened,, and you will be like God, knowing good and evil. When the woman saw that the fruit of the tree was good for food and pleasing to the eye, and also desirable for gaining wisdom, she took some and ate it. She gave some to her husband, who was with her, and he ate it. ... And the LORD God said, 'The man has now become like one of us, knowing good and evil. He must not be allowed to reach out his hand and take also from the tree of life and eat, and live forever'"* (Gen. 3:5-6, 22).

So, man was cursed and deprived of eternal existence because of his free choice to disobey God. However, this curse was reversed in Jesus Christ. Those who freely choose to obey him will drink from the water of life and live forever (Rev. 22:17). By an act of freedom (John 7:17) mankind was cursed and death entered humanity, but by an act of freedom, man can live forever (John 3:16, 36; 6:40). Would you choose to obey God and live with him forever or choose to disobey God and spend eternity in hell? It's all your choice! Your freedom will determine your eternal destiny. You are free to choose heaven or hell, but not both.

Freedom of Adam's Progeny: From the disobedience of Adam, sin entered the world, and is genetically transmitted (termed original sin or sin nature) to all of Adam's progeny. We are not only born with the potential to sin, but with the propensity to sin. It is written; *"... sin entered the world through one man, and death through sin, and in this way death came to all men, because all sinned--"* (Rom. 5:12).

All are born free yet slaves to sin;

"As for you, you were dead in your transgressions and sins, in which you used to live when you followed the ways of this world and of the ruler of the kingdom of the air [Satan], *the spirit who is now at work in those who are disobedient. All of us also lived among them at one time, gratifying the cravings of our sinful nature and following its desires and thoughts. Like the rest, we were by nature objects of wrath"* (Eph. 2:1-3).

All people (even under slavery, foreign occupation, or dictatorship/tyranny) have this fundamental freedom, except the mentally handicapped. **Every human can make personal choices no matter the external circumstances. Most of all, they can decide to follow God/Jesus. Jesus says;** *"If anyone chooses to do God's will ..."* (John 7:17). From this basic freedom, every human being is able to make whatever choice they wish to make.

Freedom from Man-made Slavery: The Bible illustrates at several instances that people could lose their freedom when they are enslaved by others or voluntarily place themselves under slave masters. Such slavery does not necessarily mean dehumanization of the slave as has been the case in modern history. A typical example of slavery is Israel in Egypt a long time after the death of Joseph (Ex. 1; 2:23-25). A modern example is the slavery practiced by Europeans from the fifteenth to the twentieth century in the Americas. Under such slavery the slaves are at the mercy of their slave owners. When the yoke of such slavery is broken, the slaves are said to have acquired freedom. That is, freedom from being under the ownership of their slave masters (The Exodus and Ex. 21).

Political Freedom: When a nation is living on its own without foreign oppression or domination, and enjoying ample civil rights (for instance, freedom of speech, press, property ownership, freedom of religion, etc.), it is said to be free. This kind of freedom is the one largely covered in the definition of *free* above. **Whether nations enjoy this freedom or not, is not God's primary concern.** Does that surprise you? When God brought the Israelites into the promised land, he granted them rest from their enemies. The law provided ample civil rights for the Israelites. Thus, in a sense, the Israelites enjoyed political freedom. However, when they sinned by worshipping other gods, God took away this freedom by allowing them to be subjected by foreign nations. This was the case during the reign of the Judges (see the book of Judges). When they continued in sin, God completely took away their political freedom by sending them into exile in Assyria and Babylon. Ever since, the Jews have never completely had absolute political freedom. It is apparent that the Jews served God more when they were under foreign domination or in exile. **Thus, political freedom had adverse or negative effects on the Jews, and only when God took it away, did they cry out to him. Political freedom bred complacency and indulgence and idolatry!** During the time of Babylon, God took away the political freedom of the surrounding independent nations by giving them over to the king of Babylon (Jer. 25:15-38; 27).

During the time of Jesus on earth, Rome was the dominant empire of the Mediterranean world, and the Jews were under their domination. It was under these conditions that Jesus lived and ministered. **In a sense, Jesus had no political freedom! He was**

constantly under the threat of the occupying Roman authorities, who eventually tried and crucified him (Matt. 2:3-18; Mark 8:15; Luke 13:31-32; John 18:28-19:16). Wait a minute, a free state crucified Jesus Christ? This illustrates to us that political freedom is not a prerequisite for spreading the gospel as many in the West think and would want us to believe. **The early church that thrived and triumphed up until Constantine, had no political freedom, yet they turned the world upside down.** Because Rome was in control, being a Roman citizen meant certain rights and privileges (Acts 16:37-39; 22:22-29; see KJV). Paul asserts that he was born free (that is, a Roman citizen), and a certain centurion stated that he had to pay a big price for his freedom (Roman citizenship), the same as many are doing today. We see therefore, that political freedom can be bought or lost. [Note: Although Paul was born free, he was a slave to sin, religion, and Satan, before his conversion.]

Political freedom can be acquired through military prowess as Rome did or as the United States did during the Revolutionary War of independence until now. We may pause to ask whether political freedom can be given? Nations can be liberated from foreign occupation or political tyranny by other nations. The question remains, would such freedom be absolute or under the shadow of the donor or liberator? In many respects, political freedom is relative. It strictly depends on who defines that freedom. Political freedom differs from nation to nation, depending on the level of socialism or government control, or even a nation's history (it is apparent that even in the Free World, British, Canadian, and an American, view freedom differently, so do other nations). Above all, political freedom comes at a price. It may involve human sacrifice through warfare. Sometimes it involves giving up free thinking to succumb to nationalistic thinking. In such instances, absolute political freedom is still slavery, that is, to the government and the nationalistic impulse or spirit. It is sometimes a trap that can lead to eternal damnation. You must be careful what price you pay for political freedom, sometimes it is your very life, even eternal life! Far from anything, freedom is not free!

Freedom Given by Christ: Jesus Christ is the only true liberator, and the freedom he gives is different in many ways to freedom given by man (especially political freedom). **All sinful mankind, even with Adamic freedom and political freedom are slaves to sin;** *"Jesus replied, 'I tell you the truth, **everyone who sins is a slave to sin'"*** (John 8:34; cf. Rom. 6:11-18). While Jesus can enable people to be freed from prison, slavery, tyranny, and other dungeons, the ultimate freedom he gives is to save sinful man from sin and give them eternal life. Jesus declared; *"The Spirit of the Lord is on me, because he has anointed me to preach good news to the poor.* ***He has sent me to proclaim freedom*** *for the prisoners and recovery of sight for the blind, to release the oppressed, ..."* (Luke 4:18). It is this freedom given by Jesus that matters. In fact, you can have this ultimate freedom from Jesus and still be under human slavery and tyranny (Eph. 6:5-8; 1 Co. 7:21-22). Anyone who does not have Jesus Christ is in bondage and needs this true freedom. Sometimes, it is possible for religionists (religion is the most deceptive and dangerous form of slavery because you think you know and serve God, while at the same time you are his enemy) to deceive themselves that they have freedom, when in fact, they are Satan's slaves. To such people Jesus declares; ***"Then you will know the truth, and the truth will set you free. ... So if the Son sets you free, you will be free indeed"*** (John 8:32,36). This clearly indicates that no matter what kind of freedom you have, if you do not know the truth (the Word; Jesus Christ; John 14:6; 17:17), you have no true freedom. Thus, there are millions in the free world (with absolute political freedom), who desperately need freedom from Jesus. Jesus made these statements to the religious people of his day, who enjoyed relative political freedom under the Romans. Yet, they were slaves to sin, religion, the Romans, and even Satan (John 8:44). Yes, you can be politically free, but at the same time, a slave of sin and hence, a slave of Satan!

True freedom was guaranteed by the death of Jesus on the cross; not the Magna Charta, not the American revolutionary war, not the Allied victory over the German Nazis and Italian Fascists in World War II, important as they might have been. It is written; *"For this reason Christ is the mediator of a new covenant, that those who are called may receive the promised eternal inheritance—**now that he*** *has died as a ransom to set them free from the sins* committed under *the first covenant"* (Heb. 9:15). The blood of Jesus is the only blood shed that can guarantee true freedom, the only ransom paid for the souls of men. No other human blood (whether of millions of soldiers) shed by men on behalf of men, can grant any freedom that matters before God. As it is written; *"No man can redeem* [grant freedom] *the life of another or give to God a ransom for him—the ransom for a life is costly, no payment is enough—that he should live on forever and not see decay"* (Ps. 49:7-9). Only the ransom paid by Jesus Christ can redeem another man's life so that they may live forever (eternal life) and not see decay! Christ also died to free men from Satan's prison cell of fear of death; *"Since the children have flesh and blood, he too shared in their humanity so that by his death he might destroy him who holds the power of death—that is, the devil—**and free those who all their lives were held in slavery by their fear of death**"* (Heb. 2:14-15).

Apostle Paul goes a great deal to elaborate on Christian freedom. In most cases he talks about freedom from the law of Moses (especially circumcision) and from human regulations or legalism (Gal. 5:1-13; Col. 2:6-23). However, he warns that Christians should not use their freedom to indulge in sin--libertinism (antinomianism), or to destroy the faith of others (1 Co. 8:9-13). We are only free to do that which is acceptable to Christ according to his word and beneficial to the church.

Apostle Peter in the context of respect and honor to governmental authorities, says to the believers; *"Live as free men, but do not use your freedom as a cover-up for evil; live as servants of God"* (1 Pet. 2:16). It would be a contradiction to go against what the Bible teaches simply because you are free.

Freedom as slavery: Peter talks about people in our days who claim to have freedom, but are sold to all kinds of sins and depravity (2 Peter 2). They are full of debauchery and;

> *"Their idea of pleasure is to carouse in broad daylight. They are blots and blemishes, reveling in their pleasures while they feast with you. With eyes full of adultery, they never stop sinning;*

they seduce the unstable; they are experts in greed--an accursed brood! ... These men are springs without water and mists driven by a storm. Blackest darkness is reserved for them. For they mouth empty, boastful words and, by appealing to the lustful desires of sinful human nature [especially the promise of wealth, affluence, ostentatious living and self-indulgence or a better life], *they entice people who are just escaping from those who live in error* [people just believing in Christ are deceived by such promises]. **They promise them freedom, while they themselves are slaves to depravity--for a man is slave to whatever has mastered him"** (vv.13-19).

One cannot read these verses and especially verse 19, without reminiscing of the Abu Ghraib scandal in Iraq. Those who were messengers of freedom committed indecent acts to demonstrate the sodomy of their homeland. These men will be judged severely. This is freedom without responsibility, which equals depravity and chaos. It is freedom that is a form of slavery—slavery to sin, religion, and Satan. People with such political freedom desperately need freedom from Jesus Christ!

Confusing Freedom Given by God/Christ with Political Freedom: Satan was a liar and trickster from the start—*"He* [The Devil] *was a murderer from the beginning, not holding to the truth, for there is no truth in him. When he lies, he speaks his native language, for he is a liar and the father of lies"* (John 8:44). Satan twists the word of God to appear as though it is the actual thing, just to get his deceptive agenda going. He guises his goals and makes them so appealing that they appear to come from God/Christ. To be sure, God wants people to be free, but political freedom is not God's primary goal. If it were, he would have made it clear when he visited earth 2000 years ago, or even in his word. Why did Jesus not fight a revolutionary war against the Romans and establish a free kingdom of God? Why did he allow the disciples under Roman domination and occupation? Because his kingdom is not of this world and his fight for freedom is different from the world's (John 18:36). While political freedom and Christ's freedom may co-exist (not mutually exclusive), they are very different! You may be politically free but lack Christ's freedom, because you are enslaved by sin. Failure to make this distinction, especially in these last days, will lead to falling into Satan's trap. The Pharisees enjoyed some Roman political freedom (see especially their alliance with Roman authorities in Mark 8:14-15, and at the crucifixion), and so did Paul before his conversion, but they lacked Christ's freedom--they were in bondage. Jesus still told the apparently politically free Pharisees and Romans that they needed freedom, which comes from the truth (John 8:32,36; 18:33-38).

Therefore, is the freedom America (political freedom) offers to the world as claimed by the American president (George W. Bush on Iraqi invasion); "Freedom is not only America's gift to the world, it is God's gift to the world," identical with God's freedom to the world? Is democracy equal to the gospel of Jesus Christ? There is a fine line of deception here that the naïve are unable to discern to their own detriment. Satan likes to imitate God and twist his word to carry out his agenda. He has no original and thus, counterfeits what is God's to deceive the myopic or short sighted (Rom. 16:17-20). Deception is dressing evil with clean apparel to make it appealing and acceptable or giving an appealing name to a hidden diabolic agenda. AMERICA'S FREEDOM TO THE WORLD IS NOT IDENTICAL WITH GOD'S FREEDOM TO THE WORLD! That is the devil's trick/bait and lie! GOD'S FREEDOM TO THE WORLD IS JESUS CHRIST, NOT IMPERIALISTIC AMERICAN DEMOCRACY! It is written; *"Then you will know the truth* [Jesus and his word], *and the truth will set you free* [from the bondage of sin and earthly burdens]." *"So if the Son* [Jesus Christ, not America!] *sets you free, you will be free indeed"* (John 8:32,36). Your eternity is at stake if you do not make the distinction. Are you free?

This Generation (The Terminal Generation)

When the doctor diagnoses your illness and tells you that it is terminal, you know that your days are up. If you do not have a will, you try to write one and start making funeral arrangements. As we shall see briefly in this section, the current generation has a terminal disease. The cancer is fierce, ruthless, and malignant, and will kill this generation within a very short time. Jesus frequently used the expression "this generation" to refer to the people of his day (a generation represents approximately 40 to 70 years). However, 2000 years ago, Jesus was seeing our days like it was in normal two days' time to him and spoke of our days then as though present. God lives in eternity future, and what will be in 1000 or 5000 years, and so on, from now exists in the presence of God now, and he can speak of it as in the present or even in the past. That is how Jesus viewed our generation—the generation that would experience and witness most of the end-time signs. To get lost in the historical distance is to miss the point. The simple question to ask is "Are these things the Bible talks about happening in our generation?" If yes, you know that we are there, it is our generation! The generation that is experiencing all these signs listed in Matthew 24: increase wars; false prophets; lack of love; earthquakes; pandemics; great distress in general.

During this distress and deception, Christ will be revealed; *"So if anyone tells you 'There he is, out in the desert,' do not go out; or, 'Here he is, in the inner rooms,' do not believe it.* **For as lightning that comes from the east is visible even in the west, so will be the coming of the Son of Man.** *Wherever there is a carcass, there the vultures will gather.* **Immediately after the distress of those days 'the sun will be darkened,** *and the moon will not give its light; the stars will fall from the sky, and the heavenly bodies will be shaken* [cf. Heb. 12:26-27; Hag. 2:6]. '**At that time the sign of the Son of Man will appear in the sky, and all the nations of the earth will mourn** [Rev. 1:7]. **They will see the Son of Man coming on the clouds of the sky, with power and great glory**. *And he will send his angels with a loud trumpet call, and they will gather his elect* [believers] *from the four winds, from one end of the heavens to the other"* (vv.26-31).

Now that the fig tree has budded (vv.32-35), that is, Israel is waking up as a nation, and the signs are all around us (wars and rumors of wars, wickedness, moral decay, famines, earthquakes, terror, and distress, etc.), we can know that it is near—it is at the door. We can be sure from Jesus' word; *"Even so, when you see all these things, you know that it is near, right at the door. I tell you the truth, this generation* [that is, the one experiencing these signs] *will certainly not pass away until all these things have happened. Heaven and earth will pass away, but my words will never pass away"* (vv.33-35). Thus, these things will happen within a single generation—the lifetime of many, that is, who have experienced or witnessed these things.

This generation is like the days of Noah (a pattern repeated); *"As it was in the days of Noah, so it will be at the coming of the Son of Man. For in the days before the flood, people were eating and drinking, marrying and giving in marriage, up to the day Noah entered the ark; and they knew nothing about what would happen until the flood came and took them all away. That is how it will be at the coming of the Son of Man"* (vv.37-39; cf. Gen. 6:1-8; Noah's days was a time characterized by universal wickedness as it is in our days—sexual immorality replete with demonism—sex with children or child molestation especially incestuous cases, rape, pornography and child pornography, crime, murder, and the like). It is written in Exodus 32:6 that the people (Israelites) sat down to eat and drink and got up to indulge in pagan revelry (entertainment). Paul expressly calls this behavior, idolatry, when he warns against this avaricious and lewd behavior; *"Do not be idolaters, as some of them* [Israelites] *were; as it is written: 'The people sat down to eat and drink and got up to indulge in pagan revelry"* (1 Co. 10:7). Yes, our generation sits down and eat and drink (gluttony and drunkenness) and get up to engage in pagan revelry and orgies (watch TV—sports, X and XXX movies, sitcoms, soap operas, and the like! Never in the history of mankind have so few corrupted the minds of so many and turn them from the Lord as in the TV or Screen age; evil communication corrupts good character! 1 Co. 15:33). We are living in the obscene, indecent, and gluttonous generation. No surprise, morals have plummeted, and even when there are famines elsewhere in the world, some nations are suffering from obesity epidemics because of gluttony! You cannot miss the signs if only you will look with spiritual eyes!

Luke 17:28-33: Our days are also like the days of Lot, with rampant sexual perversion and sodomy (the abominations of homosexuality, lesbianism, and oral sex; overfeeding, complacency, arrogance, haughtiness, and other detestable practices; cf. Ezek. 16:49-50). Jesus says, *"It was the same in the days of Lot. People* *were eating and drinking, buying and selling, planting and building. But the day Lot left Sodom, **fire and sulfur rained down from heaven and destroyed them all.** It will be just like this on the day the Son of Man is revealed."* Jesus then gives a stern warning; ***"Remember Lot's wife!*** [who loved the world (the cities and their splendor) and looked back!]. ***Whoever tries to keep his life will lose it, and whoever loses his life will preserve it."*** Billions (including professing Christians) will certainly lose their lives and eternity because they cling to worthless idols—the world and all that it offers—silver, gold, money, wealth; and comforts like cars, clothes, fine houses, the junk gadgets, just to name a few. But if you lose all for the sake of Christ, you will gain all and even more, and above all, enter the kingdom of heaven! You will have eternal life!

Luke 21:16-28: In these verses, Luke records the parallel account as that recorded in Matthew 24 as quoted above. Worthy of note is that; ***"There will be great distress in the land and wrath against this people*** [the wicked and those who forsake God]. ... *There will be signs in the sun, moon and stars. On the earth, nations will be in anguish and perplexity at the roaring and tossing of the sea* [hurricanes, tornadoes, floods, etc.]. ***Men will faint from terror*** [current terrorism], ***apprehensive of what is coming on the world,*** *for the heavenly bodies will be shaken"* (vv.23-26). Again, Jesus gives another stern warning; ***"Be careful, or your hearts will be weighed down with dissipation*** [summed up in one word, entertainment and fun, which unfortunately has overcome most, including professing Christians], ***drunkenness and the anxieties of life*** [what to eat, drink, wear, and where to live—houses, etc. (Matt. 6:25-32), which unfortunately is the very ethos of consumerism and materialistic societies], *and that day will close on you unexpectedly like a trap. For it will come upon all those who live on the face of the whole earth.* ***Be always on your watch, and pray that you may be able to escape all that is about to happen, and that you may be able to stand before the Son of Man."*** (vv.34-36). Should our societies continue the present trend, the day of Christ will trap many, even those sitting on the pews in churches. Dissipation is the order of the day and not the exception, and the frantic pursuit of happiness and dream life, has weighed down many with the anxieties of life as is visible in the psychological breakdowns rampant today. If there has ever been any time to be very watchful, it is now! If there has ever been any time to flee from the world and its idols, it is now! Will the Son of Man come and find you faithfully watching and waiting? Will the Son of man return and find faith on the earth (Luke 18:8)?

Romans 1:18-32: Here is a blueprint of vices that characterize our generation and God's attitude toward them;

> *"The wrath of God is being revealed from heaven against all the godlessness and wickedness of men* who suppress the truth by their wickedness, since what may be known about God is plain to them, because God has made it plain to them. For since the creation of the world God's invisible qualities--his eternal power and divine nature--have been clearly seen, being understood from what has been made, so that men are without excuse. *For although they knew God, they neither glorified him as God nor gave thanks to him, but their thinking became futile and their foolish hearts were darkened. Although they claimed to be wise, they became fools and exchanged the glory of the immortal God for images made to look like mortal man and birds and animals and reptiles.* Therefore God gave them over in the sinful desires of their hearts to sexual impurity for the degrading of their bodies with one another. They exchanged the truth of God for a lie, and worshiped and served created things rather than the Creator--who is forever praised. Amen. Because of this God gave them over to shameful lusts. *Even their women exchanged natural relations for unnatural ones. In the same way men also abandoned natural relations with women and were inflamed with lust for one another. Men committed indecent acts with other men,* and received in themselves the due penalty for their perversion. Furthermore, since they did not think it worthwhile to retain the knowledge of God, he gave them over to a depraved mind, to do what ought not to be done. *They have become filled with every kind of wickedness, evil, greed, and depravity. They are full of envy, murder, strife, deceit and malice. They are gossips, slanderers, God-haters, insolent, arrogant and boastful; they invent ways of doing evil; they disobey parents;*

they are senseless, faithless, heartless, ruthless. Although they know God's righteous decree that those who do such things deserve death, they not only continue to do these very things but also approve of those who practice them."

If you cannot perform sexual acts in front of others or rant sexual innuendo and verbiage, but take delight in watching it, whether in sitcoms, shows or pornography, you are equally guilty with the performers (v.32). This verse makes it categorically clear that the people who do these things *"know God's righteous decree that those who do such things deserve death,"* that is, they know that they deserve judgment and hell. In fact, Paul states in verse 18 that *"they suppress the truth by their wickedness."* Thus, they know what is true and right, and God's attitude toward their abominable actions. Yet as God-haters, they defiantly do them anyway! That is why their thinking is described as "futile" and their minds as "depraved" and their hearts as "foolish" and "darkened." They are utterly useless— they are without excuse—they will be condemned. How much of this debauchery do you participate in or approve? How much of the above description fit the society in which you live? How close do you think we are to judgment? Perhaps, as close as today is to tomorrow! How much watching do you think you have to do? Take a piece of paper and make your check list of these vices. How many of them are you guilty of or approve of? Or how many do you see in your society? The apostle Paul provides us with another check list of the terrible times of the last days in **2 Timothy 3:1-13**

It is rather striking that Paul ends this list by talking about persecution. The professing Christians who seem to portray some of the vices above, indeed, have a form of godliness but do not live in the power of the Spirit. Such people are described as evil men and impostors, who have evaded persecution and settled for a false religious freedom that is Satan's bait. They deceive others and are themselves being deceived. That is, they do not know that they are living in deception or living a lie. When you do not truly follow Christ, you are Satan's follower and Satan will not persecute you. But if, as Paul says, you want to live a godly life in Jesus Christ, Satan will persecute you. Notice that Paul does not say you may or might be persecuted, he says YOU WILL BE PERSECUTED! The true church of Jesus Christ today is undergoing persecution, but the false and apostate church is under a delusion, deceiving and being deceived. They have struck a compromise with the devil! Therefore, be watchful about your false sense of security in these terrible times.

Keeping Watch: Here are some verses that admonish the believer to be alert during these terrible times of vice and apostasy. It is a time to endure; a time to keep your lamp burning with enough reserved oil; a time to wake up from slumber and live in the light; a time to arise from the dead so that Christ might shine in you; a time to flee from any of the above mentioned vices; a time to flee from the love of the world and idols; a time to flee from Babylon; a time to look upward to the sky for the arriving Savior and not downward to the earth and the god of this age. Wake up! Watch out! (Matt. 24:42, 45-47; Mark 13:32-37; Luke 21:34-36; Rom. 13:11-14; Gal. 5:16-26; Matt. 25:1-13; Eph. 4:17- 5:20; Col. 3:1-17; 1 Thess. 5:1-8; Heb. 12:14-17; 1 Pet. 1:13-16; 1 Thess. 4:1-12; 5:1-11; 1 Tim. 6:9-11; 1 John 2:15-17; 5:18-21; Mark 13:9-13; Heb. 12:1-4; Rev. 2:10; 12:11; 18:4). You must watch because we are living in the terminally ill generation. This generation has scooped the fires of hell onto their laps; will the fire not burn? (Pr. 6:27-27).

Countdown of Moral Depravity in the West

There has always been, of course, vice in human society from time immemorial. However, the countdown to depravity in our modern era is a little bit traceable. From the Industrial Revolution, family life and life in the villages began to shift to the cities—the industrial hubs. This began the breakdown of the family and the beginning of cities as centers of sin, as those who migrated to the cities made more money and began to live avaricious lifestyles. Ever since, the decline in family and moral life has continued until it has plummeted to the biblical proportions described in Romans 1 and Second Timothy 3 above. During this period is the rapid decline of biblical Christianity in the West, and the rise in occultism and political ideologies of religious proportions. The state has virtually become a god to be worshipped. While this moral decline began early in Europe, it finally caught up with North America and other Western-influenced nations around the world. In America, in particular, science and evolution, especially after the Scopes Trial of 1925, undermined and continues to undermine Christianity and biblical morality. Then came out right moral rebellion from the 1950s, with the advent of TV, Playboy, and the sexual revolution of the 1960s, which is characterized by the feminist movement (which others closely associate with witchcraft and sex—a resurgence of ancient religions that used sex as part of worship, with shrine prostitutes, child sacrifice or abortion, which was sanctioned by the law of the land, Roe v. Wade). This, of course, is blatant prostitution. Prostitution in the biblical context is not only selling sex for money, but living a seductive life that ensnares men to hell. To be deliberately sexy or seductive outside of marriage, is to be a prostitute whether paid or not paid. It is promiscuity! The Bible defines prostitution as follows;

> "For the lips of an adulteress drip honey, and her speech is smother than oil; but in the end she is bitter as gall, sharp as a double-edged sword. **Her feet go down to death; her steps lead straight to the grave** [hell]. **She gives no thought to the way of life; her paths are crooked, but she knows it not**" (Pr. 5:3-6).

> "Say to wisdom, 'You are my sister,' and call understanding your kinsman; they will keep you from the **adulteress, from the wayward wife with her seductive words**. At the window of my house I looked out through the lattice. I saw among the simple, I noticed among the young men, a youth who lacked judgment. He was going down the street near her corner, walking along in the direction of her house at twilight, as the day was fading, as the dark of night set in. **Then came out a woman to meet him, dressed like a prostitute and with crafty intent**. (She is loud and defiant, her feet never stay at home; now in the street, now in the squares, at every corner she lurks). She took hold of him and kissed him and with a brazen face she said: 'I have fellowship offerings at home; today I fulfilled my vows. So I came out to meet you; I looked for you and have found you! ... Come, let's drink deep of love till morning; let's enjoy ourselves with love! ... **With persuasive words she led him astray; she seduced him with her smooth talk**. All at once he followed her like an ox going to the

slaughter, like a deer stepping into a noose till an arrow pierces his liver, like a bird darting into a snare, little knowing it will cost him his life. ... Do not let your heart turn to her ways or stray into her paths. Many are the victims she has brought down; her slain are a mighty throng. **Her house is a highway to the grave** [hell]**, leading down to the chambers of death"** (Pr. 7:4-27).

Both women described as prostitutes here are adulteresses, which means they were married women seeking sex with someone else other than their husbands. In Proverbs 7, **the woman dresses seductively (that is, sexy, *"dressed like a prostitute and with crafty intent"* v.10)** and entices the youth solely for the purpose of coaxing him into sex. The youth does not pay her for sex, in fact, she was ready to give him anything for sex. Thus, our legal definition of a prostitute does not match up with the biblical definition. **In short, to be intentionally seductive (sexy), or have sex outside of marriage (whether fornication or adultery), is prostitution (whether paid or not paid); it's whoredom--it's promiscuity!**

Ezekiel also underscores the issue of **seductive dress that is intended to ensnare men;** *"Now, son of man, set your face against the daughters of your people who prophesy out of their own imagination. Prophesy against them and say, 'This is what the Sovereign LORD says:* **Woe to the women who sew magic charms on all their wrists and make veils of various lengths for their heads in order to ensnare people"** (Ezek. 13:17-18). Again, *"Woe! Woe to you, declares the Sovereign LORD. In addition to all your other wickedness, you build a mound for yourself and made a lofty shrine in every public square. At the head of every street you built your lofty shrines and degraded your beauty, offering your body with increasing promiscuity to anyone who passed by"* (16:23-25; Our modern equivalents would include bill boards, Playboy, tabloids, some magazines, seductive behavior deemed fashionable, advertising half-naked, fashion parades, etc.). This sleaziness, indecency, and impropriety, stands in direct opposition to the biblical injunction for decency; *"I also want women to dress modestly, with decency and propriety, not with braided hair or gold or pearls of expensive clothes, but with good* *deeds, appropriate for women who profess to worship God"* (1 Tim. 2:9-10; cf. 1 Pet. 3:3-5).

From the 1970s in the United States, sodomy came out of the closet to the streets—lesbianism, homosexuality, oral sex, increase rape, pornography, all of which are apparently demonically influenced (who walks naked in front of others in his or her right mind except the demon-possessed or insane?). All this concupiscence, lasciviousness, lewdness, abominable and detestable practices are fed into every home and exported to the world through the Hollywood screen in theaters, movies and internet, the source of the abominations of the earth. In the past thirty or so years, child molestation especially between parent and child (and it is reported that 1 out of every 4 girls in America are likely to be molested at childhood and mostly by people who know them), has greatly increased. Sex slavery has revived with the prostitution ring from North America through Europe to the depths of Asia. Abortion is committed for any and every reason, that is, child sacrifice (shedding innocent blood) to the goddess of sex and/or career and comfort. Apparently, those who propounded in the 1960s that God was dead were well on track! For since the 1960s, the demons of hell have been parading the streets and are sweeping as many as possible to the dungeons of hell. Truth has been cast to the ground; drugs, crime, murder, kidnapping, etc., are becoming the norm rather than the exception. Indeed, we are running on borrowed time. No longer are sinners in the hands of an angry God suspended on a thin thread over the fires of hell, but men are literally playing with the fires of hell already on their laps!

New gods have been created and together with demons are being worshipped (sometimes revered stars and celebrities are involved with the demonic and occult). As it is written; *"The rest of mankind that were not killed by these plagues still did not repent of the work of their hands;* **they did not stop worshiping demons, and idols of gold, silver, bronze, stone and wood**--*idols that cannot see or hear or walk. Nor did they repent of their murders, their magic arts, their sexual immorality or their thefts"* (Rev. 9:20-21). Even in this time of distress in the world, people have not repented from revering these stars and their demons. Atheism, beginning with the French Revolution, then Communism; nationalism and militarism (Babylonians, whose strength is their god; Hab. 1:11); naturalism and evolution; materialism or wealth and money, which is paganism (Matt 6:28-32); beauty and sex (the goddess of sex; A TV commercial for women's leg shaver asserts that "In every woman there is a goddess waiting to be revealed"); have all surfaced and are burgeoning in our days. All this demonism and idolatry is done in the name of civilization and modernity. I call it de-civilization, retrogression, heathenism, or neo-paganism, as one person has called it. As earlier quoted, it was Jean Jacques Rousseau who captured this human moral retrogression guised in the name of progress and change or advancement: "According to him, what we call 'progress' is not really such, for what in truth has happened is that humankind has progressively departed from its natural state and fallen into artificiality." This artificiality has become so terrible so much so that we live like people lived 5000 years ago when God destroyed the world and saved only Noah and his family. Thus, we see that another cycle (eclipse) of destruction is at hand, right at the door! There are modern people who think they are civilized and have progressed, but all they do is what the most primitive man did thousands of years ago—for instance, tattoos, walking naked in public (no different on the screen). As Solomon concluded on the cycle of moral history;

> *"What has been will be again, what has been done will be done again; there is nothing new under the sun. Is there anything of which one can say, 'Look! This is something new'? It was here already, long ago; it was here before our time." "Whatever is has already been, and what will be has been before; and **God will call the past to account.**" "The hearts of men, however, are full of evil and there is madness in their hearts while they live, ..."* (Eccl. 1:9; 3:15; 9:3b).

Yes, God will call the past into account, even those things that we have covered with fig leaves in the name of reconciliation, in as much as the outward manifestations have not gone away. Daniel reports that thrones will be set in place and the Ancient of Days will take his seat as the court will be seated, and the books (probably history books and all that men have written) will be opened (Dan.

7:9-10). John echoes the same thing in Revelation 20:11-12, when he says; *"Then I saw a great white throne and him who was seated on it. Earth and sky fled from his presence, and there was no place for them. And I saw the dead, great and small, standing before the throne, and books were opened* [books containing the records of human deeds, good and bad; probably history books). *Another book was opened, which is the book of life* [the Bible, against which the acts of history are being judged]. *The dead* [from Cain to the last sinner to die before Christ is revealed] *were judged according to what they had done as recorded in the books."* Thus, God will call the past to account, he will judge both the living and the dead (2 Tim. 4:1).

The Fall of Europe

As a reminder once again, a closer look at Western Christianity reveals that the Galilean religion did not convert pagan Europe. But European paganism made a deal with Christianity and created a new militaristic and imperial religion known as Constantianity—a mixture of Christianity and paganism. European gods (demons) succeeded to be honored in various forms as part of Christianity as we have seen—the names of the days of the week and months of the Gregorian calendar, Christmas and Christmas tree, and many other so-called Christian traditions that owe their origin from paganism. The West again must be confronted with the man of Galilee. Out of Europe has come such destructive philosophies, ideologies, and practices such as: humanism (the worship of man and his achievement ostensible in art—statues); colonialism (the destruction, exploitation, displacement, and robbing of the rest of the world); slavery (the first universal savagery in which 35 million Blacks lost their lives, and millions more displaced); racism (despising and discriminating against people because of their skin color of whom the Black man has suffered the most); inquisition; anti-Semitism (racism directed at the Jewish people culminating in the holocaust in which 6 million Jews were gassed to death); secularism; naturalism; evolution; and Marxism/Communism, all of which are full-blown Atheism or acts of God- haters. From Europe also came the two World Wars provoked by the egomania of world domination, with political ideologies such as fascism and Nazism. From Europe has also come the birth of malignant secret societies such as the Rosicrucian, the Illuminati, and Freemasonry, with which many politicians dabble. There has been a relapse into occultism and ultimately the worship of the beast (Satan--mammon? money, and material wealth, driven by amoral capitalism). Europe has long been described as post-Christian and avowedly Postmodern. Europe is at the brink of judgment. Here are some highlights, which are just the tip of the iceberg from a few nations.

Great Britain: The once foremost nation (that has blessed the world with the English Language), the mother of modern industrialization and in a sense, the mother of global Protestantism (mindful of her son—the USA), has steadily declined as a global spiritual compass. The influence of secularism and humanism, and together with widespread disinterest in Christianity in general, and lack of contact with biblical Christianity in particular, have led to disintegration of moral values. This has led to increase violence and crime, high divorce rate and family breakdown, suicide, illegitimate rates, and drug abuse.[ccc] Freedom (without responsibility) has become a license for immoral behavior and social chaos, with promiscuity and other sexual abominations (homosexuality and lesbianism), and drug use very common. Christianity has very well become a religion of the past as statistics show;

> "The steady decline in belief and church attendance is of deep concern. About 62% of the population has belief in God, 38% that Jesus is the Son of God, 23% that the Bible is the unique Word of God, 16% visit a church during the course of the year and 11% at least once a month. Nominalism and notional Christianity are enormous challenges. A nodding acquaintance with structures and trappings of Christianity and basking in the afterglow of Christian influence anaesthetize the majority."[ccci]

That is a sad picture, especially added to the fact that many congregations are dying and churches closing. The Lion is dying or is it dead already! Will the lion roar again at the day of divine visitation?

France: France became the first secularized and humanistic society in Europe that resented biblical Christianity, especially during the Reformation era as manifested in the harsh and savage persecution and slaughter of the Protestant French Huguenots. This resentment toward biblical Christianity gave birth to the atheistic French Revolution that released an avalanche of revolutionary political violence that has never abated until today. Atheism and humanism were deified and anything biblical was trampled upon. Although traditionally Catholic, statistics show that much of the French public has little or nothing to do with biblical Christianity. "The non-religious have risen to 20% of the population and non-practicing 'Christians' have risen from 10% in 1970 to 50% in 2000 [within THE generation!]. Regular church attendance has plummeted to 6-8% of the population."[cccii] Indeed, it is a sign of the times; *"At that time many will turn away from the faith and will betray and hate each other, ..."* (Matt. 24:10). It is approximated that 50 million of the about 59 million French people have no real link with a Christian church! So where do we go from here? Repent or perish!

Germany: The birthplace of the Reformation and modern Protestantism had, in the eighteenth century, became the birthplace of the destructive biblical criticism and many faulty theologies as we saw earlier. The rapid humanization, secularization, de-Christianization, and aspiration for world domination, became the precursors for the carnage of World War I. After World War I came Nazism with its racist ideology and madness of world domination that led to the genocide of 6 million Jews and countless loss of lives. Christianity in this land has kissed its lowest ebb. In Germany; "The church is widely perceived as irrelevant and marginalized. Although 70% of the people claim to be Christian, only 45% believe in a personal God, and a mere 8% worship regularly. There is increased open hostility to anything Christian. The occult, alcoholism, Satanism and a New Age worldview are on the rise."[ccciii] In the former Communist East, 80% are un-churched! Church attendance continues to decline, and some churches are closing. On the overall, only 3% of German men are actively involved in church life! It is a sign of the times; *"Because of increase of wickedness, the love of most will grow cold, but he who stands firm to the end will be saved"* (Matt. 24:12-13). We need another Luther to address the German nation and chastise them to pick up the word and read and shout *Sola Scriptura* again!

Italy: The heart of the Roman Empire and the ultimate source of Western law, arts, and other achievements, remains the heart of Babylon and the seat of the Woman who rides the beast. As the center of world Catholicism, she has never bulged to correct her Babylonian pagan doctrines and abominations of the earth. Catholicism itself is losing grip over her faithful in the very heart of her capital;

"... it has lost 10 million to New Age thinking, cults, the occult and materialistic secularism. Church attendance is decreasing, as are the number of priests. ... Occultism is widespread, and there are reckoned to be 100,000 full-time consulting magicians—nearly three times the number of Catholic priests. Satanism is strong in the north, Turin being one of the global centers of its activities, which include praying for the removal of all evangelical missionaries from the country. The strong pre-Christian pagan powers have never been fully routed in 2,000 years. ... The infamous Sicilian Mafia and Neapolitan Camorra have infiltrated every level of society. ... Government leaders and church authorities, even in the Vatican itself, have been subverted, and the attitudes of the general population poisoned by this evil system. Murder and extortion are commonplace--"[ccciv]

This is organized evil at its worst that will probably be broken only by the fires of judgment. Like Paul addressed the Romans 2,000 years ago, those very words are as applicable today as never before to those very people (Rom. 1:18-32).

Portugal: Catholicism is a traditional religion that has less impact in the lives of the people. "The veneration of Mary is a 'Christian' veneer over the old paganism and an estimated 90% of the population consult spiritist mediums and witches. To this are added the new bondages of materialism, self-centeredness and alcohol and drug abuse."[cccv] Secularism and humanism are eating at the heart of the society also, and as many as 50% of young people have experimented with drugs.

Netherlands: Despite her "Christian" past, the Netherlands has become increasingly decadent and secularized. "There has been a dramatic decline in the number of Christians in this generation [THE generation] and today's openly permissive society is renouncing its heritage. There are few restrictions on drugs, deviant lifestyles, prostitution, homosexuality and abortion. The Netherlands is the first country to legalize euthanasia and has become a world leader in promoting New Age worldview with its values."[cccvi]

Eastern Europe: This region was plagued by years of tyrannical and atheistic communism that severely persecuted Christians. Many of the countries emerging from the thumb of communism lack biblical Christianity. Romania, for instance, with Europe's third largest population of Evangelicals, has a great moral vacuum. Every kind of social evil, drug abuse, prostitution, violent crime, and abortion (with one of the highest rates in the world).[cccvii]

Russia: Was the birthplace of the Anti-God or atheistic communism, that has plagued the globe with untold deaths from political revolutions and persecution of Christians. In the nuclear arms race with the USA (the precursors of the axis of evil), Russia stockpiled nuclear weapons that continue to spill even in the black market today. The greatest nuclear disaster in history occurred in the Soviet Ukraine at Chernobyl, and caused untold damage both to lives and the environment. The radiation still affects people today. Organized crime—the Mafia and money laundering still grips the Russian society. Alcoholism (it is estimated that 40% of men and 7% of women are alcoholics), drug abuse, and promiscuity are serious problems. Russia has lifted her pride against the living God by her atheism and the persecution of Christians and Jews. God will put the last hook in her mouth because of her treatment of the Jews and bring her to an end (Ezek. 38-39).

Mystery Babylon The Great: See the Judgment of Religious Babylon or Mystery Babylon, the Woman sitting on the Beast, that is, the Vatican or Papacy, sitting on Europe or the European Union in Revelation 13:1-5, and 17:1-6,15-18. This false religious and idolatrous system will be severely judged and brought to utter ruin. Like Babylon of old, she will be forgotten forever.

But why Europe? Why would Europe fall or be judged? Europe has given much to the modern world—Christianity in a sense, and modern civilization and technology. They have achieved great humanitarian efforts in the world and continue to do so. However, we must note that sin will cause the downfall of any people. And whosoever turns away from the Lord God, will be punished severely (Ezek. 33:12). Europe's sins have multiplied, and she has rebelled against God and his word. She polluted God's church with paganism and has never cared to repent from it. She has been rightly described as a post-Christian continent! She either must repent or face God's judgment.

The Fall of the USA

Warnings America Has Rejected or Refused to Heed: GOD NEVER SNEAKS UP ON PEOPLE! He always gives them sufficient warning and call to repentance and time for repentance before he judges them. He warned the people of Noah's day through the preaching of Noah for a long time (about a century) before destruction came and took them away. Before Israel and Judah went into captivity, God repeatedly warned them through the prophets to forsake their evil ways or face judgment, but they ignored the warnings and continued to be deceived by self-proclaimed prophets, and thus, they finally faced judgment and exile.

There have probably been countless warnings to the US to repent or face God's Judgment. I will focus on one of such warnings. In 1965, that is, about 60 years ago (within THE generation!), Billy Graham sounded a solemn and decisive warning of coming judgment, should America not repent, in his book, *World Aflame.* He categorically and painstakingly diagnosed the cancer and cankerworm that have been eating the American society since then, but it appears the situation now is even far worse than it was then, because the warning has gone unheeded. Here are some highlights of the warnings. He started by saying that the flames engulfing the world were out of control; "Our world is on fire, and man without God will never be able to control the flames. The demons of hell have been let loose. The fires of passion, greed, hate, and lust are sweeping the world. We seem to be plunging toward Armageddon."[cccviii] What was true then is even more than ten times true today. The demons are on the loose and the fires of Armageddon are already burning. Billy Graham went on to describe how the flames of lawlessness (riots and revolutions) and racism were raging across the globe. He also warned against the flames of the old immorality;

"Today every area of our lives is invaded by immoral flare, which leaves no one untouched. In many of our publications and in most of our entertainment, the emphasis is on sex appeal. ... Evidence of the moral disintegration of our society appears everywhere we look. ... Taking a look at Hollywood, editor Jones said 'Can anyone deny that movies are dirtier than ever? But they don't call it dirt. They call it 'realism.' Why do we let them fool us? Why do we nod owlishly when they tell us that filth is merely a daring art form, that licentiousness is social comment?' In the face of this legalized pornography, the conscience of America seems to be paralyzed. More serious than our fakery in art, literature, and pictures is the collapse of our moral standards and the blunting of our capacity as a nation for righteous indignation. We seem to be insensible to the rowdiness of the stage, the glorification of burlesque, the drowning of our youngsters in the violence, cynicism, and sadism that is piped into the living room and even the nursery via television. We are struck dumb in the presence of bawdyhouse literature, which fills our bestseller lists with risqué novels that belong in the brothel."[cccix]

This dirt has multiplied geometrically until we are already suspended in thin air over the fires of hell, yet we continue to amuse ourselves to death in the name of entertainment. No doubt it is written that fools make a mockery of sin and find pleasure in evil conduct (Pr. 10:23). Billy Graham also warned that preoccupation and obsession with sex (Eph. 4:17-19) in Western society was a glaring premonition that the civilization was racing toward doom. And that time of doom has come now! He said;

"It has always been the mark of decaying civilizations to become obsessed with sex. When people lose their way, their purpose, their will, and their goals, as well as their faith, like the ancient Israelites, they go a 'whoring.' It is a form of diversion that requires no thought, no character, and no restraint. One of the world's great historians told me: 'The moral deterioration in the West will destroy us by the year 2000 A.D. ...'"cccx

And whether we see it or not, destruction is here already, and we better see it and repent or it will be too late. Billy Graham continued to bemoan the West's infatuation with viewing sex displayed on the screen especially pornography;

"Our Western society has become so obsessed with sex that it seeps from all the pores of our national life. Formerly novelists wove the subject subtly into their stories as a part of life. But today ... [they] pour a stream of perverse, vulgar, and even obscene writings like the drippings from a broken sewer. Sex is front page copy everywhere. ... **Pornography is anything that depicts lewdness in such a way as to create impure thoughts and lusts.** However, the sewers continue to flow, destroying the moral fabric of our society, until they have become the greatest threat to our security. ... We are corrupting the imagination and taste of a whole generation [THE generation]. Love is perverted to Sodom lust. Sensibilities are so hardened that domestic crimes and international atrocities are accepted as matters of course. No one can doubt that dirty appetites are becoming the principal satisfaction of life. In this way we are permitting the diabolic to triumph. ... 'There has been a growing preoccupation of our writers with the social sewers, ... the bedroom of the prostitute, a cannery row brothel, ... the sex adventures of urbanized cavemen and rapists, the lovers of adulterers and fornicators, of masochists, sadists, prostitutes, mistresses, playboys. Juicy loves, ids, orgasms, and libidos are seductively prepared and served with all the trimmings.'"cccxi *(emphasis mine).*

It was true about 60 years ago and it is even worse off today. Anyone who continues to drink this sewer and filth will drink from the cup of God's wrath—everlasting dungeon in hell. He continued to say:

"We [The West] are now the possessors of moral depravity, and we seek in vain for a cure. The tares of indulgence have overgrown the wheat of moral restraint. Our homes have suffered. Divorce has grown to epidemic proportions [and now, more marriages end in divorce than those that last]. When the morals of society are upset, the family is the first to suffer. ... In every area of social life we see operating the inevitable law of diminishing returns in our obsession with sex."cccxii

They have indeed become sex gluttons—nymphomaniacs, who do not even blush in their open daylight caressing. As a result of this sexual promiscuity; "Illegitimate births are at an all-time high; venereal disease rages at epidemic proportions throughout the nation; ...."cccxiii And now the HIV/AIDS pandemic, and a multiplicity of more STDS!

Billy Graham went ahead to lament over the increase of dishonesty and the fact that Western culture is dying (and in a little while it will be dead!); "But we must not leave the impression that sexual immorality is the only sphere of moral danger in our civilization. Dishonesty has increased in our society to alarming proportions. ... The disease of dishonesty invades every profession, and its spread into the society is alarming even to the most apathetic among us."cccxiv On a dying culture he wrote;

"That moral and spiritual decadence is upon us today becomes evident at the turn of every page of our daily newspaper. We live in a day when old values are rejected and the sense of significance and purpose has disappeared from many people's lives. The Western world's sole objective seems to be success, status, security, self-indulgence, pleasure, and comfort. ... The playwright, the novelist, and the movie scriptwriter all give us unadulterated doses of violence, sex, and murder. This would indeed seem to be a sick generation [THE generation] in need of salvation. ... Yes, we cry out to be saved—saved from ourselves [how sad that now at the face of destruction, people seem to see only the enemy without], for it is the soul of a nation and a culture that is dying!"cccxv

The reality of Romans 1:18-32 has come upon this generation, and yet we seem to act as though God can no longer judge our indulgence and wickedness or as if we are above judgment. "We cannot claim to be God's pets," Billy Graham wrote, "We have no special dispensation from judgment. If we continue on our present course [and we have continued in that course for these 60 years], the moral law that says 'the wages of sin death' (Rom. 6:23) will mean ultimate death to our society."[cccxvi] He continued; "How ironic it is that a civilization that has produced the best automobiles, the best refrigerators, and the best television sets is at the same time producing some of the worst human beings. The total answer to our dilemma in this debacle is that we have forsaken God."[cccxvii] There is, therefore, no excuse but a fearful expectation of judgment by fire that will consume the enemies of God—for it is a dreadful thing to fall into the hands of the living God (Heb. 10:26-31). Again, Billy Graham went on to say; "In our knowledge, which has become foolishness, we are setting the stage for personal and national dissolution and ultimate judgment. We are heaping high for conflagration. We are building for destruction. We are begging for judgment."[cccxviii] Western culture has become trapped in licentious and wanton pleasure. They no longer blush at the obscene because it has become the norm rather than the exception. Like a toad placed in cold water and is gradually boiled to death without noticing the temperature change so that it could jump out, Western culture has for the past two centuries absorbed the obscene (from the theater) that they laugh at nudity, obscenity, and profanity, rather than weep and wail or cry out. Of this wanton generation, the prophesy of the evil last days generation is true; *"But mark this. There will be terrible times in the last days. People will be lovers of themselves, lovers of money, boastful, proud, abusive, ... unholy, ... without self-control, brutal, not lovers of the good, treacherous, rash, conceited, lovers of pleasure rather than lovers of God--having a form of godliness but denying its power"* (2 Tim. 3:1-5).

The most devastating of all this perversion is the double standard and lie the West lives. We profess to be one thing but are completely a different thing. Billy Graham called it *"doublethinking."* He lamented that; "How does a society develop the kind of psychosis that plagues us today? It is the product of many things, including the loss of religious faith, faulty education, and too much softness. ... Nationally we are in a state of double-mindedness that could endanger our very survival."[cccxix] He defined double-thinking as; "'Double-think,' or double-mindedness, means the faculty of holding two contradictory beliefs in one's mind and accepting both of them."[cccxx] The greatest danger of this double-thinking is religious hypocrisy--saying one thing and doing or being another. "We say we are a Christian nation, but much of our literature, our social practices, our deep interests are not Christian at all."[cccxxi] Quoting another author, he wrote; "'While people believe in God, they are not concerned with God. That is, they do not worry or lose sleep over religious or spiritual problems. Most people of the West say they believe in God, hence in God's principles of love, justice, truth, and humility. Yet these ideas have little influence on our behavior. Most of us are motivated by the wish for greater material, comfort, security, and prestige."[cccxxii]

Worse still, not only do the people double-think, they *"group-think."* When people lose their individual identity (even in an individualistic culture) they become naïve and susceptible to every deception and lie. They no longer have a sense of originality or reality. They let others think for them and they just follow without having a noble heart to search out the truth and the real for themselves. This is the atmosphere where Satan thrives the most and does a lot without being noticed (2 Thess. 2:9-12). People no longer ask "Why?" or "Where from?" They just do whatever thing because everyone is doing it--just following the flow! Billy Graham made a statement that sums up how deception works; "It is almost terrifying to note the way in which crowds can be swayed to believe almost anything, provided it is put in a form that travels the avenues along which they are accustomed to receive their knowledge, whether it be true or false."[cccxxiii] To make matter worse, the so-called models or stars or celebrities (who literally bring Satan and his demons into the homes), are the pacesetters of almost every facet of life and morals. Billy Graham wrote;

"From one end of the nation to the other, movie and television stars lay down the law of fashions, manners, speech, and even moral behavior. ... The movies and television with equal ease lead and change the nation's thoughts on politics, morals, and social questions of great importance. In the darkness of a living room or theater, where people sit relaxed to give undivided attention to the flashing pictures, psychological conditions are perfect for insinuating ideas into the mind. In test after test among high school and university students, it has been proven that a movie or a television program can brainwash."[cccxxiv]

The truth is that Hollywood largely sets the values for America, and only a double-minded double-thinker can fail to realize this. Hence the people live a lie, which is self-deception. Such compartmentalization is self-deceptive and very dangerous. It is a wide road that leads to destruction. Billy Graham went ahead to illustrate this satanic lie;

"We are in the midst of a generation [THE generation] whose minds have been prepared for THE LIE. The Bible speaks in II Thessalonians of the coming of the great Anti-Christ: 'It will be attended by all the powerful signs and miracles of THE LIE, and all the deception that sinfulness can impose on those doomed to destruction' (II Thess. 2:9, 10, NEB). The movies, television, radio, the sensual novel [the fiction], the cheap magazine all have combined to make it almost impossible for the masses to do any real individual thinking. With the breakdown of discipline in the home and with every source of amusement and instruction pouring poison into daily life, it is not to be wondered that the minds of people are ready to receive anything, but the truth and they are ready to believe lies and ultimately THE LIE.

It is possible that 'group-think has made individual action passe in our country. Are we becoming a robot civilization, manipulated by mass media, pressurized by conformity, and pushed by political maneuvers? Have we developed a department-store mind, where we shop for name brands of faith, politics, and a way of life? Are we collectivizing the mentality of America? ... It seems that as a nation we are in danger of losing our individuality and our personal identity."[cccxxv]

These words were prophetic then and have been fulfilled even in our very eyes. People have fallen for "THE LIE" and have boarded the dead train racing at high speed to doom. America has lost its individuality and personal identity. She may still think that her military might can sustain her, but that age of brute power is over! But no one would say now that they were never warned for this warning had been shouted loudly and clearly, and shockingly so (since 1965!).

Billy Graham also poignantly pointed out and warned against the prevailing national idolatry of America. The national gods are many and the list will shock you. Of course, idol worshippers never acknowledge their idols, especially when they have a façade of belief in God. It happened in Israel of old. The Israelites claimed to be worshippers of Yahweh while at the same time worshipping other gods (idols). Billy Graham lamented;

> "The idolatry of Western man is humanism, materialism, and sex. Idolatry has an almost automatic connotation of superstition, magic, sorcery, and physical idols; but our modern gods are sophisticated, cultured, fashionable, and intellectual. When a nation turns from the true living God of its Christian heritage, then it substitutes false gods. ... Modern Western culture has become a mixture of paganism and Christianity. We are a blend of both. We talk of God, but we often act as though we are atheists. We have developed a sort of dual personality, a schizophrenia. We have "In God We Trust" on our coins, but "Me First" engraved on our hearts. The fact is, while theoretically we believe in God, we have made unto ourselves graven images and have come to worship them. We have almost a new kind of polytheism wherein we attempt to worship both the God of the Bible and the gods of our own making at the same time."[cccxxvi]

Westerners have become like the Cretans; *"'Cretans are always liars, evil brutes, lazy gluttons.' This testimony is true.* **Therefore, rebuke them sharply, so that they will be sound in the faith.** *... In fact, both their minds and consciences are corrupted.* **They claim to know God, but by their actions they deny him.** *They are detestable, disobedient and unfit for doing anything good"* (Tit. 2:12-16).

Western gods (idols) are many, and God, that is, Yahweh, comes as an appendage; from top to bottom: nationalism, humanism (self—

the worship of man), materialism, sex (goddess of sex, beauty and shrine prostitution), freedom without responsibility, military strength (god of forces), money, success and achievement (1 John 2:15-17), science, intellectualism, and so on. At the end of these gods comes the God of the Bible, who is just an appendage to these idols. Like in the days of Ezekiel, they have set up these idols in their hearts and have no room for Yahweh (Ezek. 14:1-6). The center of the worship of material things is pride, as Billy Graham wrote; "Madison Avenue has found it profitable to direct the main thrust of advertising at that inherent trait of human nature--creature pride. ... Pride consists not in wanting to be rich, but in wanting to be richer than your neighbor. It is not in wanting to be noticed but in wanting to be the most noticed. It is not in wanting to have more things but in wanting more things than others."[cccxxvii] Billy Graham continued to write that by worshipping himself;

"Man has rejected the revelation of the Bible concerning the true and living God of his fathers, and he has substituted gods of his own making. In actuality modern man has decided to dethrone God and to enthrone himself in all his nuclear glory [god of fortresses; Dan. 11:37-38; Hab. 1:11]. ... Thus man has thrown aside the pagan deities of past civilizations, such as the sun, the moon, fire, water, and beasts—and the living God as well. Today he worships himself."[cccxxviii]

Even with these new gods, the center does not seem to hold. Billy Graham concluded this section on national idolatry by saying that; "We are losing our moral balance. America, Britain, and Western Europe are becoming nations of sitters, squatters, and malcontents, fed up and bored with all the nonsense that has been handed them. Whether they realize it or not, they are sick and tired of their man-made gods. Their little deities have utterly failed them. The joy, peace, security, and happiness they were supposed to bring are not there."[cccxxix]

He continued;

"Apostle Paul warned us not to change the truth of God into a lie (Rom. 1:25). He warned us that we are not to worship and serve the creature more than the Creator. Yet this is precisely what has been happening in much of the Western world. The Bible warns that 'idolaters … shall not inherit the kingdom of God' (I Cor. 6:9, 10). … In the sight of God, idolatry is a grave sin. 'Thou shalt have no other gods before me' (Exod. 20:3). Judgment will fall upon idolaters. Millions of Americans are guilty, and many of the guilty are churchgoers who serve God with their lips, while their hearts are far from Him [Tit. 2:16]. They are more guilty of idolatry than the savage in the jungle who bows before an image made with his own hands."[cccxxx]

The only solution to this gross idolatry is repentance or face judgment. Sixty years ago, Billy Graham said after this warning that there is still time, but since then, the West has continued in that downward idolatrous spiral to the point that, I can only say "Time no more!" Even the reprimand "Repent or perish," seems too late now. Even during divine visitation, idolaters do not want to repent; *"The rest of mankind that were not killed by these plagues still did not repent of the work of their hands; they did not stop worshiping demons, and idols of gold, silver, bronze, stone and wood—idols that cannot see or hear or walk. Nor did they repent of their murders, their magic arts, their sexual immorality or their thefts"* (Rev. 9:20-21). The sun of mercy and grace is setting, twilight is almost over, and darkness fully covers the earth (Is. 60:2). Wrath and the fires of judgment are being kindled slowly, the flames will soon engulf the West and the entire world. The last hour has come, and there is time no more!

"Then I saw another mighty angel coming down from heaven. He was robbed in a cloud, with a rainbow above his head; his face was like the sun, and his legs were like fiery pillars. He was holding a little scroll, which lay open in his hand. He planted his right foot on the sea and his left foot on the land, and he gave a loud shout like the roar of a lion. When he shouted, the voices of the seven thunders spoke. … Then the angel I had seen standing on the sea and on the land raised his right hand to heaven. And he swore by him who lives for ever and ever, who created the heavens and all that is in them, the earth and all that is in it, and

*the sea and all that is in it, and said, '**There will be no more delay!**'"* (Rev. 10:1-6).

The standing warning has been here for about 60 years and America and the West has not repented. Billy Graham warned; "The only alternative to mercy, spurned and rejected, is judgment. God has offered His love and mercy and forgiveness to men. From the cross God has said to the entire world, 'I love you.' However, when that love is deliberately rejected, the only alternative is judgment."ᶜᶜᶜˣˣˣⁱ He concluded his book by quoting Proverbs 1:24-32, and I add verse 23 and 33;

"If you had responded to my rebuke [at least the above warning in *World Aflame*]*, I would have poured out my heart to you and made my thoughts known to you. But since you rejected me when I called and no one gave heed when I stretched out my hand* [invitation to repentance]*, since you ignored all my advice* [the Bible] *and would not accept my rebuke, I in turn will laugh at your disaster; I will mock when calamity overtakes you--when calamity overtakes you like a storm, when disaster sweeps over you like a whirlwind, when distress and trouble overwhelm you* [terrorism]*. Then they will call to me but I will not answer; they will look for me but will not find me. Since they hated knowledge and did not choose to fear the LORD, since they would not accept my advice and spurned my rebuke, they will eat the fruit of their ways and be filled with the fruit of their schemes* [God cannot be mocked, a man reaps what he sows; Gal. 6:7]. *For the waywardness of the simple will kill them, and the complacency of fools will destroy them; but whoever listen to me will live in safety and be at ease, without fear of harm."*

Again, Billy Graham said; "In that great day, men will call upon God for mercy, but it will be too late. In that day men will seek God, but they will not be able to find Him. It is too late."ᶜᶜᶜˣˣˣⁱⁱ God's face of mercy and grace is turning to that of anger and wrath! Wrath and vengeance for God-haters, the defiant, and the unrepentant.

In 1988, the late Carl F. H. Henry also issued another warning against what he called Western relapse to neo-paganism, in his book, *The Twilight of a Great Civilization: The drift Toward Neo-paganism.* Although he seemed to indicate that this drift toward neo-paganism was coming from external sources, from what he called the barbarians, it is certain that Western culture has caved in from within. It has self-destruct. America is going to die by suicide, not from external attack. Even the Christian mindset has become identical with the pagan mindset. Christians have literally become Christo-pagans. Carl Henry bemoaned;

> "We live in the twilight of a great civilization, amid the deepening decline of modern culture. Those strange beast-empires of the books of Daniel and Revelation seem already to be stalking and sprawling over the surface of the earth. Only the experimental success of modern science hides from us the dread terminal illness of our increasingly technological civilization.
>
> Because our sights are fixed on outer space and man on the moon, we cannot see the judgment that hangs low over our own planet. We applaud modern man's capability but forget that nations are threatening each other with atomic destruction, that gun smoke darkens our inner cities, and that our near neighbors walk in terror by day and sleep in fear by night. We sit glued to television sets, unmindful that ancient pagan rulers staged Colosseum circuses to switch the minds of the restless ones from the realities of a spiritually vagrant empire to the illusion that all is basically well.
>
> We are so steeped in the antichrist philosophy—namely, that success consists in embracing not the values of the Sermon on the Mount but an infinity of material things, of sex and status-- that **we little sense how much of what passes for practical Christianity is really an apostate compromise with the spirit of the age.**
>
> Our generation is lost to the truth of God, to the reality of divine revelation, to the content of God's will, to the power of His redemption, and to the authority of his word. For this loss it is paying dearly in a swift relapse to paganism."cccxxxiii (*emphasis mine*).

He continued to lament that this relapse to paganism has first griped Christianity itself;

"Institutional Christianity has dropped that last barricade to the return of the pagan man; preoccupied with the changing of social structures, it muffles the call for a new humanity, and in doing so forfeits a mighty spiritual opportunity at the crossroads of modern history. ...

Disillusionment over organized Christianity is soaring; one can see it in the statistics of declining church attendance and diminishing denominational giving, and in second thoughts about the ecumenical projection of one great world-church."[cccxxxiv]

And where is this Christo-paganism taking root? Carl Henry responded; "The forerunners of these half-men are being nourished wherever a pulpit no longer preaches the commandments of God and the sinfulness of man, the ideal humanity of Jesus Christ and the divine forgiveness of sins, and the fact of saving grace."[cccxxxv]

He gave the daring warning to evangelicalism that has gone unheeded;

"Unless evangelical Christians break out of their cultural isolation, unless we find new momentum in the modern world, we may just find ourselves so much on the margin of mainstream movements of modern history that soon ours will be virtually a Dead Sea Caves community. Our supposed spiritual vitalities will be known only to ourselves, and publicly we will be laughed at as a quaint but obsolescent remnant from the past."[cccxxxvi]

I will not belabor the point again, assuming that a word to the wise is sufficient. Western culture has drifted toward paganism—paganism that was only disguised since the time of Constantine and has blossomed again. This time **only a spiritual revolution, not even a reformation, can save the West**, but having signed a dead deal with the god of this world, only one thing remains, judgment. It is here!

Typology and the USA (The USA in Bible Prophecy)

USA; Like Sodom (Genesis 18:20-21; 19:4-5): Is the outcry against America's moral decadence as grievous as it is bemoaned? Has it reached the proportions like that of Sodom? If yes, the LORD is coming down to execute judgment; *"Then the LORD said* [is saying], *'The outcry against Sodom and Gomorrah* [America] *is so great and their sin so grievous that I will go down and see if what they have done is as bad as the outcry that has reached me. If not, I will know."* Indeed, the outcry against these cities was as grievous, as it is written; *"Before they* [the angels, Lot's visitors] *had gone to bed, all the men from every part of the city of Sodom--both young and old--surrounded the house. They called out to Lot, 'Where are the men who came to you tonight? Bring them out to us so that we can have sex with them."* This scene in Genesis is reminiscent of homosexuals and lesbians in our day, parading the streets in Massachusetts, crying out "Marry us!" (cf. Ezek. 16:49-50).

USA; Like Egypt (Isaiah 19): According to this passage, the following are especially true of America as was true of Egypt: crime—murder (Americans kill each other with guns more than any other civilized nation—home grown terrorism), rape, kidnapping, parents raping their infant and minor girls, domestic violence and spousal abuse; child sacrifice or abortion with approximately 70 million murdered since Roe v. Wade (1973). And you think God is not angry at these? There is a great prevalence of the occult, spiritism, and doctrines of demons. America is headquarters to many occult and cultic groups that are spreading around the world. Even the organized Church of Satan has its center in the USA. This demonism and doctrines of demons is summed up in the eclectic New Age Movement. Consider the following statistics;

> "Certainly a large percentage of Americans are involved in some form of New Age occultism or another. Some 42 percent of American adults presently believe they have personally been in contact with someone who has died. Fourteen percent of Americans endorse the work of spirit mediums or channelers. About 67 percent of American adults claim to have had a psychic experience such as extrasensory perception. Approximately 30

million Americans believe in reincarnation. Some 67 percent of American adults read astrology columns. One out of three Americans believe that fortunetellers can actually foretell the future. There are presently 2,500 occult bookstores in the United States and over 3,000 publishers of occult and New Age books, journals, and magazines."cccxxxvii

This does not even exhaust all the occult groups in the land. With such a great percentage of adults involved in such demonism, one wonders who bows to Yahweh, Jesus Christ. One of the reasons Satan has taken over America is because he has successfully duped the people to believe that he is not present here. When one talks of spiritual warfare, an American Christian immediately thinks of some country in South America or Africa. Because of such ignorance, Satan is walking the streets unchallenged—he is at ease, if not in charge in America. Given the above, the USA qualifies as spiritual Sodom and Egypt of Revelation 11:8.

USA; Like Edom (Obadiah 2-8, 15-16):

"*'See, I will make you small among the nations; you will be utterly despised. **The pride of your heart has deceived you,** you who live in the clefts of the rocks and make your home on the heights, **you who say to yourself 'Who can bring me down to the ground? Though you soar like the eagle** [surprised about the emblem? God is very precise!] **and make your nest among the stars** [cf. Is. 14:13; ... I will raise my throne above the stars of God!], **from there I will bring you down,' declares the LORD.** 'If thieves came to you, if robbers in the night--Oh, what a disaster awaits you--would they not steal only as much as they wanted? If grape pickers came to you, would they not leave a few grapes? But how Esau [America] will be ransacked, his hidden treasures pillaged! All your allies will force you to the border; your friends will deceive and overpower you; those who eat your bread will set a trap for you, but you will not detect it. ... **The day of the LORD is near for all nations. As you have done, it will be done to you; your deeds will return upon your own head.** Just as you drank on my holy hill, so all the nations will drink continually* [plunder]*; they will drink and drink and be as if they had never been.'"*

USA; Like Tyre (Ezekiel 26-28, especially 28:2-19): The Sin of Tyre: She rejoiced against Jerusalem; therefore, Yahweh was against Tyre and would destroy her! *"She will become plunder for the nations!"* (26:5c, 12a; cf. Is. 23:18). The king of kings (Nebuchadnezzar, for ancient Tyre; and Jesus Christ for modern Tyre) will seize her goods and give them to the saints. **God pronounces the violent fall of Tyre;**

> *"This is what the Sovereign LORD says to Tyre [America]: Will not the coastlands tremble at the sound of your fall, when the wounded groan and the slaughter takes place in you? Then all the princes of the coast will step down from their thrones and lay aside their robes and take off their embroidered garments. Clothed with terror, they will sit on the ground, trembling every moment, appalled at you. Then they will take up a lament concerning you and say to you: 'How you are destroyed, O city of renown, peopled by men of the sea! You were a power on the seas, you and your citizens; you put your terror on all who live there. Now your coastlands tremble on the day of your fall; the islands of the sea are terrified at your collapse.' This is what the Sovereign LORD says: When I make you a desolate city, like cities no longer inhabited,* **and when I bring the ocean depths over you and its vast waters cover you, then I will bring you down to the pit, to the people of long ago. I will make you dwell in the earth below, as in ancient ruins, with those who go down to the pit**, *and you will not return or take your place in the land of the living. I will bring you to a horrible end and you will be no more. You will be sought, but you will never again be found, declares the Sovereign LORD'"* (26:15-21; cf. Rev. 18:21).

Ocean depths and vast waters (hurricanes, and others) are against her; and she will be brought down to the pit and will dwell in the earth below (From heaven to earth, that is, from a place of honor to that of dishonor, or in other words, from honor to disgrace. cf. Lam. 2:1).

Lament for Tyre; both old and modern (27): What she thought of herself or really was/is: perfect in beauty; domain on the high seas (from shining sea to shining sea); with good builders or architecture (with tall towers and skyscrapers); expert in international trade, that is, business with many nations.

The **taunt** [mockery] **against the king of Tyre (both old and modern--that is, the Antichrist; 28):** Those who sit on political thrones of superpowers, become demagogues, and think of themselves as superior and invincible—Satan incarnate! They usurp God's universal authority as King of kings over the nations. The king of Tyre, the great ancient economic superpower, was to be exposed by Daniel, that is, the Spirit of prophesy (Rev. 19:10). **The king of Tyre was/is proud at heart:** he says in his heart; *"I am a god,"* and sit on the throne of a god in the heart of the seas (from shining sea to shining sea); but he was/is just a man and not a god; he thought or thinks he was/is as wise as a god (all earthly wisdom, espionage and intelligence service and surveillance, even false prophetic deception). By her wisdom and understanding, Tyre had gained wealth: silver, gold (today, paper money and strong currency, and stocks!); she had great skill in trading, leading to increase in wealth, hence *". . . your heart has grown proud"* (v.5). **His condemnation or demise (vv.6-10):** the LORD brought/is bringing foreigners and the most ruthless of nations (Babylon then, and terrorists now) against her; *"They will bring you down to the pit, and you will die a violent death . . ."* (v.8).

Modern Tyre will be overthrown by foreigners NOW! The lament concerning the king in particular depicting him as Satan (Antichrist) in Eden, that is, paradise restored and extended (vv.12-19). He was/is perfect in beauty (most beautiful and sophisticated of all human civilizations); full of wisdom; he was/is in Eden (beautiful place!); he was/is the anointed or guardian cherub on the holy mount of God (that is, on eternal Zion—she was blameless at creation, like a lamb from the start, that is, determined to worship God and defend his Word; cf. Rev. 13:11); **until wickedness was found in her as a result of TRADE;** *"Through your <u>widespread trade</u> you were filled with violence, and you sinned. ... <u>By your many sins and dishonest trade</u> you have desecrated your sanctuaries* [the American Church has become an accomplice to this sin and evil *and politicization]. So I made a fire come out from you, and it consumed you, and I reduced you to ashes on the ground in the sight of all who were watching"* (vv.16,18).

[**What is wrong with trade?** False balances or scales and unbalanced currencies as we saw earlier--thus robbing other nations; there is also cheating, extortion, usury or high interest, and others. Therefore, dishonest trade = violence = sin = fall = disgrace; from heaven to earth or pit (from honor to dishonor). The pit is introduced in Revelation 9 as the bottomless pit or abyss (out of which has arisen the antichrist). Beauty and splendor/glory and wisdom have become pride and corruption, and she will therefore be thrown to earth, making it a spectacular fall before the kings of the earth. Many sins and dishonest trade have led to desecration of sanctuaries (no true doctrine in churches, which are polluted by politics and DJ Trump)]

USA; Like Babylon (Isaiah 13-14; esp. 14:12-20): Babylon was the greatest political superpower of antiquity. She became lifted up in pride and exalted her military prowess to the status of "god" (Hab. 1:11). **A taunt** [scorn] **was raised against the king of Babylon—both old** (how Nebuchadnezzar suffered for seven years with animals in the bush; Dan. 4:28-33), **and new** (Satan-inspired Antichrist; Rev. 18). Babylon's characteristics were revealed as follows: oppressor, furious, struck down the peoples, subdued nations, relentless aggression (though as God's servant! Jer. 25:9).

Isaiah 14:12-23 depicts the king of Babylon, both old and modern, as Satan incarnate, the Antichrist. God will bring the king of Babylon down (Jer. 25:12). These verses also show that Satan/his incarnate was/is the first of God's creation, the morning star, who laid low or is laying low the nations, and who played or is playing God (divine claims—all wise through spying network, all seeing through satellite surveillance and technology, almighty or military might or god of fortresses; does as he pleases; etc.); and who exalted or exalts himself above the stars (other nations) of God. The only superpower that qualifies at this moment is the USA!

Isaiah prophesied again about Babylon in chapter 21, for emphasis, because of her pride and military havoc. Isaiah also described the attack against Babylon by Yahweh's army, the Medes (in 539 BC by Darius). Again, in Isaiah 46 and 47, Babylon is exposed. **The gods or idols of Babylon (46) were:** Bel, Nebo, the images of gold and silver (that are also spread throughout modern Babylon, that is, USA) that cannot be compared with the God of prophecy, who declares the end from the beginning and brings it to pass with precision, using his chosen ones (vv.8-11; also 44:26). **Babylon was to fall and rise no more (47):** The Virgin Daughter of Babylon or Daughter of the Babylonians may very well refer to modern Babylon (Rev. 18). Think of it this way; if Rome or Europe is Babylon, then European settlers outside Europe constitute Daughters of the Babylonians! (That is, they follow old Babylon, Rome, their mother). Babylon and her daughters fell then, and will fall again, that is, the West, and eventually the whole world!

But why destroy Babylon, once called God's servant or like Satan, who was God's first creation, and hence God's prime servant? Because of her idols; she was or is a whitewashed tomb; proud as queen of the kingdoms; she felt or feels that she was or is indestructible, that is, eternal; she put or puts a heavy yoke on the elderly (elderly work!); she is a wanton creature; she trusted or trusts in false security; she acted or acts like or imitated or imitates God (47:8b, which is blasphemy; **like playing God today**—acting as Almighty, that is, military might, omniscience—satellite surveillance, unmanned aerial vehicles and drones, etc.); she trusted in wrong and misleading wisdom or misleading counsel (false intelligence and secret spying network today!); she trusted or trusts in helpless astrologers and stargazers, who made or make wrong predictions full of errors; she practices unfair trade (which equals robbery, extortion, exploitation—as has been done by the West for the past 500 years all over the world, and continue today. For instance, the G7 and the WTO, that profits industrialized nations at the expense of developing nations with unbalanced trade and currencies, that is, unjust scales, etc.). These tantamount to magic spells and sorceries, which is sin and wickedness. That is why Babylon fell and that is why her modern type, America, will fall! **When God's servant sins, especially by**

trying to play God (replacing God or trying to be like God), that servant becomes God's archenemy. That is Satan's problem! That is modern Babylon's (America's) problem!

NOTE: [God has ALWAYS destroyed proud superpowers. In our modern era, the French under Napoleon tried to rise above Europe, but their hopes were crushed at Waterloo. The Germans tried in WWI and WWII, but were consecutively brought down by the Allied Forces, especially the USA. The British reigned as the largest overseas European Empire, upon which the sun never set, but came down after WWII. The Russians tried for about 40 years but collapsed in 1989. The Americans are up, and like Babylon of old, their fall is imminent. Europe is trying to rise again (EU), but Yahweh will cut short all this rebellion! (Dan. 2:34-35, 44-45; 7:11-14, 21-27; Rev. 18; 19:11-21)]. **The only hope is to take your stand by believing in Christ Jesus! You must be born again before you enter the kingdom of heaven!**

Jeremiah on Babylon (50-51): Babylon was the Destroyer (cf. Is. 33:1; Rev. 9:1-11) and supreme power—only to be equaled by end-time Babylon as described in Revelation 18—the zenith of all human civilization. **Babylon was destroyed because of:** idols and images (Bel, Marduk); she had devoured Israel, just as modern nations do today; she was the hammer of the earth (victorious conqueror); she defiled the LORD'S temple (like political rhetoric in churches today); she was arrogant and was like Sodom and Gomorrah (Rev. 11:8); she devoured other nations like a serpent that swallowed others' delicacies through trade (cf. Rev. 12:7-9); she was proud. The LORD himself raises armies against those he intends to punish (50:14-18,21-32, 35-42; 51:1-5,11-14, 25ff), that is, for retribution (51:56). Yahweh himself will do what he has planned (50:44-46; 51:12b,2-23).

Habakkuk on Babylon; The Babylonians are described as: ruthless, impetuous, sweeping across the earth and seizing dwelling places; feared and dreaded by all; a law to themselves; promote their own honor; violent, gather prisoners, deride kings and scoff at rulers; scorn others' defenses; *"... guilty men, whose own strength* [nuclear power] *is their god,"* **that is, military worship or god of fortresses**

(1:5-11; cf. Dan. 11:37-38)! Babylon too, would be destroyed (historic Babylon was destroyed by Cyrus in 539 BC, and modern Babylon will be destroyed at the coming of the Lord Jesus Christ; Dan. 5:30-31; Rev. 18; 19). Babylon was puffed up; was not upright and had piled up stolen goods; she had made wealth by extortion; she was in debt; she had plundered many nations; shed blood; destroyed lands and cities; built his realm by unjust gain; plotted the ruin of many peoples; and established cities by crime (and so has modern Babylon).

The Lament over Babylon's (America's) fall:

"'So Babylonia will be plundered; all who plunder her will have their fill,' declares the LORD." "... your mother [mother country—Great Britain] *will be greatly ashamed; she who gave you birth will be disgraced. She will be the least of the nations--a wilderness, a dry land, a desert." "Cut off from Babylon the sower, and the reaper with his sickle at harvest* [cf. Rev. 14:14-20]. *Because of the sword of the oppressor let everyone return to his own people, let everyone flee to his own land* [America certainly has people gathered from many nations]." *"The noise of battle is in the land, the noise of great destruction* [natural disasters]! *How broken and shattered is the hammer of the whole earth! How desolate is Babylon among the nations!* **I set a trap for you, O Babylon, and you were caught before you knew it; you were found and captured because you opposed the LORD.** *The LORD has opened his arsenal and brought out the weapons of his wrath* [Ezek. 14:21; Job 38:22-23], *for the Sovereign LORD Almighty has work to do in the land of the Babylonians." "'Summon archers against Babylon, all those who draw the bow. Encamp all around her; let no one escape.* **Repay her for her deeds; do to her as she has done. For she has defied the LORD**, *the Holy One of Israel. Therefore, her young men will fall in the streets; all her soldiers will be silenced in that day,' declares the LORD.* **'See, I am against you, O arrogant one,' declares the Lord, the LORD Almighty, 'for your day has come, the time for you to be punished. The arrogant one will stumble and fall and no one will help her up; I will kindle a fire in her towns**

that will consume all who are around her.'" *"'A sword against the Babylonians!' declares the LORD-- 'against those who live in Babylon and against her officials and wise men* [secret spying network]*! A sword against her false prophets! They will become fools.* **A sword against her warriors! They will be filled with terror.** *A sword against her horses and chariots* [tanks, armored vehicles, ammunition; etc.] *and all the foreigners in her ranks* [those who fight for America but are not yet her citizens]*! They will become women. A sword against her treasures! They will be plundered. A drought on her waters! They will dry up.* **For it is a land of idols, idols that will go mad with terror."** (Jer. 50:10, 12, 16, 22-25, 29-32, 35-38)

Again, a warning to the people within her borders;

"Flee from Babylon! Run for your lives! Do not be destroyed because of her sins. It is time for the LORD'S vengeance; he will pay her what she deserves. Babylon was a gold cup in the LORD'S hand [she was My Servant!]*; she made the whole earth drunk. The nations drank her wine; therefore they have now gone mad. Babylon will suddenly fall and be broken. Wail over her!* **Get balm for her pain; perhaps she can be healed. 'We would have healed Babylon, but she cannot be healed;** *let us leave her and each go to his own land, for her judgment reaches to the skies, it rises as high as the clouds." "Lift up a banner against the walls of Babylon! Reinforce the guard, station the watchmen, prepare the ambush!* **The LORD will carry out his purpose, his decree against the people of Babylon. You who live by many waters and are rich in treasures, your end has come, the time for you to be cut off. The LORD Almighty has sworn by himself:** *I will surely fill you with men, as with a swarm of locusts, and they will shout in triumph over you."* **"'I am against you, O destroying mountain, you who destroy the whole earth** [cf. Is. 33:1; Rev. 9:1-11; 11:18]*,' declares the LORD. 'I will stretch out my hand against you, roll you off the cliffs, and make you a burned-out mountain." "'Come out of her, my people! Run for your lives! Run from the fierce anger of the LORD. Do not lose heart or be afraid when rumors are heard in the land; one rumor comes*

this year, another the next, rumors of violence [terrorism] *in the land and of ruler against ruler. For the time will surely come when I will punish the idols of Babylon; her whole land will be disgraced and her slain will all lie fallen within her. Then heaven and earth and all that is in them will shout for joy over Babylon* [Rev. 12:10-12; 19:3], *for out of the north destroyers will attack her,' declares the LORD."* (51:6-9, 12-14, 25, 45-48; cf. Rev. 18:4-5, 20)

But Why America?

Europe may be understandable, but America? No political success in modern times rivals that of the USA. And it is undisputable that she has impacted and for good many other countries of the world. She saved the civilized world for two consecutive times from political tyranny and dictatorship (WWI and WWII). She literally rebuilt Europe after WWII. The success of the modern economy largely depended on the contribution of the United Sates—technology, investment, etc. America's humanitarianism has touched almost every nation on the globe. The story of the Protestant Church is largely the story of American missionaries going into all nations of the globe with the good news of Jesus Christ—sometimes very holistic, with medicine, education, and even financial help. Wouldn't America deserve a reward rather than judgment? From the surface of things, that might be the case, but from a biblical perspective, it is judgment rather than reward, because of the obvious reasons outlined above. The USA today resembles the nations of old that were judged than those that were rewarded, if there was any rewarded. The important thing to note is that we do not live or glory in the past. Just like God warned Israel that if they forget him after prospering in the land he would destroy them (which they did and God destroyed them and sent them to exile), America has forsaken and forgotten God, and turned her back on him (Deut. 8, esp. v. 19; *"If you ever forget the LORD your God and follow other gods and worship and bow down to them, I testify against you today that you will surely be destroyed."*). Because America has forgotten the LORD, and has disobeyed his commands, she will be destroyed. God gave a stern warning through Prophet Ezekiel to any person or nation that turns its back on God; ***"But if a righteous man turns from his righteousness and commits sin and does the same detestable things the wicked man does, will he live? None of his righteous things he has done will be remembered*** [forget about past glory]. ***Because of the unfaithfulness he is guilty of and because of the sins he has committed, he will die"*** (Ezek. 18:24).

THE ONLY WAY TO AVERT JUDGMENT IS TO REPENT!

*"But if a wicked man **turns away from all the sins he has committed and keeps all my decrees and does what is just and right, he will surely live; he will not die.** None of the offenses he has committed will be remembered against him. Because of the righteous things he has done, he will live. **Do I take any pleasure in the death of the wicked? declares the Sovereign LORD. Rather, am I not pleased when they turn from their ways and live? ... if a wicked man turns away from the wickedness he has committed and does what is just and right, he will save his life. Because he considers all the offenses he has committed and turns from them, he will surely live; he will not die."** "Therefore, O house of Israel* [America], *I will judge you, each one according to his ways, declares the Sovereign LORD.* **Repent! Turn away from all your offenses; then sin will not be your downfall. Rid yourselves of all the offenses you have committed, and get a new heart and a new spirit. Why will you die, O house of Israel** [America]***? For I take no pleasure in the death of anyone, declares the Sovereign LORD. Repent and live!"*** (Ezek. 18:21-23, 27-28, 30- 32).

But if she continues to lift herself up in pride, strength, and riches, even with a façade of "Christian" nation, that will bring her downfall. And she is already on a slippery slope like sinners in the hands of an angry God. It is paradoxical that, sometimes, those who have received blessings from the LORD can turn against him, even though at the same time with the name of God on their lips.

It is possible that a nation that might have been regarded as God's servant by God himself, turns against God and fall under his judgment. Assyria was used by God as an instrument of judgment against Israel, however, because of their pride in their conquest, God in turn destroyed Assyria (Is. 8-10; then 10:5-15). Nebuchadnezzar of Babylon was called "My Servant," by God, but he was judged because of his pride, and eventually, Babylon was judged because of her many idols, sins, and pride (Jer. 25:9-14; 27:3-7; but see her condemnation in Jeremiah 50-51; and Nebuchadnezzar's judgment in Daniel 4—and eventually Babylon under Belshazzar, who desecrated the Lord's instruments, just as his modern type, the antichrist, is doing today! Dan. 5). God uses some nations (which he calls his servants) to do his will--either to spread the gospel or bring judgment to other nations (using evil to judge evil), and in turn, judges those nations because of their sin and pride. This elaborates how, Satan, God's first servant, the anointed cherub, became or has become God's archenemy. He wanted to be like God by trying to play God like America is doing—all powerful and omnipresent through satellite surveillance; doing as she pleases (Dan.11:36)—removing and installing kings; and so on. Truly, America is a lamb (began as or appears as) that is speaking like a dragon or Satan (Rev. 13:11-18).

Wealth and success are very difficult to handle, even for professing Christians. It is a test that most fail. Wealth and success are the greatest temptations that almost always bring down whoever they grip. In most cases, wealth plus success inevitably equal pride that blindfolds, and which God hates (Pr. 8:13). Also, the evil of too much power (sole superpower) was rightly asserted by one of America's founding fathers; "Power corrupts and absolute power corrupts absolutely." Absolute power almost always leads to tyranny, which is not only national, but global!

Satan's Battle for America:

A lamb turned dragon? How could this be? America, despite the slaughter of natives and turning the Negro into a beast of burden, could still be described as having a humble beginning, with zeal for God (and who does only right and does not sin? Pr. 20:9). Article VI of the American Constitution, in part states that; "… but no religious Test shall ever be required as a qualification to any Office or public Trust under the United States," and together with the First Amendment of the Bill of Rights, ensured that God's things were kept separate from

Caesar's, that is, the separation of Church and state. This was unlike in Europe, where state churches existed. However, misguided zeal of some Christians began to undermine that distinction. For instance, at the turn of the twentieth Century, the Evangelist, Billy Sunday "... claimed that 'Christianity and Patriotism are synonymous terms, ..."cccxxxviii That may seem a very patriotic statement, but the subtlety embedded in it can lead astray--right into Satan's snare and playground. To make such a claim is to equate Caesar with God, but these two must remain distinct. Christ says; *"Give to Caesar what is Caesar's, and to God what is God's"* (Matt. 22:21). Again, Christ also says; *"My kingdom is not of this world"* (John 18:36). Therefore, to equate Christ's kingdom (Christianity) with a kingdom of this world (under the domain of Satan), is to mislead, to apostatize. Would serving country be identical with serving God? The Bible seems to indicate otherwise, although we are to serve our earthly masters as though we are serving Christ.

Early in the 1900s, the words "In God We Trust" were inserted on the American currency, implying either a violation of the First Amendment, or blasphemy of God, if that stands for Yahweh, the God of the Bible. America was founded as a country where any religion was free to thrive. Was the word "God," identifying that God, whoever he is, with one religion, Christianity, or did the word simply imply the pluralistic or generic "God" as claimed by many religions? Is there legitimate freedom to call that "God," Jesus Christ, as is the case with Christianity? How many would accept the phrase if it was changed to "In Jesus Christ We Trust?" Or will it mean the same thing if so changed? If this change cannot be made, you can be sure that, the "God" of the currency is not Yahweh, revealed in Jesus Christ. Do not fall into Satan's traps.

Again, the phrase, "One Nation Under God" on the pledge (the cultic prayer of the Republic), strategically uniting God and Nation or Church and state is illegal according to the US constitution (it violates the First Amendment) and wrong according to the Bible. Both usages of the word "God" on currency and pledge tantamount to blasphemy because the "We" and "One Nation" do not stand for believers only, nor are all who say the pledge, Christians. That is, if the word "God" in both instances refers to the God of the Bible, which many claim is the case. **To say the name of the Lord in vain is blasphemy;** *"You shall not misuse the name of the LORD your God, for the LORD will not hold anyone guiltless who misuses his name"* (Ex. 20:7).

Again, does the word "God" always mean Yahweh/Jehovah or Jesus Christ, as revealed in the Bible? Satan does not reject God (he and his demons believe that God exists; James 2:19) but tries his best to insinuate his diabolic agenda by counterfeiting and using God's name and word to his own ends. Do not allow him to trick you as he did to Eve. He is crafty, cunning, and a master of intrigue, and if you do not stay with "It is written," you will easily fall into his trap. Therefore, just because the word "God" appears somewhere does not mean that it has anything to do with Yahweh (made flesh in Jesus Christ). This pluralistic God of all, which some Christians fail to distinguish from Yahweh, has caused untold and almost irreparable damage. In my culture, even the worst pagan (unbeliever) would talk about God: they will say "God bless you" or that only "God" can perform extraordinary feats. To become excited just because a pagan uses the word "God," is to be naïve and easily deceived. To be sure, Satan uses the word "God" each day more than most Christians do! You just need to be vigilant, alert and discerning.

Satan was the first to use the word "God" in the Garden during his conversation with Eve! Satan's final defeat of America has come through the erroneous and deceptive belief by some Christians that America is a "Christian" nation. I know that is a highly controversial statement, but no matter how genuine and sincere that belief is, it is highly and devastatingly misleading. As I said before, America is a Republic with its constitution, it is not a Theocracy based on the Bible. It is very appalling to claim that the laws of the land derive from the Bible. To be sure, many good laws of pagan nations coincide with some biblical laws, especially the second half of the ten commandments. Most societies call for honor of parents and elders, forbid murder, stealing, adultery, envy and extortion. For some Christians to cling to a secular Constitution, inspired by the Enlightenment and deistic philosophy, is to display ignorance on their part. There are no "Christian" nations per se. That is, a nation ruled by the Bible or biblical law like Islamic Theocracies are ruled by the Koran and Islamic law. America is a democracy within a Republic and her principles of operation are out of phase with the Bible, which teaches a Theocracy (not for nations). A DEMOCRACY OR REPUBLIC CANNOT BE A "CHRISTIAN" NATION. To the best of my knowledge, the American Congress does not sit with the Bible at the end of the table to write or discuss legislation, nor does the Supreme Court turn to the Bible for its decisions. At least, they would never have legalized the murder of innocent children, which the God of the Bible sternly forbids (Pr. 6:16-19). To confuse the American Republic with the "Christian" nation (Theocracy) is to be naïve and voluntarily ignoramus at best, and unbiblical at worst. However, if by "Christian" nation, it is meant that a nation has had or has a great percentage of its population professing Christianity, or has had a great Christian influence, let us suffer it to be so now. After all, does Europe not still see itself as a "Christian" continent (part of Christendom), yet those who are spiritually alert rightly call Europe post-Christian? Such appellations as "Christian" nation can be misleading, and Satan loves to feed and take advantage of such ignorance and confusion. He is the genius behind Babel (confusion).

Furthermore, no political entity since the coming of Jesus Christ has ever equaled the people of God. God's people are found in all nations of the earth. God's "Christian" nation is the people of God in all the earth. The resurgence in the belief in "Christian" America is misleading at best, and erroneous at worst. However, I know that this belief is written in black and white in the minds of many, and nothing can convince them otherwise. I do not intend to do that since most people have bowed and succumbed to ignorance. Like the adage goes; "Where ignorance is bliss, T's folly to be wise" That is, it is useless educating people who are happy to remain in their ignorance. They neither read the Bible nor obey the little they have been told about it (which at many times is erroneous). When the Righteous Judge is revealed, we shall know who was in error and who was right. For the mean time, there is great danger in judging a nation as a "Christian" nation or the people of God, like Israel of old. This would mean putting everything, including policies, both domestic and foreign, under the biblical microscope, which no nation will measure up to that--not even one nation comes close to that! There are many today who believed in the biblical doctrine of separation of Church and state, but who have apostatized and picked up political agendas. SATAN WOULD NEVER HAVE CONQUERED AMERICA IF THE CHURCH REMAINED SEPARATE FROM THE STATE!

Notice that Satan tempted Jesus to worship him so that he could give him the kingdoms of the world and their glory. Christ passed the test, but his supposed followers have bowed to Satan in order to control the White House and hence, control the world and its splendor! (It happened to the Church in the days of Constantine as we saw earlier). They have tested power—they have eaten the forbidden fruit! They continue to sew fig leaves and put on themselves called "values." Jesus passed the test because he stuck with the word, "It is written" (Matt. 4:1-11). Eve messed up with "It is written," and Satan got her off her feet. A large portion of professing Christians today have abandoned "It is written," and Satan has swept them off their feet (2 Co. 11:2-3, 13-14)! **The birth of the politically active groups like the Moral Majority, Christian Coalition, Christian Right, and other Christian political activist groups since 1976 represents represents a grave apostasy.** It is an aberrant form of Christianity. Since the year 2000 (and lately from 2016 with the election of Donald J Trump), this political activism has plunged American popular Christianity into chaos of apocalyptic proportions. It is a dangerous apostasy. Constantine is back on stage and mainstream Christianity has endorsed a supposed "Christian Empire," that is, "Christian America," and a "Christian Emperor [DJ Trump]." The true church (followers of Jesus Christ) is underground and if not rescued soon by the Master, an unfortunate persecution will break out from unlikely sources, even in the age of freedom!

We must also note that following Jesus Christ is not just a moral fight, important as that is. While Christianity includes morality, morality does not necessarily mean Christianity. This blind moral fight has led to the compromise of Protestant doctrine with Catholicism— Evangelicals and Catholics united together on moral issues (values; and how can you follow Donald Trump and still claim moral values!)

and paving the way back to Rome (Rev. 17; the daughters of Mystery Babylon). The Protestant Church now uses political power to achieve its ends or at least wants to do so. Indeed, the beast that looks like a lamb is now speaking like the dragon and causing people to worship or acknowledge the beast out of the sea (Rev. 13:11-18). When the Church misses her vitality and neglects the Holy Spirit (the Spirit of the LORD departing from the sanctuary; Ezek. 10; or the Spirit taken out of the way; 2 Thess. 2:3-6; cf. Rev. 3:14-19), the Church turns into apostasy. When Satan succeeds to make the Church speak for him and like him, you know that the end has come! This is the greatest deception and delusion (THE LIE) to hit the Christian Church for the 2000 years of her existence (not forgetting Constantine and the medieval Papacy). A Protestant Papacy has arisen! Some Christians have settled for a counterfeit kingdom of Christ and Millennium.

Listen to what Jesus Christ says about his sheep. His *"... sheep follow him because they know his voice.* ***But they will never follow a stranger; in fact, they will run away from him because they do not recognize a stranger's voice.*** *... I know my sheep and my sheep know me--"* *"Watch out for false prophets. They come to you in sheep's clothing, but inwardly they are ferocious wolves."* ***"My kingdom is not of this world. If it were, my servants would fight …. But now my kingdom is from another place"*** (John 10:4-5,14; Matt. 7:15; John 18:36).

When Christians identify the kingdom of the world (over which is the god of this world, Satan) with the kingdom of Christ, they are hearing a stranger's voice, a wolf's voice, a false prophet's voice (remember the beast out of the earth is also called false prophet; Rev. 16:13c) and are therefore in danger and risk of being disqualified (1 Co. 9:24-27). When Christians unite church and state, or religion and politics, they are disobeying Christ deliberately and are therefore, playing in enemy (devil's) territory. The devil always wins in his territory because he has complete jurisdiction and writes the rules of the game. **Jesus Christ strictly warns against the union of politics and hypocritical religion (yeast);** ***"'Be careful,' Jesus warned them. 'Watch out for the yeast of the Pharisees and that of Herod"*** (Mark 8:15). **It is this religious-political alliance that condemned**

Jesus Christ to death. When religion goes hand-in-glove with politics, you know that they have tossed Christ to the back bench and welcome Satan!

I am not saying that Christians cannot participate in politics or be politicians. To be sure, they can. But to put the two as one goal is to miss the point. Jesus did not mandate believers to take over political kingdoms, but to make disciples of every nation. All nations of the earth are still governed by Satan. He has the legitimate claim to them, and Jesus did not and has never disputed that fact (Matt. 4:8- 9; Heb. 2:8). Political establishments, are however, still under God's providential guidance. They protect the sinner so that he can be reached with the gospel. But, if religion takes over government (that is, before Christ is revealed), the sinner is persecuted rather than evangelized. The sinner is no longer protected. This may sound an oxymoron. But the fact is, though God carters to both institutions (the political and the religious), they do not operate under the same principles. To further confuse you, let me say the following. If I am a pastor at a church and there is an active homosexual in it, who refuses to repent, I will put him on discipline, or eventually excommunicate him if he remains unrepentant. However, if I was also in the city council (in a democracy), I would defend his right of existence no matter his lifestyle (if it is not criminal). The church excommunicates persistent and unrepentant sinners, but the government protects all sinners (mindful of criminals though)!

I have already elaborated on the countdown of moral depravity and increase secularism in America. As it is, these have always been around. In fact, God does not judge society depending on whether there are sinners or not. There are always sinners! He preserves society because of the righteous (see Abraham's pleading for Sodom; God would have spared Sodom for the sake of a few righteous). To be sure, God will judge sinners and "humanists," but it is the apostasy of the Church that has hastened judgment. The last straw that has invited judgment is the Church's seduction to go political (some may argue it has always been so historically). Satan has launched his arsenal in all fronts and is succeeding. He has decided to attack the Protestant Church right from the apparent source of her nourishment.

America for a long time has been the protestant capital of the world, the Protestant Vatican, the Protestant Mecca. And if you were Satan, where would you attack the Church of Jesus Christ? From the top or the bottom? Obviously from the top! And that is why Satan has ruthlessly attacked America (the hub of Protestant Christianity), because he knows that by so doing, he will spill his venom to all the Protestant world. But his time is up! His buttocks are now exposed! Ignorance will not prevail!

Why God Rejects Union of Church and State

In God's administration from the start, he has always maintained a balance of power since he constituted his people. Moses and Samuel were the only exceptions during which times they were both spiritual and political leaders at the same time. Even during their time of leadership, God was always the direct ruler of his people (Theocracy). There is a reason why God chose Aaron and his descendants as priests, different from the kings. Joshua succeeded Moses, then came the era of the Judges, and finally, Samuel. Political and priestly functions were always separate in Israel, at least in principle! Moses and Samuel depicted Jesus Christ, who will be both King (political) and Priest (spiritual). During the era of the Judges, God himself remained King. God's people were a Theocracy, with God as King. When the Israelites requested the Judge, Gideon (military/political leader), to be their king, he refused; *"The Israelites said to Gideon, 'Rule over us ...' But Gideon told them 'I will not rule over you, nor will my son rule over you. The LORD will rule over you"* (Jud. 8:22-23). When Israel rebelled against God and asked for a king, God condescended and gave them Saul. **But Saul, the political leader, usurped spiritual leadership reserved only for the priests and paid dearly** (1 Sam. 13:1-14). Even with David, the man after God's own heart, the royal line (Judah) was always separate from the priestly line (Levi). Nathan, the prophet, would rebuke David after he sinned. Later, **Uzziah, king of Judah, usurped spiritual leadership and paid dearly. He had become very powerful, prosperous, and renowned, but his pride led him to presumptuously go in to burn incense in the temple of the LORD, which was reserved only for the priests.** Some **courageous priests confronted him** and said; *"It* *is not right for you, Uzziah, to burn incense to the LORD. That is for the priests, the descendants of Aaron, ... Leave the sanctuary, for you have been unfaithful; and you will not be honored by the LORD.*" As a result, he was struck with leprosy, and remained in that condition until he died (2 Chron. 26:16-21). That is how terrible and abominable the union of church and state is before God. **Where are the courageous priests of our day? Have all become lying prophets and money mongers?**

Even during the prophetic era, the prophets were always separate from the kings, whom they frequently confronted and rebuked. **The danger of uniting political and spiritual leadership was almost always apostasy. This is what the false prophets and priests, who were allies of the kings, did, and were condemned by the true prophets. So, when you see politics and religion united, be sure of this, the religionists have turned false prophets!** Only God can and will unite political and spiritual leadership when he himself will be King. This exclusive privilege belongs to one person only, Jesus Christ, who is Prophet, Priest, and King! Until he is revealed, no one is permitted to hold and sway both political and spiritual powers. Anyone who unites these two is a usurper, he is an antichrist! The medieval Papacy went that route, and so has Protestant USA since AD 2000 with JW Bush, and now with DJ Trump. Cast your vote, Christ or Trump! Not both!

False Prophets at the Eve of Israel's and Judah's Captivities

There were always many false prophets, who saw their own visions, always promising victory, and peace, even when God was warning of destruction. "There is no peace, declares the LORD, for the wicked," who flee when no one pursues them. The false prophets teach for a prize and polish the people's sins (Jer. 2:8-9a; 5:30-31; 6:10, 13-15; 14:13-16; 23:1-2, 9-36)

Rather than warn of impending judgment, the prophets appeal to heritage—God cannot destroy his people or his temple. However, God gave a very hard illustration; Ezekiel's wife, the delight of his eyes, died, symbolizing the destruction of the temple, the delight of the people, that finally happened in 586 BC (Jer. 52). **God can and**

will destroy his own temple because those found in it take pride in the temple but have forgotten God and his word. Jesus Christ says to the apostate church; *"I know your deeds, that you are neither cold nor hot. I wish you were either one or the other! So, because you are lukewarm--neither hot nor cold—I am about to spit you out of my mouth"* (Rev. 3:15-16). At the end when the eagle will swoop down for prey and never rise to the sky again, the book of Lamentation will be the eulogy at her funeral. And her pastors and prophets shall be scorned for failure to warn the people and turn them from destruction; *"The visions of your prophets were false and worthless; they did not expose your sin to ward off your captivity. The oracles they gave you were false and misleading"* (Lam. 2:14).

God's Judgment of the Nations

The rest of the world: While Europe, USA and Canada, and other European daughter-nations around the world, are leading in this moral decadence and depravity, the rest of the world, even to the remotest jungle, is steeped in immorality and moral depravity as well. It may be a matter of degree (it will probably not make sense to a lot of people somewhere else in the world if you talk to them about homosexuality, lesbianism, oral sex or even pornography!), but no nation is exempt from moral chaos. This explains why the whole world stands in judgment by God.

The End Has Come!

The following passages of Scripture record a blueprint of the current divine judgment that Yahweh is executing in the world: Ezekiel 7:1-27; Ezek. 21:1-7; Is. 24; 34).

Are the nations guilty as charged in these chapters? Do they deserve God's wrath? Will God be just in judging the whole world? Let us take a brief look to add to what we have already discussed about the West.

Asia: About slightly more than half of the world's population (3.7 billion people) live in Asia, beginning from the Mid East. Only about 9 percent of these people profess Christianity! Of these peoples, 911.2 million are professing Muslims, 815 million Hindus,

394.8 Buddhists, 382.2 million of Chinese religions, 89.3 million of Traditional ethnic religions, 19.6 million Sikh, and 707.1 million non- Religious or Atheists (mostly Communists).[cccxxxix] The great hope is that during this paganism, anti-Christianity and atheism, there is a vibrant remnant, 316.5 million professing Christians. It takes only one person that trusts God, to be a cynosure of hope. Asian indigenous religions such as Shinto in Japan, Taoism, Confucianism, and Shamanism, are also on the rise. Asia has seen its own wars and conflicts (wars and rumors of war) in the last half of the twentieth Century. The Cold War struggle resulted in major conflicts in at least 32 Asian nations. In the last decade of the twentieth Century and into the twenty first Century, secessionist wars have plagued over 14 Asian nations, some of which include: "Myanmar (6 ethnic conflicts), India (3), Indonesia (4 --Timor, Papua, Aceh, Kalimantan,), China (2- Tibet, Xinjiang), Georgia (4), Thailand (Malays), Central Asian states (4), Yemen, Sri Lanka (Tamil), Iraq and Turkey (Kurds)."[cccxl] Politically, Asian nations have known little democratic leadership.

Morality has also plummeted in this region, with the prostitution ring and sex-slavery stretching from Thailand through Eastern Europe, Western Europe to North America. As a result, the AIDS pandemic is spreading at an alarming rate, especially in the countries that participate in the sex industry (the trafficking of boys and girls). Such countries include Mumbai, India, Thailand, and surrounding lands such as Nepal, Myanmar, Cambodia, and Laos. Drug production and trafficking are also terrible crimes of the region. **Hinduism, Buddhism, Islam, Chinese religions, atheistic communism, and other religions, hold about 4.5 billion out of the 6.5 billion people in the world in bondage without the Savior** [2006 statistics]. Should the trumpet sound now, imagine how many will crash! It is mostly in this part of the world that Christianity is experiencing the greatest persecution.

China: About 50 percent of China is non-Religious and a further 29 percent practice Chinese religions. The non-Religious are mostly due to atheistic communism that still has its grip on most Chinese. In short, they are God-haters. The moral decay of China is also apparent, especially due to the "One Child" policy. "The

'One Child policy is a draconian means of taming the growth of the population. Family life has been deeply impacted, shown in a higher divorce rate, 10m abortions a year (nearly all girls), suicide (40% of the world's suicide cases are in China), pampered children with poor interpersonal skills and the abandonment of baby girls and older people. ... rape, abductions, female slavery, incest, prostitution, and the rapid spread of AIDS could all be the result [of eliminating the female population]"[cccxli] China also has a high persecution index.

India: Despite two centuries of missionary effort, about 80 percent of India is still Hindu, and only about 3 percent is professing Christianity. Persecution of Christians is high and still rising. There is not a greater evil in the world than the Hindu caste system. The shortest way to describe Hinduism is that it teaches doctrines of demons, especially reincarnation and hypnotic doctrines like Transcendental Meditation (T.M.) and Yoga. The rapid spread of AIDS is a testimony to the breakdown of morality.[cccxlii]

Japan: Of the 126.7 million people, 88.2 million are either Buddhist or Shinto (69%), 31 million of New Religions (24%), 5 million non-Religious (4%), and only about 2 million Christian (1.5%). To add to the old religions (Buddhism and Shinto), New Religions are emerging geometrically. "An average of 100 new religions are started each year - based on the occult, worship of extra-terrestrial aliens and so on."[cccxliii] Materialism has eaten deep into Japanese society especially among the young. The young have turned away from the values of work ethic to materialistic pleasures, drugs and possessions. Prostitution is alive and thriving: *"Exploited women. The yakuza criminal network has an active role in importing 200,000 foreign women who become sex-slaves. There are an estimated 100,000 Thai and also Filipino women involved."*[cccxliv] Materialism, irreligion, and high suicide rate, are just few of the ills of the Japanese decaying society.

Thailand: The country is about 92.5 percent Buddhist, and worships the supposed guardian angel, *Phra Sayam Devadhiraj,* to whom a golden image has been made. "The land is in bondage to a complex web of culture, spirit appeasement, occult practices and Buddhism, ..."[cccxlv] The society in general is rotten; "Corrupt military, government and police leaders have protected the large sex trade, drug networks, crime syndicates and ecological degradation of the country. The sex 'industry' contributes 14% to the GDP of the country."[cccxlvi] Bangkok, known as city of angels and city of sin, alone has over 2 million who derive their income from the sex 'industry'. "Most of the country's 100,000 male and 700,000 female prostitutes cater to the lusts of Thai and foreign 'tourists'. Crime, drugs, and alcohol abuse are widespread. ... Many girls are kidnapped or sold at a very young age into prostitution - which includes terrible abuse and, in all likelihood, an early death. ... It is estimated that 20% of all Thai girls between 11 and 17 become involved."[cccxlvii] The AIDS pandemic will soon ravage the society if repentance does not take place.

Africa; Especially Sub-Saharan: Even though sub-Saharan Africa is reported to be 60 percent Christian (thanks to the phenomenal growth in the twentieth century), much of what happens at a practical level does not seem to portray holy living or back up the number. Having emerged from the old shadow of colonial domination and exploitation, and into the new, neocolonialism, characterized by international debt, sub-Saharan Africa has marched backwards or stagnated economically leading to much frustration. In a sense, most countries still live in political darkness as their leadership is plagued by endemic corruption (with bribery at almost every level of society) and embezzlement (leaders emptying national treasuries and banking in Western banks) at the expense of its citizens (poor education, health, economic development, and unemployment). Most African governments are plagued by these diseases coupled with despotism, nepotism and cronies, dictatorship, and tyranny. Such political immaturity has been the source of numerous wars and conflicts with devastating damage and loss of life. The 1990s alone saw more than 19 nations at war, especially civil wars in countries like Liberia, Sierra Leone, Democratic Republic of Congo, Rwanda, Burundi, Congo, and Sudan, some of which were accompanied by ethnic cleansing. The prevalence and widespread of the HIV/AIDS pandemic is a visible sign of marital infidelity, promiscuity, fornication, and adultery. This formal or informal prostitution is costing the lives of many. The Scriptures are clear on this subject; *"A man reaps what he sows. The* *one who sows to please his sinful nature, from that nature will reap destruction"* (Gal. 6:7-8). This reminds me of what happened to the Israelites in the wilderness when they indulged in sexual immorality with Moabite women. God sent a plague among them destroying as many as 24,000 people (Num. 25). (By making this analogy, I am not saying that AIDS is a plague from God). Not only so, nearly half of Africa is under the grip of Islam (about 325 million people) and as many as 11 percent are griped by Traditional ethnic religions and atheism (about 70 million Traditional ethnic and about 9 million with no religion at all). There is still widespread fetishism, ancestor worship, idolatry, sorcery, necromancy, divination, spirit mediums, black magic, witchcraft, and the like. In some cases, many who profess Christianity are also guilty of these demonic practices, which are strictly forbidden by Yahweh.

Latin America and The Caribbean: Although about 92 percent are professed Christians, there are as many evils as possible in the society that one could get lost trying to enumerate. Top on the list is drug production and trafficking that has infiltrated every facet of the society even corrupting the politicians and law enforcement officers. And of course, millions of the users are in North America especially the US. Most of the continent has known little fair leadership, only dictatorship, autocracy, despotism, and Marxism. There is beginning to be a rise in humanism and secularism. Spiritism and syncretism still plague the Catholic Church in which most of the people are trapped. Sexual immorality is rampant to the extent that in some Caribbean countries, illegitimate birth rate is above 50 percent (e.g. Bahamas, Barbados, Dominica, Grenada, just to name a few).

Brazil: In addition to the normal chain of evils—crime, violence, murder, drugs, prostitution, sexual immorality, and the like, Brazil is the largest spiritist country in the world. "In 1975 there were at least 14,000 spiritist centres guided by 420,000 mediums. There are seven million Brazilians practicing Kardecism ('high' spiritism) and millions more practicing Umbanda ('low' spiritism with African roots). A majority of Brazilians are involved—most still claiming to be Christian."**cccxlviii**

We could list every nation on earth, and it will be obvious that all nations, without exception, are hanging over the fires of hell. The prophets usually list a few nations, and then conclude with the whole earth (Is. 24; 34). Indeed, Satan is the god of this world, and has eclipsed all the nations by his schemes and strongholds. The danger for any Christian is to assume that his or her country does not deserve judgment or is better than other nations. That may be true to an extent, but judgment looms over all the nations of the earth! We are running on borrowed time—grace and mercy will soon run out and give way to wrath and judgment! Drug trafficking, money laundering, crime groups like the Mafia; sex trade and sex slavery, and the prostitution ring, are evils that provoke judgment. All of these, together with terrorism inspired by hatred and perhaps, jealousy, have eaten the fabric of our society, so much so that it can be said;

"The LORD saw [has seen] *how great man's wickedness on earth has become, and that every inclination of the thoughts of his heart was* [are] *evil all the time. The LORD was* [is] *grieved that he had made man on the earth, and his heart was* [is] *filled with pain. So the LORD said* [is saying] *'I will wipe mankind, whom I have created, from the face of the earth—for I am grieved that I have made them"* (Gen. 6:5-7).

God destroyed then with water, but he will destroy now with fire;

"If we deliberately keep on sinning after we have received the knowledge of the truth, no sacrifice for sins is left, but only a fearful expectation of judgment and raging fire that will consume the enemies of God .... How much more severely do you think a man deserves to be punished who has trampled the Son of God under foot, who has treated as an unholy thing the blood of the covenant that sanctified him, ... *'The Lord will judge his people.' It is a dreadful thing to fall into the hands of the living God"* (Heb. 10:26-31).

God does not show partially (neither to the poor nor to the rich), but judges in truth and justice;

"God is just: He will pay back trouble to those who trouble you [persecutors and God-haters] ... *This will happen when the Lord Jesus is revealed from heaven in blazing fire with his powerful angels.* **He will punish those who do not know God and do not obey the gospel of our Lord Jesus. They will be punished with everlasting destruction and shut out from the presence of the Lord and from the majesty of his power ...**" (2 Thess. 1:6-9).

Whoever does right will be accepted, but whoever does wrong will be wiped out (Rev. 22:11). God is going round and putting his mark on those who are grieving because of these evils (Ezek. 7:3-4; Rev. 7:1-3), but if you give a hand to them (or are an accomplice; Rom. 1:32), whether as an unbeliever or a professing Christian, woe on you. Fire!

Again, looking at the prophets, why will God judge the nations? Because of sin. The prophets declare why God is against both his people and the nations.

Prophet Isaiah Against Judah

Judah had become a rebellious nation (Is. 1:2-31). To rebel means to turn against your legitimate master—here, the LORD GOD. Even animals (ox, donkey) know their master, but God's children did/do not know him.

Indictment and Exposition of sin: The people were loaded with guilt, evil, corruption, (thus, faced affliction and invasion; 1:5-8); they gave meaningless sacrifices, offerings, prayers, festivals (evil assemblies), that is, **hypocritical worship,** which God hates/abhors. Judah had become like Sodom and Gomorrah. Jerusalem had become a harlot; she was full of murderers, rebellious rulers, thieves, bribery, chasers of gifts, but ignored the fatherless and widows (1:21-24).

Call to repentance: What God wanted them to do; Repent! Do right! Seek justice! (1:16-19). God always calls the people to repent after exposing and indicting them of their sins. But if the people refuse to repent, they will face God's wrath on the great day of the LORD, then and now.

The Day of the LORD (Is. 2:6-4:1): This was a time of wrath and judgment for Jerusalem and Judah for their sins by invasion. **Those to be destroyed:** eastern superstition, divination (consulting the dead), pagans (cf. Matt. 6:25-33; that is, the materialistic), the wealthy; warriors and those who trust in war weapons; idols or man-made gods and idolaters; the proud and arrogant will be humbled or brought low; those who trust in achievement or man, and do wrong economics or trade, that is, cheating in buying and selling. **The LORD, YAHWEH or JEHOVAH, will remove** food and water supply, heroes, warriors, judges, false prophets, soothsayers, elders (who mislead), captains, counselors, cleaver enchanters; children will rebel; confused and wrong leadership; those who defy the LORD'S glorious presence; Sodomites; those who have a defiant and hostile look and sin in the open without shame; women and youth lead over the people; leaders who mislead the people and crush or grind the faces of the poor; women, who trust in their fashion, beauty, perfumes, fleeting and deceptive charms; every beauty dependent thing! (3:16-4:1).

On the Day of the Lord, the day of wrath, the LORD will sound the battle cry; he will blow the trumpet blast—to declare the sins of the people (Is. 58:1-2), and to rouse the armies of the nations to assemble at Armageddon, his holy mountain or in the valley of decision. The LORD will devastate the earth and render it desolate. The LORD is against the whole earth because of its sins. Instead of going nation by nation, Isaiah shows that sinful mankind in general, all over the whole earth, will be destroyed and devastated on the Day of Wrath at the end of the age (Christ's return). Why? Mankind has defiled the earth, disobeyed the laws, violated the statutes, broken the everlasting covenant (rejecting the Bible), reveled in merrymaking--they have rejected God! Terror will overcome them, as is the case now! (Is. 24:10b-12; 16b-23a; 26:20-21). **The LORD will judge and destroy the wicked with WAR and with his NAME with burning anger; his LIPS are full of wrath; his TONGUE is a consuming fire; his BREATH is like a rushing torrent; his MAJESTIC VOICE, which he will cause men to hear** (Is. 30:27-33; What else but his Word/Jesus Christ! cf. Heb. 4:12,13; 2 Thess. 2:8; 2 Tim. 3:16; Is 11:1-4; Rev. 19:11-21; John 12:47-50), **and with raging anger—**

cloudburst, thunderstorm and hail (in short, disaster). **That was
the Day of Wrath** then, and so it is at the end of the age (now). The
LORD summons the nations and their armies in his anger, he will
destroy them! (also Rev. 19:17-19; cf. 2 Peter 3:10; Matt. 24:29ff,
Luke 21:10-28; just before Christ returns). **It is a day of vengeance;
a year of retribution, to uphold Zion's cause.**

Prophet Jeremiah

Jeremiah in chapter 5 cries out: no one in the city seeks truth,
they all swear falsely in the LORD'S name. Despite discipline,
both the poor and the leaders continued in rebellion, backsliding,
and prostitution. The prophets did not know God's word and they
prophesied lies, and the priests ruled by their own authority and
strengthened the hands of evil doers or big business (13,30,31).
The people were foolish and senseless (21). Thus, invasion was
inevitable—wrath (6:1-9, 11, 12, 24-30). **The LORD'S word was
offensive to the people just as it is today** (6:10,16-19). All were
greedy for gain! Prophets and Priests or Pastors practiced deceit yet
were not ashamed (13, 15). *"They dress the wound of my people as
though it were not serious. 'Peace, peace,' they say, when there is no
peace"* (14, cf. 1 Thess. 5:1-13; 2 Tim. 4:3-4; TODAY!). In chapters
7 and 8, Jeremiah bemoaned the worthlessness of false religion (or
hypocrisy--lip service). Jeremiah had to **stand right at the door of
the temple to confront these hypocrites** (what a difficult thing to
do)! We note here that there are people who claim to worship God,
but who still practice the following: deal unjustly with each other;
oppress the alien, the widow, and the poor; shed innocent blood;
follow other gods; steal, murder, commit adultery, and perjury
(7:6- 11). The LORD would destroy these people and his temple,
in which they trusted (fulfilled in 586 BC, when Judah was taken
into captivity, and in AD 70, when Rome sacked Jerusalem). With
increase idolatry, truth had perished and vanished from their lips
(7:12-8:3). The LORD will punish sin (8:4ff), either you hide under
Jesus Christ (who was punished on your behalf), or you pay for your
own sin— eternal suffering in hell! In chapter 9, Jeremiah continued
to list more of the people's sins: lies, slander, deception, but no truth;
they weary themselves with sinning; and no acknowledgement of the

LORD. They forsook the law, yet boasted in their wisdom, strength (individual and military), and riches/wealth/money. On the contrary;

"This is what the LORD says: 'Let not the wise man boast of his wisdom or the strong man boast of his strength or the rich man boast of his riches, but let him who boasts boast about this: that he understands and knows me, that I am the LORD, who exercises kindness, justice and righteousness on earth, for in these I delight,' declares the LORD" (9:23-24).

Ezekiel

Why God destroyed Jerusalem (chapters 21 and 22): The LORD was to bring Babylon against Jerusalem as his instrument of judgment and discipline. **Ezekiel was to PREACH AGAINST THE SANCTUARY or the APOSTATE CHURCH TODAY!** Attack on Jerusalem was inevitable because of her sins (21:6-27): bloodshed; idols; father and mother treated with contempt (family breakdown today!); oppressed and mistreated the alien, the fatherless, and the widows by neglect and denying them justice; despised holy things; desecrated Sabbaths and not keep them; slanderous men bent on shedding blood; ate at mountain shrines and committed lewd acts; dishonored their fathers' bed; violated women during their periods; adultery; another defiled his daughter-in-law; another violated his sister (incest, like child molestation today); they accepted bribes to shed blood; they practiced usury and excessive interests (just like today); unjust gain by extortion; they had forgotten the LORD (22:6-12). Therefore, the LORD would strike them in his fiery anger/wrath (17-22). The priests did violence to the law and profaned holy things, that is, making no distinction between the holy and the unholy! Officials were like wolves tearing their prey; they killed people to make unjust gain; but prophets just whitewashed their deeds! There was/is none to stand in the gap (22:30). We are no different than these people except we are more than ten times worse!

Micah also denounced the peoples' sins and evils:

"Woe to those who plan iniquity, to those who plot evil on their beds! At morning's light they carry it out because it is in their power

to do it. They covet fields and seize them, and houses, and take them. They defraud a man of his home, a fellowman of his inheritance" (2:1, 2). Because of these things, the LORD will bring disaster against them. The false prophets, whom the people prefer, commanded the true prophet not to prophesy against them. The **wickedness of the people again:** The leaders and rulers of Israel knew no justice; they hated good and loved evil; they mistreated the helpless people. The prophets and priests prophesied for gain, and led the people astray— there was bloodshed, wickedness, bribery; **yet they claimed,** *"Is not the LORD among us?"* Much like among apostate Christians today! We do evil but continue to claim we are Christians!

Zephaniah also decried the peoples' sins and why God would punish Judah:

Judah was destroyed because of Baal worship; worship of heavenly bodies (starry hosts, the sun, moon, and the planets, astrology); they swore by God and also by Molech (god of the Ammonites, worshiped by child sacrifice) at the same time; they had turned away from the LORD. There was violence, deceit, complacency, and they were only interested in trade. Therefore, the day of the LORD would overtake them.

Are we any better than God's people of old and the sinful nations? No! We are worse than they. Therefore, sinners will drink from the cup of God's wrath. The day for destroying the destroyer and those who destroy the earth (whether through global warming with greenhouse emissions or environmental pollution), a day of vengeance, a day of reckoning is upon us (Is 33:1ff; Rev. 11:18). God has done it before and will do it again—**does the LORD threaten and not bring to pass (Ezek. 6:10)? During this devastation Yahweh will preserve the righteous, he will "pass over" them.** But why call the past into the present? Because we must all give an account before the Living God, the Supreme Judge of the universe.

What Does the LORD Want from People?

In short, God wants repentance; true worship; justice in equity, mercy, and faithfulness; humility; and a contrite heart that trembles at his word. This is the call of the prophets!

ISAIAH: An Invitation to Repentance; *"'Come now, let us reason together,' declares the LORD. 'Though your sins are like scarlet, they shall be as white as snow; though they are red as crimson, they shall be like wool. If you are willing and obedient, you will eat the best from the land; but if you resist and rebel, you will be devoured by the sword.' For the mouth of the LORD has spoken"* (1:18-20).

God wants the people to proclaim a True Fast: Which is to lose the chains of injustice; to untie the cords of the yoke; to set the oppressed free; to break every yoke; to share your food with the hungry; to provide the poor wanderer (alien) with shelter; to cloth the naked; to keep the Sabbath holy (58:6-7,9b-10). **The Result will be** light, righteousness, and answer to prayer (58:9-14). Unfortunately, there are many times that Christians fast, but do not do the above-mentioned things. They fast but still practice injustice; suppress and oppress others; lay a heavy yoke on others; exploit workers; despise the aliens; remain selfish; and desecrate the Sabbath by doing as they please--seeking their own pleasure and entertainment. Such fasting is abominable before the Father--it is hypocrisy (Is. 58:1-5).

Also, the LORD declares; *"This is the one I esteem: he who is humble and contrite in spirit, and trembles at my word. ... Hear the word of the LORD, you who tremble at his word ..."* (Is. 66:2b, 5a). At the end of the day, attitude toward the word of God becomes the measure of our love for God! Has the LORD really said this or that? Has God spoken? Did God really say (Gen. 3:1)?

HOSEA: Admonition to Seek the LORD; *"Sow for yourselves righteousness, reap the fruit of unfailing love, and break up your unplowed ground; for it is time to seek the LORD, until he comes and showers righteousness on you. But you have planted wickedness, you have reaped evil, you have eaten the fruit of deception. Because you have depended on your own strength and on your many warriors"* (10:12-13).

JOEL: A Call to Return to the LORD; *"Even now, declares the LORD, return to me with all your heart, with fasting and weeping and mourning. Rend your heart and not your garments. Return to the LORD your God, for he is gracious and compassionate, slow to anger and abounding in love, and he relents from sending calamity. Who knows? He may turn and have pity and leave behind a blessing--"* (2:12-14).

God Gives a Serious Command; *"Blow the trumpet in Zion, declare a holy fast, call a sacred assembly. Gather the people, consecrate the assembly; bring together the elders, gather the children, those nursing at the breast. Let the bridegroom leave his room and the bride her chamber. Let the priests, who minister before the LORD, weep between the temple porch and the altar. Let them say, 'Spare your people, Oh LORD. Do not make your inheritance an object of scorn, a byword among the nations'"* (2:15-17).

MICAH: He Says; *"He has showed you, o man, what is good. **And what does the LORD require of you? To act justly and to love mercy and to walk humbly with your God"** (6:8).*

ZEPHANIAH: What the LORD Requires of the People; *"Seek the LORD all you humble of the land, you who do what he commands. **Seek righteousness, seek humility; perhaps you will be sheltered on the day of the LORD'S anger"** (2:3).*

HAGGAI: Consider Your Ways; *"This is what the LORD Almighty says: 'Give careful thought to your ways. You have planted much, but harvested little. You eat, but never have enough. You drink, but never have your fill. You put on clothes, but are not warm. You earn wages, only to put them in a purse with holes in it* [credit, credit, credit, debt, debt, debt!]*'"* (1:5-6).

ZECHARIAH: A Call to the People to Turn Away from Empty Religion--Hypocrisy (7:5-7, 11-14) **to;** *"This is what the LORD Almighty says: **'Administer true justice; show mercy and compassion to one another. Do not oppress the widow or the fatherless, the alien or the poor. In your hearts do not think evil of each other'"** (7:9-10; cf. Matt. 23:23; show justice, mercy, and* faithfulness). *"These are the things you are to do: **Speak truth to each other, and render true and sound judgment in your courts; do not plot evil against your neighbor, and do not love to swear falsely. I hate all this, declares the LORD." "... Therefore love truth and peace"*** (7:16-17,19).

The message of the Prophets is clear and direct. I do not need to interpret it. It is plain to whoever is seeking God and wants to do what he says—what is just and right. The message of the prophets is as relevant to us today as it was in their days. In fact, the message is more relevant to us, given that they spoke mostly of our days. Repeatedly in the New Testament, we are asked to pay attention to the prophets because all they wrote will still be fulfilled in our day. Thus, their message is as relevant, in fact, even more relevant to us upon whom the end of the ages has come, than to any other generation (Acts 3:19-21, 24; 2 Pet. 1:19-21; Rev. 19:10). The evils the prophets condemned are prevalent in our days, even to an alarming proportion. Therefore, we must heed the warning and repent, perhaps we might be spared in this day of divine visitation. Consider their message as addressed to you and to us, the church.

To round up this section, I would like to ask one question; **"Does prophesy mean that God hates the people or what does it really mean?" The very essence of prophesy is love!** If it were hatred, God would never warn the people before he brings judgment. He would rather sneak up on them and just wipe them out. But he sends prophets because he loves the people and wants them to repent and live true and righteous lives, which for the most part, is for our own good. Repentance would avert judgment because the LORD is rich in mercy and compassion, slow to anger and abounding in love. In fact, when there is sin and wickedness, the people groan and suffer, but when the people honor God, there is joy, peace, and happiness. So, God sends prophets because he loves the people, and that is why in almost all the prophets, there is always the promise of redemption or the promise to show mercy even in wrath as Habakkuk requested (3:2). Prophets are messengers of hope and not of doom. It is the people themselves who invite doom upon themselves, but not the prophets. The prophets are there to tell the people that there is a cliff ahead, and they should therefore slow down and turn around or they will all fall off the cliff and perish. The LORD is a God of compassion, slow to anger and quick to forgive. His love endures forever, and he will not always accuse, or harbor anger forever (Ps. 103:8-14). He is always slow in bringing judgment; *"Though he brings grief, he will show compassion, so great is his unfailing love. **For he does not willingly bring affliction or grief to the children of men"*** (Lam. 3:32- 33).

GOD HAS NEVER AND WILL NEVER DESTROY PEOPLE WITHOUT WARNING THEM OR SHOWING THEM MERCY. IT IS ONLY WHEN THE PEOPLE REJECT GOD'S MERCY THAT THEY ARE WIPED OUT IN JUDGMENT!

There is always grace before judgment. To him who heeds God's warning, he will be merciful. It will always be well with the righteous, even during wrath. **God always relents, if those warned repent;**

> *"If at any time I announce that a nation or kingdom is to be uprooted, torn down and destroyed, and **if that nation I warned repents of its evil, then I will relent and not inflict on it the disaster I had planned.** And if at another time I announce that a nation or kingdom is to be built up and planted, and if it does evil in my sight and does not obey me, then I will reconsider the good I had intended to do for it. 'Now say to the people of Judah* [people of the world] *and those living in Jerusalem* [now, cities of the nations]*, This is what the LORD says: Look! I am preparing a disaster for you and devising a plan against you. So turn from your evil ways, each one of you, and reform your ways and your actions"* (Jer. 18:7-11; cf. Jonah 3).

But why do the people hate the prophets and their message? Why do they always regard the prophets as messengers of doom— as unpatriotic, traitors, troublemakers, and conspirators? Here are some typical examples. In the days of Ahab, king of Israel, there were many false prophets as opposed to Micaiah, the only true prophet (1 Kings 22). Jehoshaphat, king of Judah went to visit Ahab, who wanted them to attack Aram. But Jehoshaphat said, *"First* *seek the counsel of the LORD,"* that is, before going to battle. Ahab brought in about 400 prophets (who were all false prophets) and asked whether he should attack Aram or not. All of them replied with the same thing; *"Go,' they answered, 'for the Lord will give it into the king's hand"* (v.6). Jehoshaphat sensed that something was wrong with these prophets, and then asked, *" 'Is there not a prophet of the LORD here whom we can inquire of?'"* **The king of Israel, who preferred false prophets to the true prophet, answered; *"'There is still one man through whom we can inquire of the LORD, but I hate him because he never prophesies anything good about me, but always bad'"*** (v.8). Yes, the true prophet is always hated and rejected, because the people want to do their own thing.

Throughout his ministry, **Jeremiah** was continually mistreated by the people, who did not want to repent or hear the word of the LORD.

First, the people connived together to attack him with words; *"They said, 'Come, let's make plans against Jeremiah; ...let's attack him with our tongues and pay no attention to anything he says'"* (18:18).

Secondly, when the LORD commanded him to stand in the temple and confront the people, and he did, **the people wanted to kill him;** *"The priests, the prophets and all the people heard Jeremiah speak these words in the house of the LORD. But as soon as Jeremiah finished telling all the people everything the LORD had commanded him to say, the priests, the prophets and all the people seized him and said, 'You must die!"* (26:7-8). When the officials of Judah enquired about what was going on; *"... the priests and the prophets said to the officials and all the people, 'This man should be sentenced to death because he has prophesied against this city"* (v.11ff).

Thirdly, Jeremiah was called a madman because he was filled with the Spirit and zeal of the LORD (29:26-27).

Fourthly, in Jeremiah 36, the LORD commanded Jeremiah to write down in a scroll all the prophesies he had given him until then. He wrote them down and because he was restricted from going to the temple, he sent his secretary, Baruch, to go and read it in the temple. An informant went and reported what Baruch had read in the temple to the officials, who requested Baruch to come and read in their hearing. They, in turn, reported to the king, who had the scroll read to him. **The king cut the scroll column by column as it was read to him, and burned them on the fire, until all was burned. It is written;** *"The king and all his attendants who heard all these words showed no fear, nor did they tear their clothes. ... Instead the king commanded ... to arrest Baruch the scribe and Jeremiah the prophet"* (vv.24-26). **Yes, the king not only burnt the scroll, but commanded that the prophet and his secretary be arrested.** Be mindful that all the people who attacked Jeremiah were religious people, who claimed to worship God, even in God's temple!

Fifthly, Jeremiah was accused of desertion to the Babylonians, who had laid siege around Jerusalem. **They arrested Jeremiah, had him beaten, and put into prison;** *"Jeremiah was put into a vaulted cell in a dungeon, where he remained a long time"* (37:16). Could you imagine Jeremiah's situation and ministry? The Babylonians were besieging the city, and all the LORD asked him to say to the people was, *"Pharaoh's army* [for the Egyptians had come to aid Judah], *which marched out to support you, will go back to its own land, to Egypt. Then the Babylonians will return and attack this city; they will capture it and burn it down"* (37:7-8). After repeated inquiries, his message did not change, for he kept telling the people; *"This is what the LORD says: 'Whoever stays in this city will die by the sword, famine or plague, but whoever goes over to the Babylonians will live. He will escape with his life; he will live. And this is what the LORD says: 'This city will certainly be handed over to the army of the king of Babylon, who will capture it'"* (38:2-3). **What an unpatriotic fellow, you may ask?** But this is precisely what the LORD demands at some points for the prophet--to prophesy against your own country; to tell them that they will be crushed to ashes! As a result, Jeremiah was accused of discouraging his own country's soldiers and the people, and thus, not seeking the good of the people but their ruin (38:4). Therefore, he deserved death, according to the people. **They threw Jeremiah into a cistern that had no water in it, but only mud,** and he sank down in the mud (38:6). If not for a Cushite (Ethiopian) to rescue him, Jeremiah would have starved to death, especially as there was bread shortage in the city because of the siege. **That of course, explains why all prophets, right down to Jesus Christ himself, were always slaughtered** (Heb. 11:32-38). **They were considered unpatriotic, enemies of the people and misconstrued as prophets of doom. The fate of the prophets has not changed, just that most today are false prophets** (Luke 6:22-26)!

If you think that God is hard on sinners; consider this, he is hardest on his own prophets! Consider God's charge to Jeremiah (1:9b-10, 17);

> " 'Now, I have put my words in your mouth. See, today I appoint you over nations and kingdoms to uproot and to tear down, to destroy and overthrow, to build and to plant.' ... 'Get yourself ready! **Stand up and say to them whatever I command you. Do not be terrified by them, or I will terrify you before them.**"

Again, to Ezekiel, the LORD said;

> " 'Son of man, I have made you a watchman for the house of Israel; so hear the word I speak and give them warning from me. **When I say to a wicked man, 'You will surely die,' and you do not warn him or speak out to dissuade him from his evil ways in order to save his life, that wicked man will die for his sin, and I will hold you accountable for his blood.** But if you do warn the wicked man and he does not turn from his wickedness or from his evil ways, he will die for his sin; but you will have saved yourself" (3:17-19; 33:1-9).

Thus, for the prophet, to declare the LORD'S warning to the wicked was a matter of saving his own life! So, will the prophet lose his life because of another's sin just because he failed to warn the wicked? If you were the prophet, would you keep your mouth shut, or run to Tarshish like Jonah? Even in the case of Jonah, we realize that no one can escape from the LORD! You must do your duty, no desertion! The most dreadful case of God's seriousness toward his prophets is the case of the "man of God" from Judah (1 Kings 13). This prophet had been sent by God to prophesy against the idolatry (golden calves) of Jeroboam, the first king of Israel, the northern kingdom. God had carefully instructed him not to eat or drink anything in that place or return by the way he had come. But an older prophet persuaded him (by lying) to do otherwise. So, he ate and drank water, defying the word of the LORD. As a result, he was killed by a lion!

We may note that while the prophet has the option to disobey God, to the obedient prophet, who knows God and has tasted his goodness, there is only one option—to obey God rather than men! Like Jeremiah, once the word of the LORD has griped you, you cannot keep it in (Jer. 20:7-9)! It becomes a matter of life and death, and not even your own life matters! For whoever shall save his life will lose it, but whoever loses his life for my (Jesus') sake will find it (Luke 9:23-24). Therefore, *"Do not be afraid of those who kill the body but cannot kill the soul. Rather, be afraid of the One who can destroy both soul and body in hell"* (Matt. 10:28).

The Remnant

The Remnant comes up over and over in Scripture, and stands for a group of people, who, during evil, idolatry, sinfulness, and apostasy, are preserved or redeemed by God for his own purposes (they trust and obey God, no matter the terrible circumstances). God has always had a remnant since the time that he revealed himself to mankind. Noah represented a remnant in his day during the flood, and so did Lot during the destruction of Sodom and Gomorrah. When twelve Israelites were sent out to spy out the land they would later inherit, ten of them brought back a bad report, but a remnant (two) brought a good report. In the troublesome and sinful days of Elijah the prophet, he complained that; *"I have been very zealous for the LORD God Almighty. The Israelites have rejected your covenant, broken down your altars, and put your prophets to death with the sword. I am the only one left, and now they are trying to kill me too."* But the LORD replied; *"Yet I reserve seven thousand in Israel--all whose knees have not bowed down to Baal and all whose mouths have not kissed him"* (1 Kings 19:14,18). It is hard to imagine where this seven thousand (remnant) were hiding so much so that only Elijah was visibly battling for the LORD. Nevertheless, there was this remnant that God had reserved for himself. In every generation, during idolatry, hypocrisy, and apostasy, God always keeps a remnant for himself. Therefore, there is always hope. The gates of hell cannot prevail against the Church! The existence of a remnant is not so much for their own sake or faithfulness as it is God's faithfulness and for the sake of his name that he preserves them.

Even when God denounces pagan and sinful nations, he always promises to redeem a remnant from among them to be his people. (Is. 19:19-25). Again, after denouncing Moab for her sin and pride, the LORD declares; *"Yet I will restore the fortunes of Moab in days to come"* (Jer. 48:47). Of the Cushites (Ethiopians), he says; *"Are not you Israelites the same to me as the Cushites?' declares the LORD"* (Amos 9:7). This shows to us that God is not inherently against any peoples (races or nations), but against sinners of all peoples, who violate his laws, including his chosen people, Israel. **Thus, even in the heart of Europe, North America, Asia, Africa, South America, Australia, and the islands of the seas, a banner will be raised for the glory of Yahweh!** For out of all nations, millions upon millions, will stream to the God of Jacob, they will go up to his holy Mountain, the New Jerusalem, and will worship him forever. They will celebrate the Feast of Tabernacles and the Sabbaths of the LORD (Is. 66:18-23; Zech. 14:16-17). In that day the joy of Yahweh will be the strength of the remnant of the nations. In the LORD they will put their trust and will forget their national idols forever--for surely, the gods of all the nations are idols! In that day; *"They will neither harm nor destroy on all my holy mountain, for the earth will be full of the knowledge of the LORD as the waters cover the sea"* (Is. 11:9).

Throughout church history, with the satanic attack on the church, God has always preserved a remnant in every generation, some of whom I tried to delineate in the earlier. Even in our days of the falling away (apostasy and the mystery of iniquity), there is still a strand of the Church of Philadelphia (Rev. 3:7-13), which will persevere to the end. This is what Jesus says in Matthew 24:9-13: some will persevere to the end and be saved. The book of Revelation is full of promises to those who will overcome (Rev. 2:7, 11, 17, 26-28; 3:5, 10, 12, 21; 7:13; 2 Tim. 3:12, 13), and escape the deception and delusion of the pre-tribulation rapture. **Here is the testimony of those who** overcome, and their victory over the dragon and the worship of the beasts; *"They overcame him by the blood of the Lamb and by the word of their testimony; they did not love their lives so much as to shrink from death"* (Rev. 12:11).

I have likened (typology) the fall of the free world to the fall of Satan and his angels or demons. Therefore, the remnant of the free world could also be likened to the elect angels. This remnant tenaciously and unwaveringly clings to God and his word and service, and obey him during idolatry, pride, and apostasy (Rather than pointing a finger at me, I wish you jump from your seat because you are sure you are part of the remnant. If you don't jump, be wary!). They continue to carry the gospel of salvation and hope to the nations. In all the nations of the earth, there is this remnant that God is preserving for himself and for the sake of his name. They will greet the Son of Man as he appears in his glory and kingdom. They are his bride and have kept themselves unspotted from any form of idolatry and worldliness. They are from every tribe and tongue and nation. The question is, "Are you part of the remnant or are you an enemy of God or an apostate?" Now that you have heard it all, whose side do you cast your vote, God's, or Satan's? No absentee ballot will be accepted! It will be automatically counted for Satan! Choose life (Kingdom of heaven) or death (hell) (Deut. 30:11-20).

CHAPTER 14

AH, SOVEREIGN LORD!

" There is no wisdom, no insight, no plan that can succeed against the LORD"

"The LORD foils the plans of the nations; he thwarts the purposes of the peoples. But the plans of the LORD stand firm forever, the purposes of his heart through all generations."

"I know that you can do all things; no plan of yours can be thwarted."\

"I know that everything God does will endure forever; nothing can be added to it and nothing taken from it. God does it so that men will revere him." (Pr. 21:30; Ps. 33:10-11; Job 42:2; Eccl. 3:14) AMEN!

Prayer

"Eternal and holy Father; You made the heavens and the earth, and all that is in them--the planets, the sun, the moon, the stars, the seas, the rivers, the hills and the mountains, and the valleys. They all declare your eternal divine power, nature, and wisdom, as it is written; *"For since the creation of the world God's invisible qualities—his eternal power and divine nature—have been clearly seen, being understood from what has been made, ..."* (Rom. 1:20). You set the seasons in place to refresh the earth—its ecological self-sustenance—rain, snow, dew, and sunshine. You fill the whole universe and even the highest heaven cannot contain you, as it is written; *"The highest heavens belong to the LORD, but the earth he has given to man." "But will God dwell on the earth? The heavens, even the highest heaven, cannot contain you"* (Ps. 115:16; 1 Kings

8:27). You have made heaven your throne and the clouds its support, which is the canopy over us, and the earth your footstool. As it is written; *"This is what the LORD says: 'Heaven is my throne, and the earth is my footstool. Where is the house you will build for me? Where will my resting place be?'"* (Is. 66:1). Your ways are not our ways and are beyond human understanding, and your thoughts are not our thoughts; you are far removed from us and dwell in a high and holy place (transcendence), but you have chosen to dwell with us (immanence)—to dwell with those who are humble and contrite in spirit and who tremble at your word (Is. 55:8-9; 57:15; 66:2b, 5a). Your ways are beyond human understanding, as it is written; *"Oh, the depth of the riches of the wisdom and knowledge of God! How un-searchable his judgments, and his paths beyond tracing out! Who has known the mind of the Lord? Or who has been his counselor?"* (Rom. 11:33-34). But You have freely and graciously shown to us THE WAY (JESUS CHRIST), and your (his) mind, which is your word (1 Co. 2:10-16). You are always ready to teach us your ways if we are willing (Pr. 1:22-23).

You are invisible yet visible in your word. You are the only one true and living God--without beginning and without end (*El Olam)*, the author of life and the giver of eternal life (John 1:4; 3:16,36). You create life and You bring down to the grave and bring out of the grave (1 Sam. 2:6). You are the resurrection and the life (John 11:25-26). O LORD God Almighty, You are mighty in deed and do great miracles and wonders—nothing is impossible for you. You have done countless numbers of things to those who love You. O LORD, renew them in our day, show us your awesome power (Hab. 3:2). You do as you please and no one can ask you "What is this you have done?" (Dan. 4:34-35). For; *"Our God is in heaven; he does whatever pleases him"* (Ps. 115:3). Therefore, all your creatures in heaven, on earth, and under the earth, will praise You (Rev. 4:11). They will kneel in adoration before You. They will proclaim your mighty deeds from generation to generation. They will sing forth your praise night and day; *"The heavens declare the glory of God; the skies proclaim the work of his hands. Day after day they pour forth speech; night after night they display knowledge. There is no speech or language where their voice is not heard. Their voice goes out into all the earth, their words to the ends of the world"* (Ps. 19:1-4). We are the mold of your hands—clay in the potter's hand, and we will praise You as long as You give us breath. We honor and exalt your glorious and holy Name--Yah, that powerful Name—that strong tower, which is a refuge to us and our security in times of trouble and need. We will worship you for your mighty works done on behalf of the children of men. For what we are is your doing, and it is marvelous in our eyes.

Father, before You laid the foundation of the world, your only Son was slain for our redemption. It was then that you laid the foundation of the everlasting kingdom that you have prepared for us (Matt. 25:34). Your plan, indeed, is perfect and cannot be thwarted. Your plan has been going according to schedule because no one can stop your advance. In fact, you were in eternity future even before there was time or man or anything else. You knew our days before you set the eternal clock. You know and have determined what will be a thousand years to come. Before we shall reach there, you are there. We revere You for your perfect work—for your perfect plan. You are sovereign over all the affairs of men and direct them do achieve your purposes. As it is written; *"The LORD works out everything for his own ends--even the wicked for a day of disaster"* (Pr. 16:4). No one can escape from your presence (Ps. 139), for you hold the lives (breath) of all men in your hand and direct them as you please (Dan. 5:23). You move the hearts of kings and princes to do your will, yet you judge them for their pride, folly, and arrogance. As it is written; *"The king's heart is in the hand of the LORD; he directs it like a watercourse wherever he pleases"* (Pr. 21:1). Yes, even the wrath of men will bring you praise; *"Surely the wrath of men brings you praise, and the survivors of your wrath are restrained"* (Ps. 76:10). You brought Nebuchadnezzar to the height of power and glory—you even called him your servant, yet You brought him down and made him eat grass with the animals because of the pride of his heart (Dan. 4). You brought Cyrus to power—your anointed one, even though he did not acknowledge You, to fulfill your purpose (Is. 45). You do these things to bring about your will and to bring honor to your great and wonderful Name. Do them again in our days. Bring in your everlasting kingdom.

At just the right time you brought forth your Son to show us the way, to shine the light in our dark world, to give us the truth, and to give us eternal life. You gave us your Word so that whoever wishes could take hold of this life. At just the right time again, You will reveal your Son, as he brings forth the eternal kingdom. We will see it and be satisfied. Indeed, You have worked salvation for yourself, your arm has done it for You; *"Truth is nowhere to be found, and whoever shuns evil becomes a prey. The LORD looked and was displeased that there was no justice. He saw that there was no one, he was appalled that there was no one to intervene;* **so his own arm worked salvation for him, and his own righteousness sustained him.** *" "Sing to the LORD a new song, for he has done marvelous things;* **his right hand and his holy arm have worked salvation for him.** *The LORD has made his salvation known and revealed his righteousness to the nations." "The stone the builders rejected has become the capstone; the LORD has done this, and it is marvelous in our eyes"* (Is. 59:15-16; Ps. 98:1-2; 118:22- 23).

But LORD, the enemy scoffs at You and your plan, as it is written; *"... in the last days scoffers will come, scoffing and following their own evil desires. They will say, 'Where is this 'coming' he promised? Ever since our fathers died, everything goes on as it has since the beginning of creation'"* (2 Pet. 3:3-4). The nations are united together against You and your Anointed One; *"Why do the nations conspire and the people plot in vain? The kings of the earth take their stand and the rulers gather together against the LORD and against His Anointed One. 'Let us break their chains,' they say, 'and throw off their fetters'"* (Ps. 2:1-3). The wicked mock at your patience. In their wisdom, they have trampled the blood of the covenant underfoot, they have abused your grace. As it is written; *"Though grace is shown the wicked, they do not learn righteousness; even in the land of uprightness they go on doing evil and regard not the majesty of the LORD."* Yes, LORD, they cling to worthless idols and forfeit the grace that could be theirs—idols of silver, gold, bronze, stone, wood, money! (Is. 26:10; Jonah 2:8). *"So justice is far from us, and righteousness does not reach us. We look for light, but all is darkness; for brightness, but we walk in deep shadows. Like the blind we grope along the wall, feeling our way like men without eyes. At midday we stumble as it were twilight; among the strong, we are like the dead." "... the law is paralyzed, and justice never prevails. The wicked hem the righteous, so that justice is perverted"* (Is. 59:9-10; Hab. 1:4). The wicked have worshiped and served the creature rather than the Creator; *"For though they knew God, they neither glorified him as God nor gave thanks to him, but their thinking became futile and their foolish hearts were darkened. Although they claimed to be wise, they became fools and exchanged the glory of the immortal God for images made to look like mortal man and birds and animals and reptiles. ... They exchanged the truth of God for a lie, and worshiped and served created things rather than the Creator--who is forever praised. Amen"* (Rom.1:21-25). They have profaned your name. Your name is in their lips every moment not for reverence but for profanity; *"Although they say, "As surely as the LORD lives,' still they are swearing falsely." "... You are always on their lips but far from their hearts." "They claim to know God, but by their actions they deny him. They are detestable, disobedient and unfit for doing anything good"* (Jer. 5:2; 12:2b; Tit. 1:16). They have become; *"... lovers of themselves, lovers of money, boastful, proud, abusive, disobedient to their parents, ungrateful, unholy, without love, unforgiving, slanderous, without self- control, brutal, not lovers of the good, treacherous, rash, conceited, lovers of pleasure rather than lovers of God--having a form of godliness but denying its power"* (2 Tim. 3:2-5).

Even us, O LORD, those who profess your name, have plunged into the same dissipation. We have followed the way of the world and have loved the world more than we love you (1 John 2:15-17). We have mixed the new leaven with the old one and made a mess of ourselves. We have established our own righteousness instead of the righteousness that comes from Jesus Christ. We have become conceited and trust in our own works rather than in your grace (Rev. 3:14-18). O LORD, forgive! Our hearts have become calloused and our ears dull; our eyes have become blind—we hear but do not understand; we see but do not perceive; we only see our own visions and delusions; we no longer love the truth even though your word to us is line upon line. We no longer accept rebuke from You and your word. We want our ears to be tickled and to hear only what our itching ears want to hear so that we may continue with our evil desires; *"For the time will come* [and has now come] *when men will not put up with sound doctrine. Instead, to suit their own desires, they will gather around them a great number of teachers to say what their itching ears want to hear. They will turn their ears from the truth and turn aside to myths"* (2 Tim. 4:3-4). We dress our wounds with fig leaves and whitewash our sins; *"The priests did not ask, 'Where is the LORD?' Those who deal with the law did not know me* [The LORD]*; the leaders rebelled against me. The prophets prophesied by Baal, following worthless idols." '"A horrible and shocking thing has happened in the land; the prophets prophesy lies, the priests rule by their own authority and my people love it this way." "To whom can I speak and give warning? Who will listen to me? Their ears are closed so they cannot hear. The word of the LORD is offensive to them; they find no pleasure in it." "From the least to the greatest, all are greedy for gain; prophets and priests* [pastors] *alike, all practice deceit. They dress the wound of my people as though it were not serious. 'Peace, peace,' they say, when there is no peace* [cf. 1 Thess. 5:3]. *Are they ashamed of their loathsome conduct? No, they have no shame at all; they do not even know how to blush"* (Jer. 2:8; 5:30-31; 6:10,13-15). O LORD, we are perishing for lack of knowledge; *"You stumble day and night, and the prophets stumble with you. ... my people are destroyed from lack of knowledge. 'Because you have rejected knowledge, I also have rejected you as my priests;* **because you have ignored the law of your God, I also will ignore your children.** *... '"* (Hos. 4:5-8). We deceive others and ourselves are being deceived; *"In fact, everyone who wants to live a godly life in Christ Jesus will be persecuted, while evil men and impostors will go from bad to worse, deceiving and being deceived"* (2 Tim. 3:12-13). We trust in our wealth but do not realize how wretched, pitiful, blind, naked, and desperate we are (Rev. 3:17). O LORD, have mercy, forgive us, and we will be forgiven!

But *"Why, O LORD, do you make us wander from your ways and harden our hearts so we do not revere you?"* (Is. 63:17). Why do You cover our eyes and ears and make our hearts calloused? As it is written; *"He said, 'Go and tell this people: 'Be ever hearing, but never understanding; be ever seeing, but never perceiving.' Make the heart of this people calloused; make their ears dull and close their eyes. Otherwise they might see with their eyes, hear with their ears, understand with their hearts, and turn and be healed'"* (Is 6:9-10; cf. Deut. 29:4). Why do You send us false visions and delusions? For it is written; *"... I saw the LORD sitting on his throne with all the host of heaven standing around him on his right hand and on his left. And the LORD said, 'Who will entice Ahab into attacking Ramoth Gilead and going to his death there?' One suggested this, and another that. Finally, a spirit came forward, stood before the LORD, and said, 'I will entice him.' 'By what means?' the LORD asked. 'I will go out and be a lying spirit in the mouths of all the prophets,' he said. 'You will succeed in enticing him,' said the LORD. 'Go and do it.' So now the LORD has put a lying spirit in the mouths of all the prophets of yours."* Again, about the coming of the Antichrist, it is written; *"For this reason God sends them a powerful delusion so that they will believe a lie and so that all will be condemned who have not believed the truth but have delighted in wickedness"* (1 Kings 22:19-23; 2 Thess. 2:11-12). Our false visions have blinded us and we are oblivious to the disaster that loams over us; *"The visions of your prophets were false and worthless; they did not expose your sin to ward off your captivity. The oracles they gave you were false and misleading"* (Lam. 2:14). You have covered the whole world with a veil (a shroud, a sheet) and so we grope only in darkness like drunkards in the gutters, as it is written; *"See, darkness covers the earth and thick darkness is over the peoples, ..."* (Is. 60:2a; cf.25:7). You have indeed, bound all of us over to disobedience; *"For God has bound all men over to disobedience so that he may have mercy on them all"* (Rom. 11:32). The mystery of the appearing or unveiling of the Christ, O LORD, You have shut up from our eyes—we toil and toil, but see only our shadows!

O LORD, have mercy on us; help our unbelief! Help our disobedience! Heal our blindness! Open our eyes, and they shall be opened; open our ears, and they shall be opened; enlightened our hearts, and they shall be enlightened! Bring us to your holy mountain, to Mount Zion, to New Jerusalem; fulfill your promises of long ago; as it is written; *"On this mountain he [God] will destroy the shroud that enfolds all peoples, the sheet that covers all nations; ...."*

"LORD, I have heard of your fame; I stand in awe of your deeds, O LORD. Renew them in our day, in our time make them known; in wrath remember mercy" (Is. 25:7; Hab. 3:2). O LORD, remove the veil from our eyes so that we may see our Lord. Save us from our false visions and delusions. Refine us with a refiner's fire; purify us like gold and silver, but do so in justice and mercy, or we shall all be consumed. Remember that we are but flesh, a mist that is, but soon disappears without a trace. Like flowers, in the morning we blossom, but at twilight we wither away, and are fit only to be gathered up and burned. O LORD, give us white clothes to wear so that we can cover our shameful nakedness. Give us salve to put on our eyes, so that we can see (Rev. 3:18,19b). Remove our stony hearts and give us hearts of flesh that yearn and desire You and your commandments. Give us the spirit of wisdom and revelation so that we may know You more. Open the eyes of our understanding and enlighten us so that we may know the hope to which You have called us, the riches of your glorious inheritance in the ones you have called, and your incomparably great power for us who believe in Jesus Christ (Eph. 1:17-19). Help us not to settle for the temporal and perishing things of the world, the fleeting idols that preoccupy our hearts--wealth, money, fame, strength (military might), deceptive wisdom, and the desires of the flesh. O LORD, have mercy, forgive, and heal! You are full of compassion, slow to anger and quick to forgive. Your love endures forever! For it is written; *"Yet this I call to mind and therefore I have hope: Because of the LORD'S great love we are not consumed, for his compassions never fail. They are new every morning; great is your faithfulness"* (Lam. 3:21-23). If You could reckon sin and treat us as our sins deserve, you will wipe us out completely. But we have hope because your word says; *"Blessed is he whose transgressions are forgiven, whose sins are covered. Blessed is the man whose sin the LORD does not count against him and in whose spirit is no deceit." "God made him* [Jesus Christ] *who had no sin to be sin for us, so that in him we might become the righteousness of God." "Surely he took our infirmities and carried our sorrows, yet we considered him stricken by God, smitten by him, and afflicted. But he was pierced for our transgressions, he was crushed for our iniquities; the punishment that brought us peace*

was upon him, and by his wounds we are healed. We all, like sheep, have gone astray, each one of us has turned to his own way; and the LORD has laid on him [Jesus Christ] *the iniquity of us all"* (Ps. 32:1-2; 2 Co. 5:21; Is. 53:4-6). Because of Jesus Christ, we have hope that You will forgive and cleanse us with hyssop; that You will make us to be whiter than snow, radiant with your glory. O, the riches of the mercy and compassion of our God! Who is a God like You who forgives sins and do not reject those that are contrite in spirit! As it is written; *"The LORD is compassionate and gracious, slow to anger, abounding in love. He will not always accuse, nor will he harbor his anger forever; he does not treat us as our sins deserve or repay us according to our iniquities. For as high as the heavens are above the earth, so great is his love for those who fear him; as far as the east is from the west, so far has he removed our transgressions from us. As a father has compassion on his children, so the LORD has compassion on those who fear him; for he knows how we are formed, he remembers that we are dust." "Their sins and lawless acts I will remember no more"* (Ps. 103:8-14; Heb. 10:17).

Therefore, I thank You, O LORD, for your mercy. Thank You for your forgiveness. Thank You for your grace. Thank You for working salvation for us. Thank You for bringing in your salvation. Thank You for bringing in your eternal kingdom. We will rejoice in your faithfulness. We will praise the glory of your Great Name forever. Glory, honor, power, wisdom, majesty, and all dominion be yours forever. Amen"

God's General Sovereignty Over All of History and Civilizations

So far, this book is overwhelming. It is not a pleasant thing to be the bearer of bad news, though inherent in that bad news is the good news: God has not given up on sinful mankind—he is still running after us and calling us to repent and turn to him for our own good; *"The Lord is not slow in keeping his promise, as some understand slowness.* **He is patient with you, not wanting anyone to perish, but everyone to come to repentance." "Or do you show contempt for the riches of his kindness, tolerance and patience, not realizing that God's kindness leads you toward repentance?"** (2 Pet. 3:9; Rom. 2:4). The evil and wickedness of human society is very puzzling and might lead one to begin to ask if God is in control. And if he is in control, why can he not stop such wickedness or why did he allow it in the first place. It is beyond the scope of this book to handle the origin of evil and its perpetuity down the ages. The answers to the above questions are in the Bible, it is just a matter of taking time to find them out. Although the world might not acknowledge God, he is sovereign over all the affairs of mankind from the worst to the best, and from the least to the greatest. He is as close to us as the air we breathe, if only we can recognize him or hear him (Acts 17:27)!

Unlike Deism (and other closely related philosophies and cults), which believes that a Great Being made the world and its laws and allowed it to function autonomously without any interference from this Being, God is actively involved in his creation, especially in the affairs of men. He is more closely involved than we think or realize—providence. He planned everything in eternity past, and guides, directs, oversees, and renders certain everything that goes on in the world, whether good or evil. He is directing everything towards his own ends (Pr. 16:4). We have seen the typical example of Nebuchadnezzar, whom God brought up to punish the evil nations surrounding Israel and to discipline Judah (Jer. 25:1-14). God built Babylon for him! In Daniel's words to Belshazzar, he said; *"O king, the Most High God gave your father Nebuchadnezzar sovereignty and greatness and glory and splendor"* (Dan. 5:18). By also revealing western history to Nebuchadnezzar and Daniel in dreams, God showed it clear that whatever will happen was included in his plan and he has providentially been directing it to this day. Thus, some of the events that have been highlighted in this book like colonialism, slavery, the strife for world dominance, and the like, have all been under his providential guidance. But we dare not ask him why he allowed them (Dan. 4:34-35).

God has enabled every step of human civilization, from Africa to the Mesopotamia or Babylon and to Europe, North America to South America, and to Asia, whether the peoples of these places acknowledged him or not. He gives life and breath to all mankind (2 Tim. 6:13). As it is written; *"In the beginning was the Word, and the Word was with God, and the Word was God. He was with God in the* *beginning. Through him all things were made; without him nothing was made that has been made. In him was life, and that life was the light of men. **The light shines in the darkness, but the darkness has not understood it.** ... He was in the world, and though the world was made by him, the world did not recognize him* (John 1:1- 5,10). From Babel, God dispersed mankind to inhabit the whole earth; *"... he [God] himself gives all men life and breath and everything else. From one man he made every nation of men, that they should inhabit the whole earth; **and he determined the times set for them and the exact places where they should live.** God did this so that men would seek him and perhaps reach out for him and find him, though he is not far from each one of us"* (Acts 17:25-27). Whether it is the heathen (that is, so-called animists or pagans) or the civilized (that have largely become christo-pagans and neo-pagans), God providentially guides all their affairs (Rom. 1:18-2:16). His eyes go to and fro over the whole earth; *"The eyes of the LORD are everywhere, keeping watch on the wicked and the good." "God understands the way to it and he alone knows where it dwells, for he views the ends of the earth and sees everything under the heavens"* (Pr. 15:3; Job 28:23-24). There is no mistake or accident in God's providence; it is going according to schedule and will be consummated soon with precision.

God's Particular Sovereignty Over His Chosen People

While God super-intends all human affairs, he has chosen a few (election) to carry out his specific plan in history. While he controls all of history in general, he also works in particular ways to make his presence visible. This is through particular revelation (Bible) and through the people he has chosen. From the beginning, he chose a few through whom he impacted the rest of the world. At the time of the flood, he chose Noah and his family. From the pagan Near Eastern civilizations (Mesopotamia), he chose Abraham, and promised that through him, all the peoples of the earth shall be blessed (Gen. 12:2-3). He chose Abraham's descendants, the Israelites, as his agent of salvation to the whole world. Since the coming of Jesus Christ, he has chosen the Church, and when the Church misses the way, he chooses individuals to revitalize the church and reach the world.

We have already seen that God has touched every significant human civilization since early Egypt and Mesopotamia to the present.

There is something interesting in God's particular sovereignty—ultimate success or victory always comes through the second agent. The first Adam failed and brought sin into the world whereby all are condemned, but the second Adam (Jesus Christ) passed the test and brought salvation to mankind, whereby many are made righteous (Rom. 5:12-19). Adam's firstborn son, Cain, was a murderer, but his second born, Abel, was upright and still speaks today even though he is dead (Heb. 11:4). Abraham's firstborn son, Ishmael, did not receive the promise, but his second born son, Isaac, received the promise. Esau was Isaac's firstborn son and had the right to the inheritance, but he sold his birthright for a bowl of soup to Jacob, his younger brother, who eventually became the father of the Israelite Patriarchs--the founding father of the Jewish nation. It just happened that God had predicted that the older, Esau, would serve the younger, Jacob, according to God's principle of election. The LORD had told their mother before they were born; *"'Two nations are in your womb, and two peoples from within you will be separated; one people will be stronger than the other, and the older will serve the younger'"* (Gen. 25:23). In Christ's days on earth, he frequently referred to the religious hypocrites that though being first, they would become last. This declaration seems to hold true for today. The first, that is, the West, is losing Christianity, while the last, the Third World is receiving it. Like Esau, many are selling their birthright for a bowl of soup (wealth, money, the god of the stomach—Phil 3:18-19; Heb. 12:16-17) and forfeiting their first place! What a paradox or pattern? The intricacy of God's particular sovereignty is weaved throughout the Scripture, and it could take a lifetime to delineate.

Conclusion on Part One

We are indeed already under judgment, but God is still extending his hand of mercy to those who will heed his warning and turn from their evil. His merciful hands are still wide open. He will not turn anyone away who comes to him. His grace is sufficient to the worst of sinners; as the old hymn says; "The vilest offender who truly believes that moment from Jesus a pardon receives." It is fitting here to insert the cries and petitions of the prophets when judgment loamed over Israel and Judah. You can pick up a Bible and read the petitions of Isaiah and Jeremiah (Is 59:1-20; 63:7-65:12; Jer. 5:1-31).

God Gives his Final Invitation:

*"Come, all you who are thirsty, come to the waters; and you who have no money, come, buy and eat! Come, buy wine and milk without money and without cost. Why spend money on what is not bread, and your labor on what does not satisfy? Listen, listen to me, and eat what is good, and your soul will delight in the richest of fare. Give ear and come to me; hear me, that your soul may live. I will make an everlasting covenant with you, my faithful love promised to David. ... **Seek the LORD while he may be found; call on him while he is near. Let the wicked forsake his way and the evil man his thoughts. Let him turn to the LORD, and he will have mercy on him, and to our God, for he will freely pardon"** (Is. 55:1-7).*

Should the superpowers and the nations of the world continue in defiance, God will display his glory in bringing them down just as he did to the superpowers and nations of antiquity. The world (particularly, the West and G7) should seriously consider taking Daniel's advice to Nebuchadnezzar after his judgment was revealed from heaven, perhaps, they might avert their judgment; ***"Therefore, O king** [West], **be pleased to accept my advice: Renounce your sins by doing what is right, and your wickedness by being kind to the oppressed [restitution and/or reparations] It may be that then your prosperity will continue"*** (Dan. 4:27). But as we know, Nebuchadnezzar refused to repent and to do justice and what was right, and hence, he learned justice the hard way—he walked in the bush and ate grass with animals for seven years (Dan. 4:27-37).

Will the West learn it the hard way too like this king? Will they take his words to heart? That those who walk in pride he can humble?

When God was angry with the Sodomites because of their great sin, he made his intention to destroy them known to Abraham. Abraham interceded and pleaded earnestly that God should spare them for the sake of a few righteous, but they were destroyed because they did not have any righteous nor did they repent from their abominations (Gen. 18-19; cf. 2 Pet. 2:6-10). This was a sad case indeed. Again, Jonah called Nineveh, the great and wicked city, to repentance and they repented, and God relented from punishing them for a time (Jonah 3). God is striking the world as he promised he would with judgments (pandemics and disasters), but defiance continues. What can I do but echo Habakkuk's prayers (1:2-2:3; 3)?

The one who does right will be accepted but the one who does wrong will be judged and rejected. Here are God's words to Cain, the murderer from the evil one; *"Then the LORD said to Cain, 'Why are you angry? Why is your face downcast?* ***If you do what is right, will you not be accepted? But if you do not do what is right, sin is crouching at your door; it desires to have you, but you must master it'"*** (Gen. 4:3-7).

"WHOEVER BELIEVES IN THE SON HAS ETERNAL LIFE, BUT WHOEVER REJECTS THE SON WILL NOT SEE LIFE, FOR GOD'S WRATH REMAINS ON HIM" (John 3:36). AMEN!

PART TWO

THE BRIDE OF CHRIST

Amidst the chaos and evil in the world, the Bride of Christ, the faithful remnant Church, continues to march on in triumphant victory. The gates of hell cannot prevail against her! She is continuously adorning herself as she sees the day of the bridegroom fast approaching.

The Church is metaphorically called the Bride of Christ; a woman espoused to him, who is earnestly waiting for him to return (Matt. 9:15; 25:1-13; Rev. 19:1-9). The Church is the prized possession that Jesus Christ bought with his precious blood (1 Co. 6:19-20). The Church is God's purchased possession, his treasured possession, that God has been building since Eden (Mal. 3:16-17; Eph. 1:13-14; Ps. 135:4). The arrival of the bridegroom is such an expectant event. And how ought a bride to be? Keeping herself pure and adorned with the costliest jewelry and pearls and waiting for that dream day. The bride continues to adorn herself by growing up to the stature and fullness of Christ (Eph. 4:11-16). She is eagerly waiting for that day of consummation—that ecstatic and exciting night, for the trump call. In our age of fornication or pre-marital sex, this betrothal expectation has all but disappeared. Not only is the betrothed expectant, the hour of the arrival of the bridegroom is unknown. Therefore, the earnestness of waiting increases more. But will the bridegroom arrive and find the bride waiting or committing fornication? This is precisely what a larger part of Christendom is doing. She has been cajoled by Satan, and at the eve of her wedding, a portion of the bride is committing adultery with Satan (2 Co. 11:2,3).

These idle virgins without enough oil in their lamps might very well miss the wedding (Matt. 25:6-12).

The Bride of Christ consists of all who have been "born again" by the Spirit of God through faith in Christ Jesus, wherever they are in the world. She consists of all God's faithful ones of all ages. The bride does not consist of a particular denomination, church, or group of churches—Catholic, Orthodox, or Protestant. Nor does she consist of a particular movement—Evangelicals, Pentecostals, Charismatic, or any other. Those who belong to the Bride of Christ are conscious of their identity and redemption by Jesus Christ and their betrothal to him, and hence, they stay pure from any form of contamination. They remain chaste and continue to adorn themselves for their one and only husband and do not expose their bosom to deceptive men, especially false prophets, and politicians. They are in close fellowship with him through his word by which they recognize his voice amidst myriad voices mimicking him—the pseudo-Christs. While they are found within denominations, they live above denomination with ultimate allegiance to Christ (for there is no denomination that does not falter). They follow the Spirit wherever he leads them.

CHAPTER 15

THE DIVERSE NATURE OF THE BRIDE

Trans-Ethnic

We read of the heavenly redeemed throng; *"And they sang a new song: 'You are worthy to take the scroll and to open its seals, because you were slain, and **with your blood purchased men for God from every tribe and language and people and nation"** **"After this I looked and there before me was a great multitude that no one could count, from every nation, tribe, people and language, standing before the throne and in front of the lamb.** They were wearing white robes and they were holding palm branches in their hands. And they cried out in a loud voice: 'Salvation belongs to our God, who sits on the throne, and to the Lamb'"* (Rev. 5:9; 7:9-10).

Israel might have been God's chosen people in ancient times, but from the coming of Jesus Christ, God officially opened the door and began to build a new people that consists of individuals from every single group or tribe of people all over the earth. Though this materialized with the coming of Jesus, it had always been God's intention from the beginning, to bless all the nations of the earth through Abraham's seed (Gen. 12:3). The promise was repeated several times in the Old Testament. In Hosea, God declares; *"I will plant her for myself in the land; I will show my love to the one I called 'Not my loved one.' I will say to those called 'Not my people,' 'You are my people'; and they will say, 'You are my God'"* (3:23). Also, in Isaiah 56:3, we read; *"Let no foreigner who has bound himself to the LORD say, 'The LORD will surely exclude me from his people.' And let not any eunuch complain, 'I am only a dry tree.'"*

God declared in Amos 9:7; *"'Are not you Israelites the same to me as the Cushites?' declares the LORD."* God made a unique gesture to signal his universal goal when he included some non-Israelite women, like Rahab and Ruth in the genealogy of Jesus Christ (Matt. 1:5). God declared through prophet Isaiah that his chosen one will be a light to the Gentiles (49:6).

The universal invitation to submit to God by believing in Jesus Christ is offered to all the peoples of the earth, and whosoever wills, let him believe and be saved. We are born naturally as the children of Satan, but by putting faith in Jesus Christ, we become (are adopted) children of God irrespective of our natural ethnic origin; *"You are all sons of God through faith in Christ Jesus, for all of you who were baptized into Christ have clothed yourselves with Christ. There is neither Jew nor Greek, slave nor free, male nor female, for you are all one in Christ Jesus."* Again, it is written; *"He came to that which was his own, but his own did not receive him. Yet to all who received him, to those who believed in his name, he gave the right to become children of God—children born not of natural descent, nor of human decision or a husband's will, but born of God"* (Gal. 3:26-28; John 1:11-13).

Trans-Colored

The classification of peoples into colors or races is the devil's idea to divide people, in as much as we all make up one race—humans that came from the hand of God, beginning with Adam (Acts 17:26). The Bride of Jesus Christ makes no distinction between white, black, brown, red, pink, tan, or whatever color we can think of. I am aware that there are denominations that were founded on racial lines and others who discriminate against others because of color or race. Some denominations are built not only along these lines, but many congregations are built on such lines. The history of racism or discrimination based on skin color is a sad one and some countries enshrined such evil and hatred in their constitutions. Such an attitude is sinful—even satanic. People who think and act on such racial lines have no place in the Bride of Christ, no matter how religious they may claim to be. You cannot think and act this way and pretend that there is no hatred. The Apostle John puts it bluntly concerning such hatred;

"We know that we have passed from death to life, because we love our brothers. Anyone who does not love remains in death. Anyone who hates his brother is a murderer, and no murderer has eternal life in him." "If anyone says, 'I love God,' yet hates his brother, he is a liar. For anyone who does not love his brother, whom he has seen, cannot love God, whom he has not seen. And he has given us this command: Whoever loves God must also love his brother" (1 John 3:14-15; 4:20; cf. John 13:34- 35).

Jesus had said that the two greatest commandments are to love God and neighbor. You cannot love a neighbor you despise. If you are too color conscious, maybe you do not belong to the Bride of Christ. If your identity depends primarily on your skin color, you will probably miss out the Bride of Christ, because in the Bride of Christ, identity primarily comes from believing in Christ. What are you going to do if your resurrection or transformed body shall no longer look like the body that you got your primary identity from? Do you not know that we all came from the same dust and shall return to that dust at death? Does it really matter what kind of dust you turn back to? Have you not read that God does not look on the outside appearance as man does, but looks at the heart? *"But the LORD said to Samuel, 'Do not consider his appearance or his height, for I have rejected him. The LORD does not look at the things man looks at. Man looks at the outward appearance, but the LORD looks at the heart'"* (1 Sam. 16:7). If your heart is full of discrimination because of your color, you are in direct opposition to God and have no place in the Bride of Christ. The person who built his identity around his appearance is Satan, and that led or would lead to his downfall! *"'You were the model of perfection, full of wisdom and perfect in beauty. ...* **Your heart became proud on account of your beauty,** *and you corrupted your wisdom because of your splendor. So I threw you to the earth; I made a spectacle of you before kings'"* (Ezek. 28:12b, 17). So be careful when you build your identity around color and discriminate against others that do not look like you. There is no such distinction among those who belong to the Bride of Christ. We are all the children of God by faith in Christ Jesus no matter our complexion. We are heading to the same destination—the color-blind and classless society.

Trans-Denominational

The multiplicity of Protestant denominations, with many claiming that one must belong to them to be saved, is a difficult challenge and confusion in our days. It is like the days of the Corinthian Church, where groups of believers claimed the either followed Paul, Apollos, Peter, or Christ. There are some believers who do not accept other believers until they belong to their denomination or church. We must understand that even in the days of Christ on earth, not everybody who served him followed him around. The disciples, just like many of us today, were unhappy that some who preached in the name of Jesus did not follow them. But Jesus told the disciples to leave them alone; *"'Master,' said John, 'we saw a man driving out demons in your name and we tried to stop him, because he was not one of us.' 'Do not stop him' Jesus said, 'for whoever is not against you is for you'"* (Luke 9:49-50). If only we could learn that lesson! There is no denial that there was a need for the Church to split because the main church (Roman Catholic Church) leadership had gone astray and did not want to repent. However, it is apparent that many denominations are splitting over minor issues today. The Church today is characterized more by differences than by similarities and love (John 13:34-35). This is one of the greatest weaknesses of the modern Church, especially Protestantism. Unbelievers are rather confused as to who to believe. I am mindful that there are some strengths to this splintering. Wherever it is called "church", and the Bible is preached, obeyed, and respected, there is light. Even in the darkest corners. To belong to the bride does not mean belonging to a particular denomination or church. **The underlying qualification for belonging to the bride is being "born again." Whoever is "born again," no matter which denomination or church they go to, belongs to the Bride of Christ, and will go into the millennial kingdom with Christ, and ultimately eternity. Belonging to a church or denomination does not automatically make you a member in the Bride of Christ— you must be "born again" to belong.**

The ideal for the Bride of Christ is union in one: one God, one body (Church), and one Lord. Jesus Christ earnestly prayed for this unity; *"I have given them the glory that you gave me, that they may*

be one as we are one: I in them and you in me. **May they be brought
to complete unity** *to let the world know that you sent me and have
loved them even as you have loved me"* (John 17:22-23). When the
Church is united in one—one mind and the same accord, the Lord's
glory is manifested in a magnificent way in the Church, unleashing
the power of the Holy Spirit in a unique way (Acts 4:23-33, KJV).
The call for unity was Paul's earnest urge and prayer for the Church
too (1 Co. 1:12-13, 11:17-19; Phil. 2:1- 2; 4:2). It is sad that the
Church does not have this unity today. Christians are known more
for their divisions and dislike for one another than for the unity and
love for one another, and thus, breaking Jesus' commandment in
John 13:34-35. Even where there is attempted unity, it is not based
on the word and doctrine of Christ. Nevertheless, everyone who
belongs to the bride knows that although they may be separated
from other members of the bride because of denominational barriers,
they ultimately belong to the same body. We long for the day when
this hidden Bride would be made public under her Bridegroom and
leader, Jesus Christ, the King of kings and Lord of lords. Then, there
will be a visible Bride united with a visible Bridegroom.

Trans-National

The Bride of Christ is constituted by believers of every nation
(ethnic groups and geographical nations). She is not to be identified
within a particular geographic nation, no matter how many Christians
live within that nation or how influential the nation is in Christian
matters. The appellation "Christian" nation or "Christendom" may
cause some people to begin to identify certain nations or groups of
nations (the West) as constituting the Bride of Christ. This would
be a serious mistake. To be sure, there is one "Christian Nation" or
country: "One Nation Under Jesus Christ." This nation/country is
invisible and is the destination of all believers from all the nations
of the earth. Its name is Zion—the city and presence of God! This
nation has been under construction for countless ages—from eternity
past.

A Grave Mistake: While God scattered mankind from Babel
to inhabit the whole earth and determined the times set for them
and the exact places where they should live (Acts 17:26), and

therefore, gave us our distinct ethnicities or nationalities, **we must never attach ourselves to an earthly nation more than we attach ourselves to God.** When we do that, it tantamount to idolatry. The believer's allegiance to Jesus Christ, must therefore, be stronger than his allegiance to an earthly nation. Thus, no matter your national expression of Christianity, you must avoid nationalistic Christianity and be engaged in the bridal Christianity that knows no national boundaries. It is quite easy to become blinded by nationalistic religion and lose contact with the universal body of Christ (the Bride). You must be a "universal" or an "international" Christian. Never stick your head in the sand and be absorbed by nationalistic religion because the wind will not stop blowing, nor will the reality clock stop ticking. Christianity is an international religion with equality among its members across national borders.

A brief theology of nations explains why.[cccxlix] God is sovereign over all the nations and determines their affairs, raising up kings and deposing kings (Is. 45; Jer. 25:8-14; 27:2ff; Dan. 4:17, 34- 37). However, all the nations of the earth are under the jurisdiction of Satan and do his will and biding (Matt. 4:8-9; Jesus did not dispute Satan's claim to the nations of the earth; Satan is the god of this world, the god of this age; 1 John 5:19; Rev. 12:9; 20:7-8; see also Luke 22:52-53, where Christ confirmed to those authorities who arrested him that, it was their hour (time, age) when darkness reigns upon the nations). To think or believe that there is a single nation that is not under Satan is naïve, myopic, delusional, and a great deception. **All nations, no matter their professed Christianity, are against God and conspire against him** (Ps. 2). They do not write their secret plans and policies (domestic and foreign) with God in mind—they do it for themselves and their self-interests, and for their glory and pride, no matter the public camouflage in using God's name. Do not be deceived by the appellation "Christian" nation or "Christendom." At best, these appellations are only confusing and deceptive. **All nations, no matter their greatness** (even those reaching the skies or the heavens) **will pass away.** More than 80 great civilizations (empires or nations) have risen and fallen in the brief history of mankind, and those that are now will inevitably fall as well! Here is the testimony of Scripture about the nations.

About the great and glorious ancient Babylon, it is written; *"This is what the LORD Almighty says: 'Babylon's thick wall* [security and defense] *will be leveled and her high gates set on fire; **the peoples exhaust themselves for nothing, the nations' labor is only fuel for the flames"*** (Jer. 51:58). Remember that God says he will destroy again with fire. Even the tallest skyscraper will be turned into rubble. Habakkuk echoes the same theme in chapter 2 verse 13; *"Has not the LORD Almighty determined that the people's labor is only fuel for the fire, that the nations exhaust themselves for nothing?"* **The greatness of nations means nothing to God, whether Great Britain, Great Germany, Great France, Great China, Great Russia, or Great America.** As it is written;

> *"A voice says, 'Cry out.' And I said, 'What shall I cry?' 'All men are like grass, and all their glory is like the flowers of the field. **The grass withers and the flowers fall, because the breath of the LORD blows on them. Surely the peoples are grass. The grass withers and the flowers fall, but the word of our God stands forever. ... Surely the nations are like a drop in a bucket; they are regarded as dust on the scales; he weighs the islands as though they were fine dust. ... Before him all the nations are as nothing; they are regarded by him as worthless and less than nothing"*** (Is. 40:6-8, 15-17).

Yes, all these great nations are regarded by God as worthless, as nothing; they will all be blown away by his breath, his word, that abides forever;

> *"While you were watching, **a rock** [Jesus Christ] *was cut out, but not by human hands. It **struck the statue** [human civilization, especially Western civilization from Babylon of old to New Babylon--America] *on its feet of iron and clay and **smashed them.** Then the iron, the clay, the bronze, the silver and the gold were **broken to pieces** [cf. Ps. 2:9] *at the same time **and became like chaff on a threshing floor in summer. The wind swept them away without leaving a trace.** But the rock that struck the statue became a huge mountain* [the Mountain of the LORD—Zion, New Jerusalem] *and filled the whole earth* [the Universal Everlasting Kingdom of Christ]. ... *In the time of those*

*kings, the **God of heaven will set up a kingdom** that will never be destroyed, nor will it be left to another people. **It will crush all those kingdoms and bring them to an end,** but it will itself endure forever"* (Dan. 2:34-35, 44).

Thus, all the nations of the world will be ended, but only Christ's "Christian Nation" that is invisible now, will endure and will occupy all the earth (Rev. 11:15)! The word of God is the only window or gate to the future! Where is your primary citizenship and allegiance? To Christ's nation or to an earthly nation that will soon be broken to pieces and vanish like chaff in the wind? The future belongs exclusively to the Bride of Christ, who are citizens of Christ's nation: "One Nation Under Jesus Christ." (Dan. 7:17-18, 26-27).

That is the only window to the future—citizenship in the kingdom of Christ (his Bride) as saints of the Most High.

The Christian universal brotherhood is stronger than any nationalistic bonds between citizens of the same country. Therefore, the bond between Christians of different nationalities is stronger than nationalistic bonds. We are all united in Christ. In heaven, it will not matter which country you came from, but whether you did the will of God and were a citizen of heaven. The Christian Country or Nation is not located in a particular country or continent. The kingdom of God/Christ is not of this world and must never be identified as such (John 18:36ff). We must never get comfortable in the devil's world but must always remember that we are strangers and aliens in this world and are looking forward to our heavenly country (1 Pet. 2:11-12; Heb. 11:13-16). Ours is going to be a heavenly country—Zion, the New Jerusalem (Heb. 12:22ff; Rev. 21; Jer. 33:16; Ezek. 48:35). Our citizenship in any earthly country is only temporal, our ultimate citizenship is in this heavenly country (Phil. 3:18-21).

I have watched with dismay how many from South America and Africa die attempting to cross into the USA or Western Europe, respectively. They even sell their souls to obtain citizenship in these western nations! They aspire for earthly countries that will soon vanish into oblivion, but if you were to ask them to obtain citizenship in heaven, they will obviously reject it. They have settled for the temporal. That is why the Bible says that the whole world wondered after the beast and worshipped the dragon (Satan) that gave it power (Rev. 13:8). In fact, many lie, deceive, risk their lives, betray their mother-country, and do all sorts of things just to obtain citizenship in a western country. I sometimes imagine the following scenario. Let's say, a Preacher and Consular officer from the United States are going around the world with options of either believe in Christ and wait for heaven wherever you are or reject him and obtain a visa to the States. Who do you think will make more converts in these our days? Would you prefer to be a part of the Bride or enjoy the temporal earthly pleasures that even come at such great sacrifice? On an ending note, the Bride of Christ is trans-continental. She is not located in a particular continent but is made up of people from the six inhabited continents. All are represented. Are you in the number?

The Bride: One Flock Under One Shepherd/Pastor/Master

Christ's Expectation: The Bride is a flock that hears the voice of the Bridegroom, and will not listen to another's voice (John 10). Hearing his voice means absolute obedience to him and his word— not 90 percent, not 95 percent, not 99.99 percent, but 100 percent obedience! This obedience is built on love. You cannot obey a God you do not love, and you cannot love God without obeying his commandments, and you cannot obey commandments you do not know. Therefore, you must diligently seek God in his word and obey what he commands (Zech. 6:15; Heb. 11:6; John 14:21,23-24; 1 John 3:24; 5:2-4). Christ reveals himself more to you when you obey him in what you already know. It is an oxymoron to say you love God but disobey his commands. If you say you love Jesus Christ, but spurn his word, you are on dangerous or slippery ground, you are a liar (1 John 2:3-6).

Our Failure: Christ also expects his flock to be one and united together, built on love for one another (John 13:34-35; 17). The apostle Paul expects the same unity from the flock of Christ (Phil. 1:27; 2:1-2; 1 Co. 1-3). But we have failed and continue to fail. We no longer seem to hear the voice of Christ, but only other voices competing in his place. Nor do we love one another or are united. Instead of love, we have shown hatred, and instead of unity we have practiced division. Christianity seems to be a joke to many, especially because of the multiplicity and splintering of denominations today--in their thousands! Each denomination preaches its own Christ and some claim to be the only right denomination. Inter-denominational relationships are characterized more by hatred than by love. We are strictly warned that no one who hates his brother has the Father or the Son or eternal life (1 John 3:11,14-15)! Therefore, we must try to overcome our failure as we anticipate the appearing (Tit. 2:13). Doctrinal unity built on grace and forgiveness, and not just ecumenism.

CHAPTER 16

AN INTERVIEW INTO THE KINGDOM OF GOD

God! Who Is He?

"H*ear, O Israel: The LORD our God, the LORD is one* "
*"For there is **one God and one mediator between God and
men, the man Jesus Christ.** ..." "There is **one body and one Spirit
... one Lord, one faith, one baptism; one God and Father of all,**
who is over all and through all and in all"* (Deut. 6:4; 1 Tim. 2:5;
Eph. 4:4-6).

God! Yes, who is he? Or what does that word stand for or mean?
The word God/god is a generic word that can apply to a lot of things. It
is a universal term used by all mankind. Before particular revelation,
the peoples of the earth had a concept of god. For most primitive
peoples there were always many gods— polytheism; a god for nearly
everything and activity: god of fields, streams, stones, goddess of
fertility, and others. Polytheists worship animals, trees, rivers, sun,
moon, planets (astrology--still practiced even in civilized societies
openly and in disguised forms like horoscope). As men began to
build cities, they developed city gods and then national gods.

Thus, before the One, True and Living God revealed himself in
a personal way (of course, he was known to Adam in Eden) all men
worshipped many gods, that were sometimes represented by idols
(for instance, Abram in Josh. 24:2). As we saw earlier, the idea of
gods evolved to the idea of a supreme being among other peoples,
even so-called animists. This supreme being or deity/god was far up

in the sky and transcendent (far removed). He had made everything in the universe both plants and animals. He can see all things approving and disapproving man's actions. He himself is uncreated, that is, he is eternally existent, the beginner of all things, like a first father. This thought is behind all religions— whether it is in the family, village, town, city, country, or kingdom. Many other enlightened peoples ended up with the idea of "A High God"—the originator of all things, including their customs and rituals. This High God is eternal, uncreated, and existed in the beginning; he is supreme and without equal, transcendent, yet immanent (close by). In other areas, this God was regarded as "A Supreme Spirit." The Spirit over the spirits or souls of the dead or ancestral spirits in the spirit world. Most African traditionalists believe in this supreme being or High God, but to them, he can only be reached after appeasing the malevolent spirits that stand between him and them. In Western civilization, it was the Greek philosophers, who gradually proceeded from polytheism and mythology to the idea of one supreme being or deity purely from human reason. This deity to the philosophers, was/is one, creative and divine, greatest among all gods, unlike man in form and mind.

The last constructive philosophers to appear on the scene were the deists. They believe that there is a supreme being, who can be reached by pure reason, and as such they reject divine revelation. Other major religions have their own concept of who God is and what he requires from man and how he can be reached or worshipped. Lastly, we have atheists, who believe that there is no God. The Bible calls them fools (morally deficient; Ps. 14:1)! By so doing they are declaring themselves as gods! There are also agnostics. They simply do not believe in God, whether he exists or not, is none of their business.

But, why all this universal religiosity? Must there be religion? Something rather than nothing? The answer is simple; man was made in the image and likeness of God, and there is a longing in man to fellowship with him from whom man came. Our lives are the breath of God, thus creating an affinity with him. There is something inherent in man that longs for God. Man is a religious being. His religiosity, if not fulfilled, creates a void in him. When this void is not filled by the One and True God, Satan fills the void with all kinds of false religion and philosophies, designed to keep man away from the Living God. Satan is the master planner behind all false religions, philosophies, and political ideologies that contradict the Scriptures and exalt man. He takes advantage of man's religiosity to enslave man and bid him to do his will. He has invented every religion that does not honor God and recognize his revealed will (Bible).

Therefore, does the word "God" always mean the same thing or refer to the same being whenever it is used? The word exists or is used in almost every single religion—organized/formal or unorganized / informal. Is this "God" of all religions the same as the God of the Bible? The simple answer is no!

First, the Bible acknowledges that there are many other gods (which are not gods) implicit from the warnings against idolatry (1 Co. 8:4-6). Secondly, the God of the Bible is known as the God of gods, thus, confirming the existence of other gods. Thirdly, the God of the Bible is known as "I AM" or *LORD* (in most Bible translations) or Yahweh (English transliteration) or Jehovah (German transliteration), thereby distinguishing him from other gods. While his description or qualities might co-inside with those of other gods; for instance, Creator or spirit, he, nevertheless, is different from them. All men know there is God, even those who deny him like Atheists (Rom. 1:18ff). The devil knows there is God, and that is why he wants to usurp God or be like God and is deceiving man to want to do the same (Gen. 3:1ff; Is. 14:12-14; Ezek. 28:2-10; James 2:19). Fourthly, the God of the Bible is known as Jesus Christ! This makes the distinction obvious and unmistakable. You cannot acknowledge the One True God without acknowledging Jesus Christ as God! This is where we can discern who knows or does not know the true God. Therefore, wherever you see the word "God," if it cannot be replaced by the words "Yahweh/Jehovah" or "Jesus Christ" and still mean the same thing, then "God" in that sense does not refer to the one true God of the Bible.

Jesus Christ! Who Is He?

Jesus Christ is either all that the Bible claims he is, or he is nothing at all! It is all or nothing! No one can claim to know God without acknowledging Jesus Christ as God. Jesus Christ has become the stumbling block to the world, to those who do not accept him for who he is. Ever since he arrived on earth, the world has been disturbed because of him. At his birth the Magi asked; *"'Where is the one who has been born king of the Jews? We saw his star in the east and have come to worship him. When King Herod heard this he was disturbed, and all Jerusalem with him.'"* At his presentation at the temple, Simeon said of him; *"This child is destined to cause the falling and rising of many in Israel* [and ultimately the whole world], *and to be a sign that will be spoken against, so that the thoughts of many hearts will be revealed. And a sword will pierce your own soul too"* (Matt. 2: 2-3 Luke 2:34-35). The world continues to be disturbed today and many are falling because of this Jesus. Are you rising with him or falling because of him? In these last days, the final test for mankind will not be whether there is a God or "Who is God?" but "Who is Jesus Christ?" **JESUS CHRIST is very God, yet man!** *"Let this mind be in you which was also in Christ Jesus, who, being in the form of God, did not consider it robbery to be equal with God, …" "The Son is the radiance of God's glory and the exact representation of his being, …"* (Phil. 2:5-6; Heb. 1:3).

The Mistake of Many, Then and Today: The religious leaders of Jesus' day charged him with blasphemy when he forgave sins and called himself the Son of God; *"'How can a mere man claim to be God or make himself equal with God?' they asked"* (Matt. 9:1-6; John 10:30-36). The greatest mistake of **Muhammad (founder of Islam)** and his followers is their denial that Jesus is the Son of God, and hence, a denial of his deity. They reject that he is the Son of God (Allah cannot have a Son), and reduce him to a mere prophet, even superseded by Muhammad. **Religious pluralists** (who believe all religions lead to God) say Jesus is a revelation of God no better than God's revelation through other religious leaders like Buddha and others. To them, he is not the unique Son of God, and therefore, not deity or equal with God. **Freemasons and Deists** acknowledge a

"God" known as the Great Being or Creator or Grand Architect of the universe but reject special revelation (Bible) and hence the epitome of God's revelation, Jesus Christ (Heb. 1:1-3). To them, Jesus Christ cannot be God. They are willing to accept him as a historical moral teacher, but not as deity (God). Just as a reminder, anyone who rejects the deity of Jesus (God having come in the flesh) is an antichrist (1 John 4:2-3; 2 John 7). In short, Freemasons and Deists are antichrists, and they occupy important political seats, and therefore, are ruling the world! The world is under the rulership of antichrists! There is a host of other misconceptions about and rejections of the personality of Jesus Christ which we cannot discuss here. Their general problem is that Jesus is not deity and is not the only way to God as the Bible claims (John 14:6; Acts 4:12).

So, Who is Jesus Christ? Or Yahushua Ha Mashiach" OR *"The Anointed Savior?"*

Jesus is God: Jesus Christ is all that God is. He is 100 percent God! Nothing less! **He is Yahweh or Jehovah, the Great "I AM," The Ancient of Days,** whose days are of old (Is. 9:6; 40:3,10; Zech. 14:5; Dan. 7:13, 14; Mic. 5:2; John 8:57-58; 10:30, 33; 14:8-10; 20:28; Tit. 2:13; Phil. 2:5-6). He is **Immanuel—**God in the flesh dwelling with us (Is. 7:14; Matt. 1:22-23). He is the **image of the invisible God** and the **exact representation of his being** (Col. 1:15-20; Heb. 1:3).

Jesus is the Eternal Word; The *Logos* **made flesh** (Ps. 119:89; 1 Tim. 3:16; 1 John 4:2): He is deity and equal with the Father in every way; *"In the beginning was the Word, and the Word was with God, and the Word was God. ... The Word became flesh and made his dwelling among us. We have seen his glory, the glory of the One and Only, who came from the Father, full of grace and truth" "For God was pleased to have all his fullness* [deity] *dwell in him, ..." "For in Christ all the fullness of the Deity lives in bodily form, ..."* (John 1:1,14; Col. 1:19; 2:9).

Jesus is the Unique Son of God: One of an Only Kind, Begotten by the Holy Spirit! (Is. 7:14; Matt. 1:18, 20; Luke 1:30-31, 34-35; John 3:16-17; 20:30-31; Rom 1:1-4; Gal. 4:4-5): As the unique or only begotten Son of God, he is equal with God as the religious leaders of the Jews understood; *"'We are not stoning you for any of these,' replied the Jews, 'but for blasphemy, because you, being a mere man, claim to be God.' ... Jesus answered them, ... Why then do you accuse me of blasphemy because I said 'I am God's Son?'"* (John 10:33-36).

Jesus is the Creator (Gen. 1:1; Is. 40:28; 44:24; Rev. 4:11): *"I am the LORD, your Holy One, Israel's Creator, your King." "Through him* [Jesus Christ] *all things were made; without him nothing was made that has been made." "For by him all things were created: things in heaven and on earth, visible and invisible, whether thrones* [like the Kremlin and White House] *or powers or rulers or authorities; all things were created by him and for him. He is before all things, and in him all things hold together"* (Is. 43:15; John 1:3; Col. 1:16-17). He is the center of the universe, which he upholds by his powerful word (Heb. 1:3).

Jesus is Savior, Just as the Father is Savior: The name *Jesus* means the LORD (Y*ah)* saves (Matt. 1:21; Acts 4:12; 1 Tim. 4:9,10; Is. 43:3,11; Phil. 3:20; Tit. 1:3-4). Jesus Christ is both God and Savior; *"... while we wait for the blessed hope--the glorious appearing of our great God and Savior, Jesus Christ, who gave himself for us to redeem us from all wickedness and to purify for himself a people that are his very own, eager to do what is good"* (Tit. 2:13-14). He is, therefore, the **Redeemer,** who bought us (sinners) from the slave market of sin (Is. 43:14a; 59:20; Job 19:25; Rom. 3:22-24).

Jesus is the Lawgiver and Judge, Just like the Father (Is. 32:22; Ps. 50:1-6; 75:7; 89:14; 96:10; 98:9; John 5:19-20, 22-23, 27; 8:15-16; 9:39; 12:47-48; Acts 10:42; 17:30-31; Rev. 19:15; 20:11-15): The Father loves the Son and has committed everything into his hands and has appointed him as Judge over the whole world. He appeared the first time to take away sins but will appear a second time to bring salvation to those waiting for him and judgment to his enemies (Heb. 9:26-28). He will judge the world in justice, righteousness, equity, and with impartiality.

Jesus is the Son of Man: He is 100 percent Human! (Ezek. 1:25-27; Rev. 1:12-16; Dan. 7:13; Luke 19:10; 21:27; 2:40, 51-52): The

Son of Man was Jesus' favorite title for himself. He is as human as we are except without sin. He endured every painful experience of life that we go through (suffering, thirst, hunger, fatigue, loneliness, rejection, hatred, etc.), and that is why he is our perfect model or example and can represent us before the Father (Heb. 2:5-18; 4:14-15; 5:7-9).

Jesus is The King; The Anointed (Messianic/Christ) King: He is the Son of David, who will sit on David's eternal throne forever (2 Sam. 7:11b-16; Luke 1:31-33; John 18:33-37; Acts 17:6-7; Ps. 24:7-10; 47; 98:4-6). He is **the King installed in Zion,** who will rule the whole world (the heavens and the earth, and under the earth) with the iron scepter (His Word); *"The One enthroned in heaven laughs; the Lord scoffs at them* [the kings of the earth plotting against the LORD and his Anointed One—vv. 1-3]. *Then he rebukes them in his anger and terrifies them in his wrath, saying, 'I have installed my King on Zion, my holy hill .... You* [the King] *will rule them with an iron scepter; you will dash them to pieces like pottery'"* (Ps. 2:1-9; cf. In Rev. 2:26-28, Jesus gives the same promise to believers who overcome!). He is the King of kings and the Lord of lords (Rev. 19:16).

Jesus is The Prophet; Yes, more than a Prophet! (Deut. 18:15-19; Matt. 13:57; 14:5; 21:11; John 7:40): He is the summation of all prophecy; all the word of God, the mind of Christ! (1 Co. 2:16; Luke 24:27). It is said of Christ; *"Then I said, 'Here I am—it is written about me in the scroll—I have come to do your will, O God'"* (Heb. 10:7).

Jesus is The Priest, The High Priest, in the Order of Melchizedek (Ps. 110:4ff; Heb. 4:14-5:10; 7:26): As High Priest, he offered himself once and for all for sin, and represents us before the Father. He has made all believers priests of God together with him (1 Pet. 2:5; Rev. 1:5-6; 5:10).

Jesus is The Stone, The Rock in Zion (Zech. 3:8-9; Dan. 2:34; Ps. 118:22; Acts 4:10-11): This stone will crush those it falls on and all pagan civilizations. This stone is a stumbling block to the Jews, unbelievers, and all who reject him (1 Pet. 2:4-8).

Jesus is A Sure Foundation (Is. 26:16; Eph. 2:19-20): He is the foundation rock, the cornerstone; a fortress for the oppressed, helpless, and needy people to trust in. To hear and practice the word of Jesus Christ is to be wise and to build upon this solid foundation (Matt. 7:21-27; 1 Co. 3:10-15; 2 Tim. 2:19).

Jesus is The Firstborn; The Firstborn from the Dead (Matt. 28:5-6; Acts 2:23-24; 1 Co. 15:20-23; Col. 1:15; Rev. 1:4b-5a, 18): He is alive and lives forever—the Living One. And because he lives forever, believers shall live forever also (Rom. 11:15).

Jesus is the Eternal Wisdom of God (Pr. 8:22-31; 1 Co. 1:30): By him the universe was made.

And Much More! Jesus is all in all! Do you have a problem with that? With whom Jesus Christ is? Dig a hole and hide because there will be no place for you in the world to come. In fact, even in your hole he will find you out and throw you into eternal torment (Ps. 139:7-12). You cannot escape him! Every knee must bow to him (Phil. 2:9-11)! **The Case for Jesus Christ would be the Last Test for Mankind.** As already shown, many like to acknowledge God or a Creator, or a Supreme Being, but they have a hard time acknowledging Jesus Christ for who he is—deity. The last test for mankind would not be whether there is God or not (for even Satan and his demons believe there is God), but who Jesus Christ is. He is either all the Bible claims him to be, or he is nothing at all. But why God man—the God- man? Why a human Savior? It is God's pleasure for it to be so (Col. 1:19; Heb. 2:14-18)!

The Word of God (The Bible)

What is the Bible? Just another Scripture like others? It is impossible to acknowledge God or know him without acknowledging the Bible. The Bible is the breath of God—it is God-breathed (Ps. 18:15; 33:6; 2 Tim 2:16). The Bible is the voice or speech of God. It is God speaking. The theological term for this is verbal inspiration under the leadership of the Holy Spirit;

"And we have the word of the prophets made more certain, and you will do well to pay attention to it, as to a light shining in a

dark place, until the day dawns and the morning star rises in your heart. Above all, you must understand that no prophecy of Scripture came about by the prophet's own interpretation. For prophecy never had its origin in the will of man, but men spoke from God as they were carried along by the Holy Spirit" (2 Pet. 1:19-21; cf. Heb. 3:7; 10:15; *"... the Holy Spirit says ... "*).

Inspiration involves the supernatural work of God by the Holy Spirit upon the human writers of Scripture that rendered what they wrote an account of God's revelation. God's superintendence enabled them to write without error or omission but without stamping out the personality of the individuals concerned. The superintendence of the Holy Spirit was so intense that it was verbal, even including the choice of words. This inspiration includes all the Bible (Luke 24:25-27; John 10:34-35). It was never concocted and conceived by man as Peter acknowledges; *"We did not follow cleverly invented stories when we told you about the power and coming of our Lord Jesus Christ, but we were eyewitness of his majesty"* (2 Pet. 1:16). Reading the Bible, therefore, means listening to God, listening to his voice!

The Bible self-authenticates itself. It makes us know what it is. The Bible is **the living Word of the living God** (Acts 7:38). The Word is **Life** (John 6:63). The Word is **Jesus himself** (John 1:1, 14; 1 John 1:1-3). By the power of the Word the world was created and by the same Word it is upheld (Gen. 1; Ps. 29:3-9; 33:4-11; Heb 1:3). The Word is **the mind of Christ** (1 Co. 2:16). The Word is **Truth** (John 17:17—making it identical with Jesus; John 14:6). The Word is **Alive and Powerful— authoritative** (Heb. 4:12; Matt. 7:28-29; 28:18). The Word is **the Iron Scepter** with which Christ will rule the nations (Ps. 2:9; Rev. 2:26,27). The Word is **Judge,** that is, the iron scepter of judgment, **the majestic voice of the LORD,** which he will cause men to hear (John 12:47-48; Is. 11:4; 30:30-33; cf. 2 Thess. 2:8; Ps. 110:2. Rev. 19:11-15). As Judge, the Word discerns and critiques the thoughts and intents of the hearts of men, proving them to be futile (Heb. 4:13; Jer. 12:3; Ps 19:12-13; 139:1-4). **The Word of God is described as;**

*"The law of the LORD is **perfect,** reviving the soul, The statutes of the LORD are **trustworthy,** making wise the simple. The precepts*

*of the LORD are **right,** giving joy to the heart. The commands of the LORD are **radiant,** giving light to the eyes. The fear of the LORD is **pure, enduring forever.** The ordinances of the LORD are **sure and altogether righteous.** They are **more precious than gold,** than much pure gold; they are **sweeter than honey,** than honey from the comb. By them is your servant warned; **in keeping them there is great reward"** (Ps. 19:7-11).*

If you want to feast on the value and importance of the Word of God, see Psalm 119. The Psalmist asks one important question that most neglect in our day; *"How can a young man keep his way pure? By living according to your word"* (v.9). He goes on to say; *"I seek you with all my heart; do not let me stray from your commands. I have hidden your word in my heart that I might not sin against you"* (vv.10-11). He says again; *"I rejoice in following your statutes as one rejoices in great riches. I meditate on your precepts and consider your ways. I delight in your decrees; I will not neglect your word. ... Your statutes are my delight; they are my counselors"* (vv.14-16, 24).

Does this yearning for God's word in these verses and the entire chapter reflect the attitude and motive of your heart? If not, think again! Yes, **the Word of God is eternal and will stand or last forever,** while everything else will perish (Is. 40:6-8). It will never pass away but will be fulfilled to the smallest dot—all its promises and prophecies (Matt. 5 :17-18; Luke 24:44; John 17:12; Is. 44:26; 46:11; 55:10-11). The Word of God (Scripture), therefore, cannot be broken, but must all be fulfilled (John 10:34-36), for it is impossible for God to lie or change what he has said (Tit 1:2; Heb. 6:18). God has bound himself to what he has said, he will not change his word; *"I will not violate my covenant or alter what my lips have uttered"* (Ps. 89:34). God has spoken and he proves his word (Heb. 1:1-2). God has exalted above all else his name and his word; *"I will bow down toward your holy temple and will praise your name for your love and faithfulness, for you have exalted above all things your name and your word"* (Ps. 138:2).

The Word has power to do a lot of things some of which include the following: the Word saves (James 1:21); sanctifies (John 17:17); transforms (Rom. 12:2); guides and prospers (Ps. 1:1-3); lights our path (Ps. 119:105); enlightens; et cetera. The Word of God is without error or mistake (that is, as it was given from the mouth of God); *"Every word of God is flawless; he is a shield to those who take refuge in him. Do not add to his words, or he will rebuke you and prove you a liar"* (Pr. 30:5-6). The word of God is ultimate wisdom, the encyclopedia of all knowledge (see Proverbs, especially chapter 8)! Studying the word brings ultimate knowledge, understanding, prudence, and wisdom. It brings life and eternal life!.

Holy Spirit (God at work; the Power of God at Work)

Jesus Christ declared; *"'Whoever believes in me, as the Scripture has said, streams of living water will flow from within him.' By this he meant the Spirit, whom those who believed in him were later to receive." "And I will ask the Father, and he will give you another Counselor to be with you forever—the Spirit of truth. The world cannot accept him, because it neither sees him nor knows him. But you know him, for he lives with you and will be in you. I will not leave you as orphans; I will come to you"* (John 7:38-39; 14:16-18).

Many are ignorant about the activity of the Holy Spirit because they do not know who he is. The Holy Spirit is God in action! When God works in our midst and in us, he is known as the Holy Spirit. As deity, he is equally personal as the Father and Son. He does things that we expect from a real personality: He speaks (Rev. 2:7); he intercedes (Rom 8:26); he testifies (John 15:26); he leads (Acts 8:29); he commands (Acts 16:6-7); he guides (John 16:13); and he appoints (Acts 20:28). He can be lied to (Acts 5:3-2); he can be insulted (Heb. 10:29); he can be grieved (Eph. 4:30); et al. As the Spirit of God, he is God—eternal, all powerful, omnipresent (Psalm 139), omniscient, and Creator. He fills the place of Jesus Christ in his physical absence—the Lord is that Spirit (John 14:16-18; 2 Co. 3:17-18; 1 Co. 15:45).

The Holy Spirit, as already mentioned, is God in action. As God in action, he moves people to perform extraordinary feats for God, and moves them to write the word of God through special means such as dreams and visions (Jud. 6:34; Ezek. 3:12-14; 2 Pet. 1:20-21; Rev. 1:10; 4:1-2). He can even physically transport a believer from one location to another (Acts 8:39-40). God's ministry to the world and to believers from start to finish is through the Holy Spirit. The Holy Spirit is God's operating power system. Jesus was conceived by the Holy Spirit (Luke 1:34-35); he was filled with the fullness of the Holy Spirit (John 3:34; cf. Col. 1:19; 2:9); and he ministered by the power of the Holy Spirit (Matt. 12:28). **The ministries of the Holy Spirit are summarized as follows.**

The Ministries of the Holy Spirit: restraining (helping to prevent) sin (2 Thess. 2:6,7); **reproving and convicting** the world of sin (John 16:7,8); **regenerating**--that is, causing people to be born again (John 3:3-8; Tit. 3:5); **baptizing** those believing into Christ and his body, the church (Acts 2:1ff; 1 Co. 12:13); **indwelling** (living in) the believer permanently (John 7:38-39; 14:15-17; 1 Cor. 6:19,20); **sealing** believers--God's permanent stamp or mark of approval (Eph. 1:13-14; 2 Cor. 1:21-22); **anointing** believers for ministry (1 John 2:20-27; 'Christ' means 'Anointed One'); **producing sanctification** or holiness and helping believers to participate in the divine nature (Rom. 8:9-13; 2 Pet. 1:3-8); **bestowing spiritual gifts** (1 Cor. 12:1-11); and **filling** believers--on a regular bases (Acts 4:31; Eph. 5:18). We are actually commanded to be filled by the Spirit! Anointing and especially filling are designed to give believers power for holiness and service. The believer's life must be lived under the constant filling of the Holy Spirit. Without the filling of the Spirit it is impossible to live the Christian life!

The Filling of the Spirit Produces: fruit (John 16:7, 8; Gal. 5:22, 23a); Christian **character** (2 Pet. 1:3-9); Christian **service** (1 Co. 12-14; 1 Pet. 4:8-10); **guidance and teaching** (John 16:13; 1 John 2:20ff); **praise and thanksgiving--worship** (Col. 3:15-16); **leadership and bearing witness** with our spirit that we are the children of God (Rom. 5:5; 8:14-16); **intercession** for us (Rom. 8:26,27); and **revelation and knowledge** of the deep things of God (1 Co. 2:10-16). Thus, the filling of the Spirit is the normal way of life for the believer, that is, he that is spiritual! You cannot be spiritual without the filling of the Spirit.

Therefore, Do not Grieve the Spirit (Eph. 4:29-32): To sin or continue to live in known sin is to grieve the Holy Spirit (1 Co. 6:15-

20; 1 John 3:4-10). Sin is incompatible with the filling of the Spirit. It is like living in the same house with stinking filth. But if you sin, here is the cure: confess (1 John 1:5- 2:2; James 5:16); judge or examine yourself (1 Co. 11:31-32); then repent and forsake your sin (2 Co. 7:8-11; 2 Pet. 2:20-22); and you will restore the filling of the Spirit. Here are some examples of people who repented in the Scriptures (Ps. 51:1-19; Luke 15:1-32). If you continue to sin and fail to repent, divine discipline will be applied on you (Heb. 12:3-15; Ps. 119:67, 71).

Do Not Quench the Spirit (1 Thess. 5:19-22): When a believer fails to repent and fails to heed divine discipline, he eventually quenches the Holy Spirit, that is, the Spirit no longer influences him at all. The believer is now regarded as being an apostate or in apostasy (2 Thess. 2:3; 1 Tim. 1:18-20; 4:1-3; 2 Tim 2:16-18; 4:1-5). He will be handed over to Satan for the torture of the flesh or body (1 Co. 5). The believer is thus, sinning the sin unto death (1 John 5:16). A good example of this is the first king of Israel, Saul. He disobeyed God and God rejected him. The Spirit of God left him, and he continued in rebellion and disobedience until he took his own life (1 Sam. 15; 16:14; 28; 31).

Walk in the Spirit or Keep on Living by Means of the Spirit (Gal. 5:16-25): This means that the believer should live the Christian life under the influence of the Spirit moment by moment. He needs the Holy Spirit for spiritual life every second just as the body needs oxygen every moment to survive! For any temporal circuit break because of sin, the believer should confess immediately to restore filling of the Spirit (1 John 1:9). Nothing of spiritual worth counts in the believer's life unless it is done under the filling and control of the Spirit; otherwise, it is only hay, wood, and stubble, fit only to be burned (1 Co. 3:10-15)! Walking by the spirit is technically referred to as sanctification--living a holy life that is pleasing to God by constant victory over sin (Rom. 6:11-23; 8:5-13; Eph. 4:17-5:20; Col. 3:1-17; 1 Thess. 4:1-7; 1 John 3:9). When you become a believer, the sin nature (propensity to sin) is brought under control only, but it does not go away. Therefore, the potential to sin is still there. The sin nature (or flesh) opposes the Spirit (Gal. 5:16-17). It is only by yielding to the Spirit that the believer can overcome the sinful nature and its desires and temptations (Rom. 8:12-13). **That is why we are commanded to walk constantly by means of the Spirit!** The person who does not walk by the Spirit is self-deceived and may indeed not belong to the Lord (Rom. 8:9).

Growth in the Word, the Sword of the Spirit (1 Pet. 2, 3; 2 Pet. 3:17, 18; Eph. 4:11-15; 6:17): The filling of the Spirit would mean very little if the believer does not feed constantly on the word of God. In the Christian armor, the word of God is described as the sword of the Spirit. A Spirit-filled believer who is not immersed in the word of God is like a well-trained soldier, who has no weapon to fight with. No matter how skilled the soldier is, he will not attack or defeat the enemy. The weakest enemy with a weapon will easily defeat such a soldier. It is the same with the Spirit-filled believer, who is not knowledgeable in the word of God (Pr. 19:2). The word becomes the offensive weapon. **That is why the command to grow in the word is repeatedly emphasized in Scripture.** The believer must regularly study and store the word of God in him to properly function under the Spirit's leadership. Read it; study it; meditate on it; believe it; memorize it; and use it.

Salvation

The Bible was written in Hebrew and Greek (and portions in Aramaic), and it is sometimes difficult to translate concepts from one language to the other. **What is salvation?** The *New Bible Dictionary* helps us to understand the etymology of the word "salvation." The English term is derived from Latin *salvare,* 'to save', and *salus,* 'health', 'help', and translates Hebrew '*Yeshua*' and its cognates ('breadth', 'ease', 'safety') and Greek *soteria* and cognates ('cure', 'recovery', 'redemption', 'remedy', 'rescue', 'welfare').

In most of its Old Testament usages, salvation means deliverance from danger, disease, and enemies, into safety, health, and prosperity (Ps. 3:8; 34:4; Luke 1:68-75). It also included deliverance from sin. Salvation also means preservation. The Lord not only saves but he preserves and keeps until the last day those he saves (Phil. 1:6; Jude 24; 2 Tim. 1:12). God's only command to mankind is; *"Believe in the*

Lord Jesus Christ and you shall be saved" (John 6:28-29; 3:16; Acts 16:30-31; 1 John 3:21-23).

By way of illustration, many people are willing to live under thousands of human laws but reject God's one and only law: to believe in Jesus Christ and be saved. That's all God wants from anyone; believe in Jesus Christ and he will take care of the rest by the filling of the Spirit.

CHAPTER 17

THE GOSPEL OF SALVATION

The Gospel of the Kingdom

Jesus declared his mission at the beginning of his ministry in Luke 4:18-19 as having come:

To preach the good news (gospel) to the poor, with the hope of releasing them from poverty;

To proclaim freedom to the prisoners (captives), so that they can be released from prison;

To grant recovery of sight to the blind;

To release the oppressed, and also to release or deliver from all kinds of sicknesses (Matt. 8:16, 17);

To deliver from sin (Matt. 9:1-7, 12, 13; Luke 19:1-10).

All of Jesus' ministry was a proclamation of salvation (deliverance, release, preservation) to all kinds of people, although the word salvation is not often used. Jesus said repeatedly; *"I came to seek and save that which was lost"* (Luke 19:10); to lay down his life as a ransom for many (Matt. 20:28). He came for no other reason but to save sinners. Everything he did was calculated to save sinners. That was his mission then, that is his (our) mission now!

Content of the gospel and Salvation in the Gospels: Salvation in the gospels is summarized as "believe in him whom the Father has sent," that is, the Messiah (John 5:36-43; 6:29, 35, 40). Salvation was to be consummated on the cross. Jesus said; *"Just as Moses lifted up the snake in the desert, so the Son of Man must be lifted up, that everyone who believes in him may have eternal life. For God so loved the world that he gave his one and only Son, that whoever believes in him shall not perish but have eternal life"* (John 3:14-16). **Receiving this salvation means one must be born again; one must become a new creation** (John 3:1-8; 2 Co. 5:17). To be born again includes repentance from sin. Jesus says; *"Repent for the kingdom of God is at hand"* (Matt. 3:2,17).

The Gospel in Acts: The salvation message in the book of Acts is focused on the witness to the resurrection (Acts 2:22-41; 3:11-16; 17:30-32). God had given proof that Jesus was his Son by raising him from the dead, and that by believing in him we might be saved or have eternal life (Acts 16:29-31).

The Gospel in the Epistles: Paul summarizes or defines the gospel as follows; *"For what I received I passed on to you as of first importance: that Christ died for our sins according to the Scriptures, that he was buried, that he was raised on the third day according to the Scriptures, and that he appeared to Peter, and then to the Twelve"* (1 Co. 15:3-5). Christ paid for salvation in full by his death on the cross--by his blood. He said, *"It is finished,"* (John 19:30). You cannot add and you cannot subtract from that finished work. It is all his doing! His cross is sufficient for us (Rom. 4:25). His death or atonement (sacrifice for sin) was a substitute for sinners. He died on behalf of sinners (Rom. 3:21-26; 2 Co. 5:21). His death was the maximum expression of God's love. His death was a propitiation— an appeasement of God's wrath toward sin (1 John 2:1-2). The door to heaven stands open, enter while you can--believe in the Lord Jesus Christ, and you shall be saved (John 3:36).

Who Saves People?

Salvation was one person's idea, and he ensures that that plan is accomplished. God himself conceived the idea of rescuing men from their sinful and wayward lives. Thus, he is the one who saves people. God (Father, Son, and Holy Spirit) saves sinners from sin. The Father is the one who drafted the plan (Planner); the Son is the one who accepted the Father's plan to die for sins (Executor); and the Holy Spirit is the one who applies this salvation—makes it efficacious in the lives of those believing in Jesus (Applier). God has a well-thought-out plan in respect to human salvation. The plan has many details and intricacies but can be clearly understood from the Scriptures.

God's Eternal Plan: God's overall plan is for the salvation of sinners. From eternity past in the counsel and pleasure of his will, he designed the plan of salvation. His Son, Jesus Christ, accepted to carry out that plan by accepting to die on the cross for the sins of mankind. The Holy Spirit, the power of God, has been at work since creation to apply this plan in the lives of men (Eph. 1:3-14). You were personally included in God's plan from eternity past and at the right time he saved you or if you are not saved, it is time to make up your mind for Jesus Christ.

God's Plan is Going According to Schedule: Why could God not institute his kingdom from the beginning of time with Adam and the woman? Why did he allow them to sin and bring death to the world? Why could he not do it in the days of Jesus Christ? Paul explains that the ways of God are past finding out. We may wonder and ask such questions, but everything is going according to schedule as God planned from eternity past. Paul states that at just the right time God brought forth his Son, born of a woman and under the law (Gal. 4:4,5; Rom. 5:6). The disciples were eager to know the exact time that God will bring in his kingdom, but Jesus Christ told them that it was not for them to know the times and dates that the Father has set by his own authority. Their business was to be witnesses to the lost world. Thus, everything in God's plan is going according to schedule and would be fulfilled on the exact dates (Acts 1:6, 7; 2:22-23; Rom. 9:22-24; Eccl. 3:1-8; Matt. 24:22).

How do you fit into God's plan? In the first place, you are to repent and believe in Jesus Christ for the forgiveness of sins. Secondly, you are to grow in grace to maturity and Christian service by the power of the Holy Spirit (Rom. 8:1-17; 1 Pet. 2:2).

God's Plan is Perfect: God is perfect and so is his plan. A perfect God can do only that which is perfect and reflects his character. King Solomon recognized God's perfection in respect to his plan; *"I know that everything God does will endure forever; nothing can be added to it and nothing taken from it. God does it so that men will revere him"* (Eccl. 3:14). He does as he pleases using both unbelievers and believers to accomplish his plan; *"To the man who pleases him, God gives wisdom, knowledge and happiness, but to the sinner he gives the task of gathering and storing up wealth to hand it over to the one who pleases God."* About the pagan king of Persia, who took over Babylon, God said; *"I summon you by name and bestow on you a title of honor, though you do not acknowledge me. ... I will strengthen you, though you have not acknowledged me..."* (Eccl. 2:26; Is. 45:4, 5).

God's Character in Respect to Salvation: There are certain attributes or qualities of God that directly relate to his plan of salvation toward mankind. Some of which include:

Mercy: This is God's loving-kindness that he freely shows to mankind. Mercy is the aversion of God's wrath and anger from mankind, who deserve to be punished and condemned (Deut. 4:31). Mercy is God's unmerited favor shown to sinners on account of God's pleasure and discretion (Ex. 33:19). In showing mercy, God freely forgives sinners and bestows salvation and blessing upon them (Is. 63:9). God's mercy endures forever despite man's continuous waywardness (Lam. 3:21-23).

Grace: This is God's favor that he lavishes upon undeserving sinners. It is the sum of all that God does for sinners--forgiveness, salvation, new birth, and every other blessing. Grace is almost synonymous with gift; it is all that God gives to those who do not deserve (Eph. 2:8,9). No human being has ever or will ever deserve anything from God. God gives us grace by virtue of his integrity and character.

Love: Love is God's nature and attitude toward mankind aimed at saving mankind from his sinful and depraved condition. The death of Jesus Christ on the cross is the ultimate expression of the love of God toward sinners (John 3:16; Rom. 5:6,8). Love is God's very nature; *"God is love"* (1 John 4:16). God's love is eternal and irrevocable (Ps. 136; Rom. 8:35-39; 11:29). In his love he blesses us abundantly both spiritually and materially (1 John 3:1,16-18).

Faithfulness: God will always abide by what he has promised. He does not change. Therefore, he is worthy of our trust and reliance. We can hold God to fulfill what he has promised and be sure he will do so. God is trustworthy and dependable. He is faithful and will keep to the end those he has saved (1 Co. 1:13; Phil. 1:6; 2 Tim. 3:13).

In God's plan, the Father works in full collaboration with the Son, who gave himself a ransom for many (Matt. 20:28). He declared that *"I lay down my life just to take it up again"* (John 10:17-18). Thus, the Son is the Executor of the plan. In the physical absence of Jesus Christ on earth, the Holy Spirit is doing the job of applying salvation to those believing in Jesus Christ. He is the Applier of God's plan (2 Co. 2:21-22; Eph. 1:13-14).

It is a fatal mistake to think that your salvation is your own doing or that you can save people by your own power! No one seeks God on his own (Rom. 3:9-18; Eph 2:1); our righteous deeds do not qualify (Is 64:6-7); only Jesus can draw you to himself (John 6:44; Acts16:14); and last of all, you are saved by grace (Eph. 2:8,9; Tit. 3:3-7; 2 Tim. 1:9).

How Does Someone Appropriate Salvation? YOU MUST BE BORN AGAIN!

"I tell you the truth, no one can see the kingdom of God unless he is born again" (John 3:3).

A wise man has said, and it is true, that a journey of a thousand miles begins with one step. Another wise man has said that it takes only one step to stray. The beginning of the Christian life is so important that how one begins matters a lot. What exactly happens at the moment of salvation? Some of the concepts involved at this moment include repentance, believing, receiving, conversion, and regeneration.

Repentance: *"From that time on Jesus began to preach,* **Repent,** *for the kingdom of heaven is near."* *"I tell you, no! But* **unless you repent, you too will perish."**

*"**Repent then and turn to God,** so that your sins may be wiped out and the times of refreshing may come from the Lord."*

"In the past God overlooked such ignorance, but **now he commands all people everywhere to repent"** (Matt. 4:17; Luke 13:3; Acts 3:19; 17:30).

To repent means to turn back from; to change from one course to a totally different one; to turn away from sin toward God. Repentance is a change of mind—a thorough change in the heart from sin and a turning toward God. Repentance that results in salvation is accompanied by faith in God. Such repentance involves contrition or sorrow for sin (Ps. 51); an inward repugnance to sin; it is followed by an actual forsaking of sin (Matt. 3:8; Acts 26:20); and a humble self-surrender to the will and service of God (Acts 9:6). Where there is true repentance, all life relationships are radically altered.

Who should repent? All sinners are called upon to repent. The alternative to repentance is to perish in hell. However, it is not God's wish that any should perish but that all should come to a saving knowledge of Jesus Christ (2 Pet 3:9; 1 Tim. 2:4). Repentance is so important that there is great rejoicing in heaven over one sinner who repents (Luke 15). Heaven is waiting to rejoice over your repentance. Repentance results in the forgiveness of sins and peace with God (Rom. 5:1). Only God can make repentance possible. Repentance is therefore a gift of God (Jer. 31:18-20; Ps. 80:3,19; Acts 5:31; 11:18; Rom. 2:4).

Believe: *"Whoever* **believes in the Son** *has eternal life...."*

"Jesus answered, 'The work of God is this: to **believe in the one he has sent.**'"*

"For my Father's will is that **everyone who looks to the Son and believes in him shall have eternal life,** *and I will raise him up at the last day."*

*"'Sirs, what must I do to be saved?' They replied, **'Believe in the Lord Jesus,** and you will be saved"* (John 3:16,36; 6:29,40; Acts 16:30-31).

For salvation, one must believe in Jesus Christ as Savior and Lord. Repentance that results in salvation must be accompanied by believing in Jesus. To believe in Jesus is to put one's trust in him or to rely wholly on who he is and what he has done. He is God—God in the flesh; Son of God; Son of Man; Messiah; Savior; Redeemer-- the one who died in the place of sinners so that they may be forgiven of their sins (John 1:1, 14; 3:14-16, 36; 9:35-38; 1 John 4:14; Tit. 2:13). To believe in Jesus is to have faith in him; to remain steadfast to these truths about him; to have complete confidence in him. To believe in Jesus, one must know these truths about him—knowledge precedes believing, for you cannot believe what you do not know— faith comes by hearing the word of God (Rom. 10:14-17). What you believe matters—it must be orthodox truth as revealed in Scripture, otherwise your belief is without content and therefore in vain. To believe in Jesus is to give over your life to him and to allow him to take over control. It is to allow him to be your driver or pilot.

Receive: *"He* [Jesus] *came to that which was his own* [Jews], *but his own did not receive him. Yet **to all who received him,** to those who believed in his name, **he gave the right to become children of God…**" "**He who receives you receives me**, and he who **receives me receives the one who sent me**"* (John 1:11- 12; Matt. 10:40).

Receiving Jesus Christ means to accept him for who he is as described above—He is God, Messiah, Savior, etc. It means to accept as true every scriptural teaching and claim about him; to welcome him into your heart so that he takes over total control of your life.

Conversion: *"The church sent them on their way and as they traveled through Phoenicia and Samaria, **they told how the Gentiles had been converted**"* (Acts 15:3).

Simply put: repent + believe + receive = conversion. To be converted means to turn or return; to turn away from evil or sin toward God; to turn away from idols and false gods unto God (Jer.

18:7-8; Acts 14:15; 26:20; 1 Thess. 1:9). Every sinner or unbeliever is under the control of Satan and is said to be in darkness and an enemy of God (Eph. 2:1-3). In conversion the sinner is translated from the domain of Satan or darkness to God's domain or light and is granted forgiveness (Acts 3:19; 26:18). Some prominent examples of repentance in the Bible include Zacchaeus and Saul (Luke 19:1-10; Acts 9:1-19). People who are converted, turn away from the deeds of darkness to the deeds of light (Gal. 5:19-23). They break off old habits and develop new ones that are pleasing and acceptable to the Lord. It is important to note that it is God himself who moves and causes people to be converted (Acts 9:1-19, 16:14).

Regeneration: *"Yet to all who received him, to those who believed in his name, he gave the right to become **children of God—children born not of natural descent**, nor of human decision or a husband's will, but **born of God.**"*

*"In reply Jesus declared, 'I tell you the truth, **no one can see the Kingdom of God unless he is born again** [of the Spirit]'"*

*"... he saved us, not because of righteous things we had done, but because of his mercy. **He saved us through the washing of rebirth and renewal by the Holy Spirit ....**"* (John 1:12, 13; 3:3; Tit.3:5).

Unlike repentance, believe, receive, and conversion, that seem to emphasize human action, regeneration, by meaning and implication, is the work of God by the Holy Spirit on the individual turning to him in faith through Jesus. Regeneration is the work of the Holy Spirit at the moment of salvation, whereby, the basic disposition of the sinner is transformed and redirected away from sin toward God. In regeneration, the Holy Spirit enables and moves the individual to respond to Jesus Christ in repentance and faith, resulting in a new life. Regeneration means to be born again or anew.

The word itself occurs only two times in the New Testament (Matt. 19:28; Tit. 3:5), but the concept is taught in several passages of Scripture: born of God (John 1:13, I John 3:9; 4:7; 5:1); born again or born from above (John 3:3,7); born of the Spirit (John 3:5); born again through the living and enduring word of God (1 Pet. 1:23);

saved through the washing of rebirth and renewal by the Holy Spirit (Tit. 3:5). Other related concepts include sprinkling clean water or giving a new heart (Ezek. 36:25-26); and becoming a new creature in Christ (2 Co. 5:17).

To be born again is a gift from God—born from above or born of God. It is the work of God. This emphasizes the fact that God is the source of this new birth. He is the one who initiates and performs it. The analogy of physical birth here illustrates the fact that just as a child does not contribute anything to his or her birth, so also is the sinner who is being born again. God conceives and gives birth to a believer without his or her help or contribution. Does that surprise you or make any sense to you? Many people emphasize the concept of "being born again" as though it is a human undertaking or endeavor.

What exactly happens at rebirth or at the moment of salvation? First, the Bible says that sinners are dead in sin and tress-passes, and we know that a corpse cannot move itself (Eph. 2:1). Again, the sinner is described as a natural man, who cannot discern spiritual things (1 Co. 2:14). Therefore, a sinner cannot do anything on his own to be saved. It is God who brings the preacher to preach to the sinner. When the sinner hears the word (Rom. 10:14-17), the Holy Spirit convicts the sinner (John 16:8), enabling the individual to respond by an active choice of the will in repentance and faith. Since it is the work of God, it is irreversible. It is once and for all. God gives you birth to become a child forever in his family. You cannot be unborn just as a child born into a family cannot unborn himself or herself out of the family. There are several practical implications resulting from regeneration that would require another book to explain.

"Born Again": A Controversial Phrase?

As discussed above, one must be born again before one can enter the kingdom of God. I have said that this event includes repentance, believing and receiving Jesus, and is encapsulated in the word "regeneration." Here, I want to settle the air concerning the fact that the phrase "born again" has become highly controversial in both Christian and non-Christian circles today. Does the phrase refer only to certain Christians and denominations, or to all Christians?

Is there anything like a "Born Again Church" or a "Born Again Denomination"? And is there anything like a "Born Again Christian?" And if so, can there be a Christian, who is not "Born Again?" And I would also ask, "Why is the secular world intrigued by the phrase and why do they find offense with the phrase?" It is my intention to clarify the mistakes commonly made in reference to this phrase, "Born Again."

First Mistake: Some people tend to overuse and over emphasize the phrase, sometimes emptying it of its meaning. They trivialize and spiritualize the phrase and use it at instances when its usage is not called for. Moreover, they emphasize the human aspect to the neglect of the heavenly aspect. They make it appear as though it is a human endeavor. To be "born again" is heavenly initiated and accomplished. God gives birth to those turning to Jesus Christ in faith. It's a heavenly phenomenon that cannot be completely described but only felt (John 3:8; Eccl. 11:5).

Second Mistake: Following from the above, these believers begin to refer to their Church or denomination as "born again." We must recognize that only people can be "born again." Jesus did not command synagogues or churches to be born again, he commanded individuals. A Church or denomination in a sense is an institution that cannot make such a decision and therefore cannot be born again. Whether or not its members are born again, the church or denomination cannot be referred to as such. Therefore, a church or denomination cannot be referred to as "born again," either by its members or outsiders. It is wrong in both cases. This does not deny the fact that some churches or denominations have more people in them who are born again than others. Nor am I rejecting the fact that some churches and denominations emphasize that people should be born again (which is what should be) than others do. The ideal situation is for every member of a church or denomination to be born again, but as it is, this has never and will never be the case. The wheat and tares are always together.

Third Mistake: The third mistake has to do with the pride and arrogance of some who claim to be born again. These believers fail to follow in the footsteps of Christ in humility (Phil. 2:3-5; Rom.

12:4). They often bring shame and confusion to the cause of Christ, and sometimes alienating unbelievers from him. We are reminded that; *"For it is by grace you have been saved, through faith—and this not from yourselves, it is the gift of God--not by works, so that no one can boast"* (Eph. 2:8-9).

The Fourth mistake is Hypocrisy: When the mouth says, "I am born again," while the lifestyle shows something else. Your life must match or conform to your claim of being born again.

Fifth Mistake: There are some Christians and denominations who mock the idea of being "born again." This is the greatest problem of all, as you would expect that every Christian ought to have been born again and tries to help others to become the same. Any Christian who mocks the idea of being born again, is mocking Jesus himself, who has given this exclusive clause as a prerequisite for entering the kingdom of God; *"I tell you the truth, no one can see the kingdom of God unless he is born again"* (John 3:3). There are no two classes of Christians: Christians and "Born Again Christians." One is either born again and hence a Christian, or he is nothing at all. No one can be a Christian unless he is born again. You are self-deceived if you claim to be a Christian but are not born again. You can be certain; the kingdom of God is not for you. You are a hypocrite, fit only for destruction. You better make up your mind now and be born again before it is too late.

Lastly, the phrase "born again," poses a threat to the unbeliever because it calls for separation — separation from the world of sin and pleasure to God and holiness. It challenges the sinner's character and calls for a radical change. It brings discomfort to the one who is still under the clutches of sin. In the same passage that Jesus challenged Nicodemus to be born again, he explains that those who do what is wrong hate the light and would not come to it, lest they be exposed. He said; *"This is the verdict: Light has come into the world, but men loved darkness instead of light because their deeds were evil. Everyone who does evil hates the light, and will not come into the light for fear that his deeds will be exposed"* (John 3:19-21). Thus, that phrase will continue to bring discomfort to unbelievers, who hate the light because they are evil.

Assurance of Salvation

How can I be sure I am saved? There are at least three things by which you can know for sure that you are saved: by faith (1 Pet. 1:3-9; Heb 11:1,6; 2 Co. 5:7); by the testimony of God's word (1 John 5:11-13); and by the inner witness of the Holy Spirit (Rom. 8:9-16; Gal. 5:16-25; 1 Co. 2:10-15). If you have done it you know in yourself that you did it (2 Tim. 1:12), not because of any visible sign. The Holy Spirit will confirm it and you will also know by the word of God, which says anyone who believes receives eternal life (saved). Agreement with the word of God is a positive sign that you belong to God, but disagreement with the word of God could very well be a proof that you are not born again (saved).

But what are some of the visible signs of a saved person? The one who is saved has a changed life and newness of life. He has conviction of sin and true repentance. He lives in constant victory over sin; expresses true faith, true prayer; and above all, shows a willingness to obey the Lord and the word of God. He also enjoys fellowship with other believers (Heb. 10:19-25) and has a desire to make known the salvation that Jesus provides to others (John 4). And much more!

Who can un-save you? Or take away your salvation? Nobody can take away your salvation! Not God (Rom. 11:29)! Not Jesus Christ (John 6:37-40)! Not the devil or angels or anything else (Rom. 8:31-39)! Not you (Heb. 6:4-6, 9)! God saves and preserves to the end (Phil. 1:6; Jude 24).

Some Immediate Benefits of Salvation

The one who believes receives many gifts from God, some of which include the following: forgiveness (Acts 2:38; Col. 2:13-24); no more condemnation (Rom. 8:1); change of allegiance from the kingdom of darkness (Satan) to the kingdom of light (Col. 1:13); becomes a child of God by adoption (John 1:12,13; Gal. 4:5); becomes an heir of God (Rom. 8:14-17; Rev. 2:26-28); is reconciled to God (2 Co 5:17-21); is justified or declared right with God (Rom 3:21-26; 1 Co. 6:11); receives the baptism and sealing of the Holy Spirit (Matt.

3:11; 1 Co. 12:13; Eph. 1:13; 2 Co. 1:21-22); receives the availability of divine power for holy living (2 Pet. 1:3; 2 Tim. 1:7); and much more. Salvation is a gift and was completed on the cross. You either receive it God's way and with the whole package or you receive nothing at all. Being saved is not a process. It is an act accomplished by God (Father, Son, Holy) in time, and lasts forever. It is God's doing and it is marvelous in our eyes. If you do not understand from the beginning that it is God who saves people (you), you will remain in Satan's prison of false doctrine and confusion, trying to help God to stay saved.

Growth In the Body of Christ

The first and most important service required from a saved person, is growth in the word of God. You must get acquainted with God and his ways, and his family, the church, before you can function well in your new life. You must understand what happened to you in reference to your salvation and its benefits. Jesus commands those who believe in him to continue in the Scriptures (which then referred to the Old Testament; this also includes every mention of the word Scripture in the New Testament), and in his teaching in John 8:31-32 (which referred to the gospels and the Apostles' teaching—Acts 2:42; John 17:20). The command to devour the word, which is the sword of the Spirit, is replete throughout the Bible (Eph. 6:17; 4:11-15; 1 Pet. 2:2-3; 2 Pet. 3:17, 18; 2 Tim 2:15; 3:14-15). Knowledge of the word of God is a prerequisite to properly know Jesus Christ and function in his body, the church. It is helpful in many ways. For instance, in avoiding wrong doctrine (1 Tim. 4:15-16) and effecting transformation (Rom. 12:2). Therefore, the believer must dedicate himself to the study of the word of God, both in private and under devoted and faithful ministers of the word. We will note that study means something only when you obey: if the word says it, do it. If it doesn't make sense, believe it because in due time you will know (John 14:15,21,23-24; Matt. 7:21,24-25; James 1:22-25; 1 John 2:3-6; Rev. 1:3).

God's Workmanship (Good Works and Deeds)

We are saved by grace and not by works, but we are saved to do good works (Eph. 2:8-10). We are God's workmanship, co-workers, or fellow workers with him (1 Co. 3:5-15; 1 Thess. 3:2). The first work any human can do for God is to believe in the Lord Jesus Christ, without which anything done by such a person is useless--a waste of energy and resources. As it is written; *"Then they asked him, 'What must we do to do the works God requires?'* **Jesus answered, 'The work of God is this: to believe in the one he has sent"** (John 6:28-29). The next step after believing is to continue in the word so that you can know what to do; *"To the Jews who believed him, Jesus said, 'If you hold to my teaching, you are really my disciples"* (John 8:31). That is Growth! You must be transformed to know and approve God's will (Rom 12:1-2). That is, offer self, first, then be transformed. Then find out and understand what that will of God is, and do it (Matt. 7:21,24; Eph. 5:15-18; 1 Thess. 4:1-8). It is God who does his work through us (Phil. 2:12-14; 4:13)! Growth in grace is from God but we must make every effort to grow and do good works (1 Co. 15:9-10).

Faith (believing in Jesus) must be backed by works (1 John 3:16-18; James 2:14-26). You will notice an apparent contradiction in James and Paul in Romans 4. But it is just that: *an apparent* contradiction. There is really no contradiction. Both approach the same theme from different angles. It is not as though Paul is opposed to works, rather, he wants all to understand that faith precedes work and not vice versa. Where there is faith without works there is reward but where there are works without faith (saving faith) there is no reward. The two must go together, but must always begin by one, faith. In fact, Paul commanded and recommended good works over and over (Tit. 2:11-14; 3:8,14; 2 Tim. 3:16- 17).

God will reward every good work at the end that is done for his glory. That is, everything done under the filling of the Holy Spirit with the right motive and right attitude and for God's glory alone. There are some good works done for the glory of self and family or other persons or things. These do not receive reward from God! The smallest thing done in the name of Jesus Christ will be rewarded (Matt. 10:40-42; 1 Co. 15:58; Rev. 22:12). God has a specific way by which his work or good works should be done, and if you fail to carry out that work his way, you will have no reward as Jesus warned (Matt. 6:1-4).

Paul declares in 1 Corinthians 9:24-27, that he does not fight aimlessly but as one who fights for a prize and hopes that at the end, he will be accepted rather than disqualified. Likewise, you must fight according to the rules, according to God's guidelines. It is precisely for this reason that all will stand before the *bema* (judgment) seat of Christ (2 Co. 5:9-10), so that he would examine us and our works. Our good works in this process are said to be tried by fire and only what stands the test (that built with gold, silver, and costly stones) will be rewarded, but works done wrongly (that built with wood, hay, and straw) will be burned up and the individuals will suffer loss though still saved (1 Co. 3:5-15; Matt. 25:31-46; 24:45-47). God has been building the kingdom since the foundation of the world, and this will be inherited by the believers. It is such a beautiful kingdom that the Bible describes it as; *"No eye has seen, no ear has heard, no mind has conceived what God has prepared for those who love him"* (1 Co. 2:9; cf. Is. 64:4).

Before you get too excited and start counting how great your rewards would be, bear in mind that the Father and Jesus Christ has been doing all the work through you and therefore the rewards rightfully belong exclusively to Jesus Christ (John 15: 4-8; Phil. 2:12-13). We shall all lay our crowns and rewards at his feet (Rev. 5:5-10). Consider Jesus' humbling parable to his servants in Luke 17:7-10;

"Suppose one of you had a servant plowing or looking after the sheep. Would he say to the servant when he comes in from the field, 'Come along now and sit down to eat'? Would he not rather say, 'Prepare my supper, get yourself ready and wait on me while I eat and drink; after that you may eat and drink?' **Would he thank the servant because he did what he was told to do? So you also, when you have done everything you were told to do, should say, 'We are unworthy servants; we have only done our duty."**

CHAPTER 18

THE COST OF DISCIPLESHIP: FOLLOWING JESUS CHRIST

The Call to Individuals

Who is a disciple? A disciple is one who follows a teacher or master and learns from him. A disciple is therefore a learner. A disciple follows his master closely and copies everything he does and obeys everything his master teaches (John 8:31; 14:23,24; Matt. 11:28,29). The disciple hears his master's voice and follows in his exact footsteps. He imitates his master in everything! This is what each believer (disciple of Jesus Christ) ought to do—to follow the Master in everything. The apostles were sent out to make disciples, not Christians. Christians follow a religion, disciples follow Jesus. Notice the difference.

If you have found God through Jesus Christ, follow him resolutely and completely. Seek after him and his kingdom—set your priorities straight (Matt. 13:44-45; 6:25-33). Thus, be careful about materialism (paganism), which is Satanism—having in mind the things of men (Matt. 16:23; Phil. 3:17- 19). Be careful that wealth and riches do not prevent you from entering the kingdom of God like the rich young ruler or allow riches to choke the word you have received and make you unfruitful (Matt. 19:16- 26; cf. James 4:13- 5:6; 2 Tim. 6:3-10,17-19). Now that you have put your hand to the plow, do not look back (Luke 9:57-62). Jesus must take first place among all other things in your life, including self.

Following Jesus on the one hand is very easy (Matt. 11:28-30). But on the other hand, it is a hard road to walk, because the whole world is under the sway of the devil. Following Jesus means you will be persecuted, maligned, rejected, and hated; it means suffering all kinds of trials and tribulations. Once delivered from sin and Satan's clutches, we go through all kinds of tribulations and trials. Believers go through persecution, rejection, hardships, seizure of property, no food, no clothes, no job, sickness, and even death, all for the sake of Jesus Christ (Job; Matt. 5:10-12; Acts 14:22; 2 Co. 4:8-12; 6:3-10; 11:16- 12:10; Heb. 10:32-39; 11:32-40; 1 Pet. 4). Above all, you must carry your cross daily and follow Jesus. This is radical discipleship. However, there is hope because God will deliver us from all our afflictions (Ps. 34:7,19-20). In fact, Jesus has already conquered the world (John 16:33).

Following Jesus Christ according to the following passages; Matthew 8:18-23; 10:37-39; Mark 8:34-9:1; Luke 9:57-62; 14:25-35, could mean:

1. Could mean going without a home.

2. Could mean forfeiting a lot of personal relationships and responsibilities.

3. Means minding about the things of God because to mind about the things of the world is Satanism.

4. Means to deny all, even self (not doing anything that pleases self but displeases Jesus).

5. Means to carry the cross daily (suffering, persecution and trials that come with following Jesus).

6. Means losing the whole world to gain your soul.

7. Means to hate (love less) all other relationships (father, mother, wife, child, sister, brother, self, etc.). Jesus must take first place among other things.

8. Means listening and doing all that Jesus says or commands (cf. John 14:15,21,23; 1 John 2:3-6).

9. Therefore, count the cost before you embark on the journey with Jesus.

Jesus, Paul, Peter, and the rest of the apostles, all promise us persecution (Matt. 5:11-12; 10:17-20; 13:20-21; Luke 6:22-23; 12:49-53; Acts 14:22). The words suffer, tribulation, trials, persecution, and other related words, are all over the pages of the New Testament. They are the lot of those who faithfully follow the LORD from time immemorial. Only those who deceive and are being deceived are free from such suffering; *"... In fact, **everyone** who wants to live a godly life in Christ Jesus **will be persecuted**, while **evil men and impostors will go from bad to worse, deceiving and being deceived"** (2 Tim. 3:10-13). The Apostles testified that; **"We must go through many hardships to enter the kingdom of God, ..."** *(*Acts 14:22). In fact, Paul says BELIEVERS WERE DESTINED TO BE PERSECUTED; *"We sent Timothy ... to strengthen and encourage you in your faith, so that **no one would be unsettled by these trials. You know quite well that we were destined for them.** In fact, when we were with you, **we kept telling you that we would be persecuted.** ..."* (1 Thess. 3:2-4). If you think that Paul knew Christ more than you do, pay attention to his words! But, why persecution? Because Satan is a defeated foe. Satan, disguised in atheism, politics, and religion, hates God and Jesus Christ. Satan also knows that his time is short and almost over. Political figures and religious leaders are threatened by the fact that their authority will be taken over by Jesus Christ and his followers (Matt. 2:1-3; 26:3-5,57-67; John 7:25-36,45-49; 12:45-53; Acts 17:5-8; Rev. 12:12-17). They want to be in control. Religion and politics are enemies of Christ, and when they unite, they give birth to the most odious persecution. In this light, religion becomes the greatest satanic trap (John 8:31-47). Also, persecution exists because the world rejects both the Father and Jesus Christ, and hence, the believer also (John 15:18-25).

However, persecution comes to bless the believer, therefore, be courageous and endure to the end (Matt. 5:10-12; Mark 10:32-30; Rom. 5:1-5; James 1:2-4; 5:10-11; Heb. 10:32-34; 11:32-38; 1 Pet. 4:1-3,12-19). You are fighting a battle that has already been worn by Jesus--it's just a matter of time (John 16:33). Suffering with Christ or for Christ, means you will reign with him on his eternal throne! (Rev. 2:26-27; 3:11-12, 21; 2 Tim. 2:11-12). Our present afflictions cannot be compared to the glory that will be ours when Jesus Christ is revealed (2 Co. 2:16-18).

Therefore, **Fear Not** (Matt. 10:17-33; Rev. 12:11; 21:8)! Cowards are the first group of sinners listed in the exclusion list from the city of God! Would you miss an eternal inheritance in the city of God because you are a coward—afraid to stand up for truth and Jesus Christ in this wicked and perverse generation? Jesus warns that; *"Whoever, acknowledges me before men, I will also acknowledge him before my Father in heaven. But whoever disowns me before men, I will disown before my Father in heaven"* (Matt. 10:32-33). Do not fear because Jesus walks with us—nothing can harm us beyond what he has allowed (Is. 41:10; 54:16-17). The angel of the LORD encamps around us; no pestilence or sickness will overcome us (Ps. 34:7; 91). He says, *"I will never leave you or forsake you"* (Heb. 13:5).

Satan is a defeated foe, and what is man that you should fear him? Man is but breath, a mist that now is, but soon disappears. In his greatest glory and power, man is still nothing! So do not fear, neither the devil nor man (Is. 40:6-8; 51:7,12-13; Ps. 27:1-3; 56:3-4; Pr. 29:25). To be sure, men will manhandle you and mistreat you, or even kill you, as it is written;

"Be on your guard against men; they will hand you over to the local councils and flog you in their synagogues. On my account you will be brought before governors and kings as witnesses to them and to the Gentiles. ... So do not be afraid of them. There is nothing concealed that will not be disclosed or hidden that will not be made known. ... ***Do not be afraid of those who kill the body but cannot kill the soul. Rather, be afraid of the One who can destroy both soul and body in hell"*** (Matt. 10:17-28).

Therefore, on the contrary, God is the one you are to fear. To fear God is to stand in awe of him, to keep his commandments (Ps. 111:10; 112:1). Ecclesiastes 12:13, puts it succinctly; *"Fear God and keep his commandments, for this is the whole duty of man."* The fear of God is the key to knowledge, understanding, wisdom, and eternal life—the key to eternal existence!

Do not put your trust in man or princes or any human organization, no matter how prosperous and great it might seem to be (Ps. 20:7; 28:7; 31:6, 14; 40:4; 49:5, 6; 56:3, 4; 62:8; 118:8, 9; 146:3, 4; Pr. 3:3-7; Is. 2:22; Jer. 17:5-6). According to the last quotation, you are cursed if you put your trust in man or anything else other than God; *"This is what the LORD says: 'Cursed is the one who trusts in man, who depends on flesh for his strength and whose heart turns away from the LORD.'"* Instead, you are to put your trust in God the Father and Jesus Christ (John 14:1; Is. 50:10; Jer. 17:7-8). He can never disappoint you. He will always prove faithful to those who trust exclusively in him.

The Christian walk must be in humility. Humble yourself before Jesus Christ (Matt. 11:28-30; Rom. 12:1-3). Humility is the key to understanding Jesus Christ and the way of service in his kingdom. Humility is the road to honor and exaltation. On the contrary, pride is Satan's number one sin—to be proud is to identify with Satan. It is the leading reason for Satan's fall and all who are proud at heart. Pride only breeds quarrels. Pride goes before a fall, and a haughty spirit before destruction. You can be sure, all the proud at heart will follow Satan into hell (Pr. 13:10; 15:25; 16:5,18; James 4:6-10; 1 Pet. 5:5-9). From these verses we can draw the implication that pride equals Satanism or associating with the devil. Pride is what is leading Satan to his fall! (Ezek. 28:2, 5, 12, 17; Job 41:34). **Scripture categorically states over and over that God HATES PRIDE! So have nothing to do with pride if you want to follow Jesus!** Put on humility as a necklace just as Jesus did (Phil. 2:1-11).

Baptism of Fire

John the Baptist introduced Jesus as; *"I baptize you with water for repentance. But after me will come one who is more powerful than I, ... He will baptize you with the Holy Spirit and with fire. His winnowing fork is in his hand, and he will clear his threshing floor, gathering his wheat into the barn and burning up the chaff with unquenchable fire"* (Matt. 3:11, 12). Contextually, we may say that burning up the chaff with unquenchable fire is the baptism of fire. But we must notice that those he baptizes with the Holy Spirit are the same ones he baptizes with fire, and they are not burned up. Therefore, the baptism of fire is for believers. The baptism of fire, therefore, refers to the believers' suffering for and with Christ, and sometimes death (martyrdom). Jesus spoke of his suffering and death on the cross as a baptism, which baptism the disciples also underwent—the cup (Mark. 10:38-39; Luke 22:41-44). Many believers, except hypocrites, are still undergoing such baptism today. Thus, once baptized with the Holy Spirit, be prepared, the baptism of fire is your lot!

A Time of Distress/Tribulation

While believers in all of history have been persecuted, Jesus promised that at the end of time (our time) the world will be tried—wrath for God's enemies, but deliverance for believers (Dan. 12:1-3,6,7b; Is. 24; 34; 63:1-7; Ezek. 38-39; Zephaniah; Matt. 24:5-31; Luke 21:8-36; Hag. 2:6-7; Heb. 12:26-29; Rev. esp. 2:10; 3:10; Matt. 24:10-13,42-44, 48-51; Luke 17:26-33; 21:34-36). Believers do not suffer God's wrath, but they are baptized with suffering (1 Thess. 5:1-9). This time is a time of trial, of test, of purification, of refining, and of birth pains (Dan. 3,6; 11:35; 12:10; Mal. 3:3; Ps. 66:10-12; 1 Pet. 1:6-7). Only those who will persevere to the end and overcome will be saved (Matt. 24:13; Rev. 2:7,11,17,26; 3:5; 12:11; 13:10; 14:12-13; 20:4). There is an invisible battle going on now between the commander of God's or heaven's army, Michael, the archangel, and Satan and his army (Dan. 12:1; Rev. 12:3-9). But the great news is that Michael will defeat or has defeated Satan and his angels.

A Time of Trouble for Jacob

Daniel 9:24 tells us that a definite time was given to Israel to finish transgression, put an end to sin, atone for wickedness, and bring in everlasting righteousness. At the appointed time, the atonement for sin was made (crucifixion of Jesus), but the Jews were accomplices to this act and since then, many Jews have continued to reject Jesus as the Messiah (Christ), thus not having finished transgression, or put an end to sin. Therefore, there remains a time for them to do these things (by accepting the atonement of Jesus of 2000 years ago) and this will come after a time of trouble, known as the time of Jacob's trouble (Jer. 30:7; Zech. 12:1-9; 14:1-3). After this time, the Jews will finish transgression, atone for wickedness, and put an end to sin by accepting the atonement of Jesus Christ, and by accepting him as the Messiah. The LORD God Almighty will ensure that this happens. He will give the Jews a new heart that is willing to obey him, and all Israel will be saved/delivered/restored! (Is. 10:20-23; 11:10-11; 14:1-4; 43:1-7; 45:15-17; Jer. 23:3-8; 30-31; 33; Ezek. 28:24-26; 37; 39:21-29; Joel 2:16-3:21; Zech.10:6-12; Rom. 11:11-32).

Darkness Before Dawn

The darkest hour of the day is just before dawn as we say. So, after this dark hour, the day will dawn upon us, and we shall behold and worship the Lord forever. The deliverance of the Israelites from Egypt was preceded by increased servitude. When Moses began his ministry (when God called him from the burning bush and sent him to Pharaoh), the Egyptian task masters increased the labor of the Israelites and became very ruthless to them. Eventually Egypt was judged (the ten plagues) but Israel was delivered. The world (particularly spiritual Egypt and Babylon, that is the USA) is being judged by plagues now, but believers will be delivered. Therefore, even though the hour is dark (as you see the birth pains all around us with increasing frequency; Matt. 24:8, 32-35; Luke 21:29-32, 36), lift your eyes and watch—our Savior cometh! Prepare your minds for action and stand up and get ready for flight! Just like the Israelites ate the Passover in haste and ready to go, so must we get set, for our afflictions will soon be over (Ex. 12:11; Mic. 7:15-16). Our present afflictions and trials are far less than the glory that will be revealed in us when Christ is revealed (2 Co. 4:16-18). Therefore, do not lose heart--persevere! The Lord will deliver his own (Ex. 12:12-13; Is. 26:20; 31:5; Ezek. 9:3-6; Rev. 7:1-4; 3:10; John 17:14-16; 1 Co. 10:13; 1 Thess. 5:8; 2 Pet. 2:4-9). The Lord will "pass over" his chosen ones, who have his mark on their doorposts or foreheads! The heart-searching question is, do you have the mark of God on you or the mark of the Beasts?

The Call to the Church

Let us Keep the gospel message simple and depend on the power of the Holy Spirit. Paul said to the Corinthian Christians that he resolved to know nothing among them except Christ and Christ crucified, and that he did not use cunning words or human philosophy to communicate the gospel to them (1 Co. 2:1-5). We must follow in the same footsteps. Most often, Christians relapse into dead orthodoxy and schisms that have nothing to do with the salvation message. We have neglected the Holy Spirit and as such, the glory of the Lord has departed from his church (Ezek. 10). We are relying on our power and riches (Rev. 3:14-19). Theologians have hijacked God and locked him up behind steel and iron doors (academic classroom). While the letter is important (the sword of the Spirit), the letter by itself alone kills but the Spirit gives life (2 Co. 3:6). [This, of course, is not a call to anti-intellectualism. I believe Christians should be intellectually informed as much as they are able—studious and men of learning; Ezra 8:16; 2 Tim. 2:15. We have eternal wisdom, and of all people in the world, believers should be the wisest. I am sickened by the apparent alarming biblical illiteracy in this age of apostasy]. We must be men of the word and men of the Spirit also.

The message of Christ to his followers is summed up in love for one another (John 13:34-35; 1 John 3:11-24; 4:7-21; James 2:14-17). Love, according to John, becomes a sign of whether one is saved or not—no one who hates his brother has eternal life in him! Paul sums it up that love is the fulfillment of the whole law! And that love is the only eternal virtue in comparison to hope and faith, both of which will disappear when the Lord appears (Rom. 13:8-10; 1 Co. 13). Love is one of those much talked-of virtues. And in many cases, it is stripped of its meaning to refer only to sensuality. But to understand love, we must look at it from God's perspective: God is love! Love is an essential quality of his being. In love he continues to pursue sinners (John 3:16; Rom. 5:6,8). It is only when we accept God's love that we can love God back, love our neighbor, fellow believers, friends, family members, and our enemies. Yes enemies! Jesus commands us to love our enemies and pray for them, including those who persecute us and plan to hurt us (Matt. 5:38-48; Rom. 12:9-21; 1 Pet. 3:8-9).

Do not let your love grow cold because of continuous wickedness in the world and around you (Matt. 24:10, 12). We are commanded to bear one another's burdens and to encourage one another as we see the day fast approaching (Rom.15:1-7; 1 Co. 12:12-26; Gal. 6:1-2,9-10).

Let us keep the unity of the body, which of course sounds like a nightmare in an age of continuous replication of denominations. Such disunity shows our level of immaturity and lack of love and tolerance. I really lament the fact that the church has become more and more an organization rather than the organism it was designed to be (Eph. 4:1-16).

Perseverance must be a lot of the church in an age when Christianity is battered both from within and without (Heb. 10:19-39; 11-13). As we persevere, we should serve the Lord faithfully with the gifts he has given us and with sincere devotion (Rom. 12:1-8; 1 Co. 12-14; 1 Pet. 4:10). Divisiveness over spiritual gifts seems to be the norm rather than the exception within the body of Christ today. This goes a long way to demonstrate our lack of understanding of the word of God and lack of love for each other and for the church of Christ, which we are tearing down as we promote our agendas. When we sin against the church in this way, we are putting ourselves at odds with the Lord of the church. It was Christ's prayer that we should be one just as he and the Father are one (John 17). Paul equally prays for the church to keep the unity as they grow up in the most holy faith (Eph. 1:15-23; 3:14-20).

A Message to the Churches (Rev. 2-3)

The most difficult thing a preacher can do is to preach against the Church! Not when we are strictly warned not to so (Rom. 14:4; 1 Co. 4:5). It is Christ's Church that he bought with his own blood, and who dare to stand up and point a finger! It is obvious that Martin Luther wrestled within himself before he could challenge the Roman Church, but still, it is a difficult task. However, when the Church fails to live according to the word and the faith it professes, it must be challenged. It is precisely what the LORD asked Ezekiel to do--to preach against the sanctuary, and it is a painful ordeal (Ezek. 21:1-2).

The seven churches in these two chapters of Revelation existed literally in the time of John. Jesus identifies the spiritual condition of each, commends a few things, and commands them to repent on some areas. The churches could also be taken to represent the whole of church history until the second coming. Many interpreters have divided the history of the church into seven eras. I do not intend to reproduce them here. No one knows exactly how these ages can be divided. The best divisions are only approximations. However, most agree that the Laodicean Church represents the complacent modern church today at the eve of the second coming.

Ephesus: Stands for believers at the time of the apostles and the second-generation believers. Their problem was that they had lost their first love. Christ calls on them to remember their first love.

Smyrna: Represents second generation believers up to Constantine (AD 312). They went through afflictions, martyrdom, poverty, and imprisonment by the devil—persecution (2:10). As we saw earlier, these generations of Christians suffered severely under Roman imperial persecutions.

Pergamum: Represents the imperial Roman Church from Constantine until the Protestant Reformation (from Wycliffe, Hus, and others to Luther in 1517 AD). Pergamum is introduced as the place where Satan's throne is (when the tares were officially sown in Christ's field; Matt. 13:24-30). Balaamism and sexual immorality existed in the church, and worst of all, the unfortunate marriage between the church and the Roman state, consequently introducing paganism in the church. Many unbiblical doctrines such as infant baptism, worship of Mary, purgatory, rosary, worship of Saints, seven Sacraments, crucifix, clerical celibacy (1 Tim 4:1-3), transubstantiation, tradition in par with Scripture, pope as Vicar of Christ (God on earth—Holy Father), pope's spiritual and temporal authority over kings and princes and having power to shut up heaven and open hell for dissenters (a usurpation of Christ's authority; cf. Rev. 1:18c), et cetera, were developed. Satan's throne was literally situated in this city and church, which we saw in Part I. To note is that until the Reformation, true believers, who opposed the state church (later Roman Catholic Church-RCC), were persecuted, and killed or burned at stake or labeled heretics. This strand of true believers has continued until today, not necessarily as a denomination, as some are within different denominations. The Eastern Orthodox Church broke away from the RCC in 1054 AD over the use of images. The Egyptian Coptic and Ethiopian churches remained independent from the apostate Roman Church.

Thyatira: Represents the Lutheran reformation, Anglican, and similar denominations. They rejected most of the Roman false doctrines and restored many biblical doctrines (2:19). However, Luther remained close to RCC in some areas (2:20-22), for instance, infant baptism, confirmation, view of Lord Supper, state church, et al. The woman Jezebel, the prophetess, is introduced, in as much as we know that sometimes, the head of the Anglican Church is a woman. This church is commanded to repent (2:24, 25).

Sardis: Calvin and Zwingli took the Reformation further than Luther. From them came the Reformed, Presbyterian, and similar denominations. Except for infant baptism, most of these denominations hold to the Bible as the inspired word of God and the absolute authority on matters of faith and practice. Note well their chastisement (3:1c-4) and commendation of the few who are faithful (3:4).

Philadelphia: The Anabaptists and later on, the Baptists, took the Reformation to its logical conclusion. They hold the Bible as the inspired word of God and the absolute authority in matters of faith and practice. Within these movements, biblical Christianity flourished and believer's or adult baptism by immersion, and the Lord's Supper as a symbol were restored. Doors were opened for Protestant world missionary efforts (the end-time harvest or gathering of the elect). Many other denominations that started from the late 1700s to the 1800s hold to similar doctrines and fall into this category. **Note their commendation in** (3:8-11).

The key phrase to note here is; "you have kept my word." Attitude to and obedience to the word of God becomes the true mark of following Jesus. You can't follow him and spurn or neglect his word! From this statement, each one of us can know for sure which of these churches we belong to. Have you kept the word--all of it?

Methodism, the holiness movements, Pentecostals, and the Charismatic movements, equally fall into this category, except that emphasis on the second blessing (baptism of the Holy Spirit evidenced in speaking in tongues) as a subsequent experience after conversion, has opened the door to scoffers and false prophets. A strand of the Philadelphian church will persist until Christ comes in glory.

Laodicea: This is the modern church that may date back to the 1920s or earlier, with the outbreak of modernity and liberal scholarship. This represents churches across all denominations or group of churches that have abandoned the true faith and the word. The twentieth century saw the splitting of many denominations and the formation of many new ones. Because of this wicked and adulterous generation (Matt. 12:39; 24:10-12; 2 Tim. 3:1-5), the modern church has become cold and lukewarm though "churchianity" and activism are going on as normal. It has amassed a lot of wealth, especially the Western Church, and seems to rely on these riches—the gangrene of prosperity gospel (3:16-17; 1 Tim.6:3-10).

Thus, this church at the eve of the second coming should heed Jesus' warning and repent from their lukewarmness;

"I counsel you to buy from me gold refined in the fire, so you can become rich; and white clothes to wear, so you can cover your shameful nakedness; and salve to put on your eyes, so you can see. Those whom I love I rebuke and discipline. So be earnest and repent. Here I am! I stand at the door and knock. If anyone hears my voice and opens the door, I will come in and eat with him, and he with me [the wedding banquet after Christ's arrival]*"* (3:18-20; cf. 19:7-9; Matt. 22:1-14).

This is the only church where Jesus does not commend anything and where he is outside! Nevertheless, he is still concerned about this church. He rebukes them because he still loves them (Heb. 12:5-6). The Lord Jesus had wondered; *"However, when the Son of Man comes, will he find faith on the earth?"* (Luke 18:8). Many today are deluded and are believing a lie and are following the man of lawlessness (2 Thess. 9-12). They are running after the world (wealth, money, fame; 1 John 2:15-17).

Addressing the Laodicean Church is like Ezekiel preaching against God's sanctuary in Jerusalem before it was destroyed by the Babylonians. It is not an easy thing to do. God commanded Ezekiel to preach against his very own sanctuary! **He was asked to go and stand right in front of the door of the temple and confront the people and their abominable practices** (Ezek. 16:2; 20:4; 21:2; 22:2), **the same thing that Jeremiah had also been asked to do** (Jer. 7:1-11, 20). **In our day, Ezekiel and Jeremiah would be arrested and jailed for using such a style of confrontation!** The people were loaded with sin, idolatry, and hypocrisy (Ezek. 8). They were deluded and deceived by false prophets just as is the case today (Ezek. 13; 34:1-10). **Because of these things, the glory of the LORD departed from the sanctuary--that is, the Spirit taken out of the way** (Ezek. 9:3; 10:18; 2 Thess. 2:6-8), **just like Christ is outside the Laodicean Church!** This church is void of the Spirit or the glory of God. God judged the people in the sanctuary because of their idolatry (9:5-8; 14:1-8), just like Christ will spit out the Laodicean Church from his mouth if they do not repent (Rev. 3:16). Finally, the LORD took away the sanctuary, the delight of the people, and he illustrated this by taking away Ezekiel's wife, the delight of his eyes (24:15-21, esp. 21). Christ will eventually spit out of his mouth those who refuse to repent. The Laodicean Church has become more earth bound (reliance on riches) rather than heaven bound (reliance on the word of God). It has become so earthly minded that it is no heavenly good!

The church of Laodicea is under the spell of Satan, and God has sent a strong delusion to them because they do not want to believe the truth of the word of God (2 Thess. 2:9-12). The church exists at a time when the fallen angels are loosed—like the days of Noah. They continue to regard riches as a sign of God's favor, yet they fail to realize that true riches are spiritual (3:18; cf. Ps. 1:1-3).

Whatever the case, if it is called church, and within which are those born again, irrespective of doctrinal deviations, Christ still commends it. Even without commending anything in the Laodicean church, Christ rebukes it because he still loves them, and he is at the door knocking (3:20)! His love endures forever. Will the apostate church open the door to her Bridegroom or remain on the bed of adultery (trust in wealth and politicians)?

A Message For Ministers

This is apparently the most difficult time to do ministry because of the many voices out there. But consider Titus and 1 & 2 Timothy as your direct instructions from the pastors' pastor, Paul. Devote yourself to study and teaching the word (Rom. 15:4; Phil. 1:9-11; Ps. 1:1-3; Ezra 7:10,11; Acts 6:4; 2 Tim. 3:15). As you do, beware of the warnings in the following passages (Mal. 2:1-9; Jer. 2:8; 5:13, 30, 31; 8:8, 9; 18:18; Hos. 4:5-6). Declare the whole counsel of God even if they reject you (Acts 20:27; Jer. 18:18ff; 36-38). Be the right minister at the right time, giving the sheep the right food at the right season (Matt. 24:45ff; Dan. 11:35; 12:1,3). Evangelize with all your energy in the power of the Holy Spirit; God does not wish anyone to perish but to come to repentance, and that is why he is tolerant and patient (Jude 22-23; 2 Tim. 4:5; 1 Tim. 2:4; 2 Pet. 3:9; Rom. 2:4; Ezek. 33:10-11). Teach sound doctrine and watch over your flock (1 Tim 4:1-5,11-16; 2 Tim. 4:1-5; 1 Pet. 5:1-4; Acts 20:28-32; 1 Co. 4:1-2), building up the body of Christ to its full measure (Eph. 4:7-16). Do not whitewash the peoples' sins or dress their wounds with medicine that does not cure (Jer. 6:10,13-14; 23:9-11,16-18,25-32,36; Lam. 2:14; Ezek. 3:16-21; 33 esp. 6-9; Mic. 2:6-11; Luke 6:24-26; 2 Tim. 4:1-5; 3:5-9). Rebuke, correct, and warn in love, without fear (Mic. 3:5-12; 2 Tim. 16-17). Do not work to please men or to receive praise from men, but labor to please the Father and Jesus Christ (John 5:41-44; Gal. 1:6-10; 2 Co. 10:12-18). Do not peddle the word or teach for a price or filthy lucre (Mic. 3:5; 1 Thess. 2:3-6a; 1 Co. 9:7-9; 2 Co. 2:12-3:6; 4:1-6; 1 Tim. 3:3; 5:17; 6:3-11) but be satisfied with your meat. I was surprised when I learned of the dictionary definition of a televangelist: "An evangelical preacher who appears regularly on television to promote beliefs and appeal for funds." This is sad and confirms what Peter says; *"In their greed these teachers will exploit you with stories they have made up"* (2 Pet. 2:3a). Therefore, be careful of the deceitfulness of riches (Matt. 13:22; Pr. 11:28; 23:4-5). Do not lose heart in as much as you know that the anointing the Lord gave you will lead you into all truth (John 16:13; 1 John 2:20-21), and as much as you know that the Righteous Judge will reward all your labors (1 Co. 15:58). He will keep his word!

CHAPTER 19

BEHOLD! JESUS IS COMING!

S everal New Testament words are used to refer to the second coming of Jesus Christ: presence, appearing, reveal, unveiling or apocalypse. Jesus will be physically unveiled or revealed and will be present in our midst forever.

The Messiah came for the first time to declare the year of the LORD'S favor (salvation). When he entered the synagogue in his hometown, he announced his first advent ministry by reading Isaiah 61:1-2a;

"The Spirit of the Sovereign LORD is on me, because the LORD has anointed me to preach good news to the poor. He has sent me to bind up the brokenhearted, to proclaim freedom for the captives and release from darkness for the prisoners, to proclaim the year of the LORD'S favor ... " (cf. Luke 4:18- 19).

Jesus deliberately stopped at the middle of the sentence because his first advent was to begin a time of salvation, a time of favor to all men—not judgment (John 3:16-17; 12:47). The past 2,000 years have been the time of the LORD'S favor, and they are fast ending, when grace will end! During this time, the gospel has been preached especially in the West. When Jesus will appear a second time (in our days), he will bring judgment to unbelievers (day of vengeance) and final salvation to believers. The second half of Isaiah 61:1-2 reads; **"... and the day of vengeance of our God, to comfort all who mourn, and provide for those who grieve in Zion ..."** (Is. 61:2b-3). The second part of this verse awaits fulfillment in our day. Jesus is not coming again to declare the year of the LORD'S favor but the day of vengeance, and with it, comfort, provision, and deliverance for those who wait for him. The words he spoke in his first advent will be the judge at the end (John 12:48; cf. Heb. 4:12-13; Jer. 17:10).

His appearance will be devastating to his enemies. The meek and harmless lamb of God that appeared 2000 years ago in weakness and in a manger, will arrive this time as a lion—the Lion of the tribe of Judah. He will be a warrior and a conqueror. **His appearing will be spectacular in the midst of the tribulation;**

*"For as lightning that comes from the east is visible even to the west, so will be the coming of the Son of Man. ... **Immediately after the distress of those days** 'the sun will be darkened, and the moon will not give its light; the stars will fall from the sky, and the heavenly bodies will be shaken.' At that time the sign of the Son of Man will appear in the sky, and **all the nations of the earth will mourn**. They will see the Son of Man coming on the clouds of the sky, with power and great glory"* (Matt. 24:27-30).

Again; *"Look, he is coming with the clouds, and every eye will see him, even those who pierced him; and **all the people of the earth will mourn because of him.** So shall it be! Amen"* (Rev. 1:7).

Why will the nations and peoples mourn? Because they are currently plotting against him;

"Why do the nations conspire [rage] *and the peoples plot in vain? The kings of the earth take their stand and the rulers gather together against the LORD and against his Anointed One. 'Let us break their chains,' they say, 'and throw off their fetters.' **The One enthroned in heaven laughs; the Lord scoffs at them. Then he rebukes them in his anger and terrifies them in his wrath,** ... Therefore, you kings, be wise; be warned, you rulers of the earth. Serve the LORD with fear and rejoice with trembling. **Kiss the Son, lest he be angry and you be destroyed in your way, for his wrath can flare up in a moment"*** (Ps. 2; cf. Rev. 16:12-16).

The Messiah declares; *"Behold, I am coming soon! Blessed is he who keeps the words of the prophecy in this book* [Revelation].*"*

Again Jesus says; *"Behold, I am coming soon! My reward is with me, and I will give to everyone according to what he has done. I am the Alpha and the Omega, the First and the Last, the Beginning and the End"* (Rev. 22:7, 12).

Introduction to Last Things (Eschatology)

John the Baptist and Jesus Christ began to teach and preach; *"Repent for the kingdom of God is at hand."* Prepare! For Jesus is coming again soon! In fact, he is even at the door. It is written; *"Just as man is destined to die once, and after that to face judgment, so Christ was sacrificed once to take away the sins of many people; and* **he will appear a second time,** *not to bear sin, but to bring salvation to those who are waiting for him"* (Heb. 9:27-28).

Have you come to a point in your life when you were waiting for something, and you were sure it must happen? Imagine how well prepared you must be as you wait for it. It is obvious that anything you wait for that is good, you do so with great anticipation and anxiety; being busy about it and ready for it. Take for instance, a woman waiting for her husband to take her for the first time. And to those of you already married; what kind of preparation did you make? Again, if a reliable person promises you a gift, you will be assured and certain that he will give you that gift at the appointed time. What more of God?

Your preparedness, readiness, and anxiousness toward an event is always dependent upon the importance of that event. The second coming of Jesus Christ is one of the most important events ever to happen in these last days of the age to both believers and unbelievers. It is an event that the whole world is looking forward to and wondering about with anxiety and impatience. While unbelievers may be waiting for that day in fear, doubt, and the threat of judgment and hell, the second coming of Jesus is the basis of the believers' hope. It is the goal believers are looking forward to—their final glorification— their being with the Lord forever and the cessation of all earthly troubles and sorrows!

However, some believers are curious about this event just to excite themselves and show off rather than to live holy lives. It is important to note that the intention of prophesy is not to satisfy our curiosity, but to humble us and call us to repent and live holy lives.

Jesus' teaching focused a lot on the age to come. He took a great deal of time talking about his second coming and the age to come to his disciples, who were anxious to know the exact time. The answers he gave to questions about the time of his coming again showed that he wanted believers to be watchful and prepared rather than to know the exact day or hour. Thus, it is unnecessary to make times and dates predictions. Many have tried and failed. However, he gave them (and us) characteristics of the world situation by which believers can judge for themselves what is going on, as we have examined in Part I. In view of this, here are some few questions to ponder: What do you make of the present world situation? How does the present state of the world and its people fit your view of life and man? Does it make any difference to you, or you do not care at all? Just staying and waiting for tomorrow and whatever happens? **Let's examine a few things about the second coming of Jesus Christ.**

It is a Certain Event

The Bible clearly shows to us that Jesus Christ is coming again and we can believe the testimony of the Bible. He shall come in glory, and he shall reign as King and Judge; *"When the Son of man comes in his glory, and the angels with him, he will sit on his throne in heavenly glory"* (Matt. 25:31). Also, he says; *"And if I go and prepare a place for you, I will come back and take you to be with me that you also may be where I am"* (John 14:3). The coming will be visible; *"Men of Galilee, 'Why do you stand here looking into the sky? This same Jesus who has been taken from you into heaven will come back in the way you have seen him go into heaven'"* (Acts 1:11).

The coming will be a public event; with a trumpet sound and everyone shall see him. Believers will be received and unbelievers will be rejected; *"Look, he is coming with the clouds, and every eye will see him, even those who pierced him* (even us today by our sin);

and all the peoples of the earth [unbelievers] *will mourn because of him. So shall it be! Amen"* (Rev. 1:7). Thus, we know that Jesus is coming again for his own, and this is our hope. Whether we suffer or are troubled (2 Tim. 2:11, 12), or are hungry or persecuted or whatever kind of hardship, we know that our Lord is preparing a place for us and will come back and take us with him there. Therefore, we will persevere till the end and not fall back (Matt. 24:13). We continue to wait in hope—hope does not disappoint us because we have the anointing of the Holy Spirit (Rom. 5:5).

It Will Be Sudden and Unexpected

Although we are certain that Jesus is coming again, we do not know the hour of his coming, neither the angels nor the Son of Man. When the disciples asked Jesus about the time, he began to talk to them about things that will begin to happen up to the day: false prophets shall arise, wars and rumors of wars, famines, earthquakes, persecutions, turning away from the faith, lack of love among people, children rebelling against their parents, and other things (Matt. 24:3-4; 36; 40-41). These things are all around us in a great magnitude. Furthermore, the day will come like a thief; *"But the day of the Lord will come like a thief. The heavens will disappear with a roar; the elements will be destroyed by fire, and the earth and everything in it will be laid bare"* (2 Pet. 3:10).

Therefore, in view of the above, the next thing we will examine about the second coming of Jesus is that:

It Must be Prepared For

Because the coming of Jesus will be like a thief, we need to prepare for it. We need to be always ready and watchful so that the day will not take us unaware (Matt. 24:42, 44). This does not call for idleness. (A personal principle: I am always ready as though Jesus was coming in the next minute, yet I plan as though he were not coming in my lifetime). Now, how can we watch and how can we be ready? You can watch by examining yourself whether you have truly been converted; that is, whether you have trusted Jesus Christ (and him alone) as your Savior. Are you fit in the light of the Bible before

God? If you are, continue to **learn** and **obey** God's word and **live by it always.** If not, **believe in the Lord Jesus now and receive the forgiveness of your sins.** This watchfulness involves staying away from sin and all appearance of sin and evil.

To be ready involves living a life of faithfulness, holiness, purity, and righteousness, every day and at all times of your life. No idleness or indulging in sinfulness (1 John 2:28-3:10). Thus, we must live pure lives if we are truly waiting for Jesus. To live a holy life is not an option, it is a command; *"Make every effort to live at peace with all men and to be holy; without holiness no-one will see God!"* (Heb. 13:14). The condition to see God is plainly stated here--holiness!

Dear people, if you have an opportunity to be righteous, to be holy, live as though Jesus were coming at that very moment--and that is how you ought to live your life always (as in the presence of God). Do not be like the wicked servant in Matthew 24:48-51, who turns into debauchery and dissipation because his Lord is delaying. What will the Lord come and find you doing—lying, killing, doing sorcery, committing fornication, adultery, or stealing? We must live our lives as children of light and not in the darkness (Eph. 5:3-20; Rom. 13:11-14), so that the coming of Jesus will not take us by surprise. Be watchful! Ready! And Holy!

However, the unfortunate thing is that few people in the world and even in churches today, are prepared and ready for the coming of Jesus Christ. They are living in sin and committing sin every day. Others are worried about earthly things (riches, fame, and the like), but leaving aside heavenly things; *"What good will it be for a man if he gains the whole world, yet forfeits his soul? Or what can a man give in exchange for his soul?"* (Matt. 16:26). **Because of this worldliness, this day will take them unaware, and God will assign them to HELL and ETERNAL PUNISHMENT,** where **there will be WEEPING AND GNASHING OF TEETH.** The question remains: will Jesus come and find you watching and waiting in righteousness and holiness? **The Bible tells us the end of unbelievers;** *"Do you not know that the wicked will not inherit the kingdom of God? Do not be deceived: Neither the **sexually immoral, nor idolaters, nor adulterers, nor male prostitutes, nor homosexual***

offenders, nor thieves, nor greedy, nor drunkards, nor swindlers will inherit the kingdom of God" (1 Co. 6:9-10). Where do you fall? Do not be deceived: what you sow, you will reap (Gal. 6:7-8).

Jesus tells us how the coming of destruction took people unaware in Noah's day and in Sodom and Gomorrah, because they were living in sin (Luke 17:26-30). The people were preoccupied with themselves and their earthly interests—eating, drinking, marrying, buying, selling, planting, building, etc. [Note that these things or activities are legitimate and apparently normal for any thriving society!] However, when these things become our priorities, and we are preoccupied with them to the neglect of spiritual priorities, they blind us and become a curse. What is your life worth? Just a home? Just a car? A wife or a husband? A career or a job? More money? More fame? More sex? What gives you ultimate satisfaction? If such legitimate things as mentioned above make people not to prepare for Christ's coming, what more of those living in sin? As it is written; *"For it is time for judgment to begin with the family of God; and if it begins with us, what will the outcome be for those who do not obey the gospel of God? And if it is hard for the righteous to be saved, what will become of the ungodly and the sinner?"* (1 Pet. 4:17-18). Let us be careful then, how we live our lives, so that that day will not surprise us. It is written; *"Since everything will be destroyed in this way, **what kind of people ought you to be? You ought to live holy and godly lives. ... So then dear friends, since you are looking forward to this, make every effort to be found spotless, blameless and at peace with him"*** (2 Pet. 3:11,14).

It Will Come With the Verdict of God's Judgment

When Jesus Christ appears, everyone shall be repaid according to how he prepared or what he had done. The wicked will go to hell and eternal punishment; *"But the cowardly, the unbelieving, the vile, the murderers, the sexually immoral, those who practice magic arts, the idolaters, and all liars, will be in the fiery lake of burning sulfur"* (Rev. 21:8). This will be the same fate for the hypocrites (all those who pretend to be Christians but have not repented of their sins). They will be equally rejected by Jesus Christ; *"Not everyone who says to me, 'Lord, Lord,' will enter the kingdom of heaven, but **only***

he who does the will of my Father who is in heaven. *Many will say to me on that day, 'Lord, Lord, did we not prophesy in your name, and in your name drive out demons and perform many miracles?' Then I will tell them plainly, 'I never knew you. Away from me, you evil doers!'"* (Matt. 7:21-23).

This solemn declaration ought to make us tremble and re-evaluate the state of our hearts and our motives. Everything hidden shall be exposed! Imagine some people who have spent all their lives in church but are hypocrites saying; "I was a member of this or that church;" "I sang in the choir for many years;" "I was a deacon;" "I attended church meetings and conferences;" "I prophesied in church several times!" "I drove out demons!" and so on. If you do all these things without having given your life to Jesus, he does not know you and will assign you with sinners and pagans; *"I never knew you!"* **he will say. So settle it with Jesus now!**

Let's consider the following illustration. Imagine working in somebody's farm without having begged or rented it from the owner, only to be ready to harvest and the owner drives you away with nothing. How will that be to you? You better negotiate with the owner before working. In the same way you must make things right with Jesus before working in his farm--doing church work! Without Jesus in your life, church work will amount to nothing. Do not wait to be disappointed on the last day.

Unlike what will happen to sinners and the hypocrites, believers will be received into eternity with Jesus Christ;

"When the Son of Man comes in his glory, and all the angels with him, he will sit on his throne in heavenly glory. . . . He will put the sheep on his right hand and the goats on the left. Then the King will say to those on the right, 'Come, you who are blessed by my Father; take your inheritance, the kingdom prepared for you since the creation of the world" (Matt. 25:31-34).

Again; *"For the Lord himself will come down from heaven, with a loud command, with the voice of the archangel and with the trumpet call of God, and the dead in Christ will rise first. After that, we who are still alive and are left will be caught up together with them in the clouds to meet the Lord in the air. and so we will be with the Lord forever"* (1 Thess. 4:16-17). Believers will go into eternity with Jesus and enjoy heaven forever—the ultimate hope of our salvation!

To conclude, I can write on and on about these things if I have space and time because they are true. They give me comfort and hope that Jesus will come again and take me home. How pleasing to you are the words about his coming? Are you **prepared** and **ready** for his coming? Are you **watchful** because you do not know when he is coming, or you are just **idle** and **pretending**? You have heard what the end will be for everybody. Where do you belong? Whether you want it or not, Jesus is coming again—and you will either receive blessing from him or damnation. There is no middle ground! I am burdened in my heart and even shed tears as I write these things. I implore you to make the right decision for Christ so that you will not end up in hell. **Now, this one last question: If you were to die now or Jesus were to come now, will you go into the kingdom of heaven with him?** If yes, rejoice evermore in the Lord. If no, do you want to be sure from this moment where you will go when Jesus comes? Repent and believe in the Lord Jesus Christ and you shall be saved. Then you will spend eternity with him. Please do not deceive yourself, God knows your heart.

Three Millennial Views

Students of the Word of God have tried for hundreds of years throughout the history of the Church, to interpret what the Bible says about the events surrounding the second coming of Jesus Christ. The main question is not whether he will come again, for all believers believe he will come again, but whether Jesus will come and literally reign on earth for a thousand years (millennium) before ushering in eternal states. The millennium is mentioned in Revelation 20:4-6 only. However, there is evidence in the prophets that Jesus will come and reign literally on earth for a considerable amount of time before ushering in eternity. This will be a time of universal righteousness, justice, and restoration (of the earth and Israelites). There are three prevailing views regarding the 1000-year reign of Jesus on earth.

Postmillennialism: This is the view that the millennium is already in progress and will precede the second coming. Those who hold to this view believe that the preaching of the gospel will be so successful that it will lead to the conversion of the whole world.

A-millennialism: Those who hold to this view believe that there will be no 1000-year reign of Christ on earth. They believe that when Jesus comes, he will execute judgment and usher in the final states—heaven and hell. They deny the 1000-year reign of Revelation 20:4-6. They take these 1000 years as symbolical.

Pre-millennialism: This view holds that Jesus Christ will return physically, visibly, and bodily to reign with his saints on earth for a thousand years (Rev. 20:4-6; Jer. 23: 5-6). This seems to have been the dominant, if not the exclusive view in the early church, for they expected Jesus to return very soon. In Revelation 20:4-6, two resurrections are evident, one at the second coming (believers only) and the other at the end of the 1000 years (of the rest of the dead).

A belief in the millennium leads us to what Bible students call the **Great Tribulation (GT** for short) **for a duration of approximately seven years**. Will Jesus rapture (catch away) the church at the beginning, middle or after the seven years of the GT? This sometimes proves to be a difficult point for pre-millennialism. Much has been written on the subject and I do not intend to reproduce lengthy arguments here. Why a 7-year tribulation? (see Dan 9:27). Before I answer that question, I would like to remark that from the time of Jesus Christ (that is, approximately AD 26 or AD 30) as he began his earthly ministry, his true followers have always been persecuted. That is, they are always going through trials and tribulations, and some of them pay it with their lives as Jesus did (Matt. 5:11, 12; 24:9, John 16:33; Rev. 7:14). This has happened throughout church history until today all over the world, except in the West now (Europe and North America—a rather dangerous situation; Rev. 3:14-18).

Based on the prophesy timetable of Daniel 9: 24-27, it would seem only 69 sevens were fulfilled until the crucifixion, and the last seven was postponed (so it is believed), which is believed to be the time of the GT. [The people of the ruler (Roman Empire) destroyed the Jewish temple in AD 70 marking the Diaspora (scattering of the Jewish people). Since that time wars have continued (multiplying in the twentieth century, and especially (of the earth and Israelites). Dan 9:26). There is nothing as just war—war is war (*Woe to the world because of things that cause people to sin! Such things must come, but woe to the man through whom they come!* Matt.18:7), though God is sovereign and uses wars (stronger powers and even weaker powers) to discipline the wicked and curb evil and pride.]

Three Tribulation Views

There are three major views of the tribulation in relation to rapture and the second coming.

Pre-tribulation: This is the most popular view today among prophesy students and classical dispensationalists. Pre-tribulationists hold that the rapture of the church will happen just before the GT begins. They hold that the GT will be unparallel to any in the history of mankind. The rapture will be secret and would not be seen by any unbelieving eye (1 Thess. 4:15-17). Thus, there will be two phases of the second coming—before the GT and after the GT. The church will be absent during the GT (1 Thess. 5:9). The church will be removed before the man of lawlessness is revealed (2 Thess. 2:7).

Pre-tribulationists also believe that the elect of Matthew 24:22 and 24 refers only to the Jews. To them, the Lord's return is imminent [can occur at any moment—with no signs preceding it). (This, however, contradicts 1 Thessalonians 4:16, which states that the Lord with descend with a shout, with a trumpet call; the loud voice of the archangel.] Pre-tribulationists also believe in two judgments: one at time of rapture (believers and rewards); then the other at the end of millennium (sheep and goats).

Mid-tribulation: This view holds that the church will go through the first 3 and 1/2 years of the Great Tribulation but the rapture will occur before the last 3 and 1/2 years, the terrible years of God's wrath. This view has some plausibility given that the saints are handed over to the Antichrist for three and a half years (Dan. 7:24-25), before he is revealed.

Post-tribulation: This is the view that the rapture and the second coming are two stages of the same event and happens after the Great Tribulation or somewhere within, since Jesus said that the time will be shortened (Matt. 24:21-22). Here, the elect refers to all who are chosen in Christ Jesus, not just the Jews. The church will go through the GT but will be preserved from God's wrath (1 Thess. 5:9; Luke 21:36; John 17:15; Rev. 3:10; Is. 26:20; 31:5). Notice the way Jesus puts it in Luke 21:36; *"Be always on the watch, and pray that you may be able to escape all that is about to happen, and that you may be able to stand before the Son of Man."* If the rapture must occur before the GT, it would be needless for believers to be watchful or to pray that they may be able to escape the tribulations. The believers during the GT will be like Israel in Goshen while Egyptians went through the plagues. **Jesus said that he will come immediately after the distress (GT) of those days** (Matt. 24: 29-31). There is no indication in the chronology of events in Matthew 24 or Luke 21 that the church is removed before the GT begins.

Post-tribulationists distinguish between the wrath of God and the GT. Believers do not face the wrath of God (Rom. 5:9; 1 Thess 1:10; 5:10); only unbelievers do (John 3:36; Rom. 1:18). Tribulation has been the experience of the church throughout its history (John 16:33; Acts 14:22; 2 Tim. 3:12; Rom 5:3). The GT will be of the same kind just different in degree. Within this period, though believers will experience tribulation, only unbelievers will experience wrath.

Many have said that believers will be removed before the drama of Revelation 6-19 unfolds. However, we must be careful because this drama may not refer exclusively to the 7-year period. For instance, the first beast (Roman Empire) and the second beast out of the earth (USA), span the whole of history from the time of John (in fact, it even goes back to the time of Daniel) until the second coming. The true church in Revelation is promised two things: (1) She will be kept from the moment of trial (Rev. 3:10), and (2) The second coming (Rev. 3:20). Throughout the book of Revelation, references are made to those who overcome and to saints or believers being present. There is no indication that they have been taken away (Rev. 12:11, 17; 13:9, 10; 14:12-13; 16:15). Though some believe these are tribulation believers, I disagree. The thief rapture pre- and mid-tribulation are spiritual; that is, Jesus seals his own but they are not removed (Rev. 7:1-3). This wicked generation (the one up to and during the GT) shall not be given a sign (Matt. 12:39; 16:4). Thus, removing (rapture) the believers must be a big sign because their disappearance will cause an uproar probably causing many to believe. Again, we see that those experiencing the GT and the wrath of God refuse to repent (Rev. 9:20-21;16:21). We can only conclude that Jesus will keep or protect believers from the GT and the evil one (John 17:15; Rev. 3:10).

Post-tribulationist view 1 Thess. 4:17 differently. We will meet the Lord in the air and return with him back to earth (welcome!). Elsewhere in the Bible the verb used here, "to meet," means to go out and meet (welcome) and return with to where one was (see also Matt. 25:6, 10; Acts 28:15).

If the rapture and the second coming are two parts of a single event, who is taken and who is left? (Matt. 24:40, 41; 13:24-30, 47-50). There will be a separation of believers from the wicked. Since the believers will inherit the earth (Matt 5:5; 6:10), we conclude that the wicked will be gathered up and thrown into hell (Matt. 13:30, 37-43, 49-50).

What is Christ doing now? He is interceding for the believers and laughing at his enemies because he knows that their time is almost over. As it is written; *"Therefore he is able to save completely those who come to God through him, because **he always lives to intercede for them**"* (Heb. 7:25).

"The One enthroned in heaven laughs; the Lord scoffs at them [nations/rulers raging]*"* (Ps. 2:1-4).

*"A little while, and the wicked will be no more; though you look for them, they will not be found. But the meek will inherit the land and enjoy great peace. The wicked plot against the righteous and gnash their teeth at them; but **the Lord laughs at the wicked, for he knows their day is coming**"* (Ps. 37:10-13).

"O LORD God Almighty, the God of Israel, rouse yourself to punish the nations; show no mercy to wicked traitors. They return at evening, snarling like dogs, and prowl about the city. See what they spew out from their mouths--they spew out swords from their lips, and they say, 'Who can hear us?' **But you, O LORD, laugh at them; you scoff at all those nations"** (Ps. 59:5-8).

Christ is sitting now on the right hand of Majesty on high waiting for his enemies to be made his footstool (Acts 3:21; Heb. 1:2-4, 13; Phil. 3:20-21; 1 Co. 15:24-25).

The Great Tribulation (GT)

A Time of Wrath and Judgment—The Day of the LORD/ Lord/Christ

As we saw earlier, the Day of the LORD comes up over and over in the prophets, and **refers to a day or year or period, when God punishes his children or sinful nations through invasion or war/sword, natural disaster (locusts, floods, hail, windstorms, tornadoes, hurricanes, typhoons, drought, earthquakes, etc.), famine, plague, and wild beasts** (Ezek. 14:21). While this day was fulfilled historically for Israel, Judah, and the nations, it typologically pointed forward to the final day that God/Jesus Christ will punish sinners by bringing in the final judgment and final redemption for believers. It is also called the day of Christ, and will coincide with the GT—the kind of distress going on in the world now (Ps. 50:1-6; 58:1-11; Is. 14:24-27; 22:5; 23:6-11a; 24; 33:1; 34; 40:25; 63:1-6; 65:1-16; Jer. 25:30-38; 46:10; Joel 2:28-32; 3:9-16; Zephaniah; Jude). It is a day to punish sinners and the wicked and bring down or humble all the arrogant, lofty, and proud of the earth.

A historical example of the **Day of the LORD is recorded in** Isaiah 2:6-4:1. This was **a time of wrath and judgment by invasion for Jerusalem and Judah because of their sin. Those who were destroyed include:** those who practiced eastern superstition, divination (consulting the dead), pagans (Matt. 6:25-33), the wealthy, warriors and those who trust in war weapons; those who worshipped idols or man-made gods and idolaters; the proud and arrogant were humbled or brought low (which will happen same in our day);

"The eyes of the arrogant will be humbled and the pride of men will be brought low; **the LORD alone will be exalted in that day.** *The LORD Almighty has a day in store for all the proud and lofty, for all that is exalted (and they will be humbled) ... The arrogance of man will be brought low and the pride of men humbled;* **the LORD alone will be exalted in that day,** *and the idols will totally disappear. Men will flee to caves in the rocks and to holes in the ground from dread of the LORD and the splendor of his majesty, when he rises to shake the earth"* (Is. 2:11-12, 17-19; cf. Rev. 6:15-17; Hag. 2:6,7; Heb. 12:26).

However, during wrath, in the day of the Lord, the righteous will be preserved; *"Tell the righteous it will be well with them, for they will enjoy the fruit of their deeds"* (Is. 3:10). The **LORD ALWAYS preserves the righteous from wrath**—he passes over them; *"Go, my people, enter your rooms and shut the doors behind you; hide yourselves for a little while until his wrath has passed by. See, the LORD is coming out of his dwelling to punish the people of the earth for their sins. ... "* (Is.26:20-21). *"... so the LORD Almighty will come down to do battle on Mount Zion and on its heights. Like birds hovering overhead, the LORD Almighty will shield Jerusalem; he will shield it and deliver it, he will 'pass over' it and will rescue it"* (Is. 31:5; cf. 54:16-17). The LORD will always protect his own. He shows mercy even in wrath (Hab. 3:2)!

The Day of Jacob's Trouble

As already mentioned, the GT will have a Jewish character (the seventy sevens were decreed for the Jews to finish transgression and put an end to sin and bring in everlasting righteousness). The GT is called the day of Jacob's trouble (Jer. 30:7; Is. 27-31). However, during this time there will be great distress all over the world, as in fact is the case now (Matt. 24:21; Luke 21:23,25; Dan. 11:40-12:1). The prophets also prophesied about this period of distress (Is. 24; 34; 63:1-6; Jer. 30:4-8; Ezek. 38 & 39; Zech.12:1-3; 14:1-2). Some of Revelation 6-19 will be fulfilled during this time. For the first three and a half years, the saints are handed over to the Antichrist (Dan.

7:24-25), but in the middle of the seven years they will realize his deception when the abomination that causes desolation is set up (Dan. 9:27; 12:7b). During the first half of the GT, there will be apparent prosperity and world peace or a concerted effort at achieving world peace (1 Thess. 5:1-3). The Antichrist as an agent of Satan, will use (or is using) power politics and religious manipulation to deceive the world. After the abomination of desolation is set up, Satan will be driven out of heaven and the world will face his full wrath as he knows his time is short (Rev. 12:9, 12b). There will be total chaos as Satan is bent to destroy many. This is the time of the real distress of the GT (Dan. 12:11,12).

The Reign of the Antichrist

This is the central figure during the Great Tribulation, who is in alliance with Satan (aspiration for power and world domination with religious and political control). He will be obsessed with self-glorification for himself and his empire. His empire is described as follows; *"Out of one of them came another horn, which started small but grew in power to the south and to the east and toward the Beautiful land. It grew until it reached the host of the heavens* [towers reaching heaven, number one, the greatest], *and it threw some of the starry host down to the earth* [Rev. 12:3-4] *and trampled on them. It set itself up to be as great as the Prince of the host* [imitating the kingdom of Christ]*; ... "* It should be noted that since the early church, the spirit of the antichrist has always been working in the children of disobedience (1 John 2:18; 4:3; 2 John 7). The children of disobedience are described to be under the ruler of the kingdom of the air, Satan (Eph. 2:2). **The Antichrist is called by different names in various passages.**

Another king that will arise: *"The ten horns are ten kings who will come from this kingdom. After them another king will arise, different from the earlier ones; he will subdue three kings. **He will speak against the Most High and oppress the saints** and try to change the set times and laws. The saints will be handed over to him for a time, times and half a time. **But the court will sit and his power will be taken away and completely destroyed forever**"* (Dan. 7:24-26).

A stern-faced king: *"In the latter part of their reign* [Age of Gentiles], **when rebels have become completely wicked** [current moral rebellion]*, a stern-faced king, a master of intrigue, will arise. He will become very strong, but not by his own power. He will cause astounding devastation and will succeed in whatever he does. He will destroy the mighty men and the holy people. He will cause deceit to prosper, and **he will consider himself superior.** When they feel secure, **he will destroy many and take his stand against the Prince of princes** [He will take Jesus Christ head-on]. **Yet he will be destroyed, but not by human power"** (Dan. 8:23-25; cf. 2:34-35, 44).*

The king who does as he pleases: *"The king will do as he pleases. He will exalt and magnify himself above every god and will say unheard-of things against the God of gods. He will be successful until the time of wrath* [Great Tribulation] **is completed, for what has been determined must take place.** He will show no regard for the gods of his fathers or for the one desired by women, nor will he regard any god, but **will exalt himself above them all. Instead of them, he will honor a god of fortresses** [rely on military strength, capability, and technology]; a god unknown to his fathers he will honor with gold and silver [medals of honor], with precious and costly gifts. ... He will pitch his royal tents between the seas at the beautiful holy mountain. **Yet he will come to his end,** and no one will help him"* (Dan. 11:36-45).

The Man of lawlessness: *"Don't let anyone deceive you in any way, for that day will not come, until the rebellion occurs* [current moral rebellion; Dan. 8:23 above] *and the man of lawlessness is revealed, the man doomed to destruction. He will oppose and **will exalt himself over everything that is called God** [cf. Dan. 11:37 above, that is, any god, not necessarily only the God of heaven] or is worshiped, so that he sets himself up in God's temple [amongst the people of God, the church; Is. 14:13- 14] proclaiming himself to be God [a god; cf. Ezek. 28:2,6,9] ... And now you know what is holding him back, so that he may be revealed at the proper time. For the secret power of lawlessness is already at work; but the one who now holds it back will continue to do so till he is taken out of the way* [now, the Spirit and Christ are outside the apostate and delusional church, in which this man sits; Rev. 3:14-19]. *And then the lawless one will be revealed, whom the Lord Jesus will overthrow with the breath of his mouth* [that is, without human hands or power--no military assistance] *and destroy by the splendor of his coming"* (2 Thess. 2:3-12).

Notice in all four quotations the destruction of the Antichrist: (1) *"But the court will sit and his power will be taken away and completely destroyed forever"* (Dan. 7:26). (2) *"Yet he will be destroyed, but not by human power"* (Dan. 8:25c). (3) *"Yet he will come to his end, and no one will help him"* (Dan. 11:45c). (4) *"... whom the Lord Jesus will overthrow with the breath of his mouth and destroy by the splendor of his coming"* (2 Thess. 2:3-12). It will be the spectacle of all ages.

Like Belshazzar, this man has desecrated the church of God with the gangrene of politics (Dan.5:2-6;20-28; cf. Ezek. 28:18). The handwriting is on the wall! The kingdom of the Antichrist will be taken over in one night and given to the saints (Dan. 5:30-31; cf. Rev. 11:15).

Other people have come close to describing this man—the Antichrist. One man has concluded that this usurper will be elected democratically. He will probably claim to be a Christian, perhaps even born again! Arno Froese writes;

"Don't expect the Antichrist to be an evil man, with blood dripping from his mouth, to appear on the world scene fomenting destruction and chaos. Rather, he will be a gentle, kind, compassionate, caring personality, who is dedicated to true democracy and is determined to bring peace and prosperity to the world.

I can well imagine that he will support prayer and Bible reading in schools, the political platform of the conservatives, and with a unique ability, he will appease the liberal camp as well. He will be all things to all people. Finally, the world will have a leader capable of taking care of all situations. Most importantly he shall prosper. His policies will actually work and not be empty political promises as our politicians are so fond of making in our day. He will accomplish great things.

Nevertheless, the Antichrist's work is the work of darkness. ..."[cccl]

Dave Hunt writes; "It is important to understand that the Antichrist will not claim to be God in the classical biblical sense, but a man who has achieved godhood."[ccli] He will put on a different face but in his heart he will exalt himself and will be bent on deceit. After all, Satan himself disguises or masquerades as an angel of light in order to penetrate the ranks of believers (2 Co. 11:13-15). Keith Harris also writes the following about the Antichrist;

> "He is the white-horse rider of Revelation 6:4: The Antichrist is seen as having a bow, but no arrows. He has no crown until one is given to him. The picture is that of a conqueror who conquers by means of peace, as symbolized by the white horse and an empty bow. He will dazzle the world with his strategically and governmental intelligence. This flatterer, an arch manipulator, will gain the trust of the world's political leaders.
>
> The Antichrist first comes as a man of peace (white horse rider with peaceful bow). He conquers by means of peace. ...
>
> From the beginning, the Antichrist's goal will be that of self-exaltation. Underneath his dazzling brilliance and influence for good will be a heart of lawlessness. This lawless heart will make way for the most evil, demonic activity since the expulsion of angels from Heaven at the fall of Lucifer. These fallen angels will play an important role in the book of Revelation."[ccclii]

The good news is that Jesus Christ will destroy the Antichrist with the breath of his mouth at his coming. Amen!

Christ Descends to Earth

The saints of the ages and the saints of this age are all crying out to God for justice, and he has heard their cries, and the time for vindication has come.

"Arise, O LORD, let not man triumph; **let the nations be judged in your presence. Strike them with terror** [as in fact, the world is

experiencing now], *O LORD; let the nations know they are but men"* (Ps. 9:19-20; cf. Luke 21:25-26).

"May God arise, may his enemies be scattered; may his foes flee before him. As smoke is blown away by the wind, may you blow them away; as wax melts before the fire, may the wicked perish before God. But may the righteous be glad and rejoice before God; may they be happy and joyful. ... Summon your power, O God; show us your strength, O God, as you have done before. Because of your temple at Jerusalem kings will bring you gifts. Rebuke the beast among the reeds, the herd of bulls among the calves of nations. Humbled, may they bring bars of silver. **Scatter the nations who delight in war**" (Ps. 68:1-3,28-30).

"How long will the enemy mock you, O God? Will the foe revile your name forever. ... Rise up, O God, and defend your cause; remember how fools mock you all day long. Do not ignore the clamor of your adversaries, the uproar of your enemies, which rises continually" (Ps. 74:10,22-23).

"Rise up, O God, judge the earth, for all the nations are your inheritance" (Ps. 82:8).

"O LORD, the God who avenges, O God who avenges, shine forth. Rise up, O Judge of the earth; pay back to the proud what they deserve. How long will the wicked, O LORD, how long will the wicked be jubilant? They pour out arrogant words; all the evil doers are full of boasting. They crush your people, O LORD; they oppress your inheritance. **They slay the widow and the alien; they murder the fatherless.** *They say, 'The LORD does not see; the God of Jacob pays no heed.'* **Take heed, you senseless ones among the people; you fools, when will you become wise?** *Does he who implanted the ear not hear? Does he who formed the eye not see? Does he who disciplines nations not punish? Does he who teaches man lack knowledge?* **The LORD knows the thoughts of man; he knows that they are futile.** *...* **Can a corrupt throne be allied with you--one that brings on misery by its decrees?** *They band together against the righteous and condemn the innocent to death"* (Ps. 94:1-11, 20-21).

"When he opened the fifth seal, I saw under the altar the souls of those who had been slain because of the word of God and the testimony they had maintained. They cried out in a loud voice, 'How long, Sovereign Lord, holy and true, until you judge the inhabitants of the earth and avenge our blood?" (**Rev.** 6:9-10).

Before Christ descends to the earth, he is making one more call--one more plea to mankind before descending to judge, because once he appears there will be no time for repentance--no more grace! The door will be shut forever (Matt. 25:10-12). Christ is calling out; ***"This is what the LORD says: 'Maintain justice and do what is right, for my salvation is close at hand and my righteousness will soon be revealed. Blessed is the man who does this, the man who holds it fast, who keeps the Sabbath without desecrating it, and keeps his hand from doing any evil"*** (Is. 56:1-2).

Christ will make his contact with the earth at the battle of Armageddon, on the Mountain of the LORD (Har-Magedon);

*"The sixth angle poured out his bowl on the great river Euphrates, and its water was dried up to prepare the way for the kings from the East. Then I saw three evil spirits that looked like frogs; they came out of the mouth of the dragon, out of the mouth of the beast and out of the mouth of the false prophet. They are spirits of demons performing miraculous signs, and they go out to the kings of the whole world, to gather them for the battle on the great day of God Almighty. **'Behold, I come like a thief! Blessed is he who stays awake and keeps his clothes with him, so that he may not go naked and be shamefully exposed.'** Then they gathered the kings together to a place in Hebrew called Armageddon"* (Rev. 16:12-16).

The Battle of Armageddon (Har-Magedon)

"I saw heaven standing open and there before me was a white horse, whose rider is called Faithful and True. With justice [righteousness] ***he judges and makes war. His eyes are like blazing fire*** [Rev. 1:12-18; Dan. 7:9-14; Ezek. 1:25-28], ***and on his head are many crowns. He has a name on him that no one knows but he himself. He is dressed in a robe dipped in blood*** [Is. 34:5-6; 63:1-

6], *and his name is the Word of God* [cf. John 1:1]. *The armies of heaven* [cf. Ezek. 37:1-10] *were following him, riding on white horses and dressed in fine linen, white and clean. Out of his mouth comes a sharp sword* [cf. Heb. 4:12-13; Rev. 2:12,16] *with which to strike down the nations. 'He will rule them with an iron scepter* [Ps. 2].' *He treads the winepress of the fury of the wrath of God Almighty* [cf. Rev. 14:14-20]. *On his robe and on his thigh he has this name written: KING OF KINGS AND LORD OF LORDS"* (Rev. 19:11-16).

Jesus Christ will confront the armies of Satan under the Antichrist (who also rides a white horse; Rev. 6:2) on the Mountain of the LORD and will vanquish them in a spur of a moment; *"Then the LORD will go out and fight against those nations, as he fights in the day of battle"* (Zech. 14:3). This battle is the culmination of the historic struggle between God and his ex-servant, Satan; between Good and Evil; between God's will and human will; between the city of God and the city of man. **The LORD himself will sound the trumpet for the battle** (Is. 8:9-10; 42:13-17; Zech. 9:14-15; Joel 3:9-16).

The army of Christ, with Christ at the head, will crush Babylon and her allies;

"Your [Christ's] *troops will be willing on your day of battle. Arrayed in holy majesty, from the womb of the dawn you will receive the dew of your youth" "They* [the nations under the beast and the false prophet—Antichrist] *will make war against the Lamb, but the Lamb will overcome them because he is Lord of lords and King of kings--and with him will be his called, chosen and faithful followers."*

*"Then I saw the beast and the kings of the earth and their armies gathered together to make war against the rider on the horse and his army. **But the beast was captured, and with him the false prophet** who had performed the miraculous signs on his behalf. ... The two of them were thrown alive into the fiery lake of burning sulfur. **The rest of them were killed with the sword that came out of the mouth of the rider on the horse** [cf. Rev. 2:12b,16; Is. 30:27-31; Ps. 29:3-10],*

and all the birds gorged themselves on their flesh" (Ps. 110:3; Rev. 17:14; 19:19-21; cf. Is. 13:1-22; 42:13-17; Ezek. 37:1-10).

Are you in the army of Christ or in the army of the beast and the Antichrist? The LORD planned this day of vengeance long ago and will execute it, it will not fail; *"For the revelation awaits an appointed time; it speaks of the end and will not prove false. Though it linger, wait for it; it will certainly come and will not delay."* Again, it is written, ***"The LORD has done what he planned; he has fulfilled his word, which he decreed long ago.*** *He has overthrown you without pity, he has let the enemy gloat over you, he has exalted the horn of your foes"* (Hab. 2:3; Lam. 2:17; cf. Jer. 50:45; 51:12).

The Battle Events:

Jesus Christ is described as having a winnowing fork, with which to winnow the peoples of the earth; *"His winnowing fork is in his hand, and he will clear his threshing floor, gathering his wheat into the barn and burning up the chaff with unquenchable fire"* (Matt. 3:11-12).

"'Surely the day is coming; it will burn like a furnace. All the arrogant and every evildoer will be stubble, and that day that is coming will set them on fire,' says the LORD Almighty. 'Not a root or a branch will be left to them. *But for you who revere my name, the sun of righteousness will rise with healing in its wings. And you will go out and leap like calves released from the stall. Then you will go and trample down the wicked; they will be ashes under the soles of your feet on the day when I do these things,' says the LORD Almighty"* (Mal. 4:1-3).

Thus, Christ will rescue his own but will show fury and wrath to his enemies—he will burn them up with fire;

"When you see this, your heart will rejoice and you will flourish like grass; the hand of the LORD will be made known to his servants, but his fury will be shown to his foes. See, the LORD is coming with fire, and his chariots are like a whirlwind; he will bring down his anger with fury and his rebuke with flames of fire. ***For with fire and with his sword the LORD will execute judgment upon all men and***

many will be those slain by the LORD. ... And they [the redeemed] *will go out and look upon the dead bodies of those who rebelled against me; their worm will not die, nor will their fire be quenched, and they will be loathsome to all mankind'"* (Is. 66:14-18, 24-25).

Christ will tread the winepress of God's wrath; *"I looked, and there before me was a white cloud, and seated on the cloud was one 'like a son of man'* [cf. Ezek. 1:25-28; Dan. 7:13; Rev. 1:13-15] *with a crown of gold on his head and a sharp sickle in his hand. Then another angel came out of the temple and called out in a loud voice to him who was sitting on the cloud, 'Take your sickle and reap, because the time to reap has come, for the harvest of the earth is ripe.' So he who was seated on the cloud swung his sickle over the earth and the earth was harvested. Another angel came out of the temple in heaven, and he too had a sharp sickle. Still another angel, who had charge of the fire, came from the altar and called in a loud voice to him who had the sharp sickle, 'Take your sharp sickle and gather the clusters of grapes from the earth's vine, because its grapes are ripe.' The angel swung his sickle on the earth, gathered its grapes and threw them into the great winepress of God's wrath. They were trampled in the winepress outside the city, and their blood flowed out of the press, rising as high as the horses' bridles for a distance of 1,600 stadia* [about 180 miles or 300 km]*"* (Rev. 14:14-20; cf. Is. 10:1-4; 24:1- 13; 34:1-8; 63:1-7; 66:14-16; Jer. 30:23-24).

The birds of the air will feast (the Great Supper of God) on the flesh of those slain; *"And I saw an angel standing in the sun, who cried in a loud voice to all the birds flying in midair, 'Come, gather together for **the great supper of God,** so that you may eat the flesh of kings, generals, and mighty men, of horses and their riders, and the flesh of all people, free and slave, small and great'"* (Rev. 19:17-18).

The Lord Jesus Christ would be like the kinsman Redeemer; the commander of the LORD'S army, the angel of the LORD that paves the way (Jos. 5:13-14). **No nation or king will be saved by the strength of his army, no matter its military genius and arsenal—nuclear or bioweapons or smart bombs or even A-bombs** (Ps. 33:16-17; Jer. 9:23-24). There will be complete victory

(Rev. 17:14; 19:11-21)! **The zeal of the LORD Almighty will do this** (Is. 37:32,36; where the LORD killed 185,000 Assyrian soldiers in one night!). On the battle of Armageddon, Keith Harris comments;

"The battle of Armageddon will be the meeting of the allied armies of the Antichrist and their confrontation with Christ. There is no evidence that the kings of the earth, or the beast, or false prophet launches an attack. The armies of the world are only seen gathering for the battle. **Due to the overwhelming fierceness of Christ, even if the armies of the world attack, the battle is seemingly over before it begins.** ...

The Antichrist, driven by the power of the satanic forces within him, and his cohorts, evidently expect a great war, but are ignorant of the outcome."[cccliii] *(emphasis mine)*

The Wicked or Enemies of Christ are Slain

The dragon (Satan), the first beast, to whom the dragon gave his power, great authority, and throne (Rev. 13:1-2), the second lamblike beast or false prophet that speaks like a dragon, and their foremost leader, the Antichrist, will all be captured and thrown alive into the lake of fire (Rev. 19:20- 21)! Christ will slay them and all the wicked with the breath of his mouth, the sword of his lips, that is, with the word of God (Is. 11:4b; 17:12-14; 27:1; 30:27-33; cf. Ps. 29; Job 34:20; 2 Thess. 2:8).

The Lord Jesus Christ had said; *"I saw Satan fall like lightning from heaven"* (Luke 10:18). Satan will fall in the sight of all watching, that is, the entire world (Is. 14:12,19-22; Ezek. 28:16,18-19; apparently, this will be a television event!). Paul equally said; *"The God of peace will soon crush Satan under your feet"* (Rom. 16:20). Again, we read about the arrest of Satan;

"And I saw an angel coming down out of heaven, having the key to the Abyss and holding in his hand a great chain. He seized the dragon, that ancient serpent, who is the devil, or Satan, and bound him for a thousand years. He threw him into the Abyss, and locked and sealed it over him, to keep him from deceiving the nations anymore until the thousand years were ended" (Rev. 20:1-3).

And so will come the end of Satan and the beasts that operate under his power and authority. Evil, ignorance, rebellion, disobedience, idolatry, and the like, will no longer reign over the nations. The LORD will consume his enemies and evil with fire, which is his Word, for the LORD is a consuming fire--*Yahweh Kanna* (Jer. 20:9; cf. Heb. 12:29; Deut. 4:24).

Christ's Enemies Will Become his Footstool

"The LORD said to my Lord: 'Sit at my right hand until I make your enemies a footstool for your feet.' The LORD will extend your mighty scepter from Zion; you will rule in the midst of your enemies."

"This is what the Sovereign LORD says: 'See, I will beckon to the Gentiles, I will lift up my banner to the peoples; they will bring your sons in their arms and carry your daughters on their shoulders. Kings will be your foster fathers, and their queens your nursing mothers. **They will bow down before you with their faces to the ground; they will lick the dust at your feet.** *Then you will know that I am the LORD; those who hope in me will not be disappointed"* (Ps. 110:1-2; Is. 49:22-23; cf. Heb. 2:5-8; Ps. 45:5; Dan. 2:46-47; 1 Co. 15:24-25).

Cleansing the Earth and Refining Zion:

The earth will be devastated and tried with fire (Is. 24 and 34). In fact, it will be recreated, for God will create a new heaven and a new earth (Is. 65:17-25; Rev. 20:1-3). As it is written of the original creation at the beginning; *"Now the earth was formless and empty, darkness was over the surface of the deep, and the Spirit of God was hovering over the waters. And God said, 'Let there be light and there was light. God saw that the light was good, and he separated the light from the darkness"* (Gen. 1:2-5). So also, the earth has now become formless and empty, that is, moral chaos (and will be finally devastated by the Lord), and the darkness (spiritual darkness) is over the deep (abyss—ignorance of God and his word; cf. Rev. 9:1-11) and the Spirit of God is hovering over the waters (peoples of the earth, with the Bible and Holy Spirit available to all), but they do not understand it. Once more, God will say "let there be light," and the light will overcome all spiritual darkness (sin and evil) as we enter the Millennium. As it is written about the beginning of the Millennium; *"Arise, shine, for your light has come, and the glory of the LORD rises upon you* [Christ and his followers]. *See, darkness covers the earth and thick darkness is over the peoples* [spiritual darkness—moral chaos], *but the LORD rises upon you. Nations will come to your light, and kings to the brightness of your dawn"* (Is. 60:1-3). Furthermore, like at the original creation, God will separate the darkness (moral chaos, sin and evil) from the light (millennial kingdom of light and righteousness). It is not as though the light will shine only now, it has been shining in the darkness, but the darkness has not understood it. As it is written; **"In him** [Jesus Christ] **was life, and the life was the light of men. The light shines in the darkness, but the darkness has not understood it.** *... He was in the world, and though the world was made through him,* **the world did not recognize him"** (John 1:4-5,10). Peter wrote about people's ignorance of this light that is shining in the dark place; *"And we have* **the word of the prophets** *made more certain, and you will do well to pay attention to it, as to* **a light shining in a dark place, until the day dawns** [second coming and beginning of Millennium] *and the morning star* [cf. Rev. 2:28; 22:16] *rises in your hearts"* (2 Pet. 1:19). Paul also admonishes us about this coming light in Romans 13:11-14).

Zion (both earthly and heavenly) will be thoroughly refined and cleansed forever. As it is written; *"'I will turn my hand against you; I will thoroughly purge away your dross and remove all your impurities. I will restore your judges as in days of old, your counselors as at the beginning. Afterward you will be called the City of Righteousness, the Faithful City. Zion will be redeemed with justice, her penitent ones with righteousness"* (Is. 1:25-27). The women of Zion (Is. 3:16-4:6), who are now haughty, and who walk with outstretched necks and flirt with their eyes and walk with mincing steps, and delight in fashion and beauty finery (ankle ornaments, bangles, headbands, necklaces, earrings, bracelets, veils, headdresses, ankle chains, sashes, perfumes, charms, signet rings, nose rings, fine robes, capes, cloaks, purses, mirrors, linen garments, tiaras, shawls), will be judged and humbled. The LORD will seize their beauty boxes, finery, and charms, because they delight in these things and neglect the LORD. It is written; *"Charm is deceptive, and beauty is fleeting;*

but a woman who fears the LORD is to be praised" (Pr. 31:30; cf. 1 Tim. 2:9-10; 1 Pet. 3:1-6). These fashion-and-beauty-infatuated women will be refined with fire; *"The Lord will wash away the filth of the women of Zion; he will cleanse the bloodstains from Jerusalem by a spirit of judgment and a spirit of fire"* (Is. 4:4). The Lord will rebuke and chastise the complacent women in Zion, who now feel secure and do not care about the things of the LORD (Is. 32:9-20). The LORD, the King, will terrify sinners in Zion and will consume them with fire, he will thoroughly purge them and burn up the chaff (Is. 33:10-24). Jerusalem or earthly Zion will be the holy city, it will be exalted forever, and it will be freed from all its enemies. Yes, Mount Zion will be a holy mountain to the LORD, and from it he will raise a banner for the nations (Is. 52:1-12). The LORD will shake the earth so that what is temporal should be removed and what is eternal should be established firmly (Hag. 2:6-9; cf. Heb. 12:25-27; Mal. 3:2-5). During all this cleansing, the righteous will be redeemed, and they shall receive their eternal salvation (Is. 11:10-16; 35:3-10; 59:16-21; 62:11- 12; 65:11-16).

CHAPTERS 20

THE MILLENNIUM

The millennium is the physical kingdom of God to be inaugurated on earth under the kingship of the Holy One, his Majesty, Supremacy, and Highness, Jesus Christ, The Righteous One. The kingdom will cover the whole earth and replace all the present kingdoms or nations of the world. It will destroy their evil scheming and hatred toward each other, and the remnant of the nations will serve and worship the one True God, Yahweh, God Almighty. The Millennium is the prelude to eternity, during which many things will be set right and the saved made ready for eternal worship in the kingdom of heaven. The long awaited prayer; *"Our Father in heaven, hallowed be your name, your kingdom come, your will be done on earth as it is in heaven,"* will be answered (Matt. 6:9-10).

The Kingdom of God (or The Kingdom of Heaven)

What is the Kingdom of God or the Kingdom of Heaven? The kingdom of God is the royal reign or rule of God. At present, that reign is primarily in the hearts of men, who believe in Jesus--it is not visible. When was the kingdom of God instituted on earth? The kingdom was instituted on earth by the first coming of Jesus (beginning of his earthly ministry). Jesus was the King and the kingdom of God among the people (Matt. 12:28). However, the kingdom was not instituted in its fullness, because he asked us to continue to pray; "your kingdom come." It will be fully established during the Millennium. It is here but not yet here ("already not yet," as theologians express it)!

What did John the Baptist and Jesus say about the Kingdom of God?

John the Baptist: *"In those days John the Baptist came, preaching in the Desert of Judea and saying, 'Repent, for the kingdom of heaven is near'"* (Matt. 3:1-2).

Jesus Christ: *"From that time on Jesus began to preach, 'Repent, for the kingdom of heaven is near'"* (Matt. 4:17). He instructed the disciples when he sent them out to preach; *"As you go, preach the message: 'The kingdom of heaven is near'"* (Matt. 10:7). Jesus also said: *"From the days of John the Baptist until now, the kingdom of heaven has been forcefully advancing, and forceful men lay hold of it"* (Matt: 11:12)

How does one gain entrance into the Kingdom of God? Repentance from sin and believing in Jesus Christ (you must be born again) is the only guarantee to enter and experience the kingdom of God. Jesus used many parables to teach about the Kingdom of God (Matt. 13:24-30 and 36-43; 13:31-32; 13:33; 13:44, 45). The kingdom began 2000 years ago and will soon be consummated with the inauguration of the King of kings and his Millennial Kingdom.

The Age to Come

It is important to note that Jesus focused his teaching on the present age and how it will end. He gave some promises that will be fulfilled in the age to come (Mark 10:29-30; Matt. 19:27-29). The biggest promise is in John 14:1-3, where he says he was going to prepare a place for believers. This age will be introduced after the Great Tribulation or the day of the Lord in which the whole earth will be tried and refined as previously discussed.

Entrance Into the Age to Come

The initial entrance into the kingdom of God as stated above is repentance from sins and believing in Jesus Christ alone for salvation. Jesus invites whoever wants to be saved to come to him (Is. 55:1; Rev. 22:17; Matt 11:28-30). The Bible makes it clear that we were saved, we are being saved, and we shall be saved. (1) **We**

were saved (Eph. 1:13; 2:5,8; Tit 3:5), (2) **We are being saved** (1 Pet. 1:9; Phil. 1:6; 2:12,13; 1 Co. 1:18), and (3) **We shall be saved;** that is, persevering to the end (Matt. 24:13). Believers shall inherit salvation and Jesus Christ is bringing salvation with him (Mark 10:29-30; Heb.1:14; 9:28; 1 Pet 1:5; Rom. 8:23-25; 13:11; 1 Thess. 5:9; 2 Thess. 2:13). Believing in Jesus, therefore, is the guarantee to enter the Age to Come. Those to be excluded from the age to come are listed in the following verses: 1 Corinthians 6:9-10; Rev. 21:8; and 22:15.

The Nature of the Millennium

The Bible does not give the details about the Millennium, but the most striking thing is that Jesus Christ himself will be present. He will rule as King of kings and Lord of lords and as son of David (Ps. 2, 72). He will be the ideal King and will rule the world in justice, equity, righteousness, and with an Iron Scepter, which is the Word of God (Rev. 19:15-16). The Millennium will be a time of righteousness: of righteous judgment; of peace among wildlife (perfect environment); of peace among nations (Is. 11, 12). Nations will flock to Jesus Christ for righteousness and will praise God (Is. 30:19- 26; 32:1-8). It will be a time of restoration (Is. 35; 49:8ff; 54; 62); a time of everlasting salvation (Is. 51:1-16); a time of glory in Zion (Is. 60); a time of universal knowledge of God (Is. 11:9; Hab. 2:14; Jer. 31:33-34; Heb. 10:16); a time of prosperity to all nations (Ps. 72:7, 16); a time of new creation and long life (Is. 65:17-25); and a time when God will lift the veil from his face (Is. 25:7; Ezek. 39:29).

THE KING Will Reign

THE KING; Psalm 45: His Majesty will defend the cause of **truth, humility, and righteousness**; *"Gird your sword upon your side, O mighty one; clothe yourself with splendor and majesty. **In your majesty ride forth victoriously in behalf of truth, humility and righteousness;** let your right hand display awesome deeds"* (vv.3-4). It is evident that those who love lies and tell lies, and the proud and unrighteous, will have no place in the King's Kingdom of truth and righteousness. The King himself is God; *"Your throne, O God, will* *last for ever and ever; **a scepter of justice will be the scepter of your kingdom. You love righteousness and hate wickedness;** therefore God, your God, has set you above your companions by anointing you with the oil of joy"* (vv.6-7). The king will seek justice for all, especially for the poor, who are oppressed by the rich through unjust laws, unjust trade, and exploitation.

THE KING; Psalm 72: The King will rule the whole world, and all will serve him because **he will defend the cause of the needy, the afflicted, the oppressed, and the despised. Justice and righteousness** will be his standard virtues.

THE KING: He is the LORD (I AM) or Yahweh or Jehovah; The King of Glory; The LORD God Almighty; God; Mighty God; God Almighty; LORD Most High (Ps. 9:7-10; 10:16; 24; 46; 47; 48; 75; 93; 95; 96; 97; 99; Is. 24:23; Is. 43:15; Lam. 5:19; Mic. 4:7; Zech. 14:9; 1 Tim. 1:17; Ps. 24:1, 7-8; Ps. 47).

THE KING: Is Mighty God, Everlasting Father, Prince of Peace, the Universal Governor (Is. 9:6-7).

*"For to us a child is born, to us a son is given, **and the government will be on his shoulders. And he will be called Wonderful Counselor, Mighty God, Everlasting Father, Prince of Peace. Of the increase of his government and peace there will be no end.** He will reign on David's throne and over his kingdom, **establishing and upholding it with justice and righteousness** from that time on and forever. The zeal of the LORD Almighty will accomplish this."*

THE KING: Is The Prince, The Prince of princes (Ezek. 44:2,3; 45:13-46:18; Dan. 8:23-25).

THE KING: Is My Servant David (Ps. 89:14-52; Jer. 30:9; Ezek. 37:24-28).

THE KING: Is My Servant (Is. 42:1-9; 49:1-7; 50:1-10; 52:13).

THE KING: Is Son/Branch of David (2 Sam. 7:11-16; Is. 16:4b-5; Jer. 23:5-8; 33:14-18; Zech. 3:8).

THE KING: Is The Anointed One/Lord/Son (Ps. 2:4; 110:1; Mal. 3:1).

THE KING: Is The Anointed Most Holy One (Dan. 9:24).

THE KING: Is A Leader raised from among the people (Jer. 30:21).

THE KING: Is A Son of Man (Ezek. 1:25-28; Dan. 7:9-14,21-27; Matt. 25:31; Luke 18:8; Rev.

THE KING: Is A Shepherd (Ps. 23; Is. 40:10-11; Jer. 31:10-14; Ezek. 34:7-31; Mic. 5:1-5a; 7:14-20; John 10:11-16; Rev. 7:13-17).

THE KING: Is The King of kings and Lord of lords (1 Tim. 6:15-16; Rev. 19:16).

THE KING: Is A Judge by Appointment (Ps. 2:6-7; 89:26-27; John 5:19-23,27; Acts 17:31; Heb. 1:2; 3:1-2).

THE KING: The LORD on behalf of the King (Ps. 89:19ff; Is. 60:1-18).

THE KING: His Throne (1 Ch. 29:23; Ps. 9:7-20; 45:4-6; 89:14; Is. 16:5; 66:1; Ezek. 43:7). The Throne of the LORD our God belongs to the Son, which in turn belongs to the believers! (Rom. 8:14-17; 2 Tim. 2:12; Rev. 2:26-27; 3:21).

THE KING: The Scepter; His Authority and Rule: The Iron Scepter (Gen. 49:10; Num. 24:17; Ps. 2:8-9; 45:6; 110:2; Heb. 1:8; Rev. 2:26-27). The Scepter is the Word of God (Rev. 2:12,16; 19:13, 15, 21; Heb. 4:12-13; John 12:47-48).

THE KING: All these titles referring to the same person? Yes! The LORD, the Lord, is one but with distinction! The Father and the Son are one but distinguished! As we have already seen, The LORD, and the Lord is King, Savior, Judge; in fact, the Lord (Son) is all that the LORD (Father) is (Tit. 1:13; 1 John 5:20; Rev. 1:8,17-18; Is. 44:6; John 10:30; 12:44-45; Eph. 4:5-6). God the Father and the Son/Lamb are distinguished (1 Co. 15:24,28; Rev. 1:1; 4:8-5:14). However, seeing the Son means seeing the Father (John 14:8-11).

The SON is the EXACT REPRESENTATION OF THE FATHER, his being and all his attributes (Heb. 1:3; Col. 1:19; 2:9-10). The Lord/Son comes in the name of the LORD/Father (Ps. 118:22-26; cf. Matt. 21:9; 23:39). Did you get what Colossians 2:9-10 says about believers and the fullness of Christ? *"For **in Christ all the fullness of the Deity lives** in bodily form, and **you have been given fullness in Christ,** who is the head over every power and authority* [all world powers visible and invisible]. *"* Christ has the fullness of deity (Godhead) and believers have the fullness of Christ, and hence ....

THE KING: His Character

The King grew in wisdom and strength and was in favor with men and God (1 Sam. 2:26; 3:19-21; cf. Luke 2:52; Is. 42:1-3). He is an obedient student of the Word of God, that is, he is very studious (Is. 49:1-7; 50:4-5; Ps. 119 esp. vv.97-104). His Wisdom conforms to the prophesies about him (Is. 52:13- 15; 53:2-3, 11-12). He is very dependent on the Word of God (Deut. 17:14-20; Matt. 4:1-11; John 5:30; 7:16-18; 8:15-16; 12:47-50; 14:31). He is humble and meek (Matt. 11:28-30; Phil. 2:5-11).

THE KING: His Kingdom and Mission

When heaven touches or unites with earth (or when earth is heavenized, as one man has put it)— when the King smites and sweeps away the kingdoms of men at Armageddon, he will inaugurate the physical kingdom of God on earth as recorded in the following verses (Dan. 2:34-35, 44-457:17-18, 23-27).

The Lord had asked us to pray that his will be done on earth as it is in heaven and that his kingdom should come. This time around, the kingdom would have come and the will of God in heaven will be fully realized on earth as heaven and earth are united (Rev. 11:15; 21:1-4).

Like was the case in Eden, God will dwell with men again. He will tabernacle in our midst and the mysteries of the ages will be revealed. The folly of men will be cast aside, and the righteous will shine like the brightness of the stars for ever and ever.

THE KING Will be The Universal Master and Teacher (Matt. 23:8-10): He will teach the peoples and there will be universal knowledge of God. God will remove the veil from his face and the people will all see and know him (Is. 60:2; 25:7; Ezek. 39:29). The King will teach the inhabitants of the earth, especially believers, to know Yah forever. They will be full of the knowledge of the LORD. The ignorant will understand, and rash minds will understand; the stammering lips will be fluent; fools and scoundrels will no longer be called noble (Jer. 31:31ff; Heb. 8:8-12; Is. 30:19-26; 54:13; 32:1-8). The earth will be filled with the knowledge of the LORD as the waters cover the seas (Is. 11:9; Hab. 2:14). The light will shine in the darkness (Is. 9:2; 60:1-3). Goodbye to the age of ignorance!

I have realized that in many cases, if not all, ignorance is a choice. When we (my wife and I) had our daughter in February of 2003, my father-in-law gave us a digital camera so that we could send pictures of the grand daughter to them. The camera was with us for almost three years, but I could not operate it effectively! When it got bad, a different one was bought. In less than a day after looking at the operation manual, I could do whatever I wanted with the camera. Then I turned to my wife and said; **"Dear, you know what; ignorance is a choice!"** Life has its operation manual written by the creator of life himself, God. To understand life, you must know the author's operation manual. There are millions and even billions today, who have remained ignorant even when the word of life (Bible) lies in the streets (Pr. 1:20-22; 8:1-5)! They have buried their heads in the sand like an ostrich. Ignorance, especially biblical ignorance, is alarming in our days--it can be called rightly, abysmal ignorance. This ignorance or biblical illiteracy is made worse by religion. People practice religion (traditions and works) rather than seek the righteousness of God that comes by faith alone in Jesus Christ. Yet at the same time, they sincerely think that they know already. This only makes me to lament; "The most dangerous ignorance is the ignorance of one's ignorance." That is, they don't know, and they don't know that they don't know, especially deceived by the fact that they think they know already! That is the greatest danger to mankind—religion! However, when the King is revealed, even the most ignorant will know-- they will understand.

THE KING Will be The True Shepherd: Most of the present shepherds (priest, pastors, theologians, etc.) have misled and scattered the sheep of the LORD'S pasture, but the King, when he comes, will search for them, and gather them. He will feed them good food and will never let them stray again. He will lift them on his shoulders and curdle with them and dandle them (Ezek. 34; Ps. 23; John 10). They will listen to his voice forever.

THE KING Will be The Righteous Judge: In his reign righteousness and justice will prevail, as it is written of him; *"Righteousness and justice are the foundation of your throne; love and faithfulness go before you"* (Ps. 89:14). The King will match forth victoriously on behalf of truth, humility, and righteousness, and will establish justice in all the earth (Ps. 45:4, 6-7; cf. Rev. 19:11; Ps. 95:13; Is. 11:1-5; 32:1, 14-20; 33:5-6, 15-17; 42:3-4). We had seen in previous chapters of this book that justice is one of God's greatest requirements from man, yet it is far from us. Habakkuk cried out; *"How long, O LORD, must I call for help, but you do not listen? Or cry out to you, 'Violence!' but you do not save? Why do you make me look at injustice? Why do you tolerate wrong? Destruction and violence are before me; there is strife, and conflict abounds. Therefore the law is paralyzed, and justice never prevails. The wicked hem in the righteous, so that justice is paralyzed"* (1:2-4). Today, justice is far from us and indeed, justice is paralyzed! Even when politicians demand justice, it is to favor them and their constituencies or countries in most cases. But the King will bring justice without favoritism or partiality to the weakest and most un-represented of the earth, irrespective of their ethnicity or nationality. The King has in mind all the peoples of the earth and will not favor some over others. This is the kind of justice that is demanded of those who know Jesus Christ. Jesus Christ requires us to show justice, mercy, and faithfulness. We are to do what is right and just in all circumstances, even when the right thing hurts us or makes us unpopular.

In their struggle to define justice, one of Plato's interlocutors said; "I proclaim that justice is nothing else than the interest of the stronger."[cccliv] He also stated that; "… in all states there is the same principle of justice, which is the interest of the government; and as the government must be supposed to have power, the only reasonable conclusion is, that everywhere there is one principle of justice, which is the interest of the stronger."[ccclv] We may all thrash his statements just as his other interlocutors did, but at the end of the day, we shall all realize that there is some truth in his statements, especially as concerns justice in our world today. The weak and oppressed hardly get justice and most who insist on justice, do so for some self-interest. We do not have time here to elaborate on these statements in respect to crime (certain peoples, especially those who cannot buy their way, that is, the poor, often do not get justice) and international justice, which is mostly for the interests of the strong nations. Some nations operate within international law, but others operate above international law. Thus, there is a sense of injustice in our practice of justice today. However, the King will show justice of all kinds: criminal justice—no longer will the innocent be condemned and the guilty acquitted because the guilty rich can bribe their way or are considered important; justice in trade--no more unbalanced trade because Tyre and Babylon and her allies that defrauded and robbed the nations and crushed the poor (Jer. 51:34; Rev. 18:11- 17a,23b; Ezek. 28:16-18), would have been crushed and destroyed themselves. As it is written; ***"For I, the LORD, love justice; I hate robbery and iniquity"*** (Is. 61:8). There will be no more exploitation, robbery, cheating, and such associated evils. **The King will judge the world with EQUITY or FAIRNESS—TRUE JUSTICE for ALL.**

*"Say among the nations, '**The LORD reigns**.' The world is firmly established, it cannot be moved; **he will judge the peoples with equity**." "... let them sing before the LORD, for he comes to judge the earth. **He will judge the world with righteousness and the peoples with equity**." "The King is mighty, **he loves justice--you have established equity; ...**"* (Ps. 96:10; 98:9; 99:4).

He will bring justice to the poor, the oppressed, and the exploited; for the rich of this world now trample the poor, and the spoil of the poor is in their houses (James 5:1-6; Mal. 3:5 Is. 3:13-15; Ps. 9:7-12; 12:5; 22:25-31; 72:2-7, 12-14; 82:2-4; Is. 11:4; 41:17-20; 58:6-10; Matt. 5:3-12; Luke 6:20-21). The King will free the captives, the broken hearted, the prisoners, the downtrodden, and the like (Is. 42:6-7; 61:1-2a).

The King will judge between the nations and settle disputes for many. All who mourn and are landless (especially those displaced by ruthless colonial occupiers), will at last find justice. Finally, there will be complete disarmament, beginning with the strongest and nuclear power nations. They will give up their arms and give the earth a rest from nuclear spills, radiation, and pollution (Is. 2:2-4; Mic. 4:1-5). He will separate the sheep from the goats among the nations (Mal. 3:14-18; Matt. 7:21-23; 25:31-46).

Matthew 5:3-12 will be fulfilled finally—the poor in spirit will inherit the kingdom of God; those who mourn will be comforted; the meek will inherit the earth, those who hunger and thirst for righteousness will be filled; the merciful will be shown mercy; the pure in heart will see God; and the righteous, who are now persecuted, will receive their reward.

THE KING Will be The Restorer: The King will restore and rebuild the desolated places and ruined cities (Is. 49:6-26; 61:2b-62:12; Jer. 30; 31,33; Ezek. 11:16-25; Amos 9:11-15). He will restore the LORD'S Sabbaths and the Feast of Tabernacles will be celebrated forever!

THE KING Will be The Great Physician and Giver of Eternal Life. The King will wipe away all tears from the eyes of his people and sorrows will be gone forever and there will be perfect health in the Kingdom/Zion (Is. 25:8; 35:5-6; 33:24; Mic. 4:6-8; Rev. 21:4). No barrenness or miscarriages or curse will occur again (Is 54:1; Ex. 23:25-26; Rev. 22:3). The last enemy, **DEATH, will be swallowed up in VICTORY, resulting in the final resurrection and eternal life** (1 Sam. 2:6; Is. 25:8a; 26:19; Ezek. 37:1-14; Dan. 12:1-2; Mark 10:29-30; John 5:24-26; 1 Co. 15:20-26;35-57; 1 Thess. 4:16-19; Rev. 20:4,6; 21:3-4). Men will once more live to be as old as a tree—**long Life** (Is. 65:20-22)!

THE KING: His Vice-Regents

Believers will rule together with the King as his Vice-regents. A new royalty will be introduced, with the lowliest of men exalted to the highest positions just because they trusted in Christ and humbled themselves; *"The LORD sends poverty and wealth; he humbles and he exalts.* ***He raises the poor from the dust and lifts the needy from the ash heaps; he seats them with princes and has them inherit a throne of honor"*** (1 Sam. 2:7-8a; cf. Dan. 4:17). The Vice-regents are all that the King is! He is the Son of God; they are the sons of God. He is the heir of God; they are co-heirs of God with him (John 1:12- 13; Rom. 8:13-17). Just as the Son is all that the Father is, so are the vice-regents like the Son in all things (John 14:20). The King is reigning, the vice-regents will reign with him too (2 Tim. 2:11-12; Rev. 1:5; 2:26-27; 20:4)! **Who are the vice-regents? All who are born again--all believers in Jesus Christ! Believers are not only Christ's servants, but his friends, his brothers, co-heirs of God with him** (John 15:13-15; James 2:23; Heb. 2:10-17; cf. Is. 8:16-18). What greater honor could we receive from the LORD, our God! The King is the High Priest of God and has made believers priests of God together with him to serve God upon the earth (1 Pet. 2:4-9; Rev. 5:9-10). He is The King and has made believers kings! All the duties of the King above will be executed by his Vice-regents because they all have the unique privilege of being co-workers with him; yes, believers are co-workers, fellow workers, with God—his workmanship. They will judge the world with him after they have received their judgment before his *bema* or judgment seat (Rom. 14:10-12; 2 Co. 5:9-10; 1 Pet. 4:17; 1 Co. 3:9-15; Eph. 2:10). In fact, believers will even judge the angels (1 Co. 6:3).

As co-heirs, the Vice-regents will inherit the King's Kingdom and the wealth of the nations. To inherit means to get possession of something—property; to receive or obtain by lot and own; to receive by legal right according to donor and recipient stipulations, especially by birthright. The son automatically inherits the father's property by birthright. The Son (Jesus Christ) deserves the right of inheritance of all the Father's property—the earth and all that is in it (Ps. 2:8; 24:1; Heb. 1:2). Because Jesus has given the right of sonship as

God's children to all who believe in him (John 1:12,13), all believers automatically inherit what is Jesus'. This inheritance is primarily a gift, not necessarily a right of sonship. It is the Father's pleasure to give you (believers) the kingdom. The kingdom of God will be given over to the saints/believers (Dan. 2:44; 7:26-27; Matt. 5:3-5; 25:34; Luke 12:32). The world or age to come (Millennium/Eternity) will be the inheritance of the saints/believers (Acts 20:32; Eph. 1:14,18; 5:5; Col. 3:24; Heb. 9:15; 12:28; 1 Pet. 1:4). The King will plunder the nations for the believers (Ex.12:35-36; Is. 18:7; 23:18; 45:14; 49:24-26; 60:5-9,16; Zech. 14:14; Rev. 21:26). This has been God's goal since he called Abraham (Gen. 15:13-14; Eccl. 2:24-26). Are you in the number?

Joy and Millennial Worship

The Millennial joy begins with the triumphal hymns of Revelation (15:3-4; 19:1-8). All the Psalms, especially 98 and 111-118 will be standard hymns for millennial worship. The following millennial passages also express glimpses of the joy and worship of the redeemed (Is. 12; 25-26; 27:13; 30:29; 35; 40:29-31; 42:10-17; 54-55; 60, esp. v.5; the hearts of believers will throb and swell with joy; 63:7-64:12; Ezek. 40-48; Zeph. 3:9-20). All these passages and many more will be recited in Zion as the redeemed come in with dancing before their God, the King. The saved will enter Zion with singing; *"The ransomed of the LORD will return. They will enter Zion with singing; everlasting joy will crown their heads. Gladness and joy will overtake them, and sorrow and sighing will flee away"* (Is. 51:11). Blessings will flow from Zion to the nations (Is. 2:2-3; Joel 3:17-21). The children of Zion will celebrate the Sabbaths of Yahweh (Ex. 16:23-25; 20:10-11; 31:13; Lev. 23:3; 25; Is. 58:13-13; 66:23; Mal. 4:4; the Millennium itself is the Sabbath rest of Yahweh; Heb. 4:1-11), and the Feast of Tabernacles forever (Lev. 23:33-43; Zech. 14:16-21).

New Things

The LORD will do many new things when he comes as King. It will be a totally new world with the old order gone forever. For professed believers who are comfortable with the present order of things, it will be a shock since they have allied with the world.

A New Thing For All

Yahweh is going to create a new heaven and a new earth. This is strictly in terms of the governance of the earth. All wicked rulership and evil of all forms will be eliminated! (Matt. 13:40-42; Is. 65:17-25; Rev. 21-22).

A New Thing For Israel

"I am the LORD; that is my name! I will not give my glory to another or my praise to idols. See, the former things have taken place, and new things I declare; before they spring into being I announce them to you" (Is. 42:8-9). *"This is what the LORD says— your Redeemer, the Holy One of Israel: 'For your sake I will send to Babylon and bring down as fugitives all the Babylonians, in the ships in which they took pride. I am the LORD, your Holy One, Israel's Creator, your King.' This is what the LORD says—he who made a way through the sea, a path through the mighty waters, who drew out the chariots and horses, the army and reinforcements together, and they lay there, never to rise again, extinguished, snuffed out like a wick: 'Forget the former things; do not dwell on the past. See, I am doing a new thing! Now it springs up; do you not perceive it? I am making a way in the desert and streams in the wasteland. ...' 'I, even I, am he who blots out your transgressions, for my own sake, and remembers your sins no more'"* (Is. 43:14-21, 25; Is. 48:3-11).

Salvation of Israel

The Israelites rejected Jesus the Messiah when he came to them the first time (John 1:11). They will accept him when he comes as King and Lord, to restore all things (Matt. 23:37-39; Is. 10:20-23; 11:11- 16; 14:1-3; 43:1-7; 49:8-23; 59:20-21; Joel 2:16-3:21; Zech. 10:6-12; Rom. 11:11-32). Only those who will finally reject Jesus Christ at his coming will have their part with sinners and hypocrites in the lake of burning sulfur.

A New Thing For Israel in the Grave

THE KING will **restore and rebuild their desolated places** (Is. 49:6-26; 61:2b-62:12; Jer. 30-31; 33; Ezek. 11:16-25; Amos 9:11-15). He will restore all the tribes and clans of Israel—**all Israel shall be saved** (Rom. 11:25-29; Ezek. 37:1-14). We shall see and know where Israel was exiled to. **Israel** (in the grave) **and Judah** (Jews) will be **reunited** as one kingdom as it was under David, as David is raised to take leadership again (Ezek. 37:15-28). Yahweh will pour out his Spirit abundantly upon them and will give them a heart that will acknowledge, know, and serve him forever (Ezek. 11:16-20; 39:25-29; Jer. 32:37-42).

The emphasis here is that it is God himself who will restore Israel and give them a new heart that will obey him. He will remove their stony heart and give them an undivided heart of flesh that will fear him forever. He will inspire them to fear him and give them singleness of heart. God will do this for the sake of his holy and great name and for his majestic glory.

THE KING: And the Nations (that survive his judgment)

THE KING: To Raise a banner (flag) for the Nations (Yahweh-Nissi—The LORD is My Banner; Ex. 17:15-16);

"He lifts up a banner for the distant nations, he whistles for those at the ends of the earth. Here they come, swiftly and speedily!" "He will raise a banner for the nations and gather the exiles of Israel; he will assemble the scattered people of Judah from the four quarters of the earth (Is. 5:26; 11:12; cf. Matt. 24:31).

THE KING: To be Worshipped by the Nations

*"As I looked, 'thrones were set in place, and the Ancient of Days took his seat. His clothing was as white as snow; the hair of his head was like wool. ... In my vision at night I looked, and there before me was **one like a son of man,** coming with the clouds of heaven. He approached the Ancient of Days and was led into his presence. He was given authority, glory and sovereign power; **all peoples, nations and men of every language worshiped him.** His dominion is an*

everlasting dominion that will not pass away, and his kingdom is one that will never be destroyed. ... His kingdom will be an everlasting kingdom, and **all rulers will worship and obey him"** (Dan. 7:13-14,27-28; cf. Ps. 22:27-31; 45:17; 86:9- 10; Ps. 100; Is. 66:23; Zech. 8:23; 14:16; Phil. 2:9-11; Rev. 15:2-4; 21:24-26).

We can hardly imagine what he will be called! He will be called His Eminence, Pre-eminence, Preponderance, The Most High, The Most Holy. All thrones (presidencies), powers, principalities, and authorities (all invisible powers), were created by him and for him, and he will reign above them all (Eph. 6:12; Col. 1:16-18; Rev. 4:11). He is before all things and all things were created by him and in him, they have their being, and in him all things hold together. He is the center of the created order, both visible and invisible.

THE KING: To Teach the Nations

"O LORD, my strength and my fortress, my refuge in time of distress, **to you the nations will come from the ends of the earth and say, 'Our fathers possessed nothing but false gods. Worthless idols that did them no good.** *Do men make their own gods? Yes, but they are not gods!'* **'Therefore I will teach them--this time I will teach them my power and might. Then they will know that my name is the LORD"** (Jer. 16:19-21).

THE KING: To Judge between the Nations

"He will judge between the nations and will settle disputes for many peoples. They will beat their swords into plowshares and their spears into pruning hooks. Nation will not take up sword against nation, nor will they train for war anymore" (Is. 2:4). Finally, there will be disarmament! He will scatter the nations that delight in war (Ps. 68:30).

THE KING: To Reign over the Nations

"The LORD reigns, he is robed in majesty; the LORD is robed in majesty and is armed with strength. The world is firmly established; it cannot be moved. Your throne was established long ago; you are from all eternity. ... Your statutes stand firm; holiness adorns your

house for endless days, O LORD" (Ps. 93). ***"The LORD reigns, let
the nations tremble;*** *he sits enthroned between the cherubim, let the
earth shake. Great is the LORD in Zion; he is exalted over all the
nations. Let them praise your great and awesome name--he is holy.
The King is mighty, he loves justice--you have established equity; in
Jacob you have done what is just and right. Exalt the LORD our God
and worship at his footstool; he is holy. ... "* (Ps. 99; cf. Ps. 72:8-11).

THE KING: To Rule the Nations with an Iron Scepter—The Word of God

*"I will proclaim the decree of the LORD: He said to me, 'You are
my Son; today I have become your Father. Ask of me and I will make
the nations your inheritance, the ends of the earth your possession.*
***You will rule them with an iron scepter, you will dash them to pieces
like pottery.'*** *Therefore, you kings, be wise; be warned, you rulers of
the earth. Serve the LORD with fear and rejoice with trembling. Kiss
the Son, lest he be angry and you be destroyed in your way, for his
wrath can flare up in a moment. Blessed are all who take refuge in
him"* (Ps. 2:7-12; cf. Rev. 1:5; 2:26-27; 19:15).

The Son of Man will come with great power and glory and with
his powerful angels (Matt. 24:30; 26:64; Rev. 5:12-13; 11:17). All
authority in heaven and on earth has been given to him (Matt 28:18),
and he has undisputed and unrivaled authority over the nations he
created.

THE KING: The Kings of the Nations to Bow Down Before the King and Kiss his Feet

"All kings will bow down to him and all nations will serve him"
(Ps. 72:11; cf. Is. 49:7,23; 60:10,14). *"And being found in appearance
as a man, he humbled himself and became obedient to death--even
death on a cross! Therefore God exalted him to the highest place and
gave him the name that is above every name, that* ***at the name of
Jesus every knee should bow,*** *in heaven and on earth and under the
earth, and every tongue confess that Jesus Christ is Lord, to the glory
of God the Father"* (Phil. 2:5-11).

THE KING: Those who Refuse to Worship Him Will be Afflicted with a Plague

They will perish; they will utterly be ruined; they will be dashed to pieces like pottery (Ps. 2:9). It is written;

"For the nation or kingdom that will not serve you will perish; it will be utterly ruined" (Is. 60:12). Again, *"If any of the peoples of the earth do not go up to Jerusalem to worship the King, the LORD Almighty, they will have no rain. If the Egyptian people* [prototype for all nations] *do not go up and take part, they will have no rain. The LORD will bring on them the plague he inflicted on the nations that do not go up to celebrate the Feast of Tabernacles. This will be the punishment of Egypt and the punishment of all the nations that do not go up to celebrate the Feast of Tabernacles"* (Zech. 14:17-19).

Do Not Miss the Kingdom

Amos had warned the religious hypocrites of his day of their empty worship and lip services. They were self-deceived to think that their works and religiosity will earn them favor with God. They were anxious for the day of the LORD yet lived in hypocrisy. Amos cried out;

"Woe to you who long for the day of the LORD! Why do you long for the day of the LORD? That day will be darkness, not light. It will be as though a man fled from a lion only to meet a bear, as though he entered his house and rested his hand on the wall only to have a snake bite him. Will not the day of the LORD be darkness, not light--pitch-dark, without a ray of brightness? **'I hate, I despise your religious feasts; I cannot stand your assemblies. ... Away with the noise of your songs! I will not listen to the music of your harps. But let justice roll like a river, righteousness like a never-failing stream!'"** (Amos 5:18-24).

These people were interested and passionate about religion and religious feasts: New Moon celebrations, Sabbaths; or in our day, Christmas, Easter, and the like, but were/are not interested in justice for all and righteousness. They go around crying rapture, rapture, rapture! When indeed the coming of the Lord will be wrath to them!

In the Gospels, we see a similar situation. The Jewish rulers and teachers, who were waiting for the kingdom of God, refused to enter the kingdom as presented by Jesus Christ because they had their own agendas and expectation of who the Christ should be. As a result, they missed the kingdom! Thus, the Lord warns that not all who say to him Lord, Lord, will enter the coming kingdom! There are many who are first who shall be last and many who are last who shall be first. The Kingdom will be taken away from the children of the kingdom (Christendom) and given to others, who are bringing forth fruit. The children of the kingdom will be cast out, where there will be weeping and gnashing of teeth. The Kingdom of God does not come by careful observation.

The Lord himself gave a serious warning concerning those walking the wide gate to destruction; *"Then Jesus went through the towns and villages, teaching as he made his way to Jerusalem. Someone asked him, 'Lord, are only a few people going to be saved?' He said to them, 'Make every effort to enter through the narrow door, because many, I tell you, will try to enter and will not be able to'"* (Luke 13:22-24). Why will they not be able to enter? *"Enter through the narrow gate. For wide is the gate and broad is the road that leads to destruction, and many enter through it. But small is the gate and narrow the road that leads to life, and only a few find it"* (Matt. 7:13-14). Have you found the small road and entered through the narrow gate? **Here comes the King! Come Lord Jesus!**

"Behold, I am coming soon! My reward is with me, and I will give to everyone according to what he has done. I am the Alpha and the Omega, the First and the Last, the Beginning and the End. Blessed are those who wash their robes that they may have the right to the tree of life and may go through the gates into the city. Outside are the dogs, those who practice magic arts, the sexually immoral, the murderers, the idolaters and everyone who loves and practices falsehood. I, Jesus, have sent my angel to give you this testimony for the churches. I am the Root and the Offspring of David, and the bright Morning Star" (Rev. 22:12-16)! **Amen.**

Jesus Christ says:

"I have come to bring fire on the earth, and how I wish it were already kindled! But I have a baptism to undergo, and how distressed I am until it is completed! Do you think I came to bring peace on earth? No, I tell you, but division. From now on there will be five in one family divided against each other, three against two and two against three. They will be divided, father against son and son against father, mother against daughter and daughter against mother, mother-in-law against daughter-in-law and daughter-in-law against mother-in-law" (Luke 12:49-53). **Amen!**

THE END!

Bibliography

Burke, Fred. *Africa.* Boston: Houghton Mifflin Company, 1970.

Current, Richard N., T. Harry Williams, Frank Freidel. *American History: A Survey,* 3rd ed. New York: Alfred A. Knopf Inc., 1971.

Colson, Charles, Richard John Newhaus, eds. *Evangelicals and Catholics Together.* Dallas: Word Publishing, 1995.

Douglas, J. D., ed. *The New Bible Dictionary.* Grand Rapids: Eerdmans, 1962.

Dues, Greg. *Catholic Customs & Traditions.* Mystic, CT: Twenty-Third Publications, 2000.

Fee, Gordon D., and Douglas Stuart. *How to Read the Bible for All its Worth.* 2nd ed. Grand Rapids: Zondervan, 1982.

Foxe, John. *Foxe's Book of Martyrs.* Springdale, PA: Whitaker House, 1981.

Froese, Arno. *How Democracy Will Elect the Antichrist.* West Columbia, SC: The Olive Press, 1997.

Gonzalez, Justo L. *The Story of Christianity,* Vols. 1 & 2. New York: HarperCollins Publishers, 1984.

Graham, Billy. *World Aflame.* Garden City, NY: Doubleday, 1965.

Gushee, David P. ed. *Christians & Politics Beyond the Culture Wars.* Grand Rapids: Baker Books, 2000.

Harris, Keith. *The Unveiling: A Journey Through the Book of Revelation.* West Columbia, SC: The Olive Press, 1999.

_____*The Masonic Christian Conflict Explained.* Madisonville, KY: Omega Publishing, 1993. Harrison, John B., Richard E. Sullivan, Dennis Sherman. *A Short History of Western Civilization.* 6th ed. New York: Alfred A. Knopf Inc., 1971.

Hastings, Adrian, ed. *A World History of Christianity.* Cassell, London: Wellington House, 1999.

Henry, Carl F. H. *Twilight of A Great Civilization: The Drift Toward Neo-Paganism.* Westchester, IL: Crossway Books, 1988.

Hettinga, Jan David. *Follow Me: Experience the Loving Leadership of Jesus.* Colorado Springs: NavPress, 1996.

Hunt, Dave and T. A. MacMahon. *The Seduction of Christianity.* Eugene, OR: Harvest House Publishers, 1985.

Isichei, Elizabeth. *A History of Christianity in Africa.* Grand Rapids: EERDMANS, 1995.

Johnson, John L. *The Black Biblical Heritage.* Nashville: Winston-Derek Publishers, Inc., 1994.

Johnstone, Patrick. *The Church is Bigger Than You Think.* Ross-shire, Great Britain: Christian Focus Publications, 1998.

Johnstone, Patrick, Jason Mandryk. *Operation World.* 6th ed. Waynesboro, GA: Paternoster USA, 2001.

Lazor, William Sanford, David Allan Hubbard, Frederick William Bush. *Old Testament Survey.* Grand Rapids: EERDMANS, 1982.

Mead, Frank S., Revised by Hill, Samuel S. *Handbook of Denominations in the United States.* New Tenth Edition. Nashville: Abingdon Press, 1985.

Moreau, A. Scott. *The World of the Spirits: A Biblical Study in the African Context.* Nairobi, Kenya: Evangel Publishing House, 1990.

Nash, Ronald H. *Life's Ultimate Questions: An Introduction to Philosophy.* Grand Rapids: Zondervan, 1999.

Noll, Mark A. *A History of Christianity in the United States and Canada.* Grand Rapids: EERDMANS, 1992.

Noll, Mark A., Nathan O. Hatch, George M. Marsden. *The Search For Christian America.* Colorado Springs: Helmers & Howard, 1989.

Noss, David S., John B. Noss, *A History of the World's Religions.* 9th ed. Upper Saddle River, NJ: Prentice Hall, 1994.

Olson, Roger E. *The Story of Christian Theology: Twenty Centuries of Tradition & Reform.* Downers Grove, IL: InterVarsity Press, 1999.

Rhodes, Ron. *The Challenge of the Cults and New Religions.* Grand Rapids: ZONDERVAN, 2001. Sider, Ronald J. *Rich Christians in an Age of Hunger.* Grand Rapids: Family Christian Press, 1997. Terry, John Mark, Ebbie Smith, Justice Anderson, eds. *Missiology.* Nashville: Broadman & Holman Publishers, 1998.

White E. G. *America in Prophecy.* Jemison, AL: Inspiration Books East, Inc., 1988.

Wohlberg, Steve. *End Time Delusions.* Shippensburg, PA: Treasure House, 2004.

_____*America's Fascinating Indian Heritage.* Pleasantville, New York: The Reader's Digest Association Inc.. 1978.

_____*The New Strong's Concise Concordance & Vine's Dictionary of the Bible.* Nashville: Thomas Nelson, Inc., 1997.

_____*Plato's Republic.* Jowett Translation. Clinton MA: The Colonial Press, 1968.

NOTES

[i] William Sanford Lazor, David Allan Hubbard, Frederic William Bush, *Old Testament Survey* (Grand Rapids: Eerdmans, 1982), 223.

[ii] Ibid., 164.

[iii] David s. Noss and John B. Noss, *A History of the World's Religions,* 9th ed. (Upper Saddle River, NJ: Prentice Hall, 1994), 185. (The Ten Precepts of Buddhism (only first five for laity and all ten for monks) are as follows: 1. Refrain from destroying life. 2. Do not take what is not given. 3. Abstain from unchastity. 4. Do not lie or deceive. 5. Abstain from intoxicants. 6. Eat moderately and not after noon. 7. Do not look on at dancing, singing, or dramatic spectacles. 8. Do not affect the use of garlands, scents, unguents, or ornaments. 9. Do not use high or broad beds. 10. Do not accept gold or silver.)

[iv] Ibid., 194-195. (The Eightfold Path including the following steps: 1. Right belief in the Four Noble Truths. 2. Right aspiration or purpose, resolving to overcome sensuality and all misery-producing desires. 3. Right speech. 4. Right conduct. 5. Choosing the proper occupation of one's time and energies. 6. Right effort implying untiring and unremitting intellectual alertness in discriminating between wise and unwise desires. 7. Right mindfulness—disciplined thoughts on helpful topics. 8. Right meditation or absorption—attainment of the trance-states that are advanced stages to sainthood and assurance of passage at death into Nirvana, the state of quiescence, all karma consumed, and rebirth at an end forever.)

[v] John B. Harrison, Richard E. Sullivan and Dennis Sherman, *A Short History of Western Civilization,* 6th ed. (New York: Alfred A Knopf Inc., 1971), 15.

[vi] Noss, *A History of the World's Religions,* 42-44.

[vii] Ibid., 50.

[viii] Ibid., 60.

ix   Ibid., 61.

x   Ibid., 61.

xi   Ibid., 61.

xii   Ibid., 70.

xiii   Ibid., 70.

xiv   Ibid., 72-73.

xv   Ibid., 70.

xvi   Ibid., 74.

xvii   Reader's Digest, *America's Most Fascinating Indian Heritage* (Pleasantville, New York: The Reader's Digest Association Inc., 1978), 7.

xviii   Ibid., 7.

xix   Noss, 32.

xx   Ibid., 74.

xxi   Ibid., 75.

xxii   Ibid., 76.

xxiii   Ibid., 78.

xxiv   Ibid., 79.

xxv   Ibid., 79.

xxvi   Ibid., 79.

xxvii   Scott Moreau, *The World of the Spirits: A Biblical study in the African Context* (Nairobi, Kenya: Evangel Publishing House, 1990), 100.

xxviii   Ibid., 100.

xxix   Ibid., 101.

xxx   Ibid., 102-105.

xxxi   Ibid., 102-103.

xxxii   Ibid., 104.

xxxiii   Ibid., 105.

xxxiv   Keith Harris, *The Masonic Christian Conflict Explained* (Madisonville, KY: Omega Publishing, 1993), 59.

xxxv   Justo L. Gonzalez, *The Story of Christianity, Vol. 1* (New York: HarperColins Publishers, 1984), 40.

xxxvi   Ibid., 50.

xxxvii   Ibid., 50.

xxxviii   Ibid., 51.

xxxix   Ibid., 86.

xl   Ibid., 59.

xli   Ibid., 59.

xlii   Ibid., 61.

xliii   Ibid., 161.

xliv   Ibid., 254.

xlv   Ibid., 255.

xlvi   Ibid., 257.

xlvii   Ibid., 42-43.

xlviii   Ibid., 119.

xlix   Ibid., 121.

l   Ibid., 123.

li   Patrick Johnstone, *The Church is Bigger Than You Think* (Ross-shire, Great Britain: Christian Focus Publications, 1998), 262-263.

lii   Gonzalez, vol. 1, 125.

liii   Ibid., 251.

liv   Ibid., 243.

lv   Steve Wohlberg, *End Time Delusions* (Shippensburg, PA: Treasure House, 2004), 97.

lvi   Gonzalez, vol. 1, 371-373.

lvii   Ibid., 136.

lviii   Ibid., 196.

lix   Elizabeth Isichei, *A History of Christianity in Africa* (Grand Rapids: Eerdmans, 1995), 49.

lx   Ibid., 49.

lxi   Gonzalez, vol. 1, 346.

lxii   Ibid., 347.

lxiii   Ibid., 349.

lxiv   Ibid., 349.

lxv   Ibid., 350.

lxvi   Ibid., 352.

lxvii   Ibid., 354.

lxviii   Gonzalez, *The Story of Christianity,* vol. 2, 24.

lxix   Ibid., 36.

lxx   Ibid., 52.

lxxi   Ibid., 51.

lxxii   Ibid., 56.

lxxiii   Ibid., 73.

lxxiv   Ibid., 73.

lxxv   Ibid., 77.

lxxvi   Ibid., 132.

lxxvii Ibid., 133.
lxxviii Ibid., 197.
lxxix Ibid., 198.
lxxx Ibid., 198.
lxxxi Ibid., 199.
lxxxii Ibid., 96.
lxxxiii Ibid., 107.
lxxxiv Ibid.,124.
lxxxv Harrison, *A Short History of Western* Civilization, 6th ed., 101.
lxxxvi Gonzalez, vol. 1, 366.
lxxxvii Harrison, 345.
lxxxviii Fred Burke, *Africa* (Boston: Houghton Miflin Company, 1970), 175.
lxxxix Ibid., 176.
xc Ibid., 178.
xci Ibid., 178.
xcii Ibid., 179.
xciii Harrison, 347.
xciv Ibid., 349.
xcv Ibid., 349.
xcvi Ibid., 349.
xcvii Gonzalez, vol. 1, 382.
xcviii Harrison, 603.
xcix Ibid., 613.
c Ibid., 605.
ci Ibid., 603.
cii Ibid., 352.
ciii Ibid., 603.
civ Gonzalez, vol. 1, 381.
cv Ibid., 382.
cvi Ibid., 383.
cvii Ibid., 386.
cviii Ibid., 389.
cix Ibid., 392.
cx Ibid., 392.
cxi Ibid., 393.
cxii Ibid., 394.
cxiii Ibid., 396-397.
cxiv Ibid., 406.

cxv   Ibid., 410.
cxvi   Ibid., 411.
cxvii   Gonzalez, vol. 2, 209.
cxviii   Richard N. Current, T. Harry Williams and Frank Freidel, *American History: A Survey,* 3rd ed. (New: York: Alfred A. Knopf Inc., 1971), 14.
cxix   Harrison., 436.
cxx   Current, 21.
cxxi   Harrison, 436.
cxxii   Current, 22-25.
cxxiii   Ibid., 18.
cxxiv   Ibid., 18.
cxxv   Ibid., 19.
cxxvi   Ibid., 19.
cxxvii   Ibid., 34.
cxxviii   Harrison, 439.
cxxix   Ibid., 440.
cxxx   Burke, *Africa,* 172.
cxxxi   Ibid., 174.
cxxxii   Ibid., 182.
cxxxiii   Ibid., 182.
cxxxiv   Ibid., 184.
cxxxv   Ibid., 184.
cxxxvi   Ibid., 185.
cxxxvii   Ibid., 185-6.
cxxxviii   Ibid., 181.
cxxxix   Harrison, 439.
cxl   Burke, 188.
cxli   Ibid., 189.
cxlii   Gonzalez, vol. 2, 252.
cxliii   Ibid., 253.
cxliv   Ibid., 254.
cxlv   Current, 32.
cxlvi   Gonzalez, vol. 2, 224.
cxlvii   Ibid., 202.
cxlviii   Ibid., 202.
cxlix   Current, 29.
cl   Harrison, 474.
cli   Gonzalez, vol. 2, 193.

clii   Harrison, 474.
cliii   Ibid., 487.
cliv   Albert James Dagger, "A Masonic History of America", *Midnight Call, July 2006,* 28.
clv   Ron Rhodes, *The Challenge of the Cults and New Religions* (Grand Rapids: Zondervan, 2001), 176.
clvi   Ibid., 231.
clvii   Harrison, 444.
clviii   Ibid., 444.
clix   Ibid., 469.
clx   Ibid., 469.
clxi   Ibid., 469.
clxii   Gonzalez, vol. 2, 193.
clxiii   Harrison, 469-470.
clxiv   Ibid., 473.
clxv   Gonzalez, vol. 2, 193.
clxvi   Mark A. Noll, Nathan O. Hatch, George M. Marsden, *The Search For Christian America* (Colorado Springs: Helmers & Howard, 1989), 129-130.
clxvii   Harrison, 475.
clxviii   Ibid., 628.
clxix   Ibid., 630.
clxx   Ibid., 630.
clxxi   Ibid., 630.
clxxii   Mark A. Noll, *A History of Christianity in the United States and Canada* (Grand Rapids: Eerdmans, 1992), 367.
clxxiii   Gonzalez, vol. 2, 256.
clxxiv   Ronald Nash, *Life's Ultimate Questions: An Introduction to Philosophy* (Grand Rapids: Zondervan, 1999), 37-38.
clxxv   Ibid., 39.
clxxvi   Harrison, 630.
clxxvii   Ibid., 630.
clxxviii Ibid., 552.
clxxix   Ibid., 629.
clxxx   Ibid., 630.
clxxxi   Ibid., 631.
clxxxii   Gonzalez, vol. 2, 256.
clxxxiii Harrison, 632.
clxxxiv   Noll, *A History of Christianity in the United States and*

Canada, 373.

clxxxv Noss, *A History of the World's Religions,* 571.

clxxxvi Roger E. Olson, *The Story of Christian Theology* (Downers Grove, IL: InterVarsity Press, 1999), 542.

clxxxvii Ibid., 533.

clxxxviii Ibid., 539.

clxxxix Gonzalez, vol. 2, 256.

cxc Ibid., 257.

cxci Ibid., 257.

cxcii Ibid., 321.

cxciii Ibid., 391.

cxciv Ibid., 392.

cxcv Ibid., 392.

cxcvi Harrison, 568.

cxcvii Ibid., 568.

cxcviii Noll, *A History of Christianity in the United States and Canada,* 308.

cxcix Noss, *A History of the World's Religions,* 81.

cc Ibid., 63.

cci Ibid., 66.

ccii Ibid., 68.

cciii Ibid., 70.

cciv Ibid., 72.

ccv Ibid., 72.

ccvi Ibid., 72.

ccvii Ibid., 72.

ccviii Ibid., 72-73.

ccix Greg Dues, *Catholic Customs & Traditions* (Mystic, PA: Twenty-Third Publications, 2000), 30.

ccx Ibid., 20.

ccxi Ibid., 20.

ccxii Ibid., 20.

ccxiii Ibid., 21.

ccxiv Ibid., 21.

ccxv Ibid., 22.

ccxvi Ibid., 22-23.

ccxvii Ibid., 26.

ccxviii Ibid., 26-27.

ccxix Ibid., 46.

[ccxx] Ibid., 50.

[ccxxi] Ibid., 51.

[ccxxii] Ibid., 51.

[ccxxiii] Ibid., 54.

[ccxxiv] Ibid., 56.

[ccxxv] Ibid., 98-99.

[ccxxvi] John L. Johnson, *The Black Biblical Heritage* (Nashville: Winston-Derek Publishers, Inc., 1994), 193.

[ccxxvii] Johnstone, *The Church is Bigger Than You Think*, 263.

[ccxxviii] Harrison, *A Short History of Western Civilization*, 437.

[ccxxix] Ibid., 510.

[ccxxx] Ibid., 512.

[ccxxxi] Ibid., 522.

[ccxxxii] Ibid., 580.

[ccxxxiii] Ibid., 593.

[ccxxxiv] Ibid., 595.

[ccxxxv] Ibid., 596.

[ccxxxvi] Ibid., 597.

[ccxxxvii] Ibid., 661.

[ccxxxviii] Ibid., 551.

[ccxxxix] Ibid., 618.

[ccxl] Ibid., 619.

[ccxli] Ibid., 671.

[ccxlii] Patrick Johnstone, *Operation World,* 6th ed. (Waynesboro, GA: Paternoster USA, 2001), 541-542.

[ccxliii] Harrison, 678.

[ccxliv] Ibid., 678.

[ccxlv] Ibid., 678.

[ccxlvi] Ibid., 678.

[ccxlvii] Ibid., 680.

[ccxlviii] Ibid., 680.

[ccxlix] Ibid., 680.

[ccl] Ibid., 680.

[ccli] Ibid., 693.

[cclii] Ibid., 701-2.

[ccliii] Ibid., 710.

[ccliv] Ibid., 723.

[cclv] Charles Colson, Richard Newhaus, eds. *Evangelicals and Catholics Together* (Dallas: Word Publishing, 1995), This book is a

united concerted treatise aimed at fighting the moral decline in the West, particularly in America. It virtually makes Evangelicals (those who stand with it) one with Catholics; a return to Rome.

cclvi   Harrison, *A Short History of Western Civilization,* 732.
cclvii   Ibid., 732.
cclviii   Ibid., 718.
cclix   Ibid., 719.
cclx   Ibid., 719.
cclxi   Ibid., 721.
cclxii   Ibid., 724.
cclxiii   Ibid., 745.
cclxiv   Ibid., 727.
cclxv   Noss, *A History of the World's Religions,* 594.
cclxvi   Ibid., 582.
cclxvii   Ibid., 623.
cclxviii Ibid., 586.
cclxix   Ibid., 587.
cclxx   Ibid., 588.
cclxxi   Johnstone, *The Church is Bigger Than You Think,* 264-5.
cclxxii   Noss, 630-1.
cclxxiii R. B. Thieme, *Christian Integrity* (Houston: R. B. Thieme, Jr. Bible Ministries, 1990), 168.
cclxxiv   Ronald J. Sider, *Rich Christians in an Age of Hunger* (Grand Rapids: Family Christian Press, 1997), 4.
cclxxv   Harrison, *A Short History of Western Civilization,* 443-444.
cclxxvi   Sider, 133-134.
cclxxvii Harrison, 444.
cclxxviii Ibid., 444.
cclxxix   Sider, 24.
cclxxx   Ibid., 137.
cclxxxi   Ibid., 139.
cclxxxii Ibid., 144.
cclxxxiii Ibid., 145.
cclxxxiv Ibid., 22.
cclxxxv   Ibid., 22.
cclxxxvi Ibid., 147.
cclxxxvii Ibid., 147-148.
cclxxxviii Ibid., 148.
cclxxxix Ibid., 28.

ccxc   Ibid., 29.

ccxci   Ibid., 30.

ccxcii   Ibid., 168.

ccxciii   Ibid., 114.

ccxciv   Ibid., 41-42.

ccxcv   Ibid., 61.

ccxcvi   Ibid., 64-65.

ccxcvii   Ibid., 110.

ccxcviii   Ibid., 110-111.

ccxcix   Ibid., 113.

ccc   Johnstone, *Operation World,* 651.

ccci   Ibid., 654.

cccii   Ibid., 256.

ccciii   Ibid., 270-1.

ccciv   Ibid., 365-6.

cccv   Ibid., 529.

cccvi   Ibid., 474.

cccvii   Ibid., 536.

cccviii   Billy Graham, *World Aflame* (Garden City, NY: Doubleday, 1965), 1.

cccix   Ibid., 18-19.

cccx   Ibid., 20.

cccxi   Ibid., 20-22.

cccxii   Ibid., 22-23.

cccxiii   Ibid., 24.

cccxiv   Ibid., 24-25.

cccxv   Ibid., 26.

cccxvi   Ibid., 29.

cccxvii   Ibid., 29.

cccxviii   Ibid., 29.

cccxix   Ibid., 36.

cccxx   Ibid., 36.

cccxxi   Ibid., 36-37.

cccxxii   Ibid., 37.

cccxxiii   Ibid., 38.

cccxxiv   Ibid., 39.

cccxxv   Ibid., 39-40.

cccxxvi   Ibid., 42-43.

cccxxvii   Ibid., 47.

cccxxviii Ibid., 47-48.

cccxxix Ibid., 48-49.

cccxxx Ibid., 49.

cccxxxi Ibid., 237.

cccxxxii Ibid., 243.

cccxxxiii Carl F. H. Henry, *Twilight of a Great Civilization: The Drift Toward Neo-Paganism* (Westchester, IL: Crossway Books, 1988), 15.

cccxxxiv Ibid., 16-17.

cccxxxv Ibid., 17.

cccxxxvi Ibid., 19.

cccxxxvii Rhodes, *The Challenge of the Cults and New Religions,* 129-130.

cccxxxviii Noll, *A History of Christianity in the United States and Canada,* 308.

cccxxxix Johnstone, *Operation World,* 29-41.

cccxl Ibid., 43.

cccxli Ibid., 162.

cccxlii Ibid., 310-312.

cccxliii Ibid., 372.

cccxliv Ibid., 374.

cccxlv Ibid., 619-620.

cccxlvi Ibid., 620.

cccxlvii Ibid., 621.

cccxlviii Ibid., 122.

cccxlix Jan David Hettinga, *Follow Me: Experience the Loving Leadership of Jesus* (Colorado Springs: NavPress, 1996), 30- 31.

cccl Arno Froese, *How Democracy Will Elect the Antichrist* (West Columbia, SC: The Olive Press, 1997), 237.

cccli Dave Hunt, T. A. MacMahon, *The Seduction of Christianity* (Eugene, OR: Harvest House Publishing, 1985), 57.

ccclii Keith Harris, *The Unveiling: A Journey Through the Book of Revelation* (West Columbia, SC: Olive Press, 1999), 135- 6.

cccliii Ibid., 397-8.

cccliv Plato, *The Republic, Jowett Translation,* (Clinton, MA: The Colonial Press, 1968), 35.

ccclv Ibid., 36.

www.ingramcontent.com/pod-product-compliance
Lightning Source LLC
Chambersburg PA
CBHW071658120626
46550CB00001B/24